Lecture Notes in Computer Scier

T0237742

Commenced Publication in 1973
Founding and Former Series Editors:
Gerhard Goos, Juris Hartmanis, and Jan van Leeuwen

Hee Yong Youn   Minkoo Kim
Hiroyuki Morikawa (Eds.)

Ubiquitous Computing Systems

Third International Symposium, UCS 2006
Seoul, Korea, October 11-13, 2006
Proceedings

 Springer

Volume Editors

Hee Yong Youn
School of Information and Communication Engineering
Sungkyunkwan University
Jangangu Chunchundong 300 Suwon, Korea
E-mail: youn@ece.skku.ac.kr

Minkoo Kim
College of Information Technology
Ajou University
San 5, Woncheon-Dong, Yeongtong-Gu
Suwon, Korea
E-mail: minkoo@ajou.ac.kr

Hiroyuki Morikawa
The University of Tokyo
7-3-1 Hongo
Bunkyo Tokyo 113-8656 Japan
E-mail: mori@mlab.t.u-tokyo.ac.ip

Library of Congress Control Number: 2006933414

CR Subject Classification (1998): C.2, C.3, C.5.3, D.2, D.4, H.4, H.5, K.4, J.7

LNCS Sublibrary: SL 3 – Information Systems and Application, incl. Internet/Web and HCI

ISSN   0302-9743
ISBN-10   3-540-46287-2 Springer Berlin Heidelberg New York
ISBN-13   978-3-540-46287-3 Springer Berlin Heidelberg New York

Springer is a part of Springer Science+Business Media

springer.com

© Springer-Verlag Berlin Heidelberg 2006
Printed in Germany

Typesetting: Camera-ready by author, data conversion by Scientific Publishing Services, Chennai, India
Printed on acid-free paper   SPIN: 11890348   06/3142   5 4 3 2 1 0

Preface

We cordially welcome you to the proceedings of the 2006 International Symposium on Ubiquitous Computing Systems (UCS) held in Seoul, Korea. UCS has been a symposium for dissemination of state-of-the-art research and engineering practices in ubiquitous computing with particular emphasis on systems and software. 2006 UCS was the third of this series of international symposia, and its importance is increasing as information technology industries are recognizing ubiquitous systems to be one of their top priorities. This year the symposium was organized by u-Korea Forum, Sungkyunkwan University, The Electronic Times, and UCN, Korea. It was also sponsored by the Korea Ministry of Information and Communication, KISS, KIPS, KICS, NCA from Korea and IPSJ SIGUBI, IEICE URON, and UNF from Japan.

This year we attracted 359 high-quality paper submissions from all over the world. Among them, 41 papers representing 11 countries were selected to be included in the technical program. This very low acceptance rate of about 11% clearly demonstrates the high quality of the conference, and this tradition will continue in the upcoming years. Three distinguished speakers were also invited for keynote speeches, who enlightened the audience on ubiquitous computing theory and application.

The technical program of UCS 2006 could achieve a very high quality through a precise and stringent review process. The Technical Program Committee consisted of 47 excellent members, and every submitted paper received at least 3 reviews. Most reviews were almost of journal paper review quality, and the paper selection made via Web conferences for several days was very serious and strict. This greatly contributed toward a high-quality program, and at the same time, enhanced of the quality of each respective paper submitted.

Along with the symposium, we also offered a poster session. This was for emphasizing the practical aspect of ubiquitous issues in real-world problems, especially in computing and communication. It provided the researchers and engineers with opportunities for sharing their ideas and solutions of various challenging problems in this area.

The city of Seoul is a mega-center of academia/industry for various areas of information technology. It also houses a variety of cultural and modern settings. Therefore, the participants of UCS were able to enjoy not only an interesting technical program but also a unique metropolitan atmosphere.

As General Co-chairs and Program Co-chairs, we would like to extend our appreciation to all those who took part in the symposium: the Steering Committee, Organizing Committee, Program Committee, the authors, and the reviewers. Special thanks go to Minsoo Kim from Ajou University, Korea for preparation of the proceedings and Suhee Kim from u-Korea Forum for taking care of all the chores.

Hee Yong Youn
Hideyuki Nakkashima
General Co-chairs
Minkoo Kim
Hiroyuki Morikawa
Program Co-chairs

Organization

Technical Program Committee

Jorg Baus, Saarland Univ., Germany
Michael Beigl, Univ. of Karlsruhe, Germany
Keith Cheverst, Lancaster Univ., UK
Anind Dey, Carnegie Mellon Univ., USA
Michael Evans, Virginia Polytechnic Institute and State Univ., USA
Kaori Fujinami, Waseda Univ., Japan
Masaaki Fukumoto, NTT DoCoMo Inc., Japan
Mikio Hasegawa, NICT, Japan
Paul Holleis, Univ. of Munich, Germany
Manpyo Hong, Ajou Univ., Korea
Ismail Ibrahim, Johannes Kepler Univ. Linz, Austria
Sozo Inoue, Kyushu Univ., Japan
Nobuo Kawaguchi, Nagoya Univ., Japan
Hyun-Sung Kim, Kyungil Univ., Korea
Daeyoung Kim, ICU, Korea
Kwangjo Kim, ICU, Korea
ChongGun Kim, Yeungnam Univ., Korea
Matthias Kranz, Univ. of Munich, Germany
Koichi Kurumatani, AIST, Japan
Marc Langheinrich, ETH Zurich, Switzerland
Dongman Lee, ICU, Korea
Wonjun Lee, Korea Univ., Korea
Sungyoung Lee, Kyung Hee Univ., Korea
Seon-Woo Lee, Hallym Univ., Korea
Jungtae Lee, Ajou Univ., Korea
Ben Lee, Oregon State Univ., USA
Rene Mayrhofer, Lancaster Univ., UK
Masateru Minami, Shibaura Institute of Technology, Japan
Joseph Ng, Hong Kong Baptist Univ., Hong Kong
Masayoshi Ohashi, KDDI, Japan
Young-Tack Park, Soongsil Univ., Korea
Thorsten Prante, Fraunhofer IPSI, Germany
Enrico Rukzio, Univ. of Munich, Germany
Lee Sanggoog, SAIT, Korea
Ichiro Satoh, National Institute of Informatics, Japan
Jun Bae Seo, ETRI, Korea
Itiro Siio, Ochanomizu Univ., Japan
Frank Stajano, Univ. of Cambridge, UK

Thomas Strang, DLR Oberpfaffenhofen, Germany
Martin Strohbach, Lancaster Univ., UK
Kaz Takashio, Keio Univ., Japan
Yasuo Tan, JAIST, Japan
Kristof Van Laerhoven, Lancaster Univ., UK
Woontack Woo, GIST, Korea
Kenichi Yamazaki, NTT DoCoMo Inc., Japan
Hee Yong Youn, Sungkyunkwan Univ., Korea
Chansu Yu, Cleveland State Univ., USA

Reviewers

Kensuke Baba, Kyushu Univ., Japan
Doo-Kwon Baik, Korea Univ., Korea
Urs Bischoff, Lancaster Univ., UK
Kijoon Chae, Ewha Womans Univ., Korea
Hangbae Chang, SoftCamp Co., Ltd., Korea
Young-jong Cho, Ajou Univ., Korea
Jinsung Cho, Kyung Hee Univ., Korea
Eun-Sun Cho, Chungbuk National Univ., Korea
We-Duke Cho, UCN, Korea
Seongje Cho, Dankook Univ., Korea
Sehyeong Cho, MyongJi Univ., Korea
Jong-Chan Choi, KETI, Korea
Ahyoung Choi, GIST, Kuwait
Seong Gon Choi, ChungBuk National Univ., Korea
Hyun Hwa Choi, ETRI, Korea
Eunmi Choi, Kookmin Univ., Korea
Misook Choi, Woosuk Univ., Korea
Soon Chung, Wright State Univ., USA
Ki-Dong Chung, Pusan National Univ., Korea
Matthias Dyer, TIK, ETH Zurich, Switzerland
Young Ik Eom, Sungkyunkwan Univ., Korea
Zoltan Fiala, TU Dresden, Germany
Christian Frank, ETH Zurich, Switzerland
Jeonghye Han, Chungju National Univ. of Education, Korea
Toru Hasegawa, KDDI, Japan
Paul Havinga, Univ. of Twente, Netherlands
Mike Hazas, Lancaster Univ., UK
Otmar Hilliges, Univ. of Munich, Germany
Michael Hinz, TU Dresden, Germany
Youn-Sik Hong, Univ. of Incheon, Korea
Dongpyo Hong, GIST, Korea
Kwang-Seok Hong, Sungkyunkwan Univ., Korea
Soon Hong, Samsung Electronics, Korea
Benedikt Hornler, Technische Universitaet Muenchen, Germany

Danny Hughes, Lancaster Univ., UK
Youngha Hwang, ETRI, Korea
EenJun Hwang, Korea Univ., Korea
Oh HyeongCheol, Korea Univ., Korea
Soon Hyun, ICU, Korea
Akira Idoue, KDDI, Japan
Kim Jai-Hoon, Ajou Univ., Korea
Dongwon Jeong, Kunsan National Univ., Korea
Su-hyung Jo, ETRI, Korea
Inwhee Joe, Hanyang Univ., USA
Woojin Jung, GIST, Korea
Souhwan Jung, Soongsil Univ., Korea
Kyungran Kang, Ajou Univ., Korea
Donghoon Kang, KIST, Korea
Jungwon Kang, ETRI, Korea
Keecheon Kim, Konkuk Univ., Korea
Jae-Chul Kim, ETRI, Korea
Joongheon Kim, LG Electronics, Korea
JongWon Kim, GIST, Korea
Seonhyeong Kim, Korea Univ., Korea
Jae-Gon Kim, ETRI, Korea
Sang-Ha Kim, Chungnam National Univ., Korea
Younghan Kim, Soongsil Univ., Korea
Jong Deok Kim, Pusan National Univ., Korea
Hong Kook Kim, GIST, Korea
Shin-Dug Kim, Yonsei Univ., Korea
Won-Tae Kim, ETRI, Korea
Sungwook Kim, Sogang Univ., Korea
Ung Mo Kim, SungKyunKwna Univ., Korea
Myoung Ho Kim, KAIST, Korea
Hwankoo Kim, Hoseo Univ., Korea
Jihoon Kim, Kyunghee Univ., Korea
HakMan Kim, KERI, Korea
Jin Hyung Kim, KAIST, Korea
Joon Kim, Dankook Univ., Korea
Sang-Wook Kim, Hayang Univ., Korea
Hyeokman Kim, Kookmin Univ., Korea
Sehwan Kim, GIST, Korea
Hyeon Kyeong Kim, Hanshin Univ., Korea
Moon Kim, Sungkyunkwan Univ., Korea
Teruaki Kitasuka, Kyushu Univ., Japan
Young-Bae Ko, Ajou Univ., Korea
Albert Krohn, Univ. of Karlsruhe, Germany
Kyung Sup Kwak, Inha Univ., Korea
Young Kwak, Cheju National Univ., Korea
Obyung Kwon, Kyunhee Univ., Korea
Juhum Kwon, Korea Air Force Central Computer Center, Korea

Jitae Shin ,Sunkyunkwan Univ., Korea
DongRyeol Shin, Sungkyunkwan Univ., Korea
Choonsung Shin, GIST, Korea
Kee-Young Shin, ETRI, Korea
Christian Shin, State Univ. of New York, USA
Hyoung-Kyu Song, Sejong Univ., Korea
Akihito Sonoda ,Kyushu Univ., Japan
Oliver Storz, Lancaster Univ., UK
Youngjung Suh, GIST, Korea
Hyo-Won Suh, KAIST, Korea
Son Tran, Korea Univ., Korea
Ha Nguyen Tran, NICT, Japan
Pasi Valkkynen, VTT, Finland
Arnd Vitzthum, Univ. of Munich, Germany
Harald Vogt, ETH Zurich, Switzerland
Hideaki Yamada, KDDI, Japan
Shouichi Yamazaki, KDDI, Japan
Jung-Jin Yang, The Catholic Univ. of Korea, Korea
HIdetoshi Yokota, KDDI, Japan
Seong Joon Yoo, Sejong Univ., Korea
Dongsuk Yook, Korea Univ., Korea
YoungKeun Yoon, ETRI, Korea
Hyoseok Yoon, GIST, Korea
Young-Hwan You, Sejong Univ., Korea
Taewan You, ETRI, Korea
Son Young Sung, ETRI, Korea
Jieun Yu, Korea Univ., Korea

Table of Contents

Human Computer Interaction

A Rule-Based Publish-Subscribe Message Routing System
for Ubiquitous Computing 1
  Yixin Jing, Dongwon Jeong, JinHyung Kim, Doo-Kwon Baik

Exploiting Eye Gaze Information for Operating Services in Home
Network System 13
  Kohei Mitsui, Hiroshi Igaki, Masahide Nakamura,
  Ken-ichi Matsumoto, Kentaro Takemura

A Methodology for Assessing the Level of U-Transformation
of Ubiquitous Services 28
  Ohbyung Kwon, Jihoon Kim

3D Space Handwriting Recognition with Ligature Model 41
  Dae Hwan Kim, Hyun Il Choi, Jin Hyung Kim

Scenario-Based Design of Ambient Intelligence 57
  Veikko Ikonen, Marketta Niemelä, Eija Kaasinen

Ubiquitous Multimedia Access with a Multidimensional Information
Browser 73
  Seong Joon Yoo, Yoo-Joo Choi, Soo-Mi Choi, Carsten Waldeck,
  Dirk Balfanz

OPF: A Distributed Context-Sensing Framework for Ubiquitous
Computing Environments 82
  Max Van Kleek, Kai Kunze, Kurt Partridge, James "Bo" Begole

Modeling and Social Aspects

Implementation of Telematics Services with Context-Aware Agent
Framework 98
  Kenta Cho, Yuzo Okamoto, Tomohiro Yamasaki,
  Masayuki Okamoto, Masanori Hattori, Akihiko Ohsuga

Clock Offsets in TDOA Localization 111
  Nak-Seon Seong, Seong-Ook Park

Context-Dependent Task Computing in Pervasive Environment 119
  Hongbo Ni, Xingshe Zhou, Daqing Zhang, Lek Heng Ngoh

Semantic Information Retrieval in the COMPASS Location System 129
  Frank Kargl, Günter Dannhäuser, Stefan Schlott,
  Jürgen Nagler-Ihlein

A Formal Characterization of Vagueness and Granularity
for Context-Aware Mobile and Ubiquitous Computing 144
  Hedda R. Schmidtke, Woontack Woo

An Inference Engine for Personalized Content Adaptation
in Heterogeneous Mobile Environment 158
  Seunghwa Lee, Jee-Hyong Lee, Eunseok Lee

Context-Based Cooperation Architecture for Ubiquitous Environment ... 171
  Minsoo Kim, Youna Jung, Jungtae Lee, Minkoo Kim

Affordance-Based Design of Physical Interfaces for Ubiquitous
Environments 183
  Jennifer G. Sheridan, Gerd Kortuem

Systems

Dynamic Clustering for Object Tracking in Wireless Sensor Networks.... 200
  Guang-yao Jin, Xiao-yi Lu, Myong-Soon Park

An Ultra Low Power Medium Access Control Protocol with the Divided
Preamble Sampling... 210
  Sangsoon Lim, Youngmin Ji, Jaejoon Cho, Sunshin An

A Service Conflict Resolution Algorithm Based on Virtual
Personal World 225
  Joo-Kyoung Park, Chang-Deok Kang, Kyung-Lang Park,
  Hoon-Ki Lee, Eui-Hyun Baek, Shin-Dug Kim

Experimental Evaluation of Decision Criteria for WLAN Handover:
Signal Strength and Frame Retransmission 239
  Kazuya Tsukamoto, Takeshi Yamaguchi, Shigeru Kashihara,
  Yuji Oie

Buffer Feedback Scheduling: Runtime Adaptation of Ubicomp
Applications.. 254
  Christian Decker, Michael Beigl, Till Riedel, Albert Krohn,
  Tobias Zimmer

Exploiting Passive Advantages of Sentient Artefacts 270
  Fahim Kawsar, Kaori Fujinami, Tatsuo Nakajima

Scenario-Based Programming for Ubiquitous Applications 286
  Eun-Sun Cho, Kang-Woo Lee, Min-Young Kim, Hyun Kim

JSense - Prototyping Sensor-Based, Location-Aware Applications
in Java 300
  *Silvia Santini, Robert Adelmann, Marc Langheinrich, Georg Schätti,
  Steven Fluck*

Communications I

Estimation of the Number of Competing Stations Applied with Central
Difference Filter for an IEEE 802.11 Network 316
  Jang-Sub Kim, Hojin Shin, Dong-Ryeol Shin, Woo-Gon Chung

An Emergency Message Propagation Method in Highway Traffic 331
  Sukdea Yu, Moonkun Lee, Gihwan Cho

UbiComm: An Adaptive Vertical Handoff Decision Scheme
for Heterogeneous Wireless Networks 344
  *Wonjun Lee, Eunkyo Kim, Jieun Yu, Donghwan Lee, Jihoon Choi,
  Joongheon Kim, Christian K. Shin*

Reducing Location Update Cost Using Multiple Virtual Layers
in HMIPv6 357
  Jongpil Jeong, Min Young Chung, Hyunseung Choo

Design and Emulation of Integration Framework for Heterogeneous
Wireless PAN Networks 368
  In-Yeup Kong, Won-Joo Hwang

Heterogeneous Routing Protocol Coordinator for Mobile
Ad Hoc Networks 384
  *Namhi Kang, Seongil Yoo, Younghan Kim, Souhwan Jung,
  Kihun Hong*

Communications II

DynaMoNET: Dynamic Multi-homed IPv6 Mobile Networks
with Multiple Mobile Routers 398
  Won-Tae Kim

Fast IPv6 Address Auto-configuration Using Proxy for Mobile
Environment 414
    Dongkeun Lee, Keecheon Kim

Parametric Routing for Wireless Sensor Networks 428
    Yeultak Sung, Hojung Cha

Analyzing the Effect of a Block FEC Algorithm's Symbol Size
on Energy Consumption in Wireless Sensor Networks.................. 440
    Jong-Suk Ahn, Young-Su Lee, Jong-Hyuk Yoon, Kang-Woo Lee

Minimum Dominating Sets for Solving the Coverage Problem
in Wireless Sensor Networks....................................... 454
    Babak Pazand, Amitava Datta

A Simple Scheme with Low Energy Consumption for Coverage
Maintenance in Wireless Sensor Networks 467
    Sung Ho Hwang, Minsu Kim, Tae-young Byun

Spectrum Sensing Method for Increasing the Spectrum Efficiency
in Wireless Sensor Network.. 478
    Ning Han, Sung Hwan Shon, Jong Ok Joo, Jae Moung Kim

Smart Devices and Security

Algorithm for the Predictive Hibernation of Sensor Systems 489
    Hyo Jong Lee

Encapsulation and Entity-Based Approach of Interconnection Between
Sensor Platform and Middleware of Pervasive Computing 500
    Shinyoung Lim, Abdelsalam (Sumi) Helal

Feature Selection and Activity Recognition from Wearable Sensors 516
    Susanna Pirttikangas, Kaori Fujinami, Tatsuo Nakajima

Portable Device for Bi-emotional State Identification Using Heart Rate
Variability 528
    *Sun K. Yoo, ChungKi Lee, GunKi Lee, ByungChae Lee,
    KeeSam Jeong, YoonJung Park*

An Optimizing Authenticated Key Exchange Protocol
for Self-organizing Sensor Networks 537
    Eun-Jun Yoon, Kee-Young Yoo

Author Index 547

A Rule-Based Publish-Subscribe Message Routing System for Ubiquitous Computing

Yixin Jing[1], Dongwon Jeong[2], JinHyung Kim[1], and Doo-Kwon Baik[1]

[1] Department of Computer Science & Engineering, Korea University
Seoul, 136-701, Korea
{jing, koolmania}@software.korea.ac.kr, baikdk@korea.ac.kr
[2] Department of Informatics & Statistics, Kunsan National University
Gunsan, 573-701, Korea
djeong@kunsan.ac.kr

Abstract. The ubiquitous computing produces big volume of messages as the pervasive computability is deployed in large scale. As a middleware between the message producer and message consumer, message routing system enables backend systems to efficiently acquire the interested message. A widely adopted message routing mechanism is the content-based publish-subscribe framework. Based on this paradigm, we propose a rule-based system for supporting message routing in ubiquitous computing. The novel system features in the flexibility of the message computing, which is accomplished through a set of message operators. The message consumer could select the appropriate operator and specify the operating rule to get satisfying messages.

1 Introduction

Message routing system is a fundamental element in the ubiquitous computing architecture. The ubiquitous computing faces the challenges promoted by the explosion of the context information. RFID technology enables the product tracking at the instance-level rather than at the class-level [1]. Sensor network which is monitoring the environment constantly reports the current data and any changes. Countless mobile devices generate huge numbers of unanticipated events. All of this information, including event and data, gathered from the physical world is defined as messages. The hardware or software which generates the message is so called the message producer. The message generated from the producer is called raw message, which flows from the message producer to the backend systems or applications to get treatment. Those systems or applications where the message sinks are called as message consumer.

However, the message generated from the message producer is usually of interest not only to a single consumer, but to a diverse set of consumers across an organization and its business partners. The message data must thus be broadcasted to the entities that indicated an interest in the data. On the other hand, common to all consumers that make use of the message is the desire to receive filtered and aggregated message rather than raw streams of message. Different consumers are

H.Y. Youn, M. Kim, and H. Morikawa (Eds.): UCS 2006, LNCS 4239, pp. 1–12, 2006.

however interested in a different subset of the total message captured based on the message producer. The entity which deals with the message disseminating, filtering and aggregating is a kind of middleware decoupling the message producer and consumer. The middleware like that is named as message broker. Message producer, broker and consumer form the basic elements of the message routing system, see Fig. 1.

Fig. 1. Message routing system

Publish-subscribe (pub-sub for short) is an important paradigm for asynchronous communication between the message producers and message consumers. In the pub-sub paradigm, subscribers (message consumer) specify their interests in certain message conditions, and will be notified afterwards of any message fired by a publisher (message producer) that matches their registered interests. Pub-sub systems can be characterized into several broad types based on the expressiveness of the subscriptions they support. Content-based pub-sub is a general and powerful paradigm, in which subscribers have the added flexibility of choosing filtering criteria along multiple dimensions, using thresholds and conditions on the contents of the message [2].

In the ubiquitous computing, pub-sub should be an easy process which enables un-expert subscriber to progress smoothly. However the prevailed content-based pub-sub is designed for distributed network which result in a complicated message pub-sub process. To overcome this weakness, we propose a novel content-based message routing system. The system features in a rule-based approach to cope with the message routing. Compared with other approaches, the proposed system has a clear guideline to ease the subscription. The paper is organized as the follows. Section 2 introduces the related work. Section 3 explains a XML based message expression. The rule-based routing method is present in the Section 4. Section 5 proposes the architecture of the message routing system and relative solutions. We conclude the paper in the Section 6.

2 Related Work

Publication-subscription message routing mechanism has been evolving for years [3]. Channels [4, 5] are the first generation of publish/subscribe systems. A notification is published to a specific channel specified by the publisher and delivered to all consumers that have subscribed to this channel. However, applications consuming context information do not need to maintain communication channels with individual message producer, but can simply specify which message they are interested in by submitting subscriptions to the message broker.

Subject-based publish/subscribe systems [6-8] associate with each notification a single subject that is usually specified as a string. Subjects can be arranged in a tree by using a dot notation. The drawback of this approach in ubiquitous computing is that the any change of the subject will cause the rearrange of the subject tree. In ubiquitous computing, the potential message consumers, namely subjects, are hard to anticipate, which make the messaging servers unable to afford the high cost brought by frequent change to the subject tree.

Content-based pub-sub is a more general and powerful paradigm, in which subscribers have the added flexibility of choosing filtering criteria along multiple dimensions, using thresholds and conditions on the contents of the message, rather than being restricted to (or even requiring) pre-defined subject fields. Clearly, it is the most flexible mechanism adaptive to the dynamic characters of ubiquitous computing. The research on this area produce considerable outputs including Elvin [9], Gryphon [10-12], Keryx [13], Siena [14, 15], Le Subscribe [16, 17], Jedi [18], the CORBA Notification Service [19], and Rebeca [20]. These routing systems are designed for the environments which have high demand for treating complicated message types, such as XML document. Considering the comparative simple message, an easy-to-handle content-based message routing is more suitable for ubiquitous computing. Motivated by this goal, we propose a novel rule-based message routing for efficiently delivering message to interested destinations.

3   Message Expression

We use a XML based expression to represent the message, including the input and output of the message broker. Although XML encoding adds substantial overhead, XML provides more opportunities for structure. Parsing every incoming message, constructing every outgoing message, and transmitting information in the verbose XML format, may reduce message throughput and adds latency along the event flow. However, compressing the XML reduces bandwidth consumption [21], and enhances interoperability and extensibility. In addition, most messages in ubiquitous computing have a simple structure, we exploits an XML based message representation in our system.

The message could be an event, context information from sensors, or a tag data read by RFID readers. We assume that before the message arrive the message broker, it could get formatted by message producers. Or, after the source message arrival, it could be formatted within the message broker. The issue of how to transform the heterogeneous message to the expression defined in this paper is out of scope of this paper. Part of the XML schema of the message is shown as the Fig. 2.

The message has a root element <Message>. The message information is classified into two components, viz. the basic information (such as message type and timestamp) and the message detail. The message detail is contained in <msgpara> element, which attributes consist of parameter name and data type. Fig. 3 illustrates a message example. The example is generated by sensors detecting the employee ID cards, which tells his/her location in the company.

```
...
<xs:element name= "Message">
  <xs:complexType>
    <xs:sequence>
      <xs:element name= "msgtype" type= "xsd:string"/>
      <xs:element name= "timestamp" type= "xsd:dateTime" minOccurs="1" maxOccurs="1"/>
      <xs:element ref= "msgpara" minOccurs="0" maxOccurs="unbounded"/>
    </xs:sequence>
  </xs:complexType>
</xs:element>
<xs:element name= "msgpara">
  <xs:complexType>
    <xs:attribute name="paraname" type="xs:anyURI" use="required"/>
    <xs:attribute name="paratype" type="xs:anyURI" use="required"/>
  </xs:complexType>
</xs:element>
...
```

Fig. 2. Message schema based on XML

```
<Message>
        <msgtype> employee location</msgtype>
        <timestamp>2001-10-26T21:32:52</timestamp>
        <msgpara paraname="employeeName" paratype="string">
            John
        </msgpara>
        <msgpara paraname="department" paratype="string">
            sale
        </msgpara>
        <msgpara paraname="employeeLocation" paratype="string">
            Room225
        </msgpara>
</Message>
```

Fig. 3. The message example. John, who belongs to the sale department, is in the room 225 now.

4   The Rule-Based Message Routing

In this section, we introduce the rule-based message routing. In the proposed routing approach, we adopt message operator to route the message flow according to the subscription. We first define the concept of message operator, then, explain how to define a rule based on the message operator.

4.1   Message Operators

To provide a message broker which is capable of meeting the application requirement, we define a set of message operator to complete the primitive message treatment. Three kinds of message operator are defined (see Fig. 4).

The message operator enables the message broker to deal with flexible message routing. The raw message is not generated for the particular applications (message consumer). The context information included in the message from the message

Operator	Explanation	Example
Merge	Merge several messages into one	message A, message B → ⊕ → message C = (A+B)
Split	Split one message into several smaller piece	message A → ⊖ → message A', message A"
Transform	Transform the message information, such as the measurement	message A → ⊙ → message A'

Fig. 4. Message operators

producer is probably not sufficient for the application to execute given process. To solve this problem, the application has to gather all necessary messages itself. However, this expectation is not applicable in ubiquitous computing. Since in most cases, applications are designed and developed independently from the sensor level. If the application is tightly coupled with the sensor level, it looses flexibility when used in different scenarios. In this case, the message operator in a message broker is required to enrich the raw message and possibly to inquire about more information from several context sensors. Consider the scenario in the Fig. 5 where two monitor systems are using sensors to detect the location of the employee and car in the parking lots. The location information of each employee and each car is constantly sent out through message flow. At the backend, an alert application is running by analyzing the distance between the car and its owner. If the distance exceeds a given maximum number, a car-stealing alert would be sent to the owner. To support the application, the location of the employee as well as that of the car should be merged into one message and delivered to the alert application.

On the contrast, raw messages may contain a lot of information that is not pertinent to the application. When these potentially irrelevant messages are delivered to the destination application without being tailored, the redundant data increase the network overload. In addition, when this meaningless data arrives the application, extra computing resources are consumed to digest the volume of data. In Fig. 5, two working management systems in different departments are interested in the different employees. The split operator can filter the messages, and pass the messages to the different department systems.

In some other cases, the encoding of the message information does not match the application requirement. For example, in Fig. 5, the RFID reader of the car monitor system can receive 64bit EPC of a car while the backend parking management system can only process 96bit EPC. To overcome the code set gap, a message transform operator could help to change the encoding.

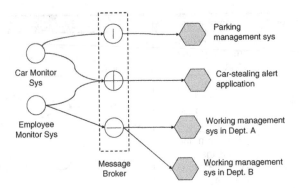

Fig. 5. Scenario of the message operator utilization

4.2 Message Operator Definition

Each kind of message operator has the input and out put message. In the operator, some rules have to be pre-defined. When the incoming messages meet the condition of the rules, the messages are merged, split, or transformed following the rules. The definition of operator is actually a XML file which restricts the input message, output message and the corresponding rules. The general structure of the operator is shown in Fig. 6. Operator information includes basic description such as creation date and subscriber. Input message depicts the message types which are going to be operated. The output message is defined for producing the message in a given format to satisfy the message consumer. In addition, the output message component contains the information of definition where the generated message be delivered. One output message can be sent to multiple consumers. Rule is a key component where the operator processor can obtain necessary conditions to check whether the input messages meet the operator requirement or not. Within the rule, a set of functions could be executed and finally return a Boolean value.

We take the merge operator for car-stealing alert application as an example. The employee location message was illustrated in the Fig. 3. Likewise, the message of the car location is defined in the similar way, which includes the type information of the car and the name of the car's owner. Fig. 7 shows the definition of the merge operator.

The merge operator defines the format type of output message as well as the rule. The operator is specified by the message subscriber, in this example, namely the alert application. During the subscription (discussed later), the alert application has to define a target message format, mycar, and specify the rule. Under the element <rule>, different conditions could be defined. Condition <equal> restricts that the value of the two elements should be the same. Only when the employee name is the same as the owner of the car, the input messages could be merged into one according to the format defined under <msgformat>. XPath [22] expressions are adopted to locate the target elements for comparison, and to fill the merged message with the value from input messages. Finally the merged message is sent to the target address depicted in the <destination> element.

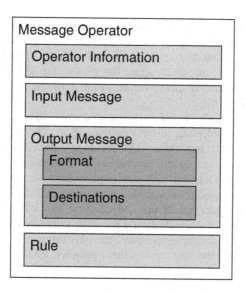

Fig. 6. The construction of operator

```
<Merge id="merge001">
        <input>
                <msgtype>employee location</msgtype>
                <msgtype>car location</msgtype>
        </input>
        <output>
                <msgformat>
                        <msgtype>mycar</msgtype>
                        <timestamp/>
                        <msgpara paraname="employeeName" paratype="string"
                                valuefrom="employee location ://msgpara[@paraname='employeeName']"/>
                        <msgpara paraname="employeeLocation" paratype="string"
                                valuefrom="employee location ://msgpara[@paraname='employeeLocation']"/>
                        <msgpara paraname="carLocation" paratype="string"
                                valuefrom="car location ://msgpara[@paraname='carLocation']"/>
                </msgformat>
                <destinations>
                        <destination>192.168.0.15:80</destination>
                </destinations>
        </output>
        <rule>
                <equal>
                        <element>employee location://msgpara[@paraname='employeeName']</element>
                        <element>car location://msgpara[@paraname='carOwner'] </element>
                </equal>
        </rule>
</Merge>
```

Fig. 7. Operator for merging context message of the employee and car

4.3 Message Operator Customization

The message operators provide a very flexible approach for subscriber to customize the subscription. This flexibility is carried out by two perspectives.

First, the structure of the message operator is easily to extend. XML-based message operator is easy to understand for non-expert users. Additionally, the message broker could provide plenty choices of functions for message subscribers to customize the operator. Within the <rule> element of operator, more predefined functions could be provided. For example, the subscriber can make the judgment on the value with <isString>, or can compare the values carried by the input messages with <greaterThan>. Whatever functions are adopted, the returned result should be a boolean value, i.e. true or false.

Second, the combination of the message operators significantly magnifies the subscriber capability of selecting interesting messages. The message operator does not must to be utilized stand alone. The message subscriber could combine the different operator types to get a more precise output . For example, a merged message can be split again depending on different requirements, or can be transformed to another encode to feed special subscriber. In this case, the message routing system needs to manage the operators in one subscription to ensure they can cooperate correctly. This process in dealt with during message subscription. When the message consumers attempt to use multiple operators, the only thing they need to do is to alter the destination denoted in the operator to other operators' ID instead of IP address.

5   Message Routing System

The section describes the implementation of the message routing system. First we will introduce the architecture of the system. Second, we present the algorithm of the message merge operator.

5.1   System Architecture

In this section we present the primitive message routing system and explain how to implement the capability enumerated in the previous section. Fig. 8 show the architecture of the system.

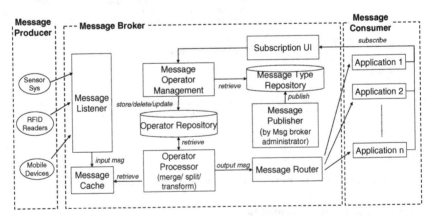

Fig. 8. The architecture of the message routing system

The entire system can be partitioned into three functions, message publish, subscribe and route. Message publisher is responsible for publishing the different types of incoming messages to a repository. The Subscription UI is an interface through which the message consumers can create, delete or update their subscription. This process is accomplished through manipulating the operator XML files. First, the message consumer has to retrieve the current message type published by the message broker. After selecting the interested message type, the message consumer has to decide the operator type. As the operator type varies, the Message Operator Manager provides different UI styles for the message consumer to complete the subscription. In the Subscription UI, the message consumer defines the message format for the output message as well as the rules. Based on the interested message content, the Message Operator Manager can formulate the subscription into a XML file and store the file in the Operator Repository. The operator file stored in the Operator Repository is referenced by the Operator Processor. The incoming messages are stored in the Message Cache first. Responding to the input message, the Operator Processor reads the predefined operator in the repository, then merges, splits or transforms the message under the guideline specified in the operator. Finally, the output message is delivered to the corresponding message consumer through a Message Router.

5.2 Algorithm for Merge Operator

Although all of three message operators have distinguished algorithms, message operator is the most complicated one due to its multiple incoming. This subsection takes the merge operator to investigate how system deals with the subscription which requires a message merging.

Two major factors influence the performance of merge operator. One is the interval time t_o at which the message subscriber wants the output message to be delivered out. The other one is the interval time t_i that the input messages arrives the message cache. Obviously when $t_o < t_i$, the message subscriber could not be sufficiently feed. Therefore, when the message broker receives the subscription, the broker has to acquire t_o from the subscriber to assure that the desired output message could be delivered in time. According to the cache size and operator processor's performance ability, an appropriate memory space is allocated to cache the constantly input messages. In our system prototype, we adopt a matrix to cache the input messages. The row number of matrix, r, equals the number of the input message going to be merged. The column number is decided by the following function.

$$c = \frac{T_h}{t_o} \tag{1}$$

Where T_h is the period time, in which the incoming messages will be stored, otherwise will be considered be expired. For example, if the system decides to save the messages received in recent 300 seconds and the message consumer wants to get merged message every 60 seconds, the $c = 300/60 = 5$. If two kinds of input messages are candidate to be merged, the matrix looks like that shown in Fig. 9.

$$t_1 \quad t_2 \quad t_3 \quad t_4 \quad t_5$$

$$M = m_1 \quad \circ \quad \circ \quad \circ \quad \circ \quad \circ$$

$$m_2 \quad \circ \quad \circ \quad \circ \quad \circ \quad \circ$$

Fig. 9. Storage matrix for incoming message

The object saved in each element of the matrix is the message content for sake of the small message size. During each 5 seconds, the cache saves the newest input message in one matrix column according to the message type. In the next 5 seconds, the cache will save the input messages to the next matrix column. When the process for saving messages meets the fifth column, it will re-begin from the first column. The old messages in the first column are replaced, i.e. treated as expired.

The processing for reading the messages from the matrix is synchronous with the process for saving. Thus, the two processes will not conflict as long as they don't access to the same column at the start time. The algorithms of the saving and reading are present in Fig. 10 a) and b) respectively.

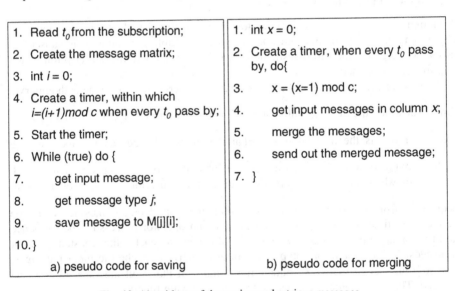

1. Read t_0 from the subscription;
2. Create the message matrix;
3. int $i = 0$;
4. Create a timer, within which $i=(i+1)mod\ c$ when every t_0 pass by;
5. Start the timer;
6. While (true) do {
7.   get input message;
8.   get message type j;
9.   save message to M[j][i];
10.}

a) pseudo code for saving

1. int $x = 0$;
2. Create a timer, when every t_0 pass by, do{
3. $x = (x=1)$ mod c;
4.   get input messages in column x;
5.   merge the messages;
6.   send out the merged message;
7. }

b) pseudo code for merging

Fig. 10. Algorithms of the saving and retrieve messages

6 Conclusion

In this paper we contributed a rule-based message routing system for ubiquitous computing. The mechanism is based on the pub-sub framework. The rule for routing the message is defined by subscribers during the subscription. Under the guideline of the rule, the incoming message could be computed by utilizing the merge operator, split operator or transform operator, to meet the message consumer interests. The system benefits from the flexibility of the message operator. In essence, message operator is an atomic message computing unit. More sophisticated message computing could be achieved by combining the different operators. The prototype implementation and experiment would be covered in our future work.

References

1. Floerkemeier, C., and Lampe, M.: RFID Middleware Design: Addressing Application Requirements and RFID Constraints. In: The 2005 Joint Conference on Smart Objects and Ambient Intelligence. ACM International Conference Proceeding Series, Vol. 121. (2005) 219–224
2. Cao, F., and Singh, J.P.: Efficient Event Routing in Content-Based Publish-Subscribe Service Networks. In: The INFOCOM 23rd Annual Joint Conference of the IEEE Computer and Communications Societies. Vol. 2. (2004) 929-940
3. Mühl, G.: Generic Constraints for Content-Based Publish/Subscribe. In: The 9th International Conference on Cooperative Information Systems (CoopIS). Lecture Notes in Computer Science, Vol. 2172. (2001)211-225
4. OMG: CORBA event service specification. OMG Document formal/94-01-01(1994)
5. Sun: Distributed event specification (1998)
6. Oki, B., Pfluegl, M., Siegel, A., and Skeen, D.: The Information Bus-An Architecture for Extensible Distributed Systems. In: ACM Symposium on Operating Systems Principles. (1993) 58–68
7. Sun: Java message service specification 1.0.2 (1999)
8. TIBCO Inc.: TIB/Rendezvous. http://www.tibco.com/. (1996)
9. Segall, B., Arnold, D., Boot, J., Henderson, M., and Phelps, T.: Content Based Routing with Elvin4. In: AUUG2K (2000)
10. Aguilera, M., Strom, R., Sturman, D., Astley, M., and Chandra, T.: Matching Events in a Content-Based Subscription System. In: The 18th ACM Symposium on Principles of Distributed Computing (PODC) (1999)53-61
11. Banavar, G., Chandra, T., Mukherjee, B., Nagarajarao, J., Strom, R. E., and Sturman, D. C.: An Efficient Multicast Protocol for Content-Based Publish-Subscribe Systems. In: The 19th IEEE International Conference on Distributed Computing Systems (1999) 262
12. Opyrchal, L., Astley, M., Auerbach, J., Banavar, G., Strom, R., and Sturman, D.: Exploiting IP Multicast in Content-Based Publish-Subscribe Systems. In: Sventek, J., Coulson, G. (eds.): Middleware. Lecture Notes in Computer Science, vol. 1795 (2000)185–207
13. Wray, M., Hawkes, R.: Distributed Virtual Environments and VRML: An Event-Based Architecture. In: The 7th International WWW Conference (1998)43-51
14. Carzaniga, A., Rosenblum, D., and Wolf, A.: Content-Based Addressing and Routing: A General Model and its Application. Technical Report CU-CS-902-00, Department of Computer Science, University of Colorado, USA (2000)
15. Carzaniga, A.: Architectures for an Event Notification Service Scalable to Wide-area Networks. PhD thesis, Politecnico di Milano, Milano, Italy (1998)
16. Fabret, F., Llirbat, F., Pereira, J., and Shasha, D.: Efficient Matching for Content-Based Publish/Subscribe Systems. Technical report, INRIA (2000)
17. Pereira, J., Fabret, F., Llirbat, F., and Shasha, D.: Efficient Matching for Web-Based Publish/Subscribe Systems. In: Etzion, O., Scheuermann, P. (eds.): The International. Conference on Cooperative Information Systems (CoopIS). Lecture Notes in Computer Science, Vol. 1901 (2000) 162-173

18. Cugola, G., Di Nitto, E., and Fuggetta, A.: Exploiting an Event-Based Infrastructure to Develop Complex Distributed Systems. In: The 1998 International Conference on Software Engineering. IEEE Computer Society Press / ACM Press (1998) 261–270
19. OMG: Corba Notification Service. OMG Document telecom/99-07-01 (1999)
20. Fiege, L., and Mühl, G.: Rebeca Event-Based Electronic Commerce Architecture. http:// www.gkec.informatik.tu-darmstadt.de/rebeca (2000)
21. Snoeren, A. C., Conley, K., and Gifford, D. K.: Mesh Based Content Routing using XML. In: ACM SIGOPS Operating Systems Review. ACM Press, Vol. 35 (2001)160-173
22. W3C: XML Path Language (XPath) 2.0, W3C Candidate Recommendation. http:// www. w3.org/TR/2005/CR-xpath20-20051103/ (2005)

Exploiting Eye Gaze Information for Operating Services in Home Network System

Kohei Mitsui[1], Hiroshi Igaki[2], Masahide Nakamura[1],
Ken-ichi Matsumoto[1], and Kentaro Takemura[3]

[1] Graduate School of Information Science, Nara Institute of Science and Technology
8916-5 Takayama, Ikoma, Nara 630-0192, Japan
{kohei-m, masa-n, matumoto}@is.naist.jp
[2] Department of Information and Telecommunication Engineering, Nanzan University
27 Seirei, Seto, Aichi 489-0863, Japan
igaki@nanzan-u.ac.jp
[3] Department of Electrical Engineering, Nara National College of Technology
22 Yata, Yamatokoriyama, Nara 639-1080, Japan
kenta-ta@elec.nara-k.ac.jp

Abstract. This paper presents a system which extensively exploits user's eye gaze information for operating services and appliances in the emerging home network system (HNS). We design and implement the system called AXELLA, which captures user's gaze, then invokes a service operation, and finally announces the response via voice. AXELLA interprets the gaze information together with supplementary information as a *gaze context*, and triggers a service module associated by a service rule. Thus, a simple gazing activity can be used for various service operations. Service developers (or even home users) can easily develop context-aware HNS services with the eye-gaze-based UI. We demonstrate a practical service called "See and Know" implemented using AXELLA, where a user can acquire the current status information of every appliance just by looking at the appliance. It was shown that the proposed system can reduce the artificial dependency significantly with respect to ease-of-learning and system scalability.

1 Introduction

With the emerging ubiquitous technologies, various objects have been equipped with network functionalities. A *home network system* (HNS) is a major application of such ubiquitous technologies. In a HNS, general household appliances, such as a TV, a DVD/HDD recorder, an air-conditioner, lights, curtains, a ventilator, an electric kettle and sensors, are connected to a LAN at home, in order to provide sophisticated services for home users. It is expected in the near future that a great variety of services and appliances for a HNS will be available. Several products are already on the market (e.g., [3][13][19]). Currently, a user interface (UI) for the HNS services is supposed to be provided with a hand-held device (e.g., a handy-phone, a PDA, a proprietary remote controller, etc.) [5][10][14], or with a built-in control panel operating GUI applications [3][8][13].

H.Y. Youn, M. Kim, and H. Morikawa (Eds.): UCS 2006, LNCS 4239, pp. 13–27, 2006.
© Springer-Verlag Berlin Heidelberg 2006

However, as the number of appliances and services grows, a user will face with the problem of *artificial dependency*. Here we mean the artificial dependency by a set of factors that the user has to comply with, in order to use the HNS services[1]. For example, to use a service the user has to be familiar with usage of the hand-held device (or the control panel). The user also has to learn how to operate services on the UI, which generally varies from appliance to appliance as well as service to service. Moreover, the UI must keep up with the new appliances and services deployed. The problem is that the artificial dependency would be accumulated exponentially in the number of appliances and services, without careful consideration. The artificial dependency always exists but can be reduced. Therefore, we consider it quite important for the future HNS to minimize the artificial dependency.

In this paper, we introduce user's *eye gaze* as a UI for HNS services, which aims to reduce the artificial dependency especially in the aspects of *ease of learning (adaptability)* and *system scalability*. Specifically, we develop a system called AXELLA (Adaptive and eXtensible Environment for Legacy and Leading Appliances), which exploits user's eye gaze for operating HNS services. We assume such scenarios that a user can use HNS services easily just by "looking" at some appliances.

We first point out the following four requirements, which are unique but essential for such an eye-gaze-based UI for a HNS: (a) appliance-wise eye tracking, (b) context-aware actions, (c) switching to service mode and (d) system response with non-visual medium. Based on these requirements, we then design and implement four sub-systems for AXELLA. Specifically, as for (a), we introduce an *eye gaze analyzer* with a face tracking system, which has been developed in our previous work. For (b), we propose a context-based *service processor*. To achieve (c), we exploit a small wireless device, called *trigger button*. For (d), we select a voice-based information presentation using a text-to-speech technology.

What most original and significant in AXELLA is that it interprets the gaze information as a context. Specifically, we use supplementary information including time, location and userID together with the gaze. Upon receiving the gaze context, AXELLA activates a service module associated by a service rule. Thus, a simple gazing activity can be used for triggering various service operations. Since the service rule is written in a simple IF-THEN format, the developer (or even home user) can create and customize context-aware HNS services easily.

As a practical example, we implement an appliance presence service called "See and Know" using AXELLA. When a user looks at an appliance, the system speaks its current status, taking the current context into consideration. Through qualitative discussion, we show that the proposed system can reduce the artificial dependency significantly with respect to ease-of-learning and system scalability.

---

[1] The original definition of artificial dependency was given in the context of service-oriented architecture (SOA) [17].

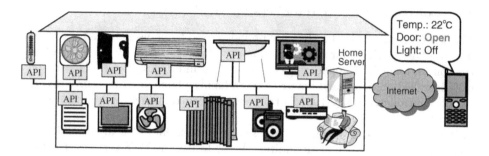

Fig. 1. Example of a home network system

2 Preliminaries

2.1 Home Network System

A home network system (HNS) consists of one or more *networked appliances* connected to a local area network at home. In general, every appliance has a set of *device control APIs*, by which users or external software agents can control the appliance via network. Figure 1 shows an example of a HNS, where various appliances are networked. In this example, a *home server* manages all the appliances in a centralized manner. It also plays a role as a residential gateway to the Internet. The communication among the appliances is performed with an underlying *HNS protocol*. Several HNS protocols are currently being standardized, such as DLNA [1], UPnP [15], ECHONET [2].

It is natural to regard each appliance in a HNS as a self-contained *distributed object* [18], since an appliance generally has an internal *state* and a set of *methods* affecting the state. For instance, let us consider a networked TV. A TV has a state consisting of *attributes* such as `power`, `channel` and `volume`. The current values of the attributes characterize the (current) state, e.g., [power=ON, channel=2, volume=15]. The device control APIs correspond to the methods. Typical methods (APIs) for the TV include `ON()`, `OFF()`, `selectChannel()`, `setVolume()`, `getState()`, etc. For convenience, we denote `A.m()` to represent an API invocation `m()` of an appliance `A` (e.g., `TV.setVolume(20)`, `Curtain.open()`, `DVD.getState()`).

2.2 HNS Services

A service for a HNS is basically implemented as a *software application* that executes the APIs with a pre-defined logic. For instance, invoking `getState()` API for every appliance implements an *appliance monitoring service*, The user can watch the current status of the appliances at any time and any place (see Figure 1). Another example is a *sleep service* that uses `OFF()` API for a set of registered appliances. The user can shut down all the appliances at once before leaving home or going to bed. The service applications are usually installed on the home server [6], which manages all the appliances in the HNS.

2.3   Conventional User Interfaces for HNS Services

The service application of a HNS are provided for a home user through a certain user interface (UI). As far as we know, most of the UIs currently available adopt the conventional GUI applications or Web-based interfaces. These UIs are typically installed on hand-held devices (e.g., a handy-phone, a PDA, a proprietary remote controller, etc.) [5][10][14] or proprietary control panels built in the house [3][8][13].

However, the conventional UIs impose a certain extent of the artificial dependency upon users, which is an additional cost to use the HNS services. First of all, a user is required to use the hand-held device or the control panel. Then, the user has to *learn* how to operate services on the UI. In general, such a UI varies from service to service. Therefore, when a new service becomes available, the user has to learn the operation for the new service. From the system point of view, the conventional UIs are not so adaptive (scalable) for *evolution* of a HNS. Basically the GUI is designed for known services and appliances, and not for future ones currently unknown.

As the number of services and appliances grows, the problem of the artificial dependency will become serious. Therefore, it is quite important for the future HNS to minimize the artificial dependency. This motivated us to investigate new UIs that can complement the conventional ones.

3   Exploiting Eye Gaze Information for HNS

3.1   Advantage and Drawback

To minimize the artificial dependency problem, our key idea is to introduce user's *eye gaze* as a UI for operating HNS services. More specifically, our goal is to achieve such an environment that a user can activate (or deactivate) a service, and can control or monitor appliances by just looking at the networked appliances.

The primary reason why we chose the eye gaze is that it is quite a simple and native activity for human beings. It is also known in the cognitive science that looking at an object reflects a human interest or attraction to the object [9]. Due to the above reasons, there has been much research work using the eye gaze for supporting UIs, although application to a HNS is few.

The major advantage in applying the eye gaze to the UI for HNS services is that it can reduce the artificial dependency drastically in the sense of *ease-of-learning*. This is due to the simple and intuitive nature of the eye gaze. Also, even if the number of appliances (or services) grows, the user can keep the same manner to operate with HNS services. That is, new appliances and services never affect the UI. Thus, the artificial dependency can be reduced with respect to *system scalability*. Thus, the problems caused by the conventional GUIs would be improved.

However, introduction of the eye gaze brings some new problems. Firstly, the HNS should be able to capture user's gaze with certain extent of accuracy. For this, we cannot force the user to use extra complex devices lest the user should feel physical and mental stress. Secondly, the activity "looking at an appliance" is so simple that it is difficult to make a variety of operations for the appliance solely with the gaze. Thirdly, it is necessary to identify whether the gaze at an appliance is for service operation or just for seeing the appliance. Finally, since user's eyes are occupied for the service operation, the user cannot *see* the system response simultaneously.

3.2 System Requirements

To cope with the drawbacks, we propose the following four requirements to be satisfied by the system with the eye-gaze-based UIs for operating HNS services.

Requirement R1 (appliance-wise eye tracking): The system must be able to track user's gaze on *every* appliance in a HNS. For this, no complex device should be worn by the user.

Requirement R2 (context-aware actions): The system must have a capability of mapping the gaze at the same appliance to different actions (operations). Preferably, the mapping should be performed based on the *context* derived from the gaze information.

Requirement R3 (switching to service mode): The system must have a means that a user can easily switch the system to a *service mode*, where the system accepts user's gaze as an operation to a HNS service or an appliance.

Requirement R4 (system response with non-visual medium): The system must notify a user of the response (or result) of a service operation via *non-visual medium*.

4 AXELLA — Proposed System

Based on the requirements in Section 3.2, we develop a system called AXELLA (Adaptive and eXtensible Environment for Legacy and Leading Appliances).

4.1 System Architecture

To satisfy the requirements, AXELLA is composed of the following four components (sub systems).

Eye gaze analyzer: To achieve Requirement R1, the eye gaze analyzer identifies which appliance the user is currently looking at, based on data polled from an external eye camera. Then, combining the appliance information with supplementary information (time, location, userID), the analyzer generates a *gaze context*.

Service processor: To satisfy Requirement R2, this system collects the eye gaze context polled from the eye gaze analyzer. Then, the service processor interprets the context, consults the user-defined service rules, and finally triggers an operation for the HNS appliances. The service processor also sends the response of the operation to the speech engine (See below).

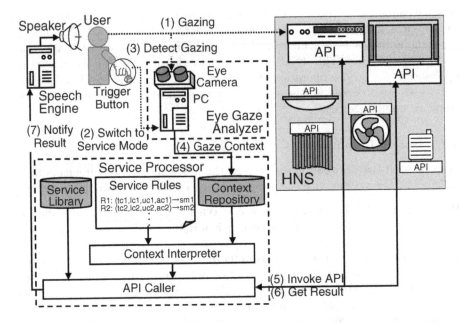

Fig. 2. Overall system architecture of AXELLA

Trigger button: This is a small wireless device for achieving Requirement R3, which is supposed to be carried by each user. When the user clicks the button, AXELLA switches to the service mode where it accepts user's eye gaze as an operation.

Speech engine: The speech engine reports the system response to the user via voice, which copes with Requirement R4. Using the text-to-speech technology, the engine dynamically synthesizes the voice from the text sent from the service processor.

Figure 2 shows overall system architecture of AXELLA. In the figure, a dotted arrow represents an interaction among a user and the system, whereas a solid arrow denotes the data flow among components. First, (1) a user gazes an appliance and (2) presses the trigger button to enter the service mode. Then, (3) the eye gaze analyzer detects the gaze and (4) sends the gaze information as a gaze context to the service processor. Upon receiving the gaze context, the service processor interprets it and chooses an appropriate service module based on a service rule. (5) The service processor invokes APIs as specified in the module, and (6) gets the results. Finally, (7) the result is sent to the speech engine to announce to the user.

For each of the four components, we give more detailed explanation in the following subsections.

Fig. 3. Screen shot of eye gaze analyzer

4.2   Eye Gaze Analyzer

The eye gaze analyzer captures user's eye gaze information. It identifies which appliance the user is currently looking at. To implement the analyzer, we employ the existing face-and-gaze measurement system [11]. The measurement system consists of a three-dimensional stereo camera and a PC. It captures user's face image, and performs an image processing to identify position of every facial organs. Then, the system calculates the direction and angle of eyes. Finally, the system identifies the object (i.e, appliance) by detecting the intersection of the eye direction and the object based on floor plan data prepared in advance. The system outputs the gaze information in a form of continuous bulk data. To cover a wider range of the gaze measurement, we assume to deploy multiple eye gaze analyzers in the HNS.

In this paper, we extend the measurement system so that it can capture a *context* from the gaze information. Here we define a *gaze context* as follows:

Definition (Gaze Context). Suppose that at the time t a user u in a location l keeps looking at an appliance a during a pre-defined period. Then, we define a quad-tuple $c = (t, l, u, a)$ as a *gaze context*.

A gaze context involves information on when, where and who in addition to the appliance, which is likely to reflect the user's intention and wish. Also, these attributes help the system interpret a simple eye gaze activity in different ways. For instance, a gaze context (7:30, bed, userA, curtain), where user A is looking at a curtain on the bed, could characterize a wish that user A wants to

```
openCurtain {
   status s = Curtain.getStatus(); /*Get the current status of curtain*/
   if (s == CLOSE) {                /*Open the curtain if closed*/
      Curtain.open();
      TTS.speech("The curtain is opened"); /*Announce the completion*/
   }
}
```

Fig. 4. Service module `openCurtain`

open a curtain. For another context (22:30, bed, userA, curtain), user A may want to close the curtain before sleeping.

The purpose of the pre-defined period in the definition is to distinguish a gaze from a *glance*. Our empirical study shows that around 1.5 seconds is its reasonable value. Figure 3 shows a screen shot of the eye gaze analyzer, where a user is currently looking at a curtain.

4.3   Service Processor

The service processor activates an appropriate HNS service upon receiving a gaze context, which plays a key role of AXELLA. It consists of five components as shown in Figure 2.

The *service library* is a collection of service modules which are reusable components to construct HNS services. More specifically, a service module is a program module that wraps invocations of appliance APIs with a certain control flow. Each service module corresponds to a self-contained action that a user performs against a HNS. Figure 4 shows an example of the service module, written in a C++-like pseudo code. This module invokes two curtain APIs to achieve user's action "open the curtain". The result is notified to the user with API of the speech engine (see Section 4.5).

A *service rule* specifies an association between a gaze context and a service module, in terms of a simple IF-THEN format.

Definition (Service Rule). A service rule r is defined as

$$r : \quad (tc, lc, uc, ac) \quad \rightarrow \quad sm$$

where tc, lc, uc, ac are *guard conditions* on time, location, user and appliance, respectively. These conditions are combined with AND semantics, which forms a *guard* over gaze contexts. A guard (tc, lc, uc, ac) is evaluated to be true or false for a given gaze context (t, l, u, a). sm is a corresponding *action*, which is given as a reference (name) to a service module. The service module sm is to be activated when the guard is satisfied.

Each of the guard conditions is supposed to be given in a logical formula. Considering that even home users can define their own service rules, our system currently supports a small set of constructs, including identifiers and operators * (don't care) and [from .. to] (range). For instance, the following `oc1` defines a service rule such that "from 6:00 to 11:00 if any user looks at curtain on the bed, then open the curtain (with `openCurtain` in Figure 4)".

```
oc1:    ([6:00 .. 11:00], bed, *, curtain) -> openCurtain
```

Corresponding to various operations using eye gaze, the service processor can have multiple service rules.

The *context repository* is a database that stores gaze contexts polled from the eye gaze analyzer. Upon a new gaze context c arrives, the *context interpreter* looks up the service rules to find a rule whose guard is satisfied by c [2]. If a service rule is found, the context interpreter passes the name of the corresponding service module to the *API caller*. Based on the name, the API caller loads a corresponding service module from the library, and executes it. The results of the API invocations can be redirected to the speech engine to notify the user via voice.

4.4   Trigger Button

The trigger button tells the system that a user initiates to execute the HNS services by the eye gaze. The button should be small and be capable of wireless communication. We assume that every user has a trigger button with a unique signature. AXELLA recognizes the signature as a user ID, and uses it in the gaze context.

Currently, we are using a small wireless mouse as the triggering button. When the user click the button, AXELLA enters to a service mode and waits for the eye gaze operation by the user. After a preset period (currently we set it 10 seconds), AXELLA automatically reverts to the normal mode in which user's eye gaze is not interpreted as an operation.

4.5   Speech Engine

As for the non-visual medium mentioned in Requirement R4, we choose voice announcement. When the service processor passes the API results in a text format, the speech engine synthesizes the voice from the text, and plays back to the user. For the task, the speech engine exhibits a speech API to the network. With the speech API, the speech engine can be used within HNS services in a similar fashion to the ordinary networked appliances.

According to a voice-based interaction guideline [4], the text-to-speech is suitable for system output, especially when (1) a user uses eyes for interactions, (2) the user frequently moves from one place to another, or (3) the user cannot easily access the PC monitor. Thus, our application reasonably fits the guideline. Compared with visual information, information delivered by voice tends to stay longer in human memory, but its information capacity is limited. Therefore, it should be careful not to send long sentences at a time to the speech engine.

[.] Our implementation returns only the *first match* found, even if there exist multiple rules matching c. This is to avoid the *feature interaction problem* [7], which is a functional conflict among multiple service modules.

5   Implementation

5.1   AXELLA

We have implemented AXELLA using the following components.

Eye Gaze Analyzer: Dell – Optiplex (Vine Linux3.2+gcc), Pointgrey Research
  – Frea x 2 (for the eye camera)
Service Processor: minipc.jp CF700 (Windows XP, JDK1.5.0_06)
Trigger Button: Logicool – V200 Bluetooth Mouse
Speech Engine: minipc.jp CF700 (Windows XP, JDK1.5.0_06, Apache Tom-
  cat5.5.12, Apache Axis1.3), PENTAX VoiceTEXT (for text-to-speech en-
  gine).

Then, we deployed AXELLA in an existing HNS developed in our previous
work [12]. The HNS is composed of legacy infrared-based appliances each of
which is networked with Web services. The networked appliances include a PDP
(Plasma Display Panel), a DVD/HDD recorder, two lights, an air cleaner, an
air circulator, a curtain, a door, a thermometer, an illuminometer, a sound-level
meter, and an airflow meter.

Figure 5 shows a picture and a floor plan of our experimental laboratory. As
seen in the floor plan, we deployed two sets of the eye gaze analyzer, in order
to capture the gaze contexts in different locations. The person in the bottom of
the picture is operating HNS services using his eye gaze.

5.2   See and Know: Appliance Presence Service

As a practical application of AXELLA, we have implemented an interesting
service, named *See and Know*. This service allows a user to acquire the current
state information (i.e., *presence*) of every appliance in a HNS, just by looking at
the appliance.

As seen in Section 2.1, a state of each appliance generally consists of multiple
attributes. However, it is not smart to present all the attributes every time,
since the status information a user wants may vary depending on the context.
For instance, suppose a situation that a user wants to check if a PDP is surely
switched off before leaving a room. Thus, nearby the door the user is interested
in only **power** attribute of the PDP. On the other hand, when looking at the
same PDP at a sofa, the user would be interested in **input** attribute to check
which contents the PDP is currently showing. In this case, the user does not
need the **power** attribute, since the power status is obvious at the sofa in front
of the PDP.

Our See and Know service achieves the *location-based* information filtering
by extensively using the gaze context of AXELLA. Figure 6 shows a list of
service rules implementing the See and Know service. In the figure, **notify_X_Y**
represents a service module that obtains the current state of appliance Y through
network, and then tells the status (current value) of attribute X via voice. In this
service, we assume the following use case scenarios.

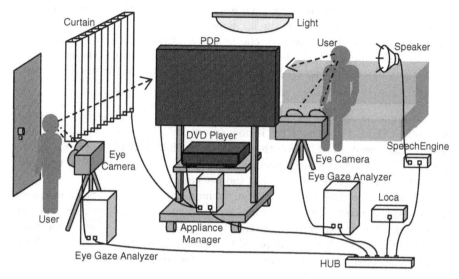

(a) Floor plan

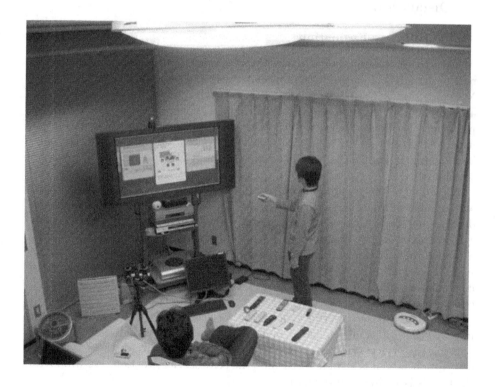

(b) Picture

Fig. 5. Our experimental laboratory for HNS and AXELLA

UC1: On the sofa in a living room, the user checks a working status specific to each appliance by looking at the appliance.

UC2: Near the exit door, the user checks power status for each appliance, to confirm that the appliance is surely turned off before leaving the room.

UC3: At any place, the user checks temperature upon looking at the thermometer.

In this implementation, when a user gazes at the PDP at the door and the PDP is off, AXELLA speaks "PDP is now power off". This is as specified in sk6 to achieve the use case UC2. Another example is that AXELLA speaks "DVD recorder still have 40GB of free space" when the user looks at the DVD recorder on the sofa. This is by sk2 involved in the use case UC1.

Through a simple usability evaluation, we have confirmed that See and Know service was quite intuitive, efficient, and easy to learn. In a cognitive sense, gazing an object and checking the object are tightly coupled with each other. Therefore, few artificial dependencies were imposed to the user. With the conventional UIs, the user would have taken more time and expertise to use the same service.

6   Discussion

6.1   Qualitative Evaluation

As seen in the example of See and Know service, AXELLA can significantly reduce the artificial dependency, especially with respect to the ease-of-learning. Note also that AXELLA is able to cope with the addition of new services and appliances quite easily, in the context of the UI. For this, the service developer just adds new lines of service rules, without re-engineering the UI. As for the user, even if new service rules are added, the operation is basically the same, i.e., looking at appliances. This fact shows that AXELLA achieves the system scalability.

According to the architecture of AXELLA (see Figure 2), a gaze context and a service module are originally independent. Therefore, the service developer can develop and deploy new service modules without assuming any link to user's gaze contexts. A gaze context and a service module are connected explicitly by a service rule. Thus, it is actually the service rules that implement a concrete AXELLA service. Due to its simple syntax, we believe that even home users can customize existing rules or define new rules. This fact implies that the users can create their own services easily.

Introducing more powerful logic in the service rules (e.g., a temporal order in guard conditions, dependency among service modules) would realize more sophisticated services. However, this increases the complexity of the service rule description, which is a trade-off against the easy service creation. We will investigate this issue in our future work.

A limitation in our current implementation is that gaze contexts can be captured only in the position where the eye camera is placed. This is due to the limitation of the eye camera of the eye gaze analyzer. To cover a wider range,

```
# See and Know Service Rules
# rule: (When, Where, Who, Appliance) -> service_module
# at sofa in living room...
sk1:  (*, sofa, *, PDP)          -> notify_input_PDP
sk2:  (*, sofa, *, DVD)          -> notify_remainingfreespace_DVD
sk3:  (*, sofa, *, LIGHT)        -> notify_brightness_LIGHT
sk4:  (*, sofa, *, AIRCLEANER)   -> notify_drivemode_AIRCLEANER
sk5:  (*, sofa, *, CIRCULATOR)   -> notify_flowlevel_CIRCULATOR
# at exit door...
sk6:  (*, door, *, PDP)          -> notify_power_PDP
sk7:  (*, door, *, DVD)          -> notify_power_DVD
sk8:  (*, door, *, LIGHT)        -> notify_power_LIGHT
sk9:  (*, door, *, AIRCLEANER)   -> notify_power_AIRCLEANER
sk10: (*, door, *, CIRCULATOR)   -> notify_power_CIRCULATOR
# for temperature
sk11: (*, *, *, THERMOMETER)     -> notify_temperature_THERMOMETER
```

Fig. 6. Service rules for See and Know service

we have to deploy many cameras in the room. However, we believe that this problem will likely be alleviated as the technology matures.

6.2   Comparison to Conventional UIs

We do *not* consider that AXELLA with the eye-gaze-based UI completely replaces the conventional UIs for a HNS. The point is that it is important to make an appropriate choice of AXELLA and/or the conventional GUIs, taking the *nature* of target services into account.

According to its eye-gaze-based UI, we consider that AXELLA is well suitable for implementing HNS services that have the following characteristics:

A1: Daily routines or operations frequently used (e.g., open/close curtains, switch on/off lights).
A2: Simple operations over multiple appliances (e.g., turn on and play TV and DVD together, group shutdown)
A3: Information presentation intuitively linked to gazing (e.g., See and Know).

On the other hand, due to the simple and intuitive nature of gazing, AXELLA is not good for dealing with the following kinds of services.

B1: Services that requires many parameter inputs and stateful operations (e.g., information search, HDD recorder setting).
B2: Operations not intuitively connected to concrete appliances (e.g., showing stock prices).

For these services, we consider it difficult to achieve solely with AXELLA. It should be complemented by the conventional or new other UIs. Further investigation on suitable applications of AXELLA is left for our future work.

6.3   Related Work

There have been a few existing research that uses the eye gaze to control appliances, although they are not for the purpose of HNS services. Takemura et al. proposed an application called *universal remote controller* [11]. In this application, the eye gaze is basically used to *select* an appliance that a user wants to control. Actual operations are issued by a user on a PC using a mouse or a keyboard. Since the user cannot see the PC monitor while gazing, the operations are limited to relatively simple ones. Also, it does not consider the gaze contexts or the link from a gaze to any service operation, as AXELLA does.

Vertegaal et al. developed a series of appliances called *media eyepliances* [16]. Each eyeplliance provides features strongly coupled with the gazing activity of human beings. For instance, an eyeplliance, called Attentive Television, plays the contents only while a user is looking at the TV. Otherwise TV pauses the contents. The approach is quite device-centric, and a relationship between a gaze and an action is fixed. This is quite different from our service-centric approach.

7   Conclusion

In this paper, we proposed a system AXELLA, which exploits user's eye gaze information extensively for services in the future home network systems (HNS). We first investigated system requirements for eye-gaze-based UIs for the HNS services. Then, based on the requirements, we designed and implemented four components: the eye gaze analyzer, the service processor, the trigger button, the speech engine. Introducing a notion of the gaze context, AXELLA allows service developers (or even home users) to create context-aware services with the eye gaze information. As a practical application, we have implemented a practical service – See and Know. Finally, we discussed and evaluated the proposed system to see its advantage and limitation.

Our future work is to analyze and enhance the expressive power of the service rule description. We also plan to clarify the service domain that makes the best use of AXELLA. Investigating human activities other than eye gaze for HNS services is also an interesting issue.

Acknowledgement

This research was partially supported by: the Ministry of Education, Science, Sports and Culture, Grant-in-Aid for Young Scientists (B) (No.18700062), Grant-in-Aid for 21st century COE Research (NAIST-IS — Ubiquitous Networked Media Computing), and Pache Research Subsidy I-A-2,2006 of Nanzan University.

References

1. Digital Living Network Alliance
   http://www.dlna.org/home/.
2. ECHONET Consortium
   http://www.echonet.gr.jp/english/.
3. Matsushita Electric Industrial Co., Ltd. kurashi-net:http://
   national.jp/appliance/product/kurashi-net/. (in Japanese)
4. Mayhew, D.J.:"Principles and Guidelines in Software User Interface Design," En-
   glewood Cliffs NJ: Prentice-Hall
5. NANO Media Inc., "App-rimo-con",
   http://www.nanomedia.jp/english/service/s02.html
6. OSGi Alliance
   http://www.osgi.org/.
7. Reiff-Marganiec, S., Ryan, M.D., editors., Proceedings of 8th International Conference on Feature Interactions in Telecommunications and Software Systems. IOS
   Press. 2005
8. Rich, C., Sidner, C., Lesh, N., Garland, A., Booth, S., Chimani, M.: "Diamond-
   Help: A New Interaction Design for Networked Home Appliances," Personal and
   Ubiquitous Computing, Springer-Verlagm ISSN: 1617-4909, Vol. 10, Issue 2, pp.
   187-190, January 2006.
9. Selker, T.:"Visual attentive interfaces," BT Technology Journal, Volume 22, No 4,
   pp.146-150, Oct. 2004.
10. SUGIYAMA ELECTRON Co., Ltd. Remocon Sauser:
    http://www.sugi-ele.co.jp/remoconsaucer.htm.
11. Takemura, K., Minamide, H., Matsumoto, Y., Ogasawara, T.: "What You Look at
    Is What You Control:A Universal Remote Control Based on Gaze Measurement
    Technology," 1st IEEE Technical Exhibition Based Conference on Robotics and
    Automation (TExCRA2004), 2004
12. Tanaka, A., Nakamura, M., Igaki, H., Matsumoto, K.: "Adapting Conventional
    Home Appliances to Home Network Systems Using Web Services," Technical Re-
    port of IEICE, IN, 2005. in Japanese
13. Toshiba Consumer Marketing Corp., "FEMINITY" :
    http://www3.toshiba.co.jp/feminity/feminity_eng/.
14. Toshiba Consumer Marketing Corp., "Life Remote Controller" :
    http://www3.toshiba.co.jp/feminity/feminity_eng/keitai/keitai_01.html.
15. UPnP Forum
    http://www.upnp.org/.
16. Vertegaal, R., Cheng, D., Sohn, C., Mamuji, A.: "Media EyePliances: Using Eye
    Tracking For Remote Control Focus Selection of Appliances," In Extended Ab-
    stract of ACM CHI 2005 Conference on Human Factors in Computing Systems.
    Portland, OR: ACM Press, 2005.
17. W3C "Web Services Glossary" :
    http://www.w3.org/TR/ws-gloss/.
18. W3C "Web Services Architecture" :
    http://www.w3.org/TR/ws-arch/.
19. ZOJIRUSHI CORPORATION "iPot" :
    http://www.mimamori.net/.

A Methodology for Assessing the Level of U-Transformation of Ubiquitous Services

Ohbyung Kwon and Jihoon Kim

School of International Management, Kyunghee University
Sochen-dong, Giheung-gu, Yongin-si, Gyeonggi-do, 446701, Korea
Tel.: +82-31-201-2306, Fax: +82-31-204-8113
{obkwon, hdlamb}@khu.ac.kr

Abstract. As the ubiquitous computing technology (uT) is prevailing, applying uT is more likely to transform the legacy way of providing services to a new service everywhere, every time, with any devices to gain more comparative advantages than the other typical services. This opportunity naturally requires a methodology to assess to what extent the legacy e-services are transformed to the uT-based services. However, research about assessing the level of u-Transformation has been still very few. Hence, this paper aims to propose a methodology for assessing the level of u-Transformation oriented by the teleology of ubiquitous services. A case study, GPS-based navigation services, is performed to show the feasibility of the methodology addressed in this paper.

1 Introduction

As envisioned by Mark Weiser(1991), one of the goals of ubiquitous computing is to provide various services by connecting multiple and embedded computing devices available around the physical environment. Another goal of ubiquitous computing is to integrate the real space with the virtual space, say cyberspace (Satoh I., 2003). To achieve the goals, assessing to what extent the systems or organizations embeds the ubiquitous features is very crucial as e-Transformation does. However, efforts to assess the degree of u-Transformation have been still very few. Moreover, even deciding what is 'ubiquitous' or not has been obscure. E-Transformation has been defined as 'the transforming processes that occur in all area of the organization such as the way of transaction, organizational structure, culture and processes by the electrification of the overall processes in the organization with introducing IT and network technology to the organization under the digital environment' (Haeckel, 1999; Deise et al., 2000; Hammer, 2001). Meanwhile, as the research about e-Transformation has been conducted at organizational level (Leem, C.S. et al., 2003; Cheung, W.K.-W., 2004), the main focus of u-Transformation should be reached at the same level ultimately. However, current usage of ubiquitous computing technologies and services is in its early stage and too pre-mature to observe u-Transformation at organizational level. In this paper, therefore, we will focus only on evaluating the level of u-Transformation at individual level: assessing to what extent an individual environment such as house, cars and pendants is transformed into ubiquitously.

H.Y. Youn, M. Kim, and H. Morikawa (Eds.): UCS 2006, LNCS 4239, pp. 28–40, 2006.

Hence, this paper aims to propose a methodology to assess the level of u-Transformation oriented by the teleology of ubiquitous service, which intends to fully make use of ubiquitous computing technology in doing new way of business.

In the remains of this paper, we review the related studies, propose an assessing methodology to identify level of u-Transformation, and show the feasibility of the methodology proposed in this paper with the example of the actually conducting Location Based Services.

2 Related Studies

2.1 Ubiquitous Computing Services

Ubiquitous computing technology has a rich potential to provide innovative computer-based information systems that enable personalized and agile services. Concepts and artifacts of ubiquitous computing leverage traditional computer-based information systems in several key areas. In particular, as information systems increase their intelligence, it will become more important for these systems to acquire knowledge and expertise in agile ways in order to provide service users with contextually relevant information. Ubiquitous computing technologies, therefore, that can be used to identify the user's current context and to recommend goods or services based on the context data, are well suited to current intelligent information systems.

Currently, researchers have proposed a variety of ubiquitous computing services. For example, in 2003, 23 services are selected from the literature and have classified them with two dimensions: technical viability and business viability (Lee and Kwon 2004). As shown in Fig. 1, the services located in the lower left area of the figure are anticipated to be appeared shortly.

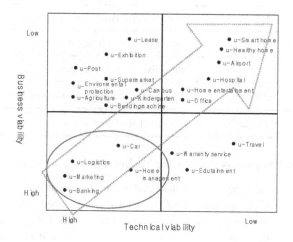

Fig. 1. Ubiquitous computing services

2.2 Location Based Ubiquitous Computing Services

Location-based services have been regarded as a promising application in the near future. Satoh categorized the LBS as the two types of approaches: 'computing devices move with the users' and 'tracking systems equipped to a space'. The categories with some example projects are listed in Table. 1.

Table 1. Categories and example projects of LBS

Approach	Research and Projects	Reference
Mobile devices	HP's Cooltown project	Chen, H. and Tolia, S. (2001)
	Stuttgart Univ.'s NEXUS	Hohl F. et al. (1999)
Embedded tracking systems	Cambridge Univ.'s Sentient Computing project	Harter A. et al. (1999)
	VNC System	Richardson T. et al. (1998)
	LocARE (CORBA-based middle ware)	Lopez de Ipina D. and Lo S. (2001)
	MS's EasyLiving project	Brumitt B.L. et al. (2000)

Even though the methodologies to assessing location-based services have been introduced, most of them are limited to evaluate the performance of the system performance itself mainly based on the technical perspective, not on the perspectives of how those location-based services are near to the basic goal and principles of ubiquitous computing technology. Only a few considerations have been conducted to evaluate how the products and services has evolved or transformed as shown in Table 2.

Table 2. LBS evaluation

Researchers	Evaluation Item
Maruyama et al. (2004)	Personal Tourism Navigation System
Burak and Sharon (2003)	Usage of Location Based System
Wu and Wu (2003)	Proactive Pushing Strategy
Rinner and Raubal (2004)	Location based Decision Support System
Pages-Zamora and Vidal (2002)	Position Estimate Accuracy

2.3 Evaluation of Ubiquitous Computing Technology and Services

Until now, there have been neither standardized nor generic criteria of evaluating the quality of ubiquitous computing services. Criteria suggested by most of the researchers also do not consider the generic issues but rather tend to focus on side issues about evaluating ubiquitous computing services solely based on their own research fields. Models and arguments for assessing ubiquitous computing systems and services are listed in Table 3.

Table 3. Evaluation of ubiquitous computing systems and services

Authors	Content
Riekki *et al.* (2004)	'Level of Calmness' of ubiquitous computing systems
Scholtz and Consolvo (2004)	attention, adoption, trust, conceptual models, interaction, invisibility, impact and side effects, appeal, application robustness
Mankoff *et al.* (2003)	evaluated ubiquitous computing focused on a specific field, such as sensing systems
Bellotti *et al.* (2002)	address, attention, action, alignment, accidence
Friedman *et al.* (2001)	human welfare, ownership and property, freedom from bias, privacy, universal usability, trust, autonomy, informed consent, accountability, identity, calmness, environmental sustainability
Spasojevic and Kindberg (2001)	interference, efficacy, design implications
Quintana (2001)	accessibility, use, efficiency, accuracy, progression, reflectiveness
Richter and Abowd (2001)	quantitative: user logs qualitative: questionnaires, interviews, observations
Burnett and Rainsford (2001)	ubiquity/pervasiveness, invisibility, connectedness, context-awareness
Basu (2001)	speed, quality, efficiency, resilience to mobility, application performance after embedding
Dey (2001)	configuration, inference, distractions/nuisance, graceful degradation, personal information, ubiquity, evolution

2.4 Level of u-Transformation

Level of u-Transformation is used to assess to what extent the legacy technologies and services are transformed to the ubiquitous ones. Since preparing the concrete methodology to evaluate the degree of u-Transformation in the companies or the organizations is in its very early stage, we will focus only on evaluating the services which adopt ubiquitous computing technology. And the level of u-Transformation gives us the state of the ubiquitous computing technology development to handle the speed of present development properly and to predict the priority and speed of development. For these reasons, the level of u-Transformation should be assessed. For example, verifying to what extent an object or service support natural interface, which is one of the primary goals of ubiquitous computing, could be a good guideline to estimate the level of u-Transformation. Hence, we evaluate the level of u-Transformation according to the two goal-oriented dimensions – level of capability and ubiquity as listed in Table 4. Based on the two assessments, level of u-Transformation (*LoUT*) is computed as (1):

$$LoUT = \begin{cases} 0, if \ LoC < \theta \\ \alpha LoC + (1-\alpha)LoU, if \ LoC \geq \theta \end{cases} \tag{1}$$

where $0 \leq \alpha \leq 1$, LoC, LoU and θ indicates level of capability, level of ubiquity and threshold whether the service is ubiquitous, respectively. Formula (1) shows that the purpose of this evaluation focuses on either LoC or LoU. α expresses to what extent LoC is more important than LoU in the assessment; if α increases, then the assessment is more focusing on how the legacy technologies and services are based on ubiquitous philosophy rather than focusing on estimating technical level, and vice versa.

Table 4. Two-layered ubiquitous service assessment

Layer	Assessment	Explanation
Infrastructure	Capability based	Assess the technical requirements that the infrastructure of the ubiquitous computing service should have.
Application	Ubiquity based	Assess to what extent the providing application of the service is ubiquitous.

3 Infrastructure Layer: Level of Capability

3.1 Finding IT Capabilities and UT Capabilities

We looked up the contents referred about capabilities of IT from all the articles published in the Communications of the ACM journal between 1994 and early half of 2004. As a result, we found 294 terms and summarized the frequency of each term. From this IT capability list revealed in the previous step, we asked the experts to choose the capabilities that related with ubiquitous computing service using focused group interview.

We made up the questionnaire for the experts in ubiquitous computing area to analyze to what extent these capabilities are important to ubiquitous computing services practically. We added the terms such as invisibility, re-configurability to the IT capability list. Even though those terms were not shown in the Communications of the ACM journal, those have been introduced continuously as developing ubiquitous computing issues. We chose 121 project managers and professors who were involving in the projects of developing the ubiquitous computing appliances or services and sent them the questionnaire through e-mail. After all, we received 35 responses (return ratio = 28.9%). According to the two surveys, capabilities which could be related to ubiquitous computing functionalities are obtained as shown in Fig. 2. We adopted the frequencies of chosen capabilities in the answers to find the weight of each capability.

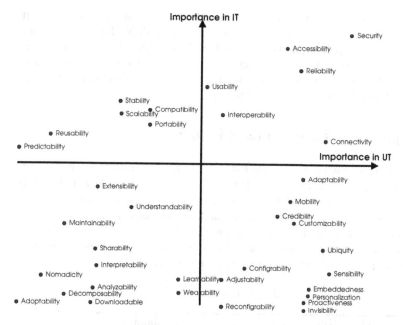

Fig. 2. Locus of capabilities

Assessment at infrastructure layer is mainly used to determine whether a service could be regarded as 'ubiquitous computing' service or not. This assessment is crucial because many 'so called' ubiquitous computing services appeared in the electronic markets may not be actually based on ubiquitous computing technology but just be mobile computing technology. Moreover, infrastructure layer model is useful to advise a ubiquitous computing service provider to find which capabilities or functionalities are omitted and hence need to be supplemented.

3.2 Evaluation Method

We conducted an assessment with the persons who are experts in the area of ubiquitous computing technology so that they understand what the capabilities appeared in the statistics derived in this layer means. Seven Likert scale is used for a certain IT-based service to identify to what extent the service can be regarded as ubiquitous computing service. The scale is represented as follows:

- Scale 1: The service definitely does not contain <a capability>.
- Scale 2: The service does not seem to contain <a capability>.
- Scale 3: It is hard to decide if the service contains <a capability>.
- Scale 4: The service a little bit contains <a capability>.
- Scale 5: The service seems to contain <a capability>.
- Scale 6: The service substantially contains <a capability>.
- Scale 7: The service definitely contains <a capability>.

For example, scale 7 for connectivity would be 'the service definitely contains connectivity.' Hence, the threshold value to decide if a specific service contains a certain capability is set to 3.0, equal or less than scale 3, in this paper. Using the scale and threshold value, the assessment procedure is as follows. First, give the point from 1 to 7 to each capability item shown in Fig. 2, and then get weighted average value, which is the final score at infrastructure layer. Second, by using a threshold (>= 3.0), which is the average of the total weight, each service is determined if the service is based on ubiquitous computing technology.

4 Application Layer: Level of Ubiquity

The weight for each criterion was same as using at application layer. The definitions of 'three keywords' are shown in Table 5. The items of three keywords are shown in Table 6. The service grounded the three keywords makes voluntary community of intelligent objects coexisting human and things, and is closely related to the realization of 'community computing', the optimal service offering by case through each member's role play. To get the weight of each item, the experts gave the weight of importance to each item and we averaged these weights.

Table 5. Definitions of three keywords

Three Keywords	Explanations
Situation Sensing /Decision	Resolves the problems based on sensing the context data and inferring the user's intention.
Autonomic Computing	Meets the goal through the autonomous cure and re-establishes commissioned authority from the user.
Self-growing Intelligence Engine	Learns the user's purposes or goals for the time being.

Table 6. Items related to evaluate the level of ubiquity

Items	
User preference	Fault tolerance
User profile	Negotiation
User context	Trust
Location tracking	Self-control
Time tracking	Authentication
Identity tracking	Authorization
Entity tracking	Usability
Context reusability	Ease of use
Inferred context	Seamlessness
Service coverage	Response time
Learning	Scalability
Reasoning	Durability
Autonomy	Standardization
Automation	

4.1 Evaluation Method

Using this evaluation method, the level of ubiquity measures as follows:

First, give points from 1 to 7 to each service item; then multiply the weight of an item to know the final score of each. Now add all final scores according to the keyword, and divide them to the sum of all weights of a keyword. With this score, get the evaluated score for each keyword: autonomy, self-growing, and community computing. For the last step, multiply the weight of a keyword to the keyword's evaluation, add all, and divide it to the sum of weights of each keyword. This is the final score of the service. The example of this evaluation appears on the next section.

5 Case Study

5.1 Service Selection

To measure the level of u-Transformation, five actual services were selected from location announcing services using GPS-based context to high value added navigation

Table 7. The selected services for evaluation

Category	Products and Services	Service Description
GPS	RoadMate Pro (http://www.road mate.co.kr)	- Backward Alarm Receiver - Road-danger Guide - Traffic Information Storage and Voice Guide - Place Register by User-Own
Navigation	ALMAP NAVI (http://www.alma p.co.kr)	- Navigation - Overspeed Area Warning and Traffic Information Guide by Voice - Driving Simulation - Track-log Management
	I-NAVI (http://www.inavi .co.kr)	- Accident-Frequent Area and Safety Speed Block Voice Guide - Buzz for Overspeed Alarm when Over Assigned Speed - Real-Time Route Voice Guide - Near Facility Search - Frequent Visit Place Setup - Route Secession Alarm and Route Re-Setup
	Nate Drive (http://drive.nate. com)	- Route Guide using Voice and Map - Watch-Camera Location Guide using Cell-phone Screen and Voice - Real-Time Traffic Information - Information Gathering about Facilities Around - Restaurant/Travel Place Recommendation
	Mozen (http://www.moz en.com)	- Burglary Alarm and Trace - Fast-Route Guide, Real-Time Traffic Information, Danger-Area Alarm - Car Remote Diagnosis, Parking Location Alarm - Restaurant/Travel Place Recommendation

services. According to the two categories, GPS and navigation, one of the services was chosen from GPS services, the remaining services from navigation services. The selected services for test are described in Table 7.

5.2 Evaluation Procedure

The domain experts are supposed to give the weight for location-based service to each item of ubiquity by observing each service. After the observation, the experts are asked to give the scores to each item of capability and ubiquity to evaluate those levels. Finally, interpret the scoring results of the assessments.

6 Results

The results of the level of capability are listed in Table 8: RoadMate is 2.9, Almap Navi is 3.54, I-Navi is 3.79, Nate Drive is 4.65, and Mozen is 5.43. Since the features such as 'Traffic Information Storage' and 'Place Register by User-Own' that RoadMate has indicate the lower level of sensibility, proactiveness, and learnability, RoadMate scores the lowest. On the other hand, since some of the features such as 'Car Remote Diagnosis' and 'Burglary Alarm and Trace' that Mozen has indicate the high level of 'Personalization' and 'Sensibility', Mozen stands on the highest place.

Table 8. Level of capability

Items	Weight	RM	AN	IN	ND	MO
Security	6.97	1	1	1	2	2.3
Connectivity	5.45	2.3	3	3	2.7	4
Sensibility	5.45	2.3	2.7	2.7	3	3.3
Ubiquity	5.15	1	1	1	1.7	2
Embeddedness	4.85	1	1.3	1.3	1.7	2.3
Personalization	4.85	1	1.3	2	2.3	4
Accessibility	4.55	2	2.3	2.3	3	3
Mobility	4.55	2.3	3.3	3.3	4.3	3.7
Reliability	4.24	2	2.3	2.3	2.3	3
Adaptability	3.94	2	1.7	2	2.7	3
	omitted					
Final Score		**2.9**	**3.54**	**3.79**	**4.65**	**5.43**

Meanwhile, the evaluation results in terms of the level of ubiquity are shown in Table 9: RoadMate is 1.54, Almap Navi is 2, I-Navi is 2.15, Nate Drive is 2.43, and Mozen is 3.16. The scores of the items such as 'Location Tracking', 'User Preference', and 'User Profile' showed the gap of the level of ubiquity between RoadMate and Mozen.

Table 9. Level of ubiquity

Weight of 3 Keywords			Items	Services				
S	A	G		RM	AN	IN	ND	MO
7.67	1.33	1	Location Tracking	1.67	3	3.67	3.67	3.67
7	2	1	Time Tracking	1	2	2	3	3
6.33	2.67	1	Identity Tracking	1	1	1	1	2
6.33	2.67	1	Entity Tracking	1.67	2.33	2.33	2.67	3
4	3	3	Inferred Context	1	2.33	2.67	2.33	3.33
4	4	2	Authentication	1	1	1	1	2
3	4	3	Authorization	1	1	1	1.67	2
3	5	2	Response Time	2.33	3	3	3.33	4
3.67	4.67	1.67	Scalability	2.33	2	2.33	2.67	3
3.33	4.67	2	Durability	3.67	2.33	2.33	2.67	3.33
2.33	4	3.67	User Preference	1	1.33	1.67	2	3.33
1.67	5	3.33	User Profile	1.67	2	2.67	3	3.67
2	3	5	Reasoning	1	2	1.33	2.67	3
2.67	4.67	2.67	Autonomy	1.67	2	2.67	2.33	2.67
1.33	7	1.67	Automation	1.67	2.67	2.67	3	3
2.67	2.67	4.67	Negotiation	1	1.33	1.33	2	2.67
2.67	3.67	3.67	Trust	1.33	1.67	2.33	3	4
1	5.33	3.67	Self-control	1.67	1.33	1.67	2	3
1.67	5.67	2.67	Fault Tolerance	1	1.33	1.33	1.67	2.33
1	2.67	6.33	Context Reusability	1	2.33	2	2	3.33
2.33	4.33	3.33	Service Coverage	4	4.33	4.33	4	5
2.33	3	4.67	Learning	1	1	1	1	2.33
2.33	4.67	3	Usability	1.33	2.67	3	2.67	3.67
3.23	3.9	2.87		1.57	2	2.14	2.41	3.1
Final Score				1.54	2.00	2.15	2.43	3.16

7 Level of u-Transformation (LoUT)

Based on the capability-based assessment (LoC) and ubiquity-based assessment (LoU) as stated in Section 6, level of u-Transformation (LoUT) is estimated as shown in Table 10 and Fig. 3.

Since the level of capability of RoadMate (2.90) is less than the threshold ($\theta >= 3.00$), RoadMate was not regarded as a kind of ubiquitous service and hence was excluded for further assessment. In case of $\alpha = 0.5$, as shown in Table 10, Almap Navi and I-Navi provide the lower level of ubiquitous service than Nate Drive and Mozen. Nate Drive runs on cell-based service and guarantees the higher level of mobility which is substantially required by the ubiquitous services. Since Mozen adopts intelligent services such as 'Restaurant/Travel Place Recommendation', 'Burglary Alarm and Trace' and 'Car Remote Diagnosis', higher level of security and ubiquity is doable.

Table 10. Level of u-Transformation ($\theta = 3.0$)

	LoC	LoU	LoUT ($\alpha = 0.5$)
RoadMate	2.90	1.54	n/a
Almap Navi	3.54	2.00	2.77
I-Navi	3.79	2.15	2.97
Nate Drive	4.65	2.43	3.54
Mozen	5.43	3.16	4.30

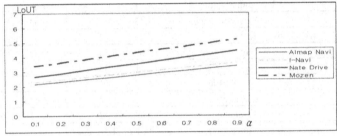

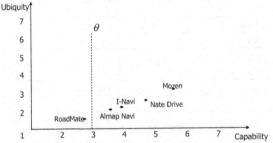

Fig. 3. Level of u-Transformation

The selected services are re-classified based on the assessment results. As the level of capability and ubiquity, 'simple-' or 'immediate-' is given. We also give the category based on the location sensors: 'GPS-', 'Navigation-', and 'Cell-'. The re-classification service results are shown in Table 11.

Table 11. LBS Service description

Category	Services	Kinds of Service
GPS	RoadMate	GPS-based Simple
Navigation	Almap Navi	Navigation-based Simple
	I-Navi	Navigation-based Simple
	Nate Drive	Cell-based Immediate
	Mozen	Navigation-based Immediate

8 Conclusion

In this paper, a methodology to assess the level of u-Transformation was proposed. A two-layered approach is considered: capability-based assessment at infrastructure layer and ubiquity-based assessment at application layer. One of the main contributions of this paper, to our knowledge, is that the need of assessing u-Transformation for developing the ubiquitous computing services is firstly suggested. Level of u-Transformation (LoUT) using the currently available services based assessment, not scenario-based assessment, is given. Even though the level of capability and ubiquity is the main factor to explain the degree of u-Transformation, further research must be conducted to explain more concretely why the two levels are representative. Moreover, enlarging the areas of evaluating services other than location-based services to justify the methodology would be necessary.

Acknowledgments

This research is supported by the ubiquitous Autonomic Computing and Network Project, the Ministry of Information and Communication (MIC) 21st Century Frontier R&D Program in Korea (2006-2008).

References

1. Bellotti, V., Back, M., Edwards, W. K., Grinter, R. E., Henderson, A., and Lopes, C.: Making Sense of Sensing Systems: Five Questions for Designers and Researchers. In: Conference of Human Factors in Computing Systems (2002) 415-422
2. Brumitt B.L., Meyers B., Krumm J., Kern A., Shafer S.: EasyLiving: Technologies for Intelligent Environments. In: International Symposium on Handheld and Ubiquitous Computing (2000) 12-27
3. Burak, A. and Sharon, T.: Analyzing Usage of Location Based Services. In: Conference on Human Factors in Computing Systems (2003) 970-971
4. Chen, H. and Tolia, S.: Steps Towards Creating a Context-Aware Software Agent System. HP Technical Report HPL-2001-231 (2001)
5. Cheung, W.K.-W.: e-Transformation Technologies: Case Studies and the Road Ahead - A Value Chain Perspective. In: e-Technology, e-Commerce and e-Service. EEE '04 (2004) 509-516
6. Deise, M.V., Nowikow, C., King, P. and Wright, A.: Executive's Guide to E-Business: From Tactics to Strategy, John Wiley & Sons (2000)
7. Friedman, B., Kahn Jr., P.H., and Borning, A.: Value Sensitive Design: Theory and Methods. In: Tech. Report 02-12-01, University of Washington, Dec. (2002)
8. Harter A., Hopper A., Steggeles P., Ward A., and Webster P.: The Anatomy of a Context-Aware Application. In: Conference on Mobile Computing and Networking (MOBICOM'99) (1999) 59-68
9. Haeckel, S.H.: Creating and Leading Sense-and Respond Organizations, Boston, Harvard Business School Press (1999)
10. Hammer, M.: The Agenda: What Every Business Must Do to Dominate the Decade, Crown Business (2001)

11. Hohl F., Kubach U., Leonhardi A., Rothermel K., and Schwehm M.: Next Century Challenges: Nexus - An Open Global Infrastructure for Spatial-Aware Applications. In: Conference on Mobile Computing and Networking (MOBICOM'99) (1999) 249-255

12. Kwon, O.B., Kim, J.H., Choi, K.H. and Kim, C.S.: A Multi-Layered Methodology for Assessing Level of Ubiquitous Computing Services. GESTS International Transactions on Computer Science and Engineering (2005) 134-142

13. Lee, H.G., Kim, K.K. and Kwon, O.B.: The 1st Annual Report on the Ubiquitous Computing Services, MOST, Korea (2004)

14. Leem, C.S., Suh, H.S., Kim, B.Y., Park, N.: A study on e-Transformation effectiveness analysis with cases in manufacturing and retail industries. Production planning & control, Vol. 14. No.8. (2003) 798-809

15. Lopez de Ipina D. and Lo S.: LocALE: a Location-Aware Lifecycle Environment for Ubiquitous Computing. In: 15th International Conference on Information Networking (ICOIN'01), IEEE Computer Society (2001) 419

16. Mankoff, J., Dey, A., Hsieh, G., Kientz, J., Lederer, S., and Ames, M.: Heuristic Evaluation of Ambient Displays. In: Conference of Human Factors in Computing Systems, ACM Press (2003) 169-176

17. Maruyama, A., Shibata, N., Murata, Y., Yasumoto, K., Ito, M.: A Personal Tourism Navigation System to Support Traveling Multiple Destinations with Time Restrictions. In: 18th International Conference on Advanced Information Networking and Applications, Vol. 2. (2004) 18-21

18. Pages-Zamora, A. and Vidal, J.: Evaluation of the Improvement in the Position Estimate Accuracy of UMTS Mobiles with Hybrid Positioning Techniques. In: 55th Vehicular Technology Conference, Vol. 4. (2002) 1631-1635

19. Richardson T., Stafford-Fraser Q., Wood K., Hopper A.: Virtual Network Computing. IEEE Internet Computing, Vol. 2. No. 1. (1998) 33-38

20. Riekki, J., Isomursu, P., and Isomursu, M.: Evaluating the Calmness of Ubiquitous Applications In: 5th International Conference of Production Focused Software Process Improvement (PROFES 2004) Kansai Science City, Japan, 5-8 April (2004)

21. Rinner, C. and Raubal M.: Personalized Multi-criteria Decision Strategies in Location-Based Decision Support. Journal of Geographical Information Science, Vol. 10. No. 2. (2004) 149-156

22. Satoh I.: Location-Based Services in Ubiquitous Computing Environments. In: ICSOC 2003, Lecture Notes in Computer Science, Vol. 2910. Springer-Verlag. (2003) 527-542

23. Scholtz, J. and Consolvo, S.: Toward a Framework for Evaluating Ubiquitous Computing Applications," Pervasive Computing, Vol. 3. No. 2. (2004) 82-89

24. Weiser M.: The Computer for the 21st Century. Scientific American, Vol. 265. (1991) 94-104

25. Wu, S. and Wu, K.T.: Dynamic Data Management for Location Based Services in Mobile Environments. In: Seventh International Database Engineering and Applications symposium (2003) 180-189

3D Space Handwriting Recognition
with Ligature Model

Dae Hwan Kim, Hyun Il Choi, and Jin Hyung Kim

Korea Advanced Institute of Science and Technology,
373-1 Guseong-dong, Yuseong-gu, Daejeon, Korea
{kimdh, hichoi, jkim}@ai.kaist.ac.kr

Abstract. 3D space handwriting is a gesture-like character written in the air, and it is a promising input method for its portability. In this work, we propose a practical development of 3D space handwriting recognition system by combining 2D handwriting and the ligature of 3D handwriting based on that the most different part between these handwritings is the shape of ligature. We designed a ligature model not to depend on each character shape but to depend only on incoming and outgoing vectors. Therefore with a few ligature models, various ligature shapes are modeled. By using 2D space handwriting models and data, we can use existing models for various writing styles, and overcome the problem of the lack of data.

Keywords: ligature model, 3D space handwriting, online handwriting recognition, Bayesian network.

1 Introduction

A hand gesture is often used to communicate with remotely located people. Since the gesture is intuitive and familiar with human being, it can be a good interface between human and computer. Previously, a hand gesture was tracked by cameras [1]. In this system, they used skin color to segment a hand from background. Therefore, when there are skin-colored objects such as furniture, or when the user wears gloves, the tracking system does not work properly.

Recently, with development of MEMS (micro-electromechanical systems) sensors, inertial sensor based hand tracking began [2] [3] [4] [5]. In this system, we need a sensor-equipped device in hand while we need nothing to hold in the camera based system. However, the sensor based system gives more detail information to the extent that complex shapes such as handwriting characters can be described properly. If a character recognition system is applied to this tracking system, a new interface - handwriting in the air - is made.

From now on, for convenience, we will call 3D space handwriting for handwriting in the air, and 2D space handwriting for existing handwriting inputs with pen and tablet. The advantages of 3D space handwriting are as following. First, compared to the 2D handwriting input system, users can write characters freely without the limitation that writing should be on a specific plane such as tablet. Second, the 3D

H.Y. Youn, M. Kim, and H. Morikawa (Eds.): UCS 2006, LNCS 4239, pp. 41–56, 2006.
© Springer-Verlag Berlin Heidelberg 2006

input device can be designed in small size since it needs only small inertial sensors. Third, it is a one-hand input interface.

There are already some inertial sensor based applications. A mobile game phone is developed, which uses the orientation of the phone as an additional input of the game [6]. A motion sensing phone is introduced, which recognizes gestures for digits, and simple commands of the phone [7].

If the 3D handwriting character input system can recognize not only digits, but also letters, such as alphabets, Hangul, and so on, it can take the place of the keyboard input system. For example, an Internet TV, which has many channels, searches the Internet, and finds movies, is a promising home appliance in the near future. The remote controller of the TV has to understand complex commands such as web addresses and movie titles. If we use buttons for inputs, the remote controller should have as many buttons as a keyboard has. However, if we use 3D handwriting input system, what we have to do is drawing commands with the controller. The size of the controller will be even smaller than that of a current TV controller. Likewise, 3D space handwriting can be a promising interface between human and computer for its portability and ability of understanding complex input, in the age of Ubiquitous computing. Figure 1 shows the examples of current 3D input device.

(a) Magic Wand [5]   (b) 3D Smart input Device [8]

Fig. 1. Examples of 3D input devices that track 3D hand movements. The devices are small and portable.

3D handwriting is, however, hard to recognize. First, the shapes of 3D handwriting have large variance since users have difficulty in getting visual feedback. Second, 3D handwriting characters have no distinction between pen-downs and pen-ups. A pen-down means a pen state when the pen is touched to the writing surface such as a paper, and draws some parts of the character, and a pen-up means a case when the pen is up and moving to another position to be written. The natural shape of 3D space handwriting is a connected stroke. You can see the shape differences between 2D space handwriting and 3D space handwriting in Figure 2. Third, currently there are only small amount of 3D handwriting data.

In order to recognize 3D space handwriting, Oh et al. and Cho et al. defined recognition target trajectory [4] [5]. The trajectory was, so called, graffiti which is in the form of uni-stroke, and has a similar shape to the character. By restricting the number of the shapes of target traces, the recognition problem was simplified. This policy, however, forces user to use only pre-defined shapes of characters, and moreover, when the user writes a multiple stroke character such as '4', the user have to learn a new uni-stroke shape which he/she has never seen.

Fig. 2. 2D space handwriting and 3D space handwriting. 3D space handwriting is drawn with one connected stroke.

In this paper, we propose a connected stroke character recognition system in order to recognize 3D space handwriting. We do not place a limitation on writing styles. We use character models in Bayesian network framework to recognize characters that have large variance. Bayesian network based character models dynamically predict the whole shapes of characters given various inputs [9]. In order to solve the problem from no distinction between pen-downs and pen-ups, we construct a 3D handwriting ligature model which describes the shapes of pen-up movements. For the problem of lack of data, we utilize existing 2D handwriting models and data.

The rest of this paper is organized as following. In chapter 2, we introduce character models in Bayesian network framework. In chapter 3, we describe a ligature model. In chapter 4, we describe the implementation of our system. In chapter 5, we evaluate the performance of our system. Finally in chapter 6, we conclude the work and discuss future work.

2   Character Models in Bayesian Network Framework

The Bayesian network based recognizer shows high recognition performance since it models character components and their relationships explicitly. In this framework, a character model is composed of stroke models with their relationships, and a stroke models is composed of point models with their relationships [9]. We focus on the stroke model since it is applied to the ligature model to be explained in the next chapter.

A stroke is assumed to be set of points, and the stroke model is represented by point distributions approximated by Gaussian distributions and their relationship which is represented in Bayesian network. Figure 3 (a) shows various stroke examples of a stroke and their end points are displayed with points. Figure 3 (b) shows the scatter plot of positions of end points, and Figure 3 (c) shows the Gaussian distributions approximating the scatter plot. The point distribution is displayed with one node as random variable in Bayesian network structure in Figure 3 (d).

The middle point of a stroke can be represented in the same way. The distribution of the middle point, however, depends on the positions of two end points. This dependency can be represented by an arc in Bayesian network structure as you see in Figure 4.

For representing dependency, it is impossible to find all distributions corresponding to possible values since the position of the point has continuous values. However by adopting conditional Gaussian distribution [10], we can settle this problem. Conditional Gaussian distribution assumes that the mean of the distribution is the linear combination of values of dependent variables and a constant, but covariance does not depend on other values. For example, the matching probability of the middle point in Figure 4 given that two end points are observed is as following.

Let O be the instance of IP, O_1 instance of EP_1, O_2 instance of EP_2, $\mathbf{W}$ be coefficient matrix

$$P(IP = O \mid EP_1 = O_1, EP_2 = O_2) \tag{1}$$

$$= (2\pi)^{-1} |\Sigma|^{-1/2} \exp\left[-\frac{1}{2}(O - \mu)^T \Sigma^{-1}(O - \mu)\right]$$

$$\mu = \mathbf{W}[x_1 \ y_1 \ldots x_n \ y_n \ 1]^T$$

As above, we can represent point distribution by finding coefficient matrix $\mathbf{W}$ and covariance matrix Σ.

A stroke model is defined as a joint distribution of point distributions. In Figure 4, matching probability of stroke is as follows.

$$P(S = s(O_1, O, O_2)) \tag{2}$$
$$= P(EP_1 = O_1, IP = O, EP_2 = O_2)$$
$$= P(EP_1 = O_1)P(EP_2 = O_2) \times$$
$$P(IP = O \mid EP_1 = O_1, EP_2 = O_2)$$

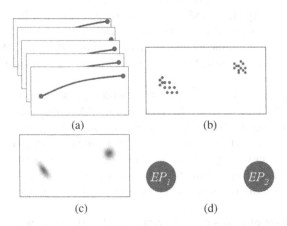

(a)   (b)

(c)   (d)

Fig. 3. Modeling of end points. (a) end point examples of strokes. (b) scatter plot of end points. (c) Gaussian distribution approximating end points distribution. (d) Bayesian network representation.

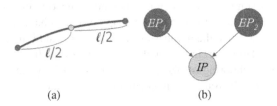

Fig. 4. Modeling of a middle point. (a) An example of a middle point. (b) Bayesian network representation of the middle point distribution.

3 Ligature Model

3.1 Need of Ligature Model

A ligature is a trajectory drawn in moving from the previous stroke to the next stroke, and it is the most different part between 2D space handwriting and 3D space handwriting. As we see in Figure 2, in 2D space handwriting, ligatures are usually drawn with pen-up, and therefore it is relatively easy to find the ligature parts from the entire trajectory of a character. Since the device cannot track the movement of the pen when the pen is up, a ligature is assumed to be a straight line connecting the end point of the previous stroke and the start point of the next stroke, and this kind of assumption ignores the detail shape of the ligature. On the other hand, in 3D space handwriting, it is not easy to find the ligature because there is no pen-up/pen-down concept. The shape of the ligature is cursive since the device gives full trajectory information including strokes and ligatures.

3D space handwriting trajectory except ligature part is similar to 2D space handwriting. Therefore by modeling the ligature of 3D space handwriting, we can efficiently adapt 2D space handwriting model to 3D space handwriting.

3.2 Characteristics of Ligature Model

The shape of a ligature has two characteristics.

First, the shape of a ligature does not depend on each character but depends on the incoming vector and the outgoing vector of the ligature. As you see in Figure 5, the ligature shape of the first consonant 'ㄷ' of Hangul – the Korean alphabet – is similar with that of the vowel 'ㅜ'. Although characters are different, only if the incoming vectors and the outgoing vectors of the ligatures are almost same, the ligature shapes are similar.

Second, as you see in Figure 6, a ligature is composed of two strokes which are nearly straight. We can assume that there is boundary which divides a ligature into two strokes, and the boundary is displayed in Figure 6 as one point. Let it called as a segmentation point. The shape of the first stroke of the ligature, that is, the stroke from the start point of ligature to the segmentation point, depends more on the incoming vector than the outgoing vector, and the shape of the second stroke depends more on the outgoing vector.

From this observation, we can model the ligature as the shape which is composed of two segments and which is affected by the shape of the previous stroke and the next stroke. In this assumption, the ligature does not depend upon a character shape itself. If the ligature is much affected by the shape of each character, the number of ligature models is bigger than the number of the characters, and it means that we need extremely much data. However, in this model, the shape of the ligature is dynamically determined by the neighboring strokes, so the number of ligature models is one. Therefore, the model can be trained with small amount of data.

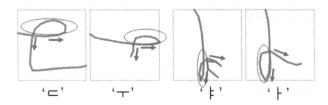

Fig. 5. Ligature shapes according to incoming vector and outgoing vector. The ligature shape is much dependent on the shape of input/outgoing vectors.

Fig 6. A ligature is composed of two nearly linear strokes. Segmentation point displayed as one big dot divides one stroke to two nearly linear segments.

3.3   Structure of Ligature Model

Based on characteristics of ligature shape, we form the Bayesian network structure of ligature as Figure 7 (a). Figure 7 (b) shows the points in a consonant 'ㅈ' that corresponds to the nodes in the structure. The proposed ligature model is composed of 9 point distributions, one incoming vector distribution, and one outgoing vector distribution. First stroke which is from the start point EP_1 to the segmentation point $SegP$, and second stroke from $SegP$ to EP_2, have symmetric structure. The distributions of the middle points in each stroke depend on their end points. The distributions of all middle points in first stroke and the segmentation point depend on starting point EP_1 and incoming vector $IVec$, and this represents the fact that the shape of first stroke depends on incoming vector. The distributions of the middle points in second stroke and the segmentation point depend on end point EP_2 and outgoing vector $OVec$, and this reflects that the shape of second stroke depends on outgoing vector.

The segmentation point is different from the middle point of a stroke in that segmentation point is not positioned in the middle of strokes, but positioned where it can divide ligature into two nearly straight strokes. The distribution of segmentation point is determined by two end points of ligature and incoming/outgoing vectors.

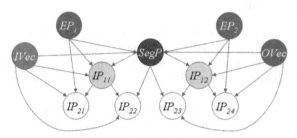

EP: end point
IP: middle point
IVec: incoming vector
OVec: outgoing vector

(a) Bayesian network representation

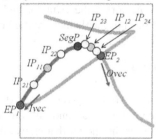

(b) Corresponding points in the consonant 'ㅈ'

Fig 7. Structure of a ligature model

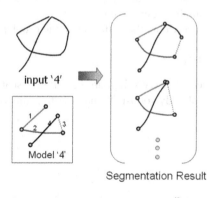

Fig. 8. Ligature extraction procedure

3.4 Ligature Extraction

Ligature extraction is a step where ligatures are extracted from an input trajectory, and this is a data collection step in ligature modeling. Ligature extraction is performed with algorithm, not with hand, by finding the part of trajectory that is most likely to be ligature by using Bayesian network based 2D space handwriting recognizer.

When a connected trajectory is inputted, the ligature extractor finds all possible segmentation results. The system segments input trajectory into N strokes. N is the number of strokes the 2D handwriting character model has. For each segmentation result, the ligature extractor finds the stroke that corresponds to ligature in the model, and makes the stroke straight. Making straight line ignores the detail shape of ligature and makes the input trajectory adapted to the 2D space handwriting model. The ligature extractor finds the segmentation result that has the maximum matching probability with the model. From the resulting trajectories, the extractor finds the linearized part, and the original shape of the part is the most probable ligature (See Figure 8).

4 System Implementation

Recognition step is as following. For a given handwriting input, evaluate all the matching probabilities between the input and all the character models that the recognizer has. Return the label of the model that shows the maximum probability as recognition result.

Therefore, in order to recognize a character, we need a corresponding character model. As the number of characters to recognize and the number of writing styles increase, the number of character models increases. We need many data to train the models, but we have only small amount of data.

In this chapter, we propose two methods that solve the problem of lack of data.

4.1 Combination of Models

3D space handwriting trajectory except ligature has similar shape to 2D handwriting trajectory. Since there are already robust 2D handwriting models for large variation

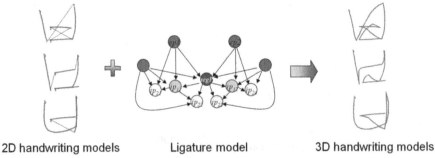

2D handwriting models   Ligature model   3D handwriting models

Fig. 9. Combination of models

and various writing styles, we can reduce the time and the efforts for constructing 3D space handwriting models by adding 3D space ligature models to existing 2D space handwriting models.

In Figure 9, we see that 2D models for various writing styles of first consonant 'ㅂ' in Hangul is combined with a ligature model to make 3D handwriting models. As you see, training data that we need to make various 3D models are only the 3D ligature data for the ligature model. However, there is one week point that the 3D model except ligature part only reflects the shapes of 2D handwriting.

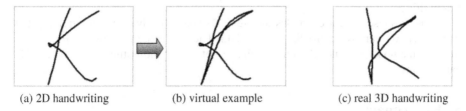

| (a) 2D handwriting | (b) virtual example | (c) real 3D handwriting |

Fig. 10. Virtual example and real 3D handwriting

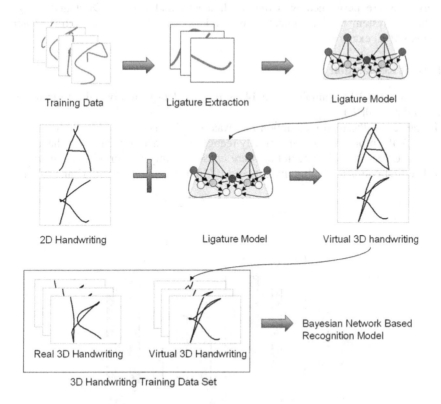

Fig. 11. Flow of the system using virtual examples

4.2 Use of Virtual Examples

Since the research on 2D space handwriting recognition has been done widely, we have much amount of 2D space handwriting data, and a large part of the data is available on the Internet. Since we know the 2D space handwriting and 3D space handwriting are quite similar, we can make enough data for training by making virtual 3D handwriting data from 2D handwriting.

It is possible to generate virtual 3D space handwriting by adding ligatures generated by the ligature model to existing 2D space handwriting examples. As you see in Figure 10, generated virtual 3D handwriting looks very similar to real 3D handwriting.

By using these virtual examples and real 3D space handwritings for training the recognizer, we can overcome the lack of data. The procedure is shown in Figure 11. In this method, 3D models reflect shapes of 3D handwriting as well as 2D handwriting.

5 Experiments

Experiments are performed with digits, alphabets, and Hangul. Digit and Hangul recognition system used combination of models, and alphabet recognition system used the virtual examples.

5.1 Digit Recognition

Digit data has 3,100 examples from 14 users. The data were divided into train data and test data with 2:1.

In the result, the total recognition rate was 95.4% (See Figure 12). As you see in Figure 13, the proposed system correctly recognize characters even if they have large variance. Errors in digit recognition were caused mainly two problems (See Figure 14). The first one is the ambiguity between '0' and '6', and between '1' and '9'. This

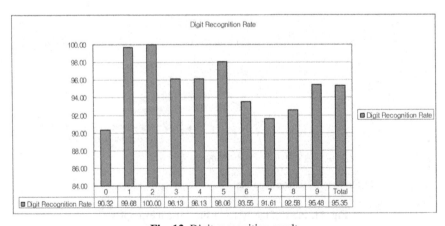

Fig. 12. Digit recognition result

Fig. 13. Examples of correct recognition. In each pair, left one shows an input trajectory and its label. Right one is the shape after ligatures are detected and removed.

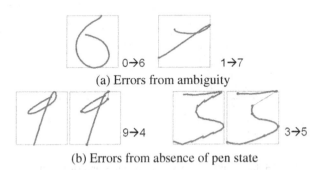

(a) Errors from ambiguity

(b) Errors from absence of pen state

Fig. 14. Examples of errors in digit recognition

kind of problem is basic, and often observed even in 2D handwriting recognition. This ambiguous trajectory is hard to recognize even with human eyes. Second one is the ambiguity from the absence of pen-up/pen-down. According to where the ligature is assigned, the recognition result can be different.

5.2 Alphabet Recognition

In Alphabet recognition, we used real 3D handwriting and virtual 3D handwriting for training the recognizer. The data were composed of 2,600 capital letters and 2,600 small letters. The half of the data was used in modeling the ligature, and the rest was used in test. Though Alphabet is composed of 26 capital letters, and 26 small letters, we used 46 handwriting models for capital letter and 42 models for small letters in order to recognize the handwriting with various styles.

As a result, the recognizer showed 97.8% recognition rate for capital letters, and 93.8% for small letters. By increasing the number of the recognition candidates, the recognition rate reached over 99% (See Figure 15). We see that this system can be also used in word recognition by adopting a language model or word set.

Figure 16 shows the examples correctly recognized. Although the input traces have large variance, the system can recognize them correctly. Most of the errors are caused by the ambiguity from the absence of pen state. In Figure 17, 'K' and 'R' have a same writing order, and their shapes are so similar that even human eyes cannot determine whether the trace is 'K' or 'R'. Small letter 'i' shows same trace as that of 'l'. This ambiguity cannot be dissolved by shape models, but by using the context or using writing speed, this kind of ambiguity can be reduced.

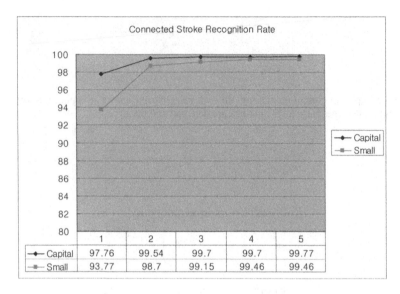

Fig. 15. Recognition rate of capital letters and small letters

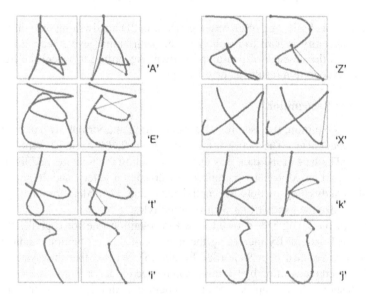

Fig. 16. Examples of correct recognition. The left one of each pair is an input trajectory, and the right one is the shape after ligatures are detected and removed.

5.3 Hangul Recognition

Since the number of Hangul characters is over ten thousand, making a handwriting model for each character needs many data to collect and many models to evaluate. Hangul is, however, composed of graphemes – first consonant, vowel, and last

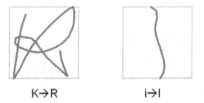

K→R   i→l

Fig. 17. Errors from the absence of the pen state

consonant – from its forming rule. By recognizing graphemes and by combining the recognition result, we can reduce the number of parameters of models. The state of the art of 2D space online Hangul recognizer adopts this grapheme recognizing policy [9] [11]. We implemented a Hangul character segmentator which segment a Hangul character into first consonant, a vowel, last consonant, and between-grapheme ligatures. We constructed a Bayesian network based model for each component using the model combination method explained in chapter 4.1 (See Figure 18).

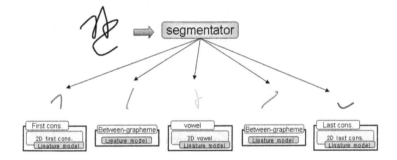

Fig. 18. Components of a Hangul character model

Hangul data has 3,600 examples from 9 users, and the data were divided into train data and test data with 2:1. Experiments are performed in two categories according to recognition targets. Recognition targets of first experiment were 900 best frequently used characters, and those of second experiment were 2,350 characters in 'Wansung-hyung' set.

Recognition rate was 78.6% and 64.0% for 900 characters and 2,350 characters respectively (See Figure 19). In Figure 20, we see that even for complex characters, the proposed system correctly finds grapheme boundaries and ligatures. Errors are mainly from two problems. First one is the error from segmentation. If character segmentator does not give correct grapheme boundary, Bayesian handwriting model cannot recognize it, and these errors are about a half of total errors. Second one is the error from ambiguity by absence of pen-up/pen-down. As you see in Figure 21, the first trajectory can be any one of the second trajectory or the third trajectory by assigning ligature. This kind of error will not be fixed by modeling since the trajectory is hard to recognize even with human eyes. In order to reduce this ambiguity, context information such as language model is required.

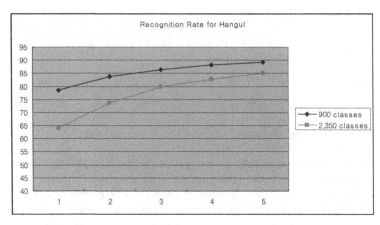

Fig. 19. 5 best recognition rate of Hangul recognition

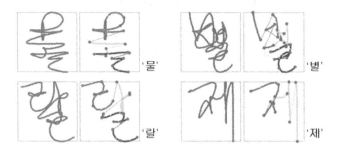

Fig. 20. Examples of correct recognition

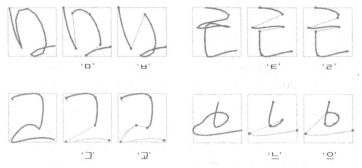

Fig. 21. Errors from absence of pen state. In each group, left most one is input trajectory. It can be either of middle and right most one.

6 Conclusion

3D space handwriting is a gesture-like character that a user writes in the air, and it is promising input method for its portability and ability of understanding complex and various inputs.

In this work, we proposed a 3D space handwriting recognition system by adapting 2D space handwriting models and data to 3D handwriting, based on that the most different part between 2D and 3D handwriting is the shape of ligature.

We designed ligature model not to depend on each character but to depend only on incoming and outgoing vectors. Therefore, with a few ligature models, various ligature shapes are modeled.

With the ligature model, we proposed two kinds of method of constructing 3D space handwriting character models. First one is combining 2D handwriting models and a 3D ligature model. It is useful when we have a robust 2D handwriting character recognizer. We can use existing models for various writing styles with only ligature modeling. Second one is using virtual 3D handwriting data in training. Virtual 3D data are generated by the ligature model and 2D handwriting data. This method is useful when we have much amount of 2D handwriting data. In either method, we can construct 3D handwriting character models with small amount of 3D data.

Recognition experiments are performed for digits, alphabets, and Hangul characters. The proposed system showed high recognition rates for digits, and alphabets. In Hangul recognition, many errors are from Hangul segmentation and various case of ambiguity. It is needed to use additional information such as writing speed and context information in order to solve ambiguity problem.

Acknowledgement

This research is partially supported by the Ubiquitous Computing and Network (UCN), one of the 21st century frontier R&D programs supported by the Ministry of Information and Communication (MIC) in Korea. The sub-project we participate in is "Agent Situation Awareness for Mobile Community Computing".

References

1. Hyeon-Kye Lee and Jun H. Kim, "An HMM-Based Threshold Model Approach for Gesture Recognition", IEEE Transactions on Pattern Analysis and Machine Intelligence, vol. 21, no. 10, October 1999
2. D. Reynaerts and H. Van Brussel, "Design of an Advanced Computer Writing Tool," Proc. of the 6th Int. Symposium on Micro Machine and Human Science, pp. 229-234, 1995
3. Won-Chul Bang, Wook Chang, Kyeon-Ho Kang, Eun-Seok Choi, Alexey Potanin and Dong-Yoon Kim, "Self-contained Spatial Input Device for Wearable Computers," Proc. of the 7th IEEE Int. Symposium on Wearable Computers, pp. 26-34, 2003
4. Jong K. Oh, Sung-jung Cho, Won-Chul Bang, Wook Chang, Euseok Choi, Jing Yang, Joonkee Cho, Dong Yoon Kim, "Inertial Sensor Based Recognition of 3-D Character Gesture with an Ensemble of Classifiers", Proceedings of the 9th international Workshop on Frontiers in Handwriting Recognition, 2004
5. Sung-jung Cho, Jong Koo Oh, Won-Chul Bang, Wook Chang, Eunseok Choi, Yang Jing, Joonkee Cho, Dong Yoon Kim, "Magic Wand: A Hand-Drawn Gesture Input Device in 3-D Space with Inertial Sensors", Proceedings of the 9th International Workshop on Frontiers in Handwriting Recognition (IWFHR-9), 2004
6. www.cyon.co.kr, "LG-SV360 / LG-KV3600", 2005

7. www.sec.co.kr, "SCH-S310", 2005
8. www.minfinity.co.kr, "3D Smart Input Device", 2005
9. Sung-Jung Cho and Jin H. Kim, "Bayesian Network Modeling of Strokes and Their Relationships for On-line Handwriting Recognition," Pattern Recognition, vol. 37, no.2, pp. 253-264, 2004
10. Kevin P. Murphy, "Inference and Learning in Hybrid Bayesian Networks", Report No. UCB/CSD-98-990, 1998
11. Bong-Kee Sin, Jin H. Kim, "Ligature Modeling for Online Cursive Script Recognition", IEEE Transactions on Pattern Analysis And Machine Intelligence, vol. 19, no. 6, pp.623-633, 1997

Scenario-Based Design of Ambient Intelligence

Veikko Ikonen, Marketta Niemelä, and Eija Kaasinen

VTT Ambient Intelligence
Sinitaival 6, P.O.Box 1206
FIN-33101 Tampere, Finland
veikko.ikonen@vtt.fi

Abstract. In this paper scenario-based design approach for development of Ambient Intelligence (AmI) is described. Design of any concept is based on communication between different stakeholders. Furthermore design of these concepts should be grounded heavily to the real user needs. Scenarios offer a flexible tool for these purposes and extremely well scenarios seems to be fitting to the early concept definition of AmI solutions. In this paper we describe our experiences of using scenario-based design approach in the MIMOSA project.

Introduction

The goal of MIMOSA project is to make Ambient Intelligence a reality. MIMOSA achieves this by developing a personal mobile-device centric open technology platform to Ambient Intelligence. Besides technological development MIMOSA stakeholders aim to ensure that the development of the MIMOSA core technology is based on the needs of the users, and that the resulting technologies will be easy-to-use, useful and acceptable from the end user's point of view, as well as applicable from the application developers' point of view. [7]

In the MIMOSA project, scenarios are stories or descriptions of usage of MIMOSA technology in the selected application areas. The scenarios also aim to describe the common vision of the MIMOSA project: first, what added value MIMOSA technologies provide to the end user and second, how the technology will look and feel. Furthermore, scenarios are used as a design instrument for the human-centred design process of MIMOSA technology and applications: the scenarios form the ground for user and application requirements. [7]

AmI becomes reality after a careful and a widely accepted definition of several open interfaces in hardware, software, protocols and user interface paradigms. These facts are recognised and fully taken into account in the MIMOSA vision of AmI. In this vision, personal mobile devices act as the principal gateway to ambient intelligence. Mobile devices provide trusted intelligent user interface and a wireless gateway to sensors, networks of sensors, local networks and the Internet. The technology platform for AmI consists of the present telecommunication technology platform augmented with the following new key building blocks: wireless sensors exploiting the RFID technology at several ISM bands, highly integrated readers/writers for RFID tags and sensors, low-power MEMS-based RF components

H.Y. Youn, M. Kim, and H. Morikawa (Eds.): UCS 2006, LNCS 4239, pp. 57–72, 2006.

and modules, low-power short-range radios, advanced integration technology, and novel MEMS sensors for context sensitivity and intuitive, user-friendly interfaces. [7]

Scenario-Based Design

Product development process has different phases where scenarios in general can be utilised in many ways. During the early phases of the design process scenarios can for instance consolidate different stakeholders' view of the project and the future. This scenario usage refers to future studies where scenarios are used for predicting the possible futures in various areas. Scenarios can further be used to build up a common vision or a starting point for the forthcoming activities and procedure in the system development project. In this way scenarios are applied as a tool to assemble a common picture of the project's goals and aims as well as possibilities and limitations of the work to be done. [4]

Scenario building is a way to generate design ideas for new products and to identify potential user groups and contexts of use for the product. The design team can generate one or more ideas (or system concepts) for the new system. The most feasible concepts can then be selected for further elaboration toward user and application requirements specification. The value of scenarios is that they make ideas more concrete and describe complicated and rich situations and behaviours in meaningful and accessible terms. [7]

As a design instrument scenarios are stories about people and their activities in a particular situations and environments (contexts). Scenarios can be textual, illustrated (for example picture books or comic strips), acted (for example dramatised usage

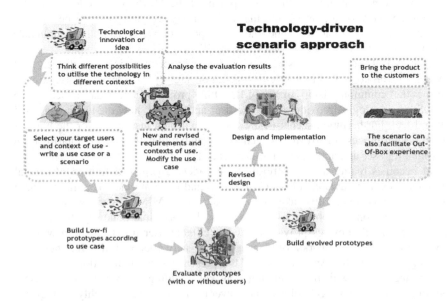

Fig. 1. Scenarios in product development cycle[4]

situation) or filmed (for example videos) descriptions of usage situations. The users in these descriptions are usually fictional representatives of users (personas) but might also be the real ones. [7]

Scenarios have been used actively in system design in past decades.[3, 6, 9, 10 12]. Besides using scenarios as a design tool for product development, scenario-based methods have often been used to enhance user involvement to design e.g. system, appliances or work. [1, 8, 11] Go and Carrol have distinguished four different areas that have had a rather different approach and purpose for using scenarios in design: strategic planning, human-computer interaction, requirements engineering, and object-oriented analysis/design [2]. In Mimosa we have tried to integrate these approaches for the design of AmI solutions. Our starting point is more technology driven than user driven but still our goal is to involve users strongly to the whole cycle of product development (Figure 1)[4]. In Mimosa the latest technology is to be developed for the applications that are co-designed and accepted by the potential users of these applications. In other words the user requirements and user driven approach are effecting in the very beginning of the technological development process.

MIMOSA Scenarios

The initial MIMOSA scenarios were produced with the contribution of all MIMOSA partners, both technology and application developers. First, preliminary scenarios were collected by e-mail. Second, the scenario ideas were analysed and refined and new scenarios created in a MIMOSA scenario workshop with partners. These scenarios were later analysed to identify usage and application requirements, which lead to some refinements in the scenarios. The resulted 35 scenarios are described in short in table 1.

Evaluation of the Scenarios

The initial scenarios were evaluated by potential user groups (focus groups) as well as the MIMOSA partners – altogether 32 focus groups involving some 96 people. VTT evaluated all the scenarios in Finland in summer 2004 with contributions of Suunto (Sports scenarios), Nokia (Fitness scenarios), Legrand (Housing scenarios and one Health care scenario in France), and Cardiplus (Health care scenarios in Spain). The partner evaluation took place in summer 2004 as well.

Focus Group Evaluation

The main evaluation method was focus groups, which refers to structured group interviews. The groups consisted of users of two kinds: first, potential end users of the to-be-developed AmI applications, and second, application field experts, such as doctors, nurses, professional athletes and trainers. In some groups (e.g. sports), we also had designers of current and future applications.

Table 1. Summary of the scenarios

Everyday scenarios	Description
Movie poster I	Jussi notices an interesting poster of a new movie at the bus stop. He points his phone at the poster and presses a button. The tag responds with an URL to a web page. The phone immediately launches a web browser and loads and displays the page. The page contains links to the movie's web page, to a local theatre and to a sample video clip.
Movie poster II	Johanna is at town and sees an interesting movie poster. Johanna points the soundtrack tag in the poster and downloads it to her phone. She sets the soundtrack as the ringing tone. After this she points another tag in the poster, which responds by sending an alarm of the movie's premier to her mobile phone's calendar. Later on, at the premier day, Johanna's mobile phone will remind her of the movie.
Where did I park?	Parking places are equipped with smart tags and mobile phone as a tag reader. User puts the phone next to car park's public UI appliance screen and drops the tag there. Now he knows where his car is - all he has to do is to follow the car park's signs.
At the bus stop	Intelligent bus stop and information access: mobile phone in "read tag" –mode and pointing bus number on the bus shelter's wall.
Product information	Picking up the tag information from the chair with the phone. User moves to her home computer where she transfers the tag information.
Comparing products	In the store all the vendible household machines are tagged. In order to compare the machines' features, one can download an application from the store's main hall. User downloads the application to his mobile phone and reads the tags from the machine labels with his phone
Conference lecture	In a large conference room, by the door there is a large sign indicating to switch the mobile phone to silent –mode. Thomas sets his phone silent by simply touching the sign and then confirming the action by clicking just one button on his phone.
Laundry service	A new kind of laundry service, which is based on the usage of tags. User has a tagged bag, which he has received from the laundry service company, and takes the bag to the laundry service's pick up box. He reads the tag of his laundry bag before throwing it into the box. Then he reads the tag of the laundry box as well, and makes an order with his mobile phone.
Kindergarten and clothes	Smart tags are inserted to children's clothes as name labels. Tag writer application is used to mark the names on the clothes.
With children at doctor's	"RFID desk" for downloading e.g. electronic short stories, magazines, newspapers, cartoons and short animations. Microprojector for watching films.
Match making	User has created a profile to his phone. Another user can read his profile (in tag) with her mobile phone.

Fitness scenarios	Description
Fitness centre	Fitness application, which is worked up together with the trainer and installed onto the mobile device. Monitoring physical condition and registering how the user has been practising. Based on this information, the Fitness application will advice the trainee in setting up the equipment, practising and also keeps count of the amount of practise.
Treating and preventing injuries	Specific training shirt with multiple embedded small sensors. The sensors measure the movements and the personal mobile device collects and analyses the measurement data. Micro projector to recall the correct movements.
Preventing sunburns	Mobile phone monitors the amount of UV radiation by getting measurement information from sensors.
Ville the weight watcher	New energy balance meter. User just has to install the inertial and pressure sensors onto his shoes and then his personal mobile device is all the time aware of what he has done and how much energy has been consumed. The other part of the system is about monitoring what the user eats and drinks.
Measuring the trainee	The smart plaster: measures lactate level and sends the information to the mobile and measures the levels of different micronutrients in her blood, e.g., iron, magnesium, chrome.
Motion altered tempo	The tempo of the music is time stretched according to her running speed. When she jogs slower, the music's tempo will slow down and if she jogs faster, the tempo will speed up. With the time stretched music the trainee can keep steady running speed and the stretching music makes also a nice effect – much more pleasant than the "click" sound.
Motion generated music	When Joakim skates, he exploits different kinds of sensors as his musical instruments. Heartbeat generates the tempo, temperature creates clear-voiced sound, step (or skate movement) creates the drums sound and arm movements generate some pre-selected vocals.
Exercise programs with acceleration sensors	Special training trousers and a T-shirt that include embedded motion sensors. Mobile phone based stretching application.

Health care scenarios	Description
Traveller's' health care on holiday – extended family going to ski resort	*Smart plaster in diabetes care*: The Smart Plaster analyses the glucose level of the blood sampled by the micro needles of the plaster. This information is sent via Bluetooth to the mobile phone (or possibly some other device). The mobile phone warns if the blood sugar level starts to be seriously offset. In addition, the information is sent to a server, which stores the data for later analysis. *Pharmacy services*: Prescriptions in mobile terminals, in pharmacy it is easy to find the right medicine because there are intelligent tags on medicine packages. User profiles. *Fidel's accident*: Medical record in mobile terminal, medical record transfer and translation. *Fidel's follow-up monitoring*: body temperature, blood pressure, ECG rhythm, body liquid and oxygen saturation (SPO2), smart plasters with necessary sensors, automatic measurements and data delivery.

Jorge – learning independent living	*Rehabilitation programme*: Jorge is paralytic and uses his mobile device to get guidance for his daily rehabilitation programme. He uses the micro projector of the device to get the display on the wall anywhere. *Remote monitoring*: Jorge has at home a system that monitors his condition. He has inertial sensors attached to his body for indicating how he is moving. Correlation with other contextual measurements for monitoring. *Home automation*: universal remote control with which he can give input to different applications e.g. just by pointing them. Using environmental measurements, the remote control can conclude Jorge's situational context and provide him with situationally relevant services.
Rosalita – stressed business lady	*Remote monitoring with smart plaster*: monitored by biosensors for some days while living her normal busy life *Self monitoring with smart plaster*: Results of health monitoring would in this case be available only to the user herself via her mobile device *Calming music or sound application*: new application for emotional computing where voices and music relax her via miniature loudspeaker whenever she is feeling depressed or stressed. *Pet (Jimmy) monitoring and care*: system (including miniature microphone, IMU and biosensors) to monitor Jimmy while sleeping, pharmacy experience with the help of RFIDs

Housing scenarios	*Description*
Housework and entertainment	RFID tagged clothes and the washer-dryer. Intelligent and automatic shopping-list: as empty RFID tagged packages have been thrown to the garbage equipped with RFID reader, they are added to the shopping list in the home computer. Automatic environment and intelligent door: video entry door system, lighting and shower adjustment according the user presence and profiles.
Safety and security	Monitoring Grandma's location in the apartment (RFID tags and sensor embedded in the apartment, mobile terminal as a reader) and intelligent damage detection system (e.g. fire or water leakage detection)
Universal terminal device	Microprojector for a quick look of forthcoming weather. Baby's intelligent diaper. Lost items functionality: pre-selected objects are equipped with RFID active tags. Mobile device as a baby alarm: miniature microphone on baby's crib and parent/nurse can hear the cry from his mobile device's miniature loudspeaker
Identifying the inhabitants or visitors	Intelligent housing system. For example the house system identifies the cleaning lady's mobile device and gives her access to predefined parts of the apartment along with access to predefined domestic appliances House system checks the status information of windows, doors, lights and so on according the information.

Sports Scenarios	Description
Golf	Marie is practising golf on a practice field. She has a golf rehearsal program with wristop computer and she has sensors in her shoes and inertial measurement unit, tags and sensors in her club. The wristop computer analyses and saves the data and sends feedback to Marie. Marie can share and read the data later on e.g. at home on PC.
Tennis	Jens has a rehearsal program for Tennis. The system is also used for collecting the actual game by overhead camera. The highlights of the game can be viewed later on using the projector in the mobile phone.
Running	Application for long-distance runners. Pierre is using running shoes with sensors, wireless earplug miniature loudspeaker in his ear, smart plaster on his arm and microphone-equipped shirt, smart plaster and wristop computer The system can measure heart rate, breathing and lactate level. After finishing his exercise, Pierre downloads speed data from his running shoes
Downhill skiing	Sensors in skiing boots, earplug loudspeaker, and inertial navigation unit in snowboard wireless connection between the accessories and mobile phone. Mobile phone reads the sensors via RFID tags and calculates balance, transmitting voice directions into the earplug loudspeaker of the skier. The location of the skiers can be estimated based on RFID tags sewed on their skiing coats.
High-risk sports	A parachute check up application. Mobile phone reads all RFID tags embedded into the straps of the parachute and checks that all the locks are closed by checking that the correct tags at the locks are touching each other.

Fig. 2. Focus group discussion

The scenarios to be evaluated were posted to the participants two weeks before the discussions. The participants were instructed to become acquainted with the scenarios before coming to the group discussion. In the actual evaluation (Figure 2), the participants discussed of each individual scenario in a freeform manner and also guided by some scenario-specific questions presented by the moderator. After showing all the scenarios, the group discussed all scenarios in general. The participants were asked to fill a questionnaire form consisting of six statements considering credibility, ethicality, pleasurability, usefulness, usability, and adoptability of the service described in scenarios.

Table 2. Assessment of individual scenarios (scale –50 to + 50; where 0 is undecided)

TOP SCENARIOS FOR PARTNERS

1.	At the bus stop	27.78
2.	Running	27.40
3.	Golf	23.70
4.	Where did I park?	23.52
5.	Safety and security	23.26
6.	Movie poster I	22.78
7.	Housework and entertainment	22.31
8.	Tennis	21.36
9.	Fitness centre	20.21
10.	Universal terminal device	19.00
11.	Going to the ski resort	18.33
12.	Movie poster II	17.77
13.	Identifying the inhabitants or visitors	17.54
14.	Kindergarten and clothes	17.41
15.	Jorge, learning independent living	16.88
16.	Treating and preventing injuries	16.81
17.	Measuring the trainee	15.97
18.	Follow-up monitoring	15.83
19.	Travelling diary	15.00
20.	At the ski resort	14.52
21.	Product information	14.20
22.	Laundry service	13.18
23.	Downhill skiing	12.95
24.	Preventing sunburns	11.20
25.	Some game scenarios	9.66
26.	Conference lecture	9.42
27.	With children at doctor's	8.85
28.	Comparing products	8.20
29.	Ville the weight watcher	6.52
30.	Exercise programs with acceleration sensors	6.25
31.	Rosalita, stressed business lady	4.60
32.	High risk sports	4.32
33.	Motion altered tempo	-0.65
34.	Motion generated music	-1.30
35.	Match making	-1.54

Partner Evaluation

The MIMOSA partners' scenario evaluation was conducted with an internet evaluation form. The form included both general ranking of the scenarios regarding how well they corresponded to the goals of MIMOSA project and detailed assessment of each individual scenario. The respondents were asked to rate how good or bad the scenarios are in illustrating the goals of the MIMOSA project. They were also asked to assess the time scale within which they thought that the described technological solutions could be implemented. The detailed scenario evaluation included six Likert-scale statements similar to the user evaluations. In addition, the respondents could write comments about the scenario to a free text field.

The most common comment from the partners was "why use this solution instead of existing solutions". Another common comment was "it will be expensive". The respondents pointed out that excess data transfer costs a lot and solutions with many tags would also be expensive. There were also doubts about the technical feasibility of the solutions. The respondents thought that some solutions could not be made reliable enough. Some scenarios presented simplified vision; actual implementations would require more versatile measurements than presented in the scenario. The respondents also commented that audio feedback only is not precise enough for instructions regarding sports performance. Quite many scenarios presented solutions that were stated to be "beyond MIMOSA technology". However, although MIMOSA is developing only some of the sensors presented in the scenarios, MIMOSA architecture should be open for other sensors as well.

The scenarios presented useful solutions to serious application fields. Some respondents were missing fun and enjoyment that also could be provided with the solutions.

Evaluation Results

The results of the evaluation indicate that health care is a promising application field. With suitable sensors, the users can be provided with systems that monitor their condition continuously, and report and alert with the user's personal mobile device. This is valuable especially for people with chronic diseases. Self-care systems are easy to deploy, as they do not require any special infrastructure. A self-care system can collect data that the patient takes to his/her doctor the next time (s)he visits the doctor. These systems will presumably indicate no needs to change current work routines of health care professionals. If the systems include continuous monitoring or on-call duty by health care professionals, it should be studied in details how these systems will fit to the work routines of the professionals and related organisations, as well as existing information and communication systems. The interviewees could point out several practical problems in using the smart plaster such as allergy, infections and moisture-impenetrability. Medical dosage via the plaster was assumed to introduce practical, judicial and ethical problems.

With housing systems the main challenge is co-operation with existing house information systems. Also, the users will probably not carry mobile phones with them at home, so the mobile phone centric system at home has to be based on the mobile phone connecting to the existing house network. An important function of the mobile device is to transfer information from the outside world to home and vice versa. [6]

With both fitness and sports applications, extreme ease of use is critical. The system setup before the exercise must be simple enough so that the user has time and motivation to do it. Context monitoring can be used to identify the need to start an application or to change the application mode. This is naturally valid regarding to other application fields as well. Monitoring sports performance by motion monitoring was expected to be quite complicated but useful in (professional) training and coaching.

Key requirement regarding the MIMOSA architecture is the need to use the same personal mobile device for several different purposes such as health monitoring, sports assistant and fitness control, both parallel and by turns. Also, the user should have the possibility to use different devices in turns for the same tasks and be able to synchronise them easily.

The tags and the readers should be visualised in a consistent way so that the user can notice and find them easily. The reading should take place easily, without any extra efforts.

User interface technologies such as the audio user interface, micro-projector and gesture-based user interfaces were felt useful in some applications but they did not raise many comments. They may have their most potential application field in everyday applications.

The users had doubts about the technical reliability of the proposed systems, for instance, about the suitability for outdoor use. Applications such as the access control to home presented in one of the scenarios would require extreme reliability. Also the reliability of the measurements made was doubted. The interviewees were unsure how much they could trust the recommendations the system offers on the basis of measurements. The user should be able to ensure somehow whether the system has all the necessary data to make conclusions and whether it is possible to analyse the situation by and large. The system in an assisting role (e.g., warning if something is wrong) instead in a controlling role (taking care of everything) is more acceptable to the users.

The system should respect personal privacy, and the user should be aware and able to control, who has access to the user's personal data. An interesting question is, whether a patient has the right to refuse of health-related measurements ordered by the doctor. Furthermore, it was pointed out that excess information may cause harm, such as too intensive observation of one's health condition may lead to hypochondriac symptoms.

The technology should not be used to substitute human contacts and care, especially in the case of children and elderly people. The users also worried about whether overly supportive technology makes disabled people passive and too dependent on technology. Excess automation was not only seen useless but also scary, if technology is making decisions for the user. At least the user should be allowed to override the rules set by the system.

From Scenarios to the Proof-of-Concepts

Five Proof-of-Concepts were selected and evaluated in the second phase: Physical Browsing by VTT, Housing by Legrand (evaluated by VTT), Fitness by Nokia (evaluated also by VTT), Sports Proof of concept by Suunto (evaluated by VTT) and Intelligent medicament Detection by Cardiplus. The first evaluations were carried in spring and summer 2005 as interviews and experiments with altogether 47 non-expert test users. In addition, six health and fitness experts were interviewed for the Fitness

Proof-of-Concept. Sports Proof-of-Concept was evaluated with eight golf-playing users in spring 2006. The scenarios were implemented to the proof of concept evaluations as a frame story.

Evaluation Results

The Physical Browsing interaction paradigm turned out to be intuitive to the users, easy to learn and use. Touching was found to be somewhat easier to use than pointing. However, the users were reluctant to make any extra effort – they don't want to take extra steps to move closer to the tag to touch it if the tag is not within arm's reach. Some objects, such as dome lamps are not reachable for touching. Therefore, pointing is an important complementary interaction method, in addition to touching (Figure 3).

Fig. 3. The Physical Browsing Proof-of-Concept

In the evaluations it became clear that in some situations touching a tag can directly trigger an action but in other situations user confirmation is needed. The need for confirmation depends both on user preferences and the task at hand. Touching was perceived to be more reliable than pointing in this regard. Confirmation may be related to the reading of the tag as in our evaluations but it can also be implemented within the application in question.

In the Housing Proof-of-Concept evaluation (Figure 4), the users accepted the idea of a control access system used by a mobile phone. Especially the idea of a temporary door-unlocking license in the mobile phone of occasional visitors such as a maintenance man was appreciated. The unlocking in general should be as effortless as possible. The users preferred automatic identification of the person approaching the door and automatic unlocking (and in some cases also opening). The security of the system (including practical issues such as a lost mobile phone) is important.

The Fitness Proof-of-Concept evaluation (Figure 5) showed that there is much potential in the domain of health and fitness measurements, and room for a MIMOSA type platform that can be flexibly used with different sensors and applications. However, the evaluations also revealed threats in implementing welfare applications, especially relating to easiness of interpretation and reliability of both measurement data and interpretation of it. Sometimes the analysis made by the computer is not felt trustworthy enough, but human professional interpretation is needed.

Fig. 4. The Housing Proof-of-Concept

Fig. 5. The Fitness Proof-of-Concept

Long-term measuring of health-related parameters was particularly promoted. This kind of data would support a person's medical diagnosis and rehabilitation in an effective way. In addition, the data would be useful for research purposes. Long-term monitoring cannot be based on the user carrying a mobile phone with him/her all the time. The users were reluctant to carry the phone even during short-term exercises such as jogging. Instead, solutions in which an easy-to-wear sensor unit collects measurements and transfers the collected data to the personal mobile phone whenever it is available should be considered.

Having fun and being a part of a social network are important for motivating the users for permanent changes in life. Getting started is especially difficult, and the users would appreciate solutions that could motivate the user by showing the small changes in the beginning. The feedback to the user should be as concrete as possible, such as butter packages for Weight Watchers, and given in time so that the user is able to make corrective actions.

The Intelligent Medicament Detection Proof-of-Concept (Figure 6) was found to be valuable for helping people in the medication issues. The Proof-of-Concept easily provides the user with different useful information of medicines in demand and even instructions, such as warning the user for a harmful medicine. The automatic call for medical guidance if the system detects a potentially harmful medicine was not accepted.

Privacy issues should be taken into account, especially in the health care domain. Personal clinical and medication history are perceived as private and sensitive information. Users should be able to control sharing of information as well as to protect information stored possibly in the mobile phone from viruses or other ways of misuse. Privacy considerations are essential also as tags get more common and are found not only at home but in public places, at work, in wearables and so on. The users may wear or carry objects with tags, which they do not want to be read from a distance. In public places, the user may not want to show to others where (s)he is pointing at, for example.

Fig. 6. The Intelligent Medicament Detection Proof-of-Concept

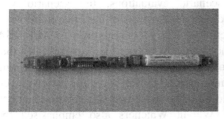

Fig. 7. The Mcard (on the left) and as partly placed into a shaft of a golf club

Sport proof-of-concept was a golf application for measuring and analysing golf swings (Figure 7). The application is based on the scenario "Golf with friends". We evaluated the proof-of-concept with eight golf-playing users to identify and understand user needs and preferences that relate to automatic, continuous, and wireless measurement of sports activity with a personal mobile device with the possibilities to store and analyse long-term data and share data with others.

The users found the golf proof-of-concept for measuring and analysing golf swing parameters useful. The system helps to see the reality of the performance, as one's own experience or feelings do not often correspond to it, and so helps to optimise performance. Automatic and uninterrupted measuring is appreciated, as users do not want to concentrate to the performance itself. In this evaluation, the users clearly preferred the activation of the application to be in the control of the user. This is partly due to the golf context. The system was seen most useful for practicing and for non-novices, in general, for those who practice a lot. People who are eager to make progress are willing to use different instruments and methods. They also want to be able to control and adjust the system themselves, for instance, by setting performance criteria by themselves. If measurements can be made in such an easy and effortless way as the golf proof-of-concept promises, the users don't see why measuring should be limited to a few parameters only. Receiving the measured data to a personal mobile device immediately, automatically, and wirelessly even during the actual performance was highly valued by the users. The solution also enables effortless social data sharing with people in the same situation for comparison or guidance, for instance. However, even if the users liked social data sharing, and did not keep their swing-related measurement data as private, they were rather doubtful about sending their data to a friend's mobile or vice versa.

Conclusions

The initial MIMOSA scenarios were updated, modified and selected for further development based on the scenario evaluations with potential end users and MIMOSA partners, as well as the evaluations of the MIMOSA Proof-of-Concepts. On the basis of the evaluations, it is evident that fitness, in addition to health-care, is a very potential domain for AmI applications. In particular, the fitness scenarios were designed to point out the call for a MIMOSA type platform that can be flexibly used with different sensors and applications. Although the users evaluated the weight watching scenario negatively in the scenario evaluations, the scenario was nevertheless selected for the next phase, because on the basis of the Fitness Proof-of-Concept evaluation, weight watching activity clearly benefits from a MIMOSA fitness application. The interviews with the Weight Watchers members revealed that those people who are in real need of losing weight are motivated for collecting weight-related data, such as energy consumption, food intake, and daily activity level. In addition, a game type application would motivate these people to exercise and so provide value beyond monitoring. The Weight Watchers also emphasised the importance of social support from peers. The social aspects in addition to fun features have been taken into account in the other scenario of Fitness game, in which physical activity of the player helps to success in the game.

Another promising AmI application field is health-care, which is also a difficult field because of the importance and sensitiveness of personal health information. Housing was seen as a problematic field for MIMOSA. Users feel that there is no need for excess technology at home, excluding home entertainment and household devices, which are outside MIMOSA's focus. In addition, people do not want to carry a mobile phone with them at home.

The next phase updated MIMOSA scenarios are based on initial MIMOSA scenarios that have been analysed and evaluated for credibility, acceptability and technical feasibility by potential end-users, field experts, and technology and application developers. Certain parts of the scenarios will be implemented as MIMOSA technology demonstrators. Other scenarios describe the MIMOSA vision of Ambient Intelligence in a complementary way.

The scenarios still emphasise the user control and the user's feeling of being in control of Ambient Intelligence. In most cases, the user actuates the interaction with the ambient intelligence. If the environment is the actuator, rather than acting automatically, the ambient intelligence applications provide the user with justified suggestions that the user can approve or refuse. Automatic actions are based on profiles and personalisation and the user has the control to easily activate and deactivate them.

The potential of the MIMOSA approach to Ambient Intelligence is three-fold. First is the mobile-centric user interface paradigm to interact with a tagged Ambient Intelligence environment, which requires somewhat light infrastructural and user-behavioral changes and enables the user be in control of Ambient Intelligence. The second potential is in applications monitoring, collecting and analysing personal data for different purposes, such as the MIMOSA health-care and fitness applications. Third, the MIMOSA approach to create a short-range personal network for communicating information between personal equipment such as golf club or jogging shoe and the terminal device open possibilities for advanced performance in different domains.

The scenario approach has suited well to the purposes of MIMOSA project. Scenarios were used in various ways in the phases of the design process. Scenarios offered a flexible communication and design tool for different stakeholders. Scenario-based design approach seems to be a suitable method for ubiquitous computing system design. As the design of these kinds of systems is very complex already in the early phase of concept definition, the scenarios can relief this complexity of intelligent environments in its entirety in a more common and understandable manner.

Acknowledgments

We wish to thank all our colleagues in the MIMOSA project that has contributed to this work. The scenario-based design approach has been further developed in the project Ecological Approach to Smart Environments (EASE).

References

1. 1.Bødker S. and Iversen, O.: Staging a Professional Participatory Design Practice-Moving PD beyond the Initial Fascination of User Involvement. *Proceedings of Second Nordic Conference on Human-Computer Interaction.* (2002) 11 – 18.
2. Go, K and Carroll J,M.: The Blind Men and The Elephant: Views of Scenario-Based System Design. *ACM Interactions.* Volume XI.6. (2004). 44-53.
3. Hertzum, M. Making use of scenarios: a field study of conceptual design. *International Journal of Human-Computer Studies.* 58.(2003). 215-239.
4. Ikonen, V. (2005) Scenarios in Ubiquitous Computing System Design: User-driven vs. Technology-driven Usag es. *in The 11th International Conference on Human-Computer Interaction* (HCII 2005), Lawrence Erlbaum Associates. (2005)
5. Ikonen, V., Sweet Intelligent Home - User Evaluations of Mimosa Housing Usage Scenarios. *Proceedings of 2ⁿᵈ IET International Conference on Intelligent Environments 2006.* Athens. Vol.2. (2006). 13-22.
6. Jarke, M.: Scenarios for Modelling. *Communications of the ACM.* January 1999/Vol.42, No.1. (1999).pp. 47-48.
7. Kaasinen, E., Rentto, K., Ikonen, V. and Välkkynen, P.: MIMOSA Initial Usage Scenarios. Retrieved July 14, 2006, from. http://www.mimosa-fp6.com/cgi bin/WebObjects/MIMOSA.woa/wa/default. (2004)
8. Löwgren, J.: Animated Use Sketches as Design Representations.*ACM Interactions.* Volume XI.6 22-27. (2004).
9. Rosson, M.B. and Carrol, J.M.: Usability Engineering. Scenario.Based Development of Human- Computer Interaction. Morgan Kaufman. (2002)
10. 10 Sotamaa, O. and Ikonen, V.: Picturing the Future Personal Navigation Products and Services by Means of Scenarios. *Mobile Data Management, 4th International Conference, MDM 2003.* (2003). Melbourne, Australia.
11. Strömberg, H., Pirttilä, V., and Ikonen, V. : Interactive scenarios -- building ubiquitous computing concepts in the spirit of participatory design. *Personal and Ubiquitous Computing.* Vol. 2004 No: 3 - 4, (2004). 200 – 207
12. Weidenhaupt, K., Pohl, K., Jarke, M., & Haumer, P.: Scenarios in system development: Current practice. *IEEE Software* 15(2), (1998). 34-45.

Ubiquitous Multimedia Access with a Multidimensional Information Browser

Seong Joon Yoo[1], Yoo-Joo Choi[2,3], Soo-Mi Choi[1],
Carsten Waldeck[4,5], and Dirk Balfanz[4]

[1] School of Computer Engineering, Sejong University, Seoul, Korea
{sjyoo, smchoi}@sejong.ac.kr
[2] Institute for Graphic Interfaces, Ewha-SK telecom building
11-1 Daehyun-Dong, Seodaemun-Ku, Seoul, Korea
choirina@ewhain.net
[3] Department of Computer Application Technology, Seoul University of Venture and
Information, Seoul, Korea
[4] ZGDV Computer Graphics Center, Dept. Mobile Information Visualization,
[5] Infoverse.org, Darmstadt, Germany
{carsten.waldeck, dirk.balfanz}@zgdv.de

Abstract. This paper suggests a framework for ubiquitous multimedia access
with multidimensional information browsing interfaces and service migration
technique. In order to achieve this goal, we propose a multi-dimensional liquid
browsing concept, which facilitate browsing of comparably large amounts of information on the various types of devices. Furthermore, the service migration
concept among the various types of devices is proposed and experimental results for the image information are shown.

1 Introduction

In the ubiquitous environment, heterogeneous multimedia resources and various types
of computing devices coexist. The integration of heterogeneous multimedia resources
is required to search the multimedia information in the distributed heterogeneous
environment. Moreover, it is necessary to effectively browse and arrange large
amounts of the retrieval results in various types of devices. This paper aims at the
design of the prototype framework for ubiquitous multimedia information retrieval
and visualization, which can search various types of multimedia data and effectively
arrange the retrieval data in distributed heterogeneous environments.

As related work, Roantree [1] describes a metadata management scheme for
federated multimedia systems. He adopted an object oriented common model for
integrating metadata and proposed a high-level query interface for the ODMG schema
repository. Most of recent research [2-6] proposes ontology based approaches for
multimedia information systems. Tsinaraki et al. [5,6] propose a framework which
allows transforming OWL ontology to MPEG-7 and TV-Anytime. However, they
have not showed an integrated metadata with which access MPEG-7 and TV-Anytime
metadata. Tsinaraki et al. transforms OWL to MPEG-7 and OWL to TV-Anytime

H.Y. Youn, M. Kim, and H. Morikawa (Eds.): UCS 2006, LNCS 4239, pp. 73–81, 2006.

respectively. The approach of transforming OWL to each metadata is not flexible enough to support non-standard metadata. Song and Yoo [7] proposed a universal metadata that will support non-standard multimedia metadata as well as the standard multimedia metadata. In this paper, we propose the multimedia resources integration framework based on this universal metadata.

We present the integration approach of heterogeneous multimedia resources based on the universal multimedia metadata in Section 2. Section 3 describes the multi-dimensional information browsing technology and Section 4 presents the liquid effect to overcome the drawback of previous browsing and service migration to support the seamless mobility among various types of computing devices. Section 5 shows the implementation results of our prototype system. We conclude the paper in Section 6.

2   Integration of Heterogeneous Multimedia Resources

An integrated multimedia information retrieval system shown in Fig. 1 has been developed for ubiquitous multimedia access. This system is developed in cooperation with the context broker development group and is aimed to be embedded into the multimedia context broker for ubiquitous multimedia access. The framework basically uses universal media access (UMA) metadata [7] that have been defined for ensuring compatibility with the current international metadata standards such as MPEG-7 Multimedia Description Scheme[8] and TV Anytime metadata[9].

The proposed integration framework is composed of three layers as shown in Fig. 1: application layer, mediation layer and resource layer. The web service APIs provided by the mediation layer and the resource layer are used for data transfer between layers.

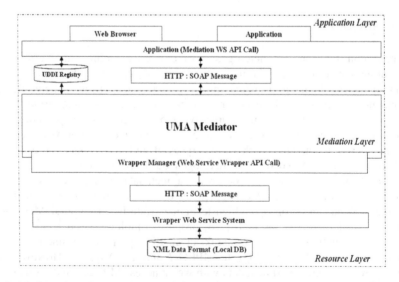

Fig. 1. Mediator based Architecture for Integrating Heterogeneous Multimedia Information Resources

2.1 Application Layer

The application layer transfers a query and receives the results. For example, a user can input a general query concerning to name, genre, ID, or keyword through an application query window in order to search movies that she or he wants to watch. The application layer calls the web service API provided by the mediation layer to transfer the query to the mediation layer in XML format using SOAP protocol. The web service API of the mediation layer is also called to get the results of the query from the mediation in XML format.

2.2 Mediation Layer

The mediation layer includes a core engine to integrate heterogeneous multimedia data in the ubiquitous environment. The query from the application layer can be defined based on various multimedia metadata such as MPEG-7 MDS or TV-AnyTime. In the mediation layer, the query is translated to various types of metadata queries by using the UMA metadata mapping table and broadcasted to resource servers in the local query form to be translated for each resource server. The results from resource layer of each resource server are integrated and transferred to the application layer. The mediation layer is composed of query processor, rule manager, and global schema manager as shown in Fig. 2.

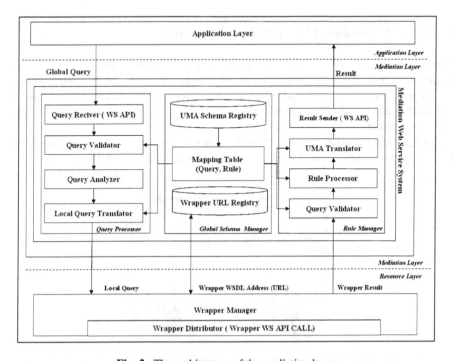

Fig. 2. The architecture of the mediation layer

The query processor receives the query from the application layer and validates the query. If the query is valid, the query processor analyzes the composed elements of the query and translates to the local query forms for MPEG-7 MDS or TV-AnyTime using the mapping table in the global schema manager. The global schema manager includes the core mapping table based on the UMA schema. The mapping table defines the matching relations among MPEG-7 MDS, TV-AnyTime and UMA. The global schema manger also managers the locations of the local resource DBs. The web service API of the mediation layer allows the wrapper of the resource layer to register the wrapper information of each resource server. The rule manager collects, validates and integrates the results of the query. Finally the integrated query results are transferred to the application layer.

2.3 Resource Layer

The resource layer is connected to a local DB through wrappers. Each resource server includes a local DB which stores the multimedia data to be represented in the form of MPEG-7 MDS or TV-AnyTime metadata et al. This layer retrieves relevant data from the local DB on which the XML-type metadata are saved. The resource layer is composed of a wrapper manager and multiple wrappers. The wrapper manager searches multimedia data by choosing and communicating with the proper wrapper among MPEG-7 wrapper, TV-AnyTime wrapper and UMA wrapper. Since the major functions are provided with web services APIs, users can build their own wrapper with ease.

3 Multi-dimensional Information Browsing

In the application layer, we apply the multi-dimensional information browsing technique in order to effectively and dynamically rearrange results of the query according to user's criteria. The multi-dimensional information browsing technique is especially suited to the small mobile devices which have spread fast in the ubiquitous environment.

A table view is very popular to browse information records, but the common table view on a mobile device such as PDA allows users to only look at 10-20 records at a

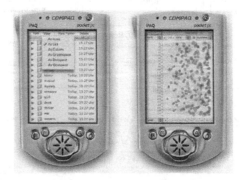

Fig. 3. Comparison of Table view(left) and multi-dimensional view (right). 15 vs. 250 information objects are displayed on table and multi-dimensional views respectively.

time without scrolling while allowing to sort and compare according to one single criterion. A multi-dimensional information browsing approach allows much larger amounts of information to be visualized and is simultaneously sortable based on two criteria. The proposed approach represents an information record by a bubble in an interactive 2D scatter plot space. Fig. 3 compares the table view and multi-dimensional view in sorted display of large amounts of information. In the multi-dimensional view approach, positions of information bubbles in an 2D scatter space are interactively changed according to user's selection to two axes criteria, i.e, x-axis and y-axis criteria.

4   Liquid Browsing and Service Migration

One disadvantage of a 2D scatter plot approach however, is the possibility of the information objects to overlap to some extent hindering readability and perceptibility of the information or, worst case, even making it impossible. To solve this problem, zoom and lens functions[10] have been implemented, which allow the (partial) enlargement of the information to counter this problem. Still, browsing high information densities in this way is a very challenging task, because a simple enlargement based fisheye lens does not reduce the overlapping and very often has to deal with heavy distortion issues.

To address this problem, we apply a distance manipulation based expansion lens[11]. The overlapping of information bubbles can be solved much more effectively

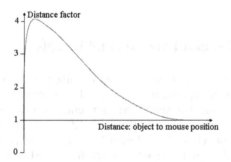

Fig. 4. Adaptive distance factor according to the distance to mouse position

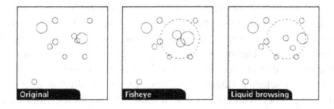

Fig. 5. Comparison of fisheye approach and liquid browsing. (Left) overlapping information bubbles, (Middle) the fisheye approach, (Right) the liquid browsing approach.

by no enlarging the information objects themselves, but rather the spaces between them. The space between information bubbles is decided by applying the Gaussian distance filter in the circle lens area which is defined by the current stylus pens or mouse position. The Gaussian distance filtering controls the distance factor of information bubbles according to the distance of objects from the current mouse position. That is, near distant objects from the mouse position move far to the boundary of a circle, while far distant objects move in the relatively less distance. The distance filtering shows oil- or liquid-like moving effect of information bubbles according to the interactive mouse movement. Fig. 4 shows the distance factor to be controlled by the distance between the information object and the mouse position. Fig. 5 shows the results of fisheye approach and liquid browsing approach to solve the overlapping of information bubbles. The overlapping bubbles can not be separated from each other even though bubbles are magnified by the enlargement lens in fisheye approach, while the distance based Gaussian lens makes the overlapping bubbles to be separated.

As various types of computing devices have widely spread, users want to immerse in a multi-platform environment with the possibility of interacting with an application while freely moving from one device to another. That is, when user moves from one device to another device in use of an application, he or she wants to resume the application from the stop point without any manual interface initialization. We call this function the service migration. The service usage history for each user is managed by the manager to support the service migration. That is, the service information such as the interface parameters and the current selected data is notified to the service manager whenever user changes the application status. Therefore, the service server can trace which kind of device is used by a user or from which point should the service be resumed.

5 Implementation and Experimental Results

The prototype framework for integration and visualization of the heterogeneous multimedia information was implemented using the Java platform for the device platform independence. That is, this framework was implemented using Java 2 Platform Standard Edition(J2SE) for the devices of Windows XP, Linux and MAC, and using Java 2 Platform Micro Edition(J2ME) for PocketPC devices such as PDA.

A user generates the initial query to collect the wanted multimedia data. The collected multimedia data are transferred to the proposed liquid browser in the XML format including the MPEG-7 MDS metadata and user-defined metadata. The multidimensional liquid browser analyzes the XML file that includes a lot of multimedia information. Each multimedia object to be read from the XML file, such as image or movie, is displayed as a bubble in the interactive 2D scatter space. Fig. 6 shows 250 or more image bubbles to be spread in the 2D scatter space that is defined by the title and the preference fields. The image bubbles can be interactively rearranged according as a user changes criteria for the X-axis, Y-axis, the bubble size and the bubble title. A user can also select a subset of bubbles by using filtering query. The Fig. 6 depicts the filtering query windows in which a user can input the filtering queries for the user defined metadata items. Users can access the multimedia objects that they want more easily and rapidly by rearranging them in two user-defined criteria.

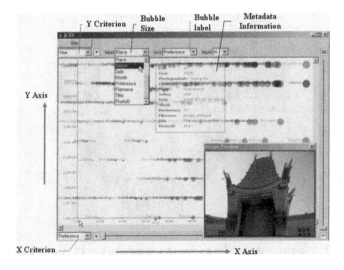

Fig. 6. The photo data bubbles to be displayed by the multi-dimensional liquid browser

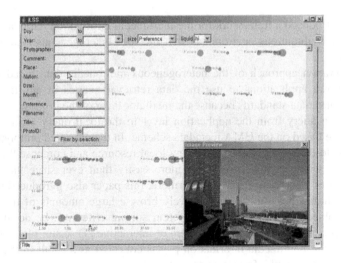

Fig. 7. Input window for the filtering query

The service server for the service migration was also implemented based on J2SE platform and the service migration was experimented among three different H/W platforms, i.e, laptop(1280 x 1024), PDA(640 x 480), and tablet PC(800 x 600). Fig. 8 shows results of the service and interface migration when a user moves from a laptop to PDA and tablet PC. Users can resume the multimedia data retrieval task without nuisance interface resetting affairs after moving to different computing device.

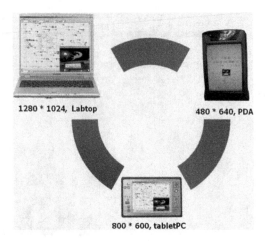

1280 * 1024, Labtop

480 * 640, PDA

800 * 600, tabletPC

Fig. 8. The results of the service migration among a laptop, PDA and tablet PC

6 Conclusions

This paper introduced a framework for the multimedia information retrieval and visualization in the ubiquitous environment that includes heterogeneous local databases and devices.

The integration approach of the heterogeneous multimedia data based on UMA metadata allows applications to use the data retrieval queries in any international multimedia metadata standards because the mediator layer of the proposed framework translates each query from the application layer to the local query forms using the mapping table based on the UMA metadata scheme. In the proposed prototype system, users can build their own wrappers for new local resource and compose the relationship between wrappers and a mediator more easily than ever since the prototype system provides web service API. Furthermore, this paper also introduced the multidimensional liquid browsing to interactively browse large amounts of the collected multimedia objects according to two different sorting criteria to be decided by the user, while solving the overlapping problem of interactive 2D scatter plots. Users can easily access the multimedia information that is collected as a result of the query by rearranging the retrieved information according to two user centric criteria.

Acknowledgements

We would like to thank So-Young Bu and Hyun-Joo Yun for giving useful help and comments. This work was supported in part by the grant no. 05A3-F3-10 from the National Center of Excellence in Ubiquitous Computing and Networking (CUCN). This research was also supported in part by the Seoul R&BD (Research and Business Development) program.

References

1. Roantree, M. : Metadata Management in Federated Multimedia Information Systems. Proceedings of the thirteenth Australasian Conference on Database Technologie, Vol. 5 (2002) 147-155.
2. Hunter, J. : Adding Multimedia to the Semantic web-Building an Mpeg-7 Ontology. International Semantic Web Working Symposium (SWWS) Stanford, (2001) 261-283
3. Chotmanee, A., Wuwongse, V., Anutariya, C. : A Schema Language for MPEG-7. LNCS Vol. 2555 (2002) 153-164
4. Troncy, R. : Integrating Structure and Semantics into Audio-visual Documents. In 2nd International Semantic web Conference (ISWC '03), LNCS Vol. 2870 (2003) 566-581
5. Tsinaraki, C., Polydoros, P., Christodoulakis, S. : Integration of OWL ontologies in MPEG-7 and TV-Anytime compliant Semantic Indexing. In the proceedings of the 3rd HDMS, Vol. 3084 (2004) 398-413
6. Tsinaraki, C., Polydoros, P., Christodoulakis, S. : Interoperability Support for ontology Based Video Retrieval Applicatons: LNCS Vol. 3115 (2004) 582-591
7. Song, C. W., Yoo, S. J. : UMA Metadata for Integrating Hetefogeneous Multimedia Resources. Asia Information Retrieval Symposium (AIRS), Oct. 13-15 (2005)
8. Martinez, J. M. : Overview of the MPEG-7 Standard(version 5.0), ISO/IECJTC1/SC29/ WG11 N4031, Singapore, March(2001): http://www.cselt.it/mpeg/standards/mpeg-7/ mpeg-7.htm
9. TV-Anytime Forum : http://www.tv-anytime.org/
10. Sarkar, M., Brown, M : Graphical Fisheye Views of Graphs. Proc. Of CHI 1992, ACM, New York:pp 317-324
11. Waldeck, C., Balfanz, D.: Mobile Liquid 2D Scatter Space (ML2DSS) : A Visual Interactive Information Space (ispace) for Displaying Large Amounts of Information and Allowing Simple Vision-based Knowledge Discovery on Small Screen Sizes. Proc. of Conference Information Visualization (IV) (2004) 494-498

OPF: A Distributed Context-Sensing Framework for Ubiquitous Computing Environments

Max Van Kleek[1], Kai Kunze[2],
Kurt Partridge[3], and James "Bo" Begole[3]

[.] MIT Computer Science and
Artificial Intelligence Laboratory (CSAIL),
32 Vassar St.
Cambridge, MA 02139
emax@csail.mit.edu

[.] Institute for Embedded Systems (IES) University Passau,
Innstrae 43
D-94032 Passau, Germany
kai.kunze@uni-passau.de

[.] Palo Alto Research Center,
3333 Coyote Hill Rd.
Palo Alto, CA 94304
{kurt.partridge, bo.begole}@parc.com

Abstract. This paper describes the *Obje Perception Framework* (*OPF*), a distributed software architecture for context sensing and inference in ubiquitous computing environments. *OPF* provides flexibility, scalability, and robustness even as the sensor configuration changes. For flexibility, *OPF* supports many context inference tasks, ways of achieving those tasks, and heterogeneity in sensor types. With respect to scalability, *OPF* accommodates the needs of a large number of applications simultaneously while conserving power and reducing the amount of data transmitted over the network. And to support robustness to dynamism, *OPF* constructs context inference pipelines to satisfy each applications' needs in a goal-directed fashion. The value of *OPF* is demonstrated by a case study of an end-user application that helps users establish and manage connections among the various digital resources in their environment.

1 Introduction

Throughout the past decade, a number of projects have demonstrated that sensed context about the user and his or her environment can greatly improve the user experience of many types of software applications [27,10,14,16,29,3]. The vision sought by ubiquitous computing [30] is attractive for the future of further context-enabling applications, as it provides a way by which this context might be captured. Yet, despite the proliferation of mobile digital devices and wireless communications technology, we are still far from having the computation, bandwidth, and sensing capabilities embedded at a sufficient density to

H.Y. Youn, M. Kim, and H. Morikawa (Eds.): UCS 2006, LNCS 4239, pp. 82–97, 2006.
© Springer-Verlag Berlin Heidelberg 2006

be able to sense all of a user's activities. To compensate for the lack of sensing resources, we feel that it is important to consider ways to 1) make efficient use of the relatively scarce resources of embedded processors, while leveraging more plentiful resources elsewhere in the environment 2) improve sensing capabilities by combining information from multiple sensors within the environment, and 3) reuse available sensor resources for as many different context inference problems posed by applications as possible.

In this paper, we present the *Obje Perception Framework*, or *OPF*, a software architecture that facilitates distributed context-sensing within ubiquitous computing environments. *OPF* is an extension to *Obje*, a middleware framework for device interoperability [19], and distinguishes itself from other context-sensing architectures in the following ways:

1. *Goal-directed construction of distributed inference pipeline* - Applications can request high-level contextual information, the framework automatically constructs an inference pipeline distributed across computational devices to meet its needs, out of available sensors and inference algorithms.
2. *Dynamic instantiation of components* - The framework dynamically instantiates components when they are necessary for an inference task, and releases components when they are no longer needed to conserve power.
3. *Opportunistic inference through service discovery* - At each stage of the pipeline, the framework uses service discovery to see if any existing sensors or algorithms can reused to help achieve the inference task.
4. *Programming sensors to filter at the source* - Pushing code for performing filtering, feature extraction and event detection to the sensors to allow high data-rate capture while reducing the amount of data sent over the network.
5. *Two-phase publish-subscribe* - Reducing data sent over the network by sending only short messages to subscribers and answering further queries.

As a motivating application of our framework, we consider the problem of helping users orchestrate interactions among the various digital resources in their environment. In Sect. 4 we present the Perceptual Orbital Browser, or *POB*, a context-aware application that dynamically arranges components in its user interface according to how likely it is that the user will need each particular resource. The *POB* relies on the *OPF* to supply sensed physical proximity readings among the devices in the user's environment to infer which resources to prioritize.

The paper is laid out as follows: Sect. 2 describes previous systems related to the work in this paper. Section 3 describes the design of *OPF* in detail. Section 4 presents the *POB*, including implementation of acoustic proximity sensing in the *OPF*. Section 5 concludes the paper with a discussion of limitations, alternative designs, and future work.

2   Background and Related Work

Obje, (a derivative of Speakeasy [19]) simplifies the management of inter-device communication by bridging the various platforms, operating systems, and applications that comprise the ubiquitous computing environment. Similar to other Distributed Mobile System (DMS) frameworks such as [6,24,21], it allows the creation of applications that integrate the capabilities of resources offered on heterogeneous devices available within an environment [9]. Like a number of other systems such as DWARF [2], *Obje* employs a point-to-point distributed dataflow metaphor for inter-device communications, resolving data format inconsistencies through the use of transcoding and mobile code.

However, like other DMS frameworks, *Obje* does not incorporate support for context-sensing. Other frameworks dedicated to sensing and context inference [26,1] contain signal processing and inference algorithms designed to transform continuous streams of sensor information into semantic models that generate discrete events that are handled by the application. However, these frameworks typically have limited support for interoperability, mobility, or distributed processing, which are essential capabilities for components of ubicomp environments. The *OPF* thus seeks to bridge DMSes and context sensing toolkits, by demonstrating how middleware frameworks can be extended to support distributed context-sensing.

3   The *Obje Perception Framework*: Architectural Support for Context-Awareness

As articulated initially by Schilit [27] and further formalized by Dey, et al. [26], providing common architectural support for context sensing and interpretation eases the burden on application writers for context-enabling applications. In ubiquitous computing settings, architectural support becomes a necessity, as the context-aware application and the sources of the contextual information become increasingly dissociated.

With the Context Toolkit, Dey, et al. propose a context sensing architecture based on a hybrid widget/network-service model. Sources of context such as sensors are logically mapped to *context widgets* which are made queryable and subscribable by applications over the network. To map low-level context from widgets to a form that is more suitable for applications, Dey et al. introduced the notion of *interpreters* and *aggregators* for abstracting events from widgets to higher-level, more convenient representations for applications, respectively.

OPF builds on the basic ideas proposed in the Context Toolkit, but is more optimized for sensor networks. *OPF* handles situations in which network and power resources are scarce compared to computational and memory resources—this coincides with observations that even as advances in processing speed and memory capacity have followed exponential growth, battery life has followed only linear growth. Reducing the amount of data transmitted over the network can dramatically help conserve energy, as data transmission often accounts for a significant fraction of the total power consumed by wireless devices [11].

The following sections describe *OPF* in greater detail, starting from how high-level requests for context are resolved from the available low-level sources of context. Then, we describe in detail how *OPF* reduces the amount of data that

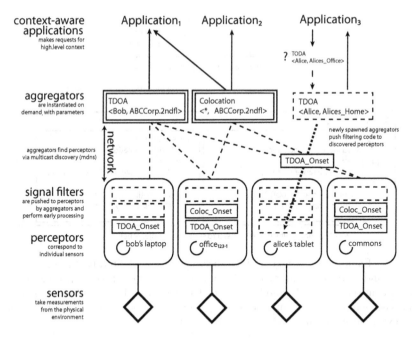

Fig. 1. Illustration of typical instantiation of *OPF* architecture. Applications request a context-inference task from *OPF*. *OPF* determines (via multicast discovery) whether an aggregator already exists that can fulfill the application's needs. If not, it instantiates an aggregator from its library with appropriate parameters. The aggregator contacts its appropriate perceptors and, if necessary, uploads signal processing code to the perceptors.

needs to be transmitted over the network—perceptual filtering at the source of context, and two-phase publish and subscribe. Finally, we provide a summary comparing *OPF* to similar context sensing architectures.

3.1 *OPF* Concept and Architecture

Figure 1 illustrates the high-level architecture of *OPF*. *OPF* comprises two types of resources: *perceptors* and *aggregators*. Perceptors in *OPF* are most similar to *widgets* in the Context Toolkit; they embody low-level contextual information sources tied to sensors in the environment. Aggregators serve the role of the Context Toolkit's *combiners* and *interpreters*, and can contain signal processing and inference algorithms that transform data from one or more lower-level sources of context into a fused, filtered, or higher-level representation.

3.2 Goal-Directed Context Pipeline Generation

Context inference tasks in *OPF* are initiated by the end-user application, which makes a request to the framework for a specific type of context using a tuple that contains *context identifiers*. These identifiers describe the types of context needed

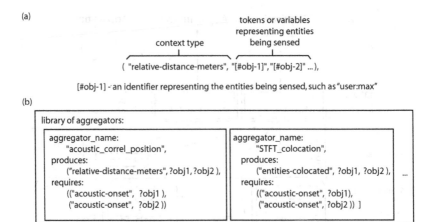

(a)

tokens or variables
representing entities
context type   being sensed

("relative-distance-meters", "[#obj-1]", "[#obj-2]" ...),

[#obj-1] - an identifier representing the entities being sensed, such as "user:max"

(b)

library of aggregators:

aggregator_name:	aggregator_name:
"acoustic_correl_position",	"STFT_colocation",
produces:	produces:
("relative-distance-meters", ?obj1, ?obj2),	("entities-colocated", ?obj1, ?obj2),
requires:	requires:
(("acoustic-onset", ?obj1),	(("acoustic-onset", ?obj1),
("acoustic-onset", ?obj2))	("acoustic-onset", ?obj2))]

?obj1 - variable which may be used to stand in for objects being sensed

Fig. 2. (a) Example of a context identifier, consisting of literals comprising a context type and associated parameters. Parameters typically represent people, places or objects being sensed. (b) Example of context literals used in two different aggregator definitions, including use of variables to tie parameters in outputs and inputs. Variables in context identifiers can match any single literal.

and the entities(s) to which the sensing pertains. Examples of such tuples are illustrated in Fig. 2. Although the current design of *OPF* uses a flat set of context identifiers (and string-matching to identify compatible context types), a hierarchical ontology would feature a number of advantages, as discussed in Sect. 5.

When an application submits such a tuple to the *OPF* framework, *OPF* attempts to satisfy the request in two ways. First, it determines whether the request can be satisfied by any of the existing perceptors or aggregators that are already instantiated on the local network. As described in Sect. 3.5, this is accomplished through multicast service discovery; instantiated aggregators and perceptors announce their availability via multicast DNS (mDNS). If an aggregator or perceptor with a matching set of context-identifiers is active, mDNS obtains a reference (i.e., a URL) to it, which it returns to the requesting application.

If no such aggregator is found, *OPF* consults a library of aggregator definitions to try to dynamically spawn one that might fit its needs. These definitions include a context identifier for the output type (i.e., type of context produced by) the aggregator, and a set of identifiers specifying the input context types required by the aggregator. Parameters among the inputs and output identifiers may be tied using Prolog-like variables, as illustrated in Fig. 2. Instantiation is performed in a progressive-deepening, backward-chaining fashion, by first matching aggregator's output identifier with the desired context type and then unifying the parameters. When this succeeds for a particular aggregator, the framework then attempts to jointly satisfy all its input requirements using the same process. This may, again, in turn involve discovering and/or instantiating more aggregators and perceptors. The chaining ends at the perceptors, which have no input requirements and are assumed to be already instantiated. Progressive deepening (using a visited list) ensures that the shortest possible pipeline is always found first, and that the algorithm always terminates.

During aggregator initialization, each aggregator subscribes itself to its data sources' outputs, using the remote references provided to it by the framework. When the application's need for the particular type of context subsides, it once again uses this reference to unsubscribe itself from the aggregator or perceptor. Each aggregator, in turn, unsubscribes itself from its data sources, down to perceptors. Signalling to the aggregator or perceptor that its services are no longer needed permits it to power down and conserve its energy until it is once again needed.

3.3   Perceptual Filtering at the Source

Due to its sheer volume, it is infeasible, or at least extremely inefficient, for perceptors to transmit all captured sensor data in raw form over the network. Therefore, it may be beneficial to have the perceptors perform some signal pre-processing locally, at the source of the signal. This is promising because the first stage in sensor interpretation algorithms usually involves some combination of preprocessing, such as filtering or de-correlation, followed by feature extraction of the raw captured signal. The result of this process usually yields a much smaller amount of data than the amount of raw data actually captured from the sensor.

However, no single method of processing the signal can yield a universally useful set of features that satisfy the needs all possible aggregators. Therefore, our design solution is to allow aggregators to dynamically program perceptors for particular inference tasks. More specifically, we have opted to allow aggregators to push arbitrary signal processing, feature extraction and filtering code, which we call perceptual filters, to the perceptors. This filtering code remains active at the perceptor for only as long as aggregators that need the filtered features are active. It gets unloaded subsequently. While a perceptual filter is active, it announces the availability of the filtered output, as described earlier with aggregators, to allow other aggregators to subscribe to the filtered output as well. Such reuse allows the system to scale for a large number of aggregators performing similar tasks. We have found this to be a common situation, as it is typical for multiple people in a space to be running the same application on their portable machines simultaneously.

Pushing perceptual filters to perceptors is particularly effective because a wide class of applications requires perceptors to monitor incoming environmental signals at a high sampling rate in order to effectively detect events that occur relatively rarely. It would be infeasible due to the bandwidth required for perceptors to transmit the raw signals to all interested subscribers. We have devised a special type of perceptual filter known as an *onset detector* to handle this common case.

Onset Detection. *Onset detectors* are designed to watch an incoming signal to identify the beginning of some sort of significant event. This type of filter is useful where the measured signal is "uninteresting" most of the time (and thus can be discarded), but then fire when the signal changes significantly. Probabilistic onset detectors typically form a model of the typical distribution over features extracted from the signal, and detect events when the probability of the observed signal given this model leaves a specified confidence interval. Examples of uses for onset detectors are microphones "listening" for the presence of sound, or pressure, thermal, break-beam, and motion sensors looking for the presence of activity.

For our acoustic proximity detection algorithms described in Sect. 4.1, we devised a onset detector that uses cepstral coefficients for features. These features are then clustered in an unsupervised manner (using a simple k-means technique). Our implementation averages the signal power amplitude over a 50ms window, and assigns each window average to the more probable class of "signal" (high amplitude) or "noise" (low amplitude). Class parameters are subsequently updated to represent the 5000 most recent samples of each. Whenever a sample is assigned to class "signal," the onset detection code fires a short event announcing that a noise has been heard. Aggregators that have interest in this event can then request more information from the perceptor by directly calling the perceptor, as described in Sect. 3.4.

3.4   Conserving Bandwidth with Multi-stage Publish-Subscribe: Announce, Buffer and Request

While the process just described of filtering and detection effectively reduces the amount of data transmitted by perceptors, it is impossible for these perceptual filters to predict with perfect accuracy events that the aggregator can use, as perceptors lack information regarding events arriving from other perceptors. Therefore, most of these filters should be tuned to be conservative with their filtering, to transmit events which have any potential of being of interest to the aggregator. Unfortunately, this means that, in general, some energy is going to be wasted on transmitting events that the aggregator cannot use.

To minimize this energy expended on these events, we have optimized our publish-subscribe mechanism to only broadcast short messages consisting of the type of event, the time the event occurred, as well as (optionally) a small set of features extracted from the sensed data at the event. Perceptors then save a window of raw data surrounding the detected event to a ring buffer. When the aggregator receives the short description of the event, it determines whether it is worth asking for the entire set of features for the event, and remotely fetches the data from the perceptor directly. From our experience with our acoustic localization algorithms described in Sect. 4.1, less than 10 percent of events generated by our onset detector are usually of interest to the aggregator.

3.5   *OPF* Implementation

When considering platform and programming language choices for *OPF*, we sought a number of features that were often seemingly contradictory; first, we wanted relative platform independence, so that *OPF*, like *Obje*, could work on a wide variety of devices, from both servers and workstations to embedded and

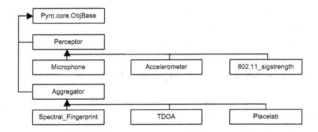

Fig. 3. Structure of the current opf implementation

mobile devices. An interpreted platform would also make it possible to, as *OPF* does, push code to perceptors (without requiring complex recompilation), and to support rapid prototyping of perceptors and aggregators. At the same time, we needed reasonably low-level access to device I/O, particularly for allowing perceptors to capture data reliably, taking advantage of device features and with minimal latency. Finally, many of the sorts of signal filtering and processing operations we envisioned performing on both aggregators and perceptors would greatly benefit from processor-optimized parallel linear algebra primitives.

Although we were initially pessimistic about finding a platform that was adequate, we discovered an option that met our needs extremely well. We first considered python because it was a popular, well-supported high-level interpreted language that had a small interpreter footprint, and could run on a wide array of computational devices. In addition, we identified that the base python environment already supported a number of native I/O devices such as audio capture, and provided a simple way by which the environment could be extended (for specific platform hardware support) in C. We were pleased to then discover the SciPy [28] and numarray [20] projects, which provided python with a set of linear algebra primitives that could be accelerated with the presence of optimized BLAS and LAPACK libraries. This ended up greatly simplifying our development process, reducing and simplifying the amount of code we had to write. As SciPy offers encapsulations and method calls similar to Matlab, it helped us a lot in the prototyping.

For communications among distributed *OPF* components and with *Obje*, we initially relied exclusively on python's native support for XML-RPC. However, we found that there seemed to be a great deal of overhead in XML-RPC calls, and therefore switched to using PyRO *pyro* remote object protocol for communications among *OPF* components. This made it possible for aggregators and perceptors to more easily transfer larger blocks of information among each other, such as raw audio clips, for which XML-RPC encoding was extremely expensive. However, we maintained XML-RPC support for cross-platform interaction, and for interfacing with *Obje*. Finally, we found and modified a python port of mDNS to support multicast object discovery and publishing.

Figure 3 depicts the class diagram of the current *OPF* implementation. All aggregators and perceptors are subclasses of the PyRO remote base object. As already elaborated earlier we have a mobile filter class that holds an interface for any mobile processing code an aggregator or application wants to push to perceptors. So far, only code for variable onset detection and static thresholding are supported here. An aggregator interfacing with Intel Placelab is in development.

3.6   Comparison with Previous Approaches

As described above, the *OPF*, like the Context Toolkit, eliminates the need for application writers to concern themselves with what actual sensors should be used by the application or how to process raw information from sensors into a form that a context-aware application can use. Another architectural approach designed to accomplish this goal is the blackboard [7] or tuple-space architecture, as used in the *Event Heap* of Winograd et al. [31], and in the Equip Component Toolkit (ECT) of Greenhalgh et al. [12]. Unlike in the Context Toolkit, where the process of transforming the data is prespecified, using a fixed set of combiners and interpreters, Winograd's architecture supports *opportunistic inference*, where any set of available knowledge sources can contribute to the inference process as appropriate. The design of the *Event Heap* reflects the observation that transforming the low-level data to a form that is usable by the application usually depends on both the application's needs and on the nature and quality of data available from the sources, two factors that change frequently.

One drawback of Winograd's approach is that their blackboard is implemented as a centralized tuplespace, which forms both a single point of failure and an obstacle to scalability. Furthermore, by being centralized, blackboards create strict logical boundaries at the periphery of the ubiquitous computing space; devices either have access to all the messages in the tuplespace or do not. For example, if one installs an event heap-based interactive workspace in the conference rooms and offices within an workplace, a separate mechanism would be needed to transfer data between the spaces, which would happen in situations such as when a user walks from one space to the next.

Like the *Event Heap*, ECT uses a shared data space to transfer data between modules. ECT's emphasis is on the componentization of the data producers and consumers. It provides a number of mechanisms for transfering data between components that developers can use depending on the level of control they desire. The mechanisms include simple component property access for low-bandwidth access, publish/subscribe mechanism and custom component-specific APIs for high-bandwidth interactions.

Extensions to the *Gaia* middleware architecture by Ranganathan et al. [22] for supporting context inference most closely resemble the goals of *OPF*. The two projects differ in emphasis but are largely complementary; Gaia's context infrastructure emphasizes simplifying the task of building new *Context synthesizers* (i.e., inference algorithms) by providing support for inference in first order logic, bayes nets, and fuzzy-logic within the middleware. *OPF*, on the other hand, remains agnostic to the potentially wide variety of sensor fusion or inference techniques that can be used to build aggregators, and primarily focuses on

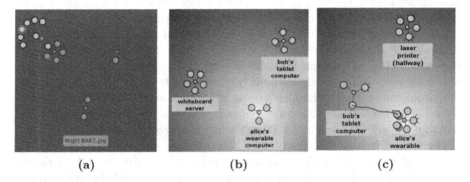

Fig. 4. The original orbital browser and perceptually enhanced versions, respectively. (a) In the original *OB*, components are placed geometrically in fixed positions around the display. Actions may be taken by expanding resources, appearing as children of individual components, and making connections among them. (b) The *POB*, which positions components on the screen relative to the user. Here, Alice (running the *POB*) on her wearable, approaches Bob in the hallway near a printer. (c) The browser recalls that the last time Alice ran into Bob in this hallway, Alice took a snapshot of the whiteboard and showed it to Bob on his tablet. *POB* recalls this action as she approaches him, and faintly suggests that she may want to perform this action again by drawing a dashed line from her notes to his display.

the problem of constructing and maintaining context inference pipelines within frequently-changing ubiquitous computing environments. A difference in the philosophy between Gaia and *OPF* is that Gaia's eventing and query mechanism aims to provide a uniform and consistent view of the state of the world across components, so that components can maintain updated local knowledge bases, while *OPF* aims to minimize energy expenditure and bandwidth consumption by delivering context information to consumers only of the type needed upon request.

OPF also resembles iCAP [8], an end-user programming system for context-aware applications. iCAP is built on top of the Context Toolkit, and therefore operates at a level similar to applications of OPF. Compared to the Orbital Browser described below, iCAP allows users to specify rules for how arbitrary functionality should be triggered, whereas the Orbital Browser provides a clean, simple interface for allowing the user to immediately assess the system state and combine arbitrary components together.

4   Case Study: An Adaptive UI for Service Composition

In this section, we describe an end-user application known as the *Orbital Browser* or *OB*, designed to help users orchestrate resources in device-rich environments. We first describe the our first version of the *OB* designed prior to the *OPF*, which provides the user with a static user interface for configuring devices in their environment. We then describe how we integrated *OPF* into the *OB* to transform it into a dynamic, context-aware user interface.

The *Orbital Browser* (*OB*) [18] is an experimental service composer user interface for *Obje*, designed to make it easy for users to establish connections and configure the digital resources available in their environments. The *OB* was originally designed to allow the user to quickly achieve arbitrary configurations of their ubiquitous computing environments using a variety of unusual input devices, such as the Griffin PowerMate[13], mobile phone keypads, or directional joysticks common to phones, PDAs and tablet PCs. The original *OB* UI is visible in Fig. 4a.

The main difficulty with the original *OB* interface surrounded its scalability; as the number of active devices and potential capabilities of each available device increased, the number of components likewise grew. The *OB* became quickly too crowded or required an unmanageable amount of screen real estate usually beyond a dozen or so devices (each with sub-resources).

4.1   Just Add OPF: Achieving Adaptivity Through Context Sensing

Schilit, et al. [27], Gellersen, et al. [10], and others have suggested using location in context-aware systems to prioritize access to resources. We take this idea and directly apply it to the *OB* to arrange components in the *OB* UI according to approximately how close they are to the user, and to each other. The enhanced *OB* interface, called the *Perceptual Orbital Browser*, or *POB*, is visible in Fig. 4.

If the location of the user running the *POB* can be deduced by *OPF*, the *POB* places the user at the center of the display, to create an ego-centric fish-eye view of resources in the world. As the user walks around in the physical environment, components fluidly rearrange themselves to reflect their relative physical positions to the user. Components are actuated by a simple kinematics model that adds pairwise forces to maintain a distance between graphical components that is proportional to physical distance between devices. Other forces ensure that components do not overlap with one another, or from leaving the bounds of the user interface.

Learning from Past Connections - During an initial trial period, we realized that although it was often the case that physical proximity correlated well with probability of use for particular resources, we were inconvenienced by the fact that there were a few often-accessed digital resources that were *not* physically nearby, like the user's desktop machine, or centralized file and print servers. With the behavior of *POB* just described, their desktops were relegated to the periphery, and it was difficult to locate them repeatedly.

This inspired us to modify our original kinematics model for *POB* to bring frequently used resources closer to the center of the UI in situations that they were most likely to be used. We wished the system to learn automatically which resources were relevant on a per-user and situation basis. This turned out to be simple to implement using *OPF*; we simply saved the 50 most recent service composition actions made by the user, along with corresponding distance readings representing the user's physical distance to resources at the time the composition was made. Then, whenever the user's position changed significantly, the historical record of compositions were consulted for situations that most closely resembled the user's active situation, measured by their proximity to all known resources around them. Resources that were involved in these compositions were brought closer to the center, at a distance proportional to their "importance" (measured by the number of compositions in which they were involved).

Proximity Sensing in the OPF - In order to achieve proximity sensing needed by *OPF*, we needed to implement aggregators which could provide the approximate physical proximity of devices in the environment. There has been a huge amount of work in localization, ranging, and proximity sensing using a large variety of physical phenomena [17]. We chose acoustic ranging for several reasons. First, walls that form natural space boundaries also isolate audio signals well, generally better than radio-frequency signals. Second, many mobile and embedded devices already contain microphones.

Time Difference of Arrival (TDOA) aggregator - The first proximity algorithm estimates the location of a sound source using the time difference of arrival of a sound to different microphones located in the environment. When an array of fixed microphones whose locations are known are used, the *TDOA* technique can usually be used to precisely triangulate the source of a sound [5]. In our application, however, the locations of the perceptors may be unknown, and we do not have, in general, as tight a synchronization among the clocks in our perceptors (since microphones are usually connected to separate machines, synchronized via NTP to a local timeserver on our LAN). Therefore, it is, impossible using our setup to locate the user precisely. Instead, we use *TDOA* to gain only a rough measure of the proximity of the user to various microphones attached to devices in the environment. Our implementation computes the difference in signal arrival times through normalized cross-correlation of 100ms windows around noise bursts (detected onsets). Unfortunately, this simple approach was unreliable, due to problems arising from reverberation and resonance of sound in the room. Rui et al. [25] describe how a maximum-likelihood or PHAT weighting function may help counter some of these effects. We employed a simpler workaround: rejecting readings where multiple candidate correlations are ambiguous (where the ratio between peaks was low) as recommended by Bian [4], and by five-sample median-filtering the output. This worked well enough to determine the user's location within a radius of approximately 2 meters.

Spectral fingerprinting aggregator for co-location - Instead of trying to determine the proximity between two receivers, this second algorithm determines merely whether the receivers are within "earshot" of one another, i.e., located within the same acoustic space. This algorithm calculates a "signature" for detected noise events, computed by taking the amplitude of the short-time Fourier transform (STFT) over the signal. Each window is further subdivided into 4 sub-windows, each of which is analyzed using a coarse 32-band FFT. The magnitudes of the respective spectra of each of these windows is then concatenated to form the feature vector of the window. After these features are calculated, they are returned to the aggregator, which performs a sum-correlation between the fingerprints to determine whether it is likely that both perceptors heard the same sound.

This algorithm has a number of advantages over the *TDOA* version. First, as this algorithm does not intrinsically rely on timestamps, it can operate with much looser time synchronization. Second, by extracting features that "summarize" heard audio, the algorithm reduces the amount of information that needs to be preserved and transferred over the network for comparison. We have also found that this algorithm performs more robustly than our *TDOA* approach through noise, and often even works even when the microphone is placed in the user's pocket. Our method of extracting features from the audio has the additional feature of improving privacy, by discarding the phase component in the frequency spectrum of all captured audio; this makes recovering content such as speech difficult.

5   Discussion and Future Work

While our implementation of *OPF* is preliminary, we have demonstrated that the task of transforming low-level sensor data into high-level context in ubiquitous computing environments can be effectively accomplished by constructing custom context inference pipelines at runtime, based on applications' needs and the set of available sensors in the environment. In Sect. 3.6, we describe how our approach offers advantages over static inference pipelines and blackboard approaches.

An essential aspect of the design of *OPF* is the ability to push detection, signal processing and feature extraction code to perceptors, without which it would not be possible to process high-bitrate sensor streams. Buffering raw sensor data locally at the perceptor and allowing aggregators to access it remotely only when necessary provides additional savings in bandwidth by eliminating wasted transmissions of full feature sets for "uninteresting" onsets. Our experience with the *TDOA* and co-location algorithms shows that the largest proportion of onsets fired are of this type. We also found multicast service discovery (mDNS) to be singularly useful towards allowing the system to be entirely decentralized, and for handling many aspects of dynamism—registering new devices on the network and enabling reintegration after migration or failure. Multicast service discovery also made the reuse of components for multiple inference tasks extremely trivial to implement.

To reiterate a point made in Sect. 4.1, one limitation we encountered with using separate machines as perceptors was how closely the internal clocks within perceptors could be synchronized. Particularly when perceptors were wirelessly connected, only coarse synchronization could be achieved. This limit in many cases may directly affect the algorithm's performance, as we witnessed with the *TDOA* algorithm. Therefore, we are currently seeking context inference and sensor fusion algorithms which are more robust to bias in timestamps across readings from perceptors.

A number of incremental improvements to *OPF* are planned in the short term. First, supporting a more expressive set of context descriptors would allow applications to more precisely specify their sensing requirements, and would similarly allow perceptors and aggregators to more concisely express their capabilities. For example, if an application sought information regarding the user's presence, the framework could identify that this request was related to determining the user's location, and invoke inference algorithms for the latter to serve the former. The Gaia perception framework described earlier uses context predicates grounded in a DAML+OIL ontology, and employs a theorem-prover to resolve whether predicates were entailed by a particular sensed context. However, there are many computational challenges to such an approach [23].

A second improvement to context descriptors would be to support extra metadata that would help the framework better resolve ties among alternative sensing techniques when there were multiple ways to satisfy a particular context sensing task. Such metadata might include the technique's cost of use, expressed in terms of number of perceptors required, estimated power consumption, network traffic, or estimated accuracy. This metadata might help the framework perform load balancing among perceptors and aggregators. This is important as it is likely that perceptors or aggregators may become swamped as the number inference tasks and devices in the environment are increased to support more users.

The most important work to be done, of course, surrounds integrating new perceptors to support different types of sensing, and inference algorithms for new types of context. We are currently investigating how to interpret accelerometer data from sensors worn on the body, for the purpose of detecting the user's activities, such as walking [15]. Each type of sensor and context inference task has so far presented a whole series of new challenges, and has illuminated us to the limitations in the design of *OPF*. We look forward to seeing how our design for *OPF* evolves in the future.

References

1. D. Bannach, K. Kunze, P. Lukowicz, and O. Ampft. Distributed modular toolbox for multi-modal context recognition. Accepted at ARCS, 2006.
2. M. Bauer, B. Bruegge, G. Klinker, A. MacWilliams, T. Reicher, S. Ri, C. Sandor, and M. Wagner. Design of a component-based augmented reality framework. In *ISAR: International Symposium on Augmented Reality*, New York, NY, USA, 2001. ACM Press.
3. M. Beigl, A. Krohn, T. Zimmer, C. Decker, and P. Robinson. Awarecon: Situation aware context communication. In *Ubicomp*, 2003.
4. X. Bian, G. D. Abowd, and J. M. Rehg. Using sound source localizaiton in a home environment. In *Pervasive 2005, LNCS 3468*, pages 19–26. Springer-Verlag, 2005.
5. M. Brandstein, J. Adcock, and H. Silverman. A closed-form method for finding source locations from microphone-array time-delay estimates.
6. M. Coen, B. Phillips, N. Warshawsky, L. Weisman, S. Peters, and P. Finin. Meeting the computational needs of intelligent environments: The metaglue system. In P. Nixon, G. Lacey, and S. Dobson, editors, *1st International Workshop on Managing Interactions in Smart Environments (MANSE'99)*, pages 201–212, Dublin, Ireland, December 1999. Springer-Verlag.
7. D. Corkill. Blackboard systems. *AI Expert*, 6:40, 1991.

8. A. K. Dey, T. Sohn, S. Streng, and J. Kodama. icap: Interactive prototyping of context-aware applications. In *Proceedings of the Fourth International Conference on Pervasive Computing*, May 2006.

9. C. Endres, A. Butz, and A. MacWilliams. A survey of software infrastructures and frameworks for ubiquitous computing. *Mobile Information Systems Journal*, 1(1):41–80, January–March 2005.

10. H. W. Gellersen, A. Schmidt, and M. Beigl. Multi-sensor context-awareness in mobile devices and smart artifacts. *Mob. Netw. Appl.*, 7(5):341–351, 2002.

11. J. Gomez, A. Campbell, M. Naghshineh, and C. Bisdikian. Conserving transmission power in wireless ad hoc networks. In *Proc. of IEEE Conference on Network Protocols (ICNP'01)*, Nov 2001.

12. C. Greenhalgh, S. Izadi, J. Mathrick, J. Humble, and I. Taylor. Ect: A toolkit to support rapid construction of ubicomp environments. In *UbiSys '04, System Support for Ubiquitous Computing Workshop at the Sixth Annual Conference on Ubiquitous Computing*, 2004.

13. Griffin technology powermate. http://www.griffintechnology.com/products/powermate/.

14. K. Hinckley, J. Pierce, E. Horvitz, and M. Sinclair. Foreground and background interaction with sensor-enhanced mobile devices. *ACM Trans. Comput.-Hum. Interact.*, 12(1):31–52, 2005.

15. H. J. Kai Kunze, Paul Lukowicz and G. Tröster. Where am i: Recognizing on-body positions of wearable sensors. In *LOCA'04: International Workshop on Location- and Context-Awareness*, London, UK, 2005. Springer-Verlag.

16. J. Krumm and K. Hinckley. The nearme wireless proximity server. In *Proceedings of Ubicomp*, September 2004.

17. A. LaMarca, Y. Chawathe, S. Consolvo, J. Hightower, I. Smith, J. Scott, T. Sohn, J. Howard, J. Hughes, F. Potter, J. Tabert, P. Powledge, G. Borriello, and B. Schilit. Place lab: Device positioning using radio beacons in the wild. In *Proceedings of the 3rd International Conference on Pervasive Computing (Pervasive 2005) Munich, Germany.* Springer-Verlag, May 2005.

18. M. Newman, N. Duchenaut, K. W. Edwards, R. E. Grinter, and J. Sedivy. The art of the boring: using ubiquitous computing to support mundane practices. Submitted for publication, 2006.

19. M. W. Newman, J. Z. Sedivy, C. M. Neuwirth, W. K. Edwards, J. I. Hong, S. Izadi, K. Marcelo, T. F. Smith, J. Sedivy, and M. Newman. Designing for serendipity: supporting end-user configuration of ubiquitous computing environments. In *DIS '02: Proceedings of the conference on Designing interactive systems*, pages 147–156, New York, NY, USA, 2002. ACM Press.

20. Numerical library for python. http://www.stsci.edu/resources/ software_hardware/numarray.

21. S. Ponnekanti, B. Lee, A. Fox, P. Hanrahan, and T. Winograd. Icrafter: A service framework for ubiquitous computing environments. In *UbiComp '01: Proceedings of the 3rd international conference on Ubiquitous Computing*, pages 56–75, London, UK, 2001. Springer-Verlag.

22. A. Ranganathan, J. Al-Muhtadi, and R. H. Campbell. Reasoning about uncertain contexts in pervasive computing environments. *Pervasive Computing, IEEE*, 3(2):62–70, 2004.

23. A. Rangnanathan and R. Campbell. An infrastructure for context awareness based on first order logic. *Personal Ubiquitous Comput.*, 7:353–364, 2003.

24. M. Roman, C. Hess, R. Cerqueira, A. Ranganathan, R. H. Campbell, and K. Nahrstedt. Gaia: a middleware platform for active spaces. *SIGMOBILE Mob. Comput. Commun. Rev.*, 6(4):65–67, 2002.

25. Y. Rui and D. Florencio. New direct approaches to robust sound source localisation. In *Multimedia and Expo 2003, ICME '03 International Conference*, volume 1, pages 737–40. IEEE, July 2003.

26. D. Salber, A. K. Dey, and G. D. Abowd. The context toolkit: aiding the development of context-enabled applications. In *CHI '99: Proceedings of the SIGCHI conference on Human factors in computing systems*, pages 434–441, New York, NY, USA, 1999. ACM Press.

27. B. N. Schilit. *A System Architecture for Context-Aware Mobile Computing*. PhD thesis, 1995.

28. Scientific tools for python. http://www.scipy.org/.

29. I. Smith, S. Consolvo, A. LaMarca, J. Hightower, J. Scott, T. Sohn, J. Hughes, G. Iachello, and G. D. Abowd. Social disclosure of place: From location technology to communication practices. In *Proceedings of the 3rd International Conference on Pervasive Computing (Pervasive 2005) Munich, Germany*. Springer-Verlag, May 2005.

30. M. Weiser and J. S. Brown. The coming age of calm technolgy. pages 75–85, 1997.

31. T. Winograd. Architectures for context. *Human-Computer Interaction Journal*, 16, 2001.

Implementation of Telematics Services with Context-Aware Agent Framework

Kenta Cho[1], Yuzo Okamoto[1], Tomohiro Yamasaki[1], Masayuki Okamoto[1], Masanori Hattori[1], and Akihiko Ohsuga[1]

TOSHIBA Corporation
1 Komukai-Toshiba-cho, Saiwai-ku, Kawasaki-shi, 212-8582, Japan
kenta.cho@toshiba.co.jp

Abstract. With the development of a car-mounted navigation system and an in-car network, improved information services for creating drive plans automatically have been realized. We propose a method of developing telematics services through combination of a context-aware agent framework and a planner that provides the predicted feature situation to the framework and creates drive plans composed of POIs (Points Of Interest) proposed by the framework.

1 Introduction

Context-aware applications are attracting attention as an approach to distinguishing important data from a large amount of contents spread on a network. A context-aware application recognizes the user's situation and offers information that may be useful for the user in that situation. Telematics, that is, advanced information services based on in-car embedded devices and networks, has become widely used. Services providing information in a mobile environment are realized with a network enabled car navigation system [1] [2]. When using a car navigation system to create drive plans from a starting point to a destination, user have to select stop-off points from among many POIs (Points of Interest). Since there are many POIs in the real world, it is difficult to select appropriate stop-off points unaided. A POI recommendation function may help a user in creating drive plans, but existing recommendation functions offer little variation in plans, lack adaptation to the user's preference and can't consider if a whole drive plan is appropriate for the user. Our approach is to apply context-aware applications to telematics to address these issues. In this paper, we propose an architecture to implement telematics services as a context-aware application. We use a reactive context-aware framework that outputs recommendation contents according to inputs such as a preference and a situation of a user. We also implemented a drive planner that simulates travel corresponding to recommended drive plans to predict a feature situation.

Section 2 of the paper explains problems in applying a context-aware application to a telematics service. Section 3 describes the architecture of Ubiquitous Personal Agent (UPA), our reactive context-aware framework. In Section 4, we

H.Y. Youn, M. Kim, and H. Morikawa (Eds.): UCS 2006, LNCS 4239, pp. 98–110, 2006.

provide a detailed explanation of Smart Ride Assist @ Navi (@Navi), which is a telematics service implemented with UPA. In Section 5, we evaluate if the combination of a drive planner and UPA is more effective in creating suitable plans than in the case of using only a reactive context-aware framework. We present related work in Section 6.

2   Applying Context-Aware Application to Telematics Service

In creating a drive plan that contains stop-off POIs, existing telematics services force a user to select a point from a catalog of a large number of POIs. To avoid the burden of selecting points, a telematics service should satisfy the following conditions.

– Creating drive plans that considers a user's preference, a user's situation on the drive, a drive route and a time constraint.
– Use interaction with a user as feedback to the system and personalize behavior of the system.

We propose a method to realize a service that satisfies these conditions by applying a context-aware application to a telematics service. We define "context" as follows.

– Context is information to characterize a situation, preference and objective of a user. That information must be abstracted for ease of use for an application. A situation includes spatial information (e.g. location), temporal information, physiological measurements (e.g. emptiness, fatigue) and activity.

A context-aware application is defined as an application that provides information or performs services according to inputs of context [6][11]. Most existing context-aware applications [7][12][5] work reactively and provide information in response to inputs from sensors.

Context-aware telematics service can recommend a POI at which a user should stop in a certain situation at a certain moment. But such a reactive service has the following problems.

– Such a reactive service recommends a POI only with an estimation at a certain moment, even if there are more appropriate POIs in the feature, a service can't recommend them. For example, a service recommended a restaurant at a certain point and a user had lunch at that restaurant. After that, even if there is another restaurant that is more to the user's taste, the service can't recommend it, and so the total satisfaction rating of the drive plan becomes lower.

For solving this problem, there is an approach in which a static user's preference is used to select POIs. But this approach still has a problem.

- Since each POI is recommended according only to a user's preference, dynamic situations of the user, such as hunger and sleepy, are not reflected in a drive plan.

We solve these problems with a prediction of a user's feature context. In our proposed architecture, a drive planner simulates an itinerary and provides a predicted car's location to a reactive context-aware framework, and recommended POIs are passed from the framework to the planner. The planner creates a drive plan by combining recommended POIs. A drive planner predicts a feature context and evaluates a comprehensive satisfaction rating of drive plans to cover the shortcomings of a reactive context-aware framework.

3   Ubiquitous Personal Agent

We have implemented our reactive context-aware framework, Ubiquitous Personal Agent (UPA) [9]. UPA has the following features.

- UPA abstracts data acquired from a ubiquitous sensor network with using context recognition rules.
- Service selection rules evaluate user's context and output appropriate contents and services for the user in that context.

3.1   Entity, Context and Module

UPA works as follows:

1. Data from various sensor devices are stored in UPA. UPA handle these data with a structure called "Entity". Entity includes data such as a current date and a user's location.
2. "Context" is derived from entity by context recognition rules. Context includes data such as a user's preference and neighboring POIs. Examples of context recognition rules are presented in Section 4.
3. "Module" is derived from context by service selection rules. Module represents services that should be provided to the user in a certain context. Examples of service selection rules and modules are presented in Section 4.

UPA handles entity, context and module with a structure called 'Node'. Node is an architectural component in UPA and it contains a common data set for handling entity, context and module. Rules in UPA fire when a specific combination of nodes is stored in UPA, and output other nodes. Each node and each rule has a weight that represents its importance. A weight of the output node is calculated with weights of rules and nodes that derive the output node.

3.2   Feedback

Each node has information from which rule it is derived. So if a context or a module is considered to be inadequate by a user, UPA can reduce weights of rules derived for that context or module. It works as a feedback to the system to reduce a probability of providing inadequate information to the user.

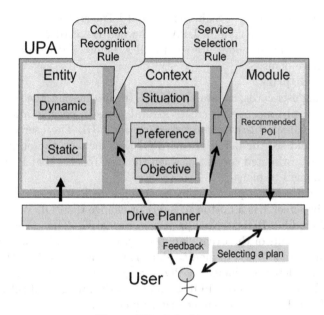

Fig. 1. @Navi Architecture

4   Creating Drive Plans with UPA

In this section, we describe our telematics service @Navi that creates drive plans for a leisure trip with UPA. @Navi recognizes a user's preference and context with rules in UPA, and recommends stop-off POIs. @Navi has a drive planner that covers the shortcomings of reactive action of UPA, obtaining the measure of recommended POIs through the viewpoint that the whole drive plan is appropriate for the user.

4.1   Architecture of @Navi

Fig. 1 shows the outline of the architecture of @ Navi. A drive planner provides time and location to UPA as entities. UPA derives contexts and modules from entities. A drive planner receives modules that contain information about recommended POIs and creates several plans with combinations of these POIs. The user can select and modify the proposed drive plans. Interactions with the user in selecting plans and making changes to stop-off POIs are used as feedback to rules in UPA.

4.2   Using @Navi

In this section, we show how @Navi is used to create a drive plan.

1. Inputting user's preference with user cards
   User cards are data that contains the user's preference and an objective of a drive. For example, user cards have a description like 'A taste for Japanese

food", "Outdoors type", "Sightseeing" and "Travel deluxe". Each card is related to the context node in UPA, and when the card is selected by the user, related context nodes are set to UPA before a drive planner starts creating drive plans.

2. Showing drive plans

   After setting user cards, the starting point, the destination, the starting time and the arrival time, @Navi create several plans in consideration of these constraints. Created drive plans are shown on GUI. The user can select a drive plan and see the detail of each POI that includes the outline of that POI and the estimated context of when the user reaches that POI.

3. Making changes to plans

   The user can select a plan and make changes to POIs in a drive plan. A POI details screen has a button to insert or change the POI. When the user inserts or modifies POIs, @Navi proposes alternative POIs in the drive plan graph. The details of the drive plan graph are described below. Interaction between user and @Navi to modify plans is used as feedback to the system. If the user deletes or changes a POI, weights of rules deriving that POI decrease. If the use selects a POI as an alternative, weights of rules deriving that POI and POIs in the same category increase.

Designing UPA nodes and rules for @Navi. In this section, we describe the details of nodes and rules for @Navi.

Designing nodes. Nodes are classified into entity, context and module. Table 1 shows types of nodes used in @Navi. A node is defined by a name and types of attributes. These nodes have a same weight when they are entered into UPA. All POIs are input as entities to UPA, and these contain genre information as an attribute. By genre information, POIs are classified into 300 categories.

Designing rules. Rules are classified into context recognition rules and service selection rules.

– Context recognition rule

  A context recognition rule derives context such as neighboring POI, time zone, season and hunger. A neighboring POI is derived from entities of a current location, information of POI and threshold distance. Time zone, season and hunger are derived from entities of a current time.

– Service selection rule

  A service selection rule recommends POI according to the user's context. Genre information described in attributes of POI is used for POI recommendation. Service selection rules are created from the mapping table from the user's context to the POI's genre.

Example of a context recognition rule. Fig. 2 shows an example of a context recognition rule. UPA provides a feature to define enumeration rules. Since each enumerated rule can be assigned a different weight, enumeration rules

Table 1. Nodes Used in @Navi

Entity		
Dynamic	Current Location(Coordinate)	
	Current Time(Date)	
	Threshold for Neighboring POI	
	(NearbyThreshold)	
	Stop-off POI(VisitingPoint)	
Static	POI(POI)	
Context		
Situation (Spatial)	Neighboring POI(NearbyPOI)	
Situation (Temporal)	Time Zone(Time), Season(TimeOfYear)	
Situation (Physiological)	Hunger(Hungry), Fatigue(Thirsty) Sleepy(Sleepy), Urinary(Urinary)	
Situation (Activity)	Searching POI(SearchedPOI) Visiting POI(VisitingPoint)	
Preference	Gender(UserGender)	
	Generation(UserGeneration)	
	Passenger(Passenger)	
	Estimated cost(Budget)	
	Food Preference(FoodPrefrence)	
	Outdoors or Indoors type(ActivityType)	
Objective	Objective(Purpose)	
Module		
	Recommended POI(RecommendPOI)	

can define time-varying weights by defining multiple rules corresponding to hours of a current time entity and genre-varying weight with rules corresponding to the genre of a POI entity.

- Defining enumeration rule

  An enumeration rule is defined with an identifier and a set of values. Each expanded rule can has a different weight. In Fig. 2, the enumeration rule has an identifier 'Hour' and a set of values from 0 to 23. The expanded rules that have a value 7, 12, and 19 have a weight of 2.5, rules that have a value 6, 8, 11, 13, 15, 18 and 20 have a weight of 1.5, rules that have a value 9, 10, 14, 16, 17 have a weight of 0.5, and other rules have a weight of 0.1. These rules emulated the hunger context of each hour.
- Defining fire condition

  The fire condition is defined with output context name, input entity name and condition description. In Fig. 2, huger context is derived from Date and VisitingPoint entity.

Example of a service selection rule. Fig. 3 shows an example of a service selection rule. By this rule, RecommendPOI module is derived from user's food

```
rule DeriveHungryState {
 // Defining enumeration rule
 Hour = [0 1 2 3 4 5 6 7 8 9
         10 11 12 13 14 15 16
         17 18 19 20 21 22 23];
 // Defining weights
 weights[Hour hour] {
    [*] = 0.1;
    [9,10,14,16,17] = 0.5 ;
    [6,8,11,13,15,18,20] = 1.5 ;
    [7,12,19] = 2.5; }
 // Defining fire condition
 Hungry hungry
 (Date[maxCardinality=1] date,
  VisitingPoint[maxCardinality=1]
   visitingPoint*[large_class==
     "eating"]) {
       --- snip ---
```

Fig. 2. Example of a Context Recognition Rule

preference and neighboring POIs. RecommendPOI module contains information about the name and the ID of the recommended POI.

4.3   Drive Planner

A drive planner simulates an itinerary of drive plans from the starting point to the destination, and provides predicted situation such as a location and time to UPA. UPA provides recommended POIs to a drive planner, and a drive planner sorts out an appropriate POI and creates a drive plan within constraints of an arrival time and a geographical route. To create variations in plans, a drive planner uses a data structure called a drive plan graph.

Drive plan graph. A drive plan graph is a data structure to manage drive plans from the starting point to the destination. A drive plan graph has nodes that represent each stop-off POI. A path from the node of the starting point to the node of the destination represents a drive plan. A drive plan graph is created as follows (Fig. 4).

1. Creating an initial drive plan graph that contains only the starting point and the destination, and searching the geographical route.
2. Simulating a drive along the route and providing a location and time to UPA at intervals. UPA recommends POIs to a drive planner with a Recommend-POI module.
3. Connecting n POIs next to the node of the starting point as stop-off POIs. These POIs are selected from recommended POIs ranked with weights of corresponding UPA modules.
4. Searching routes from each stop-off POI to the destination.

```
rule DeriveRecommendPOI {
      --- snip ---
weights[FoodGenre foodGenre,
        POIClass poiClass] {
  [* *] = 0.1 ;
      --- snip ---
  ["Japanese" "Curry", "Ramen"]
    = 0.5; }
RecommendPOI recommendPoi
 (NearbyPOI nearbyPoi,
  FoodPreference foodPref) {
  if(nearbyPoi.class   == poiClass &&
   foodPref.type == foodGenre ) {
   recommendPoi.id   = nearbyPoi.id;
   recommendPoi.name  = nearbyPoi.name;
      --- snip ---
```

Fig. 3. Example of a Service Selection Rule

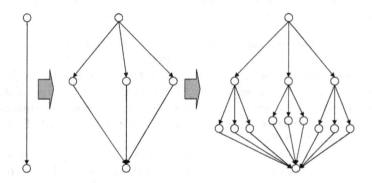

Fig. 4. Creating a Drive Plan Graph

5. Repeating 2 - 4 as long as a user can reach the destination before the arrival time with the recommended drive plan. We assume that the user stays for an hour at each POI.

Drive plans are selected from the drive plan graph as follows.

1. Adding all weights of POIs for each path from the starting point to the destination. Weights of POIs correspond to weights of modules recommending that POI. Total of weights is used as the evaluated value for the drive plan.
2. Selecting the drive plan that has the highest value.
3. To minimize the inclusion of duplicate POIs between plans, if there are POIs in a drive plan graph that are included in the selected plan, weights of these POIs are reduced to half.
4. Repeating the above operations until a predetermined number of plans is selected.

5   Evaluation

In this section, we evaluate if a drive planner can create better plans for a user than in case of only using a reactive context-aware framework. Also, we evaluate if the feedback from the user's operations can improve created plans.

5.1   Creating Better Plans by Using a Planner

To evaluate if the proposed architecture using a combination of a drive planner and a reactive context-aware framework can create better plans than in case of only using a reactive context-aware framework, we experimented with two methods of creating a drive plan with UPA, and checked an evaluated value of each method.

- Planning method: Creating drive plans with a drive planner and UPA. UPA uses the user's feature information predicted by a drive planner. (the method proposed in this paper)
- Reactive method: Stopping at POIs recommended by UPA one after another. UPA uses only the user's current location.

In the reactive method, the system inputs a current location and a current time as an entity to UPA, and stops at the POI that has the highest weight.

An evaluated value of the drive plan is calculated by adding the weight value of each stop-off POI. The weight value of POI is the same as that of its corresponding module. Each method creates a plan that can reach the destination before the arrival time. For each method, we created drive plans with the settings in Table 2 with 4929 POIs.

Fig. 5 shows evaluated values of plans. In most plans, the planning method got a higher value than the reactive method. In drive plans 2 and 8, the reactive method got a higher value, but it was attributable to the larger number of POIs contained in a plan. Fig. 6 shows an average calculated by dividing an evaluated value by the number of POIs in a plan. This figure shows the planning method got a higher value even in plans 2 and 8. We evaluated another 20 plans. Table 3 shows the average value of each method with 30 trials. Table 4 shows P values in a Wilcoxon matched-pairs signed-rank test. P values show that there are statistically significant differences between two methods with significant level $\alpha = 0.01$. So the result shows that the planning method can create the plan that has a higher value and is suitable for the user.

5.2   Improvement Through Feedback

@Navi uses interactions with user as feedback to UPA. In this section, we evaluate that @Navi can make an improvement with feedback and create more appropriate plans. We use the user model to simulate the user's behavior that changes according to preference and context. The user model has a mapping table from user's context and genre of POI to the satisfaction rating of user, and evaluates plans recommended from @Navi. The user model interacts with UI of @Navi,

Table 2. Settings of Evaluated Drive Plans

	Date	Starting - Destination	Time	User Card
1	2004/8/4	Sontoku Memorial	12:00	Alone, Japanese food, Refresh, Deluxe
		Ashinoko Lake	18:00	
2	2004/10/10	Hakone Museum	9:00	Asian food, Sightseeing
		Kanakawa Suisan	15:00	
3	2004/11/18	Sontoku Memorial	12:00	Alone, Japanese food, Refresh, Deluxe
		Ashinoko Lake	18:00	
4	2004/11/18	Odawara Castle Park	9:00	Family vacations, Experience
		Ashinoko Park	15:00	
5	2004/12/20	Tohi Castle	13:00	Reflesh, With friends, Outdoors type
		Hakuundo Teahouse	20:00	
6	2005/1/1	Gotenba Sports Guarden	10:00	Shopping, Italian food, Chinese food
		Kamakura Station	17:00	
7	2005/4/5	Hakone Kougen Hotel	9:00	With lover, Youth, Indoors type
		Dynacity West	14:00	
8	2005/6/21	Kodomo Playground	12:00	Female, Sight scenery, With children
		3D Dinosaur World	18:00	
9	2005/7/7	Hakone Sekisho	10:00	Economy, Sightseeing, Youth
		Katufukuzi Temple	16:00	
10	2005/8/10	Ohkurayama Memorial	14:00	Adult, Chinese food
		Odawarazyou Muse	20:00	

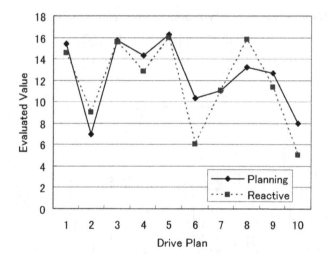

Fig. 5. Evaluated Values of Plans

by selecting a plan and modifying POIs according to the evaluated value of each
POI. Table 5 shows a setting of the evaluation. In this evaluation, we set the
user card of 'A taste for Japanese food', 'male', and 'adult'. For the user model,
we set the preference of 'A taste for Japanese food', 'dislike foreign food' and

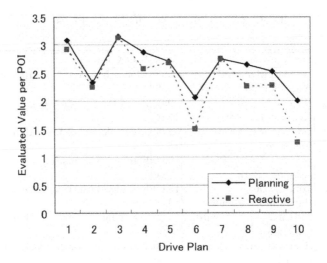

Fig. 6. Evaluated Values of POIs

Table 3. Average of the Evaluated Values

	Value of Plans	Value of POIs
Plannning	11.54	2.49
Reactive	10.27	2.25

Table 4. P values in a Wilcoxon matched-pairs signed-rank test

	Value of Plans	Value of POIs
P value	0.00028	0.00001

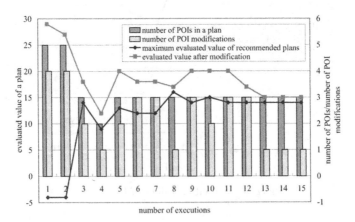

Fig. 7. Evaluated Value and Number of Modifications

Table 5. Settings of Evaluation of Feedback

User Card	Japanese food, Male, Adult
Date	2004/2/1
Starting	Odawarazyo Castle 11:00
Destination	Hakone Prince Hotel 18:00
User Model	A taste for Japanese food,
	Dislike foreign food and hot spring

'dislike hot springs'. Since some preferences are more detailed descriptions than the user card, we can check if the system can suit the user's detailed preference by using feedback. Fig. 7 shows a result of 15 trial runs of creating plans and simulating a drive. The horizontal axis shows the number of executions and the vertical axis shows the evaluated value of a plan and the number of POI modifications. This result shows the evaluated value is improved by feedback and the number of modifications decreases. So by using feedback, @Navi can adapt to the user model.

6   Related Works

For creating a context-aware application in the ubiquitous environment, pervasive middleware is proposed [4]. Context Toolkit [7] is one of these middleware that provides the widget for hiding the complexity of sensors and providing a common interface to the application and the interpreter for abstraction of context. The developer should implement an algorithm in the interpreter to abstract context. In contrast, UPA provides the framework of rule-based abstraction. SO-CAM [12] is another middleware that provides a context model based on ontology and the context interpreter that abstracts the context. The context interpreter has a rule-based reasoning engine like UPA, but rules in SOCAM do not provide a function to handle the importance of rules that is realized with a weight of rule in UPA. SOCAM is used with the telematics service based on OSGi [5]. TRM [3] is another middleware for developing a context-aware telematics service. TRM emphasizes finding and gathering information in a wireless network. TRM provides a language called iQL [10] to abstract data. iQL also describes a function that outputs a abstracted data for a specific input in the same manner as the context recognition rules in UPA, but that function can't handle the feedback from the user. The importance of precision of the user's context has been discussed regarding the context-aware application of wireless mobile devices [8]. The application to support travelers is considered for instance, to explain the advantage of use of context precision to improve the response time. In this paper, we also discussed about the context precision, but our main purpose is to create a drive plan that can adapt to the user.

7   Conclusions

We developed a drive plan recommendation system @Navi with the context-aware application framework UPA. We evaluated that a combination of a reactive context-aware application framework and a drive planner can create appropriate drive plans by using the predicted user's situation. We intend to implement automatic generation of rules based on integration of many users' activities.

References

1. G-book http://g-book.com/pc/.
2. internavi premium club http://premium-club.jp/pr/.
3. C. Bisdikian, I. Boamah, P. Castro, A. Misra, J. Rubas, N. Villoutreix, D. Yeh. Intelligent pervasive middleware for context-based and localized telematics services. *Proceedings of the second international workshop on Mobile commerce, ACM Press*, pages 15–24, 2002.
4. D. Saha, A. Mukherjee. Pervasive computing: A paradigm for the 21st century. *IEEE Computer, IEEE Computer Society Press*, pages 25–31, 2003.
5. Daqing Zhang, Xiaohang Wang, et al. Osgi based service infrastructure for context aware automotive telematics. *IEEE Vehicular Technology Conference (VTC Spring 2004)*, 2004.
6. Dey A.K., Abowd G.D. Toward a better understanding of context and context-awareness. *GVU Technical Report GIT-GVU-99-22, College of Computing, Georgia Institute of Technology*, 1999.
7. Dey A.K., Abowd G.D. The context toolkit: Aiding the development of context-aware applications. *Workshop on Software Engineering for Wearable and Pervasive Computing , Limerick, Ireland*, June 2000.
8. Brown P.J. Jones G.J.F. Exploiting contextual change in context-aware retrieval. *Proceedings of the 17th ACM Symposium on Applied Computing (SAC 2002), Madrid, ACM Press, New York*, pages 650–656, 2002.
9. Masanori Hattori, Kenta Cho, Akihiko Ohsuga, Masao Isshiki, Shinichi Honiden. Context-aware agent platform in ubiquitous environments and its verification tests. *First IEEE International Conference on Pervasive Computing and Communications (PerCom'03)*, 2003.
10. Norman H. Cohen, Hui Lei, Paul Castro, John S. Davis II, Apratim Purakayastha. Composing pervasive data using iql. *Fourth IEEE Workshop on Mobile Computing Systems and Applications*, 2002.
11. Schilit B.N., Adams N.I. and Want R. Context-aware computing applications. *Proceedings of the Workshop on Mobile Computing Systems and Applications. IEEE Computer Society, Santa Cruz, CA*, pages 85–90, 1994.
12. Tao Gu, H. K. Pung, et al. A middleware for context aware mobile services. *IEEE Vehicular Technology Conference (VTC Spring 2004)*, 2004.

Clock Offsets in TDOA Localization

Nak-Seon Seong[1] and Seong-Ook Park[2]

[1] Electronics and Telecommunications Research Institute,161 Gajeong-dong, Yuseong-gu, Daejeon, 305-700, Korea
[2] Department of Electronic Engineering, Information and Communications University, 119 Munjiro, Yuseong-gu, Daejeon, 305-732, Korea
nsseong@etri.re.kr, sopark@icu.ac.kr

Abstract. Time based TDOA localization systems require time or clock synchronization between receivers such as cellular base stations, satellites, and sensor nodes. Imperfection of time synchronization causes degradation in positioning accuracy. However if we know about its characteristics and how to estimate the clock offsets, the localization system can be properly calibrated to provide good quality of services. In this paper, hence, we present how to derive a localization error vector with independent clock offset, and illustrate its effect on the positioning errors, and then, provide a simple method of TDOA clock offset estimation from the observation of error vectors.

1 Introduction

Many researches on source localizations have been addressed in many applications including sonar, radar, mobile communications, and, more recently, wireless sensor networks [1]-[6]. The approaches to the solution of the source location problem include iterative least-squares [7], [8] and maximum likelihood (ML) estimation [9]. Closed-form solutions have been given in [10]-[11], using "spherical intersection" and "spherical interpolation" methods, respectively. Fang gave an exact solution when the number of TDOA measurements is equal to the number of unknowns [12]. Meanwhile, Chan suggested a non-iterative general solution which is an approximation of maximum likelihood (ML) estimator of achieving optimum performance for arbitrarily placed sensors [5], [9]. But most of the previous works have focused on location estimation techniques. Major sources of errors in time-based localization detection schemes are the receiver time synchronization offset, the wireless multi-path fading channel, and the non-line-of-sight (NLOS) transmission. In theses, although NLOS problem is most significant, time synchronization offset (or clock offset) is primarily required to be resolved, which is our focus in this paper.

Even a few nano-seconds of clock offset can make position error of up to several meters in triangulation, which is ferocious performance for high resolution positioning systems. However, it can be mitigated by system calibration by way of observing localization error vectors and estimating the time differences of clock offset. Literatures about estimating and canceling the clock offsets in wireless sensor networks and how to self-calibrate the unknown clock offsets was recently addressed [15]-[16]. Patwari suggested joint ML estimation of clock-offsets and node

H.Y. Youn, M. Kim, and H. Morikawa (Eds.): UCS 2006, LNCS 4239, pp. 111–118, 2006.
© Springer-Verlag Berlin Heidelberg 2006

coordinates [15], and Rydström, more recently, two ML estimators of linear preprocessing operations to remove the effect of unknown clock-offsets from the estimation problem in [16].

In this paper, first, a matrix equation with independent parameters of clock offset is derived for the estimation, and the effects on the localization is illustrated, and then, finally, a simple method of how to extract the difference of clock offsets in three-receiver case is presented.

2   Effects of Clock Offset

2.1   Theory

The localization error depends on the all of the clock offsets in the receivers. Most previous works and articles provide TDOA techniques on time difference, however, this paper presents simple equation with independent clock offset parameters, and then illustrate how they causes in localization. To obtain the matrix equation, we first investigate effect of clock offset in a single receiver, and then all of the contributions from three receivers are put together.

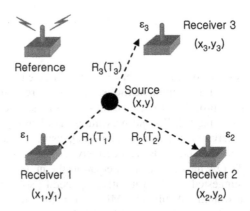

Fig. 1. Two-dimensional TDOA source localization geometry with three receivers

It is assumed that localization geometry is two-dimensional to simplify the problem, and that there are three receivers at locations (x_i, y_i), and that signals propagate in line-of-sight (LOS) without multi-paths as in Fig. 1. All the three receivers are to be synchronized to the reference clock. When the true source location is at $P(x, y)$, the range R_i (i=1,2,3) between the source and the sensor i is given by

$$R_i = \sqrt{(x_i - x)^2 + (y_i - y)^2} = CT_i \tag{1}$$

where C is the signal propagation speed and T_i is the signal flight time from the source to the receiver i according to the distance. Hence, the range difference R_{ij} between the receivers i and j is

$$R_{ij} = R_i - R_j$$
$$= \sqrt{(x_i - x)^2 + (y_i - y)^2} - \sqrt{(x_j - x)^2 + (y_j - y)^2} \tag{2}$$

so that R_{ij} is a function of x and y

$$R_{ij} = f(x, y). \tag{3}$$

and

$$\Delta R_{ij} = \frac{\partial f}{\partial x} \Delta x + \frac{\partial f}{\partial y} \Delta y \tag{4}$$

where ΔR denotes range estimation error and Δx, Δy are source location errors in x and y coordinates respectively. Substituting the partial derivatives in (4) and combing (2), (3), and (4) gives

$$\Delta R_{ij} = \frac{-1}{R_i}[(x_i - x)\Delta x + (y_i - y)\Delta y]$$
$$+ \frac{1}{R_j}[(x_j - x)\Delta x + (y_j - y)\Delta y]. \tag{5}$$

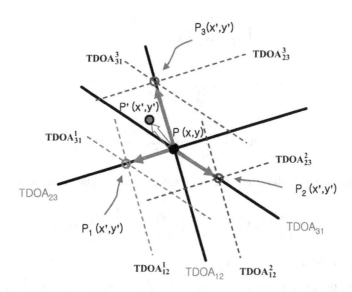

Fig. 2. Shift of hyperbolic curves due to time synchronization offset at receiver 1

Since R_{ij} can be obtained from time difference of two propagation delays of T_i, T_j, it has a relation of $R_{ij} = CT_{ij} = C(T_i - T_j)$, hence, when the offsets are small, the variation of range difference is given by

$$\Delta R_{ij} = C(\Delta T_i - \Delta T_j) = C(\varepsilon_i - \varepsilon_j) \tag{6}$$

where $\varepsilon_i, \varepsilon_j$ denote clock offset of receiver i, j from global or local reference clock.

To find individual contribution to the position error by a single clock offset at a receiver, we need to first start with $\varepsilon_i \neq 0, \varepsilon_j = 0$ in (6) and then all the contributions will be summed up. When $\varepsilon_1 \neq 0, \varepsilon_2 = \varepsilon_3 = 0$, then, in Fig. 2, the two location curves $TDOA_{12}$, $TDOA_{31}$ move to $TDOA_{12}^1$, $TDOA_{31}^1$ respectively along the $TDOA_{23}$ curve. From the two new curves, a new intersection $P_1(x',y')$ is obtained. Combining (5) and (6) gives a set of linear equations about $\mathbf{u}_1 = [\Delta x_1 \quad \Delta y_1]^T$ and ε_1 as

$$[\frac{-(x_1 - x)}{R_1} + \frac{(x_2 - x)}{R_2}]\Delta x_1 + [\frac{-(y_1 - y)}{R_1} + \frac{(y_2 - y)}{R_2}]\Delta y_1 = C\varepsilon_1 \tag{7}$$

$$[\frac{-(x_2 - x)}{R_2} + \frac{(x_3 - x)}{R_3}]\Delta x_1 + [\frac{-(y_2 - y)}{R_2} + \frac{(y_3 - y)}{R_3}]\Delta y_1 = 0 \tag{8}$$

where suffix 1 in Δx, Δy means the error from time synchronization offset at receiver 1. Combining (7) and (8) gives a matrix equation with a single independent parameter ε_1

$$\begin{bmatrix} A_{12} & B_{12} \\ A_{23} & B_{23} \end{bmatrix}\begin{bmatrix} \Delta x_1 \\ \Delta y_1 \end{bmatrix} = C\begin{bmatrix} \varepsilon_1 \\ 0 \end{bmatrix}$$

where

$$A_{ij} = \frac{-(x_i - x)}{R_i} + \frac{(x_j - x)}{R_j}$$

$$B_{ij} = \frac{-(y_i - y)}{R_i} + \frac{(y_j - y)}{R_j} (i = 1,2,3). \tag{9}$$

From (9), we can obtain the effect of clock offset due to ε_1 on the location estimation as

$$\begin{bmatrix} \Delta x_1 \\ \Delta y_1 \end{bmatrix} = C\begin{bmatrix} A_{12} & B_{12} \\ A_{23} & B_{23} \end{bmatrix}^{-1}\begin{bmatrix} \varepsilon_1 \\ 0 \end{bmatrix} = \frac{C}{D_1}\begin{bmatrix} B_{23} \\ -A_{23} \end{bmatrix}\varepsilon_1 \tag{10}$$

where D_1 is defined as $A_{12}B_{23} - A_{23}B_{12}$.

Similarly, the error vectors $\mathbf{u}_2 = [\Delta x_2 \quad \Delta y_2]^T$ and $\mathbf{u}_3 = [\Delta x_3 \quad \Delta y_3]^T$ due to ε_2, ε_3 can be also obtained as in (11) and (12)

$$\begin{bmatrix} \Delta x_2 \\ \Delta y_2 \end{bmatrix} = \frac{C}{D_2}\begin{bmatrix} B_{31} \\ -A_{31} \end{bmatrix}\varepsilon_2 \tag{11}$$

$$\begin{bmatrix} \Delta x_3 \\ \Delta y_3 \end{bmatrix} = \frac{C}{D_3} \begin{bmatrix} B_{12} \\ -A_{12} \end{bmatrix} \varepsilon_3 \qquad (12)$$

where D_2, D_3 are defined as $A_{23}B_{31} - A_{31}B_{23}$ and $A_{31}B_{12} - A_{12}B_{31}$ respectively.

Since each error vector $\mathbf{u}_i$ (i=1,2,3) is independent, the integrated location error of the source can be expressed as sum of individual error vector, $\mathbf{S}_b = \mathbf{u}_1 + \mathbf{u}_2 + \mathbf{u}_3$, and we obtain as in (14)

$$\begin{bmatrix} \Delta x \\ \Delta y \end{bmatrix} = C \begin{bmatrix} \dfrac{B_{23}}{D_1} & \dfrac{B_{31}}{D_2} & \dfrac{B_{12}}{D_3} \\ -\dfrac{A_{23}}{D_1} & -\dfrac{A_{31}}{D_2} & -\dfrac{A_{12}}{D_3} \end{bmatrix} \begin{bmatrix} \varepsilon_1 \\ \varepsilon_2 \\ \varepsilon_3 \end{bmatrix}. \qquad (13)$$

From (13), the source position error vector $\mathbf{S}_b$ is obtained in a simple matrix form of $\mathbf{S}_b = \mathbf{CHT}_b$, where $\mathbf{S}_b = [\Delta x \quad \Delta y]^T$, $\mathbf{T}_b = [\varepsilon_1 \quad \varepsilon_2 \quad \varepsilon_3]^T$, and

$$\mathbf{H} = \begin{bmatrix} \dfrac{B_{23}}{D_1} & \dfrac{B_{31}}{D_2} & \dfrac{B_{12}}{D_3} \\ -\dfrac{A_{23}}{D_1} & -\dfrac{A_{31}}{D_2} & -\dfrac{A_{12}}{D_3} \end{bmatrix}. \qquad (14)$$

Hence, the final location error ΔL is given by $\Delta L = \sqrt{\Delta x^2 + \Delta y^2}$.

2.2 Results and Discussions

Fig. 3 shows how time error of a receiver affects on the source localization. In this paper, we assume that three receivers are placed in triangular shape. We can find the fact that when a receiver is out of synchronization from a global or local reference clock but the others are not, then the localization error contours shift to the direction of the defective receiver. This means localization accuracy near the defective receiver is ironically better than other service area with perfect receivers. Direction of the error vectors reverses depending on the polarity of the clock offset [Fig. 3-(b), (c)]. However, Fig. 3-(d)-(i) gives us additional information about the movement of accuracy region. In Fig. 3-(d)-(f), error contours shift to a perfectly synchronized receiver when only one receiver is synchronized but the others have clock offsets of the same magnitudes. Fig. 3-(g)-(i), however, illustrates that the accuracy geometry moves to the opposite direction of Fig. 3-(d)-(f) when the polarities of the clock offsets of the two receivers are different each other. Hence, summing up, the information above puts the fact that localization accuracy of geometry moves the direction where a receiver has a different clock offset from the others with similar magnitudes whether or not the receiver is in a good synchronization with the reference clock.

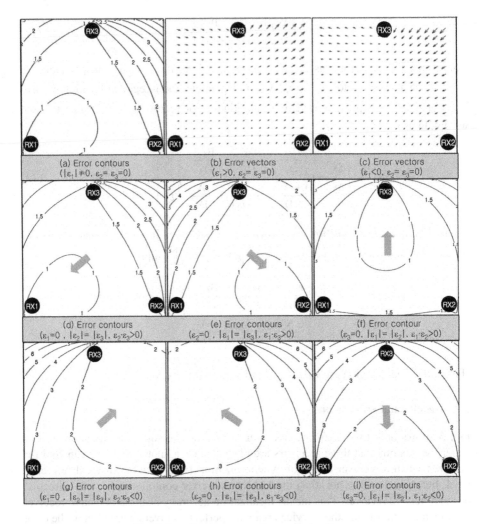

Fig. 3. Localization errors due to clock offsets

3 Estimation of Clock Offsets

In the previous section, we derived a TDOA error vector equation in a form of independent clock offset parameters as in (14). But, since matrix **H** is not a square matrix, we can not directly obtain $\mathbf{T}_b$ from (14). Using (5)-(6) again gives a simple form of solution in difference of time offsets as in (15)

$$
\begin{bmatrix}
\dfrac{-(x_1-x)}{R_1}+\dfrac{(x_2-x)}{R_2} & \dfrac{-(y_1-y)}{R_1}+\dfrac{(y_2-y)}{R_2} \\[2mm]
\dfrac{-(x_2-x)}{R_2}+\dfrac{(x_3-x)}{R_3} & \dfrac{-(y_2-y)}{R_2}+\dfrac{(y_3-y)}{R_3}
\end{bmatrix}
\begin{bmatrix}
\Delta x \\ \Delta y
\end{bmatrix}
= C
\begin{bmatrix}
\varepsilon_1-\varepsilon_2 \\ \varepsilon_2-\varepsilon_3
\end{bmatrix}
\tag{15}
$$

So we obtain $\Delta \mathbf{T}_b = \mathbf{C}^{-1}\mathbf{G}\mathbf{S}_b$ where

$$\Delta \mathbf{T}_b = \begin{bmatrix} \varepsilon_1 - \varepsilon_2 \\ \varepsilon_2 - \varepsilon_3 \end{bmatrix}$$

and

$$\mathbf{G} = \begin{bmatrix} \dfrac{-(x_1 - x)}{R_1} + \dfrac{(x_2 - x)}{R_2} & \dfrac{-(y_1 - y)}{R_1} + \dfrac{(y_2 - y)}{R_2} \\ \dfrac{-(x_2 - x)}{R_2} + \dfrac{(x_3 - x)}{R_3} & \dfrac{-(y_2 - y)}{R_2} + \dfrac{(y_3 - y)}{R_3} \end{bmatrix}. \qquad (16)$$

Measurement of $\mathbf{S}_b$ in several positions gives more accurate estimation of difference of clock offsets $\hat{\mathbf{T}}_b$ for the receivers. Since the estimation matrix is given by $E[\Delta \mathbf{T}_b] = \mathbf{C}^{-1}\mathbf{G}E[\mathbf{S}_b]$, the solution for estimated difference of clock offsets is

$$\Delta \hat{\mathbf{T}}_b = \mathbf{C}^{-1}\mathbf{G}\hat{\mathbf{S}}_b. \qquad (17)$$

4 Conclusion

We derived a new solution of independent clock offset matrix in TDOA localizations to see how each offset of a receiver affects on the source localization, and how to measure the difference of clock offsets by measuring position error data. Hence localization systems can be monitored and calibrated by simply observing error vectors and thus compensating for them.

References

1. Y. Rockah and P.M. Schultheiss, "Array Shape calibration using sources in unknown location Part I: Far-field source," IEEE Trans. Acoust., Speech, Signal Processing, vol. ASSP-35, No. 3, pp. 286-299, Mar. 1987.
2. Y. Rockah and P.M. Schultheiss, "Array Shape calibration using sources in unknown location Part II: Near-field source and estimator implementation," IEEE Trans. Acoust., Speech, Signal Processing, vol. ASSP-35, No. 6 , pp. 724-735, Jun. 1987.
3. Y.M. Chen, J.H. Lee, and C.C. Yeh, "Two- dimensional angle of arrival estimation for uniform planar array with sensor position errors," Proc. IEE Radar, Signal Processing, vol.140 No. 1, pp. 37-42, Feb. 1993.
4. W.H. Foy, "Position-location solution by Taylor series estimations," IEEE Trans. Aerosp. Electron. Syst, vol. AES-12, pp.187-194, Mar. 1976.
5. Y.T. Chan and K.C. Ho, "An efficient closed-form localization solution from time difference of arrival measurements," in Proc. IEEE ICASSP, ICASSP 94 vol. ii, , pp. II/393-II/396 Apr. 1994.
6. Xiang Ji and Hongyuan Zha, "Robust sensor localization algorithm in wireless ad-hoc sensor networks," in Proc. IEEE ICCCN 2003, pp.527 – 532, Oct. 2003.

7. R. Schmidt, "Least squares range difference location," IEEE Transactions on Aerospace and Electronic Systems, 32, 1, Jan. 1996.
8. R. Schmidt, "A new approach to geometry of range difference location," IEEE Transactions on Aerospace and Electronic Systems, AES-8, 3, Nov. 1972.
9. Y.T. Chan and K.C. Ho, "A simple and efficient estimator for hyperbolic location," IEEE Transactions on Signal Processing, 42, 8 Aug. 1994.
10. H.C. Schau and A.Z. Robinson, "Passive source localization employing intersecting spherical surfaces from time-of-arrival differences," IEEE Transactions on Acoustics, Speech, and Signal Processing, ASSP-35, Aug. 1987.
11. J.O. Smith and J.S. Abel, "Closed-form least-squares source location estimation from range-difference measurements," IEEE Transactions on Acoustics, Speech, and Signal Processing, ASSP-35, 12, Dec. 1987.
12. B.T. Fang, "Simple solutions for hyperbolic and related location fixes," in IEEE Transactions on Aerospace and Electronic Systems, vol. 26, Issue 5, Sep. 1990.
13. A. Nasipuri and K.Li, "A Directionality Based Location Discovery Scheme far Wireless Sensor Networks," SNA'O2, pp. 105-111, 2002.
14. E.D. Kaplan, "Understanding GPS: Principles and Applications," Artech House Published, 1996.
15. M. Rydström, E.G. Strom, and A. Svensson, "Clock-offset cancellation methods for positioning in asynchronous sensor networks," International Conference on Wireless Networks, Communications and Mobile Computing, vol.2, pp.981 - 986, June 2005.
16. N. Patwari, A.O. Hero III, M. Perkins, N.S. Correal, amd R.J. O'Dea, "Relative location estimation in wireless sensor networks," IEEE Transactions on Signal Processing, vol.51, Issue 8, pp.2137 – 2148, Aug. 2003.

Context-Dependent Task Computing in Pervasive Environment

Hongbo Ni[1], Xingshe Zhou[1], Daqing Zhang[2], and Ngoh Lek Heng[2]

[1] School of Computer Science, Northwestern Polytechnic University, China
{nihb, zhouxs@nwpu.edu.cn}
[2] Context Aware System Department, Institute for Infocomm Research, Singapore
{daqing, lhn}@i2r.a-star.edu.sg

Abstract. Pervasive computing environments need to exhibit highly adaptive behavior to meet the changing personal requirements and operational context of environment. Recently, task computing (TC) paradigm has gained acceptance as the choice computing model for pervasive computing environment. One of the key components of TC is a task model that provides an adequate high-level description of user-oriented tasks. This paper presents a novel context-sensitive task modeling approach capable of supporting complex, user-oriented task definitions, and proposes an algorithm to discover a task and a method to execute it. This work is motivated by the fact that whilst current TC systems allow users to interact with their ambient environments in terms of high level tasks, existing task definitions are still relatively simple, and do not include user-centric and environmental contextual information in the task definition. This paper elaborates the proposed task model through a smart home application example to illustrate steps in context-dependent task modeling, service provisioning and resource organization.

1 Introduction

In pervasive computing environments, users are immersed in a triad of sensors, invisible servers and mobile devices, offering plentiful and complex services and resources for users to access and utilize. This has resulted two critical challenges for building pervasive computing systems. One is how to stay user-focused by understanding user's goal, and the other is how to achieve these goals and activities adaptively with the available services and resources. Obviously, pervasive computing systems should enable paradigm shift from technology-oriented to user-centered, that is, they should recognize user's intentions and then autonomously fill in any technical details that user left out and assist its users in performing a suitable task from a particular set of tasks.

Recently, task computing (TC) paradigm has gained increasing acceptance as the choice computing model for pervasive computing environments [10, 11]. The key idea behind TC is that the system should take over many low-level management activities of computing resources, so that users can interact in a pervasive computing environment

H.Y. Youn, M. Kim, and H. Morikawa (Eds.): UCS 2006, LNCS 4239, pp. 119–128, 2006.

in terms of high-level, user-centric tasks (i.e. WHAT) that they wish to accomplish, rather than on the actual mechanisms (i.e. HOW) to perform those tasks. Another attraction of TC is its ability to manage the tasks in runtime by having the capability to suspend from one environment and resume the same task later in a different environment. This is made possible by the way that a task is often specified independent of both the actual underlying computing services and resources, and its surrounding environmental conditions. The underlying TC software infrastructure achieves this feature by providing the necessary support to maintain and manage task-associated context information in the form of task states (e.g. user preferences) from one environment to another. Despite its promises, however, there a number of challenges in TC that is still to be addressed fully (see Related Work section). One of these key challenges is in the modeling of user-centric tasks, its context information, and how a task can be associated with the underlying service. In this paper, we propose such a task modeling solution and the approach for supporting context-dependent task definition. In particular, we recognize the importance that in a smart pervasive computing environment, the nature of a user's task is closely associated with the context of external physical environment, as well as the particular user's profile.

Our key contributions in this paper include the definition of a context-dependent task modeling solution, proposed a partial matching scheme for the discovery of *active-tasks* based on prevailing context information, and introduce the notion of *task contract* to organize the resources and to compose available services in order to a task to be performed. Throughout this paper, an example of a smart home application is used to illustrate the modeling approach.

The remainder of this paper is organized as follows. Section 2 summarizes the current related works in TC. In section 3, we propose and elaborate the rational behind our work. Section 4 presents the details of our context-dependent task modeling solution, active task discovery scheme, and illustrates the relationship between task, context-information and underlying services through an example of a smart pervasive computing environment. Finally Section 5 summarizes this paper and highlights the future directions.

2 Related Work

There are a number of related works in pervasive computing focusing on context-aware. However, most attempts to use context-awareness in pervasive environments have been centered on the physical aspects of the user context (e.g. number, time, location) and the environment context (device proximity, lighting condition) [2]. This is despite the fact that many authors have long recognized the importance of using the cognitive aspect of the user context (such as users' goals, preferences and emotional state etc.)[3], to date, very little work has been done to develop such models and apply those models in building context-aware applications [4]. On the other hand, user context modeling has long been adopted for use in: recommendation based systems [5], adaptive information retrieval systems [6], and systems for coaching/teaching users [7, 8], and user preference and user historical information has been well utilized [9]. However, the research in exploiting both the physical and cognitive user context in those fields is still in the early stage. Our proposed modeling solution attempts to capture both these two categories of context information in defining a task.

Earlier research in the TC area has defined task-driven computing [10] and task computing [11], and demonstrated applications in a computing-oriented environment. These earlier works simply treated a task as merely binding together a set of relevant computing applications (called virtual services) in a hierarchical or otherwise fashion, with task defined as the top-level virtual service. The fundamental problem with this approach is that it is too application-centric; and since these applications are only a means to carry out a task; they are not suited to represent the task itself, nor to capture user-related context information. Furthermore, all resources within the task computing are realized as services available to the task computing clients, and it is up to the client to co-ordinate the use, and to monitor these resources. In these systems, the manually configured/defined tasks can then be executed as atomic tasks or can be used for further task compositions. Unfortunately, this is a time-consuming activity and usually means the user needs to be familiar with the environmental conditions and the available computing resources himself. This laborious process could often take longer than executing the intended tasks. This also means the user must have a reasonably in-depth knowledge of how to configure services based on his/her requirements. To solve this bottleneck, we choose instead to look beyond the applications, and focus on the user's goals and prevailing context, using the notion of context-dependent task model, couple this with an automatic TC execution framework. In another word, with our proposed solution, TC can truly be a user-oriented computing model that lets users accomplish complex tasks on-the-fly over an open, dynamic and distributed set of underlying resources/services automatically.

3   Context-Dependent Task Model

The context-dependent task modeling approach uses the abstraction of tasks in order to separate logical relations of relevant items from the services realizing and fulfilling the intended goals. This approach is able to support human requirements and preferences better because of the following reasons:

(1) Task definition models human preferences and requirements better than service-orientation models adopted in earlier works;
(2) Separation of tasks and services would allow for greater flexibility of changing the tasks without changing the services and vice-verse;
(3) It hides the complexity of compositing embedded services in pervasive environment from the users.

As mentioned above, a task is tightly related to the current context, this means that a task is highly context-dependent and this relationship must be captured in the model definition. This interpretation can for example be suitable for the development of a smart home environment, where complex cognitive tasks (e.g. "to relax at home") serving a user's need and preference are to be performed. This is in contrast to the more straight-forward computing task (e.g. "to do a presentation") in the earlier TC work [10]. We elaborate this in the rest of this section.

3.1 Basic Idea

Man is a creature of habit, and he will perform a certain activity at a particular situation as a routine. When interacting with a pervasive computing system, the user is often involved in performing a task that is shaped by his need for information, or other user-centric goals. The exact fulfillment and nature of a task is, however, heavily influenced by the actual environment context information (e.g. location, time), coupled with user's cognitive context information (e.g. preference etc). We called this task model a *context-dependent task model*, and the actual task, a *contextual-task*.

In terms of previous definition of context [12], the situation or entity we are considering is the performance relationship that links a particular user, to a particular task at a particular environment, as shown in Fig. 1.

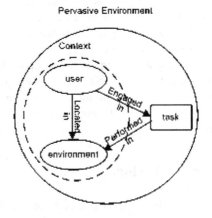

Fig. 1. A Context-dependent Task in Pervasive Environment

In Fig. 1, we illustrate that a task is dependent on the current context (including the user's state), but at the same time the context often determines the exact task to be executed, and it remains dynamic over the entire period of a particular task.

3.2 Hierarchical of Tasks and Contexts

So far we have explained the rational and established the notion of a contextual-task. In this section, we attempt to generalize this notion to cover a wide range of possible task definitions. Generally speaking, a task can be as broadly defined as, *serving the elderly*, or as narrowly defined as *making tea*. Similarly, how different task-specific context information will apply depending on the task itself. The actual scope of the task is therefore defined by its intended use, and thus to generalize, we can further define a set of related tasks and their dependency on context information in a hierarchical manner as seen here in Fig. 2.

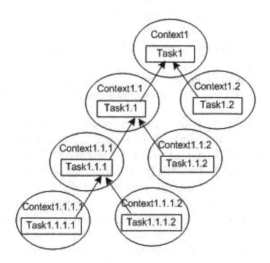

Fig. 2. Hierarchical Representations of Contexts and Tasks

To elaborate, in Fig. 2, Task1 (e.g. task "eldercare"), for instance, can be refined by Task1.1 (e.g. "activities at home") and Task1.2 ("health-care in hospital"), and Task1.1 can also be further refined by Task1.1.1 (e.g. "relaxation"), and Task1.1.2 (e.g. "bite and sup"). At the lowest level is the real task which can't be decomposed, such as Task1.1.1.1 (e.g. "watching TV") and Task 1.1.1.2 (e.g. "listening to radio"). As shown in Fig. 2, there are three types of tasks the hierarchy: an overall and generic task (root node), composite tasks (intermediate nodes) and atomic tasks (leaf nodes).

On the other hand, the context relevant to individual tasks can be similarly defined using the task hierarchy. However, the relevance of context to a task is also applicable to all the sub-tasks of a particular task. Hence, in Fig. 2, Context1 (e.g. in Singapore), would be relevant to Task1, as well as all the sub-tasks associated with Task1. Similarly, Context1.1 (e.g. apartment 01-12 in BLK567 in Clementi town) and Context 1.2 (e.g. Raffles Hospital) are related with Task1.1 and Task1.2 and their subtasks respectively. Notice that the applicability of context is necessarily from a task to its sub-tasks and not the other way round, therefore Context 1.1.1.1 (e.g. "7:00 pm in living room") is only related to Task1.1.1.1 and not Task 1.1.1, likewise, context1.1.1.2 (e.g. "8:00 am in living room") only related to Task1.1.1.2. In summary, whenever a task is decomposed into more objective sub-tasks, the related contexts will similarly be more and more specific with a sub-task automatically inherits the context of its parent tasks.

4 Discovering and Executing a Context-Dependent Task

In this section, we will address few basic issues of our proposed solution: first, how to model a task and second, given a set of context information, how to determine a suitable task to execute (i.e. *active task*, see section 4.1). Further, we show how services are related to the task model in section 4.2.

We model tasks and their relations from the idea of the context-dependent task hierarchy explained previously, where each can be further decomposed into a set of sub-tasks (in the case of a composite task), or in the case of atomic task, a set of sequential activities. A task can be described by a union of the following vocabulary:

Task-ID (TI): a unique identifier of a task in a pervasive computing application;
Task-Name (TN): a string to distinguish a task and easy to understand for a user;
Condition (C): a set of preconditions, or context information, that must be met before the task can be performed. Two kinds of conditions are included. The first is information on the user cognitive context (i.e. knowledge of habits, emotional state, physiological conditions etc.), and the other is information related to physical environment, such as location, time, weather, infrastructure (e.g. surrounding resources for computation, communication etc.), as well as physical conditions (e.g. noise, light, pressure etc.), and such information is expressed as parameters for a given task. The condition is specified in the form of parameters, and we will illustrate the use of these parameters in section 4.1.
Priority (Pr): this field denotes the importance and exigency of a task to further facilitate the execution, suspension and re-scheduling of tasks at runtime. For tasks that have the same priority their relative importance will be determined by the priority of their respective parent-tasks.
Task-Contract (TKC): this is a crucial element for our task definition. Task contract has two roles: one is to discovery necessary resources and services for the task; the other is to organize and guide the steps of executing a task. The detail of TKC is further elaborated in section 4.2.

In summary, based on our explanation above, each task is denoted by a nested 5-tuple, for example, Task1.1 can be denoted as follows:

T1.1= (TI1.1, TN1.1, C1.1, Pr1.1, TC1.1).

4.1 Active-Task Discovery

As we noted earlier, more often than not, a suitable task is determined only by considering the related context-information. To see why this is the case, let us consider following two scenarios.

Scenario A: "At 9:00 am, Mr. Brown enters the living room; he sits down on a sofa in front of the TV, Smart Home automatically recognizes the inhabitant's context, such as time, location, interests etc, and then the TV is turned on and the weather news report channel is tuned."

Scenario B: " At 8:00 pm, Mr. Brown enters the living room; he sits down on a sofa in front of the TV, and then the TV is turned on and his favorite teleplay channel is tuned. Meanwhile, Mrs. Brown is sleeping in the bedroom; the volume of TV is turned down automatically."

Hence active- task discovery refers here to the process of identifying the relevant tasks out of the entire task definitions, given the prevailing contextual information specified in the Condition clause as explained in section 4. Here, we will discuss how to discover an active task with our proposed task model. The key idea is to match the Condition parameters to the value dynamically aggregated from the environmental and user contexts. To formalize this process, let us define each Condition to be a context tuple, i.e. C=<c1,c2,...,cn>, c1...cn are a set of context attributes. In an actual system, Context tuple values are sampled periodically. In these tuples, there may be many types of attribute values according to various tasks, such as string, numerical value and Boolean. Each kind of attribute values has its own similarity calculation method, which can be expressed in a general form as follows:

$$dis(v(ci), v'(ci)) = \frac{|v(ci) - v'(ci)|}{dom(ci)} \tag{1}$$

where ci means a context attribute, v(ci) is an expected value, v'(ci) is the real-time value, and dom(ci) means the maximal difference of two values v(ci),v'(ci). Obviously, for any attribute ci, the value dis(v(ci),v'(ci)) is within[0,1]. The Condition's similarity is the combination of all evaluated attribute similarities. We further take into consideration that given it is likely that different attribute has different contribution to the overall Condition's similarity, an *attribute weight* is used for this purpose. Hence for example, location, and time can have a higher weight that others. The Condition similarity is evaluated as follows:

$$dis(T(c), T'(c)) = \sum_j wjdis(v(cj), v'(cj)) \tag{2}$$

where $\sum_{j=1} wj = 1$. The range of dis(T(c),T'(c)) is [0,1], a value of zero means perfect

match and 1meaning complete mismatch.

4.2 Task Contract

In this section, we elaborate the notion of a task contract (TKC) first mentioned in section 4 above. The main purpose of a task contract is to relate underlying resources and services to a composite or atomic task. A task contract can be defined in terms of following vocabulary:

Contract-ID (CI): unique identifier of a contract, equal to Task-ID;
Contract-Name (CN): to distinguish a contract and easy to understand for a user;
Parent-Task (PT): to describe the relationship among different tasks, especially the parent-son tasks;

Requirement (R): to express the necessary material, services (abstract of software or devices). Notice that the Requirement field is very different from Condition field in task model for two reasons. First, Condition depicts a situation surrounding a task (i.e. What), but Requirement describes the resources will be utilized in performing a task (i.e. How). Second, Condition contains an encoding of all relevant aspects about the current environment while Requirement only contains a tailored description of the relevant resources within the environment. To some extent, Condition is more generic than Requirement.

Procedure (P): this field can contain two different sets of values depending on whether the task is composite or atomic nature. In the case of an atomic task, Procedure field will include a sequence of actions that will be executed by some services associated to either some automatic devices and/or software. On the other hand, if this TC belongs to a composite task, then this field will contain information of its "leaf" tasks instead.

Using the above explanations therefore, a task contract can be defined as shown in Fig. 3. In general, however, we say a TKC is denoted by a 5-tuple, for example, the task contract of Task1.1 in Fig. 3 above can be denoted as follows:

TKC1.1= (CI1.1, CN1.1, PT1.1, R1.1, P1.1).

```
Contract ID: 1.1.3
Contract Name: WatchingTV;
Parent Task:
  Amusement;
Requirement:
  Light, Blind, TV, DVD, Hi-Fi Speaker;
Procedure:
Begin {
        ( User sitting down on a sofa in front of TV) --user-initial-event
          1. turn on the light-1 or the blinds; --sensor-ready-event
          2. turn on the TV; --TV-done-event
          3. tune to the favorite channel at the period of time; --Channel-ready-event
        if --user-rejecting-event
        then   { 3' turn on the DVD --DVD-done-event
                      4' search a popular movie--movie-ready-event
                   }
          4. adjust the volume of Hi-Fi Speaker according to the style of movie;
                                        --Speaker-done-event
} End
```

Fig. 3. An Example of a Task-contract in a Smart Home

4.3   Task Execution

Having defined the task contract in the previous subsection, we shall now focus on the steps involving in executing a task through the procedure field defined as part of the task contract. As mentioned, for an atomic task, the procedure field within the task contract will contain one or more discrete action steps. These steps specify the sequential actions to be taken during task execution, along with a number of discrete events that may happen during the execution (see Figure 4.). Conceptually, a procedure can be regarded as a finite automaton, with each state corresponds to a step during task execution, and an event which might occur during the execution. An event can come from outside user or from inside devices, sensor and software. Hence, a procedure can be defined as a directed acyclic graph (DAG) in which the nodes represent primitive actions and arcs between two nodes indicate temporal dependencies between them.

We further propose the basic algorithm for procedure execution to be based upon Firby's Reactive Action Packages (RAPs) reactive execution system, used in earlier robotics research [13]. The RAP system takes tasks and refines them into commands to enable appropriate primitive steps (similar to our actions defined above) for situation encountered at runtime [14].

In summary Fig. 4 shows a graphical representation of the relationships among the various context-dependent task model components elaborated so far. The first table is the set of tasks, and the second one is a current task derived from the context information. The third table is a corresponding task contract, and the actual procedure (i.e. actions) of performing the task illustrated in the last table. Finally, on the extreme right is the set of events that the current action in the procedure is either producing or waiting for.

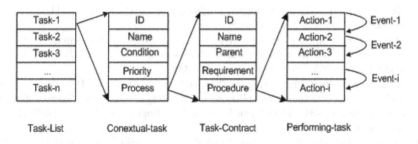

Fig. 4. Task Model and the Relationship between Task and Task Contract

5   Conclusions

This paper proposed a novel context-dependent task model suitable for task computing (TC). Our task model focuses on modeling user-centric goals and requirements, and not the numerous complex underlying system services. Furthermore, being context-sensitive, the model is capable of describing a wide range of tasks using contextual-task hierarchy, and with the ability to perform active-task discovery based on the runtime physical environment and user's context information. Furthermore, by using the task contract defined as part of the task model, the proposed model bridges and solves issues of underlying service requirements for a specific task. We believe that the proposed model is more general and is able to support a wider range of task-based computation applications than current related works. We are currently evaluating the proposed model for elderly care applications in a smart-home environment, using OWL [15] to define ULCO (Upper Level Context Ontology). Finally, the work here represents the authors' initial attempt to unravel the complexities of user's goal recognition, task-based computing, together with infrastructural service support and adaptation, which are the critical issues in pervasive computing environments.

References

[1] M. Weiser, "Some Computer Science Issues in Ubiquitous Computing. Communication," *Communications of the ACM,* 1993, vol. 36, no. 7, pp. 75-84.

[2] P.Castro and R. Muntz, "Managing Context Data for Smart Spaces," IEEE Personal Communications, 2000, vol. 7, pp. 44-46.

[3] Paul Prekop and Mark Burnett, "Activities, Context and Ubiquitous Computing, Computer Communications", 2003, vol. 26, no. 11, pp. 1168-1176.

[4] Heckmann, D., "Introducing Situational Statements as an integrating Data Structure for User Modeling, Context-Awareness and Resource-Adaptive Computing", ABIS Workshop on adaptivity and user modeling in interactive software systems, 2003.

[5] Tiffany Y. Tang and Gordon McCalla, "Smart Recommendation for an Evolving E-Learning System", AIED2003, Vol10, PP. 699-711.

[6] Charles Seger Jakobsen and Simon Warthoe, "Adaptive Design Implications for Knowledge Organization and Information Retrieval Systems", Nord I&D, Knowledge and Change, 2004, PP. 58-61.

[7] Kay J., "The um toolkit for cooperative user modeling", User Modeling and User-Adapted Interaction, 1995, Vol 3, pp. 149-196.

[8] Shareef A. F. & Kinshuk, Student Model for Distance Education System in Maldives. In A. Rossett (Ed.) Proceedings of E-Learn 2003 (November 7-11, 2003, Phoenix, Arizona, USA), Norfolk, VA, USA: AACE, pp. 2435-2438.

[9] Zhiwen Yu, Daqing Zhang, Xingshe Zhou, and Changde Li, "User Preference Learning for Multimedia Personalization in Pervasive Computing Environment", in Proc. of 9th Int. Conf. Knowledge-Based Intelligent Information & Engineering Systems (KES'2005), , September 2005, pp. 236-242.

[10] Zhenyu Wang and David Garlan, "Task-driven computing", Technical Report, NO. CMU-CS-00-154, http://www-2.cs.cmu.edu/~aura/docdir/wang00.pdf, Carnegie Mellon University, May 2000.

[11] R. Masuoka, et al., "Task computing - the Semantic Web meets Pervasive Computing", 2nd International Semantic Web Conference, ISWC2003, pp. 866-881.

[12] A. K. Dey and G. D. Abowd, "Towards a Better Understanding of Context and Context-Awareness," College of Computing, Georgia Institute of Technology, Atlanta GA USA, Technical Report GIT-GVU-99-22, 1999.

[13] Firby, R. J.; Kahn, R. E.; Prokopowicz, P. N.; and Swain, M. J., "An architecture for vision and action", In Fourteenth International Joint Conference on Artificial Intelligence, 1995, pp. 72-81.

[14] R. J. Firby, "Task networks for controlling continuous processes", In Proceedings of the Second International Conference on Artificial Intelligence Planning Systems, 1994, pp. 49-54.

[15] X.H. Wang, D.Q. Zhang, H.K. Pung, "Ontology Based Context Modeling and Reasoning using OWL", In *Workshop Proceedings of the 2nd IEEE Conference on Pervasive Computing and Communications (PerCom2004),,*2004, pp. 18–22.

Semantic Information Retrieval in the COMPASS Location System

Frank Kargl, Günter Dannhäuser, Stefan Schlott, and Jürgen Nagler-Ihlein

Ulm University, Media Informatics Institute, Ulm, Germany

Abstract. In our previous work, we have described the COMPASS location system that uses multiple information sources to determine the current position of a node. The raw output of this process is a location in geo-coordinates, which is not suitable for many applications. In this paper we present an extension to COMPASS, the so called Translator, that can provide facts about the location like city name, address, room number, etc. to the application. These facts are represented in the Semantic Web RDF/XML language and stored on distributed Geo RDF Servers. The main focus of this paper is a location-based service discovery mechanism which allows a node to find all services that can provide facts about its current location. This discovery service is built upon a structured Peer-to-Peer system implementing a distributed hash table.

1 Overview

In our previous work, we have presented the COMPASS location system [1] which merges the results of different location sensors like GPS or WLAN signal positioning and thus provides a more accurate and available positioning solution. The delivered geo-coordinate of the current position is then used to search for location-based services (LBS) that provide additional information about that position. In this paper we present these mechanisms and focus on the mechanisms to discover the LBS in a decentralized and self-organizing manner.

The paper is structured as follows: In Section 2, we give a brief overview on the COMPASS architecture. Section 3 describes the Geo RDF Service (GRS), a server that provides semantic information on specific locations. In Section 4 we outline general mechanisms for location-based service discovery and develop the idea of a distributed directory for GRSs using a quadtree index mapping to a structured peer-to-peer network. The concepts and implementation of our discovery solution is presented in detail in Section 5. Section 6 considers related work in this domain before we close in Section 7 with a summary and give an outlook on the further development.

2 Introduction to COMPASS and Motivation

Figure 1 shows the overall architecture of COMPASS. As shown, it includes multiple sensors which each provide location information to the Locator. The

H.Y. Youn, M. Kim, and H. Morikawa (Eds.): UCS 2006, LNCS 4239, pp. 129–143, 2006.

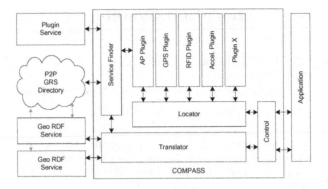

Fig. 1. COMPASS architecture

output of each sensor is a so called Probability Distribution Function (PDF) which is based on ideas presented by Angermann, Wendlandt et al [2, 3].

PDFs are 2- or 3-dimensional probability distributions that represent the measurements of single sensors or a combined measurement of multiple sensors. Figure 2 shows an example of a PDF which might represent a user that is inside a building with crossing corridors. This information can e.g. be the result of sensors which detected that the mobile user entered this corridor and has not left it since.

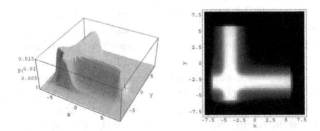

Fig. 2. Example of Probability Distribution Function (from [2])

Additionally, a PDF contains the origin expressed as WGS-84 coordinates. When multiple sensors output PDFs, these can easily be combined to a joined PDF. In the architecture, it is the job of the *Locator* to manage all the different sensor plugins and to collect and combine the PDFs. Using the Control API, applications can retrieve the combined PDF and determine the position with the highest probability.

For many applications, a position given as geographic coordinates is not very useful. Instead, a semantic form of position representation is needed, e.g. in terms of city, building, room, etc.

Given a specific geographic position discovered by the Locator, the Translator component is responsible for collecting this kind of information from the network.

In our previous paper [1] we implemented and described only a minimum version of the Translator. Position information was given as text strings of the form "germany.ulm.university.main_building.o27.3303" and the storage and retrieval of this information was done via a simple and centralized web service that took a WGS-84 coordinate as input and returned the information string as output.

Of course, this approach has a number of severe drawbacks. First, only one fixed string as output is much too restricted. Given a location, lots of information about this place may be given. So, a more flexible format to represent location information is needed. We now have implemented a system where we use a RDF vocabulary for that purpose. RDF, the "Resource Description Framework", is an XML application proposed by the W3C as part of their Semantic Web initiative [4]. RDF represents facts as simple triples of the form *subject, predicate, object*. The following RDF document shows an example, where for the subject "http://informatik.uni-ulm.de/o27/h20" a type and some properties are given; its location is defined by some coordinates and also semantically by a certain street address.

```
<?xml version="1.0" encoding="iso-8859-1" ?>
<rdf:RDF
    xmlns:rdf="http://www.w3.org/1999/02/22-rdf-syntax-ns#"
    xmlns:loca="http://uni-ulm.de/rdfschema/location#"
    xmlns:room="http://uni-ulm.de/rdfschema/room#" >
  <rdf:Description rdf:about="http://informatik.uni-ulm.de/o27/h20">
    <rdf:type rdf:resource="http://uni-ulm.de/rdfschema/auditorium" />
    <room:label>H20</room:label>
    <room:seats>150</room:seats>
    <loca:validIn>
      <rdf:Description>
        <loca:north>48252117N</loca:north>
        <loca:west>009572634E</loca:west>
        <loca:south>48252008N</loca:south>
        <loca:east>009572758E</loca:east>
      </rdf:Description>
    </loca:validIn>
    <loca:Address>
      <street>Albert-Einstein-Allee</street><number>11</number>
      <city rdf:resource="http://ulm.de/" />
    </loca:Address>
  </rdf:Description>
</rdf:RDF>
```

One big advantage of using RDF is that facts from different sources can easily be combined by a mechanical inference systems. So, an application that receives the above RDF from the COMPASS location system can try to query public RDF databases in the semantic web for facts on *http://ulm.de/* and discover additional information on that city which it can present to the user.

A second drawback of our earlier Translator implementation lies in the fact that we used a centralized and pre-configured service for getting the information. In reality, such a centralized service is unlikely to become widely accepted.

Instead, several institutions or even individual companies or private persons will run servers that provide information for certain areas like countries, cities or individual buildings.

This raises the question, how these services are to be found, if they are not configured statically. One solution to this problem is the main focus of this paper.

3   Geo RDF Service

As shown in Figure 1, the so called Geo RDF Services (GRS) store the RDF information for certain locations. Each Geo RDF service provides information on one or more areas. These areas can be of an arbitrary form, for simplicity reasons, our prototype implementation only supports rectangle areas, where the corners are given in WGS-84 coordinates.

The service has a simple SOAP interface, where a client (the Translator component in COMPASS) connects, provides its WGS-84 coordinate as argument and receives as result an RDF document, containing all the facts that the service knows for this location.

Internally, the GRS stores the RDF statements in an RDF database and uses the RDF Query Language RDQL [5] for retrieval of suitable facts. The area where a fact is valid is again given by geometric primitives, like rectangles, circles or polygons[1]. This area is stored as a *validIn* property with the RDF facts and is called fact validity area (FVA). The minimum bounding box (MBB) of all fact validity areas is the service coverage area (SCA), i.e. the area where a service might be able to provide facts for locations lying inside. These concepts are illustrated in Figure 3.

So in order to find information on its current location, COMPASS only needs to find a suitable list of GRS servers, or more precisely a list of service URIs for these servers. This process is commonly called service discovery. In our special case we need to find all services where the SCA includes our current location. We call this special case location-based service discovery. In the next section we review a number of mechanisms that may be helpful in this location-based service discovery (LBSD).

4   Mechanisms for Location-Based Service Discovery

4.1   General Mechanisms

Ahn et al [6] lists several forms of queries that can be used to access multidimensional data. In our case, we do a so called *Point Query*, where a node wants to find all objects, that cover a given point. More precisely, we want to find the URIs of all Geo RDF Servers where the SCA includes the given location.

The most simple form of a location-based service discovery mechanism to support this is a *centralized directory server* that stores the SCAs and URIs of

---

[1] Again, the prototype implementation only supports rectangles.

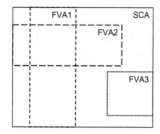

Fig. 3. Fact Validity Areas and Service Coverage Area

all Geo RDF Servers worldwide. Obviously, this approach creates huge scalability and organizational problems.

Another approach would be a *local service discovery mechanism*, where clients send a broad-, multi-, or anycast message to the local network. Local Geo RDF Servers can then respond to that query, providing their access information. To prevent overloading the whole network, the flooding is usually restricted by means of a time-to-live counter or similar mechanism. The problem with this approach is the limited reach of the service discovery. It will only find GRS in the local network or at least in the vicinity. On the other hand, if a local node is currently attached to a wireless access point of provider A, a GRS operated by provider B may well provide information for the same physical area, although the networks of the two providers have no direct peering and are far away from each other in terms of network connectivity. So relying on vicinity in network topology for location-based service discovery is not really a wise choice.

To overcome the restrictions of both approaches many systems use distributed directories, where a set of servers stores the data, eventually replicating all or a part of it. Examples of systems that support distributed service directories include INS [7] or SSDS [8]. Whereas the first one supports full replication in a small domain of servers, the latter is an example of a hierarchical system.

Both approaches again have problems in scalability, as either the number of servers is restricted or the organization of the servers demands manual administration. Peer-2-Peer (P2P) systems that allow the distributed storage and retrieval of data in a self-organizing manner offer a solution to this problem. In a (pure) P2P network, there are no special nodes, all nodes (the so called peers) can perform the same tasks and operations.

4.2 Structured Peer-to-Peer Systems and Distributed Hash Tables

So called Distributed Hash Tables (DHT) allow the storage and retrieval of arbitrary data in a P2P network. For indexing, a unique key is used that is usually generated by hashing an identifier like the filename. In contrast to the well known unstructured P2P systems like Napster or Gnutella, structured P2P systems do not flood requests throughout the network but organize the P2P nodes in a way so that the (storage or retrieval) requests can be routed toward a destination.

A prominent example of a DHT system is Chord [9], where the peers are organized in a ring structure. Each peer and each data object needs an unique identifier which is generated by hashing e.g. its IP address or the filename with a hash function like SHA-1. Peer- and Data-IDs must have the same size. Each peer node manages the keyspace from its predecessor to its own Peer-ID.

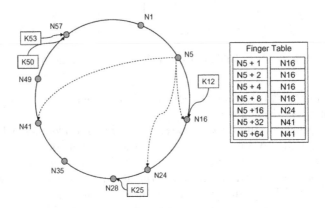

Fig. 4. An example of a Chord Ring

Figure 4 shows an example of such a Chord ring. This ring uses 6 bit key length and currently contains nine nodes. Each node knows its pre- and successor. When new nodes are inserted into the ring, they need to find their correct position and update the pre-/successor relationships accordingly. When data is to be stored in the ring, the storing node first calculates the Data-ID. Then it starts with an arbitrary node in the ring and sends a query to the node which is then forwarded along the ring until it reaches the responsible node with the next higher Peer-ID. So in this example, data with the Data-ID 25 is stored on node 28. As navigating through the ring would require $O(N)$ messages, each node stores a so called finger table which contains pointers to the next $\lceil \text{NodeID}+2^i \rceil$ nodes. Using these finger tables, routing can take shortcuts, reducing the message overhead to $O(\log N)$. So when e.g. node 5 wants to send a message to node 49, it can use its finger table to directly send the message to node 41 which can forward it to node 49.

A system similar to Chord is Pastry [10] where nodes are also structured in a ring, but routing is organized slightly different.

Bamboo is an open-source implementation of a slightly re-engineered Pastry DHT [11]. OpenDHT [12] is a free, public DHT service running the Bamboo implementation on PlanetLab [13]. "PlanetLab is a geographically distributed overlay network designed to support the deployment and evaluation of planetary-scale network services."

By using a DHT service like OpenDHT, we are now able to store and retrieve key-value pairs in a world-wide distributed, self-organizing, and scalable database consisting of peer nodes. Geo RDF Services that want to register at the discovery service simply use their URIs as values. The next problem is the construction of keys: when COMPASS clients want to retrieve GRS servers for their location, the discovery system should return only the URIs of these servers that actually cover the node's location with their service coverage area.

What we need is a way to map an area to a key in the keyspace of the DHT system. DHT systems like OpenDHT usually use flat keyspaces of fixed size, e.g. 160 bit (the output of a SHA-1 hash function).

4.3   Point and Spatial Access Methods

Our first idea was to use space-filling curves like the Hilbert- or Z-curves to construct the keys. Using e.g. a 2-dimensional Z-curve [14] partitions the area to cover with a grid where each x- and y-coordinate can be transformed to an index value using bit interleaving. For each grid cell covered, a Geo RDF Server could then insert an entry to the DHT, mapping the index value to the URI of the server[2].

Unfortunately, these indexing methods need a pre-determined grid resolution. When using the maximum available keyspace and given the 160 bit keyspace of the DHT, we have a resolution of 80 bits per axis. Mapped on geo coordinates, this allows a longitude resolution of $3*10^{-17}$ meters at the equator. Well enough for most applications. On the other hand this means that a service that covers only an area of 1 square meter needs to set $9*10^{32}$ DHT entries. Reducing the resolution can of course lessen this problem. But even when we set the resolution to 1 meter per axis (which is pretty reasonable for indoor applications), a service that e.g. covers whole Germany still needs about 10^{17} entries in the DHT.

So we clearly need a more flexible mechanism that adapts to the size and resolution requirements of the service and its covered area. We found that space partitioning trees like Quadtrees and R-Trees are good candidates for use in COMPASS.

Quadtrees were introduced 1974 by Finkel and Bentley [15]. They can easily be extended to also cover 3D data and are then called Octrees. A special form, the so called MX-CIF Quadtree [16] is presented later.

Figure 5 gives an example of a Quadtree. As you can see, the depth of the tree controls the resolution of areas. In areas where only a coarse-grained resolution is necessary, the tree is not as deep as in areas where fine grained resolution is needed.

A variant of the Quadtree is the MX-CIF Quadtree [16]. The MX-CIF Quadtree is used to store and retrieve references to arbitrary sized areas. Figure 6 shows areas labeled from A to G. For each area, the algorithm determines the Minimum Bounding Box (MBB), which is the smallest Quadtree partition that completely encloses the area. The area data is then stored in the respective position in the tree as shown in part a).

When you want to retrieve data for a certain position, you simply descend the tree based on the globally-known partitioning scheme until you reach a leaf

---

[2] OpenDHT allows to store multiple entries per key, so multiple GRS could announce their service for the same cell.

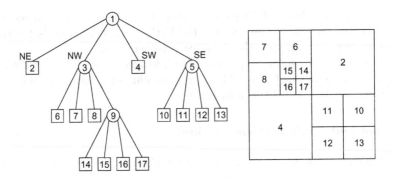

Fig. 5. An Example of a Quadtree

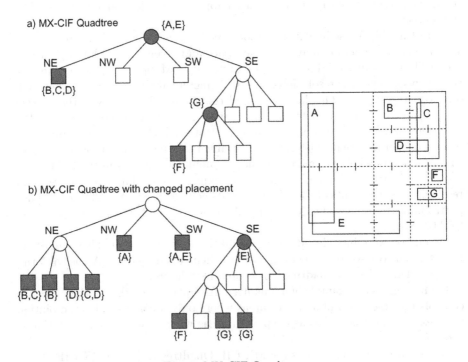

Fig. 6. MX-CIF Quadtrees

node. All references found in this process are potential hits and need a separate check whether the referenced area actually includes your position.

As you can see in the example, area D is referenced from the north-eastern quarter which encloses a much larger area than just D. Therefore, many clients will do the check and find that the location is not inside D. In order to balance between storage and retrieval overhead, one can modify the placement scheme for the MX-CIF Quadtree.

In tree b) we have done this and added a rule where each area reference is pushed down one tree level. This can lead to area separation, so the same area is stored at multiple tree nodes as you can again see for area D. So the storage costs have increased, but the retrieval gets more efficient, as clients checking locations in the northern half of the north-eastern quarter will not find the irrelevant references to D.

Further tuning options are maximum and minimum storage height. In order to prevent too many results or too deep trees, one could set a minimum and maximum threshold for the tree-level where no data is stored above or below this level respectively.

Another potential data structure for spatial data access are R-Trees [17] which are an extension of the well-known B-Trees. As these trees may need a tree reorganization when data is inserted or deleted, they are not well suited for usage in a distributed P2P system. For this reason R-Trees are not considered further.

5   The COMPASS Translator Service

Based on the mechanisms shown above, we now describe the design and implementation of the Translator mechanism in COMPASS.

In our system, Geo RDF Services (GRS) are Web Services with a well known interface that take a location as input and respond with an XML document that contains RDF facts that are true for that position.

5.1   The P2P GRS Directory

In order to be found, these services need to register with the P2P GRS Directory. This mechanism is implemented using the Bamboo Distributed Hash Table. For the purpose of our prototype, we used the OpenDHT service that runs on top of PlanetLab. Bamboo and OpenDHT provide simple put and retrieve commands where one can either put a key-value pair to the DHT or retrieve all values that are stored for a certain key. As entries expire after some time, the registration needs to be updated regularly. This prevents stale entries from services that become unavailable.

We use a distributed MX-CIF tree to store the index for the areas. Nodes in the tree are mapped to the DHT in the following way:

1. We call P_S a *partition section* where S is a string that determines the precise position in the area partitioning. $S = (s)^i | s \in \{1, 2, 3, 4\}, i \in \mathbb{N}$. i denotes the tree level and for each level, the value of s gives the quarter to select. 1 stands for north-east, 2 for north-west, 3 for south-west and 4 for south-east. Each partition section corresponds to a node in the MX-CIF tree.
2. Let x_{P_S} be the longitude and y_{P_S} the latitude of the center of the partition section P_S. $C_{P_S} = (x_{P_S}, y_{P_S})$ denotes this center position. All coordinates are given as WGS-84.

3. The covered area and the center of this area C_P is well known. When using COMPASS in a worldwide context, $C_P = (0°, 0°)$. The area covered is the whole world. The above steps uniquely determine the partitioning scheme. All the sections on all levels are fixed and can be calculated by all involved parties without storing any partitioning information in the DHT.

4. $h(C_{P_S})$ is used as a key for the DHT where h is a hash function that delivers the correct key size (SHA-1 in the implementation).

5.2   GRS Registration

Each GRS has a list of covered areas A_j. For simplicity, our prototype only supports rectangular, 2-dimensional areas. The extension to arbitrary shapes (e.g. polygons) and 3 dimensions (taking height as 3rd coordinate) is straight forward, but not implemented yet.

For each A_j, the GRS determines MBB_{A_j}, the Minimum Bounding Box(es) and next the partition P_S that completely includes MBB_{A_j}. Let $k = h(C_{P_S})$. It then calls the P2P GRS Directory and issues a

$$\text{put}(k, "COMPASS\_URI\_" + < \text{URI} >)$$

where URI is the URI of the Web Service. The string in front of the URI is used to distinguish entry types. This registration needs to be done in regular intervals to prevent expiration of entries in the DHT.

There is no explicit tree stored in the DHT. In order to determine if there are child nodes, a client that received results for a certain node in the tree would need to send queries for child node keys and see whether the DHT delivers a result or not. To prevent this unnecessary overhead, the GRS sets flags that let clients determine whether additional tree levels are available. So for all elements

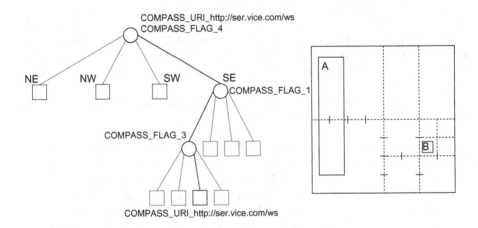

Fig. 7. COMPASS Tree

$s \in S$ in P_S, the GRS also sets a flag of the form "COMPASS_FLAG_s" on the next higher tree level.

Figure 7 shows an example, where a service located at http://ser.vice.com/ws registers for two areas A and B and sets the corresponding keys in the DHT. This example uses the original MX-CIF placement without modifications whereas the actual implementation uses the optimizations as described earlier.

There is no explicit mechanism for deleting entries; instead services simply wait for the expiration of entries. If a GRS goes offline in the meantime, this will result in stale requests to the web service in the worst case.

5.3 Service Discovery

When the Translator wants to find a suitable GRS, it uses the PDF from the Locator to find its current position. It simply takes the position with maximum probability in the PDF.

All the functionality for searching suitable services is located in the Service Finder. The Service Finder traverses the MX-CIF Quadtree from the root to the current position. For each level it calculates $h(C_{P_S})$, queries the DHT for that key, collects all COMPASS_URI_* results and COMPASS_FLAGS and descends one level, if the corresponding COMPASS_FLAG_s flag is set.

As this may lead to a lot of wrong URIs returned, esp. on the higher levels of the tree, we also implement the MX-CIF Quadtree modifications described at the end of Section 4.3.

5.4 Service Access

After the URIs are collected and the tree has been traversed down to its bottom, the Translator tries to access all the discovered GRS in turn, asking for information on the current position. GRS that do not have information on that position simply return an empty document.

The Translator then merges all the returned RDF statements into one RDF document and returns that to the application.

5.5 Implementation

We have implemented the described system as a prototype and have run a number of preliminary tests that showed that our approach is usable in practice. A first test case was to register and lookup an average sized object (on level 17 of the distributed quadtree) in the P2P GRS Directory. We did runs in 1-hour intervals over one day, each run with 10 consecutive registration and lookup processes. Although most get-requests were answered within one second, the distribution of response times showed a long tail with single response times above 10s. To reduce the total time needed by the Translator, we implemented OpenDHT-requests as well as Geo RDF (Web) Service requests to be executed concurrently in thread pools (default 10 threads). To allow for load distribution among OpenDHT-gateways and further optimizing the performance, clients maintain a list of reachable gateways. For each put/get-request, the gateway to be used is chosen from this list on basis of its ping-latency, the latencies observed in previous requests and the number of concurrent requests by the respective client.

The median time measured for single gets was 650ms. In an example scenario, the median time for the complete process of translating a discrete coordinate into semantical information for a auditorium at our university was 2.7s.

For single put-operations, we observed a somewhat higher median latency of 1.2s. A 95 percentile of "stragglers" had response times of 3.5s and we even observed response times above 50 seconds. Thus, the median time for registering a Geo RDF Service in our example scenario rose to 8.5s.

As the information of GRS is not expected to be very dynamic, these median values would be feasible for COMPASS. The main problem lays with "stragglers" – slow nodes in the OpenDHT-network – that may introduce delays of dozens of seconds to the registration or lookup-process of GRS. The OpenDHT authors are aware of this problem and are working on solutions [18]. Another solution would be to drop OpenDHT and use Bamboo on a dedicated P2P infrastructure.

6   Related Work

Many recent approaches target mainly range- and nearest-neighbor queries on one-dimensional data in Peer-to-Peer networks. Particularly work on Sensor Networks and Mobile Ad-hoc Networks [25, 26] contributed useful ideas to this related problem domain. In contrast, COMPASS deals with point-queries on multi-dimensional data, i.e. objects with spatial (geographical) extent. There are a number of similar systems that also try to develop a spatial access method for Peer-to-Peer systems.

One is P2PR-Tree [19], which uses R-Trees for building the index. As the authors want to limit the overhead of tree reorganization, they use a static partitioning for the first two levels and an R-Tree with reorganization on the lower levels. Nevertheless, the system will have a substantial reorganization overhead, once the tree gets deeper.

Tanin, Harwood, Samet et al presented several solutions that use distributed Quad- or Octrees to do spatial indexing of objects in a Cartesian space [20, 22, 23]. In "A serverless 3D World" [21] they implement a distributed Octree on basis of their "Open P2P Network" architecture using a modification of Chord for an online multi-participant virtual-world systems. In contrast to that, we decided to abstract from the underlying DHT utilizing the OpenDHT service, which also frees us from the need to deploy and maintain our own DHT infrastructure.

Intel Research's Place Lab Project also uses a OpenDHT based system for a distributed storage and retrieval of their beacon database[24]. They achieve locality-preserving hashing of geographical coordinates to the OpenDHT keyspace using space-filling curves and "Prefix Hash Trees" – a distributed trie-like data structure. Though one goal of this solution was a strictly layered implementation on top of OpenDHT, potential race conditions made it necessary to introduce additional functions to the OpenDHT API.

In "Exploiting Location Awareness for Scalable Location-Independent Object IDs" [27], the authors develop a distribution mechanism for the workload of a wide-area location service that tracks the location of mobile and replicated objects. They partition the underlying network into a hierarchy of geographical domains and try to minimize network communication paths by exploiting the knowledge of the geographical location of nodes. Directory nodes that store location information for all objects within the associated domain form a distributed search tree. Routing is based on shortest distances of physical nodes to the locations stored with object references in the tree. For that purpose, they employ a location-mapping table based on a quadtree. Prerequisite for this approach is the knowledge of physical node locations of P2P nodes, an assumption we consciously avoided.

7   Summary and Outlook

In this paper we have presented the Translator component of the COMPASS system. It uses a location-based service discovery mechanism that is based on structured Peer-to-Peer systems, Distributed Hash Tables, and MX-CIF Quadtrees. For the semantic representation of facts on a location we use an RDF vocabulary.

The system has been implemented in a prototype which uses OpenDHT as DHT implementation and has shown its basic practicability. Our next steps will be to test and enhance the performance further. Another idea is to implement some kind of fact cache. At the moment facts are retrieved freshly on each request. But as facts are also labeled with properties that express the area where they are valid in, this information could be used to temporarily cache the RDF statements in the translator and add them to future queries as long as the client stays in the valid area. Finally, we are developing an in-door navigation system as example application for COMPASS.

References

1. Kargl, F., Bernauer, A.: The compass location system. In: Location- And Context Awareness, First International Workshop, LoCA 2005. Number 3479 in LNCS (2005)
2. Angermann, M., Kammann, J., Robertson, P., Steinga¯, A., Strang, T.: Software representation for heterogeneous location data sources within a probabilistic framework. In: International Symposium on Location Based Services for Cellular Users, Locellus (2001) 107–118
3. Wendlandt, K., Ouhmich, A., Angermann, M., Robertson, P.: Implementation of soft location on mobile devices. In: International Symposium on Indoor Localisation and Position Finding, InLoc 2002, Bonn, Germany (2002)
4. W3C: The resource description framework (rdf). http://www.w3.org/RDF/ (2005)
5. W3C: Rdql - a query language for rdf. http://www.w3.org/Submission/2004/SUBM-RDQL-20040109/ (2004)
6. Ahn, H.K., Mamoulis, N., Wong, H.M.: A survey on multidimensional access methods. Technical report, Institute of Infomation and Computing Sciences, Utrecht University, The Netherlands (2001)

7. Adjie-Winoto, W., Schwartz, E., Balakrishnan, H., Lilley, J.: The design and implementation of an intentional naming system. In: SOSP '99: Proceedings of the seventeenth ACM symposium on Operating systems principles, New York, NY, USA, ACM Press (1999) 186–201
8. Czerwinski, S.E., Zhao, B.Y., Hodes, T.D., Joseph, A.D., Katz, R.H.: An architecture for a secure service discovery service. In: MobiCom '99: Proceedings of the 5th annual ACM/IEEE international conference on Mobile computing and networking, New York, NY, USA, ACM Press (1999) 24–35
9. Stoica, I., Morris, R., Liben-Nowell, D., Karger, D.R., Kaashoek, M.F., Dabek, F., Balakrishnan, H.: Chord: a scalable peer-to-peer lookup protocol for internet applications. IEEE/ACM Trans. Netw. **11**(1) (2003) 17–32
10. Rowstron, A.I.T., Druschel, P.: Pastry: Scalable, decentralized object location, and routing for large-scale peer-to-peer systems. In: Middleware 2001: Proceedings of the IFIP/ACM International Conference on Distributed Systems Platforms Heidelberg, London, UK, Springer-Verlag (2001) 329–350
11. Rhea, S., Geels, D., Roscoe, T., Kubiatowicz, J.: Handling churn in a dht. In: Proceedings of the USENIX Annual Technical Conference. (2004)
12. Rhea, S., Godfrey, B., Karp, B., Kubiatowicz, J., Ratnasamy, S., Shenker, S., Stoica, I., Yu., H.: Opendht: A public dht service and its uses. In: Proceedings of ACM SIGCOMM 2005. (2005)
13. Bavier, A., Bowman, M., Chun, B., Culler, D., Karlin, S., Muir, S., Peterson, L., Roscoe, T., andMike Wawrzoniak, T.S.: Operating system support for planetary-scale services. In: Proceedings of the First Symposium on Network Systems Design and Implementation (NSDI). (2004)
14. Boehm, C., Klump, G., Kriegel, H.P.: XZ-Ordering: A space-filling curve for objects with spatial extension. In: Proceedings of Advances in Spatial Databases, 6th International Symposium, SSD'99, Hong Kong, China (1999) 75–90
15. Finkel, R., Bentley, J.: Quad-trees: a data structure for retrieval on composite keys. Acta Informatica **4** (1974) 1–9
16. Kedem, G.: The Quad-CIF tree: A Data Structure for Hierarchical On-line Algorithms. In: Proceedings of the Nineteenth Design Automation Conference, Las Vegas (1982) 352–357
17. Guttman, A.: R-trees: a dynamic index structure for spatial searching. In: SIGMOD '84: Proceedings of the 1984 ACM SIGMOD international conference on Management of data, New York, NY, USA, ACM Press (1984) 47–57
18. Rhea, S., Chun, B.G., Kubiatowicz, J., Shenker, S.: Fixing the embarrassing slowness of opendht on planetlab. In: Proceedings of USENIX WORLDS 2005. (2005)
19. Mondal, A., Lifu, Y., Kitsuregawa, M.: P2pr-tree: An r-tree-based spatial index for peer-to-peer environments. In: Current Trends in Database Technology - EDBT 2004. Volume 3268 of Lecture Notes in Computer Science. (2004) 516–525
20. Tanin, E., Harwood, A., Samet, H.: Indexing distributed complex data for complex queries. In: Proceedings of the National Conference on Digital Government Research, Seattle, WA (2004) 81–91
21. Tanin, E., Harwood, A., Samet, H., Nutanong, S., Truong, M.T.: A serverless 3d world. In: GIS '04: Proceedings of the 12th annual ACM international workshop on Geographic information systems, New York, NY, USA, ACM Press (2004) 157–165
22. Tanin, E., Harwood, A., Samet, H.: A distributed quadtree index for peer-to-peer settings. In: ICDE '05: Proceedings of the 21st International Conference on Data Engineering (ICDE'05), Washington, DC, USA, IEEE Computer Society (2005) 254–255

23. Tanin, E., Nayar, D., Samet, H.: An efficient nearest neighbor algorithm for p2p settings. In: dg.o2005: Proceedings of the 2005 national conference on Digital government research, Digital Government Research Center (2005) 21–28
24. Chawathe, Y., Ramabhadran, S., Ratnasamy, S., LaMarca, A., Shenker, S., Hellerstein, J.: A case study in building layered dht applications. In: SIGCOMM '05: Proceedings of the 2005 conference on Applications, technologies, architectures, and protocols for computer communications, New York, NY, USA, ACM Press (2005) 97–108
25. Demirbas, M., Ferhatosmanoglu, H. Peer-to-peer spatial queries in sensor networks In: Proceedings of the 3rd IEEE International Conference on Peer-to-Peer Computing (P2P '03), Linkoping, Sweden, (2003)
26. Cai, M., Frank, M., Chen, J., Szekely, P. MAAN: A Multi-Attribute Addressable Network for Grid Information Services In: 4th International Workshop on Grid Computing (GRID 2003), Phoenix, AZ, USA, IEEE Computer Society (2003) 184–191
27. Ballintijn, G., Van Steen, M., Tanenbaum, A. S. Exploiting Location Awareness for Scalable Location-Independent Object IDs In: Proceedings of the Fifth Annual ASCI Conference, Heijen, The Netherlands, (1999) 321–328.

A Formal Characterization of Vagueness and Granularity for Context-Aware Mobile and Ubiquitous Computing*

Hedda R. Schmidtke and Woontack Woo**

GIST U-VR Lab.
Gwangju 500-712, Republic of Korea
{schmidtk, wwoo}@gist.ac.kr

Abstract. In this article, a formal approach for modeling central concepts of context-awareness in ubiquitous and mobile computing is introduced. The focus is on an appropriate handling of issues of vagueness and granularity in ubiquitous computing environments. A formalization of perceptual and sensory uncertainty and a characterization of granularity are applied for modeling three central aspects of context-awareness: context as retrieved from sensors, context for representing relevance, and context as unfocussed background information. The notions are developed and demonstrated with respect to the special case of spatial contexts, but are sufficiently general to also cover other types of context. Use of the characterized concepts is motivated with an example of ongoing work on ontology design for ubiquitous computing environments.

1 Introduction

Vagueness and uncertainty arising from limited sensory accuracy and the dynamic of an environment flexibly adapting during user interaction pose central challenges to context modeling and ontology design for ubiquitous computing environments. Several definitions for context and context-awareness exist [5, 10, 25, 26] resulting in different perspectives and approaches to establishing context-awareness in computing environments. Nevertheless, central aspects and challenges have been identified. Three aspects of context constitute the conceptual basis for this article: context as retrieved from sensors, context for representing relevance, and context as unfocussed background information.

Context retrieved from sensors provides information about the context of the user in the physical world [26]. A central challenge in modeling information from sensors in an application is how to model the uncertainty resulting from the inevitable limitations of accuracy.

Context for representing relevance makes advanced human-computer interface techniques, such as *proximate selection* [25], possible. A representation of

---

* This work was supported by Seondo project of MIC, Korea, by the UCN Project, the MIC 21st Century Frontier R&D Program in Korea, and by the BK 21 Project in 2006.
** Corresponding author.

H.Y. Youn, M. Kim, and H. Morikawa (Eds.): UCS 2006, LNCS 4239, pp. 144–157, 2006.
© Springer-Verlag Berlin Heidelberg 2006

relevance in a context can help anticipate which objects are more likely to be desired next by a user, so that the user needs less effort for retrieving information that is closely related to the currently displayed information. Additionally, a representation of relevance can be used to improve efficiency of an application.

Context as unfocussed background information is information of which a user is aware, but which is currently not in the focus. Similarly to irrelevant information, background information can be disregarded in processing. This is used in AI systems to reduce complexity [14]. However, a change in background information entails a change of context, whereas a change in irrelevant information is inconsequential.

The aims of this article are to present a formal modeling for granularity and vagueness as core concepts underlying these three central aspects, and to use this modeling to reveal formal links that can be used in future context-aware applications. The formal concepts described in the article can be applied to different types of context [26]. However, spatial context was chosen as an example domain of special relevance, since it is not only a parameter for interaction with a user but also influences effectivity and efficiency of ubiquitous computing environments conceived as systems for (spatially) distributed computing [30]. Consequentially, spatial context has been a focus of interest with respect to technical [15] as well as application-oriented questions [8], and the representation of spatial context has emerged to be a problem of sufficient complexity to justify a more detailed theoretical analysis.

Structure of the Article. In Sect. 2, formal properties common to uncertainty resulting from limited sensory accuracy and perceptual vagueness are studied. Uncertainty is represented as an interval on a scale, which can be computed from a sensor reading and a range of accuracy, given a desired precision. Section 3 gives an outline of a theoretical framework for modeling spatial contexts, which is based on a mereotopological notion of regions. The formal notions of context for representing relevance and of context as unfocussed background are then illustrated for the example of spatial contexts in Sect. 4. In Sect. 5, a method for developing and modifying a granular spatial context representation for ubiquitous computing environments is sketched. A summary and an outlook on ongoing research are given in Sect. 6.

2   Sensory Input and Perceptual Vagueness

Vagueness resulting from the limited accuracy of sensors is not only a problem for ubiquitous computing and robotics, the human perceptual system has to handle similar restrictions. In this section, formal links between sensory uncertainty and perceptual vagueness are traced back to results from basic measurement theory. Applicability of the formal notions is demonstrated with composition tables for qualitative reasoning[1] about uncertain perceptions and measurements.

---

[*] For an introduction to qualitative reasoning cf. Cohn and Hazarika [9], Galton [13]; for a discussion on the role of composition tables for ontologies cf. Eschenbach [12].

2.1 Perceptual Vagueness

Vagueness in the human perceptual systems has been studied in psychophysical experiments on distinguishability, e.g., of colors or lengths (for an overview cf. [22], p. 671): subjects were shown two lines successively or in horizontal alignment, so that direct comparison of lengths was not possible, and were then asked to judge, whether the lines had been of the same lengths or of different lengths. The experiments showed that lengths of less than a certain difference could not be distinguished. In comparison with a line of 10 cm, e.g., a line of 10.5 cm was judged to have the same length, and subjects could not indicate which of the two lines was shorter, whereas a line of 11 cm was noticeably longer. Accordingly, this difference is called the *just noticeable difference* (JND).

The mathematical properties of the relations *perceivably smaller* and *of indistinguishable length* as given by the experiments can be formally characterized by a semiorder ($\prec$) and an indistinguishability relation ($\approx$), respectively. Axioms A1–A4 give the characterization proposed in [31]. Semiorders are irreflexive (A1). Given two ordered pairs of values, either the smaller of the first is smaller than the larger of the second pair, or the smaller of the second pair is smaller than the larger of the first pair (A2). If three values are ordered according to $\prec$, then every further value is smaller than the largest of the triple or larger than the smallest (A3). Two values are indistinguishable, iff they cannot be ordered (A4).[2]

$$\forall x : \neg x \prec x \tag{A1}$$
$$\forall x_1, x_1', x_2, x_2' : x_1 \prec x_1' \wedge x_2 \prec x_2' \rightarrow x_1 \prec x_2' \vee x_2 \prec x_1' \tag{A2}$$
$$\forall x_1, x_2, x_3, x : x_1 \prec x_2 \wedge x_2 \prec x_3 \rightarrow x_1 \prec x \vee x \prec x_3 \tag{A3}$$
$$\forall x, x' : x \approx x' \leftrightarrow \neg(x \prec x' \vee x' \prec x) \tag{A4}$$

The relations $\approx$, $\prec$ and its inverse relation $\succ$ are mutually exclusive and exhaustive relations on the domain of possible lengths. For reasoning about these relations, the composition table 1(a) can be used, e.g.: if x is unnoticeably smaller than y (row: $x \prec y$) and y is indistinguishable from z (column: $y \approx z$), then we can infer that x must be perceivably smaller than, or indistinguishable from z (entry: $\prec, \approx$; to be read as: $x \prec z \vee x \approx z$).

A particularly interesting property of semiorders is that we can obtain more certain information from uncertain information by subsequent observations: if x_1 in reality is smaller than x_2, then, given all possible lengths, there is an x that is large enough to be distinguishably larger than x_1, but still not perceivably different from x_2; cf. van Deemter [32] for a discussion of this property and its usage with respect to linguistic notions of context. Using this property, the relation $\approx$ can be split up into three relations $=$, $\preccurlyeq$ (*unnoticeably smaller*) and its inverse relation $\succcurlyeq$, so that also inferable relations between lengths can be

---

[.] In order to abbreviate formulae and to reduce the number of brackets, the scope of quantifiers is to be read as maximal, i.e. until the end of a formula, or until the closing bracket of a pair of brackets containing the quantifier. Additionally, the following precedence applies: $\neg, \wedge, \vee, \rightarrow, \leftrightarrow, \overset{def}{\leftrightarrow}$.

Table 1. Composition table with three relations: smaller ($\prec$), indistinguishable ($\approx$), larger ($\succ$) (a) and composition table with more specific inferred information (b) derived from Tab. 2. The asterisk ($*$) represents a situation in which no information can be inferred, i.e., any of the relations is possible.

	$\prec$	$\approx$	$\succ$
$\prec$	$\prec$	$\prec,\approx$	$*$
$\approx$	$\prec,\approx$	$*$	$\approx,\succ$
$\succ$	$*$	$\approx,\succ$	$\succ$

(a)

	$\prec$	$\approx$	$\succ$
$\prec$	$\prec$	$\prec,\precsim$	$*$
$\approx$	$\prec,\precsim$	$*$	$\succsim,\succ$
$\succ$	$*$	$\succsim,\succ$	$\succ$

(b)

represented. The relation $\precsim$ holds between two values x_1 and x_2, iff the two are indistinguishable, and there is a third value that is noticeably larger than x_1 but still indistinguishable from x_2; in this case, x_1 is smaller, but not noticeably smaller, than x_2 (D1):

$$x_1 \precsim x_2 \overset{def}{\Leftrightarrow} x_1 \approx x_2 \wedge \exists x : x_1 \prec x \wedge x_2 \approx x \tag{D1}$$

Accordingly, we obtain a composition table of five exhaustive and mutually exclusive relations between lengths (Tab. 2). Comparison of (a) and (b) in Tab. 1 shows how the use of $\precsim$ contributes to the elimination of vagueness in continued observation and inference: in four cases in which (a) contains indistinguishability, inference of more specific information is possible in (b).

Table 2. Composition table with five exhaustive and mutually exclusive relations: smaller ($\prec$), unnoticeably smaller ($\precsim$), equal ($=$), unnoticeably larger ($\succsim$), larger ($\succ$). The asterisk ($*$) represents a situation in which no information can be inferred.

	$\prec$	$\precsim$	$=$	$\succsim$	$\succ$
$\prec$	$\prec$	$\prec$	$\prec$	$\prec,\precsim$	$*$
$\precsim$	$\prec$	$\precsim,\prec$	$\precsim$	$\succsim,=,\precsim$	$\succsim,\succ$
$=$	$\prec$	$\precsim$	$=$	$\succsim$	$\succ$
$\succsim$	$\prec,\precsim$	$\succsim,=,\precsim$	$\succsim$	$\succ,\succsim$	$\succ$
$\succ$	$*$	$\succsim,\succ$	$\succ$	$\succ$	$\succ$

2.2   Uncertainty from Sensors

We can now compare uncertainty from perception with uncertainty from sensors by showing that accuracy intervals are a model of the axiomatic characterization presented above.

The vagueness associated with sensory input can be specified by an interval of accuracy and a precision expressed as a percentage [15], e.g.: a temperature sensor giving $10\,°C$ with an accuracy of $\pm 1\,°C$ at a precision of 95 % means that the true temperature is in the interval $[9\,°C, 11\,°C]$ with a probability of 95 %. Conversely, we could state that a value of $10\,°C$ in the world will in 95 % of all cases result in a sensory reading in the interval $[9\,^\circ C, 11\,^\circ C]$. For simplifying the following discussion, the two perspectives are called *sensor perspective* and *world perspective*, respectively. In the specification of the accuracy of a sensor reading, a sensor perspective is assumed; the notion of indistinguishability in Sect. 2.1, in contrast, indicates a world perspective, as it refers to objects in the world. Furthermore, the discussion focusses on accuracy, with precision being regarded as a fixed value specifying overall reliability of a system. A more detailed treatment is beyond the scope of this article.

For sensors such as the thermometer described above, the domain of possible sensor readings can be given as the set I_T of closed, convex intervals of unit length within a range $[t_{\min}, t_{\max}]$ on $\mathbb{R}$:

$$I_T = \{[t - 1, t + 1] \mid t \in [t_{\min}, t_{\max}]\}$$

Chalmers et al. [7], assuming a sensor perspective, present a similar approach for reasoning about context in the presence of uncertainty, which is based on arbitrary intervals. However, the full set of 13 interval relations [1] is not necessary for the domain of I_T, since no interval of I_T can contain another interval of I_T. In fact, the five relations, which correspond to the relations $\prec, \preccurlyeq, =, \succcurlyeq, \succ$ are sufficient, as I_T can be shown to be a model of the axiomatic characterization presented above with the following interpretations for $\prec$ and $\preccurlyeq$:[3] $\prec_{I_T}$ holds between two unit intervals iff the first ends before the second begins, $\preccurlyeq_{I_T}$ holds iff the second interval starts after, but within the duration of the first interval.

$$\prec_{I_T} \overset{def}{=} \{([t_1 - 1, t_1 + 1], [t_2 - 1, t_2 + 1]) \mid t_1 + 1 < t_2 - 1\}$$
$$\preccurlyeq_{I_T} \overset{def}{=} \{([t_1 - 1, t_1 + 1], [t_2 - 1, t_2 + 1]) \mid t_1 - 1 < t_2 - 1 \leq t_1 + 1\}$$

The differences between the two perspectives show, if we look at the relations between values in the world which can be inferred from sensory readings. The statement $[t_1 - 1, t_1 + 1] \preccurlyeq [t_2 - 1, t_2 + 1]$ under a world perspective means for the actual values t_1 and t_2 in the world: $t_1 < t_2$. Under a sensor perspective the statement $[t_1' - 1, t_1' + 1] \preccurlyeq [t_2' - 1, t_2' + 1]$ for sensor readings t_1' and t_2' entails only vague information about the actual values in the world: $t_1' < t_2'$ and thus $[t_1' - 1, t_1' + 1] \preccurlyeq [t_2' - 1, t_2' + 1]$ in the domain of sensory values entails only $[t_1 - 1, t_1 + 1] \approx [t_2 - 1, t_2 + 1]$ for the measured actual values. Using composition table (b) of Tab. 1, knowledge regarding $\preccurlyeq$ in the world domain can be obtained with multiple measurements. For actual applications, however, imprecision limits the maximally usable number of measurements.

Uncertainty resulting from limited sensory accuracy is not only a critical challenge for the representation and processing of information about the physical context of a user in ubiquitous and mobile computing. Likewise, knowledge about contextual parameters that are assumed by a user is accessible only indirectly to an application. Accordingly, the relations of semiorder and indistinguishability were employed to model granularity as a dynamically changing parameter

---

[.] The proof follows along the lines of the one given in [31]. Cf. also [29].

of context in human-computer interaction [29]. In [29], the example of temporal granularity was examined. An extension to the more complex case of spatial granularity is described in Sect. 4.

3   Spatial Context

Two models of location are employed in ubiquitous and mobile computing [8]: *geometric* and *symbolic* location models. This distinction has both technical and semantic aspects. Hightower and Borriello [15] accordingly differentiate between two types of spatial information a location system may provide: the coordinate-based information provided, e.g., by GPS is called *physical position*; *symbolic location* information, in contrast, is used in location systems that employ sensors that only determine whether or not objects are in a certain stationary or mobile area. Concerning information processing, the retrieved information is numerical in the first case and boolean or textual – e.g. the ID of an object detected by the sensor – in the second case.

This technical distinction is mirrored on the semantic level: coordinate-based information can directly be interpreted spatially, if the used reference system and resolution are known; in contrast, the spatial information in symbolic location systems – i.e. how different sensor areas are spatially related – has to be provided externally, either during installation of the system or via inference from coordinate-based information. Concerning resolution, coordinate-based information, e.g. obtained from GPS, has a certain limited accuracy, whereas symbolic location systems, such as the system described by Schilit and Theimer [24], can be organized in a hierarchical manner based on the relation of spatial containment, so as to provide arbitrarily fine spatial distinctions. However, the spatial notion of resolution or size is usually not represented in symbolic location systems.

Location-aware systems for heterogeneous environments need to incorporate both sources of location information. Hybrid location models have been specified to address this need [18, 21]. The formal framework proposed in the following sections is related to these approaches, and provides a theoretical foundation for improving hybrid location models. The characterization of regions given in Sect. 3.1 provides the basic relations of containment and overlap used in the symbolic location model; in Sect. 3.2, rudimentary notions of resolution or grain-size are added to this framework, in order to make it compatible with coordinate-based location models and to allow stratification according to grain-size. The resulting framework for hybrid location models, similar to the one of Leonhardt [21], is based on the relations of containment and overlap, but additionally contains representations for resolution and size. A location model equipped with methods to handle granularity (Sect. 4) can be key to improving scalability and interoperability of location-aware systems. Section 5 illustrates this claim with the sketch of a non-partitioning stratification methodology.

3.1   Regions

A mereotopological framework is chosen as a foundation for characterizing regions [2, 6, 23]: the basic relation C of mereotopology, stating that two regions are connected, can be characterized as a reflexive (A5) and symmetric relation (A6); the relation $\sqsubseteq$ holding between a region and its parts can then be defined in terms of C (D2): x is part of y, iff every region that is connected to x is also connected to y.

$$\forall x : C(x, x) \tag{A5}$$

$$\forall x, y : C(x, y) \rightarrow C(y, x) \tag{A6}$$

$$x \sqsubseteq y \overset{def}{\Leftrightarrow} \forall z : C(x, z) \rightarrow C(y, z) \tag{D2}$$

This rudimentary foundation suffices for present purposes, as $\sqsubseteq$ gives the basic ordering constraints on the sizes of regions that are used in the following: it can be shown that $\sqsubseteq$ is a reflexive, antisymmetric relation. For a thorough treatment of mereotopological ontological questions, however, a more elaborate framework would be needed [2, 6, 23].

3.2   Extended Locations: Regions with a Unique Size

In order to develop a notion of grain-size, an ordering relation $\leq$ (*smaller or of equal size*) describing basic size constraints between two regions is used. Following Dugat et al. [11], a suitable relation $\leq$ can be axiomatized as a reflexive (A7) and transitive relation (A8) holding, inter alia, between a region and its parts (A9). The relation can be used to define a notion of congruence of a special class of regions – here called: *extended locations* –, upon which Dugat et al. following Borgo et al. [4] then build a geometry of spheres. Extended locations are characterized with a predicate L as a special class of regions on which $\leq$ yields a linear order (A10):

$$\forall x : x \leq x \tag{A7}$$

$$\forall x, y, z : x \leq y \wedge y \leq z \rightarrow x \leq z \tag{A8}$$

$$\forall x, y : x \sqsubseteq y \rightarrow x \leq y \tag{A9}$$

$$\forall x, y : L(x) \wedge L(y) \rightarrow x \leq y \vee y \leq x \tag{A10}$$

Additional relations $\equiv$ (*same size*) and $<$ (*smaller*) can be defined:

$$x \equiv y \overset{def}{\Leftrightarrow} x \leq y \wedge y \leq x \tag{D3}$$

$$x < y \overset{def}{\Leftrightarrow} x \leq y \wedge \neg y \leq x \tag{D4}$$

Spheres are one example of a class of regions that adhere to the requirements for extended locations L, since two spheres can always be ordered according to their diameter. In contrast to the spheres of Dugat et al. [11] however, the extended locations are not restricted further in shape or topology. Additionally, the notion of size is used here for illustrating the partial order $\leq$ on regions, but a formal characterization of size as related to distance in a metric sense would require further restrictions and is beyond the scope of this paper; for geometric characterizations cf. [4, 11, 27, 28]. The main advantage of the less restrictive formalization chosen here is that it encompasses a broad range of models and therewith modeling alternatives for developers of location aware systems, as illustrated in Sect. 5 below.

4   Spatial Relevance and Spatial Background

Notions of context for representing relevance and of context as unfocussed background information can be formally specified based on a characterization of granularity [29]. Mechanisms for representing, and reasoning about, granularity are a means to filter and simplify complex domains, so as to focus on the currently relevant objects and attributes [16]. Spatial granularity is largely determined by the concept of grain-size. It can be used to restrict the set of objects under consideration to the subset of objects having at least a certain minimal size. A further component of spatial relevance is proximity. Objects which are within a certain range of currently relevant objects are more likely to be relevant than remote objects. This concept is fundamental for the interface technique of proximate selection [25]. Linking the concept of ranges of proximity to the notion of grain-size, we can ensure that the number of objects currently under consideration can be kept small: as we focus on a smaller area, i.e. *zoom* into a scene, objects further away become irrelevant, and smaller details become relevant.[4]

Based on the notion of extended locations, a stratification of space into an ordering of levels of granularity can now be characterized. The characterization is based upon the primitive relation $\vartriangleleft$ between extended locations, with $x \vartriangleleft y$ denoting that x is a grain location of the context location y. The grains thus represent the smallest possibly relevant locations, whereas the context location provides the maximal range of proximity and determines the background: an object that is contained in a location smaller than a grain can be classified as irrelevant; an object containing the context location can be classified as a background object, since all objects relevant in the context lie within its region.

Axiom A11 states that grains are ubiquitous within a context location: every region connected to a context location that has a grain is also connected to a grain. It is worth noting that this axiom is the only ontological axiom in a narrow sense, as it actually guarantees existence of regions under certain conditions. From an application point of view, the axiom demands minimum requirements on availability of fine-grained location services. The second axiom (A12) states that grains and context locations are extended locations, and that the grains of a context location are contained in the location. Axiom A13 gives the central restriction on the ordering of levels of granularity: grains are ordered in the same way as their respective context locations and vice versa. As a consequence, all grains of a context location have equal extension (1).

---

[*] For a discussion on the photo metaphor see §1.6 in [13]; for empirical evidence regarding phenomena of granularity in spatial imagery see Kosslyn [20].

$$\forall c, g, x : C(x,c) \wedge g \lhd c \rightarrow \exists g' : g' \lhd c \wedge C(x,g') \tag{A11}$$

$$\forall c, g : g \lhd c \rightarrow L(g) \wedge L(c) \wedge g \sqsubseteq c \wedge g \neq c \tag{A12}$$

$$\forall c_1, c_2, x_1, x_2 : x_1 \lhd c_1 \wedge x_2 \lhd c_2 \rightarrow [c_1 < c_2 \leftrightarrow x_1 < x_2] \tag{A13}$$

$$\forall c, x, y : x \lhd c \wedge y \lhd c \rightarrow x \equiv y \tag{1}$$

The ordering on levels of granularity can be characterized with relations $\prec$ and $\approx$: c_1 is of *finer granularity* than c_2, iff there is a grain of c_2 that is larger than c_1 (D5); c_1 is of *compatible granularity* with c_2, iff c_1 is not smaller than any grain of c_2 and c_2 is not smaller than any grain of c_1 (D6). The predicate *CL* (*proper context location*) selects those extended locations which have grain locations (D7).

$$c_1 \prec c_2 \overset{def}{\leftrightarrow} \exists g : g \lhd c_2 \wedge c_1 < g \tag{D5}$$

$$c_1 \approx c_2 \overset{def}{\leftrightarrow} \forall g_1, g_2 : g_1 \lhd c_1 \wedge g_2 \lhd c_2 \rightarrow g_1 \leq c_2 \wedge g_2 \leq c_1 \tag{D6}$$

$$CL(x) \overset{def}{\leftrightarrow} \exists g : g \lhd x \tag{D7}$$

It can be shown (Sect. A) that, if restricted to the class of *CL*-locations (D7), $\prec$ actually is a semiorder with $\approx$ as a relation of indistinguishability, as the use of the symbols suggests. The axiomatization thus supports representation of the vagueness associated with the notion of granularity as a parameter of interaction with a user: the actual granularity conceptualized by the user, like the actual values measured by a sensor, can be modeled as an indirectly accessible parameter.

The above axioms are neutral with respect to the question whether space is partitioned by grain locations. Axiom A11 demands that context locations having a grain location are completely covered by grains, but allows for grains to overlap. Axiom A13 does not restrict this either. For a partitioning approach to modeling spatial granularity cf. Bittner and Smith [3].

5 Application: Stratification of a Ubiquitous Computing Environment

With the ordering on levels of granularity being anchored in the containment hierarchy, a context management system that keeps containment information can be modified to handle information about levels of granularity: first, constraints on the sizes of regions have to be extracted; second, sizes which are particularly important throughout the whole domain of application have to be identified; these sizes are then used in the third step to stratify the domain. If the third step has been performed in a consistent way, further regions and strata can be flexibly incorporated into the system, when new location sensing components are to be added to an environment.

Step 1: Size Constraints. A consistent hierarchy of sizes on which to base the stratification of a domain can be obtained from a given containment hierarchy.

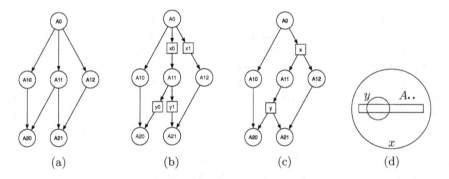

Fig. 1. A containment hierarchy (relation $\sqsubseteq$) describing a set of symbolic locations (a) can be enriched with extended locations representing possible coordinate-based locations based on knowledge about the extension of regions (b). After unification of equally extended locations ($\equiv$), we obtain a corresponding hierarchy of sizes (relation $\leq$, c). The region $A..$ is an example of a region that is contained in an extended location x, but neither contains nor is contained in any location of the same extension as y (d).

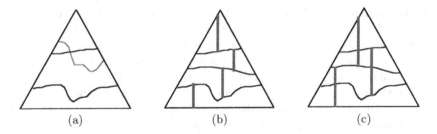

Fig. 2. Schematic of the graph of a containment hierarchy (horizontal lines indicate extended locations of the same equivalence class with respect to $\equiv$, vertical lines illustrate the extent of strata): alternative (gray) for stratifying the upper part of the hierarchy (a), partitioning stratification (b), and non-partitioning stratification (c).

All necessary information on size constraints, as specified by the above axioms, can then be derived by replacing every occurrence of $\sqsubseteq$ with $\leq$ as justified by (A9). Figure 1(a) shows a simple example for a containment hierarchy.

Step 2: Extended Locations. The procedure of the first step is sufficient for modeling arbitrary fixed containment structures. The need to introduce extended locations arises when mobile devices and location sensors providing coordinate-based locations are used. The region representing a specific GPS-signal, for instance, can be specified as a circle corresponding to the accuracy of the signal around the currently measured GPS-coordinate (Sect. 2). If this accuracy and with it the size of the region does not change with the place where it is measured – or if the accuracy changes, but is known – the mobile device provides an absolute measure for comparing disjoint spatial regions. If the extensions of the regions collected in step 1 are known, we can compute the regions corresponding to possible measurements of a coordinate-based location sensor as the extended locations and enter these into the hierarchy of sizes (for a discussion of methods cf. Leonhardt [21] on semi-symbolic location hierarchies). Since the extended locations have to be linearly ordered with respect to $\leq$, the classes of regions that are extended locations of the same equivalence class with respect to $\equiv$ have to be selected carefully, so as to avoid inconsistencies. Figure 2(a) shows a schematic of a $\leq$-hierarchy with two possible alternatives (crossing lines) for separating the upper part of the hierarchy, between which a developer would have to chose.

Step 3: Stratification. With the extended locations entered in the $\leq$-graph, a stratification of the domain of sizes can be derived. Figure 2 illustrates two possible options for stratifying a containment hierarchy with three size levels: in (b), four non-overlapping levels of granularity were generated, whereas, in (c), three overlapping levels of granularity were chosen. A non-overlapping stratification has the advantage of providing smaller strata; an overlapping stratification allows for modeling smooth transitions between levels of granularity [29].

Step 4: Modification. A difficult problem in software development is how to ascertain a sufficient flexibility of used representations, so that later refactoring can be avoided or kept to a minimum. The proposed formal structure supports this effort in so far as results from previous steps are not affected when the structure is changed: a change in the stratification (step 3) does not entail re-developments at earlier steps. In fact, new strata of granularity can simply be added to an existing granularity structure, because the strata are not required to partition the domain of sizes. Likewise, adding new fixed regions (step 1) or mobile sensors (step 2) requires only local updating in the $\leq$-graph.

6   Outlook and Conclusions

This article presented a formal comparison of perceptual and sensory vagueness and a characterization of granularity applied to the domain of spatial contexts. The characterizations were used to model central aspects of context-awareness: uncertainty of contextual information was modeled using the notion of indistinguishability; context-dependent relevance was represented with the concept of granularity. Granularity provides the notion of grain-size – determining the smallest represented details – as well as the notion of context location – specifying a maximal range of proximity and the unfocussed background of current interactions with a user.

The proposed spatial framework can be used for reasoning as well as for specification purposes: as a characterization of space as obtained from sensors in a heterogeneous ubiquitous computing environment, it can be employed in specifying, checking, and proving availability and reliability of spatially distributed services, e.g., for safety critical applications; as a logical language for describing spatial layouts, it can be used for reasoning, e.g., in tools for diagnosis and automatic configuration of ubiquitous computing environments.

With respect to semantic web applications and related developments, the proposed language can be employed for describing the local spatial ontology of a ubiquitous computing environment, so that the configuration of an environment can be communicated to a user's devices. Both availability of services in the environment and necessary devices on the user's side contribute to the actual spatial configuration of which the user's mobile devices and services in the environment can make use.

Future work includes the application of the specified concepts and methodology for defining a flexible and extensible ontology for Ubiquitous Smart Spaces. This ontology has to incorporate a broad variety of different location sensing technologies, such as: a stationary IR-based sensor system for location and orientation tracking [19], and a computer vision based system for gesture recognition [17].

Nevertheless, application of the proposed framework is not restricted to modeling spatial context. The mereotopological basis is neutral with respect to dimensionality, so that spaces of arbitrary dimensionality can be represented. The formalization can be applied for any context modeling domain that uses both coordinate-based information with fixed resolutions and symbolic information in a containment hierarchy.

References

[1] J. Allen. Towards a general theory of action and time. *Artificial Intelligence*, 23: 123–154, 1984.

[2] N. Asher and L. Vieu. Toward a geometry for common sense: A semantics and a complete axiomatization for mereotopology. In C. Mellish, editor, *Proceedings of the Fourteenth International Joint Conference on Artificial Intelligence*, pages 846–852, San Francisco, 1995. Morgan Kaufmann.

[3] T. Bittner and B. Smith. A theory of granular partitions. In M. Duckham, M. F. Goodchild, and M. F. Worboys, editors, *Foundations of Geographic Information Science*, pages 117–151. Taylor & Francis, London, New York, 2003.

[4] S. Borgo, N. Guarino, and C. Masolo. A pointless theory of space based on strong connection and congruence. In L. C. Aiello, J. Doyle, and S. Shapiro, editors, *KR'96: Principles of Knowledge Representation and Reasoning*, pages 220–229. Morgan Kaufmann, San Francisco, California, 1996.

[5] P. Brézillon. Context in problem solving: A survey. *The Knowledge Engineering Review*, 14(1):1–34, 1999.

[6] R. Casati and A. C. Varzi. *Parts and places: the structure of spatial representations*. MIT Press, 1999.

[7] D. Chalmers, N. Dulay, and M. Sloman. Towards reasoning about context in the presence of uncertainty. In *Proceedings of the Workshop on Advanced Context Modelling, Reasoning And Management at UbiComp*, Nottingham, UK, 2004.

[8] G. Chen and D. Kotz. A survey of context-aware mobile computing research. Technical Report TR2000-381, Dept. of Computer Science, Dartmouth College, November 2000. URL ftp://ftp.cs.dartmouth.edu/TR/TR2000-381.ps.Z.

[9] A. G. Cohn and S. M. Hazarika. Qualitative spatial representation and reasoning: An overview. *Fundamenta Informaticae*, 46(1-2):1–29, 2001.

[10] A. K. Dey and G. D. Abowd. Towards a better understanding of context and context-awareness. In *Workshop on The What, Who, Where, When, and How of Context-Awareness, as part of the 2000 Conference on Human Factors in Computing Systems (CHI 2000)*, 2000.

[11] V. Dugat, P. Gambarotto, and Y. Larvor. Qualitative geometry for shape recognition. *Applied Intelligence*, 17:253–263, 2002.

[12] C. Eschenbach. Viewing composition tables as axiomatic systems. In *FOIS '01: Proceedings of the international conference on Formal Ontology in Information Systems*, pages 93–104. ACM Press, 2001.

[13] A. Galton. *Qualitative Spatial Change*. Oxford University Press, 2000.

[14] R. Guha and J. McCarthy. Varieties of contexts. In P. Blackburn, C. Ghidini, R. M. Turner, and F. Giunchiglia, editors, *Modeling and Using Context*, pages 164–177, 2003.

[15] J. Hightower and G. Borriello. A survey and taxonomy of location systems for ubiquitous computing. *Computer*, 34(8):57–66, 2001.

[16] J. Hobbs. Granularity. In *Proceedings of IJCAI-85*, pages 432–435, 1985.

[17] D. Hong and W. Woo. A 3d vision-based ambient user interface. *International Journal of Human Computer Interaction*, 20(3):271–284, 2006.

[18] C. Jiang and P. Steenkiste. A hybrid location model with a computable location identifier for ubiquitous computing. In G. Borriello and L. E. Holmquist, editors, *Proc. UbiComp*, pages 246–263, Gothenburg, Sweden, 2002. Springer.

[19] W. Jung and W. Woo. Indoor orientation tracking using ubiTrack. In *Proc. ubiCNS*, 2005.

[20] S. Kosslyn. *Image and Mind*. The MIT Press, Cambridge, MA, 1980.

[21] U. Leonhardt. *Supporting Location Awareness in Open Distributed Systems*. PhD thesis, Imperial College, London, UK, 1998.

[22] S. E. Palmer. *Vision science—photons to phenomenology*. MIT Press, Cambridge, MA, 1999.

[23] D. Randell, Z. Cui, and A. Cohn. A spatial logic based on region and connection. In *Principles of Knowledge Representation and Reasoning: Proc. 3rd Intl. Conf. (KR'92)*, pages 165–176. Morgan Kaufmann, 1992.

[24] B. N. Schilit and M. M. Theimer. Disseminating active map information to mobile hosts. *IEEE Network*, 8(5):22–32, 1994.

[25] B. N. Schilit, N. I. Adams, and R. Want. Context-aware computing applications. In *Proceedings of the Workshop on Mobile Computing Systems and Applications*, pages 85–90. IEEE Computer Society, 1994.

[26] A. Schmidt, M. Beigl, and H.-W. Gellersen. There is more to context than location. *Computers and Graphics*, 23(6):893–901, 1999.

[27] H. R. Schmidtke. A geometry for places: Representing extension and extended objects. In W. Kuhn, M. Worboys, and S. Timpf, editors, *Spatial Information Theory: Foundations of Geographic Information Science*, pages 235–252, Berlin, 2003. Springer.

[28] H. R. Schmidtke. Aggregations and constituents: geometric specification of multigranular objects. *Journal of Visual Languages and Computing*, 16(4):289–309, 2005.

[29] H. R. Schmidtke. Granularity as a parameter of context. In A. K. Dey, B. N. Kokinov, D. B. Leake, and R. M. Turner, editors, *Modeling and Using Context*, pages 450–463. Springer, 2005.

[30] T. Strang and C. Linnhoff-Popien. A context modeling survey. In *Workshop on Advanced Context Modelling, Reasoning and Management as part of UbiComp 2004 - The Sixth International Conference on Ubiquitous Computing*, 2004.

[31] P. Suppes and J. Zinnes. Basic measurement theory. In R. Luce, R. Bush, and E. Galanter, editors, *Handbook of Mathematical Psychology*, pages 1–76. John Wiley & Sons, New York, 1963.

[32] K. van Deemter. The sorites fallacy and the context-dependence of vague predicates. In M. Kanazawa, C. Pinon, and H. de Swart, editors, *Quantifiers, Deduction, and Context*, pages 59–86, Stanford, Ca., 1995. CSLI Publications.

A   Proof: Definition D5 Defines a Semiorder on *CL*-Locations

$$\forall c : CL(c) \to \neg c \prec c \tag{2}$$

$$\forall c_1, c_1', c_2, c_2' : CL(c_1) \land CL(c_1') \land CL(c_2) \land CL(c_2') \land c_1 \prec c_1' \land c_2 \prec c_2'$$
$$\to c_1 \prec c_2' \lor c_2 \prec c_1' \tag{3}$$

$$\forall c_1, c_2, c_3, c : CL(c) \land CL(c_1) \land CL(c_2) \land CL(c_3) \land c_1 \prec c_2 \land c_2 \prec c_3$$
$$\to c_1 \prec c \lor c \prec c_3 \tag{4}$$

$$\forall c, c' : CL(c) \land CL(c') \to (c \approx c' \leftrightarrow \neg(c \prec c' \lor c' \prec c)) \tag{5}$$

Irreflexivity (2) follows by transitivity (A8) from the irreflexivity of $<$.

Proof (3). Assume four *CL*-locations c_1, c_1', c_2, c_2' with $c_1 \prec c_1'$, $c_2 \prec c_2'$, and $\neg c_1 \prec c_2'$ given. Then by (D5), there are grain locations g_1' of c_1' and g_2' of c_2' with $c_1 < g_1'$ and $c_2 < g_2'$. With the third condition $\neg c_1 \prec c_2'$, we know that no grain of c_2' is larger than c_1, and thus particularly $\neg c_1 < g_2'$. By linearity of $\leq$ (A10) on extended locations and (D4) follows $g_2' \leq c_1$. Using transitivity (A8) the following order can be inferred: $c_2 < g_2' < g_1'$. And thus (D5): $c_2 \prec c_1'$.

Proof (4). Assume four *CL*-locations c_1, c_2, c_3, c with $c_1 \prec c_2$, $c_2 \prec c_3$. Then there exist grain locations g_2 of c_2 and g_3 of c_3 with $c_1 < g_2$ and $c_2 < g_3$ (D5). Using linearity (A10), we know that $c \leq c_2$ or $c_2 \leq c$ holds.

For the case $c \leq c_2$, we infer from $c_2 < g_3$ by transitivity (A8) that $c < g_3$ and thus $c \prec c_3$.

For the case $c_2 \leq c$, we infer by (A13) and the requirement that c be a *CL*-location (D7), that c has a grain location g, so that $g_2 \leq g$. By transitivity (A8) and $c_1 < g_2$ this entails that $c_1 < g$ and thus $c_1 \prec c$.

Proof (5). Assume c and c' are *CL*-locations. We then know that they have grain locations g and g', respectively, and that for all such grain locations follows: $g < c$ and $g' < c'$ (A12) and (A9), since by (A13) all grains of a context location have the same size, i.e. behave in the same way with respect to $\leq$. The theorem then follows directly from (D6) and (D5), since $g \leq c'$ and $g' \leq c$ holds iff $\neg c' < g$ and $\neg c < g'$ (D4).

An Inference Engine for Personalized Content Adaptation in Heterogeneous Mobile Environment*

Seunghwa Lee, Jee-Hyong Lee, and Eunseok Lee[**]

School of Information and Communication Engineering, Sungkyunkwan University
300 Chunchun Jangahn Suwon, 440-746, Korea
{shlee, jhlee, eslee}@ece.skku.ac.kr

Abstract. In order to overcome the various constraints of wireless environments and provide content according to device specifications and user preference, research relating to content adaptation is gaining in significance. For content adaptation, existing research either prepares content in advance, a reflection of client types which may have access to server, or describes the adaptation rules for dynamic content conversion. However, these require a lot of effort from the content author or system developer, and prospecting the appearance of a new device is a difficult work in today's rapidly changing computing environment. This paper proposes an intelligent adaptation system that automatically extends adaptation rules. The system classifies users into basic categories, then dynamically converts content according to the rule mapping category, offering this result to the user. Then, the system monitors the user action, and performs learning based on this feedback. Moreover, the system has characteristics of offering more personalized content as well as reducing the response time due to reuse of the content generated by same group category. A prototype was implemented in order to evaluate the proposed system in terms of system maintainability, by automatic rule extension, correctness of generated rules, and response time. The effectiveness of the system is confirmed through the results.

1 Introduction

Wireless Internet and various handheld devices are becoming increasingly widespread, due to the rapid development in Information Technologies. Information accessing in mobile environments is gaining in popularity, multimedia content such as Digital Multimedia Broadcasting, and E-learning are now possible. The capacity of handheld devices is continually increasing and new devices of various types are being developed. However, in order to reduce its size and weight, these devices still suffer from various limitations such as small display size, relatively low computing power, and limited battery.

---

[*] This work was supported in parts by *Ubiquitous Autonomic Computing and Network Project*, 21th Century Frontier R&D Program, MIC, Korea, ITRC IITA-2005-(C1090-0501-0019), Grant No. R01-2006-000-10954-0, *Basic Research Program* of the Korea Science & Engineering Foundation, and the *Post-BK21 Project*.
[**] Corresponding author.

H.Y. Youn, M. Kim, and H. Morikawa (Eds.): UCS 2006, LNCS 4239, pp. 158–170, 2006.

Thus, research relating to an adaptation system is currently becoming an important issue, in order to overcome various constraints in mobile environments and offer web content according to the characteristics of device and preference of users. The cleanest method to customize the web contents is having content for every possible version, on the server. However, this method requires much effort by the content author, and can incur a heavy storage burden. In addition, prospecting or corresponding with the appearance of a new device is difficult in current rapidly changing computing environments. Hence, adaptation is better performed dynamically, based on understanding the context of the user. Likewise, such dynamic adaptation must build adaptation rules in various client situations. The preparing of adaptation services in advance and the characteristics of new devices is extremely difficult.

This paper proposes an intelligent adaptation system. The system classifies users according to basic classification category, and dynamically converts content using an adaptation rule mapped to the category. Then, it is offered to the user and the system extends group categories and adaptation rules through user feedback. Therefore, users can accept suitable content depending on the situation. Moreover, the proposed system has other characteristic which reuse the adapted contents in order to reduce the time required for adaptation and consumption of computation resources.

A prototype is built in order to evaluate the viability of the proposed approach in terms of system maintainability, automatic rule extension, suitability of generated rules, and required time for adaptation.

The paper is organized as follows: Section 2 introduces related work for the context-adaptive system. Section 3 describes the overall structure and behaviors of the proposed system, designed in order to cope with the weak points of related work. Section 4 describes prototype implementation of the proposed approach and the various evaluation results of using this approach. Finally, Section 5 concludes the paper and identifies possible future work.

2   Related Work

In research relating to adaptation, overcoming the various constraints in a mobile environment, is currently the focus of considerable research in many laboratories. This adaptation can be classified into server side, intermediate, and client side, depending on the location of the adaptation being performed [1].

First, server side adaptation is a method of performing adaptation on the server. A representative study is CARMEN of P. Bellavista et al. [2] and research of A. Pashtan et al. [3]. This method has the advantage is that it can create very suitable content, because adaptation is performed by the author who has a great understanding of the meaning of the content. This method can also be classified *multiple authoring,* which creates a different version in advance, and *single authoring* which is dynamically creates a new version, according to user context, using the single version [4].

Although the multiple authoring method can create a very suitable version, which applies the intent of the author, such accomplishment is actually difficult due to the increased workload of the author. Unlike, the single authoring method, this can reduce the workload of author because it dynamically converts the single version in advance, using rules created by the expert. However, if this conversion is performed on the server, it will increase the response time because it increases the computation burden on the server.

Second, intermediate side adaptation is method for performing adaptation between server and client. This typically refers to a proxy server, it has effectiveness in distributing the computation load. In addition, this method is applied in many existing work such as WebSphere Transcoding Publisher of IBM [5] and research of T. Laakko et al. [6], because it has more characteristics as an *adapter,* even if the server does not offer adaptation functions. However, it suffers from the weak point where it can generate an incorrect result if it is not offered detailed metadata about the contents from the server.

Third, client side adaptation is a method performing adaptation in the client device. A representative research is research of D. Billsus et al. [7]. This method can solve issues relating to privacy which transmit the attributes of the device or data of users externally. In addition, it can embed a function, effectively coping with dynamic resource variation of client devices. However, generally, the client side means a portable device with poor computation power, thus the converting of web content is hard work, and when web content arrives at the client, the conversion contents may not be efficient, because the size of content is not reduced. Hence, this method is used to reconfigure internal components, or for partial content adaptation relating to 'display' via an embedded *stylesheet* [8] or function offered by the browser.

In most existing research, the client transmits context information with a request message when the client requests information from the web server. Then, the server or intermediate side dynamically converts content according to the context of the client. The adaptation rules must be constructed be considering various client situations. However, it is challenging and requires much effort of the content author or system developer. The goal of the proposed system is solving these problems, thus the system has a characteristics which automatically extends adaptation rules using user feedback. Moreover, the research to improve low response time due to adaptation work is in progress, using methods which stores/reuses adapted contents in the cache [9][10]. The proposed system is designed to offer more suitable contents in accordance with integrating a function using the cache which is reusing used contents by users classified with similar characteristics. In addition, the system is designed to structure adaptation processing is distributed between the server and the intermediate side, to make up for the weak points of existing systems previously mentioned.

In the next section, the proposed system designed for efficiently adaptation is introduced in detail.

3   Proposed System

The proposed system is aimed at automatically extending adaptation rules to dynamically convert the content, in order to cope with existing difficult problems, which generate rules by considering various situations. Moreover, the system improves the low response time, due to dynamic content adaptation through reusing the used contents by other users classified as similar characteristics.

3.1 The Proposed System Architecture

The proposed system consist of three parts, Client Module (CM), Intermediate Server Module (ISM), and Server Module (SM). The overall structure is presented in Figure 1. Each module is discussed in greater detail in Section 3.2, the overall behavior is as follows.

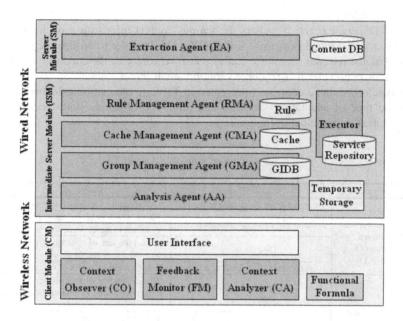

Fig. 1. Proposed system architecture

First, when the client request content, the CM transmits profile information, which is converted with this request message to the ISM. The ISM classifies the user to the most similar category using this information, and searches adapted contents for request in the cache. If an appropriate content should exist, it would be immediately transmitted to the user. Otherwise, the ISM forwards the request message to the original destination server.

The SM extracts the required portion from origin content, and rebuilds the structure of the content as layout. Then, origin image and video, which are embedded in content, are transmitted to the ISM. The ISM receives it, and then performs adaptation according to the adaptation rules mapped to the category. The ISM transmits the adapted contents to the client, and stores it in the cache.

After this, the CM monitors the user's action. If a user should use the adapted content as it is, this is transmitted to the ISM and regarded as positive feedback. The ISM adds the score to the equivalent adaptation rule based on this feedback. However, if users adjust the intensity of service via adjusting the option supported by the application, this is transmitted to the ISM and regarded as negative feedback. The ISM reduces the score of the corresponding adaptation rule, based on the feedback message, and adjusts the position of nodes in the group category. Therefore, the nodes are continually distributed by feedback, and re-clustering is performed. Thus, classification categories are gradually fractioned, and the adaptation rules are automatically extended accordingly. A user accessing the system applies a more specific classification criterion.

3.2 System Components

(1) Client Module
- *Context Observer (CO)*: It gathers the various context information of the user and generates a well-formed document using RDF [11]. In order to reduce the computation burden, the renewal period for static context representing the capability of device and dynamic context such as resource variation are different.

The type of available context is presented in Table.1, and can be extended according to the type of adaptation services. The prototype of the proposed system uses partial context as presented in Figure 2.

Table 1. Type of applicable context

Acquisition method	Context Type	Application
The context information is automatically gathered by the Context Observer (CO)	Acceptable media format of device	Convert the format of original media
	CPU-RAM capacity, current usage	Raise the degrade intensity of service, when usage exceeds the threshold
	Display size	Adjust the size of content into the size of the display
	Acceptable color depth of device	Reduce the color depth of true color media
The context information is explicitly obtained via the user interface	User's preference for each adaptation service	Decide binding of specific services such as *text_to_audio*, when user be exercising or driving
	Preference for language	Parameter of adaptation service as translator
	Preference for color depth	Decide the weight value when convert the color
	(E-learning) Content's degree of difficulty	Form content

- *Context Analyzer (CA)*: It performs regularization which converts it to the score via comparison with a mapping table. As a result, each context is converted to values between 0 to 1, and is represented in the vector set. The generated vector set is transmitted to the ISM when a user requests content via the interface. Hence, the system can slightly reduce the amount of the transmitted messages.

The dynamic context is computed using each formula, and the static context such as *cpyType*, cannot compute using formulae, is obtained by a mapping table. It is assumed that the formulae for the computation and the mapping table are updated by experts.

$$ramFreeSpace = Rnd\left(\frac{ramainedMemory}{totalMemory} \times 10\right) \tag{1}$$

* In this operation, the *Rnd* mean that a functional symbol for rounding.

In related work, the method to inform the state of client to server side uses the HTTP header [12], or CC/PP [13] information, which is described in the RDF. The server can use the information in order to grasp the characteristics of the client. However, the former suffers from the disadvantage that it is insufficient offered information from the server. The latter makes the amount of messages between client and server slightly increase, although the profile repository is used on the network if the size of the profile is long or just refers to changed parts. For reduction, the proposed system transmits the score as in Figure 2.

User_id = {displaySize, cpuType, ramSize, batteryLife, networkBandwith, cpuUsage, ramFreeSpace}

Example) *User_jb = {3, 4, 5, 7, 8, 5, 4}*

Fig. 2. Example of generated score to represent the user context

- *Feedback Monitor (FM)*: It is embedded in the client device, monitors the user action for adapted contents. The monitoring is accomplished by monitoring the key input of the interface. The essential keys in the feedback message are presented in Figure 3.

```
MessageType = feedback
User_id = 203.252.53.156
ContextScore = {3, 4, 5, 7, 8, 5, 4}
SenderAppType = ClientModule
InterfaceVer = 1.0
FContent = {(image_size_adjust, -10)}
```

Fig. 3. Essential elements of feedback message

The *MessageType* is used to identify the common and feedback messages, and the *User_id* uses the IP address to identify the user. The *FContent* represents the content of the feedback. If user uses the adapted contents as it is, this is regarded as positive feedback, the message is attached as 'positive'. If a user controls the key relating to the adaptation service offered from the interface, this is regarded as negative feedback, this information is concretely attached to *FContent* key.

(2) Intermediate Server Module
- *Analysis Agent (AA)*: It identifies the type (i.e., Request, Feedback) of message from client. For the request, the request and profile component are detached by message parsing

- *Group Management Agent (GMA)*: It manages the group category. Firstly, it compares similarity between the user context set and group category. The similarity is applied with the extended Euclidean distance [14], which is used to compare the similarity of two vectors. The applied formula is as follows.

User Context Set: $U = (u_1, u_2, u_3 \cdots u_n)$, *Group Category:* $G_i = (g_1, g_2, g_3 \cdots g_n)$
* where, i : the index of group categories, $i \geq 1$.

$$app(U,G_i) = sim_{G_i \in T} \sqrt{\sum_{n=1}^{m} (u_n - g_n)^2} \tag{2}$$

* where, $app(U,G_i)$: measurement of the similarity between user profile and group category

$sim_{G \in T}$: each group category included in total category set T

m : the number of context information

If similarity result is duplicated, the duplicated values are computed as shown in formula (3), by assigning weights from the first context.

$$
\begin{array}{c|l}
 & w, \quad w{-}1, w{-}2 \cdots \\
\hline
G'_1 & g_{11}, g_{12}, g_{13}, \cdots g_{1n} \\
G'_2 & g_{21}, g_{22}, g_{23}, \cdots g_{2n} \\
\vdots & \quad \vdots \\
G'_k & g_{k1}, g_{k2}, g_{k3}, \cdots g_{kn}
\end{array}
\tag{3}
$$

* where, k: the number of group categories which have duplicated result. $k \leq |T|$

w: weight factor. $w = |n|$

n is the number of context factors

- *Cache Management Agent (CMA)*: This agent searches adapted contents in the cache, generated from group and classified in the cache as similar to the user. If appropriate content should exist, it would be immediately transmitted to the user. Otherwise, the request is forwarded to the original destination, and it is informed to the RMA.

Table 2. Table to manage the cache

Group type	Resource ID	Applied Service list
3334444	http://selab.skku.ac.kr/test1.html	(image_size_converter, 30), (image_degrader, ...
5554444	http://selab.skku.ac.kr/test2.html	(image_size_converter, 10), (image_degrader, ...
3334444	http://jbmania.netcci.org/sample..	(video_size_converter, 15), (frame_rate_degr ...
:	:	:

- *Rule Management Agent (RMA)*: This agent searches the list of adaptation service mapping with the group category in the rule database.

- *Executor*: It converts the received media source from the SM, based on the adaptation list. The components for adaptation exist in the service repository. The executor uses it by calling with parameters as intensity. The adapted content is transmitted to the user, and is stored concurrently to the cache by the CMA. In addition, the executor temporary stores adaptation information such as user id, group category, content URL, adapted service list, and its intensity, in order to analyze feedback.

(3) Server Module

- *Extraction Agent (EA)*: It generates the new content with extraction of required elements from the source file in the original content DB, and decides on the content layout using a *stylesheet* and transmits the original video or audio which will be included in the document to the ISM. The transmission of the original content may result in network traffic increasing, however, the proposed system is designed to preferentially distribute the server's workload. However, other research is in progress, the workload is dynamically distributed by reflecting each state of resources among server, proxy, and neighboring proxy.

3.3 Extension of Rule Using Feedback

The FM embedded in the client device, monitors the application control of users about the adapted content, and informs this to the ISM. Monitoring can be accomplished by analyzing the inputted key values. The AA informs the feedback message to the GMA with the stored information in temporary storage. If the message is negative feedback, the GMA moves the user node to the intensity as presented Figure 4.

Then, the nodes are continually distributed by feedback, and system re-clustering is performed via the k-means algorithm. Hence, group categories fractionize. A specification for the appropriate number of categories is required.

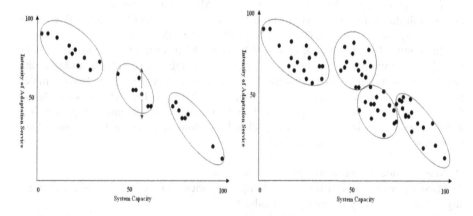

Fig. 4. Movement of nodes in the feedback and re-clustering phase

The RMA inherits adaptation rules of the previous category in order to generate the adaptation rule mapping with the new generated category. The new adaptation rules are then generated by adjusting the intensity of adaptation. This method is not customization for the specific user, but it is suited to similar majority users. However, eventually the result reflects the preference of real users unforeseen by the developer, and user satisfaction increases.

The rules managed by RMA, are presented as Table.2. In this table, all service lists and the score for each service are omitted. If positive feedback is detected, the score of corresponding rules increases. Through this score, generated groups and rules from

Table 2. Table to manage adaptation rules

Group type	Image	video
3334444	(image_size converter, 30), (image_degrader,....)	(video_size_converter, 15), ...
5554444	(image_size converter, 10), (image_degrader,....)	(video_size_converter, 10), ...
7774444	(image_size converter, 5), (image_degrader,...)	(video_size_converter, 5), ...
→ 3457854	(image_size converter, 25), (image_degrader,...)	(video_size_converter, 15), ...

irrelevant feedback are automatically removed after a period of time, and adaptation services classed as acceptable by the majority of users are maintained.

4 Experiments and System Evaluation

In this section, the proposed approach is evaluated in terms of system maintenance by automatic rule generation, suitability of generated rules, and the required time for adaptation. The performance of the system was measured, based on prototype implementation. The specification of the devices used for the implementation of prototype is as follows. Firstly, the SM and ISM were implemented on desktop PCs equipped with an 3GHz Intel Pentium-4 processor, 1Gbyte RAM, and connected over a wired LAN which has a speed between 14Mbps and 28Mbps. The client device used a desktop pc with the same specifications at above, notebook pc, and HP 5500 PDA which has a display size of 240 * 320, a 400MHz CPU, and 128M RAM.

The module for PDA is implemented by Embedded Visual C++, and the another modules are implemented in Java with JADE and JADE-LEAP [15]. In addition, the adaptation service used in evaluation used the image_converter, which was implemented in Jimi [16] and Java Advanced Imaging (JAI) [17]. This service is an adaptation service which takes parameters such as filename, width, height, and quality then handles the image. In addition, XML related technologies such as DOM and XPath were used to handle web documents.

(1) Maintenance by automatically rule generation
The first test was to confirm that the group categories and the adaptation rules (intensity) are automatically extended by feedback.
The three basic categories are created in the GIDB, and the adaptation rule and intensity are mapped to these categories, Multimedia content is made as the target content such as relatively large image files required for adaptation, and documents.

- image1.gif: display_size 2264 * 1448, file_size: 418kbytes
- image2.gif: display_size 1948 * 1216, file_size: 167kbytes
- :

We made one group which is composed of 10 users having different device, access and download to these content. This result, all users suffer from negative feedback, adjusting the option of the application because categories are insufficient. Hence, the classification category is increased, and the adaptation rule is extended according to the adjusting of option. Then, when the same group requests content again, it can be

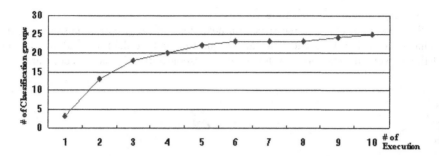

Fig. 5. Number of classification categories extended

known that the number of classification categories was increasing to small range because the categories subdivide.

As a result of the repeat of this process, the increase range is approximately the number of categories, and is therefore relatively low, flattening when reaching higher values such as 20. Through this result, it is confirmed that the number of categories according to the number of users, has not increased to infinity. In addition, the number of categories may not increase by irrelevant feedback because developers define the number of categories and manage this value via the score. This result removes concern for the system, which is massively increasing the number of categories, and indirectly verifies the system can cope with new devices emerge. Moreover, the suitableness of rules is confirmed through the result of decreased of negative feedback.

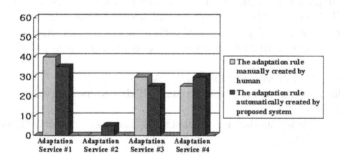

Fig. 6. Evaluation result for fitness of rules generated by the system

(2) Suitableness of automatically extended rules

Secondly, the adaptation rules are generated manually for 10 clients, which will access to the system in order to evaluate the suitability of automatically extended adaptation rules. These rules and the adaptation service rules generated by the system are compared. This comparison is possible due to the intensity of adaptation service rules represented as a numerical value. In the results, the required parts are almost consistent, it can be confirmed that automatically generated rules by feedback are suitable. The evaluation result is presented, as presented in Figure 6.

(3) The reduction of response time
The third test is to evaluate the structural advantage of the proposed system and the advantages of using the cache. The same request is made to the proposed system and existing server side adaptation system, and the response time for these is compared.

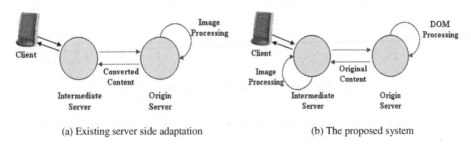

(a) Existing server side adaptation   (b) The proposed system

Fig. 7. Comparison of existing server side adaptation with the proposed system which is distributed processing of the adaptation job

The server side adaptation is a method where main adaptation work is processed in the server side as Figure 7-a. This is in contrast to the proposed system, which has structure as Figure 7.b, that the adaptation work relating to composition of content is processed on the server side; the converting work consumes considerable resources, and is processed in intermediate server.

The content from proxy to server is requested, and the response time is measured, without the request part of the client which is unnecessary in this test. In this test, a jpg image file having a 680 * 500pixel, and 177kbytes size is used. It is converted to 400 * 300 pixel, and quality is degraded 50%. The converted image is decreased to 19kbytes. The response time for these files presents average results as follows:

- The time for image processing: 1300 ms
- The time for transmitting the adapted content (19kbytes) from server to proxy (existing method): 30 ms
- The time for transmitting the original content (177kbytes) from server to proxy (proposed method): 40 ms

In the test result, it can be known that the content before adapting and the content after adapting do not have much difference in transmission in a wired environment. In ordinary situations, performing all adaptation work on the server side has more efficient results. In addition, generally, the web server has higher performance than the proxy, but, in this test, we use the systems having identical specification.

However, when a considerable workload occurs in the server, the result is very different. The *process_generator* generating the dummy process in the server is executed in order to simulate situations where the number of users connecting to the server is increasing. This developed application uses the log which records the number of accessing users and the usage of resources on the server, in order to simulate the increasing number of users. In test processes, the response time of existing server side adaptation system increases sharply according to increasing workload, unlike the

Fig. 8. Comparison of response time along with workload of the server

proposed system, which maintains consistency. The evaluation result is presented in Figure 8.

Through this result, the efficiency of the proposed system in terms of distributing adaptation work is confirmed. In addition, another result is verified, where response time is reduced through reusing content.

The quantitative measurement of user satisfaction is omitted due to the difficulty of determining this value. It can be known that more suitable content is offered due reusing the adapted contents generated by the same category.

5 Conclusion

In existing work, in order to offer the content adaptation service, the creation of multiple content forms, or rules for dynamic adaptation are made in advance, by considering the device characteristics of various users. However, this process is extremely difficult. The proposed system automatically extends adaptation rules depending on user feedback, in order to solve this problem.

A prototype was implemented in order to evaluate the proposed system in terms of fitness of automatically extended rules and system efficiency. Through the result, negative feedback decreases, and adaptation rules are automatically extended to a positive form for user satisfaction, and it is verified that automatic adaptation to a new device is possible. Moreover, by comparing with the server adaptation system, the structural efficiency of the proposed system is evaluated, which distributes the processing of adaptation work, in order to avoid excessive workload on one system.

As future work, the public owned function for information among the ISMs will be integrated, in order to solve the 'learning speed' problem of the system. In the future, a new adaptation strategy mechanism will be generated, based on the meaning of content, in order to realize increasingly suitable adaptation mechanisms.

References

1. Margaritis Margaritidis and George C. Polyzos, "Adaptation techniques for Ubiquitous Internet multimedia", Wireless Communication and Mobile Computing, vol.1, no.2, pp.141-163, Jan.2001
2. Paolo Bellavista, Antonio Corradi, Rebecca Montanari, and Cesare Stefanelli, "Context-Aware Middleware for Resource Management in the Wireless Internet", IEEE Trans. on Software Engineering, vol.29, no.12, Dec.2003
3. Ariel Pashtan, Shriram Kollipara, and Michael Pearce, "Adapting Content for Wireless Web Services", IEEE Internet computing, vol.7, no.5, pp.79-85, Sep.2003
4. Rotan Hanrahan, Roland Merrick, Candy Wong, Michael Wasmund, Rhys Lewis, and Tayeb Lemlouma, "Authoring Techniques for Device Independence", World Wide Web Consortium, Note, NOTE-di-atdi-20040218, Feb.2004
5. IBM WebSphere® Transcoding Publisher, http://www-306.ibm.com/software/pervasive/transcoding_publisher
6. Timo Laakko and Tapio Hiltunen, "Adapting Web Content to Mobile User Agents", IEEE Internet computing, vol.9, no.2, pp.46-53, Mar.2005
7. Daniel Billsus, Clifford A. Brunk, Craig Evans, Brian Gladish, and Michael Pazzani, "Adaptive Interfaces for Ubiquitous Web Access", Communication of the ACM, Vol.45, No.5, pp.34-38, May.2002
8. Mark Butler, Fabio Giannetti, Roger Gimson, and Tony Wiley, "Device Independence and the Web", IEEE Internet Computing, Vol.6, No.5, pp.81-86, Sep.2002
9. Cheng-Yue Chang and Ming-Syan Chen, "On Exploring Aggregate Effect for Efficient Cache Replacement in Transcoding Proxies", IEEE Trans. Parallel and Distributed systems, vol.14, no.6, pp.611-624, Jun.2003
10. Claudia Canali, Valeria Cardellini, Michele Colajanni, Riccardo Lancellotti, and Philip S. Yu, "A two-level distributed architecture for efficient Web content adaptation and delivery", Proc. SAINT 2005, pp.132-139
11. W3C – Resource Description Framework (RDF), http://www.w3.org/RDF/
12. W3C – Hypertext Transfer Protocol (HTTP 1.0), http://www.w3.org/protocols/http/
13. W3C - Composite Capability/Preference Profiles (CC/PP), http://www.w3.org/Mobile/
14. Michael J. A. Berry, Gordon S. Linoff, "Mastering Data Mining: The Art and Science of Customer Relationship Management, Wiley, 2000
15. Telecom Italia Lab - Java Agent DEvelopment Framework (JADE), http://jade.tilab.com/
16. Sun Microsystems – Java Image Management Interface API, http://java.sun.com/products/jimi
17. Sun Microsystems – Java Advanced Imaging (JAI) API, http://java.sun.com/products/java-media/jai/
18. Yu Chen, Xing Xie, Wei-Ying Ma, and Hong-Jiang Zhang, "Adapting web pages for small-screen devices", IEEE Internet computing, vol.9, no.1, pp.50-56, Jan.2005
19. Wai Yip Lum and Francis C.M. Lau, "A context-aware decision engine for content adaptation", IEEE Pervasive computing, vol.1, pp.41-49, Jul.2002

Context-Based Cooperation Architecture for Ubiquitous Environment

Minsoo Kim, Youna Jung, Jungtae Lee, and Minkoo Kim

Graduate School of Infromation and Communication, Ajou University,
Suwon, Korea (South)
{visual, serazade, jungtae, minkoo}@ajou.ac.kr

Abstract. Context-awareness which provides relevant information and services to situation using context is an important issue to solve problems in ubiquitous environment. In addition, many problems in ubiquitous environment are solved by interaction between computational elements rather than by performing individual actions. Therefore, it needs to approach context-awareness from in a cooperative point of view. In this paper, we discuss about context model for cooperation system in ubiquitous environment and describe context ontology focused on interaction process with general context. Moreover, we propose cooperation architecture based on context ontology supporting ontological processes. This architecture introduces community as an organization of elements solving common problem and provides context-aware mechanism within community.

1 Introduction

A dynamic and changeable ubiquitous environment gives rise to unpredictable and complex problems. Most of them are solved by interacting between elements rather than performing individual actions. Considering this issue, cooperation is an important issue to satisfy user's requirements and to provide intelligent service in ubiquitous environment. Cooperation system provides primitives for interaction with one another: interaction environments, common goals, interaction protocols, and so on. Elements in cooperation system are strongly dependent on environments and other elements to provide own and/or common services, so essentially, they must recognize the relevant information surrounding them - called *context*. However, because of the complex and dynamic features of ubiquitous environment, it is difficult to recognize or aware context. So to avoid increasing complexity and to ensure context-aware service, system and elements need to be capable to maintain well-defined context model and to provide efficient mechanism for context-awareness.

Context, generally, is referred to 'any information that can be used to characterize the situation of an entity (i.e. whether a person, place or object) that are considered relevant to the interaction between a user and an application, including the user an applications themselves'.[1] Many approaches attempt to do context modeling and context-awareness service in ubiquitous environment, and most of them have focused on the physical entities of the environment(e.g. the person or users, the devices) and little work has been done to develop models to support cognitive entities[2][3].

H.Y. Youn, M. Kim, and H. Morikawa (Eds.): UCS 2006, LNCS 4239, pp. 171–182, 2006.

Information of physical environments, naturally, is important to determine element's activity and service, but cognitive context such as element status, activities and services is also important to build ubiquitous computing system efficiently.

Many cooperation systems are developed for ubiquitous computing environment with supporting context-awareness, and most of them are based on multi-agent system (MAS). Features of MAS such as adaptability, pro-activeness and reactivity, help to build cooperation system. Especially, in many approaches [4][5][6][7][8][9], interactions between agents can be defined using role, introducing the concept of 'role' as a *set of rights* in MAS. This can derive some advantages: separation of issues related to agent algorithmic and interaction with other agents, solution reusability (since roles apply to specific context, so they can be successfully adopted similar areas), and so on. In recent works for role-based system [10][11][12], researchers emphasize the social (organizational) structure and social role to build ubiquitous computing system efficiently. In fact, a role reflects social activities of users or devices, so roles should be comprehensible when they are embedded in social context. Since ubiquitous environment and elements are highly dynamic and changeable, cooperation system for ubiquitous computing environment must support dynamism to operate seamlessly. In other words, system gives proper roles to elements dynamically, and elements can also take the role and can perform a required action.

We think that the following Requirements must be met to build cooperation system for ubiquitous computing environment:

- Context-awareness: providing intelligent service and interaction between elements in system. Context is modeled focusing on cooperative environments with general context (i.e. information of physical environments)
- Role-based interaction: separation of concerns between element's algorithmic logic and interaction logic
- Organizational structure: considering role as required social activity. Organizational structures may provide interaction environment and context-aware mechanism.
- Dynamism: providing methods to solve unpredictable problems in ubiquitous environment, dynamically.

To satisfy upper requirements, we discuss context model for cooperation system in ubiquitous environment and describe context ontology focused on interaction process with general context. We also propose cooperation architecture based on context ontology supporting ontological processes. This architecture introduces community as an organization of elements solving common problem and provides context-aware mechanism within community. This architecture provides mechanism to solve unpredictable problems in a dynamic way which we will discuss later.

The remainders of the paper are structured as follows. Section 2 describes existing role-based system and analyzes role required to ubiquitous computing system. Section 3 introduces some ontological approaches for context modeling, and section 4 specifies our context ontology. Section 5 proposes cooperation architecture and cooperation mechanism supporting system dynamism based on context ontology introduced in section 4. In Section 6, we introduce a new approach 'Community Computing' for developing ubiquitous computing system, and apply context ontology and cooperation mechanism to community computing. At last the conclusions and future works are made in section 7.

2 Cooperation Systems for Ubiquitous Computing

There are many approaches to cooperate between computational elements or agents. The purpose of them is to achieve common goal or to solve common problem shared elements in cooperation system. Most of approaches are based on the concept of 'role'. Even if role is defined as various ways in different systems or approaches, generally, role is defined as a set of rights. Comparison between some role-based approaches is shown in [7]. It is important to compare 'roles at runtime' and 'openness' phase for the ubiquitous computing. But we also consider organizational structure supporting role-based cooperation, because supporting 'roles at runtime' and 'openness' is a social or systematic capability rather than role's own. In this section, we analyze some role-based approaches and social-concept centered approaches.

2.1 Role-Based Approaches

AALADIN [4] is a meta-model for multi-agent system and focuses on the organization rather than agent in himself. It assumes that the idea of collective structure permits two levels of analysis – concrete level and abstract, methodological level. Concrete level describes the actual agent organization through core concept of model: *agent, group* and *role*. Agent is member of one or more group, and group contains roles performing by agent. AALAADIN introduces methodological concept to serve analysis and design MAS. Organization is composed of overlapping groups, and group structure is introduced to partition organization and to specify the group information. Actually, group structure defines roles and interaction protocol between agents performing roles in the group. The organizational structure defines the group structure in the organization and the correspondences between them. In extended work for AALAADIN [5], dynamic aspect of an organization is added: it describes creation of group, entering and leaving of a group by an agent, and role acquisition.

BRAIN [6] is a frame work for Flexible Role-based Interactions in MAS. Role in BRAIN is defined *set of the capabilities* and an *expected behavior* corresponding to the main feature of agent: *pro-activeness* and *reactivity*. BRAIN introduces XML-based XRole notation to describe roles. XRole consists of three main parts to define a role: basic information, allowed action and recognized action. XRole can be translated into appropriate representations, so the different phases of the development of applications relies on the same information, granting continuity during the entire development. At last, RoleSystem in BRAIN is an interaction infrastructure that implements the interaction model of BRAIN. RoleSystem is composed of tow layer: subject layer is platform-independent part of system and wrapper layer is the platform-dependent (e.g. JADE) implementation entity in charge of supporting the subject layer.

Gaia [8][9] introduced a methodology for agent-oriented analysis and design to capture an agent's flexible, autonomous problem solving behavior, the richness of an agent's interactions, and the complexity of an agent system's organizational structures. In Gaia, role is defined a well-defined position in the organization with an associated set of expected behaviors. MAS is regarded as a collection of computational organizations consisting of various interacting roles in Gaia.

2.2 Social Concept Centered Approaches

Cooperation system including MAS makes the design of system less complex reducing the conceptual distance between system and real-world application. In internal view of each agent, agent (or role) solves problem or achieves goal interacting with other agents. In external view, agents are organized to achieve common goal, and organization provides interaction environment to agents and can play a coordinator or negotiator for agents. Organizational or social view of cooperation system can make private agent's behavior to social one, not isolated behavior. And some methodology related to organize agents such as dynamic organization and role binding are efficient way to solve dynamic and changeable problem. In that point, to solve unpredictable problem in ubiquitous computing system, organization or agent society plays an important role.

A number of approaches for building MAS take social concept into consideration. Organizational model for agent society by using contracts [10] takes a collectivist view on agent societies and defines organizational framework consists of three models: organizational model, social model and agent (interaction) model. This approach aims to build MAS and to specify interaction between agents defining contract as a statement of intent that regulates behavior among organizations and individuals. Another approach is based on social role-aware [12]. This approach emphasizes social role-aware as a key feature for ubiquitous computing and proposes multi-agent architecture being aware of social role. The roles are assigned dynamically based on both sensor-data from the environments and role ontology described human designer.

As mentioned above, role means not only agent capability for interacting with others, but also social activity to achieve common goal in the society or organization. In order to take a role as a social activity, cooperation system must support a organizational architecture which can bind a role to proper agent and provide interaction environment for assuring agent activities.

3 Context and Context Modeling

Context is general term adopted in different areas of the computer science and definition of context is also general – any information related a problem implicitly or explicitly. But generality of definition makes difficult to build context model, so smart method must be required to model and use context efficiently. In this section we capture the context in ubiquitous environment and describe method to build context model.

3.1 Scenario in Ubiquitous Environment

The Following famous scenario is staring part of Berners-Lee's article that has introduced the semantic web.[14] It is very short and simple, but we imagine internal process and also capture context required by that process. The scenario has the electronic devices, the agents, the person, and also some actions (i.e. send message, sound down).

> *The entertainment system was belting out the Beatles' "We Can Work It Out" when the phone rang. When Pete answered, his phone turned the sound down by sending a message to all the other local devices that had a volume control. His sister, Lucy, was on the line from the doctor's office: "Mom needs to see a specialist and then has to have a series of physical therapy sessions. Bi-weekly or something. I'm going to have my agent set up the appointments." Pete immediately agreed to share the chauffeuring.*

3.2 Context

To capture and aware context, system requires information to be exchanged and used between different elements, and obviously that information is related element or problem. In scenario, some physical information can be captured: telephone calls, devices location. This information is recognized related elements, and then system can provide intelligent service. Most of the context modeling or context-awareness approaches capture this kind of information as context, including device location, time, temperature and all physical or sensing information. This information is important and very useful for context-aware application in various domains.

But, to complete upper scenario, other information is needed. For Pete's calling with Lucy, sound of silence is required, and device 'phone' must send message to all devices to turn the sound down. In classic approaches, this situation is resolved through interactions or communication between related elements rather than by using context model. In other words, messages from others or interactions in themselves is not information in context model. But, we think that these are also considered as information modeled context. The action 'send message' is enable aware context 'telephone calls' and similar the action 'sound down' is performed by recognizing context 'message from phone'. Moreover, an action in itself is also context: to send message, 'phone' must know whether receiver is capable 'sound down' or not. Finally, Social information as interaction environment is also important: which elements are in the group or community, who is performing a specific role, or what is a common goal that elements achieve by interacting with others.

Thus we regard both information from physical environments and cooperative or social information of system as context. By maintaining context model with them, it is possible to provide an efficient context-awareness and intelligent services.

3.3 Ontological Approach for Context Modeling

To model and aware context in the system, many methodologies is used – key value, mark-up scheme, graphical, object oriented, logic based and ontology based.[13] We choose ontology based approach to context model with following reasons: (i) ontology provides uniform way for specifying the model's core concepts, (ii) ontology enables to have a common set of concepts about context while interacting with one another, (iii) system can exploit reasoning mechanism with explicit semantic based on ontology, (iv) By reusing ontology, system can compose large-scale context ontology.

Some context-aware system for ubiquitous or pervasive computing are proposed with context-model based on ontology. SOUPA [15] ontology has proposed for pervasive computing, and SOUPA vocabularies adopted from a number of different consensus ontologies(time, person, places etc,.). CONON [16][17] ontology provides a vocabulary for representing knowledge about a domain and for describing specific situations in a domain. In a CONON's view, context has two categories: direct context that is acquired from a context provider directly such as sensed context and defined context, indirect context that is acquired by interpreting direct context through aggregation and reasoning process. By introducing classification and dependency, CONON allows the properties of entities to be associated with quality constraints that indicated the quality of context. GAS[18][19] ontology that provides common language for the communication and collaboration among eGadgets defines an architectural vocabulary and configuration rules including eGadget's roles and relations between them.

Our context ontology, will discuss next section, is based on similar idea of these approaches – context model that aims to ubiquitous or pervasive computing - , but we focused on context for cooperation between elements in the ubiquitous computing systems. Classic ontological approaches well-define for information of physical environments, but they have weakness to represents cooperative and social information. GAS ontology aims to communicate and collaborate between elements, but it strongly depends on centered their plug and synapse methodology, that is, it is limited to a little domain and difficult to use general cooperation system.

4   Context Ontology for Ubiquitous System

In this Section, we describe context ontology for cooperation system for ubiquitous computing. We assume that user or system can define domain specific ontology using well-defined ontologies, and system can perform a reasoning or inference process using them together with our context ontology.

Fig. 1 shows context ontology with major concepts and properties. We will write context ontology using OWL (Web ontology Language) recommended for describing web ontology by W3C (World Wide Web Consortium). OWL provides rich expressive power compared other ontology language such as RDF(S), DAML+OIL, and has capability of supporting semantic interoperability to exchange and share context or domain knowledge. Our context ontology is composed of three sub-ontologies. First, Physical Ontology is similar to SOUPA core ontology or CONON upper ontology. In fact, we do not explicit define concepts in physical ontologies, because we think that physical ontologies such as place, time are already well-defined by many researchers. For example, DAML-time ontology is good to conceptualize time and related many services. Moreover, in reusable point of view that is major advantage of ontology, reusing ontologies for information of physical environments is an efficient way to build context ontology.

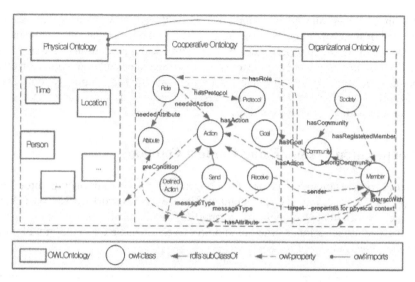

Fig. 1. Context ontology is composed of three sub-ontologies: Physical ontology, Cooperative ontology and Organizational ontology

Second, however, we define explicit the Cooperative Ontology related cooperative part of system. By using this ontology, developers describe interaction process and organizational structure. Cooperative ontology includes the following concepts: the role, the protocol, the action and the other concepts to explain the first three concepts. Role represents interaction between computational elements and social activity to support dynamism of system (see next section to get detail description). Therefore, description of role has protocols describing interaction process, and must include required capabilities (actions and attributes) to perform the role. Protocol that describes sequence of actions is an interaction process between roles. Action represents element's activities with pre-condition, inner-action, activate-time and other properties. Action has special two sub-actions 'Send' and 'Receive' for communication between elements: these actions have properties to enable working on network – 'target', 'sender', 'messageType' (It follows message type proposed by FIPA - Foundation for Intelligent Physical Agent), contents, and so on. 'target' property can have multiple elements. Moreover, actions can have special properties such as 'parallel' in programmatic point of view.

Finally, we define social ontology represented core elements in our cooperation architecture: Society, Community, and Member. Society manages all communities and members, but it is not necessary maintain all information they have. Basically, society represents 'hasCommunity', 'registeredMember' property. Community has 'goal' and 'role' properties and member has 'action', 'attribute' and properties related physical ontology. Member status in cooperation system is necessary context to interact with one another. In cooperation system based on MAS, agent status is represented by using general terms such as 'activate', 'busy', 'idle', but it is not enough to explain an agent to system or other agents. We need more concrete description: for example, agent 'A' can perform 'move' and 'run' actions and is located in a garden, and he is communicating with radio. We emphasize concrete description of member status, because by grasping a member status, other elements in the system can decide and perform a proper action without additional interaction to get his status. In order words, describing status of member and community or other cooperative information can improve the performance of cooperation system. Thus, organizational ontology is designed to satisfy for describing elements of system in concrete way with cooperative ontology.

5 Cooperation System Using Context Ontology

We define organizational structure for cooperation system introducing three core concepts: society, community and member. Each elements works based on context ontologies with some components supporting ontological process and system functionality. Organizational structure and processes to enable cooperation with three core concepts is shown in Fig. 2.

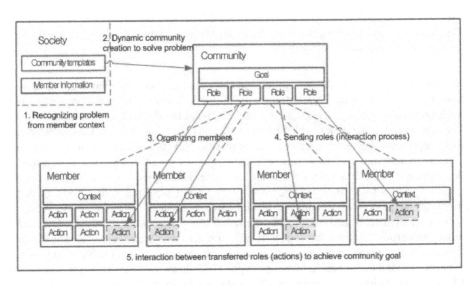

Fig. 2. Organizational structure and cooperation process

Society is an administrative concept of system and an abstraction of ubiquitous environment. Society must belong all elements and manages them using context ontologies – member ontologies and community ontologies. It is not a space occurring interaction between members to solve problem, but an environment that occurs unpredictable problems, exists members independently, is created community to solve problem.

Community is a cooperative group composed of related members to solve a problem. Problems occurred in ubiquitous environment are not static, but unpredictable and dynamic. Therefore, community does not always exist, but dynamically created by society when problem occurs. Society recognizes the occurrence of a problem using context ontology, then creates community which can solve that problem according to community ontology. Community is created with following information: (i) goal that will be achieved, and (ii) roles implying participants in community, and (iii) interaction process to achieve community goal. With this information, community can dynamically cast members and also dynamically transfer interaction processes to each cast members. Transferred interaction process is an instance of 'Protocol' class in context ontology described previous section. When goal is achieved, community is finalized dynamically, and members belonged to community leave the community and perform their own actions.

Member is a basic element in the system, representing person, device, hardware or software, similar to agent in MAS. Member provides services (actually member actions and described using 'Action' class) when satisfying 'precondition' property in 'Action' class. In Fig. 2, transferred interaction process is added as member action. We consider both alone-action and interaction between members as same kind of thing, since all actions are performed when satisfying precondition of themselves by recognizing context. Fig. 3 shows an internal architecture of member that enable this process based on context-awareness.

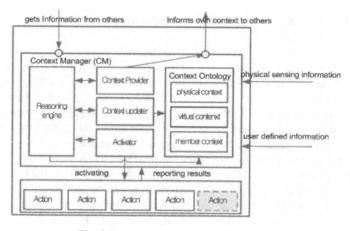

Fig. 3. Internal architecture for member

Context Manager (CM) contains a number of components including context ontology. CM gets information from other members (message), physical sensors, users and results for own actions, and then context updater updates context ontology with reasoning engine. Note that messages from other members are also information for context, not just message in traditional cooperation system. The reasoning engine provides reasoning process to other components in CM: checking pre-condition of an action, interpreting ontology, and other useful reasoning. Context provider informs own context to other elements including society and community in system. Note that 'send' action for interactions between members is performed by context provider ('receive' action is performed by CM). In other words, 'Send' and 'Receive' are not special action; they just decide target/send and type of message, and so on. Actuator activates actions that satisfy precondition by reasoning context ontology with reasoning engine.

Developers describe cooperative and organizational ontology as a program or set of rules, then system interprets this ontology and performs proper actions. For example, member 'm1' performs action 'a1' when receiving message 'msg1' from member 'm2', and after performing 'a1', send message 'msg2' to 'm3', 'm4', and 'm5'. When receiving message 'msg1', first, context updater updates context ontology with 'msg1', then CM checks preconditions of actions through reasoning engine. If 'msg1' come from 'm2', that is, satisfying precondition of 'a1', actuator activates 'a1'. When 'a1' performed, 'a1' reports result to CM, and CM updates context ontology again. Finally, context provider sends context 'msg2' to 'm3', 'm4' and 'm5'.

Society and community have similar to member architecture shown in Fig. 3. In order words, all elements in system work based on context management and context awareness, including to interaction with one another through CM, not individual action. Implementation of actions is portion of developer in difference platform, so we do not consider specific platform or implementation method in real-world applications.

6 Related Work - Community Computing

Community Computing [20] is the community-based service development methodology, proposed to develop ubiquitous spaces. Community computing focuses on how ubiquitous spaces satisfy their requirements with cooperation between predefined entities while the existing distributed object approaches focus on what entities are needed to satisfy the requirements. A community computing system means that a service providing system developed using the community computing model. A ubiquitous space can be developed as a community computing system, and the requirements of a ubiquitous space are fulfilled by communities.

To development a community computing system, community computing takes the development process with the MDA (Model Driven Architecture) approach. The MDA is an approach to system development, which increases the power of models in that work. It proposes to start the process by building high-level abstraction models obtained by requirement analysis, and then refine them until obtain models that directly represents the final system. For applying MDA approach to the development process of the community computing systems, three different abstraction model is proposed: Community Computing Model (CCM) as the most high-level abstraction model, Platform Independent Community Computing Implementation Model (CIM-PI) as implementation model without platform specific features, and Platform Specific Community Computing Implementation Model (CIM-PS) as complete implementation model as real-world application.

Social concept of Community computing is similar to describing in this paper. But, not yet, context modeling and context-awareness do not provided in community computing model. Since context-awareness is essential element to realize ubiquitous computing system, community computing must meet the context. We believe that community computing can more powerful model to develop ubiquitous computing system with context-awareness using context ontology proposed in this paper.

7 Conclusion

In this paper, we describe context ontology for cooperation system in ubiquitous computing environment, and propose organizational structure and cooperation processes based on context ontology. Context ontology represents not only information of physical environments, but also cooperative or organizational information required when cooperating between members. By using this ontology, cooperation system can provide context model and context-awareness improving the performance of system. Based on our context ontology, we also present Organizational architecture composed of society, community and members. This architecture supports a dynamic way to solve unpredictable problem in ubiquitous environment. However, there are several issues that need to be considered in future works.

- Completion of context ontology and writing in OWL: current context ontology has some weakness for organizing physical ontologies with cooperative and social ontologies. And to develop real-world application with context ontology for sharing and reusing context, it is good to publish context ontology using recommended ontology language OWL.
- Explicit description of ontology reasoning: main component of proposed architecture is the reasoning engine supporting various ontological processes. As yet, we describe reasoning process implicitly, but for completion of context management and cooperation system, we need to explicit reasoning mechanism with well-performed reasoning engine.
- Practical uses with Community Computing: community computing introduced in previous section is good to be exploited context ontology. With context ontology, community computing will have ability to manage context, and then will solve context-related problems such as resolving conflict.

Acknowledgments. This research is supported by the ubiquitous Computing and Network (UCN) Project, the Ministry of Information and Communication (MIC) 21st Century Frontier R&D Program in Korea.

References

1. Anind K. Dey, "Understanding and Using Context", Personal and Ubiquitous Computing, Special Issue on Situated Interaction and Ubiquitous Computing, vol. 5(1), 2001
2. Paul Prekop and Mark Burnett, "Activities, Context and Ubiquitous Computing", Computer Communications, vol. 26, p.p.1168-1176, 2003
3. A. Schmidt, M. Beigl, and H.W. Gellersen, "There is more to Context than Location", Computers and Graphics, vol. 23, p.p.893-901, 1999
4. J. Ferber and O. Gutknecht, "A meta-model for the analysis and design of organization in multi-agent systems", In Proceedings of 3rd International Conference on Multi-agent Systems (ICMAS'98), 1998
5. J. Ferber, O. Gutknecht, F. Michel, "From Agents to Organizations : An Organizational View of Multi-agent Systems", In Proceedings of AOSE 2003, Australia, 2003

6. G. Cabri, L. Leonardi, F. Zambonelli, "A Framework for Flexible Role-based Interactions in Multi-agent System", In Proceedings of the 2003 Conference on Cooperative Information Systems (CoopIS), Italy, 2003

7. G. Cabri, L. Ferrari, L. Leonardi. "Agent Role-based Collaboration and Coordination: a Survey About Existing Approaches", In Proceedings of the 2004 IEEE systems, Man and Cybernetics Conference, Netherlands, 2004

8. M. Wooldridge, Nicholas R. J. "The Gaia Methodology for Agent-oriented Analysis and Design", Autonomous Agents and Multi-Agent Systems, 3, p.p. 285-312, 2000

9. R. Jennings, et. al. "Developing Multiagent Systems: The Gaia Methodology", ACM Transactions on Software Engineering and Methodology, 12, 3, p.p. 317-370, 2003

10. Xinjun Mao and Eric Yu, "Organizational and Social Concepts in Agent Oriented Software Engineering", 5th International Workshop, AOSE 2004, New York, USA, July 19, 2004.

11. V. Dignum, J-J. Meyer, H. Weigand, and F. Dignum, "An organizational-oriented model for agent societies" In Proceedings of International Workshop on Regulated Agent-Based Social Systems: Theories and Applications (RASTA'02) at AAMAS'02, 2002.

12. Akio Sashima, Noriaki Izumi, Koichi Kurumatani, Yoshiyuki Kotani, "Towards Social Role-Aware Agents in Ubiquitous Computing", Proceedings of ubicomp2005, Japan, 2005

13. T. Strang and C. Linnhoff-popien, "A Context Modeling Survey", In Proceedings of 1st International workshop on Advanced Context modeling, Reasoning and Management UbiComp2004, 2004

14. T. Berners-Lee, J. Hendler and O. Lassila, "The Semantic Web", Scientific American, p.p.35-43, 2001

15. Harry Chen, Tim Finin, and Anupam Joshi, "The SOUPA Ontology for Pervasive Computing", Ontologies for Agents: Theory and Experiences, Springer, July 2005

16. Xiao Hang Wang, Tao Gu, Da Qing Zhang, Hung Keng Pung, "Ontology Based Context Modeling and Reasoning using OWL", In Proceedings of Workshop on Context Modeling and Reasoning(CoMoRea 2004), In conjunction with the Second IEEE International Conference on Pervasive Computing and Communications (PerCom 2004), Orlando, Florida USA, March 2004

17. T. Gu, X. H. Wang, H. K. Pung, D. Q. Zhang. "An Ontology-based Context Model in Intelligent Environments", In Proceedings of Communication Networks and Distributed Systems Modeling and Simulation Conference (CNDS 2004), pp. 270-275. San Diego, California, USA, January 2004.

18. Christopoulou E., Kameas A., "GAS Ontology: an ontology for collaboration among ubiquitous computing devices", Protégé special issue of the International Journal of Human – Computer Studies, 2004

19. Eleni Christopoulou, Christos Goumopoulos, Achilles Kameas, "Context-aware systems: An ontology-based context management and reasoning process for UbiComp applications", In Proceedings of the 2005 joint conference on Smart objects and ambient intelligence: innovative context-aware services: usages and technologies sOc-EUSAI '05, 2005

20. Youna Jung, Jungtae Lee, Minkoo Kim. "Multi-agent based Community Computing System Development with the Model Driven Architecture", In Proceedings of 5th International Conference on Autonomous Agents and Multiagent Systems (AAMAS), Japan, 2006.

Affordance-Based Design of
Physical Interfaces for Ubiquitous Environments

Jennifer G. Sheridan and Gerd Kortuem

Lancaster University
Computing Department
Lancaster, UK
{sheridaj, kortuem}@comp.lancs.ac.uk

Abstract. Physical interfaces have been proposed as a way to realize natural interactions with ubiquitous computing environments. The successful design of such interfaces requires design approaches that integrate aspects of our world which are usually treated separately in traditional system development approaches. This paper describes a design approach based on Gibson concept of affordance. We demonstrate an experimental method for studying object affordance and show how it can be applied to the design of a concrete physical interface artefact.

1 Introduction

Ubiquitous computing promises a computing infrastructure that seamlessly aids users in accomplishing their tasks and that renders the actual computing devices and technology virtually invisible and distraction-free. Mark Weiser formulated this vision by describing a computer "so imbedded, so fitting, so natural, that we use it without even thinking about it" [1]. One way of realizing this vision is by building task-specific information appliances [2] and physical computer interfaces [3,4,5]. In fact, in recent years a number of toolkits kits for physical computer interfaces have appeared, including Phidgets [6], iSuff [7], SWEETPEA [8], Papier-Mâché [9] and MetaCricket [10]. While these toolkits provide adequate guidance during the construction phase of a physical interface, they do not provide any help in how to design a usable and intuitive physical interface.

The key idea of physical interfaces is to capitalize on our familiarity with the physical world. The design of such interfaces requires design approaches that incorporate different aspects of our world that are usually treated separately in traditional system development approaches. In particular, the actual physical form of an interface has rarely been considered in the context of physical interfaces and ubiquitous computing. This is in stark contrast to the fields of ergonomics and industrial design which have long recognized the importance of physical form for creating usable and appealing artefacts and products. One of the first researchers to systematically investigate the relationship between physical objects and people was the perceptual psychologist J. J. Gibson who introduced the theory of *affordance* [11]. This theory states that physical objects suggest by their shape and other attributes what actors can do with them. Yet, theories of affordance are predominantly used as analytical tool and

H.Y. Youn, M. Kim, and H. Morikawa (Eds.): UCS 2006, LNCS 4239, pp. 183–199, 2006.

applied after the design stage. We believe that a thorough investigation of object affordance should be a key component of the physical interface design process.

In this paper, we present our experiences with an affordance-based design method. Our approach focuses on three key dimensions: *affordance*, *capability* and *control*.

- *Affordance*: We propose that the design of physical interfaces should begin with an investigation of the object itself in relation to human perception and motor skills, because physical form fundamentally shapes the kinds of interactions users can perform. The goal is to identify the types of actions humans can perform on an object. We formulate the results of this study as *non-verbal dynamics*, a vocabulary of significant object-specific manipulations such as gripping, squeezing, rubbing and rotating.
- *Capability*: The second component in the design process is the investigation and specification the technical capabilities of the interface artefact in terms of sensing and actuation. Technological capabilities affect which object manipulations can be recognized and how feedback is realized. As well, technology affects the form or physical properties of the device, such as shape and size.
- *Control*: The ultimate purpose of a physical interface is determined by the control it gives users over an application or service. For example, a mobile phone interface needs to provide controls for initiating and terminating a call. The set of controls needs to be mapped to non-verbal dynamics and realized by object capabilities.

We believe that these design dimensions are not separable, but must be investigated together. Understanding and applying the relationships between these three dimensions is the key to modelling and creating computer interfaces that are useful and appropriate for the ubiquitous world.

In the remainder of this paper we present our experiences in applying affordance-based design to the design of a concrete physical interface artefact for a mobile phone. We focus on one particular object type, namely the cube. We demonstrate an experimental method for studying the affordances of objects and use the results to inform the design of the technology and interaction aspects of the interface artefact. Finally, we discuss results of a usability study and relate our approach to existing design frameworks from tangible and physical computing.

2   Case Study

To illustrate our affordance-based design approach we chose to design a physical interface for a mobile phone. As physical form we chose a six-sided cube. The goal was to design an interface that makes use of basic object manipulation skills rather than buttons. The cube interface is only used for input; output is presented on a separate (wrist-mounted or heads-up) display. We refer to our interface artefact as *Cubicle*.

The decision to use a cube-shaped object was based on the fact there is extensive prior work on using cubes as tangible or physical interface objects (for example BUILD-IT [12], Flip Bricks [13], ActiveCube [14], Cognitive Cubes [15], Navigational Blocks [16] and CUBIK [17]). While many experiments use six-sided objects, very few explain why they chose this particular physical form over others, and none reports on experimentation with other shapes. One of the reasons cubes are attractive is that most people have an intuitive and immediate understanding of how it can be manipulated [16]. While some studies report that cubes provide a higher flexibility in operations [18, 19] there is little discussion about why cubes are particularly well suited for this capability. Ullmer [20] states that cubes were chosen because of the intended application, yet there is no discussion as to why cubes offer an advantage as compared to other shapes. Cohen et al. [21] alludes to Scrabble™ as a possible influence for the design of the "dominos" in LogJam but does not explicitly state this. While Rekimoto [29] discusses evaluating various shapes for the ToolStone application, he leaves this open as a future research direction.

The reason to use a mobile phone as application was based on the fact that most users are familiar with it. A mobile phone provides a familiar context for both a large majority of the local population and our design team. Rather than designing a complete interface for a fully functional phone we decided to concentrate on core functions of everyday mobile phone use. Using informal discussion and self-examination, we determined that the most common uses of a mobile phone are to make and receive phone calls as well as checking left messages. Furthermore, we selected call making rather than call receiving as our core task, as it causes users to interact more physically with the phone. Additionally, we discovered that a good number of people had a need to adjust the volume of their phone according to context, so we included this functionality in the design. We finally settled in the following functional repertoire: 1) *select entry in address book and make phone call,* 2) *select message and listen to it,* 3) *switch device on,* 4) *switch device off,* 5) *turn volume up,* and 6) *turn volume down.*

3   Studying Affordance

Our design process begins with an experimental investigation of cube affordances. The study focuses on human perception and motors skills and is an attempt to understand how people "naturally" interact with physical artefacts. Using the cube as example, we set out to explore the following questions:

- How do physical properties (such as size, shape and form) affect affordance?
- What types of manipulations are possible with cubes of various designs?
- What types and range of actions do humans naturally perform?

The primary goal of the affordance design study was to identify the types and range of actions humans naturally perform on an object. Our underlying hypothesis is that each artefact has its own *non-verbal dynamics* [31], a set of natural and object-specific object manipulations such as squeezing, rubbing and rotating. Furthermore, we expected to be able to group cubes according to non-verbal dynamics. To limit the scope of our investigation, we chose to ignore gestures such as waving and concentrate on grasp.

3.1   Study Overview

To measure the variance of non-verbal dynamics we designed several cube-like artefacts (Figures 2a - f).

Each artefact had a unique set of characteristics:

- Size: finger-sized cubes (Figure 2a), various small, medium and large cubes (Figure 2b).
- Texture: cube covered in various smooth (paper, lacquered) and rough (burlap, textured card) materials as well as squishable (Figure 2c) and organic, clay cubes (Figure 2f).
- Colour/Pattern: cubes with 2 colours placed in different arrangements on each face of the cube to create various patterns (Figure 2e).
- Weight: from heavy clay cubes (Figure 2f) to light paper cubes (Figure 2e).
- Shape: rhomboid (Figure 2f), star (Figure 2d).
- Sound: clay beads were added inside various cubes. As well, the squishy cubes caused a wheezing sound when being squeezed (Figure 2c).

We realized that some of our cubes were not cubes at all but rather "deformed" cubes, such as the star and rhomboid. However, we felt that it was necessary to include shape as one of our variables.

Fig. 2a. Finger-sized cubes resting on a large cube

Fig. 2b. Large, medium and small sized cubes

Fig. 2c. Large-sized squishy cube

Fig. 2d. Finger-sized star cube

Fig. 2e. Patterned cubes

Fig. 2f. Rhomboid

3.2 Methodology

Participants were given the various cubes and asked to answer a set of questions. The questions were designed to provoke volunteers to manipulate the cubes – the specific answers given by the participants are of lesser importance compared to our ability to observe participants in action. The following five questions were used:

1. If you had to pick one cube, which cube would you pick and why? Where would you keep it?
2. If you had to carry one of the cubes with you at all times, which one would it be? Why that one? How would you carry it?
3. One of the cubes is to be used as a control mechanism. Which cube should it be and show me how it works.
4. Create your own cube. Describe its form, functionality and the experience you would gain from using it. Describe in words, on paper or by drawing a picture what your cube would look like.
5. If one of the cubes were an alien life form, which one would it be? Describe how it lives.

This is certainly not an exhaustive set of questions however, we attempted to design questions that would yield a high amount of physical manipulation and prolong action with the cubes.

The design study took place over one week at a new media art gallery in the UK [22]. We solicited volunteers through a local new media centre via email and posted a call for participation on their website. To record our data, we used qualitative procedures, including observations and questionnaires. We recorded observations with a video camera.

3.3 Results

Our results are grouped into four categories: observed manipulations helped us develop a classification of non-verbal dynamics; a classification of handling; user preferences; and, generalizations concerning grasp.

3.3.1 Non-verbal Dynamics

Non-verbal dynamics are the manipulations (gripping, not gesture) that take place when participants grip a cube (Table 1, see also [31]). We classify these dynamics according to action (manipulation), description of the action, whether an action is discrete or continuous, and events. The event is the type of action particular to that manipulation. For example, rotate is classified as a TURN event and is one that is dependent on the speed of turning, and possibly by the number of exposed sides.

The actions *Place* and *Pick up* appear in the table since they begin and end most events and they include the grasping actions *Hold* and *Press*. The column "Properties" describes the kinds of cubes that participants favoured for executing a particular dynamic. For example, participants would *roll* cubes with high malleability, soft textures, and a larger size. Not all dynamics were used to the same extent; particular cube properties suggested particular dynamics.

Programming the events describe in non-verbal dynamics will require that algorithms recognize the subtle differences between certain actions. This is an enormous task. For example, rotation consists of two-fold axis (vertex), three-fold axis (edges) or four-fold axis (faces) as well as speed. To detect rotation, physical interfaces would

Table 1. Non-verbal dynamics of cubes

Dynamic	Description	Discrete/ Continuous	Events	Property
Rotate	To turn cube about an axis or centre in a continuous, fluid motion exposing three sides of the cube at one time.	Continuous	TURN + (exposed sides) + (speed)	All
Roll	Impelling cube forward by causing it to turn over and over on a surface.	Continuous	TURN + (surface contact) SPIN + (surface contact)	High malleability, soft textures, large cubes
Twist	To rotate cube while taking a curving path or direction using the wrist.	Continuous	TURN + curve path	Rhomboid, patterned cubes, large cubes
Turn	To cause cube to move around an axis or a centre, exposing one side at a time.	Discrete	TURN (right, left, up, down)	All but particularly large cubes
Throw	To propel cube through the air by a forward motion of the hand and arm.	Continuous	TURN + (no contact with hands) TURN + (no contact with hands)	High malleability, soft textures
Flip	One fluid movement to cause cube to turn over to expose the opposite side of the cube.	Discrete	FLIP (top → bottom) FLIP (front → back) FLIP (side → side)	Large cubes, wooden, harder textures
Spin	To revolve the cube in a fast, fluid movement where all sides are exposed very quickly.	Continuous	SPIN (forward) SPIN (reverse)	Highly angular, particularly medium and large cubes
Hold	To have or maintain cube in the grasp.	Discrete	HOLD (no movement)	All
Shake	Sharp, fluid movements up and down.	Continuous	SHAKE (up→down→up) SHAKE (down→up→down)	Audio properties (cubes with beads)
Shake	Sharp, fluid movement side to side.	Continuous	SHAKE (left→right→left) SHAKE (right→left→right)	Audio properties (cubes with beads)
Place	To put cube in or as if in a particular place or position.	Discrete	PLACE→HOLD PLACE	All
Squeeze	Exert strong pressure on cube with hands or fingers.	Discrete	PRESS + (force)	High malleability, soft textures
Press	Steady pushing or thrusting force exerted in contact with cube.	Discrete	PRESS + (force) + (time)	High malleability, wooden cubes

Pick up	To take hold of and lift up.	Discrete	PRESS→ (up)	All
Tap	Strike cube quickly and lightly so that strike produces a slight sound.	Discrete	PRESS + (force) + (time) + (sound)	Wooden cubes, harder textures
Rub	To move hand or fingers along the surface of the cube with pressure.	Continuous	PRESS + (force) + (temperature) + (area)	Rhomboid, high malleability, soft textures
Fiddle	To move the hands or fingers around the cube restlessly.	Continuous	Ambiguous movements	Star-shape, high malleability, soft textures, small cubes

need to determine both the axis type and the speed at which cube is being rotated. However, research has begun on possible implementation [23].

3.3.2 Handling

How a participant handles a cube determines the non-verbal dynamics that are available to them. We describe "handling" as *managing with the hands by touching, feeling and moving*. All handling is impactive, in that action occurs only when hands come in contact with a cube. We divide handling into four categories:

- One-handed manipulation: using one hand to perform dynamics (Figure 3a).
- One-handed finger manipulation: using one hand and fingers to perform dynamics (Figure 3b).
- Two-handed manipulation: using two hands to perform dynamics (Figure 3c).
- Two-handed finger manipulation: using two hands and fingers to perform dynamics (Figure 3d).

Fig. 3a. One-handed manipulation **Fig. 3b.** One-handed finger manipulation **Fig. 3c.** Two-handed manipulation **Fig. 3d.** Two-handed finger manipulation

We can apply each of the four handling categories to the dynamics described in Table 1 to develop handling conventions.

3.3.3 Preferences

Every user is physically different and will have a unique set of preferences. However, our results suggest that there are certain attributes that are general to all physical interfaces and that may possibly make one physical interface more desirable than another. We discuss some of these here.

Break from usual form. Participants were drawn to cubes that broke from the usual form of a cube, such as a rhomboid and one with an extruded edge. As well, participants were able to explore more freely cubes that didn't already contain some conventional meaning or function. For example, participants rejected cubes that simply looked like gift boxes.

Feedback prolongs interaction. Some of the cubes "reacted" to user interaction. For example, cubes with beads in them produced rolling sounds and soft cubes retained a deformed shape after squeezing them. Participants interacted with these cubes more often than the other cubes and would hold them for long periods of time.

Wider multi-sensory experience prolongs interaction. Visual quality is not enough to sustain attention. Cubes that offered two or more types of sensory experience were favoured. Clay cubes felt organic and left a residue on hands would appeal to users' sense of touch and smell. Multi-sensory experiences blend visual and tactile texture, colour, smell, sound, size, form, and weight.

Some degree of weight is desirable. Having some degree of weight is desirable. Interfaces must be heavy enough that users are *aware* of the object but light enough that it can carry it for long periods. Weight allows people greater control over manipulation. Hinckley[36] suggests that weight contributes to an ease-of-use physical manipulation paradigm: weight can damp instabilities in hand motion; provide kinaesthetic feedback through inertia and the force of gravity; and, constrain manipulation.

Size is relative to the user and application. In terms of handling, the bigger something is the harder it is to carry but easier to find. Conversely, the smaller something is the easier it is to carry and the harder it is to find. Like weight, we need to design the interface so that it does not impinge too much on users' space. Participants suggested that smaller cubes could be attached to a key fob or worn as jewellery. Larger cubes could be useful for low-mobility users. If the application required that the user carry the cube in their pocket, then smaller cubes were favoured.

3.4 Summary

Conducting an affordance design study allowed us to develop a preliminary classification of non-verbal dynamics particular to grasp for cube-shaped objects as well as pointing to some general preferences. It seems as though varying the properties of objects constrains the actions users can perform on an object; object affordance changes the interaction between user and artefact.

4 Designing Interface Controls

Having investigated object affordances of a cube we went on to the design of the interface. This includes a) defining a appropriate manipulation vocabulary and b) investigating and realizing technical capabilities for sensing these manipulations. These two steps were done in parallel. In this section, we describe the interface design; the technology investigation is reported in the next section.

To design the interaction wit the phone interface we used scenarios, diagrams and storyboarding (Figure 4).

We decided to use three non-verbal dynamics as the manipulation vocabulary of our cube interface: *rotate*, *squeeze* and *shake*. The decision was based on our observations during the affordance study. The three selected dynamics seemed to offer the most natural and robust manipulation vocabulary and they could be recognized reliably with the available technology (see Section 5). Having decided on ROTATE, SHAKE and SQUEEZE as the non-verbal dynamics to be employed, we designed an interface based on a pared down version of a conventional mobile phone. The Cubicle phone featured an address book, a message centre, volume controls and power on/off. Each of these functions was mapped to a particular side of the cube as depicted in Figure 5. The top-level visual interface is matched to each cube face. Sub levels map closely to a standard mobile phone interface. However the phone book sub level varied slightly from a standard mobile phone interface in that names are listed alphabetically, one letter at a time.

Fig. 4. Storyboard

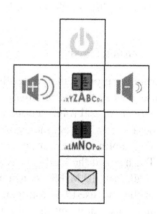

Fig. 5. Sides of the physical Cubicle interface

Table 2. Mapping of Non-verbal dynamics to control

Non-verbal dynamics	1st level Control	2nd level Control
Rotate	Switch between phone functions: 1. Message centre 2. Address book (letter a) 3. Address book (letter n) 4. Volume up 5. Volume down 6. Power on/off	In message centre: - Previous / next In address book: - Previous / next
Squeeze	SELECT / ENTER	In Volume up / down: - turn up / down by 1
Shake	CANCEL / BACK	

In our first iteration, we determined that unidirectional scrolling through the alphabet was time consuming. We redesigned our interface to allow entry at letter A and letter N.

The mapping of non-verbal dynamics to controls is listed in Table 2. The user selects a function by rotating the cube such that the chosen function is on top and then squeezes the cube. Once the message centre or phone book has been selected, rotating the cube scrolls up and down in the list. Shaking the cube cancels a function and goes back up to the main level.

5 Realizing Object Capabilities: The Cubicle Artefact

Having investigated object affordances of a cube we investigated technical capabilities for a digitally enhanced cube and implemented a prototype (Figure 6). The Cubicle is a foam covered wooden block with an embedded microchip and sensor hardware. Buttons placed underneath the foam enable the detection of SQUEEZE actions.

5.1 Sensing Hardware

During the prototyping phase, the choice of hardware is important, since it has direct consequences for the remainder of the system design. The cube as an object has to remain small and robust enough for the users to handle it, and its "digital self" needs to be accurate and autonomous so it can work properly for long periods without requiring cabling for power and communication.

The heart of the hardware is a Microchip PIC microprocessor (PIC18F252), which is small, fast (10 MIPS), consumes little energy (25 µA / 0.2 µA standby). The microcontroller we used has fourteen inputs for binary sensors and a built-in analogue-to-digital conversion unit that allows five analogue sensors to be attached. Our objective, however, to keep the hardware as simple and low-cost as possible without giving in too much on performance, means that we kept the number of sensors low:

- Two dual-axis accelerometers (ADXL311) measure both dynamic acceleration (e.g., vibration) and static acceleration (e.g., gravity) in a plane. The sensors' ability to measure gravity gives us the opportunity to discriminate in contexts where acceleration may be zero (such as different positions of the cube). We used two accelerometers to get acceleration in three dimensions (X-Y and X-Z).
- One capacitive sensor (QT110) measures whether the user's hand is nearby (i.e., whether the user is holding the cube or not), mainly to wake up the microcontroller from standby.

The system consists of two modules: the first estimates which is the top side of the cube, the second uses this information with prior states to estimate the direction to which all other sides are pointing.

Fig. 6. Cubicle Interface Artefact

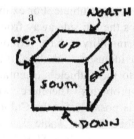
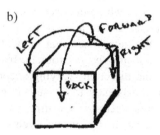

Fig. 7. a) A diagram of the six parameters for defining the cube's state from the user's view. b) The defined set of four possible transitions. The labels for the sides in both views are relative to the user's perspective.

5.2 Sensing Capabilities

The Cubicle implementation has the capability to recognize which side is facing up and in which direction it is rotated. The recognition capabilities are based on the definition of *states* where a state is defined as an arrangement of sides according to the following directions *from the view of the person holding it* (see Figure 7a for an illustration):

- *Top / Up*: the side that faces upward
- *Bottom / Down*: the side that faces downward
- *West*: the side that faces to the left
- *East*: the side that faces to the right
- *North*: the side that faces away from the user
- *South*: the side that faces toward the user

With these definitions in place, two important remarks can be made about the notation of a state: First, in general, for a person holding the cube without knowing or observing any labels of the sides, there are twenty-four possible states. Second, by exploiting the cube's structural properties and labelling each face of the cube as mentioned in the previous section, a given cube's state can be described by knowing only the direction of *two* adjacent faces. It is therefore sufficient to take two fixed directions (Top and South, for instance), rather than describing a state by all six directions.

Using the definition of states, we can define six possible 90-degree rotations between those states (two per axis, for positive or negative rotation).

- *Forward*: rotating the cube so that the Top side becomes the North side
- *Back*: rotating the cube so that the Top side becomes the South side
- *Left*: rotating the cube so that the Top side becomes the West side
- *Right*: rotating the cube so that the Top side becomes the East side

These states and transitions define a finite state machine that models the complete sensing capabilities of the Cubicle. The complete recognition algorithms and implementation of the state machine are described in [23].

5.3 Sensing Limitations and Design Implications

The Cubicle prototype is limited in that it is not able to identify how it is rotated which respect to where the user is in relation to the Cubicle. For example, the Cubicle is not able to determine if the user rotates the top side away from the body or towards it. We determined that the Cubicle's inability to have reliable directional scrolling is a major design problem. If we provide users with the ability to scroll in more than one direction (varying according to the Cubicle's orientation), we expect this inconsistency to cause navigation problems. Therefore, we decided to implement unidirectional scrolling. While it is possible for the Cubicle's accelerometer to sense many of the events described in the Table 1, we questioned whether we could distinguish between similar events such as TURN, ROTATE and TWIST. Because of time constraints, we determined that to implement reliable recognition of similar actions was unrealistic and so avoided actions with similar manipulation. Given the common occurrence of the TURN/ROTATE events in the design study, we decided to couple navigation with rotation. We mapped ROTATE to scrolling and SHAKE and SQUEEZE were chosen as additional inputs, as they were commonly observed in the design study, particularly with cubes that gave audio feedback when shaken or with cubes that were pliant. Consequently, we ensured that our interface provided audio feedback and that the cube was pliant.

6 Usability Study

To understand the usability issues of the Cubicle phone interface we conducted a qualitative usability study. The aim was not to arrive at a final verdict about the Cubicle interface because we expected that there would be errors in the use of the phone and that some of these would be caused both by hardware and software issues, as the Cubicle phone is at an early stage of development. However, we expected to see a device that fulfils basic usability criteria.

The study involved 10 people and used two different set-ups: In the first condition, the Cubicle was connected to a regular desktop computer; in the second condition participants were asked to repeat the tasks whilst wearing a head mounted display (HMD) and walking around a lab. We collected data by observation, questionnaires and video camera.

6.1 Results

Most participants described the Cubicle as easy to learn and none reported that they had found it difficult. Most criticism on learnability was directed at the unreliability of input recognition. Many participants like the novel nature of the Cubicle, describing it as "fun" or "cool". Almost 20 percent of participants described the Cubicle as "intuitive" while several others referred to it as "simple" or "easy to use." The biggest criticism with the Cubicle phone was not related to its form at all. Of the participants, 75% complained about the unreliability of input recognition in one way or another. Other criticisms were its large size and difficultly in squeezing it. Participants suggested that a decrease in size, improved pliability, and an increase in reliability of input recognition would enhance its appeal. Another suggestion was the use of haptics (touch perception) to assist participants in knowing which side should face upwards. Some participants recommended embedding the display in a cube face or replacing the visual display with audio. In terms of scrolling, participants suggested that scrolling should relate to the direction of the cube, and to map the rate of scrolling to the speed of rotation. Types of applications included control device for household appliances, as an alternative input device for children, or for gaming applications. The majority of responses suggest that the Cubicle is best suited to applications involving simple selection tasks. Task completion for all participants followed the expected pattern very closely. Although there was some two-handed finger rotation, over 80% of participants used two-handed rotation to navigate. Interestingly, during certain tasks over 10% of participants used one-handed rotation; participants would use a desk as a supporting surface and roll the Cubicle across the desk to achieve rotation. These participants tended to press the top surface of the Cubicle to initiate SQUEEZE. Since the bottom Cubicle face was pressed against the desk, this strategy did work but required a fair amount of force. Pressing the top of the cube was quite common and a lot of the participants seemed to think that they needed to press the face related to a given function rather than just squeezing the cube. Some participants failed to return to standby mode and ignored this part of the instruction and several participants had trouble working out how to delete a message, and several participants accidentally deleted a message. A number of participants tried to use the action ROTATE to change the direction of scrolling. As well, many participants tried to rotate quickly or slowly when trying to scroll a long distance or short distance. If input was not recognized, participants shook or squeezed the Cubicle harder.

6.2 Usability Summary

The Cubicle is an easily learned interface that provides some degree of user satisfaction. However our results indicate that future iterations require:

- Improved reliability of input recognition
- Better mapping to understanding of the physical world, particularly directional scrolling
- A decrease in size
- An increase in pliability
- Improved consistency in the visual interface

In its current form, the Cubicle seems best suited to relatively simple applications, particularly those that involve selection. Whether a more reliable Cubicle with more varied input will be useful for more complex applications is a question for future study. However such study seems worthwhile from the tentative findings of this evaluation.

7 Discussion and Related Work

A thorough understanding of how we as humans interact with the physical world is of great importance when designing tangible artefacts and interfaces. We thus believe that understanding and applying the relationships between object affordance, object capability and control is key for modelling and creating computer interfaces that are useful and appropriate for the ubiquitous world.

The case study reported in this paper has provided us with insights into the usefulness and effectiveness of our approach. We believe that our approach has the following key advantages:

- It introduces a systematic empirical method for discovering and representing object affordances. The result of studying affordances as suggested by our approach is a sound foundation for the two subsequent design phases, the specification of object capabilities and controls. In particular, the affordance study helps designers to discover non-verbal dynamics and basic sensing requirements.
- Our approach integrates three key design aspects that are usually considered distinct. This is achieved by using a unified terminology for representing key design aspects that enables designers to link design decisions from more than one design dimension.
- The approach assists designers in evaluating and identifying design problems and suggests entry points for systematic redesign.

The results from the case study suggest that following our approach leads to usable and desirable physical interfaces. Our approach, however, does not guarantee superior interfaces, it is simply a way for interaction designers and technology experts to communicate and work together towards a satisfactory design. The point we are trying to make in this paper is not that the particular interface we designed is optimal in any sense, but that the process we followed is useful and effective. More design iterations will be necessary to improve the Cubicles mobile phone interface. Although we have applied our approach only to cubes and cube-like shapes, we believe that it applies to physical objects in general.

7.1 Related Work

There are many theories explaining our perception and interaction with the physical world, but it is less clear how we can apply these theories in a constructive way for the design of concrete physical interfaces.

In recent years, the theory of affordance has been applied to human-computer interaction and the design of user interfaces. While Norman popularized the idea of affordance in *The Design of Everyday Things* [24] his approach focused on designing for usability and for error, in particular for "everyday" things. More recently Benford *et al* [25] have developed the sensible/sensable/desirable framework which focuses on the affordances of ubiquitous devices and how affordance can suggest opportunities for manipulation and extending the physical-digital mapping. They identify three key areas of interest in the design of a physical interface; what is sensible, sensable and desirable. They suggest that in addition to considering these areas on their own, there is value in looking at the overlap between them in order to provide designers with problems and/or opportunities.

The area of tangible computing has produced a number of descriptive frameworks for linking the physical and digital realms. Ishii and Ullmer [3] introduced a model-control-representation (MCRpd) interaction framework. Similarly, Holmquist et al. [26] introduced a common vocabulary for describing physical objects that are linked to digital information. Holmquist bases the schema on three types of physical objects: containers, tokens and tools, and pays particular attention to token-based access systems. More recently, Koleva et al. [27] makes a first attempt at classifying existing tangible interface systems based on the "degree of coherence" between physical and digital objects, which is further broken into links and a set of underlying properties. Marshall et al. [28] are first to cite a lack of conceptual frameworks for applying design decisions when designing physical interfaces, particularly for play and learning.

These models and frameworks are mainly descriptive, rather than prescriptive: they are useful for understanding the nature of physical and tangible interfaces and for classifying them, but they do not define concrete techniques, activities, or processes that we can use to design physical interfaces in a systematic and repeatable manner. It seems likely that human beings who have evolved and lived within the physical world should be well equipped to use and understand physical objects. The concept of affordance, and the immediate understanding of objects that it proposes, suggest this. Our approach for the first time operationalises the concept of affordance and makes it accessible to designers of physical interfaces.

8 Conclusions

Physical interfaces have been proposed as a way to realize natural interactions with ubiquitous computing environments. The successful design of such interfaces requires design approaches that integrate aspects of our world which are usually treated separately in traditional system development approaches. In this paper, we presented an affordance-based design approach for physical user interfaces. In particular, we demonstrated an experimental method for exploring object affordance using cube-shaped objects as type example. Our approach integrates three key design dimensions (affordance, capability, and control) in a systematic way. Our results suggest that following our approach leads to usable and desirable physical interfaces. It also assists designers in evaluating and identifying design problems and suggests entry points for systematic redesign. Although we have applied our approach only to cubes and cube-like shapes, we believe that it applies to physical objects in general.

References

1. Mark Weiser, Creating the Invisible Interface, Proc. 7th Ann. ACM Symposium on User Interface Software and Technology, ACM Press, 1994.
2. Norman, D.A. The Invisible Computer. MIT Press, 1998.
3. H. Ishii and B. Ullmer, Tangible Bits: Towards Seamless Interfaces between People, Bits and Atoms, Proc. of CHI '97, ACM Press, 1997.
4. P. Wellner, Interacting with paper on the DigitalDesk, Communications of the ACM, 1993, vol. 36, no. 7.
5. Ullmer, B., Ishii, H. and Glas, D.(1999) mediaBlocks: Physical Containers, Transports, and Controls for Online Media. Proc. of the 25th Annual Conf. on Computer Graphics.
6. Greenberg, S. and Fitchet, C. (2001) Phidgets: Easy Development of Physical Interfaces through Physical Widgets. Proc UIST 2001.
7. Anderson Ballagas, R., Ringel, M, Stone, M., Borchers, J, iStuff: A Physical User Interface Toolkit for Ubiquitous Computing Environments, CHI 2003.
8. Kaminsky, M., Dourish, P., Edwards, K. LaMarca, A., Salisbury, M. and Smith, I. (1999) SWEETPEA: Software Tools for Programmable Embodied Agents. Proceedings of ACM CHI 99 Conference on Human Factors in Computing Systems, 1999.
9. Scott R. Klemmer, Jack Li, James Lin, and James A. Landay, Papier-Mâché: Toolkit Support for Tangible Input. CHI Letters, Human Factors in Computing Systems: CHI2004. 6(1).
10. F. Martin, B. Mikhak, and B. Silverman. MetaCricket: A designer's kit for making computational devices. IBM Systems Journal, Volume 39, Numbers 3 & 4, 2000.
11. J. J. Gibson, The Theory of Affordances, The Ecological Approach to Visual Perception, Lawrence Erlbaum, Hillsdale, 1979.
12. M. Fjeld, M. Bichel and M. Rauterberg, "BUILD-IT: An Intuitive Design Tool Based on Direct Object Manipulation, In Gesture and Sign Language in Human-Computer Interaction, vol. 1371, Wachsmut and Frohlich, eds. Springer-Verlag, 1998.
13. G. Fitzmaurice, H. Ishii and W. Buxton, Bricks: Laying the Foundations for Graspable User Interfaces, Proc. of CHI'95, 1995.
14. Y. Kitamura, Y. Itoh, T. Masaki and F. Kishino, ActiveCube: A Bi-directional User Interface using Cubes, Fourth International Conference on Knowledge-Based Intelligent Engineering Systems & Allied Technologies, 2000.
15. E. Sharlin, Y. Itoh, B. Watson, Y. Kitamura, L. Liu and S. Sutphen, Cognitive Cubes: A Tangible User Interface for Cognitive Assessment, Proc. of CHI'02, 2002.
16. K. Camarata, E. Yi-Luen Do, B. R. Johnson and M. D. Gross, Navigational Blocks: Navigating information space with tangible media, Proc. of IUI'02, 2002.
17. S. Lertsithichai and M. Seegmiller, CUBIK: A Bi-Directional Tangible Modeling Interface, Proc. of CHI'02.
18. B. Ullmer, H. Ishii and D. Glas, mediaBlocks: Physical Containers, Transports, and Controls for Online Media, Proc. of SIGGRAPH'98.
19. J. Rekimoto, Tilting operations for small screen interfaces, Proc. of UIST'96, 1996.
20. B. Ullmer and H. Ishii, Emerging Frameworks for Tangible User Interfaces, In Human-Computer Interaction in the New Millennium, John M. Carroll, ed., 2001.
21. J. Cohen, M. Withgott and P. Piernot, Logjam: A Tangible Multi-Person Interface for Video Logging, Proc. of CHI'99, ACM Press, 1999.
22. folly. folly new media centre. http://www.folly.co.uk Last visited October 28, 2005.
23. K. Van Laerhoven, N. Villar, A. Schmidt, G. Kortuem and H. Gellersen, Using an Autonomous Cube for Basic Navigation and Input, Proc. of ICMI/PUI, 2003.

24. D. A. Norman, The Design of Everyday Things. Doubleday, 1998.
25. Benford, S et al. Sensible, sensable and desireable: a framework for designing physical interfaces, Technical Report Equator-03-003, Equator, February 2003.
26. L. Holmquist, J. Redström and P. Ljungstrand, Token-Based Access to Digital Information, Proc. of Handheld and Ubiquitous Computing, 1999.
27. B. Koleva, S. Benford, Kher Hui Ng and T. Rodden, A Framework for Tangible User Interfaces, In workshop Proc. on Real World User Interfaces, Mobile HCI Conference 03, 2003.
28. P. Marshall, S. Price and Y. Rogers, Conceptualising tangibles to support learning. In Proc. of Interaction Design and Children, ACM Press, 2003.
29. J. Rekimoto, B. Ullmer, and H. Oba, ToolStone: Effective use of the physical manipulation vocabularies of input devices, Proc. of UIST'02, 2000.
30. K. Hinckley, R. Pausch, J. C. Goble, N. F. Kassell, A Survey of Design Issues in Spatial Input, Proc. of UIST'94, Symposium on User Interface Software & Technology, 1994.
31. J. G. Sheridan, B. W. Short, G. Kortuem, K. Van-Laerhoven, N. Villar. Exploring Cube Affordance: Towards A Classification Of Non-Verbal Dynamics Of Physical Interfaces For Wearable Computing. Proceedings of IEE EuroWearable 2003, 4-5 September, Birmingham, UK, IEE Press.

Dynamic Clustering for Object Tracking in Wireless Sensor Networks

Guang-yao Jin, Xiao-yi Lu, and Myong-Soon Park[*]

Dept. of Computer Science and Engineering, Korea University
Seoul 136-701, Korea
{king, felicity_lu, myongsp}@ilab.korea.ac.kr

Abstract. Object tracking is an important feature of the ubiquitous society and also a killer application of wireless sensor networks. Nowadays, there are many researches on object tracking in wireless sensor networks under practice, however most of them cannot effectively deal with the trade-off between missing-rate and energy efficiency. In this paper, we propose a dynamic clustering mechanism for object tracking in wireless sensor networks. With forming the cluster dynamically according to the route of moving, the proposed method can not only decrease the missing-rate but can also decrease the energy consumption by reducing the number of nodes that participate in tracking and minimizing the communication cost, thus can enhance the lifetime of the whole sensor networks. The simulation result shows that our proposed method achieves lower energy consumption and lower missing-rate.

1 Introduction

Recently, the development of the technology for embedded processor and low energy cost sensors which are equipped with RF communication module, make the killer application for object tracking in wireless sensor network possible. Because of the sensor's low price and its ability of detecting at anytime and anywhere, the object tracking sensor network has great potential of being widely used in many domains like business and military area. But the limitation of sensor's powers, which are usually un-rechargeable batteries, as well as the attribute of highly distributed collaborated work, the instability of wireless communication and application specific requirements, really contribute the complexity to the design of a sensor network.

There have already been many researches on using sensor network to monitor the environment, and many of them can reach effective result. But however, the characteristic of the sensor network used for object tracking is completely different from the one used for simple environmental monitoring and thus we should take deep (special) research into this area.

In sensor network, many sensor nodes need to keep on collaborating with other nodes in order to track the moving target. For an important characteristic of sensor network is its limited power source, the most important issue for developing object

---

[*] Corresponding author.

H.Y. Youn, M. Kim, and H. Morikawa (Eds.): UCS 2006, LNCS 4239, pp. 200–209, 2006.

tracking sensor network is to track the target with lowest energy consumption, especially prevent some certain nodes over consuming energy, while maintain low missing-rate, thus prolong the lifetime of the whole sensor network.

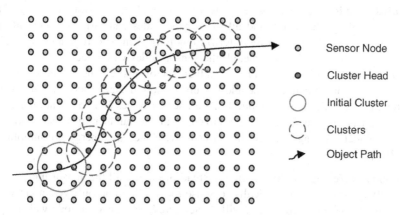

Fig. 1. Object traverses the sensor network and results the detection

Recently, the researches focus on object tracking sensor network become very active. These researches may be induced into 3 following aspects:

1. Using the position of the sensor which is the nearest to the target to be approximate position of the target's actual location.
2. Dynamically form cluster along the target's moving direction using several sensor nodes near the target.
3. Predict the next possible position of the target and check the information of the sensor nodes on the moving route of the target.

The second part of this paper gives the example of target tracking and analyzes the existing methods for it in sensor network and shows their problems. In the third part, we proposed a Dynamic Clustering mechanism base on the travel status of the target. We are going to prove the efficiency of the proposed mechanism in part 4 through simulations.

2 Related Work

Existing researches about the object tracing in wireless sensor networks can be mainly classified into the 5 following schemes, which are Naïve, Scheduled Monitoring, Continuous Monitoring, Dynamic Clustering and Prediction-based. Among them, the Continuous Monitoring, Dynamic Clustering and Prediction-based are specially studied for solving the object tracking problem in wireless sensor network while both the Naïve and Scheduled Monitoring are just focus on general applications of wireless sensor network. Each scheme can be described as follows:

Naive: In this scheme, all the sensor nodes stays in active mode and monitor their detection areas all the time and sends the detected data to the base station periodically. Therefore, the energy consumption is high. [1]

Scheduled Monitoring: This scheme assumes that all the sensor nodes and base station are well synchronized, and all the sensor nodes can turn to sleep and only wake up when it comes to their time (turn) to monitor their detection areas and report sensed results. Thus, in this scheme, all the sensor nodes will be active for X second then go to sleep for (T − X) seconds. The advantage of this scheme is that it minimize the time for sensors in active mode and let sensors stay in sleep mode as long as they can. However, actually the assumption that all sensor nodes and base station are well synchronized is very difficult to be realized. And the number of sensor nodes involved in object tracking is more than necessary. Hence the energy consumption is high. [2][3]

Continuous Motoring: In this scheme, instead of having all the sensor nodes in the sensor network wake up periodically to sense the whole area, only one node which has the object in its detection area will be activated. Whenever a node wakes up, it will keep on monitoring the object until it enters a neighboring cell. The advantage of this scheme is that it involves only one sensor node to monitor each moving object while other sensor nodes turn to sleep and thus save energy. However, because there is only one node monitor the object, the missing rate will be high when the object moves with a high speed. In order to reduce the missing rate, the active sensor has to stay awake as long as the object is in its detection area. This causes the unbalanced energy consumption among the sensor nodes and thus reduces the network lifetime. [4]

Dynamic Clustering: The network is formed with powerful CH nodes and low-end SN nodes. The CH node which has the strongest sensed signal of target becomes the cluster head and organizes nearby SN nodes to form a cluster. The SN nodes in the cluster transmit the sensed data to the cluster head, and then the cluster head sends the digested data to the base station after data aggregation. In order to prevent missing the target, all CH nodes need to monitor continuously. Since only the CH nodes can be the cluster head, object tracking becomes very difficult in some areas where the CH nodes are sparsely distributed. And after a cluster is formed, there is no rotation of the cluster head, so the higher speed the target object travels at, the higher energy the cluster head would consume. So in this scheme, the energy consumption among the CH nodes is unbalanced, and thus reduces the network lifetime. [5][6][7][8]

Prediction-based: In this scheme, a sensor node uses prediction model to predict the next location of the target object. Then, based on the prediction result, the sensor uses the Wake-up Mechanism to wake up an adjacent sensor node before the target leaving its own detection field and entering the adjacent field. If the system misses the target object, it would perform the recovery throughout the whole sensor network. According to the different requirements of the application, the Wake-up Mechanism will be chosen from followings.

- Awakes only one sensor nearby the destination.
- Awakes all the nodes on the route of the moving object from current location to the destination.
- Awakes all the nodes on and around the route of the moving object from current location to the destination.

However, different problems exist with different Wake-up Mechanisms. The problem with the first Wake-up Mechanism is that it is difficult to guarantee high accuracy of the prediction in reality, so the missing rate would be very high as well as the overhead caused by recovery procedure. And even if the prediction of the target location is 100% accurate and the awaked sensor can provide enough information for monitoring the target object, it would still have a problem of un-balanced energy consumption among the nodes, for there is only one sensor monitor the target and the energy consumption of this node would be high. In the second Wake-up Mechanism, though it has relatively smaller missing rate than the first one, there still will be un-ignorable increase of missing rate when the target change its moving direction beyond the prediction, because only the sensor nodes which are on the predicted route of the target would wake up and monitor the target continuously. If the missing rate increases, the overhead caused by missing recovery will increase too. And for all the sensor nodes on the object's traveling route are supposed to be active to monitor the target, the energy consumption would be high. In the case that the third Wake-up Mechanism is chosen, since all the sensor nodes surrounding the route of the target's movement would wake up to monitor the target at the same time, although it can reduce the missing rate, the energy consumption would be higher.

Different from other researches, the goal of our paper is to reduce the missing rate and improve energy efficiency in wireless sensor network by performing clustering dynamically along the route that the target moves, and thus prolong the lifetime of the whole network.

3   Dynamic Clustering with Considering the Moving Information

The dynamic clustering mechanism proposed in this paper, as shown in figure 1, performs the clustering along the route of the target movement with minimum numbers of sensor nodes to track the target object, thus can reduce the energy consumption and prolong the lifetime of the whole sensor network. The proposed mechanism consists of the 3 following functionalities.

3.1   Efficient Clustering Mechanism

Although there have been many researches on object tracking in wireless sensor networks, most of them are based on static clustering, hence it is difficult to apply them to object tracking application. The existing dynamic clustering mechanism in object tracking sensor networks is a kind of mechanism which first selects a sensor node with the strongest sensed signal strength to be the cluster head, and then form the cluster at the cluster composition stage. Sensor nodes need to communicate with each other several times to determine which one has the strongest sensed signal strength and can be selected as the cluster header. However, these methods could not be very useful without guarantying the optimal communication cost of the sensor nodes. And also in order to track a fast moving object, a simple, rapid and energy efficient clustering mechanism is needed.

In this paper, we considered all these features of the object tracking sensor networks and developed an energy efficient clustering mechanism which forms the cluster with optimal communication cost. The procedure of clustering consists of two stages which are initial clustering stage and re-clustering stage.

3.1.1 Initial Clustering

At initial time, all sensors in the network are in sleeping mode. After receiving a tracking command from the server, all the sensors wake up and do the sensing for a short time period. The sensor nodes which can not detect the target will go to sleep again as soon as possible, and those with the detection of the target will form a cluster and enter the target tracking state.

We define the collection of the sensor nodes which detected the target as D. All the sensor nodes in collection D will do sensing twice again, which means every sensor node in D would do sensing three times continuously. For a sensor node can know the distance, which is defined as d here, between the target and itself after doing sensing one time, by doing sensing three times, we can get three relationships between the distance d and time t, here we use R to stand for the collection of the three relationships. All sensor nodes in D which have finish sensing three times and successfully get collection R will wait for a short random time, and the first one, we say S1 whose timer expires will broadcast a solicitation packet, which contains its resident energy, its location and its collection R to the neighboring nodes and then go into listening mode. Other sensor nodes which receive the solicitation packet from the S1 will wait for another short random time, and then the second node, we say S2, whose timer first expires within these nodes will broadcast another solicitation packet to the neighboring nodes and then go into listening mode. The procedure is similar with S1. In this way, all the sensor nodes in D except S1 and S2 will get R collections, two from S1 and S2 and one from themselves. Then all nodes except S1 and S2 in D would then wait for another short random time, and the first one whose timer expires will broadcast a notification message to its neighbors and elect itself as the cluster head. It is easy to know that, a target location can be estimated from the data sensed by three different nodes at the same time, so the cluster head can get three locations of the target at three different times using the three R collections received, and thus the moving speed and acceleration of the target can be estimated. Then, with the moving information of the target, the cluster head can get the next possible location of the target by prediction. For every node is supposed to know the location information of all its one-hop neighbors, the elected cluster head will then go into schedule mode and send scheduling information to its neighbors to form a cluster.

3.1.2 Cluster Re-forming

Cluster re-forming is a little different from the initial cluster forming procedure. When initialing a cluster, all the sensor nodes in the sensor network are active and can detect the target location after receiving an object tracking command from the base station, and then they will calculate the target moving information by collaborating with other adjacent sensors and volunteer themselves as cluster head to form the cluster. In cluster re-forming procedure, after a new cluster head is successfully elected, a new cluster will be formed around it. The new cluster head is selected by the former cluster head through broadcasting a confirming packet. The sensor nodes of the old cluster which receive the confirming packet will first check out whether they are the neighbor nodes of the new cluster head, if so, they would go into listening mode and wait for getting new scheduling information from the new cluster head and if not they would go to sleeping mode immediately. After receiving the confirming packet from the former cluster head, the new cluster head will wait for a short random time, and when its timer expires it will broadcast a re-clustering command packet which contains the new scheduling information to the neighboring sensors and then go into listening mode. The neighboring nodes will use the new schedule to detect after receiving this packet, and thus a new cluster is formed.

3.1.3 Cluster Head Election

Cluster head election is one of the core issues of clustering in wireless sensor networks. How to elect the cluster head directly affects not only the cluster's energy efficiency, but also the lifetime of the whole network. In most of the existing papers related to clustering in general wireless sensor networks, a sensor node with the highest residual energy will be selected as the cluster head after a cluster has been already formed, with considering the routing information and the distribution of the sensor nodes. And most of the researches on clustering in object tracking sensor networks just simply select a node with the strongest sensed signal strength to be the cluster head. However, in the real environment, a target may travel at a varying speed all the time, so the existing methods may not be suitable for object tracking applications in real sensor network.

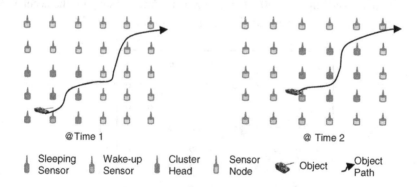

Fig. 2. New cluster head election

As shown in figure 2, this paper is focusing on the object target which moves at a varying speed. A cluster head is selected with the consideration of the next possible location of target gained by prediction, the distribution of the sensor nodes which participate in tracking and the residual energy of these sensors. When the predicted location of the target is on the boundary of the current cluster, the current cluster head would send a solicitation packet to the sensor nodes around the predicted location, and select the first one which replies the message to be the new cluster head, and send it a confirming packet. After the new cluster head receiving the confirming message, it will broadcast the re-clustering command to the neighboring sensor nodes.

4   Experimental Results

We set up simulation environment in NS2. In the simulation, there is a 100m x 100m square area with sensors uniformly and randomly deployed. The radio model adopted in this experiment is based on [12]. Thus, to transmit k-bit message a distance d, the radio expends:

$$E_{Tx}(k,d) = E_{Tx-elec}(k) + E_{Tx-amp}(k,d)$$

$$= \begin{cases} E_{elec}*k + \varepsilon_{friss-amp}*k*d^2, d < d_{crossover} \\ E_{elec}*k + \varepsilon_{two-way-amp}*k*d^4, d \geq d_{crossover} \end{cases}$$

and to receive this message, the radio expends:

$$E_{Rx}(k) = E_{Rx-elec}(k) = E_{elec}*k$$

For the experiments in this paper, we adopted the same value given in [12] as

$$E_{elec} = 50nJ/bit, \varepsilon_{friss-amp} = 10pJ/bit/m^2 \ and \ \varepsilon_{two-way-amp} = 0.0013pJ/bit/m^4$$

and each node is initialed with only 2J energy. The radio range of sensors is 10m and the distance between each sensor is 5m.

In order to simplify the experiment without losing generality, we suppose an object is moving into the surveillance area from the left bottom with an initial speed of 1m/s, and the initial speed angle is 150 relative to X-axis. And we suppose the acceleration of the target changes after every Δt, but stays as a constant within Δt.

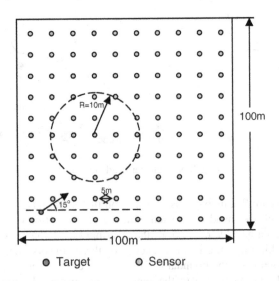

Fig. 3. Simulation Environment Setting

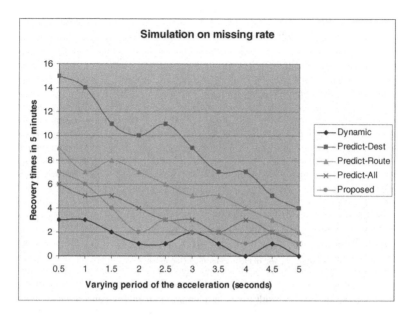

Fig. 4. Simulation result for experimentation on missing rate

In object tracking sensor network, the energy consumption is proportional with the missing rate, that is to say, the higher the missing rate is, the more missing recovery would take place, and thus the energy consumed by recovering the tracking will be higher. So in the simulation, we compare our proposed mechanism with the existing dynamic clustering mechanism and the prediction-based mechanism which can be categorized as Predict-Dest, Predict-Route, and Predict-All, and we evaluate our proposed mechanism by comparing the missing rate caused in 5 minutes and the total energy dissipation in 5 hours.

From figure 4 we can see the existing dynamic clustering method can achieve the lowest missing rate, and the result is not much influenced by the changing of target movement status. That is because in this method, all the sensors keep on sensing continuously no matter whether the target is in their sensing area. However, for all the nodes in the sensor network, including those which are far from the target are involved in tracking continuously, although it can reach low missing rate, the energy consumption will be high as shown in figure 5.

Among the three categories of prediction method, Prediction-Dest is under the strongest affection by the changing target's movement status. Comparing figure 4 with figure 5 we can see that, when the target's movement status changes smoothly, the missing rate will relatively decrease and the energy consumption will decrease too.

When using prediction-based mechanism, the whole energy consumption will be less if the target's moving status changes smoothly, for the accuracy of prediction is affected by the changes of target's movement status. Because our proposed mechanism is also based on prediction, so the energy consumption will be less when target

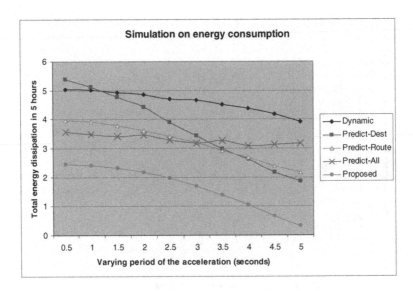

Fig. 5. Simulation result for experimentation on energy consumption

travels with a smoothly changing status, that is to say, our proposed mechanism is more suitable for tracking the target with smoothly changing movement status. In our simulation, we use the changing of acceleration to indicate the changing of target's movement status.

As shown in figure 4 and figure 5, the advantage of our proposed mechanism is more obvious when the acceleration of the target changes smoothly.

5   Conclusions and Future Work

In this paper, we proposed an efficient dynamic clustering mechanism which can reduce missing rate by prediction and prolong the lifetime of the whole sensor network by minimizing energy consumption. And the energy consumption is mainly reduced in two ways: first, minimizing the number of nodes involved in tracking by constructing cluster dynamically along the target's traveling route. Second, minimizing the communication cost between sensor nodes when forming a cluster.

For future work, we are going to study an energy efficient scheduling method based on the known moving information of the target, which can minimize both the missing rate and the energy consumption in dynamic cluster structure.

Acknowledgement

This work was supported by the Korea Research Foundation Grant funded by the Korea Government (MOEHRD) (KRF-2005-211-D00274).

References

1. W. Heinzelman, A. Chandrakasan, and H. Balakrishnan; "Energy-Efficient Communication Protocol for Wireless Microsensor Networks". Proceedings of the Hawaii Conference on System Sciences, Jan. 2000.
2. Arati Manjeshwar et al.; "TEEN: A Routing Protocol for Enhanced Efficiency in Wireless Sensor Networks". Proceedings of Wireless Networks and Mobile Computing, 2001.
3. Arati Manjeshwar et al.; "APTEEN: A Hybrid Protocol for Efficient Routing and Comprehensive Information Retrieval in Wireless Sensor Networks". Proceedings Of Parallel and Distributed Processing Symposium(IPDPS'02), pp.195-202.
4. Balasubramanian, S.; Elangovan, I.; Jayaweera, S.K.; Namuduri, K.R.; "Distributed and collaborative tracking for energy-constrained ad-hoc wireless sensor networks". Proceedings of WCNC 2004. Page(s):1732 - 1737 Vol.3
5. Xiang ji; Hongyuan Zha; Metzner, J.J.; Kesidis, G.; "Dynamic cluster structure for object detection and tracking in wireless ad-hoc sensor networks". Proceedings of Communications, 2004 Page(s):3807 - 3811 Vol.73
6. Wei-Peng Chen; Hou, J.C.; Lui Sha; "Dynamic clustering for acoustic target tracking in wireless sensor networks". Proceedings of Mobile Computing, IEEE Transactions 2004 Page(s):258 - 271
7. Wei-Peng Chen; Hou, J.C.; Lui Sha; "Dynamic clustering for acoustic target tracking in wireless sensor networks". Proceedings of Network Protocols 2003 Page(s):284 - 294
8. Vercauteren, T.; Dong Guo; Xiaodong Wang; "Joint multiple target tracking and classifica-tion in collaborative sensor networks". Proceedings of Selected Areas in Communications, IEEE Journal on Volume 23, Issue 4, 2005 Page(s):714 - 723
9. Yingqi Xu; Winter, J.; Wang-Chien Lee; "Prediction-based strategies for energy saving in object tracking sensor networks". Proceedings of Mobile Data Management, 2004 Page(s):346 - 357
10. Yang, H.; Sikdar, B.; "A protocol for tracking mobile targets using sensor networks". Proceedings of the First IEEE. 2003 Page(s):71 - 81
11. Xu, Y.; Winter, J.; Lee, W.-C.; "Dual prediction-based reporting for object tracking sensor networks". Proceedings of MOBIQUITOUS 2004. Page(s):154 - 163
12. Jain-Shing Liu; Lin, C.-H.P. "Power-Efficiency Clustering Method with Power-Limit Constraint for Sensor Networks". Conference Proceedings of the 2003 IEEE Interna-tional , 9-11 April 2003.

An Ultra Low Power Medium Access Control Protocol with the Divided Preamble Sampling*

Sangsoon Lim, Youngmin Ji, Jaejoon Cho, and Sunshin An

Dept. of Electronics & computer Eng., Korea University,
1, 5-Ga, Anam-dong Sungbuk-ku, Seoul, Korea, Post Code: 136-701
{lssgood, yangsamy, jjj, sunshin}@dsys.korea.ac.kr

Abstract. This paper proposes DPS-MAC (Divided Preamble Sampling-MAC), a carrier sense Medium Access Control (MAC) protocol with ultra low power operations for wireless sensor networks. Due to battery-operated computing and sensing devices in wireless sensor networks, the development of MAC protocols that efficiently reduce power consumption is an important issue. DPS-MAC is a novel energy efficient protocol based on sampling preamble segments that have preamble offsets and next hop addresses. By using these parameters, DPS-MAC can overcome the drawbacks of long fixed preambles and overhearing in B-MAC. The divided preamble sampling technique provides not only very low power consumption when the channel is idle, but also a chance to avoid over-hearing without additional overheads compared to B-MAC. This technique makes it possible to extend the lifetime of the wireless sensor networks that contain a large number of nodes. The experiment results show that DPS-MAC protocol reduces much energy consumed by receiving compared to B-MAC and can support various features of wireless sensor networks efficiently.

1 Introduction

Wireless sensor networks are generally composed of a large number of sensor nodes deployed to measure a variety of physical information and a few data collectors, which are called, sink nodes. Wireless sensor networks have recently become of significant interest due to cheap single-chip transceivers and micro controllers. They consist of many tiny devices, powered by small-sized batteries, and operate unattended for prolonged duration. Because sensor nodes may be deployed in remote locations, it is likely that replacing their batteries will not be possible. Therefore power efficient protocols at each layer of the communications are very important for wireless sensor networks [1]. In this paper, we will focus on the medium access control layer.

Conventional Medium Access Control protocols have been optimized for maximum throughput and minimum delay. Because of the target, they are not suitable for

---

* This research was supported by the MIC (Ministry of Information and Communication), Korea, under the ITRC(Information Technology Research Center) support program supervised by the IITA(Institute of Information Technology Assessment).

H.Y. Youn, M. Kim, and H. Morikawa (Eds.): UCS 2006, LNCS 4239, pp. 210–224, 2006.

wireless sensor networks. To reach a major requirement of wireless sensor networks, several energy conserving MAC protocols have been proposed. For example, S-MAC employs the RTS/CTS/DATA/ACK signaling scheme, periodic listen and sleep to collision and overhearing avoidance, and message passing [2]. T-MAC is another example that dynamically adapts a listen and sleep duty cycle through fine-grained timeouts [3]. This protocol improves on S-MAC's energy usage by using an active period. The IEEE 802.15.4 uses periodic sleep to reduce energy consumption and requires synchronization to decide on suitable schedules [4]. B-MAC employs not only Clear Channel Assessment (CCA) and packet backoffs to avoid collisions, but also Low Power Listening (LPL) and preamble sampling to reduce duty cycle and minimize idle listening [5].

In this paper we present DPS-MAC protocol that provides ultra low power operation using the divided preamble sampling mechanism. It tries to reduce the waste of energy consumed by reception overheads. To achieve overhearing avoidance and efficient reception, DPS-MAC employs a node recognition algorithm without additional overheads, while considering wireless sensor communication patterns and hardware limitations. The remainder of the paper is organized as follows. Section 2 summarizes and reviews related work on MAC protocols and energy-saving solutions in WSNs. Section 3 elaborates on the design of the DPS-MAC protocol. Section 4 evaluates through numerical analysis. Section 5 provides conclusions and recommendations.

2 Related Work

Because of various limitations and the characteristics of wireless sensor networks, low power consumption is the main criterion for protocol design at every layer. The medium access control layer is one of the interesting research areas, and provides large opportunities for energy savings by dealing with the situations among nodes. There are several major sources of energy waste in wireless sensor networks: [2]

- *Collision* occurs when two nodes transmit at the same time and interfere with each others transmission. Hence, retransmissions increase energy consumption.
- *Control packet overhead* such as RTS/CTS/ACK can be significant for wireless sensor networks that use small data packets.
- *Overhearing* occurs when there is no meaningful activity when nodes receive packets or a part of packets that are destined to other nodes.
- *Idle listening* is the cost of actively listening for potential packets. Because nodes must keep their radio in receive mode, this source causes inefficient use of energy.

To reduce energy consumption by these factors, Polastre et al. develop a versatile low power MAC protocol called B-MAC, which is used as the default MAC for Mica2. By comparing B-MAC to Conventional Media Access Control (MAC) protocol, e.g., IEEE 802.11 Distributed Coordinated Function (DCF), we know that B-MAC is more suitable for sensor networks, for it is optimized to conserve energy. In

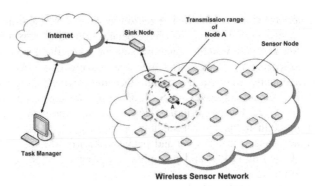

Fig. 1. The general architecture of Wireless Sensor Networks

addition, B-MAC's flexibility results in better packet delivery rates, throughput, latency, and energy consumption than other MAC protocols in WSNs such as S-MAC, T-MAC. However, B-MAC suffers from the waste in energy consumed by a long fixed preamble and overhearing. Although every node using B-MAC needs a long preamble to synchronize each other, it is a main source of energy consumption in B-MAC. Moreover, increasing the sample rate or neighborhood size increases the amount of traffic in the network. As a result, each node consumes much energy by overhearing. There is an example related to the overhearing problem in figure 1. Figure 1 shows the general communication architecture of WSNs [1]. When node A sends its physical information to the sink node, some neighboring nodes near node A overhear packets that they do not need. These activities on the channel reduce energy efficiency of WSNs.

3 Design of DPS-MAC Protocol

Energy dissipation includes three parts: energy dissipation on the sensor transducer, energy dissipation for communication among sensor nodes, and energy consumed by the microprocessor in computation. Since the part of communication consumes more power than other parts, the mechanism, which reduces transmission and reception energy, is a necessary factor for MAC protocol design in WSNs. Our goal for the protocol design is to provide an efficient preamble sampling scheme and to implement the appropriate MAC protocol that can support various features of WSNs. DPS-MAC is based on the divided preamble sampling technique, which achieves low power operations by reducing idle listening, avoiding collisions, and eliminating both protocol overhead and packet overhearing. Although DPS-MAC is motivated by low-rate, low-power wireless sensor networks, it can extend the scope through its flexible features. The details of the implementation steps for DPS-MAC protocol are described in the sections below.

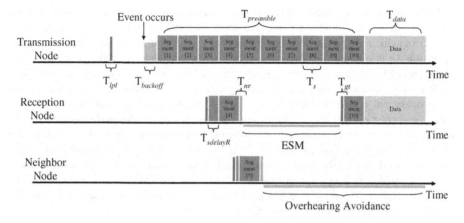

Fig. 2. Data Transmission and Reception with DPS mechanism

3.1 DPS-MAC

Figure 2 shows the basic operations of DPS-MAC protocol. When the transmissions of each node are requested from some event, the node checks for a pending packet in its queue. If a pending packet is detected, transmission fails and the information related to the state of transmission is reported to upper layer that deals with retrying the operation. If the node can immediately transmit a message, it saves the packet to the buffer and sets the value of the initial backoff time. After the operation, the algorithm of the transmission puts the node into active mode to send the packet and uses Clear Channel Assessment (CCA), which is the process of checking the status of the channel and reporting the result, in order to avoid collisions among neighboring nodes. If there is no activity, the node constructs the MAC frame that consists of several preamble segments and data payload at once and sends the message to the destination node or the next hop node. After transmission, the node turns on the timer related to the check interval and returns to sleep mode. This transmission mechanism is similar to a traditional carrier sense multiple access scheme; however, it returns to sleep mode to reduce energy consumption used by idle listening and eliminates inefficient control packet overheads. Although this mechanism has a long preamble, an efficient length of entire preamble can be obtained by controlling some bidirectional interfaces related to the check interval time on which the size of the entire preamble depends. In the case of a high-rate, the wake-up duration and the length of the preamble will be shorter to increase throughput.

To achieve low power operation of reception, DPS-MAC employs a variety of techniques such as DPS, CCA, and Low Power Listening (LPL). Each node usually keeps up a sleep state to minimize power consumption caused by idle listening and wakes up on a timer interrupt, named Check Interval Timer. If the channel is active during check period, the node decodes a preamble segment to perform the energy efficient algorithms by using the field of preamble offset and next hop address. After receiving a correct preamble segment completely, the node compares its address to the next hop address. If the incoming message is destined to this node, the number of the remaining preamble segments can be calculated by the field of preamble offset and the information of check interval. This scheme is called NR (Node Recognition) algorithm. After obtaining the value, the node immediately enters Energy Save Mode (ESM) in which the node quits an unnecessary reception to attain ultra low power operation for computed duration. The node changes the status of radio to active mode at the end of ESM duration and regularly receives the last preamble segment and data payload. By completing these procedures, each node accomplishes the entire receiving process and returns to sleep state to avoid an additional idle listening. However, there are other operations in some neighboring nodes. If the node address is not matched to the next hop address, it drops the remainder of the packet to eliminate overhearing problem. From this algorithm, a lot of energy waste consumed by reception is reduced efficiently. To implement the NR algorithm, the structure of long fixed preamble, which is proposed in WiseMAC [7] and B-MAC, must be changed. The novel structure of the preamble header and the NR algorithm are discussed more detail in section 3.2 and section 3.3 respectively.

3.2 The Divided Preamble Sampling

Every node that uses B-MAC usually suffers from long and inefficient preambles. In order to overcome this drawback, we propose more effective structure and sampling algorithm. The structure of DPS-MAC's entire preamble consists of several preamble segments and data field as shown in figure 3.

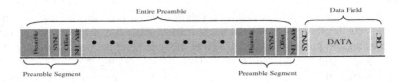

Fig. 3. The Structure of DPS-MAC Frame

A preamble segment has four kinds of fields. The first is preamble field that consists of the minimum length of bit pattern. Although a preamble is necessary for the bit synchronizer to synchronize correctly, a long fixed preamble is not an essential factor for transmitting packets. The minimum length of a preamble depends on the acquisition mode selected and the settling time. Typically, the minimum length is recommended by the manufacturer [6]. We employ the length in this field. The second is SYNC field that notifies the end of short preamble for correct synchronization. Preamble field is generally made up of regular bit sequences (0, 1, 0, 1 ...). When the node meets some different bit patterns like 00 or 11, it realizes that the receiving preamble field has ended completely. The third field is the preamble offset. While performing the NR algorithm, the node is able to know whether the message is destined to this node or not. In the case of former, an offset field provides the current position in the entire preamble. The last field is the next hop address field, which becomes a resource to eliminate overhearing. When the node constructs a preamble segment, it fetches the information of next hop node from upper layer and adds the information to a segment. When a node has a packet requested from upper layer, it constructs the MAC frame with several preamble segments consisting of all of these values to reliably receive data. The divided preamble sampling not only gets free from the inefficient structure of receiving no meaningful bit streams continually, but also allows the node to have the opportunities for ignoring a large insignificant part of the entire preamble through NR algorithm.

3.3 Node Recognition Algorithm

B-MAC provides low power operation, effective collision avoidance, and high channel utilization through a flexible interface. DPS-MAC can run NR algorithm without destroying these advantages. It can also have flexible interfaces proposed in B-MAC and provide an additional interface related to the divided preamble sampling. As described in Section 3.1, a node wakes up every check interval and detects activity on the channel, and receives message. At that time, the node that receives incoming packet does not need to listen to all parts of the packet through the NR algorithm if it is not a destination or next hop node or has many remaining preamble segments. When the node sees a busy channel at starting point of reception, it cannot always meet the preamble field in the preamble segment. Each node has to wait for $T_{sdelayR}$ duration, which is the time of preamble segment detection after waking up on a timer. Every node, which employs DPS-MAC, needs to receive the preamble at least during the minimum time recommended by the RF chip provider for stable synchronization. As shown in figure 4, the time to detect preamble segment becomes $0 \leq T_{sdelayR} < T_s$.

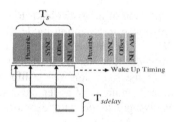

Fig. 4. Delay of preamble segment detection

After the delay of segment detection, each node is able to receive one preamble segment and runs the NR algorithm for ESM and overhearing avoidance in reception mode. In this case, we normally do not care about T_{nr} duration since the status of the radio is active and the node performs only a few comparisons and basic operations during that period. The receiver can compute the time of ESM duration by using a subtract operation between the total number of preamble segments and the current preamble offset. In addition, we need to consider other delays in all aspects when the node wakes up at the end of ESM. Every clock has the slow drift caused by quartz inaccuracy on each node, and radio module also has a delay of turning on radio and shifting the radio in reception state. DPS-MAC must guarantee these kinds of times on each node in order to achieve reliable communications and reduce energy waste caused by the recognition failure. Therefore DPS-MAC provides enough guard time, called T_{gt} before receiving the last preamble segment. Although T_{gt} is made up of clock drift and radio delay, actually radio delay is a large part of the duration. The entire preamble length must be matched to the check interval in order to check for activity on the channel reliably. If the channel is sampled every 100 ms, the entire preamble for detecting the activity must be at least 100 ms long according to the pigeonhole principle. The sender has the initial backoff to avoid collisions and the receiver needs the minimum time to prepare its reception. As a result of these factors, the length of the entire preamble is defined as

$$\text{Preamble}_{entire} \times T_{txbyte} \geq T_{interval} + \alpha \tag{1}$$

where Preamble_{entire} is the length of the entire preamble, T_{txbyte} and $T_{interval}$ are the time of sending 1 byte and the check interval time respectively, and α is the minimum delay made up of packet backoff time and the time of setting the radio. After Manchester encoding in the CC1000 used in Mica2, the data rate is 19.2kbps [6]. Because we can get the value of T_{txbyte} from the data rate, $T_{interval}$ and α from the bidirectional interface, we are able to calculate the suitable length of the entire preamble.

4   Performance Evaluation

Basically, wireless sensor networks are able to support scalability of the network since the number of sensor nodes deployed in the field widely may be on the order of hundreds or thousands. In a case of S-MAC, the complexity of the synchronization of each virtual cluster increases when the network is enlarged by much. This phenomenon decreases the efficiency of the protocol and causes many control packet overheads. When using B-MAC, the expansion of networks leads to the increase of the total overhearing overhead and energy waste in reception mode. Besides, in order to the offer fault tolerance feature of WSNs, the engineer have to provide the high density networks. For this reason, more nodes that employ B-MAC suffer from serious overhearing problem, which results in the reduction of the lifetime of network in the end. Therefore, if the traffic load or the number of nodes increases owing to various circumstances, B-MAC-applied-WSNs get to be with exhaustion caused by receiving no meaningful parts of packets. DPS-MAC is, however, able to shorten energy exhaustion in some different ways, for it has accepted the properties of the existing B-MAC.

In this section, we derive analytical expressions for the energy consumption. In order to provide an absolute benchmark, we define an ideal protocol and show the efficient factors of DPS-MAC from various equations and results. We focus on comparing DPS-MAC and B-MAC since B-MAC is shown to have higher throughput and better energy efficiency than S-MAC and T-MAC. In this analysis, we consider a system composed of N interfering nodes. Traffic arrival is assumed to be a global rate λ and all of the protocols discussed in this section do not consider an acknowledgement packet since it is an option. In addition, one operation time including a transmission and a reception is less than one second to calculate sleep energy simply.

4.1   Energy Consumption Analysis

First, we derive the expression for the power consumption of the ideal case. Ideal protocol assumes that the sender is able to forward the packet immediately on the radio channel at the time of event arrival. If the transmitter is busy at arrival time, the packet is buffered in a single FIFO queue. In absence of traffic transmitted to them, sensor nodes are sleeping. In the ideal protocol, the receiver can wake up exactly on time, listen the packet, and go back to sleep mode. In this model, each node receives one packet of T_D duration every $1/\lambda N$ seconds, which is an average packet inter-arrival time. The model includes three parts: reception cost, transmission cost, and sleep cost. The energy consumption cost of reception side is $\bar{E}_{rx}(T_{ron} + T_{rx/tx} + T_D)$. In this part, $\bar{E}_{rx}T_{ron}$ and $\bar{E}_{rx}T_{rx/tx}$ are the energy to prepare communications and $\bar{E}_{rx}T_D$ is the energy consumed by receiving one packet. The energy consumption cost of transmission side is $\bar{E}_{rx}(T_{ron} + T_{rx/tx}) + \bar{E}_{tx}T_D$. This part is almost similar to the case of reception. However, the average rate of each event is different from each other because a node generates one packet with a rate λ and receives one packet from all of its neighboring nodes. The average inter-arrival time of reception is proportional to neighboring nodes. To simplify the equation, we use $\bar{E}_{rx}$ and $\bar{E}_{tx}$ as the increment in energy consumption caused being in the reception and transmission mode. During the time except reception and transmission, a node keeps its radio in sleep mode and reduces the waste of energy. We are not able to neglect the time to set up a transceiver and change a radio status since they are important parts of node operations. From these factors, the energy consumption of ideal model in average is given by

$$E_{ideal} = E_{sleep}T_{sleep} + \lambda N \left[\bar{E}_{rx}(T_{ron} + T_{rx/tx} + T_D) \right] + \lambda \left[\bar{E}_{rx}(T_{ron} + T_{rx/tx}) + \bar{E}_{tx}T_D \right] \quad (2)$$

where

$$T_{sleep} = 1 - RX_{time} - TX_{time} = 1 - \lambda N(T_{ron} + T_{rx/tx} + T_D) - \lambda(T_{ron} + T_{rx/tx} + T_D) \quad (3)$$

The Equation (2) is the base line of power consumption in the paper.

Second, we analyze the energy consumption of B-MAC. The energy consumption model of B-MAC is composed of the sleep energy, the channel sampling energy, the reception energy, the overhearing energy, and the transmission energy. From these elements, we can obtain

$$E_{bmac} = E_{sleep}T_{sleep} + \frac{\bar{E}_{rx}(T_{ron} + T_{rx/tx} + \frac{1}{B})}{T_{interval}} + \lambda \bar{E}_{rx}(T_{bPR} + T_D)$$

$$+ \sum_{i=1}^{N-1} \lambda \bar{E}_{rx}T_{overhearRi} + \lambda \left[\bar{E}_{rx}(T_{ron} + T_{rx/tx}) + \bar{E}_{tx}(T_{bP} + T_D) \right] \quad (4)$$

where

$$T_{sleep} = 1 - Sample_{time} - RX_{time} - Overhear_{time} - TX_{time}$$

$$= 1 - \left(\frac{\left(T_{ron} + T_{rx/tx} + \frac{1}{B} \right)}{T_{interval}} \right) - \lambda(T_{bPR} + T_D)$$

$$- \sum_{i=1}^{N-1} \lambda T_{overhearRi} - \lambda(T_{ron} + T_{rx/tx} + T_{bP} + T_D) \quad (5)$$

In Equation (4), the first term is the energy consumed in the doze mode. The time to keep up doze state is calculated by Equation (5) since every node returns the doze state if a transmission or a reception does not occur. The second term, $\overline{E}_{rx(T_{ron}+T_{rx/tx}+1/B)}$, represents the energy used by sampling the medium. This event occurs every check interval time. The third term is the energy caused by receiving a packet. To receive one packet completely, a node have to listen the long preamble and data. T_{bPR} is the random duration of listening the entire B-MAC preamble. Therefore, the total reception energy becomes $\overline{E}_{rx(T_{bPR}+T_D)}$ with an average reception inter-arrival time $1/\lambda$. The fourth term is the overhearing energy. After waking up on a timer, the receiver must listen the entire packet from all of neighboring nodes except a child node. Although each duration of overhearing is different, the reception node listens the duration of $T_{overhearRi}$ per node at least. The fifth term represents the trans-mission energy. This part consists of radio setup time and packet transmission time. In this sum, $\overline{E}_{tx}T_{bP}$ is the energy to send an entire B-MAC preamble, which guarantees reliable communications between sender and receiver.

Finally, we compute the energy consumption of DPS-MAC. In a case of DPS-MAC, we derive the equation through the same manner of B-MAC model to compare each other easily. The average energy consumed by DPS-MAC is defined as

$$E_{dpsmac} = E_{sleep}T_{sleep} + \frac{\overline{E}_{rx}(T_{ron}+T_{rx/tx}+\frac{1}{B})}{T_{interval}} + E_{RECEPTION}$$
$$+ \sum_{i=1}^{N-1} \lambda \overline{E}_{rx}(T_{sdelayRi}+T_s+T_{nr}) + \lambda\left[\overline{E}_{rx}(T_{ron}+T_{rx/tx})+\overline{E}_{tx}(T_{dpsP}+T_D)\right] \quad (6)$$

where

$$T_{sleep} = 1 - \left(\frac{\left(T_{ron}+T_{rx/tx}+\frac{1}{B}\right)}{T_{interval}}\right) - RX_{time} - \sum_{i=1}^{N-1}\lambda(T_{sdelayRi}+T_s+T_{nr})$$
$$- \lambda(T_{ron}+T_{rx/tx}+T_{dpsP}+T_D) \quad (7)$$

The first term represents the energy consumed by a sleep state. This part is composed of the same elements as B-MAC; however, the elements have different values except the channel sampling duration owing to different operations. Each element will be explained in the next terms. The second term is the energy used by channel sampling. It is the same quantity as the sampling energy of B-MAC. The third term is the energy consumed by reception of a data packet. By using the energy save mode, DPS-MAC can have two kinds of reception values. After waking up and checking the channel activity, the receiver calculates $\hat{T}_{remain}$ using T_{dpsPR}, which is the random duration of listening to the remaining preamble. $\hat{T}_{remain}$, the number of remaining preamble seg-ments, represents the maximum integer of $\lfloor T_{dpsPR}/T_s \rfloor$. In the case of Equation (8), if $\hat{T}_{remain}$ is equal or less than $T_{threshold}$, the node does not enter the ESM because it can-not expect the energy efficiency from this algorithm. In this comparison, $T_{threshold}$ means the threshold line to achieve the energy efficiency of the ESM. On the other hand, as shown in Case (ii), if $\hat{T}_{remain}$ is larger than the left part, the node immediately enters the ESM and saves the reception energy during T_{ESM}. T_{ESM} considers the time of preamble detection, the running time of NR algorithm, and the guard time during T_{dpsPR}.

(i) $T_{ron} + T_{rx/tx} + T_{threshold} \geq \hat{T}_{remain}$

$$E_{RECEPTION} = \lambda \overline{E}_{rx}(T_{dpsPR} + T_D) \tag{8}$$

(ii) $T_{ron} + T_{rx/tx} + T_{threshold} < \hat{T}_{remain}$

$$E_{RECEPTION} = \lambda \overline{E}_{rx}(T_{dpsPR} + T_D - T_{ESM}) \tag{9}$$

where

$$T_{ESM} = T_{dpsPR} - T_{sdelayR} - T_{nr} - T_{gt} - 2T_s \tag{10}$$

The fourth term represents the energy exhausted by overhearing. DPS-MAC provides overhearing avoidance scheme through NR algorithm. For this reason, a lot of overheads in overhearing are reduced like this part and the receiver needs the minimum energy to decode one preamble segment completely. The fifth term is the transmission energy and similar to B-MAC's one. Table 1 lists the range of all random values described in this section.

Table 1. Ranges of random parameters

Parameter	Description	Values used in simulation
T_{bPR}	The duration of listening B-MAC preamble	$0 \sim T_{bP}$
$T_{overhearR}$	The duration of B-MAC overhearing	$0 \sim T_{bP} + T_D$
T_{dpsPR}	The duration of listening DPS-MAC preamble	$0 \sim T_{dpsP}$
$T_{sdelayR}$	The duration of preamble segment detection	$0 \sim T_s$
$T_{backoff}$	The duration of initial packet backoff	$0 \sim 10ms$

4.2 Preamble Comparison

Prior to comparing the energy consumption, we must think about the difference of the preamble length between B-MAC and DPS-MAC. In a case of B-MAC, it considers simply both the check interval time and the radio setup time. However, DPS-MAC has a fixed size of preamble segment and must receive one preamble segment at the end of the entire preamble at least. Because of these reasons, the length of the entire preamble is different between B-MAC and DPS-MAC. We can calculate both of them by applying Equation (1). For example, we assume that the check interval time is 100ms, the maximum packet backoff time is 10ms, and the radio setup time is 1.75ms. The minimum value of B-MAC preamble will be 269 bytes.

On the other hand, the length of DPS-MAC preamble will be 288 bytes since the entire preamble is increased as a multiple of preamble segments and one preamble segment must be added to implement the ESM. The increase energy consumed by additional bytes is a small quantity of energy compared to the advantages of DPS-MAC.

4.3 Energy Comparison

To illustrate the effectiveness of DPS-MAC, we compare the power consumption of the ideal, B-MAC, and DPS-MAC protocols using various parameters in this section. We assume that most of random values have uniform distributions and the remaining parameters have been chosen as shown in Table 2.

Table 2. Parameters for comparing DPS-MAC and B-MAC

Parameter	Description	Values used in simulation
N	Neighborhood size	10 nodes
B	Data rate	19.2kbps
C_{batt}	Battery capacity	2000 mAh
C_{sleep}	Current used in sleep mode	0.03 mA
C_{tx}	Current used in tx mode	15 mA
C_{rx}	Current used in rx mode	15 mA
V	Voltage	3 V
T_{ron}	The time of turning on radio	1.5ms
$T_{rx/tx}$	The time of switching rx and tx	250us
T_D	The time of sending one packet	16.7ms (40Bytes)
T_{bP}	The time of sending entire B-MAC preamble	125 Bytes (40ms check interval) ~
T_{dpsP}	The time of sending entire DPS-MAC preamble	144 Bytes (40ms check interval) ~
$T_{threshold}$	The minimum time for ESM	$2 * T_s$
T_s	The time of sending one preamble segment	5ms (12Bytes)
T_{gt}	Guard time	1.5ms

Figure 5 shows energy consumption as a function of check interval with $\lambda = 0.01$. Ideal model uses a very low power because of the magical timing and the minimum operations. DPS-MAC and B-MAC use more energy than ideal case due to some additional operations for real communications. When the check interval time increases, DPS-MAC consumes less energy than B-MAC. This result shows that DPS-MAC can eliminate the inefficiency of a long fixed preamble caused by the increase of the check interval time in B-MAC. At the point of 200ms, DPS-MAC saves approximately 42 percent of the total energy. The increase of energy efficiency results from overhearing avoidance and the ESM. Every node, which uses B-MAC, can reduce more energy caused by idle listening by increasing the check interval time suitably. However, overhearing energy is also increased by the long preamble of the protocol. Figure 6 shows how much overhearing and reception time is reduced by DPS-MAC compared to B-MAC. We can see that DPS-MAC reduces more overhearing time than reception time. This illustrates the biggest weak point of B-MAC.

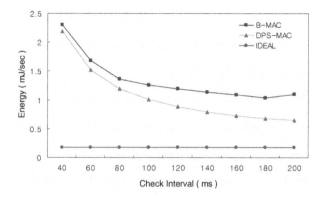

Fig. 5. Energy consumption of ideal, B-MAC, and DPS-MAC as a function of check interval

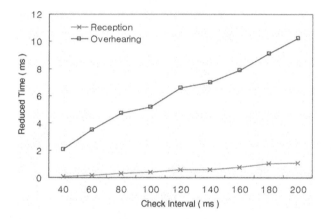

Fig. 6. Reduced time by using NR algorithm

In Figure 5 and Figure 6, we have considered only constant average traffic with $\lambda =$ 0.01. From now on, we maintain check interval = 200ms constant and vary the traffic λ from 10^{-4} to 10^{0} in order to analyze the relationship between traffic rate and energy consumption. As shown in Figure 7, DPS-MAC and B-MAC consume a similar quantity of energy when the traffic rate is very low. If the traffic rate increases, B-MAC consumes more energy than DPS-MAC because each packet used in B-MAC has a greater amount of overheads. Although the original purpose of WSNs is to support low-rate applications, some applications need to perform their jobs fast such as an emergency application or a real-time application. Therefore, the protocols for WSNs have to apply various new features of WSNs easily. From this point of view, DPS-MAC can be widely employed well. Figure 8 compares the energy consumption of three protocols as a function of node density. According to Figure 8, the overhearing problem in energy consumption of B-MAC is proportional to the number of potential overhearers. On the other hand, DPS-MAC has the uniform energy whether the neighboring nodes increase or not. This shows that the energy efficiency of DPS-MAC gets even better when node density in a specific area gets higher for fault tolerance.

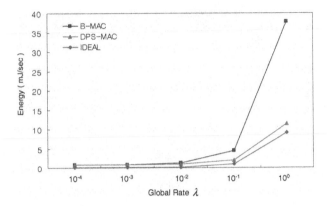

Fig. 7. Energy consumption of ideal, B-MAC, and DPS-MAC as a function of traffic rate

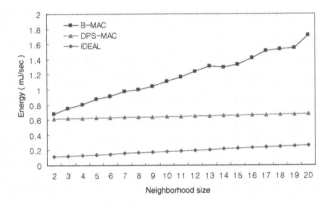

Fig. 8. Energy consumption of ideal, B-MAC, and DPS-MAC as a function of node density

In general, we are interested in the lifetime of the node when designing the sensor network applications. The lifetime of the node is dependent on the total consumed energy and the battery capacity as shown in Equation (11).

$$\text{Lifetime(Days)} = \frac{C_{batt} \times V}{E} \div 24 \qquad (11)$$

If we set the available capacity of battery and vary waking up point, we can evaluate the affect of the check interval time on node lifetime. By solving Equations (4 through 11) with $\lambda = 0.01$ and $\lambda = 0.001$, we can determine the lifetime of each node on B-MAC and DPS-MAC. The comparisons of the node lifetime between DPS-MAC and B-MAC shows in Figure 9 that the former can extend more node lifetime in each check interval time than the latter.

Consequently, it is obvious that DPS-MAC is a whole lot more efficient than B-MAC to support the properties of general WSNs efficiently. Overhearing can be reduced in the existing B-MAC when using RTS-CTS mechanism. Nevertheless, it is not efficient to reserve channels using RTS-CTS mechanism in B-MAC. Because the

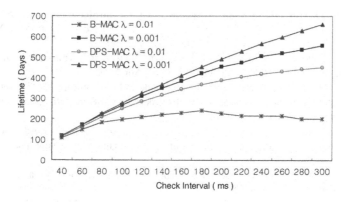

Fig. 9. Comparison of node lifetime between DPS-MAC and B-MAC

reception node has to listen to the channel status during a certain period to let the receiver hear RTS, the energy efficient operations of the node turn to be inefficient.

5 Conclusion

An energy-efficiency MAC protocol in Wireless Sensor Networks (WSNs) is an open research area in which we are conducting further studies. To solve the problem of inefficient operations and reach our goal in WSNs, we have proposed the DPS-MAC protocol that employs NR algorithm. This protocol uses a novel idea, called Divided Preamble Sampling to implement the algorithm. The structure of preamble segment provides various opportunities to improve energy efficiency. The performance results have shown the DPS-MAC protocol is more suitable for general WSNs and can achieve much conserving energy in reception compared to B-MAC protocol.

This novel protocol is the subject of an ongoing study, and we plan to implement the DPS-MAC protocol on the node that we have created. Therefore, we expect more results related to energy efficiency, latency, and throughput in the future.

References

[1] Akyildiz, W. Su, Y. Sankarasubramaniam, and E. Cayirci, A survey on sensor networks, IEEE Communications Magazine, Volume: 40. Issue: 8, pp. 102-114, August 2002.
[2] W. Ye, J. Heidemann, and D. Estrin. An energy-efficient mac protocol for wireless sensor networks. In In Proceedings of the 21st International Annual Joint Conference of the IEEE Computer and Communications Societies (INFOCOM 2002), New York, NY, June 2002.
[3] T. van Dam and K. Langendoen. An adaptive energy-effcient MAC protocol for wireless sensor networks. In Proceedings of the First ACM Conference on Embedded Networked Sensor Systems (SenSys), Los Angeles, CA, November 2003.
[4] IEEE, Wireless Medium Access Control (MAC) and Physical Layer (PHY) specifications for Low Rate Wireless Personal Area Networks (LR-WPANS), IEEE 802.15.4-2003, 2003.

[5] J. Polastre, J. Hill, and D. Culler. Versatile low power media access for wireless sensor networks. In Proceedings of the Second ACM Conference on Embedded Networked Sensor Systems (SenSys), Baltimore,MD, November 2004.

[6] Chipcon Coporation. Single Chip Very Low Power RF Transceiver. http://www. chipcon.com/files/CC1000_Data_Sheet_2_1.pdf, Apr. 2002

[7] El-Hoiyi, J.-D. Decotignie, and J. Hernandez. Low power MAC protocols for infrastructure wireless sensor networks. In Proceedings of the Fifth European Wireless Conference, Feb. 2004.

[8] El-Hoiydi, Aloha with Preamble Sampling for Sporadic Traffic in Ad Hoc Wireless Sensor Networks, in Proc. IEEE Int. Conf. on Communications, New York, USA, Apr 2002, pp. 3418–3423.

[9] University of California, Berkeley. TinyOS CVS Repository at SourceForge. http://sf.net/projects/tinyos/, 2005.

[10] Injong Rhee, Ajit Warrier, Mahesh Aia, and Jeongki Min, Z-MAC: a Hybrid MAC for Wireless Sensor Networks, in ACM Sensys 2005.

A Service Conflict Resolution Algorithm Based on Virtual Personal World

Joo-Kyoung Park[1], Chang-Deok Kang[1], Kyung-Lang Park[1], Hoon-Ki Lee[2],
Eui-Hyun Baek[2], and Shin-Dug Kim[1]

[1] Super Computing Lab, Department of Computer Science, Yonsei University 120-749,
134 Shinchon-Dong, Seodaemoon-Gu, Seoul, Korea
{jkpark, niceguy, lanx, sdkim}@yonsei.ac.kr
http://supercom.yonsei.ac.kr
[2] Electronics and Telecommunications Research Institute, Digital Home Research Division
161 Gajeong-dong, Yuseong-gu, Daejeon, 305-350, Korea
{lhk, ehbaek}@etri.re.kr
http://www.etri.re.kr

Abstract. In this paper, we introduce a service framework using the VPW (Virtual Personal World) and its associated service conflict resolution algorithm based on the VPW. In this new service model, users can manage their own spaces that include all things to support their services. Previous service frameworks are focused on designing adaptive software applications by using heterogeneous devices and softwares. However, these service frameworks have some problems to provide adaptive services to the users. To resolve the limitation that is caused by multi-user environment, we propose a service conflict resolution algorithm. Therefore, our proposed service framework based on the VPW can support more user-centric services, reduce the number of service conflicts, and improve the number of conflict resolutions. The experiment result shows that almost 40% resolution rate can be achieved comparing with the location based system and 30% work time can be improved comparing with the location based system.

1 Introduction

Ubiquitous computing environment allows a lot of different computing resources to be performed cooperatively for autonomous service initiation without any specific handling and interest [1, 2]. Recent computing technologies have changed the existing computing paradigm and eventually opened the ubiquitous computing paradigm.

In ubiquitous computing environment, computers can collect and analyze the contexts that relate to the situations of users to initiate any specific service to users [3]. To achieve this goal, computers need to collect contexts that represent the situation status of a user. The context is the information to describe the characters of an 'entity', where the entity includes user, application itself, person, space, and physical devices that interact each other [5]. In ubiquitous computing environment, intelligent applications can recognize their environments around a user, collect various physical contexts, process them through a proper computing mechanism, and

H.Y. Youn, M. Kim, and H. Morikawa (Eds.): UCS 2006, LNCS 4239, pp. 225–238, 2006.
© Springer-Verlag Berlin Heidelberg 2006

have to provide any specific service to the user. Therefore, many application service models that manipulate heterogeneous devices and information are being developed now [3, 8]. However, these service models have some problem to provide adaptive services to the users. First, these service models are just focused on how to adapt application services and how to manage many devices and software components to support a specific service to the user under a particular situation. Thus, only software components and hardware devices are considered to provider services rather than users. Second, multi-user environment, where many users want to use some specific services, are not considered.

In this research, we propose a new service model and its associated service confliction resolution algorithm based on the VPW(Virtual Personal World). In this new service model, users can manage their own spaces that include all things to support their services. The VPW can be expressed as a set of tasks, VOs(Virtual object), and proxies. The important characteristics of the VPW aren't fixed by any physical boundaries and specific virtual objects. Thus, we can derive many strong points of our service model from the VPW, which can represent the current status of a user's computing environment. Also, the VPW can represent what the user wants in this computing environment. To resolve the limitation that is caused by multi-user environment, we propose a service conflict resolution algorithm. The algorithm is based on many parameters to keep objectivity by using the VPW, the information related to the user and VOs from service framework. For example, if many users want to use specific VOs, the service conflict resolution algorithm effectively manipulate this contention situation by using the VPW related to confliction. Thus, it can reduce the number of service conflicts and increase the number of conflict resolutions. The experimental result shows that service conflict resolution algorithm increases resolution rate by around 20% compared to simple VPW management that tries to simply find alternate virtual objects. Also, our system shows almost 40% resolution rate can be achieved comparing with the location based system. Also, another result shows that 30% work time can be improved comparing with the location based system because if service conflicts are not occurred, service providing system can support many services at the same time.

Rest of the paper is organized as follows: Section 2 introduces related work on service models and frameworks of ubiquitous computing. Section 3 describes conceptual model. The proposed system is presented in Section 4. Section 5 focuses on service conflict resolution algorithm. Section 6 shows several experimental results. Conclusion is provided in Section 7.

2 Related Work

In previous service models, they have proposed the location-based service that provides services when the user is positioned at a specific location. However, these service models have many limitations, namely it is difficult to define proper location range to provide services and cannot concern many situations except specific user's location [4]. And then, the context-aware application model [5, 6] is devised from location-based model. Dey et al. defined that "Context is any information which can be used to characterize the situation of an entity and suggest a structured model to make applications utilize contexts [5, 6]. However, research in this category tends to focus on how to acquire, represent, and deliver contexts efficiently rather than service models [7].

Based on these service models, advanced service models are devised from context-aware application model. These service models can cover many weak points of previous service models.

AURA is the middleware to provide the seamless service considering the situation of users (movement and alteration of environment) [8]. To support these functions, AURA adopts the context perception techniques that gain the contexts of environment for the users and task manager to provide the service that is being provided continually notwithstanding change of environment of users. Besides, AURA uses the abstract description about the service and the framework automatically maps proper devices, software components that can provide required services over the user requirements. Also, AURA takes utility function that can make the best configuration to provide adaptive services. GAIA project [3] establishes the Active Space that manages the entity to provide the service and provide various adaptive services with the change of the contexts related to the service providing environment. Users can develop application by using abstract service model named by Olympus Programming Model [9]. It can describe detailed actions that are determined in runtime in order to suit the active space. This GAIA showed well-defined frameworks and application models for ubiquitous computing. However, it is based on fixed physical boundary named Active Space. Thus, it cannot support user-centric service providing mechanism. Some approaches [10, 11] are focused on generating user interfaces for the device that can provide service rather than make proper service providing component. Recently, some researchers have tried to define user private space that is ranged by user-centralism [12, 13, 14]. However, these service models define user private space as wireless communication coverage or just simple location. It is difficult to find any differences from previously we mentioned framework.

To overcome these weak points, we take high-level abstract programming models and dynamic configuration according to various situations such as user movement, software failure, service requirement changes, and user private space that supports user centralism. Therefore, we use the VPW that can represent user status, include virtual objects that can use to provide service, and include all the information around the user. Thus, our proposed framework can provide adaptive service totally based on the user rather than devices or location.

3   Virtual Personal World

In this section, we describe the conceptual model of VPW to provide user centric adaptive services. User specific contexts are required to support any user centric adaptive service. Contexts around a particular user are not simply physical information about user, but all the information related to the user centric services. For example, if a user wants a music play service, the information required to perform that service is necessary devices, software components, user status, and so on. The VPW can represent the current state of a user's computing environment. As mentioned, it consists of a set of tasks, virtual objects, and proxies. Task is regarded as an activated service that a user wants to use especially in terms of user's view. Virtual object is a software component that can be performed via a uniform interface.

Also it can access other software components through their uniform interfaces. Thus, all objects in service providing environment can be specified as virtual objects. Proxy is defined as other user's VPWs that may be related to a particular VPW. Figure1 shows the basic concept of VPW, where V, P, and T in Figure 1 represent virtual object, proxy, and task respectively.

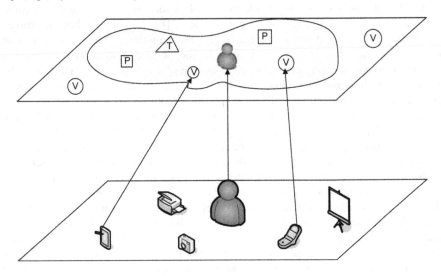

Fig. 1. The basic concept of VPW (Virtual Personal World)

Any service based on VPW can be represented as an abstract description. In this approach, a service can be reformed based on a given user's VPW adaptively to initiate any user centric adaptive service. When providing personalized services to the users, those have to be configured for the user's VPW adaptively. Service configuration based on a VPW has three meanings; 1) do not disturb other users in using a specific service 2) do not make any conflicts with other tasks in the VPW 3) use virtual objects in its own VPW. Service configuration is defined as a function which can get the VPW of a specific user requesting a service and can generate a service instance for the user. It is denoted by Eq. 1 and Figure 2 shows this concept.

$$Configured\ Service_A = S(VPW_A)\ . \qquad (1)$$

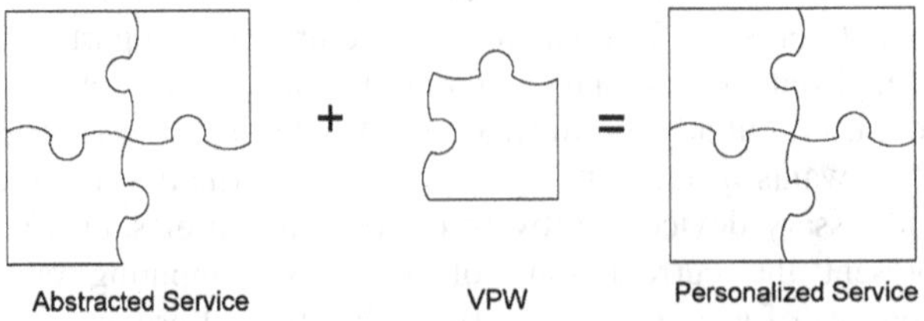

Abstracted Service   +   VPW   =   Personalized Service

Fig. 2. The concept of personalized service

4   System Framework

In this section, we introduce a software framework for providing adaptive personal service based on VPW and we focus service conflict resolution algorithm in Section 5.

Basically, service framework consists of five components, i.e., VPW manager, service manager, VO repository, and service hosting engine as shown in Figure 3.

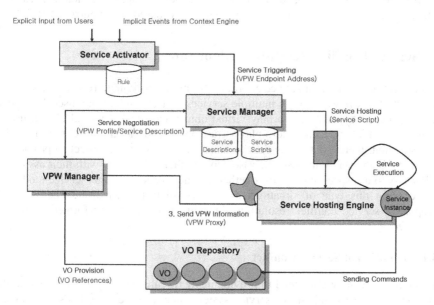

Fig. 3. Service framework for adaptive service providing

VPW manager is to maintain each user's VPW and is regarded as a personal server that collects many information related to service initiation and transfers them to the proper service manager or service hosting engine. VO repository is to manage the instance of any virtual object that can provide tangible services or operations to the user. Service activator is to trigger any specific service to the user according to defined service providing conditions. When a service is triggered by service activator, service manager negotiates to find a proper VPW with VPW manager by using service description and it sends service script to the service hosting engine. Finally, service hosting engine interprets a service script to generate executable program code to a proper virtual object and the user can take their services.

4.1   Characteristic and Advantage of Service Providing Using VPW

Our service framework can support user centric services using the VPW that includes useful information related to any service requested. Also virtual objects can represent physical hardware or software component to provide services. As mentioned in Section 3, our service framework uses an abstract service model and the VPW to personalize services. Thus, our service framework has many advantages to provide services. First, it can provide personalized and flexible services that can reflect a user's status because the VPW is constructed to represent a user status and situation around that user. Specifically the VPW is not restricted to any physical boundary or any limitation. Second, it can improve software reusability. Software components are not specified to a user or others but can be changed for personalized services according to its given VPW. Finally, service manager can support adaptive and polymorphic services. Also, service manager can serve adaptive services according to situation because it can select suitable virtual objects based on the current VPW.

5   Service Conflict Resolution Algorithm

In this section, we focus a service conflict resolution algorithm to resolve the situation that multiple users want to use multiple services. For example, when user-A wants to listen to music by using audio play virtual object and speaker virtual object, user-B tries to watch TV by using audio play virtual object and visual play virtual object. In this situation, there exists a conflict in using audio play virtual object to provide the service to both user-A and user-B. Also suppose that many users with their associated VPWs try to use specific services together. As mentioned, previous service models do not concern this type of situations causing conflicts to each user. Therefore, we propose a service conflict resolution algorithm that can be performed at service manager.

5.1   Definition of Service Conflict

Recently, most of systems tend to provide many resource sharing methods and multi-tasking. Also many ubiquitous service systems may use these methods to share the limited resources. In this point of view, service confliction concept has been resolved in some sense. However, when many users try to use some specific resources for providing services, the performance given by using these resources tends to be decreased. Thus, the quality of service(QoS) become worse and worse. This situation may be caused by service conflicts occurring among users in the same management space. A service conflict occurs when services are provided to multiple users and performing a service for a user can disturb the use of other user's service and further service invocations. Thus, the competition to acquire specific virtual objects and resources can cause any service conflict. We consider this competition situation to design our service conflict resolution. If the QoS level is higher than user's need, services can be shared up to the QoS limitation.

5.2   Concept of Service Conflict Resolution

In Section 3, services can be represented as Eq. 1. Service conflicts can be occurred in situation that multi-users try to use the same service by using their own VPWs. Also, this situation can be defined as a function which inputs each user's VPW to use same the service as denoted by Eq. 2. S_{conf_A} is defined as the resulting service instance configured for multiple user environment.

$$S_{conf\_A} = S(VPW_A, VPW_B, \cdots, VPW_n) \ . \tag{2}$$

This means that when multiple users want to use a specific service by using each user's VPW, service confliction can be caused. Also, it means that triggered services from VPW_B have not to disturb the tasks or services using VPW_A. The basic concept of service conflict resolution is performed to generate a reconfigured service instance by using neighboring VPW information.

In addition to this basic concept of service conflict resolution algorithm, several service conflict modes such as exclusive mode, group mode, and single mode are defined. In the exclusive mode, when user-B wants to use any specific service by using virtual objects that also belong to the user-A's VPW, a service triggered from the VPW_B has not to disturb the tasks or services using VPW_A. The result in exclusive mode is to subtract virtual objects that are overlapped in VPW_A from those in VPW_B. This can be represented as in Figure 4.

$$S(VPW_A, VPW_B\text{"--"})$$

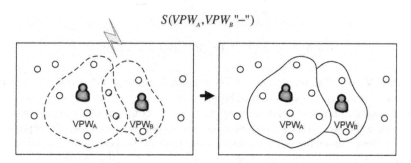

Fig. 4. An example of exclusive mode

In group mode, each VPW can be merged together to provide services. Group mode can be used when each user well knows other user's service or task, requesting the same services. This group mode is shown as in Figure 5.

In the single mode, other VPWs that can disturb other users' services need to apply service conflict resolution algorithm. Basically, the single mode is regarded as exclusive mode and represented as Eq. 1. To perform in the single mode, we need to

$$S(VPW_A, VPW_B\text{"+"})$$

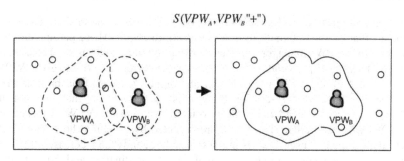

Fig. 5. An example of group mode

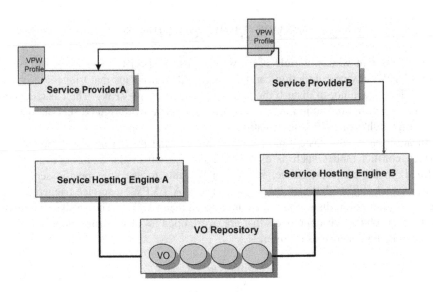

Fig. 6. An example of the VPW resolution algorithm

find other VPWs. To find other VPWs that may cause conflicts, a VRP (VPW Resolution Protocol) is designed as in Figure 6.

In the single mode, when service manager-A configures a service with its corresponding VPW$_A$, it tries to connect service hosting engine-A and VO repository. VO repository maintains virtual objects required to provide services. If service manager-A wants to use the virtual object A and also it is used to provide a service by the service manager-B, service manager-A can find the service manager-B by using the connection path from the VO repository to the service manager-B and it has the VPW profile too. Thus, service manager-A can trace any link to the service manager-B. And then, service manager-A sends its address to the service manager-B and it can obtain the VPW$_B$ maintained by the service manager-B. As the result of the VRP, service manager-A can obtain VPW$_B$ and can apply service conflict resolution algorithm with the VPW$_B$.

5.3 Parameters of the Service Conflict Resolution Algorithm

To increase objectivity, the service conflict resolution algorithm uses many parameters that can be obtained from the service framework. These parameters can be obtained from VPW manager, service hosting engine, and user. Thus, several attributes of virtual objects can be used to clarify the current size of the given VPW. If the current size of any VPW grows bigger and bigger, it means that the user tries to use some complicated services or there exist some service that are not used consistently. Thus, we need to define priority for the current VPWs by comparing user VPWs with each other. This can be represented by checking the sizes of VPWs to determine whether users use some services frequently and consistently or not. Figure 7 shows conceptual model of virtual object coordination and Eq. 3 to obtain the size of a VPW.

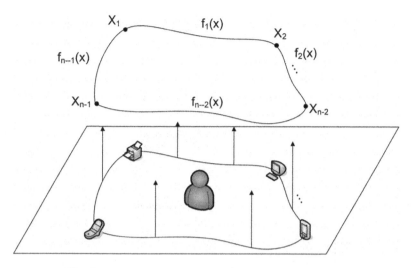

Fig. 7. The conceptual model of virtual object coordination

$$Size\ of\ VPW = \sum_{i=1}^{n-1} \int_{x_i}^{x_{i+1}} f_i(x)dx\,,\ x_1 = x_n \tag{3}$$

$$f_i(x) = \frac{f_i(x_{i+1}) - f_i(x_i)}{x_{i+1} - x_i}(x - x_i) + f_i(x_i)$$

Also, we can get the virtual object distance from the VO repository. Virtual object distance is ranged as from 1 to 10 and calculated from virtual object ontology. Virtual object ontology and calculate method is not addressed because this topic is beyond the scope of this paper. If virtual object distance is closer to one, this means each virtual object is considered as the same object. On the contrary, if it is closer to 10, each virtual object cannot be substituted with another virtual object. We can use alternate virtual object with in distance 5. Finally, we can take required QoS requirement and sharing intention of specific virtual object from the user.

5.4 Service Conflict Resolution Algorithm

Figure 8 shows the operation flow of the service conflict resolution algorithm.

Basically, this operation flow is used to apply exclusive mode. If user wants to use group mode, service conflict resolution is not required need because each user only uses group mode in the situation that they know other VPWs. First of all, when the ranges of the VPWs are conflicted, service manager should collect the specific conflicted VPWs. In single mode, service manager uses the VRP to obtain the conflicted VPW. Then, service manager calculates the size of each VPW and maintains priority between them. As mentioned, if any VPW has a big size, this VPW has higher priority because the big VPW means user doesn't use some services consistently. After this operation, service manager calculates the distance between

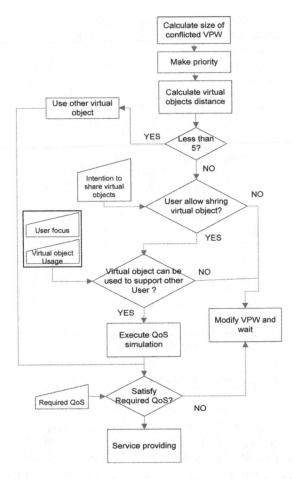

Fig. 8. Operation flow of the service conflict resolution algorithm

virtual objects. If any virtual object distance is higher than 5, each virtual object cannot be substituted. At this situation, service manager requests the intention of sharing virtual objects of the user from VPW manager. If the user wants to share specific virtual objects, service manager calculates possibility that can guarantee the required QoS level of any occupant user by using the user focus and the virtual object usage. To calculate possibility, the service conflict algorithm use Eq. 4. P_{vl} is the performance as the throughput of the VO1(virtual object) per time unit and F_{vl} is the focus rate of the VO1 per time unit, and is the weight factor. In the service conflict resolution algorithm, user focus is an important factor to resolve any conflict. Thus we apply weight factor to the user focus rate. User at the service manager can set this R value to decide whether virtual object can be used to support other users. If R value has lower value, it means that user don't concentrate on a specific virtual object and service. If R value has lower value than any set point, service manager simulates QoS level to provide service to users. As a result of simulation, service can be provided over required QoS level and service manager starts service to users. On the contrary, service manager modifies the VPW that may cause any virtual object conflict.

$$R = P_{vl} + F_{vl} \times \omega \qquad (4)$$

$$P_{vl} = \frac{Average Vir tualobject\ Usage}{Time Unit}, \quad F_{vl} = \frac{Average Use rFocus}{Time Unit}$$

6 Performance Evaluation

To demonstrate the proposed service framework and service conflict resolution algorithm, we implement a prototype of software component to perform several experiments. For experiments, ten types of virtual objects are defined. Each type has three to five random qualities and each quality has one to ten discrete levels. Then, we randomly generate a hundred of virtual objects that have different levels of qualities. We assume a 2-dimension virtual space to deploy virtual objects to the space. Finally, we randomly generate scenarios and execute them on the space. Then, we add multiple users in the scenario. If users are increased, a lot of service conflicts could be occurred. For instance, if many users want to use specific virtual objects, they cannot be used to perform any service together at the same time. At this situation, if service manager finds alternate virtual objects or shares them based on the level of object sharing for many users, we can say that service conflict can be resolved.

We measure the number of service conflicts and the number of conflict resolutions for the location based model and the VPW model where service conflict resolution algorithm is performed based on the VPW. Figure 9 shows the experimental results. For the location-based systems, services can be provided by using service components within any restricted specific location. However, our system isn't restricted by any

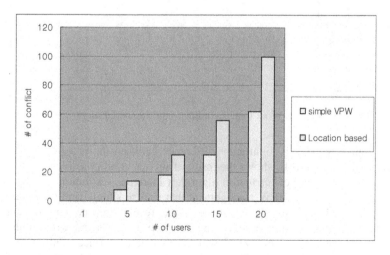

Fig. 9. Number of conflict according to the number of users

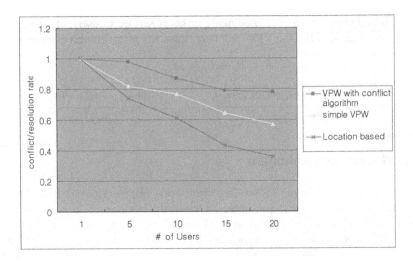

Fig. 10. Conflict/resolution rate according to the number of users

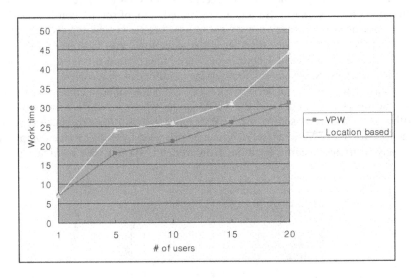

Fig. 11. Work time according to the number of users

physical boundary. This is significant difference between the proposed system and previous systems. Figure 10 shows the result of service conflict resolution. The result shows that service conflict resolution algorithm increases resolution rate by around 20% compared to simple VPW management that uses to simply find alternate virtual objects. Also, our system shows almost 40% resolution rate can be achieved comparing with the location based system. Figure11 shows the work time in the location based system and the VPW with its associated service conflict resolution algorithm. The result shows that 30% work time can be improved comparing with the location based system because if service conflicts are not occurred, service providing system can support many services at the same time. Therefore, the overall work time can be improved in the VPW system.

7 Conclusion

We propose a service framework that uses VPW and its associated service conflict resolution algorithm based on the VPW. Our system framework can support user-centric service by using the VPW and service conflict resolution algorithm based on the VPW. Using VPW, user can use more delicate service that is optimized and user isn't restricted any boundary or limitation. Also, using service conflict resolution algorithm can softly support multiple users. Experimental result shows that service conflict resolution algorithm increases resolution rate by around 20% compared to simple VPW management that uses to simply find alternate virtual objects. Also, our system shows almost 40% resolution rate can be achieved comparing with the location based system. Another experimental result shows that 30% work time can be improved comparing with the location based system because of decreasing the number of conflicts. Therefore, we can see that our frame work is suitable to provide ubiquitous services to many users.

References

1. M. Weiser.: The computer for the 21st Century, Scientific American. 265(3). 66-75.
2. Hua Liu, Manish Parashar, and Salim Hariri.: A component based programming framework for autonomic applications. Proceedings of international conference on Autonomic computing(ICAC'04)
3. Roman M, Hess C, Cerqueira R, Ranganathan A, Campbell R.H, Nahrstedt K.: A middleware infrastructure for active spaces. Pervasive Computing. IEEE,Volume 1 (2002) 74-83, Oct.-Dec.
4. Roy Want, Andy Hopper, Veronica Falcao, Jonathan Gibbons.: The Active Badge Location System. ACM Transactions on Information Systems. (1992) 91-102
5. A. K. Dey, D. Salber, G. D. Abowd.: A Conceptual Framework and a Toolkit for Supporting the Rapid Prototyping of Context-Aware Applications, Human Computing Interaction. Vol. 16. (2001) 97-166
6. B. N. Schilit, N. L. Adams, R. Want.: Context-aware computing applications. Proc. of Workshop on Mobile computing systems and applications, Santa Cruz, CA. (1994)
7. Kyung-Lang Park, Chang-Soon Kim, Shin-Dug Kim.: A Programmable Context Interface to Build a Context Infrastructure for Worldwide Smart applications. IFIP International conference on Embedded and Ubiquitous Computing, Nagasaki, Japan, LNCS 3824, (2005) 795-804
8. João Pedro Sousa, David Garlan.: Aura: an Architectural Framework for User Mobility in Ubiquitous Computing Environments. Proceedings of the 3rd Working IEEE/IFIP Conference on Software Architecture, (2002) 29-43
9. Anand Ranganathan, Shiva Chetan, Jalal Al-Muhtadi, Roy H. Campbell, M.Dennis Mickunas.: Olympus : A high level programming model for pervasive computing Environments, International Conference on Pervasive Computing and Communications (2005)

10. S.R. Ponnekanti, B. Lee, A. Fox, P. Hanrahan, T. Winograd.: ICrafter: A Service Framework for Ubiquitous Computing Environments, UbiComp 2001.(2001)
11. Giulio Mori, Fabio, Paterno, Carmen Santoro.: Design and Development of Multidevice User Interfaces through Multiple Logical Descriptions, IEEE Transactions on Software Enginering, Vol. 30, No. 8. (2004)
12. K. El-Khatib, Zhen E. Zhang, N. Hadibi, G. v. Bochmann.: Personal and Service Mobility in Ubiquitous Computing Environments, Wireless Communications and Mobile Computing 2004. (2004)595-607
13. Tatsuo Nakajima, Ichiro Satoh.: A software infrastructure for supporting spontaneous and personalized interaction in home computing environments, Personal and Ubiquitous Computing 2006.(2006)
14. Peifeng Xiang, YuanChun Shi,.: Resource Management based on Personal Service Aggregation in Smart Spaces, Proc. Of the 3rd workshop of Software Technologies for Future Embedded and Ubiquitous Systems. (2005)

Experimental Evaluation of Decision Criteria for WLAN Handover: Signal Strength and Frame Retransmission

Kazuya Tsukamoto[1,2], Takeshi Yamaguchi[1], Shigeru Kashihara[3], and Yuji Oie[1]

. Department of Computer Science and Electronics, Kyushu Institute of Technology
(KIT), Kawazu 680-4, Iizuka, Fukuoka, 820-8502 Japan
. Japan Society for the Promotion of Science (JSPS) Research Fellow (PD)
{kazuya, yamaguchi}@infonet.cse.kyutech.ac.jp, oie@cse.kyutech.ac.jp
. Graduate School of Information Science, Nara Institute of Science and Technology
(NAIST), Takayama 8916-5, Ikoma, Nara, 630-0192 Japan
shigeru@is.naist.jp

Abstract. In ubiquitous networks, Mobile Nodes (MNs) may often suffer from performance degradation due to the following two reasons: (1)
reduction of signal strength by an MN's movement and intervening objects, and (2) radio interference with other WLANs. Therefore, quick
and reliable detection of the deterioration of a wireless link condition is
essential for avoiding the degradation of the communication quality during handover. In our previous works, we focused on a handover decision
criterion allowing MNs to maintain communication quality and stated
the problems of existing decision criteria. Furthermore, we showed the
effectiveness of the number of frame retransmissions through simulation
experiments. However, a comparison between signal strength and the
number of frame retransmissions could not be examined due to the unreliability of signal strength in simulations. Therefore, in this paper, by
employing FTP and VoIP applications, we compare signal strength and
the number of frame retransmissions as a handover decision criterion
with experiments in terms of (1) and (2) in a real environment. Finally,
we show the problems of signal strength in contrast to the effectiveness
of the number of frame retransmissions as a handover decision criterion.

Keywords: Wireless LAN Handover, Handover Decision Criterion, Signal Strength, Frame retransmission, FTP, VoIP.

1 Introduction

WLANs based on IEEE 802.11 [1] have gained popularity due to their low cost,
ease of installation, and broadband connectivity. WLANs are being set up not
only in private spaces such as homes and workplaces, but also as hotspots in
public spaces such as waiting areas and hotel lobbies. Furthermore, WLANs
that are independently managed by different organizations are starting to com-
plementarily cover not only one spot but a wide area, such as a city, by using

H.Y. Youn, M. Kim, and H. Morikawa (Eds.): UCS 2006, LNCS 4239, pp. 239–253, 2006.
© Springer-Verlag Berlin Heidelberg 2006

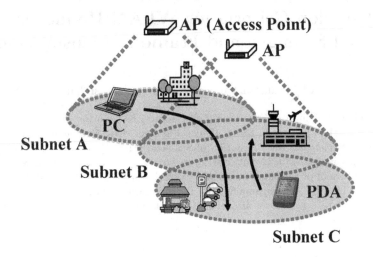

Fig. 1. Future ubiquitous mobile network based on WLANs

multiple access points (APs). Many of these deployments [2][3][4] have already been progressing around the world. In the near future, WLANs will continue to spread until they overlap to provide continuous coverage over a wide area, and then they will serve as the underlying basis of ubiquitous networks.

In a ubiquitous network, mobile nodes (MNs) are very likely to traverse different WLANs (i.e., perform a handover) divided into different IP subnets during communication because of the relatively small coverage of individual WLANs, as shown in Fig. 1. When an MN moves between different WLANs, the signal strength received from the connected AP is reduced drastically due to the distance and/or any intervening objects between the MN and the AP. Thus, the communication quality may be degraded due to the reduction of signal strength. Furthermore, in such a network, radio interference with other WLANs frequently occurs due to the wide spread of WLAN services. In this case, the communication quality may also be degraded, even when the MN does not move.

To provide transparent mobility for MNs in a ubiquitous network, it is necessary for the MNs to seamlessly execute handovers between different WLANs, which are independently managed by different organizations. In other words, quick and reliable detection of the deterioration of WLAN link quality and the execution of the handover to a better WLAN are essential for achieving seamless and efficient communication. As a result, the handover decision criterion can play an important role in executing handovers by reducing the degradation of the communication quality due to (1) reduction of signal strength, and (2) radio interference with other WLANs.

In our previous works [5][6], we showed that communication quality is significantly degraded before handover in many of the existing mobility management schemes (e.g., Mobile IP (MIP) [8]), when upper layer (higher than Layer 3) information such as packet loss and round-trip-time (RTT) is employed as the handover decision criterion. Furthermore, we also showed through simulation experiments that the degradation of the communication quality before handover could be avoided by exploiting the number of frame retransmissions obtained from MAC layer (Layer 2): thus, the number of frame retransmissions has the potential to serve as a handover decision criterion. However, although some recent studies have employed signal strength as a handover decision criterion, a qualitative evaluation of signal strength was not performed in our previous works [5][6], because it is difficult in simulation experiments to consider the fluctuation of signal strength due to various effects such as multi-path fading, radio interference, intervening objects, and movement. That is, an investigation of the effectiveness of signal strength through simulation is exceedingly hard due to the unreliability and complexity of radio transmission.

In this paper, by employing FTP and VoIP applications in a real environment, we examine the effectiveness of these two criteria, i.e., signal strength and the number of frame retransmissions, in terms of performance degradation due to (1) the reduction of signal strength and (2) radio interference. Finally, we show that the performance degradation due to both (1) and (2) can be effectively avoided by utilizing the number of frame retransmissions, whereas it cannot be inherently avoided by utilizing the signal strength.

2   Handover Decision Criteria of Existing Studies

In a ubiquitous network, the most critical issue of handover arises from the change in IP address. When an MN moves between WLANs managed by different companies or organizations (i.e., different IP subnets), the IP address of the MN changes. As a result, the communication is terminated or interrupted by the handover. Many mobility management schemes such as MIP [8], mobile Stream Control Transmission Protocol (mSCTP) [9], and others [10][11][12] have been proposed to solve this problem, and the MN employing these existing schemes can maintain the communication during handover between different WLANs regardless of the various types of applications, such as FTP and VoIP communications.

However, these existing mobility management schemes, which make the handover decision based on upper layer (Layer 3 or 4) information such as packet loss [8] and RTT, could cause drastic performance degradation of the MN before handover. In our previous work [5], to investigate the effectiveness of upper layer information (packet loss and RTT) as a handover decision criterion, we used simulation experiments to evaluate the TCP goodput performance around handover. As illustrated in Fig.2, an MN establishes a TCP connection for file transfer with a Corresponding Node (CN) via 802.11b WLAN, and moves away from an AP. Figure 3 shows that the TCP goodput performance significantly degrades before the packet loss ratio begins to increase. Furthermore, because the packet loss ratio changes dynamically due to various factors, such as congestion in a wired network and frequent and sudden transmission errors in a wireless network, the setting of an optimal threshold for a handover decision is quite

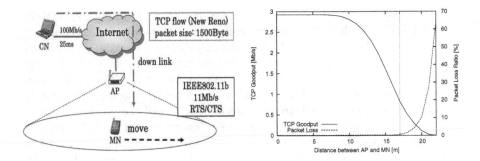

Fig. 2. Simulation model

Fig. 3. TCP goodput and packet loss ratio

Table 1. Received Signal Strength Indicator

Vendor	RSSI Range
Atheros	0-60
Cisco	0-100

difficult. Therefore, the degradation of WLAN link quality cannot be promptly and reliably detected by exploiting this information; that is, upper layer information should not serve as a handover decision criterion.

To solve the above issue, some new enhanced methods have been developed which base the handover decision on information obtained from a lower layer. In particular, the majority of these methods employ the signal strength obtained from Layer 1 as the handover decision criterion [13]. Received Signal Strength Indicator (RSSI), shown as an integer value from 0 to 255, is a common index of signal strength. The maximum RSSI value obtained from each WLAN card depends on the vendor, as shown in Table 1 [14]. The RSSI is also used as a handover decision criterion for the intra-domain handover called roaming [15]. However, RSSI fluctuates abruptly due to various and complicated events such as multi-path fading, intervening objects, and movement. Because of this fluctuation, setting the optimal threshold for RSSI as a handover decision is very difficult; therefore, it also should not serve as a handover decision criterion.

Our previous studies [5][6][7] focused on the number of frame retransmissions obtained from Layer 2 as a new handover decision criterion. We evaluated the TCP goodput performance and the behavior of the number of frame retransmissions through a simulation experiment (Fig. 2). As shown in Fig. 4, the frame retransmissions begin to occur at a distance around 8 m between the AP and the MN, and the TCP goodput also begins to decrease soon after the occurrence of the frame retransmissions. This result shows that the degradation of TCP goodput performance begins even when a frame retransmission occurs at least once. As a result, we showed that the number of frame retransmissions has the potential to serve as a handover decision criterion to effectively avoid TCP

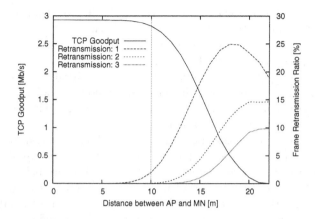

Fig. 4. TCP goodput and frame retransmission ratio

performance degradation. However, in [5][6], the comparison between the number of frame retransmissions and signal strength was not examined in detail because of the unreliability and complexity of signal strength, as described above; that is, the signal strength was not evaluated as a handover decision criterion.

Existing studies, including our previous works, focused only on the performance degradation due to the reduction of signal strength caused by movement and/or intervening objects. In a future ubiquitous network, many APs will be deployed to provide continuous coverage over a wide area. In such a network, performance degradation may also arise from radio interference with nearby APs. As a result, the handover decision criterion is required to detect the performance degradation due to (1) the reduction of signal strength and (2) radio interference with other APs. Therefore, in this paper we actually examine the effectiveness of signal strength and the number of frame retransmissions as a handover decision criterion in terms of (1) and (2) through extensive experiments in a real environment.

3   Wireless LAN

In this section, we briefly describe the mechanism of frame retransmission and the problems caused by radio interference, which may occur in a future ubiquitous mobile network.

3.1   Frame Retransmission Mechanism

Frame retransmission occurs for the following two reasons: (i) deterioration of signal strength and (ii) collision with other frames. In a WLAN, a sender can detect successful transmission by receiving an ACK frame in response to a transmitted data frame in the stop-and-wait manner. Therefore, when a data or an ACK frame is lost, the sender retransmits the same data frame until the number of frame retransmissions reaches a predetermined limit. Note that, with Request-to-Send (RTS)/Clear-To-Send (CTS), collisions between data frames, namely a hidden terminal problem, never occur due to the exchange of the RTS/CTS frames. If RTS/CTS is applied, the retransmission limit is set to 4 in the IEEE 802.11 specification [1]: A data frame can be retransmitted a maximum of four times (the initial transmission and three retransmissions), if necessary. Note that collisions may occur in an interference environment, which will be described in next section, even if RTS/CTS is applied.

If the sender does not receive an ACK frame within the retransmission limit, the data frame is treated as a lost packet. Considering the above discussion, we can see that data frames are inherently retransmitted before being treated as a lost packet. Therefore, the number of frame retransmissions can allow the MN to quickly perceive the deterioration of the condition of a wireless link, and may enable the MN to determine when the handover process should be started before packet loss actually occurs.

3.2   Radio Interference

In the near future, many different organizations will begin to provide WLAN services. Each WLAN occupies a single channel to provide communication between an AP and the MNs connected to the AP. In such a network, an overlap of channels among nearby APs may frequently occur. Therefore, preventing the performance degradation due to radio interference will be a critical issue for effective communication in future ubiquitous networks.

In the IEEE 802.11b specification [16], 13 channels are offered between 2400 MHz to 2483 MHz at 5 MHz intervals. However, because 802.11b uses the DSSS (Direct Sequence Spread Spectrum) modulation technique at the 2.4 GHz band, the frequency band spreads to 20MHz. Therefore, a "clear" channel (without any interference) should be at least 20 MHz (for five channels) away from neighboring channels. Otherwise, the frequency band overlaps with other channels, thereby causing packet losses due to the radio interference. In Japan, channel 14 (from 2471 MHz to 2497 MHz) is also available and is independent from channel 11, and thus, we have four clear channels at the maximum.

WLAN, based on the IEEE 802.11 specification, employs CSMA/CA (Carrier Sense Multiple Access with Collision Avoidance). CSMA/CA is responsible for the access control of a wireless channel. When MNs try to transmit data over the wireless channel, they first search the channel state, and then determine if a data frame can be transmitted. If the channel state is *idle*, that is, other MNs are not transmitting any frames over the wireless channel during some fixed interval, these MNs can transmit the data frame in the Collision Avoidance (CA) manner. On the other hand, if the channel state is *busy*, i.e., one of the MNs occupies the channel for data transmission, other MNs have to wait until the channel state turns to *idle*.

If the search of the wireless channel fails, collisions with other frames transmitted from other MNs may occur and the number of packet losses may increase drastically. In the WLAN specification, because an MN can search only within the same channel, collisions with other frames will also occur in the situation where nearby APs use close channels (within five channels). Thus, the number of collision frames due to radio interference increases, with the increase of the number of transmitted frames over both in use channel and close channels. As a result, the radio interference can affect communication performance. Therefore, MNs are essentially required to detect the performance degradation due to radio interference.

4 Experimental Evaluation

WLANs will begin to spread to outdoor environments, such as urban areas. Because a lot of intervening objects often exist in both indoor and outdoor environments, radio characteristics such as multi-path fading, noise, and radio interference are obviously more complex than that of an open space environment. Thus, reliable evaluation of the communication performance under an MN's movement, intervening objects, and radio interference is difficult through simulation experiments. Therefore, in this paper, we execute an experimental evaluation to take into account the multiple and complex radio characteristics in a real environment. More specifically, we focus on the communication performance in an indoor environment with a lot of intervening objects; in this environment, the radio characteristics are more notable than those of urban areas.

In experiments employing FTP and VoIP applications, we compare the following two criteria, i.e., signal strength and frame retransmission, in terms of (1) reduction of signal strength and (2) radio interference with other WLANs in a real environment. Through the experiments, we show the problems of signal strength as well as the effectiveness of the number of frame retransmissions as a handover decision criterion.

4.1 Effect of Reduction of Signal Strength

In this section, we examine how the signal strength and the number of frame retransmissions can promptly and reliably detect the performance degradation due to the reduction of signal strength by an MN's movement and intervening objects in the indoor environment. In this experiment, we investigate the behavior of signal strength and the number of frame retransmissions.

As illustrated in Fig. 5, an MN communicates with a Corresponding Node (CN) via WLAN (802.11b). The transmission rate of the WLAN is fixed to 11 Mb/s, and the RTS/CTS mechanism is employed. An Analyzer Node (AN) captures the frames transmitted on the WLAN by using Ethereal 0.10.13 [17]. "ORiNOCO AP-4000" of Proxim Co. [18] is used for the Access point (AP) and "ORiNOCO 802.11a/b/g Combo Card Gold" of Proxim Co. [18] is used for the WLAN card. Both the MN and the AN are equipped with this WLAN card for communication and frame capture. In this paper, by employing FTP (TCP) and VoIP (UDP) applications, we examine the characteristics of both

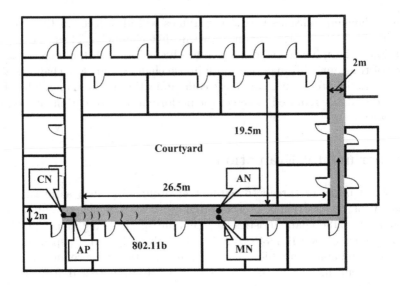

Fig. 5. Experimental environment (for reduction of signal strength)

signal strength and the number of frame retransmissions in detail by analyzing the captured frames. TCP goodput is used as the performance measure of the FTP application, and packet loss ratio is used as the performance measure of the VoIP application. In this experiment, because a WLAN card with an Atheros chipset is employed, the RSSI value, which is used as an index of the signal strength, varies from 0 to 60 [14], as shown in Table 1.

Case 1: Effect of distance from the AP
We examine how communication quality (TCP goodput performance for FTP and packet loss ratio for VoIP, the number of frame retransmissions, and the signal strength) changes with the increase of distance between the MN and the AP. Note that, in Case 1, we examine the stable and average communication performance at several distances; that is, the MN does not actually move through the environment. First, we focus on the FTP application and investigate the TCP communication performance when an MN downloads a 10 MByte file from the CN (an FTP server).

Figure 6 shows the change in the TCP goodput performance and the RSSI, and Fig. 7 shows how the TCP goodput performance and frame retransmission ratio change for 16 fixed points (2, 5, 10, 20, 27, 30, 35, 37, 39, 40, 41, 42, 43, 44, 45, 46 m). Note that "Retransmission: n" indicates the ratio of packets that experienced frame retransmissions "n" times to all the captured packets. In Fig. 6, the TCP goodput begins to decrease just after 27.5 m, where the MN turns a corner, i.e., the AP cannot view the MN directly. Beyond that, the TCP goodput performance drastically drops and then fluctuates abruptly beyond 40 m. On the other hand, the signal strength begins to decrease with the increase of the distance from the AP and also drastically drops beyond 27.5 m.

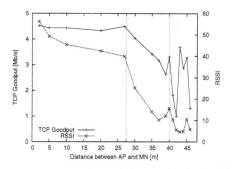
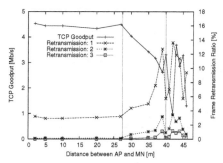

Fig. 6. TCP goodput and signal strength (FTP)

Fig. 7. TCP goodput and frame retransmission ratio (FTP)

However, it remains at a low value regardless of the drastic change of the TCP goodput beyond 40 m. From these results, we can see that quick detection of TCP goodput performance degradation is difficult when signal strength is used as the handover decision criterion.

In contrast, Fig. 7 shows that the frame retransmission ratio stays at a low level until 27.5 m. Beyond that, the frame retransmission ratio begins to increase with the decrease of the TCP goodput. In particular, "Retransmission: 2" and "Retransmission: 3" begin to increase in response to the decrease of TCP goodput performance, even though they stay nearly zero until 27.5 m. Then, after 40 m, the frame retransmission ratio just corresponds to the fluctuation of the TCP goodput. These results show that degradation of the TCP goodput performance begins when the frame retransmission ratio increases. That is, degradation of the TCP goodput performance due to the reduction of signal strength by an MN's movement and intervening objects can be detected by exploiting the number of frame retransmissions. Therefore, we suggest that the TCP goodput performance degradation before handover could effectively be avoided by utilizing the number of frame retransmissions.

Next, we focus on the VoIP application. The MN communicates with the CN using VoIP for 60 seconds. We employ Gphone 2.0 [19] as the VoIP application using G.711 codec, so that the consumed bandwidth for one direction is 80 kb/s.

Figure 8 shows the change in the packet loss ratio and RSSI, and Fig. 9 shows how the packet loss ratio and frame retransmission ratio change for 13 fixed points (2, 5, 10, 20, 27, 30, 32.5, 35, 37.5, 40, 42.5, 45, 46 m). From Fig. 8, we can see that the signal strength decreases continually, as indicated by the decrease of RSSI, even though packet loss rarely occurs until 40 m. Then, the packet loss ratio suddenly exceeds the upper bound loss rate of 3 % [6] that can maintain the VoIP communication quality at around 42.5 m and 46 m, thereby decreasing the VoIP communication quality. However, the signal strength still stays at a low value (8-10), even when the VoIP communication quality is degraded beyond 42.5 m. From this result, we can see that it is difficult to detect the occurrence of packet losses by exploiting signal strength.

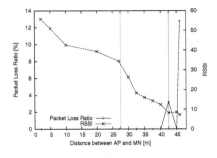 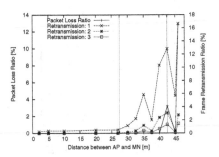

Fig. 8. Packet loss ratio and signal strength (VoIP)

Fig. 9. Packet loss ratio and frame retransmission ratio (VoIP)

In contrast, frame retransmission rarely occurs until 27.5 m. After that, the frame retransmission rate gradually increases in response to the degradation of the VoIP communication quality. In particular, "Retransmission: 2" and "Retransmission: 3" begin to increase around 38 m, soon before the VoIP communication performance actually degrades. That is, degradation of the VoIP communication performance due to the reduction of signal strength by an MN's movement and intervening objects can be promptly and reliably detected by exploiting the number of frame retransmissions. Therefore, we suggest that the degradation of the VoIP communication quality before the handover could effectively be avoided by exploiting the number of frame retransmissions.

Comparing Fig. 6 and Fig. 8, we can explain the characteristics of signal strength and the number of frame retransmissions for FTP and VoIP applications. The value of RSSI when the communication quality begins to degrade depends on the applications, i.e., FTP is 40 and VoIP is 10. Therefore, signal strength cannot detect the difference of the communication quality between applications. On the other hand, as shown in Fig. 7 and Fig. 9, the number of frame retransmissions begins to increase just before the degradation of communication quality occurs, irrespective of the FTP application and VoIP application. From these results, we can state that the number of frame retransmissions can detect the degradation of communication quality due to the reduction of signal strength. Therefore, the number of frame retransmissions satisfies the first requirement for a handover decision criterion.

Case 2: Effect of actual movement

In Case 1, we evaluated how the stable and average communication performance of the MN changes for the number of fixed points. In Case 2, we investigate the communication performance as the MN actually moves away from the AP at a walking speed (approximately 4 km/h). Figure10 shows the change in the TCP goodput, signal strength, and the number of frame retransmissions under FTP communication. Figure 11 shows the change in the packet loss ratio, signal strength, and the number of frame retransmissions under VoIP communication. Note that the horizontal axis quantity is travel time, and "Retransmission :n" indicates the occurrence time of a packet that experienced frame retransmissions "n" times.

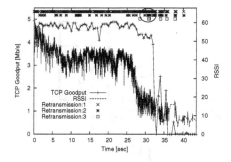

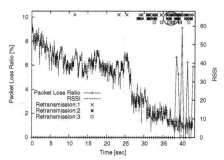

Fig. 10. FTP communication performance (actual movement)

Fig. 11. VoIP communication performance (actual movement)

From Fig. 10 and Fig. 11 and comparing these with the results of Case 1, we can see that RSSI fluctuates abruptly and drops drastically with the MN's movement. In Fig. 10, under FTP communication, the value of RSSI when the TCP goodput begins to decrease fluctuates approximately from 10 to 22. On the other hand, in Fig. 11, under VoIP communication, the value of RSSI ranges approximately from 4 to 8. That is, the value of RSSI when the communication quality begins to decrease differs depending on the application. As a result, setting a threshold is necessary for each application when signal strength is used as a handover decision criterion. In contrast, frame retransmissions frequently occur soon before the communication quality is degraded. Especially, "Retransmission: 3" occurs just before the communication quality actually decreases. From these results, the number of frame retransmissions can be used to detect the deterioration of the condition of communication quality, even if the MN actually moves. Through these experiments, we demonstrate that the number of frame retransmissions has the potential to serve as an optimal handover decision criterion for detecting the degradation of communication quality due to reduction of signal strength by an MN's movement and intervening objects, irrespective of the type of application.

4.2 Effect of Radio Interference

In this section, we examine how signal strength and the number of frame retransmissions can detect the performance degradation due to radio interference with other APs, as shown in Fig. 12. The distance between AP1 and AP2 is set to 25 m, and the distance between each AP and MN (AP1-MN1 and AP2-MN2) is set to 5 m in order to keep the communication quality and signal strength in good condition. Frame collisions due to radio interference frequently occur depending upon the number of frames transmitted over these wireless channels, as described in Sec. 3.2. Therefore, in this experiment, we focus on FTP communication, which commonly transmits a large number of frames. We investigate the communication performance when MN1 communicates with CN1 via AP1. In this case, the communication between MN2 and CN2 via AP2 causes the radio interference.

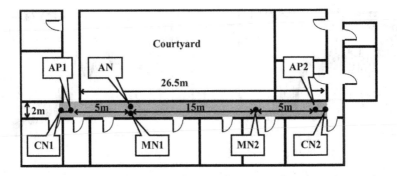

Fig. 12. Experimental environment (for radio interference)

The transmission rate of both of WLANs is fixed to 11 Mb/s (the *fall-back* function is off), and RTS/CTS is employed. We investigate how the communication performance of MN1 varies due to the effect of radio interference with AP2. The channel of AP1 is fixed at 14. On the contrary, the channel of AP2 varies from 11 to 14 in each experiment. Note that the strength of radio interference increases according to the closeness of the channels between AP1 and AP2. We examine how the radio interference caused by AP2 affects the communication performance of MN1, when MN1 downloads a 10 MByte file from CN via AP1. In other words, we investigate the TCP goodput performance, signal strength, and the number of frame retransmissions in the following two cases: (a) without data transmission (only Beacon messages) and (b) with data transmission. That is, in (a), MN2 does not send/receive any data frames, and in (b), MN2 downloads the file.

Figures 13-15 show the change in the TCP goodput, signal strength, and "Retransmission: 1". In case (a) in all three figures, we can see that TCP goodput, signal strength, and the frame retransmission ratio still remain approximately constant, because a frame collision rarely occurs due to no data transmission between MN2 and AP2; In such a case, collisions can still occur due to the beacon messages.

In Fig. 13, when the channel of AP2 is set to 11, the TCP goodput can be maintained even for case (b), which does have data transmission. This is because frame collisions due to radio interference do not occur between the channel of AP1 (14 ch) and the channel of AP2 (11 ch). On the other hand, the TCP goodput drastically drops as the channel of AP2 is set close to the channel of AP1 (14 ch). However, from Fig. 14, we can see that the signal strength does not decrease at all, even with the strong radio interference. As a result, we can state that signal strength cannot detect the degradation of TCP goodput due to radio interference, as mentioned in Sec. 3.2. In contrast, from Fig. 15, we can see that the number of frame retransmissions increases when the channel of AP2 approaches the channel of AP1. In particular, when the channel of AP1 and AP2 is the same (14 ch), the number of frame retransmissions drastically increases due to the failure of the CSMA/CA function.

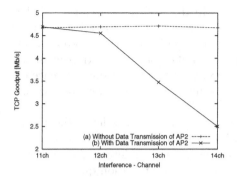

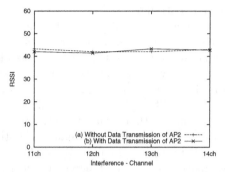

Fig. 13. TCP goodput performance   **Fig. 14.** Signal strength

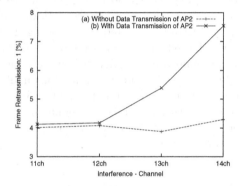

Fig. 15. Frame retransmission ratio

From these results, we demonstrate that signal strength absolutely cannot detect the performance degradation due to radio interference. On the other hand, we also demonstrate that the number of frame retransmissions can promptly and reliably detect the degradation due to radio interference with other APs. An MN employing the number of frame retransmissions as the handover decision criterion can promptly and reliably detect the radio interference and can execute handover to the AP without radio interference. Through these experiments, we can state that the number of frame retransmissions can be an optimal handover decision criterion allowing MNs to detect the degradation of communication quality due to radio interference.

5   Conclusion

In a future ubiquitous network environment, MNs are very likely to traverse different WLANs during communication. Thus, to avoid the degradation of communication quality during handover, a handover decision criterion is necessary for detecting the degradation of communication quality due to (1) reduction of signal strength and (2) radio interference. In this study, we investigated the communication quality, signal strength, and the number of frame retransmissions through experiments in a real environment and clarified the problems of signal strength and the effectiveness of the number of frame retransmissions as a handover decision criterion. Furthermore, we investigated the difference of the characteristics of signal strength and the number of frame retransmissions between FTP and VoIP communications.

We showed that signal strength cannot promptly and reliably detect the degradation of communication quality in both FTP and VoIP communications when signal strength is reduced by an MN's movement and/or intervening objects. Moreover, the value of signal strength when the communication quality begins to be degraded is different between FTP and VoIP communications. Therefore, the experimental results demonstrated that it is difficult to set the optimal threshold for handover using signal strength. In contrast, we showed that the degradation of communication quality of a wireless link due to an MN's movement and intervening objects can be detected by exploiting the number of frame retransmissions. Next, we showed that signal strength absolutely cannot detect the degradation of the communication quality due to radio interference. In contrast, we showed that this degradation of communication quality can be detected by exploiting the number of frame retransmissions. Therefore, we conclude that the number of frame retransmissions, unlike the signal strength, can promptly and reliably detect the performance degradation due to (1) reduction of signal strength and (2) radio interference.

Acknowledgment

This work was supported in part by the Japan Society for the Promotion of Science, Grant-in-Aid for Scientific Research (S)(18100001) and JSPS Fellows (17-6551), in part by a grant from the Cisco University Research Program Fund at Community Foundation Silicon Valley, and in part by the Ministry of Public Management, Home Affairs, Posts and Telecommunications, Japan.

References

1. IEEE 802.11, 1999 Edition, Available at http://standards.ieee.org/getieee802/download/802.11-1999.pdf
2. Wireless Philadelphia, http://www.phila.gov/wireless/
3. Wireless London, http://wirelesslondon.info/HomePage
4. WIFLY (Taipei), http://www.wifly.com.tw
5. K. Tsukamoto, R. Ijima, S. Kashihara, and Y. Oie., "Impact of Layer 2 Behavior on TCP Performance in WLAN," *Proc. of IEEE VTC2005-fall*, CD-ROM, Sep. 2005.
6. S. Kashihara and Y. Oie, "Handover Management based upon the Number of Retries for VoIP in WLANs," *Proc. of IEEE VTC2005-spring*, CD-ROM, May 2005.

7. S. Kashihara, K. Tsukamoto, Y. Kadobayashi, Y. Oie, "A simple heuristic for handover decisions in WLANs," Internet Engineering Task Force, Internet Draft, draft-shigeru-simple-heuristic-wlan-handover-00.txt, March 2006.

8. C. Perkins (Ed.), "IP Mobility Support for IPv4," IETF *RFC3344*, Aug. 2002.

9. S. J. Koh, et al, "Mobile SCTP for Transport Layer Mobility," *draft-reigel-sjkoh-sctp-mobility-04.txt*, Internet draft, IETF, Jun. 2004.

10. S. Kashihara, K. Iida, H. Koga, and S. Yamaguchi, "Multi-path Transmission Algorithm for End-to-End Seamless Handover across Heterogeneous Wireless Access Networks," *IEICE Trans. on Commu.*, Vol. E87-B, No. 3, pp.490-496, Mar. 2004.

11. S. Kashihara, T. Nishiyama, K. Iida, H. Koga, Y. Kadobayashi, and S. Yamaguchi, "Adaptive Selection among Heterogeneous Wireless Access Networks for End-to-end Handover," *Proc. of IEEE/IPSJ The 2004 International Symposium on Applications and the Internet (SAINT2004)*, pp. 273-276, Jan. 2004.

12. K. Tsukamoto, Y. Hori, and Y. Oie, "Mobility Management of Transport Protocol Supporting Multiple Connections," *Proc of ACM MobiWac2004*, pp. 83-87, Oct. 2004.

13. M. Chang, et al., "Transport Layer Mobility Support Utilizing Link Signal Strength Information," *IEICE Trans. on Commu.*, Vol. E87-B, No. 9, pp. 2548-2556, Sep. 2004.

14. Kavitha Muthukrishnan, et al., "WLAN location sharing through a privacy observant architecture," *COMSWARE2006*, Jan. 2006.

15. Pejman Khadivi, et al., "Handoff Trigger Nodes for Hybrid IEEE 802.11 WLAN/Cellular Networks," 2004.

16. IEEE 802.11b, 1999 Edition, Available at http://standards.ieee.org/getieee802/download/802.11b-1999.pdf

17. Ethereal, http://www.ethereal.com/

18. Proxim, http://www.proxim.com/

19. VL Inc, http://www.vliusa.com/

Buffer Feedback Scheduling: Runtime Adaptation of Ubicomp Applications

Christian Decker[1], Michael Beigl[2], Till Riedel[1],
Albert Krohn[1], and Tobias Zimmer[1]

Telecooperation Office (TecO), University of Karlsruhe
Distributed and Ubiquitous Computing (DUS), University of Braunschweig
{cdecker, riedel, krohn, zimmer}@teco.edu, beigl@ibr.cs.tu-bs.de

Abstract. In this paper we propose an operating system design for Ubicomp applications that are implemented on embedded sensor platforms. The OS provides support for both periodic sensor sampling and sequential appliation logic. Core component is a lightweight real-time runtime system guaranteeing predictable real-time behavior of periodic sampling processes. The design utilizes a novel method, called buffer feedback scheduling (BFS), to adapt the system under unpredictable workload. Processes are automatically coordinated and expensive hardware accesses are reduced when the feedback indicates that the results do not contribute to the application. Real-time behavior is guaranteed throughout the entire runtime. Theoretical analysis and implementation in a Ubicomp application study on the Particle Computer sensor platform demonstrate a significant performance step-up when utilizing BFS.

1   Introduction

Within Ubicomp, small, battery powered embedded sensor devices are a state-of-the art technology for detecting activity and situation information on an object or in the environment. Adding embedded sensor devices to things converts "dumb" and passive objects to smart and reactive subjects. A first example of such an object was the Mediacup[1], a coffee cup with embedded tiny sensor electronics. The cup was able to recognize conditions within the cup - e.g. if cup is full, coffee is cold etc. - and to react accordingly - e.g. reporting to the coffee machine the coffee consumption status. In general, embedded sensor systems are able to process raw sensor information to high-level situation information directly on the object and to trigger reactions. Software performing such processes must be able to handle

- periodic sampling of sensor information - e.g. the amount of liquid in a cup,
- processing of sensor information - e.g. to conclude on liquid status,
- reaction on events - e.g. to trigger further actions like start a new brew.

The quality of typical applications on embedded sensor systems is highly dependent on the correct recognition of situations. It requires the correct periodic execution of the sensor sampling since those samples provide the information

H.Y. Youn, M. Kim, and H. Morikawa (Eds.): UCS 2006, LNCS 4239, pp. 254–269, 2006.
© Springer-Verlag Berlin Heidelberg 2006

basis for the recognition. Fragmented sets of sensor information would otherwise require an additional resource intensive pre-processing for the applications. An OS supporting applications on embedded sensor devices must therefore be able to handle two general sets: Periodic processes and data-driven processes. This paper will introduce an OS concept that enables optimized coordination between the two process sets through feedback scheduling. It will contribute to the quality of the data processing and recognition algorithms and therefore provides an optimal basis for Ubicomp applications on embedded sensor devices.

The paper is organized as follows: In section 2, we analyze the behavior of Ubicomp applications on embedded sensor systems. Therefrom, we derive our system design in section 3. Section 4 and 5 introduce the formalization and theoretical model of feedback scheduling. The paper demonstrates the new system design in an implementation in section 6 and a case study in section 7 of the Remembrance Camera - a multi-sensor application for an embedded sensor platform. It follows a view on related work before the paper concludes in section 9.

2   Ubicomp Application Analysis

This section will briefly analyze typical Ubicomp applications based on experiences collected with several Ubicomp applications. It allows us to derive requirements for an OS approach supporting such applications. We found that applications like MediaCup, DigiClip[2], eSeal[3] and AwareOffice[4] incorporate continuous sensor perception of environmental conditions and activities - e.g. movements patterns - with data processing for context and in-situ recognition. Only periodically acquired sensor data and their processing enable accurate, detailed reaction in a timely fashion, especially in very mobile settings where an overarching processing back-end is not permanently available. For such applications, we conclude on the following common characteristics:

- the complete application runs on an embedded sensor device
- inputs are obtained from multiple, periodically sampled sensors
- data-driven processing implements context recognition and reaction

While periodic sensor samplings are under control of the developer, data-driven processing depends on acquired sensor input. An example is a rule-based expert system: The number of cycles to evaluate the rule base and each single rule's evaluation runtime depends on the facts coming in. The overall runtime behavior is not known at the design time and sensor samplings from unpredictable environmental conditions consequently cause a highly dynamic data processing behavior. An appropriate OS concept for Ubicomp applications has to separately support the different natures of periodic and data-driven processes. Runtime management of both is a primary design goal. Therefore, we derive the following requirements: Firstly, periodic sensor sampling is required to be guaranteed without any interference. This is usually referred to as a non-preemptive real-time scheduling. Interference or interruption while accessing hardware might have fatal consequences, e.g. deadlocks, distorted sampling, and assertion violations. Secondly, since data processing is highly varying, coordination between periodic and data processing parts needs runtime support. Thirdly, the application's runtime behavior needs to be adapted to the current data-dependent computation effort through feedback into the scheduling process.

3   System Design

Based on the application analysis, we decompose a Ubicomp application in a periodic part - responsible for the access to the sensor hardware - and an application logic part. This separates the two concerns: periodic sensor data acquisition and data processing. At the lower layer of our system design (figure 3) services acquire

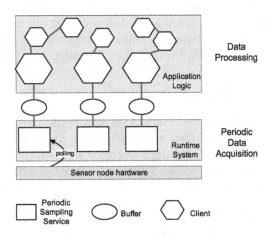

Fig. 1. System design of a Ubicomp application on a wireless sensor node

the sensor data. Services are executed periodically and encapsulate the access to the sensor hardware. Services are non-preemptive, i.e. once started a service runs to completion. A service cannot be called by another service or any other part of the application logic. Hence, a runtime system is responsible to drive services. Independent from application logic, the runtime system is required to strictly guarantee that services are executed according to a given period. This imposes real-time constraints on the services. The higher layer of the design comprises data-driven client functions that process input data from periodic services. A client is bound to one service via an intermediate buffer. Clients may form complex applications structures by calling other client functions that are not bound to a service. Clients are non-periodic, but run due to the availability of data. The buffers between the two layers decouple periodic processes from the data-driven application logic. Consequently, buffers form a data-based platform abstraction for the application.

Our system design yields the following advantages: The system clearly separates periodic processes from data driven processes. Independent, periodic real-time services guarantee a steady data acquisition process of the environment.

Data-driven application processes can be seamlessly combined through buffers forming a data-based abstraction. Finally, the design eases the application development since periodic tasks can be delegated to services and let the developer focus on the actual application logic.

4   Formalizing the System

The runtime system should guarantee periodic execution of all services. As a consequence, real-time scheduling is applied. In this section will introduce terminology and formal background. Services are equivalent to non-preemptive real-time tasks. We use the term service, because we want to emphasize their role as mediators between the hardware platform and the application.

A periodic service s_i is described by tuple (C_i, T_i) (C_i: computation time, T_i: period). C_i is assumed to be the service's worst-case execution time (WCET) and known in advance. $D_i = T_i$ is the deadline of each service, i.e. a service has to run to completion before its next period begins. Services should not be preempted by other services. A service execution begins at a first arrival time $a_{i,0}$ and is repeated every period at $a_{i,n} = nT_i$. If no arrival time is given, the set of services S_p is said to be non-concrete. From every non-concrete set any concrete one, where services are associated with arrival times, can be generated.

Client functions f_j consume the data produced by the services. They poll the buffers and continue their execution due to the availability of data. Decoupling through buffers makes the clients independent from periodic services and allows preemption by services. The clients' computation time is unknown. Their minimum period is $T^f = \sum_j C_j^f$, where C_j^f is the jth client's unknown computation time.

Problem Formulation. From the highly dynamic computation times of clients two problem cases arise. The first case is data dropping. This situation appears in an overload situation where the clients' computation times become larger. As a consequence, a client cannot serve its buffer until the next service execution begins. The previously sampled data from the associated service is then not processed and consequently dropped. In figure 2 service s_i produces data for long running client f_j. The client is interrupted and finally misses to process its buffer content. The problem is avoided if the condition $\forall i, j : \sum_j C_j^f < T^f \leq T_i$ holds. Otherwise, the service with the minimum period will recur before its buffer content could be processed. The second problem case is client idling (figure 3). When clients' computation times decrease, they access the buffers several times until new values are provided by services. The idle case can be avoided for any client by fulfilling the following condition: $\forall i, j : T^f \geq T_i > \sum_j C_j^f$. Consequently we state the following problem:

Problem 1. In unpredictable environments, where computation time C_j^f is unknown and highly dynamic, find periods T_i of the real-time services, that following conditions hold:

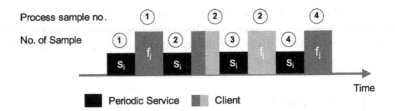

Fig. 2. Data drop: Sampling no.3 is not processed due to large computation time of f_j

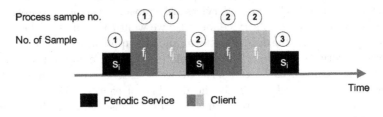

Fig. 3. Client idling: f_j processes samplings no.1&2 repetitively until a new value arrives

1. $\forall i, j : \min_i \{T_i\} = T^f > \sum_j C_j^f$ (period adaptation)
2. $\forall i : s_i$ finishes at latest at its deadline $D_i = T_i$ (preserve real-time)

The varying computation times of the clients require an adaptation of the services' periods. Our approach is to *expand* and *compress* a service period according to the change of the client computation time. An additional component - a controller - performs this adaptation during the system's runtime.

5   Buffer Feedback Scheduling

Data drop and client idling can be efficiently measured at the buffers between the periodic services and the clients. Each buffer is annotated by a single bit, which flips between 1 and 0 when the service and the client alternately access it. The bit remains in its current state, if a service or a client repeatively access the buffers in a non-alternating sequence. In this case, a counter is incremented for data drops and idling periods respectively. The counter values are fed back in the runtime system where a controller adapts the services' periods for the scheduler. Therefore, we call this adaptation method buffer feedback scheduling (BFS). The goal of BFS is to keep both counters at 0. The figure 4 depicts the basic principle of the BFS. The problem statement from section 4 requires, that the period adaptation preserves the real-time capability of the system. As a consequence, we firstly analyze the scheduling behavior under adaptation. Secondly, for the feedback adaptation itself, we have to close the loop between the actual buffer performance and the service period and synthesize an appropriate controller for implementing the period adaptation.

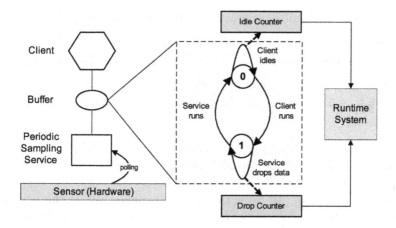

Fig. 4. Buffer drives 1-bit automaton. Feedback on idling and drops via counters.

5.1 Scheduling Analysis

Scheduling of real-time tasks is a well-investigated research topic. This section will extend this research by our approach of adapting service periods. We show, that this does not alter any statements about schedulability and the schedule. Consequently, period adaptation does not impose any scheduling overhead and is therefore well-suited for resource-constrained sensor node platforms.

The authors in [5] proved two conditions that are sufficient and necessary for scheduling a set of non-concrete, non-preemptable periodic tasks. Our considerations in section 4 show that this can be directly applied to our service approach. We will formulate all results using the term services instead of tasks. With the prerequisite that the set of periodic services $S_p = \{(C_1, T_1), (C_2, T_2), ..., (C_n, T_n)\}$ is sorted in non-decreasing order, i.e. $T_i \geq T_j$ if $i > j$, conditions from [5] are

(1) $\sum_i \frac{C_i}{T_i} \leq 1$

(2) $\forall i, 1 < i \leq n; \forall L, T_1 < L < T_i : L \geq C_i + \sum_{j=1}^{i-1} \left\lfloor \frac{L-1}{T_j} \right\rfloor C_j$

The condition (1) requires that the processor is not overloaded. The inequality in the condition (2) provides a least upper bound for processor demand, which can be realized in the interval L. As a consequence, we state the following corollary.

Corollary 1. *If the set of periodic services* $S_p = \{(C_1, T_1), ..., (C_n, T_n)\}$ *is schedulable according to condition (1) and (2), then the new set* $S_p^* = \{(C_1, T_1 + k), ..., (C_n, T_n + k)\}$, *where each period is increased by a constant time k, is schedulable according to condition (1) and (2).*

To prove the corollary, we first prove the following lemma.

Lemma 1. *If* $g(k), h(k)$ *are two linear functions with* $\frac{\partial g}{\partial k} = \frac{\partial h}{\partial k}$ *and* $\forall k, k > 0$, *then* $\frac{g(k)}{h(k)}$ *is monotonic.*

Proof. We prove this lemma constructively utilizing derivation $\frac{\partial}{\partial k}\frac{g(k)}{h(k)}$. Let $g(k)=$ $k+x$ and $h(k)=k+y$, then $\frac{\partial}{\partial k}\frac{g(k)}{h(k)} = \frac{y-x}{(x+k)^2}$. For $x,y > 0$ and $x < y$, $\frac{\partial}{\partial k}\frac{g(k)}{h(k)} > 0$ and therefore $\frac{g(k)}{h(k)}$ is monotonically increasing. For $x,y > 0$ and $x > y$, $\frac{\partial}{\partial k}\frac{g(k)}{h(k)} < 0$ and therefore $\frac{g(k)}{h(k)}$ is monotonically decreasing. For $x,y > 0$ and $x = y$, $\frac{\partial}{\partial k}\frac{g(k)}{h(k)} = 0$ and therefore $\frac{g(k)}{h(k)}$ is simultanously monotonically increasing and decreasing.

Proof. First, we prove condition (1) of corollary 1:
From $T_i + k > T_i$ it follows directly that $\frac{C_i}{T_i} > \frac{C_i}{T_i+k} \forall k, k > 0$. As a result $\sum_i \frac{C_i}{T_i+k} < \sum_i \frac{C_i}{T_i} \leq 1$.
We now prove condition (2): Note, that k is also applied to L in this condition, so that the constraint changes to $\forall L, T_1 + k < L + k < T_i + k$. It is enough to focus on the expression $\left\lfloor \frac{L-1}{T_j} \right\rfloor$ for the following cases:

Case 1:$(L-1 < T_j)$ Increasing the periods T_j by a constant k leads to following: $\forall k, k > 0 : \lim_{k \to \infty} \frac{L-1+k}{T_j+k} = 1^-$, i.e. for all k with $k > 0$, the expression $\frac{L-1+k}{T_j+k}$ converges to 1 from the left side. With lemma 1, it converges monotonically increasing. As a result, $\left\lfloor \frac{L-1+k}{T_j+k} \right\rfloor = 0$ for all $k > 0$.

Case 2:$(L-1 > T_j)$ Increasing the periods T_j by a constant k leads to following: $\forall k, k > 0 : \lim_{k \to \infty} \frac{L-1+k}{T_j+k} = 1^+$, i.e. for all k with $k > 0$, the expression $\frac{L-1+k}{T_j+k}$ converges to 1 from the right side. With lemma 1, it converges monotonically decreasing. As a result, $\left\lfloor \frac{L-1+k}{T_j+k} \right\rfloor < \left\lfloor \frac{L-1}{T_j} \right\rfloor$ for all $k > 0$.

Case 3:$(L-1 = T_j)$ Increasing the periods T_j by a constant k leads to $\left\lfloor \frac{L-1+k}{T_j+k} \right\rfloor = \left\lfloor \frac{L-1}{T_j} \right\rfloor$ for all $k > 0$.

As a result we find (properties on S_p, i, L as stated in condition (2)): $L \geq C_i + \sum_{j=1}^{i-1} \left\lfloor \frac{L-1}{T_j} \right\rfloor C_j \geq C_i + \sum_{j=1}^{i-1} \left\lfloor \frac{L-1+k}{T_j+k} \right\rfloor C_j, \forall k, k > 0$ meaning S_p^* is schedulable.

In the last step we have to prove that the schedule will not change after the transition from $S_p \to S_p^*$. According to Jeffay et al. in [5], the non-preemptive earliest deadline first (EDF) scheduling algorithm will schedule any concrete set generated from an unconcrete one. We apply this to the set S_p^* and state the following corollary:

Corollary 2. *If the unconcrete sets of periodic services S_p and S_p^* are schedulable according to condition (1) and (2) and the EDF algorithm has created a schedule $sched_{S_p}$ out of a concrete set generated from the unconcrete S_p one, then the same schedule is also valid for S_p^*, i.e. $sched_{S_p^*} = sched_{S_p}$.*

Proof. At the end of a service execution the global time is $t = a_{i,n-1} + C_i$. EDF selects then a service s_j with the closest deadline, i.e. s_j must fulfill the following condition: $\forall j, n : t < \min_{j,n} \{a_{j,n} + T_j\}$. Remember that we set $D_i = T_i$. The absolute deadline of the nth instance of s_j is $D'_{j,n} = a_{j,n} + T_j$ and therefore the EDF condition becomes to $t < \min_{j,n} \{D'_{j,n}\}$. In S^*_p, the absolute deadline of s^*_j is $D^{*'}_{j,n} = a_{j,n} + T_j + k$. Therefore, $t < \min_{j,n} \{D^{*'}_{j,n}\} = \min_{j,n} \{a_{j,n} + T_j + k\} = \min_{j,n} \{a_{j,n} + T_j\} + k$. Since $k = const.$, EDF selects the same service as it would do for S_p and we obtain $sched_{S^*_p} = sched_{S_p}$.

To conclude, we have proven that a period adaptation preserves the real-time behavior of the system. It guarantees that condition (2) of the problem formulation holds. It even does not impose any overhead because corollary 2 proves that adaptation will not alter the schedule. This is the fundament for controller synthesis in the following section.

5.2   Controller Synthesis

The controller is responsible for the services' periods adaptation. The adaptation is required to hold $\min_i \{T_i\} = T^f$ from condition (1) of the problem formulation. Figure 5 shows the placement of the controller within the runtime system. The

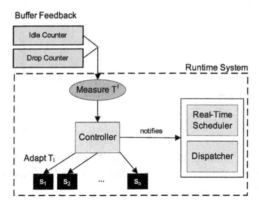

Fig. 5. Feedback controller within the runtime system

controller is triggered by non-zero drop and idle counters from the buffers. It then starts to measure the actual client period T^f and adapts the services' periods according to condition (1). Afterwards, it notifies the dispatcher for computing the new arrival times of the services before the real-time scheduler enqueues them for the next execution. In detail, the controller will compute the new period T'_i as follows:

$$T'_i = T_i + k \text{ with } k = T^f - \min_i \{T_i\} \text{ (expansion, drop counter > 0)} \quad (1)$$

$$T'_i = \max\{T_{min}, T_i - k\} \text{ with } k = \min_i \{T_i\} - T^f \text{ (compr., idle counter > 0)} \quad (2)$$

The constant T_{min} marks the lower bound of the period for that the scheduling analysis guarantees that all services will hold their deadlines. In case of compression, the periods should never set below this bound.

5.3   Controlled Buffer Feedback Scheduling

In this section we will compare the controlled BFS system with the non-controlled system under variable client workloads. The results were achieved through simulations using the Ptolemy II framework[1]. We vary the clients' computation times by applying step loads - a sudden change of the computation time. The behavior is investigated for both step-up and step-down loads in both the controlled and non-controlled case. Results are compared using the following definition of the accumulated data drop ratio: $DropRatio(t) = \frac{\sum_t dropCounter(t)}{\sum_t serviceExecutions(t)}$. We define the cumulative idle ratio as the time spent for idling in relation to the runtime of the system: $IdleRatio(t) = \frac{\sum_t idleCounter(t) \cdot clientTime(t)}{t}$. In both figures 6 and 7 the

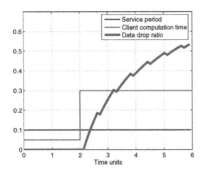
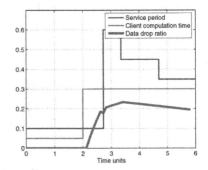

Fig. 6. Non-controlled step-up behavior. Service period remains constant and the drop ratio increases.

Fig. 7. BFS-controlled step-up behavior. Service period is expanded and the data drop decreases.

step load occurs at time 2 and changes from 0.05 to 0.3. The services' periods are initially set to 0.1. The system was previously analyzed according to the conditions in section 5.1 in order to ensure that services will hold their deadlines. When the step occurs, the drop ratio increases shortly afterwards. In the non-controlled case, the service period remains at 0.1, data drop occurs causing an increasing drop ratio. In this example, the services run 6 times until one date is processed by the clients. As a result, the drop ratio will asymptotically approach 0.83. On the other side, the controlled BFS system adapts to the new situation and expands the services period. It reaches the final period of 0.35 at 4.7 time units. The reaction to the step is delayed because the measurement of T^f firstly starts after the first data drop is detected. Since the step occurs at an arbitrary point in time, the T^f-measurement is biased due to the overlap of the original

---

* http://ptolemy.berkeley.edu/ptolemyII/

and the increased clients' computation times. This causes the overshot. Maximum drop ratio in this example is 0.24 and is reached at time 3.4 and decreased afterwards. For comparison: At the same time the non-controlled system had a drop ratio of 0.31. Although, there is no data drop anymore, the drop ratio is still positive, but approaching 0. This is due to the drop ratio definition because it represents the accumulated drop ratio throughout the entire runtime. The

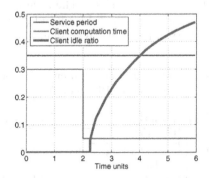 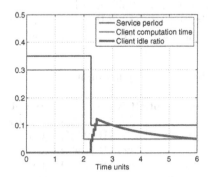

Fig. 8. Non-controlled step-down behavior. Service period remains constant and idle ratio increases.

Fig. 9. BFS-controlled step-down behavior. Service period is compressed and idle ratio decreases.

figures 8 and 9 depict the client idling in the non-controlled and controlled case. The step-down from 0.3 to 0.05 is applied at time 2. In the non-controlled case, the idle ratio increases shortly after the step and remains increasing. According to the chosen parameters, the system executes 6 times the clients before a new value is produced by the services. In this example, the idle ratio will asymptotically reach 0.71. In the controlled BFS system idling is handled by compression of services' periods. There is no undershot of the period because services should keep a minimum period of 0.1 to be still real-time schedulable (see equation (2)). Although the BFS controller denotes idling very early, reaction is delayed because the services were already scheduled and had to wait until their next period. Meanwhile, the idle ratio grows up to 0.12. The system has then adapted and the idle ratio decreases. However, it is still positive because it represents the cumulative idling ratio.

6   Implementation

We implemented the real-time runtime system and the BFS controller on the Particle Sensor platform [6]. The implementation was carried out using the Small Devices C Compiler (SDCC) for the PIC18 platform. Services contain parameters like their period, arrival time, states (ready, waiting), pointers to their output buffers and service functions. Latter actually implement the service functionality. The runtime system manages all services in two queues for waiting and ready services. A service is waiting, if it has not yet reached its arrival time. Once it has reached it, the scheduler enqueues it in the ready queue according to the EDF policy. The dispatcher brings a service to its execution by calling the service function of the first service in the ready queue. When no service is ready, the control is given to the clients for data processing. The buffers manage the access automaton and provide feedback for the BFS controller which is triggered as soon as dropping or idling is detected. Dispatcher, scheduler and BFS controller all work on a 32bit time format of the Particle's real-time clock. The accuracy is limited by the 32kHz clock to about 31 microseconds. The tables 1 and 2 list the memory footprint and the computation effort of the runtime system.

Table 1. Memory footprint of the runtime system

Component	ROM	RAM
Scheduler	5.556 kB (4.2%)	0.161 kB (4,0%)
Dispatcher	3.600 kB (2.7%)	0.052 kB (1.3%)
Queue	2.498 kB (1.9%)	0.022 kB (0.6%)
Controller	1.870 kB (1.4%)	0.021 kB (0.5%)
Byte-Buffer		34 bit
Service		104 bit
Sum	13.524 kB (10,5%)	0,256 kB (6.4%) excl. services and buffers

Table 2. Computation effort in cycles on the PIC18f6720

Function	Cycles
Dispatcher	
insert_waiting, 5 services	1250
getTime	670
timeGreater	140
Scheduler	
schedule_EDF, 4 services	1903
compareDeadlines	421
BFS Controller	
Compression, 5 Services	7371
Expansion, 5 Services	6481

7   Case Study: Remembrance Camera

The Remembrance Camera can be considered as a typical example for an embedded sensor system in Ubicomp. The Remembrance Camera is a camera-based device that is worn by a person throughout the day as a personal wearable device and automatically takes pictures of interesting events experienced from that person. The camera consists of two components: An embedded sensor board for recognition of activities and for data processing and a miniature digital camera to record pictures under control of the sensor board. We used the Particle Computer platform as a typical candidate of an embedded sensor system with ultra-low power consumption for continuous monitoring of activities through sensors. Low power design was required because of usability since the camera should be of a very small outline and able to operate throughout the day without battery recharging. The sensor hardware is attached to a small digital camera, the Apitek PenCam, and can be worn in a shirt's pocket or on a necklet (total size about 4.5x4x15 cm, see figure 10). The aim of the Remembrance Camera system is to enable a person to recall all important events of a day using taken pictures. Rather than having a continuous recording of all pictures of events - which would require a user to scan through a lot of pictures - we liked to

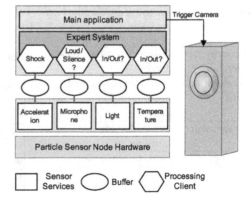

Fig. 10. Remembrance Camera (with Particle sensor node)

Fig. 11. Remembrance Camera recognition architecture

present only the most important pictures of the day to the user based on a recognition of important events of a day. This recognition was performed stand-alone by the camera device using sensors and activity recognition methods. At synchronization points pictures and recognition information could be uploaded and viewed on a PC. Events are detected through sensor recognition methods using embedded sensor hardware, sensor detection firmware and higher-level activity recognition and fusion methods (see figure 11). Acceleration, light, microphone and temperature sensors are used as inputs. These sensors are connected to *sensor services* performing the periodic sampling of sensor data. Sensors are used as input to the data *processing clients* performing the recognition algorithms. The recognition in each of the clients uses a rule-based expert system[7]. It operates on a ring-buffer of time-stamped sensor data acquired by sensor services and performs various operations under varying computation times depending on sensor input. As a consequence, the periods of clients are different due to variations of the sensor data. Output of the clients, listed in table 3, is finally used by the main application for recognizing the person's situation (table 4). The Remembrance Camera main application uses a change in the situation to detect an important event, which then triggers the camera to take a picture. The complete system is written in C and embedded on the Particle sensor node (CPU:PIC18F6720@20MHz, 4kRAM, 128kFlash).

Scheduling performance using the BFS controller. The Remembrance Camera application is sensitive to continuous and regular sensor detection. Missing information or large delays within the recognition affects the application and may lead to misinterpretation of the situation. Handling such exceptions requires more time and memory intensive algorithms that would have exceeded the platform's performance. Therefore, it is important for the quality, that the recognition runs on a frequent basis and that (almost) no samplings are dropped. This is achieved by the BFS controller. In figure 12 we have included a scheduling trace for the detection of a situation change from *working* to *work interruption*.

Table 3. Sensors on the Particle platform and extracted information

Sensor service	Client output (Activity)
acceleration	shock, calm/excited
light	inside/outside a building
temperature	inside/outside a building
microphone	loud, talking, silence

Table 4. Situations and activities used by the main application for taking a picture

Situation	Inputs Activities
working	{calm, inside, silence}
meeting	{inside, talking}
running	{shock, outside}
standing (outside)	{outside, calm}
work pauses	{shock, inside}
work interruptions	{excited, inside, talking or loud}

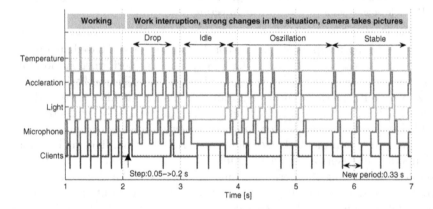

Fig. 12. Scheduling trace of BFS controlled services when situation changes from *working* to *work interruption*

The situation recognition is handled by the processing clients while the sensor input is provided by the sensor services. All services run every 0.18 seconds (s) - the initial service period. The new situation *work interruption* arising at time 2s leads to a higher effort for recognition. For this reason, the clients' computation time increases from 0.05s to 0.2s and therewith the clients' period. As a result, services run faster than data processing, data drop occurs and the system starts to adapt the period of the services. After 3.7s the BFS controller stabilizes the new period at 0.33s. Figure 13 depicts the progression of the period adaptation in more detail. When the clients' period change, the services' period follows until both reach their final period of 0.33s. During the adaptation the periods overshoot the correct ones. This is compensated by the reverse reaction. As a result, the periods are temporarily unstable causing an oszillation until the final value has been stabilized. Nevertheless, the scheduling analysis in section 5.1 shows that the real-time contraint is never violated. Figure 14 shows both periods when the controller is disabled: Clients, which are responsible for the Remembrance

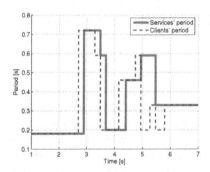 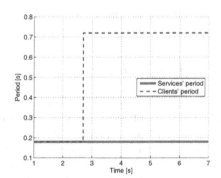

Fig. 13. BFS controlled services' and clients' periods during the adaptation. After adaptation the situation recognition (clients) runs with period 0.33s.

Fig. 14. Non-controlled services' and clients' periods. The situation recognition (clients) runs with period 0.72s more than twice as slow as in the controlled case.

Camera's situation recognition, are called more seldom - every 0.72s. As a result, we find that when utilizing the BFS controller the clients are executed more than twice as often as in the non-controlled case. For the Remembrance Camera application, the BFS controller yields a significant performance step-up.

User study. The overall quality of the Remembrance Camera application is highly dependent on underlying technical constraints, especially the expert systems that itself is very dependent on quality of the scheduling and operation of the sensor services. We evaluated the overall quality in a small initial user study and will report a short excerpt of this study. In the study 7 persons from 20 to 50 years, all of them with only minor knowledge of computer systems, were asked to carry the Remembrance camera during the daytime. Candidates were interviewed 3 days after performing the test on the value of the system. Among the questions there were 1) if they think the system performs as expected, especially if it draws a good picture of the day and if the collection of pictures contains unnecessary information and 2) if they found the information useful. All candidates found that the system draws a good picture of the day while almost half of them mentioned that there are unnecessary pictures taken while the day. All users agreed that the information is useful and most of them would wish to use the system on a daily basis. Although overall this is a very good result for the Remembrance Camera application, we were curious to see why half of them found unnecessary information among the pictures. From an additional analysis we found that in these cases the person was in a home environment all the day and not in an office environment like the other users. A more in depth analysis revealed that our initial expert system was not trained to this environment and therefore performs non-optimal. We therefore assume, that the underlying sensor service and scheduling system performed optimal like in the cases with persons in the office environment and that our service scheduling approach provides a good basis for activity recognition systems like the Remembrance Camera.

8 Related Work

Besides of our work other scheduling approaches are already implemented on embedded sensor systems. OSs like TinyOS[8] and SOS[9] incorporate non-preemptive FIFO schedulers, where tasks are sorted in order of their calling by the application logic. The system is kept responsive to various inputs by deferring procedure calls that are invoked through periodic processes. Several OSs for microcontrollers like FreeRTOS[10] and XMK[11] guarantee preemptive real-time scheduling. However, none of these approaches copes with the dynamic nature of data processing on sensor devices. WCETs need to be specified in advance leading to a static runtime behavior for dynamic workloads. Furthermore, decomposing the application in periodic-only tasks is generally not suited for data-driven processing. Our approach of separation of periodic and data-driven processes preserves the sequential semantic of the application. Varying processing loads are handled dynamically by feedback scheduling. Stankovic et al. investigated feedback scheduling for real-time OSs[12]. The model was completely periodic and adapted the computation time of the tasks according to service levels. In contrast, Buttazzos elastic task model [13] is closer to our approach since it compresses and expands tasks periods in order to handle over- and underutilization of the system. Apart from purely periodic modelling, the system is limited to preemptive tasks. With buffer feedback scheduling (BFS) we have extended this feedback control research on data driven processes with no a-priori knowledge on the computation times.

9 Conclusion and Outlook

In this paper we presented a new OS concept for supporting Ubicomp applications on embedded sensor systems utilizing adaptation through feedback scheduling. Adaptation can accurately modify parameters, e.g. service periods, in order to automatically coordinate processes and achieve a better performance under uncertain or unknown conditions. Our approach - buffer feedback scheduling (BFS) - modifies service periods and especially addresses dynamic and unpredictable workloads caused by the data processing parts of an application. BFS achieved a significant performance step-up for an Ubicomp applicaion allowing a two times faster recogition rate. BFS automatically coordinates periodic and data-driven processes based on runtime information and does not rely on any a-priori specification of the coordination behavior.

Future work includes research on new controllers incorporated in the runtime system. Feedforward controllers are an interesting option, because they act preventively before the system runs in a data drop or idling situation. The system would change from reactive to proactive enabling a distributed coordination between diverse applications on embedded sensor systems within a network.

Acknowledgments

The work presented in this paper was partially funded by the EC through the project CoBIs (contract no. 4270) and by the Ministry of Economic Affairs of the Netherlands through the project Smart Surroundings (contract no. 03060).

References

1. Beigl, M., Gellersen, H.W., Schmidt, A.: Mediacups: experience with design and use of computer-augmented everyday artefacts. Computer Networks 35(4) (2001)
2. Decker, C., Beigl, M., Eames, A., Kubach, U.: Digiclip: Activating physical documents. In: 4th IEEE IWSAWC. (2004) 388–393
3. Decker, C., Beigl, M., Krohn, A., Robinson, P., Kubach, U.: eseal - a system for enhanced electronic assertion of authenticity and integrity. In: Pervasive. (2004)
4. Zimmer, T., Beigl, M.: AwareOffice: Integrating Modular Context-Aware Applications. In: 6th IEEE IWSAWC. (2006)
5. Jeffay, K., Stanat, D.F., Martel, C.U.: On non-preemptive scheduling of periodic and sporadic tasks. In: Proceedings of 12th IEEE RTSS'91. (1991) 129–139
6. Decker, C., Krohn, A., Beigl, M., Zimmer, T.: The particle computer system. In: ACM/IEEE Information Processing in Sensor Networks (IPSN). (2005) 443 – 448
7. Fischer, M., Kroehl, M.: Remembrance camera. Term Thesis (2006)
8. Hill, J., Szewczyk, R., Woo, A., Hollar, S., Culler, D.E., Pister, K.S.J.: System architecture directions for networked sensors. In: ASPLOS. (2000)
9. Han, C.C., Kumar, R., Shea, R., Kohler, E., Srivastava, M.: A dynamic operating system for sensor nodes. In: Proceedings of MobiSys '05, New York, NY, USA, ACM Press (2005) 163–176
10. Barry, R.: FreeRTOS - a free RTOS for small embedded real time systems. http://www.freertos.org/ (2006)
11. Shift-Right Technologies: eXtreme Minimal Kernel (xmk) - a free real time operating system for microcontrollers. http://www.shift-right.com/xmk/ (2006)
12. Stankovic, J.A., He, T., Abdelzaher, T., Marley, M., Tao, G., Son, S., Lu, C.: Feedback control scheduling in distributed real-time systems. In: Proceedings of RTSS'01. (2001)
13. Buttazzo, G.C., Lipari, G., Abeni, L.: Elastic task model for adaptive rate control. In: Proceedings of IEEE RTSS '98, Washington, DC, USA, IEEE Computer (1998)

Exploiting Passive Advantages of Sentient Artefacts

Fahim Kawsar, Kaori Fujinami, and Tatsuo Nakajima

Department of Computer Science,
Waseda University, Tokyo, Japan
{fahim, fujinami, tatsuo}@dcl.info.waseda.ac.jp

Abstract. Sentient artefacts are our everyday life objects augmented with various sensors for value added services. We have been exploiting these artefacts for perceiving user context and proving proactive context aware services while keeping their natural appearances and roles intact. From our observations of these artefacts we have identified two passive advantages besides their explicit value added functionalities. The first is a profile-based participation of the artefacts in the application scenarios thus making the artefacts generalized, independent of the applications and reusable in various scenarios. The second one is the role of the static artefacts in identifying the location of the mobile artefacts thus eliminating the requirement of any dedicated location infrastructure for proactive services. In this paper we have discussed these two issues with illustrations of our findings.

1   Introduction

The task of identifying user context is perhaps the central component of ubiquitous computing research. This research put forth several questions regarding understanding, extraction, modeling, management, distribution and representation of context. Our research focus is to answer some of these key issues through an approach that we call Sentient Artefact. Sentient artefacts are everyday life objects like a chair, a mirror, a door, a lamp, etc. augmented with sensors to provide value added services that include identifying human context and providing proactive services. By augmenting sensors, we make these belongings (micro component of the environment) smart. Eventually, this process recursively makes our environment smart and context aware in a bottom up approach. Furthermore, because of these artefacts natural role in our everyday lives, computing becomes invisible, a goal that Weiser envisioned one and a half decades ago [25]. We have been developing various proactive applications using these smart artefacts [14, 15, 8]. However, during our application development we have encountered couple of issues that seek for further focuses.

- How to determine the sentient artefacts participation in context aware applications in a generic way? We must not develop application or scenario dependent sentient artefacts, rather we have to come up with generalized

H.Y. Youn, M. Kim, and H. Morikawa (Eds.): UCS 2006, LNCS 4239, pp. 270–285, 2006.
© Springer-Verlag Berlin Heidelberg 2006

artefacts that can be used in various scenarios and are independent from the applications.

- How sentient artefacts location can be acquired? It is expensive and to some extends impractical to use dedicated sensor infrastructure for location sensing in domestic environment. We confronted the fact that we need some alternative approaches that can provide the location information in an inexpensive and natural way.

Although these two issues are not contradictory with the primary functions of the sentient artefact (perceiving user contexts and providing proactive services), but for the success of our approach the resolutions are very important. Form our observations of the sentient artefacts characteristics; we have come up with the idea of using sentient artefact for the resolutions, which further increases the technical advantages of sentient artefact. These passive advantages were not in our design goals initially but later came into focus from our experiences with sentient artefact based application development. Basically we have identified two specific characteristics:

- Profile based participation of Sentient Artefacts. This is very important for supporting application independent artefact development. Artefacts can implement one or multiple profiles where each profile specifies a role. Profile based approach directly contributes in making artefacts reusable, loosely coupled with proactive applications and in supporting runtime artefact replacement feature.
- A sentient artefact based location system for sentient artefacts. From our observation we have identified there are various artefacts in our environment that are static in nature and designated in static places and we rarely move them, for example a refrigerator, a cooking oven, a room door/window etc. We can exploit this static nature of these artefacts by using them as a reference point for identifying their peer mobile artefacts. We believe this approach is feasible, practical and economical in context aware environment as it eliminates the requirement of any dedicated sensing infrastructure.

In this paper, we have discussed about these two issues and their implementation in a generic context aware middleware. Considering the view points, the contribution of the paper is purely intellectual, as we propose two notions that are very essential in context aware computing domain. However, we have also shown our findings and performance of the applications that exploited these notions.

The rest of the paper is structured as follows: for giving readers a better understanding of our approach we have introduced the sentient artefact in section 2. Section 3 presents the profile-based approach for sentient artefacts. In section 4 we have introduced the second topic of the paper: location system by sentient artefacts. Section 5 discusses in brief the implementation of these two concepts. In section 6 we have presented several applications that we have developed using sentient artefacts and our findings. Section 7 discusses on various aspects of this two issues and a comparison study with related works is presented in section 8. Finally section 9 concludes the paper.

2   Sentient Artefact

Sentient artefact is a mere everyday object without any noticeable features. We augment sensors to it to make it aware of its environment. By doing so we extend its functional advantages as it can provide value added services beyond its primary role. For example, consider a chair, it is primarily used for sitting. We can put a few sensors on it and we can identify when it is used or even who is using it. So from the functional point of view, a mere chair now serves as a source of context information of an entity. But it does not conflict with its primary role of providing support for sitting. This is the basic concept of sentient artefact; keeping its primary role intact as an artefact while allowing it to provide additional services. In the case of the chair it can provide its state of use, and if we know the identity of the person we can infer that the person is sitting (activity) and he/she is at a specific location(chair's location). In Figure 1 we show some of the sentient artefacts that we have developed.

Sentient table provides ambient display service

Sentient Chair provides state of use information like sitting/not sitting

Sentient Tray can identify objects it carries

Sensor augment PDA provides variety of physiological and environmental sensor data

AwareMirror provides ambient display service

Sentient Toothbrush provides state of use information and identifies user

Sentient lamp provides ambient light level with light service

Sentient Clock can identify Alarm setup timing

Sentient Door can identify opening/closing event

Fig. 1. Array of Sentient Artefacts

Usually these artefacts differ from the explicit sensors in three ways:

- They require a small operating software/device driver that captures values from the multiple sensors embedded in the artefacts and processes these values in a logical way to provide information about their state of use, position or any contextual information that the designer wants to provide.

– Instead of providing only analog/digital sensor value, sentient artefacts can provide a statement to the interested applications, like state of use. That means the sentient artefact developer can provide the logic for generating abstract context information from low-level sensor data.
– Finally, a sentient artefact can also be an actuator in some cases. For instance, a mirror can be used to display some information. Web services like news provider or weather forecast monitor, etc. can also contribute to identify context and are considered as soft sentient artefact.

Sentient artefacts have some strict and specific design principles that have been mentioned in [9, 10, 14]. We have been developing sentient artefacts based applications for providing various proactive services. From our experiences of application development we have come up with one interesting property of sentient artefact: the role specification. That is how to make these artefacts loosely coupled with the applications. Artefacts must not be developed for specific applications; rather artefacts should have the flexibility to be used in various applications as long as they serve the purpose. Accordingly, as a resolution, we have come up with an idea of using a profile-based approach for artefact development. In the next section this approach is discussed.

3   Profile Based Approach

Sentient artefacts can provide various functionalities according to an artefact designers intuitive understanding. It is not logical to consider that each artefact should have only one functional role beyond its primary role. For instance, consider a mirror, we can use the mirror as an ambient display. Simultaneously, the mirror can provide position information (whether some one is in front of it or not) if we embed proximity sensors into it. Similarly a stand light can provide lighting service or the ambient light level of the environment. The software component that is representing the light or the mirror must handle these multiple functionalities within the same artefact space. That means it must not be tightly coupled with the underlying functionality, like for each function, one soft component. Instead it should provide loose coupling among artefacts functional features while at the same time decoupling the functional spaces for each function within the artefact. For instance, one application may use the display service of the mirror where another application may have interest in the position information that it provides. In such case we must not implement two software components, instead one artefact with two functional features. Similarly two different applications may be interested on a single profile that several artefacts implement. In such case the application can select any artefact that is suitable for the scenario. Considering these, our proposition is to use a profile based approach for artefacts; an artefact can provide multiple functionalities and each functionality is encapsulated into one profile. All the profiles are finally integrated into single software instance that represents the physical artefact in the digital space.

Profile notion is commonly used for defining roles, for example: Bluetooth Profile, J2ME Profile etc. Our profile notion has the same meaning. This is very crucial for ubiquity as sentient artefacts' roles can be manifold. It is feasible to have loose coupling within the artefact's functional space. From a very broad point of view we can say that there are two types of categories for profile: Input profile and Output profile, as sentient artefacts role can be either context source or service actuator. However we cannot confine the profile number, because the sentient artefacts' functionalities are not confined in the first place. Designers are independent to come up with a new functionality by embedding some kind of sensors in a daily life objects to acquire context or actuate service. However in Figure 2 we have given some example profiles that artefact can implement.

Input Profile	Output Profile
- Time (Explicit or Symbolic like Evening etc.)	- Sound/Noise
- Location (Symbolic like meeting room or Geometric with longitude, latitude)	- Display
- Position (Front, Back, Right, Left, In front etc)	- Vibration
- Voice	- Lighting
- Tag Reader	- Movement
- Authentication	- Controlling (On, Off, Up, Down, Open, Close etc)
- Proximity and Distance	- Leveling (Darker, Stronger, Weaker, Lighter etc)
- Information (Weather, News, Schedule etc)	- Sending Message (Email/SMS)
- State of Use	- GUI Event (Display) etc.
- Emotion	
- Activity	
- Environment Attribute (Temperature, Light Level, Humidity etc)	
- Physical State (Height, Weight, Color, Shape, Size, Temperature, Face Up/Down, Held, etc)	

Fig. 2. Example of Profiles

We have adopted this profile-based approach for managing the roles of the artefacts. Usually developers can use any design principle for implementing the profiles. However, we have used the approach mentioned in [9, 10] to implement a profile considering the functional focus and the containment relationship among the underlying sensors. We have developed a middleware component presented in later section that the developer can use for defining the artefact profiles. The component manages distinct spaces for each profile within the artefact thus providing systematic client management at the artefact level. In section 6 we have demonstrated how this profile based approach provides various advantages for the application development.

In the next section we will focus on the second issue of this paper: sentient artefact based location system for sentient artefacts.

4   Spreha: Sentient Artefact Based Location System

Sentient artefact based application often requires the location information of the underlying artefacts. However, one of the design principles of sentient artefact based computing is to avoid dedicated sensing infrastructure. To satisfy this issue, we have developed a simple lightweight location system Spreha, where the artefact itself acts as a reference point for location information. The basic concept here is that: there are several artefacts in our environment that are static in nature and we rarely move them; for example Refrigerator, Cooking Oven, Room Door/Window etc. These artefacts can act as a reference point for identifying their mobile peers like chair, lamp, coffee mug etc. Spreha exploits this particular nature of the artefacts. Also from our experience with the application development we have observed that the "centimeter level" accuracy is not needed for the development of contextual services, actually identifying proximity even within few meters is enough for utilizing the sentient artefacts in domestic environments. So, instead of accuracy our essential design principles are flexibility and simplicity.

4.1   Design Decisions

While designing Spreha we have considered several important characteristics that are essential for pervasive environments. Following are enumerations of the guidelines that we have considered in Spreha:

- *Transparency:* The location provider should gather location information in a transparent way without any interference from the applications. Application will only be notified for location change event and must not be responsible for any network management related to location identification.
- *Abstraction:* Heterogeneity is a common characteristic of pervasive environment. The location providers should cope with this heterogeneity issue of the underlying artefacts and should provide the location information in a unified way.
- *Availability:* The location information should be available to the applications all the time regardless of the operating status of one or more location providers.
- *Privacy:* The location information should be protected from malicious client applications.

Based on these principles, we have designed Spreha that composes of some logical components that we have presented in the next subsection. Spreha uses Bluetooth as underlying technology for sensing the artefacts. A 48 Bit Bluetooth device address is used as the location identifier in Spreha, however a higher-level friendly name can also be used. The static location of the artefact is always a higher-level name such as Meeting Room, Fahims Workspace etc. This static location is the identifier of the artefacts location. For resolving the conflict (when two or more hosts see the same artefact in their territory) currently Time of Flight (TOF) is used, however Radio Signal Strength Indicator (RSSI) can also be activated where available.In Spreha there is a predefined trust policy, which contains two attributes: public policy and private policy. Public policy means location information of the artefacts can be published publicly, whereas private policy means the opposite. Artefacts can provide their preferred policy during deployment time.

4.2   Logical Components

As shown in Figure 3 few logical components participate in Spreha; their roles are discussed in the following:

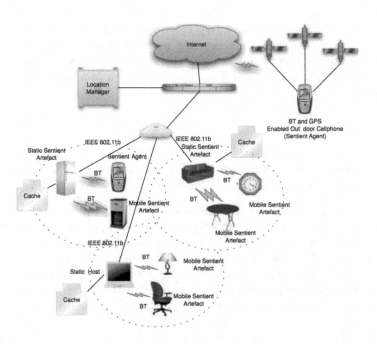

Fig. 3. Logical Architecture of Spreha

Location Manager: This is the central component that manages the location information of the artefacts. (Also each static host and static artefact manages location information locally) During deployment each artefacts register themselves to the manager. Each static artefact and static hosts periodically notify the manager about the artefacts information available to them. Application can query location manager for location information or can register for notification. On receiving new location information, it notifies the interested applications. Location manager resolves conflict when two or more hosts see the same artefact in their pico net by simply considering the minimum TOF and/or maximum RSSI for deducing artefacts location. However in case of out door sentient agents it communicates directly to receive the GPS information.

Static Sentient Artefact: This component acts as both a reference point and a location provider. Any sentient artefact that is considered to be stable in its location like a mirror, a cabinet, a couch, etc. can be considered as static artefact. These artefacts are augmented with bluetooth tag reader. It contributes to location sensing system by maintaining a cache of nearby sentient peers that is periodically updated by running the discovery service embedded in it. The discovery service discovers the nearby peers within its pico net. The cache also contains the RSSI and/or TOF. Whenever the cache state is changed it notifies the location manager and to the applications subscribed to them. During the deployment of the artefact it specifies its name, role as a location provider, static location and security policy to resource manager.

Mobile Sentient Artefact: This component is the ordinary sentient artefact that is mobile in nature like a chair, a watch, etc. A bluetooth tag is embedded in it. Static artefacts and/or the static hosts identify these tags and notify the location manager. During deployment these artefacts specifies their mobile role, name and security policy.

Static Host: This component is an ordinary location provider embedded with a bluetooth tag reader and runs the discovery service periodically and maintains a cache of seen artefacts. Whenever cache state is changed, location manager and the subscribed client applications are notified. During deployment it specifies its role as static host and its static location.

Sentient Agent: This is a special component that assumes to be run in a handheld device owned by a person. Spreha assumes that a person will carry this device. During initial deployment the agent should register its name, IP address, and security policy. Hosts identify this agent when it is in their designated pico net and notifies location manager. However if the agents location information is missing when queried by applications, then location manager communicates directly with the agent running in the handheld, and agent uses the GPS to retrieve its location information and notifies the manager. Thus locating nomadic people is supported in Spreha.

5   Implementation

The two concepts presented in the previous two sections have been implemented as modules of a generic middleware for context aware computing titled Prottoy [16, 13]. For clarity here we are introducing the middleware components in a summarized way.

- *Resource Manager:* Responsible for resource discovery, managing location information and reconfiguration of the underlying environment.
- *Artefact Wrapper:* Responsible for encapsulating artefacts and offering artefact service and context information to applications.

– *Virtual Artefact:* Responsible for providing unified interface to applications for interacting with the underlying layers.

The artefact wrapper component provides all the support to implement the concepts presented in this paper. The location manager component of Spreha is a module of the Resource Manager of Prottoy that notifies location information to clients and responses to the applications' query.

An artefact can implement one or more profiles based on the roles and functionalities it can provide. Developers use the artefact wrapper component to encapsulate the profiles of artefacts. The developers should implement a profile handler using the interfaces of artefact wrapper for each profile that the developer wants the artefact to support. However, they only need to provide the data acquisition and service provision logic, other functionalities like communication, data management, storage, representation, deployment, etc. are handled by the artefact wrapper internally. We have assumed that developers are responsible for providing the quality of service of each profile. Artefact wrappers have interfaces through which developers can specify the quality of service information. However, we do not prescribe any guideline for defining the quality of service. This quality of service can later be exploited by the application to select the best artefact with similar profile.

While participating in the Spreha, a static artefact can implement the location profile, in addition to its other profiles. For participating in the location system, application developers only need to manipulate the deployment tool to provide artefacts bluetooth information and willingness to participate in the location system. Developers do not need to write any code for this, as it is already implemented in the artefact wrapper components. The artefacts (static artefact, static host, mobile artefacts and sentient agents) are deployed in the environment using the artefact wrapper internal deployment tool. For detail of the artefact wrapper and Prottoy implementation please check the references [16, 13].

6   Experiences with Sample Applications

We have developed several context aware applications integrating multiple sentient artefacts on top of Prottoy middleware. In this section we will mention about four applications. Furthermore, our observations and experiences regarding the two focal issues of this paper are discussed.

6.1   SoLite

This is a simple application that employs only two mobile artefacts namely a stand light, a chair and a static artefact: a desk as shown in Figure 4(a). If the chair and the stand lights are in the desks location, the light is automatically turned on/off based on the ambient light sensitivity of the surrounding and the presence of the user sensed by the state of use of the chair (sitting/not sitting).

Fig. 4. Sample Applications

The desk implements location profile; the chair implements state of use profile and the lamp implements lighting profile.

6.2 Byte N Dine

This application as shown in figure Figure 4(b) , runs in a public/private dining space where the dining table acts as an ambient display. The table displays information/news about topics based on users preference. We have assumed that the user will carry a RFID tag that reflects his/her preferred topic. This application uses chairs to identify users presence by chairs state of use, and the table, which is embedded with a touch screen display and augmented with RFID Tag reader and proximity sensors (used to measure the proximity of the table and chair). The chair implements state of use profile and the table implements display, location, proximity and tag reader profile.

6.3 Auto Presenter

This application is designed for assisting conference attendees in the poster sessions at conferences as shown in Figure 4(c). The basic idea is to provide the attendees with a handheld device, which can run a small video clip about the nearby poster content. Since the posters are usually static in nature, we have used it as a static artefact with location profile. The attendees handheld implements a display profile. The handheld is augmented with bluetooth tag that is identified by the poster and accordingly the video is rendered.

6.4 Aware Mirror

AwareMirror, (the initial version was presented in [8]) is a smart mirror installed
in a washroom as shown in Figure 4(d). In addition to its primary task of reflecting some ones image it can also show some information related to the user
like schedule, weather forecasting, transportation information etc. based on the
presence of a user. The mirror is constructed using acrylic magic mirror board
through which only bright color can penetrate. A toothbrush (embedded with
a 2D accelerometer) is used as an authenticator and also as an indicator of the
users presence when co-located with mirror. Also proximity sensors embedded in
the mirror are used to measure the users distance from the mirror. The mirror
implements location, proximity and display profiles. The toothbrush implements
the authentication profile. The mirrors static location is used to identify the presence of a person who is carrying the toothbrush.

6.5 Findings and Observations

Considering the two focus issues we will mention the findings into two parts, first
we will mention about the profile based approach and then the location system.

Profile Based Approach: Our basic concern was to monitor the performance
of three features through the profile based approach.

- *Reusability:* Since in profile-based approach, each artefact implements one or
  multiple profiles rather than an applications requirement, artefacts become
  reusable. For example: we have used the same chair in Byte N Dine and in
  SoLite applications. Similarly the profile itself can be reusable. That means
  once a profile is implemented it can be used in different artefacts that have
  similar properties. For example: the display profile is used in the mirror and
  in the table in AwareMirror and Byte N Dine applications respectively.
- *Replacement:* Our next concern is the artefact replacement functionality.
  Because of the profile-based approach, we have found that artefacts can be
  replaced anytime with another similar artefacts as long as they implement
  the same profile. For example: in AwareMirror, we have found that if we use
  a comb instead of a toothbrush, that implements authentication profile, the
  application runs smoothly. Similarly in Byte N Dine we have seen that if we
  use coffee mugs that implement the state of use profile, the application has
  no functional effect. We have tried using different artefacts at different runs
  also, and found the applications to be stable.This finding supports the fact
  that application has no effect on the replacement of similar profiled artefacts.
- *Loose Coupling and Independence:* This feature is the conjugal effect of the
  previous two advantages of profile-based approach. Because of the reusable
  and replacement facilities, the artefacts are completely independent of the
  application/scenario requirement. We have found in all four applications that
  applications are interested in the context information or service provision
  (in profile in our approach) but not on the artefact itself. So artefacts have
  been developed in an adhoc manner considering the design issues of sentient

artefacts and the best alternatives are selected for the applications based on requirements and availability. Our findings validate the fact that profile based approach provides the generalization for managing sentient artefacts.

Spreha Location System: Exploiting the static sentient artefacts for locating the mobile sentient artefact is the primary goal of Spreha. From this point of view we have found from the developed applications that Sprehas logical components can contribute to the location sensing tasks successfully. However, from the performance point of view, a few issues have been identified. In a real environment we have found that bluetooth performance was not always satisfactory. Especially if the static hosts and static sentient artefacts are located in congested manner than it is very difficult to infer the actual location of the mobile artefacts. For example, in Auto Presenter since the posters are closely arranged differed by 2 3 meters, it is very difficult to identify the location of the attendee (in front of which poster the user is). Furthermore, if two static hosts/artefacts are located nearby (6-8 meters) it is difficult to select the proper one by only calculating the TOF, because sometimes it leads to wrong prediction. However, in other applications where the static hosts are arranged in disperse manner (artefacts' locations are differed by more that 12 meters), Sprehas performance is satisfactory. Since in other applications we have used only one static artefact, the identification was correct.

From this observation, it can be said that it is necessary to arrange the static hosts and static artefacts in a disperse manner for proper location sensing. However, this is not a shortcoming of the proposed concept because we can distribute the artefacts in a way that they do not conflict with each other and it is logical. For instance: consider a kitchen, we can have several sentient artefacts that are static in nature like a cooker, a refrigerator, a cabinet, etc. that are closely arranged. However, we can use only one of them as a reference point in the kitchen for location discovery. The same is true for other locations like a TV in the living room, a bed in the bed room etc (Even there may be multiple static artefacts in these locations, but we can implement location profile in one of them only). This approach is practical and economical. So the only constrain to use Spreha is that we need a prior design and layout of the environment for deciding the artefacts that can play the role of static host or static sentient artefact. So in a larger environment that includes several spatial location, Spreha can easily be used for location identification as long as the static artefacts are arranged in a disperse manner.

7 Discussion

In this section, we will focus on some specific issues of the two concepts presented in the paper.

7.1 Focus of Profile-Based Approach

We believe the Profile-Based approach for artefact development is one step towards realizing sentient artefacts as a successful context information provider for proactive services. We have shown that sentient artefacts roles can be manifold and all these roles are reusable. So it is feasible to consider the implementation of different artefact independently. This approach leads to high reusability and cost effectiveness, since one artefact can participate in multiple applications. We can generate a profile and use the profile in various artefacts that can support that profile. Similarly we can develop an artefact with specific profiles and can use the artefact in various applications. This leads to the loose coupling between artefacts and applications. This is very important for sentient artefact based application development, and in general in context aware computing. Several research groups have used several augmented artefacts for identifying context [22, 5, 1, 2]. Unfortunately, most of those artefacts are tightly coupled with the scenario in hand so can not be reused in other applications. This fact is further validated in the related work section. One interesting extension of this profile-based approach may be a wizard for artefact developers to generate artefact wrapper on the fly. If we follow the context pattern proposed in [21], the profile type and numbers, we can come up with an assistive tool that can recommend the artefact developer about the wrappers possible implementation.

7.2   Focus on the Spreha Location System

From design principle point of view Spreha satisfies the transparency and abstraction requirement by using the artefact wrapper component of Prottoy [16, 13]. In Spreha location information is stored centrally in location manager and each static host and static sentient artefact also host their own location information. From this point of view Sprehas approach is a hybrid one between centralized and distributed data storage. Because of this hybrid organization in Spreha the location information is always available either from location manager or from static location providers. Spreha does not exploit any dedicated sensing infrastructure for location sensing. We use sentient artefacts with augmented services for location sensing in an adhoc manner. From this point of view: readers may be confused about what we mean by dedicated. Our proposition here is that each artefact has its primary role in our everyday life. We are keeping that role intact while using it for location sensing. So the underlying infrastructure is the sentient artefacts not any sensor nodes deployed only for location sensing like active bat, ubiSense or cricket [24, 3, 18]. The strength of Spreha is not the sensing technology but the idea of using sentient artefacts as a location reference point.

We consider dedicated infrastructures are not applicable in a domestic environment. Our claim is further justified by the recent proliferation of Place Lab approach [20] of using existing networks for location detection.

Cost of Location Node is minimal in Spreha as no external sensing system is necessary. The value added services of sentient artefact nullifies the location system cost as the location system components (bluetooth tag and reader) are parts of the sentient artefacts. If the artefacts are not bluetooth enabled, then the cost of the system is the summation of the Bluetooth configuration cost for each mobile and static artefact.

Another important issue is that Spreha does not implement any location model on top its sensing system. Any suitable location model can be used on top of Spreha to represent the physical world, for instance: we have mentioned in section 6 that it is necessary to do a prior layout design before deploying Spreha, if each static host and static artefacts static location is organized in a predefined hierarchical manner we can easily represent any virtual model of the physical world.

8   Related Work

Most of the context aware projects use artefacts that are either traditional general purpose computing platforms ranging from small handheld to large sized high end computers like ParcTabs, or dedicated artefacts designed for providing specific contextual information Using sensor augments artefact for contextual service provision is common practice in context aware literature. Unfortunately, till now no work has been tried to generalize the roles of these artefacts so that they can be used in multiple application scenarios. For example, consider the Digital Dcor [22] project where augmented traditional drawer and coffee pots are used as a smart storage and a media for informal communication respectively. Since the profile notion is missing in their artefacts, these artefacts can not be used in any other applications, or these artefacts functionality can not be ported in other artefacts. Same is true for Phillips Home Labs initiatives [2], where they have been developing various smart artefact similar to ours like Smart Mirror, Smart Shaver etc. But due to the tight coupling with the end applications these artefacts are not reusable in other application scenarios. MediaCup [5] project is perhaps the first work that presented the augmented artefact notion, but it did not specify anything about the specific roles that the similar artefacts can implement. Some other works on augmented artefacts are, Tangible Bits [12] , Paradisos work [17] or MIT Media Labs commercial initiatives Ambient Devices [1] But all these works lack from the generalization feature that we have tried to achieve through the profile based approach in this work.

Considering Sprehas proposition, comparing Spreha with other location sensing system may seem ambiguous. The reason is Spreha introduces sentient artefact in location provider dimension but it is using bluetooth as underlying sensing technique. And using bluetooth for indoor location sensing is not a new observation as it has already been explored in [4, 11]. So from this point of view we cannot actually compare Spreha with other indoor sensing. Sprehas contribution is in introducing the novel notion of sentient artefact as reference point. On the other hand Spreha does not implement any location model as proposed in numerous literature [7, 19, 23, 24, 6]. The distinction of Spreha with other indoor location system is an intellectual one because of the utilization of sentient artefact instead of dedicated infrastructure. For example there are numerous indoor location system that make use of ultrasonic [18, 23], infrared [24], ultra-wideband radio [3]. All these systems require a hardware infrastructure be installed in the environment. Most importantly these systems are generally expensive, costing thousands to tens of thousands of US dollars for a 1000 square meter installation. These systems primarily focus on optimizing accuracy rather than wide-scale deployment. We consider these systems are not suitable for sentient artefact based computing because of such inherent dependency on infrastructure. Place Lab proposes using RF/WiFi base stations as reference points [20]. Basically we can think, Spreha augment their idea by embedding the base station in the sentient artefacts that are static in nature. Though using RF access points as reference is inherited from Place Lab, Spreha introduces few features that are missing in Place Lab, like artefact end security policy, distribution of location information in static hosts and artefacts, role of location manager and the notion of sentient agent for seamless change between bluetooth to GPS usage.

9   Conclusion

In this paper we have presented two passive advantages of using sentient artefact based approach for developing context aware applications. we have provided a illustrative explanation of our approach by providing its direct implications in the developed applications. We believe the proposed notions are very important for realizing the ubiquitous computing environment. Profile based approach is specially essential for exploiting the physical computing feature of ubiquitous computing. Also the light weight location system poses interesting findings that may be helpful for the community to further investigate the issue for better resolutions.

References

1. Website of AmbientDevice. http://www.AmbientDevics.com.
2. Website of Philips Home Lab Reserach. http://www.research.philips.com.
3. Website of UbiSense. http://www.ubisense.net.
4. G. Anastasi, R. Bandelloni, M. Conti, F. Delmastro, E. Gregori, and G. Mainetto. Experimenting an Indoor Bluetooth-Based Positioning Service. In *23rd International Conference on Distributed Computing Systems Workshops (ICDCSW'03)*, 2003.
5. M. Beigl, H. W. Gellersen, and A. Schmidt. Media Cups: Experience with design and use of Computer Augmented Everyday Objects. *Computer Networks, special Issue on Pervasive Computing*, 35-4, 2001.
6. M. Beigl, T. Zimmer, and C. Decker. A location model for communicating and processing of context. *Personal and Ubiquitous Computing*, 6(56), 2002.
7. M. Burnett, P. Prekop, and C. Rainsford. Intimate location modeling for context aware computing. In *Workshop on Location Modeling for Ubiquitous Computing, in UbiComp2001*, 2001.
8. K. Fujinami, F. Kawsar, and T. Nakajima. AwareMirror: A Personalized Display using a Mirror. In *3rd International Conference on Pervasive Computing*, 2005.
9. K. Fujinami and T. Nakajima. Augmentation of Everyday Artefacts for Context-Aware Applications' Building Blocks. In *Workshop on Smart Object Systems (sobs05) in conjunction with Ubicomp 2005*, 2005.

10. K. Fujinami and T. Nakajima. Sentient Artefacts: Acquiring User's Context through Daily Objects. In *The 2nd International Workshop on Ubiquitous Intelligence and Smart Worlds (UISW2005)*, 2005.
11. J. Hallberg, M. Nilsson, and K. Synnes. Positioning with Bluetooth. In *10th International Conference on Telecommunications (ICT 2003).*, 2003.
12. H. Ishii and B. Ullmer. Tangible Bits: Towards Seamless Interfaces between People, Bits and Atoms. In *CHI 1997*, 1997.
13. F. Kawsar. An architecture for sentient artefact based computing. Master Thesis, Computer Science Department, Waseda University, Japan, 2006.
14. F. Kawsar, K. Fujinami, and T. Nakajima. Augmenting Everyday Life with Augmented Artefacts. In *Smart Object and Ambient Intelligence Conference*, 2005.
15. F. Kawsar, K. Fujinami, and T. Nakajima. Experiences with Developing Context-Aware Applications with Augmented Artefacts. In *1st International Workshop on Personalized Context Modeling and Management for UbiComp Applications, A Workshop in conjunction with UbiComp2005, the 7th International Conference on Ubiquitous Computing*, 2005.
16. F. Kawsar, K. Fujinami, and T. Nakajima. Prottoy: A Middleware for Sentient Environment. In *The 2005 IFIP International Conference on Embedded And Ubiquitous Computing*, 2005.
17. J. A. Paradiso. A. Interfacing the Foot: Apparatus and Applications. In *CHI 2000 Extended Abstracts*, 2000.
18. N. B. Priyantha, A. Chakaraborty, and H. Balakrishnan. The Cricket Location-Support System. In *MOBICOM 2000*, 2000.
19. I. Satoh. A Location Model for Pervasive Computing Environment. In *Third Annual IEEE International Conference on Pervasive Computing and Communications (PerCom 2005)*, 2005.
20. B. Schilit, A. LaMarca, G. Borrirllo, W. Griswol, E. L. D. Mcdonald, E. Balachandran, and J. A. Hong. V. Challenge: Ubiquitous Location-Aware Computing and the Place Lab Initiative. In *First ACM International Workshop on Wireless Mobile Applications and Services on WLAN (WMASH)*, 2003.
21. A. Schmidt. *Ubiquitous Computing-Computing in Context*. PhD thesis, Computer Science Department, Lancaster University, 2002.
22. I. Siio. Digital Decor: Augmented Everyday Things. In *Graphics Interface 2003*, 2003.
23. R. Want, A. Hopper, V. Falcao, and J. Gibbons. The Active Badge Location System. *ACM Transactions on Information Systems*, 91-102, 1992.
24. A. Ward, A. Jones, and A. Hopper. New Location Technique for the Active Office. *IEEE Personal Communications*, 42-47, 1997.
25. M. Weiser. The Computer for the 21st Century. *Scientific American*, 265, 1991.

Scenario-Based Programming for Ubiquitous Applications

Eun-Sun Cho[1,*], Kang-Woo Lee[2], Min-Young Kim[2], and Hyun Kim[2]

[1] Dept. of Computer Science & Engineering, Chungnam National University
220 Gung-dong Yusong-gu, Daejeon, Korea, 305-764
eschough@cnu.ac.kr
[2] Electronic and Telecommunications Research Institute,
161 Kajong-dong Yusong-gu, Daejon, Korea, 305-350
{kwlee, hkim}@etri.re.kr, tristan88@hanmail.net

Abstract. Ubiquitous applications usually involve highly interactive context data management. Traditional general-purpose programming languages are not sufficient for use in this domain, as they do not have the capability to manage such data effectively. We have developed a scenario-based programming language that we call 'PLUE (Programming Language for Ubiquitous Environment)', which is a Java-based prototyping language for ubiquitous application development. PLUE supports ECA (event-condition-action) rules and finite state automata-based (FSA-based) interactive responses to dynamic situations. In addition, PLUE programmers are able to manage heterogeneous data with a uniform view of path expressions. We have implemented PLUE on top of CAMUS (Context-Aware Middleware for Ubiquitous Robotic Companion System), a framework for context-aware applications that was originally developed for network-based robots.

1 Introduction

Ubiquitous computing systems must handle context data from various sources, including mobile devices and sensors. These systems usually have services that are widely distributed over networks and devices. However, they must also be highly interactive with their surrounding environments.

Since they run on top of such systems, ubiquitous applications usually consist of a number of complicated commands that handle various kinds of context data. Well-designed event handling is necessary to cope with changing situations [1, 2]. Transforming scenarios that are conceived by designers into programs in C or Java takes far too long using currently available tools.

This paper describes our new language, PLUE (A Programming Language for Ubiquitous Environments), a prototyping language for ubiquitous applications. PLUE was developed in accordance with the following preliminary attributes:

---

* This work was supported in part by MIC & IITA through IT Leading R&D Support Project.

H.Y. Youn, M. Kim, and H. Morikawa (Eds.): UCS 2006, LNCS 4239, pp. 286–299, 2006.

- Handy structures for describing situation flows: a designer must always visualize the scenario of a ubiquitous service before he can proceed with the development of applications. As an example of such a scenario, consider a speaker giving a presentation at a conference. The room lights would automatically dim at the beginning and a slide show would start once the speaker has begun his talk. This will happen repeatedly for each speaker, but only until the last speaker has finished. Therefore, the whole task forms a sequence of actions with patterns and can be represented as a kind of finite state automaton. PLUE supports the description of the flow of such scenarios through its state transition facilities.
- Transparent context management: since context data usually forms a tree in a ubiquitous environment, PLUE provides path expressions for context access. The path traversal is transparent using the usual dot notation of member access in object-oriented languages. It may involve automatic context data matching provided by any third-party services. To manage context data from diverse sources uniformly, we have defined a minimal data model called the 'UDM (Universal Data Model)'. PLUE offers path expressions for UDM data access.
- Prompt responsiveness: prompt reaction to their surrounding environments is important for ubiquitous applications. PLUE allows programmers to generate ECA rules (event-condition-action) in order to encode the necessary actions in a straightforward manner.
- User-friendly language facilities: we assume that most programmers do not want to waste time learning a new language. To achieve user friendliness, PLUE is based on Java, a popular language. A PLUE program has very little dependence on its underlying system because the transparent distributed object invocation hides the complex system architecture. With simple event-handling features, interactions between the dynamic situations can be described easily.

Our current version of PLUE is implemented on top of CAMUS (Context-Aware Middleware for URC System) [3], a framework for context-awareness applications. It was originally developed for a network-based robot infra-system called 'URC (Ubiquitous Robotic Companion)' that requires software infrastructure to enhance the intelligence and context-awareness of network-based robots. CAMUS has been successfully deployed in 'Ubiquitous Dream Hall' [4] as a middleware to demonstrate future ubiquitous cities.

Fig. 1. Ubiquitous Dream Hall: the living room of u-Home (left) with a home-care robot (middle), a girl kicking imaginary balls at u-Street (right)

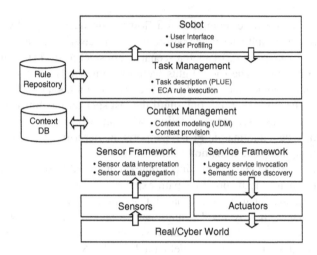

Fig. 2. CAMUS Architecture

Fig. 2 shows an abstract architecture of CAMUS. CAMUS receives the information from sensors installed in the real world. The information is delivered in the form of events that are in turn fed into the 'Sensor Framework'. The Sensor Framework gathers the events and interprets/aggregates them to generate high-level context information that is then sent to the 'Context Manager' in UDM form. Any change of context information triggers the Context Manager to transfer corresponding events to the 'Task Manager'. When an event is raised, the Task Manager searches for task rules that are interested in the event and invokes the rule action if it satisfies the condition. While performing an action, the task invokes services that make changes on the real/cyber world.

In the next section, we present a brief survey of related work. Section 3 shows how to manage context data in PLUE programs. Section 4 introduces the task description mechanism in PLUE, with ECA rules and the state transition mechanism. Section 5 shows the underlying architecture of PLUE. Finally, section 6 includes a discussion of our work and our conclusions.

2 Related Works

Compared to other topics in ubiquitous systems, the design of new tools and languages that can be used to help develop programs have not been actively pursued by the research community. In this section, we will skip RMI (remote method invocation)[5], XPath [6], and ECA (event condition action) rules [7]. While they are definitely related to our research, they are adequately described elsewhere.

In RCSM [8], and Salsa [9], script languages based on ECA rules are used to describe the behavior of agents. The behavior of an agent consists of a set of ECA rules that permit prompt responses to context changes. Such languages are useful for non-centralized agent systems, where task execution must necessarily consist of both communication between agents and the execution of the agents. However, this approach is too platform dependent, since script languages are too weak to describe sizable programs in other than an autonomous agent platform. This is especially true in centralized controlled systems that require the description of entire tasks.

COP (Context Oriented Programming) [10] from the University of Queensland is based on ambient calculus [11]. It is widely known for its theoretically appealing context management mechanism using dynamic scoping variables for context data. A COP program executes self-adjustable behaviors as the current context is changing, while also focusing on context matching and dynamic function binding. Despite the excellent manner in which it can manipulate context and context-dependent code fragments, COP does not concentrate on the task description. It also lacks the capability to handle scenarios and events.

One world [12], one of the famous pervasive computing systems developed at the University of Washington, provides a programming model with nested 'environments' each of which contains 'components' and 'tuples'. Applications are composed from components that exchange events. The flow of control for the application consists of several instances of event handling. Remote event passing, operation migration, object sharing, and querying are also supported, all of which can be designed using Java API's without transparency. This technique was founded on the premise that since ubiquitous computing has so many context changes, it would be dangerous for them to be hidden from programmers. Given this insight, programmers would then be able to handle them correctly, with their own scenarios. However, this is not necessarily true since it is likely that such detailed implementation and maintenance information would distract programmers from the task at hand. This well-known proposition has been proven true several times in the past in the field of software engineering. In addition, the language provided by one world is not suitable for prototyping.

'Olympus [13]', a high-level programming model suggested by University of Illinois at Urbana Champaign, allows a developer to specify entities and operations in ubiquitous computing environments at abstract level. Despites its entity abstraction facilities and excellent service discovery scheme, Olympus lacks support for task description based on the flow of scenarios.

3   Context Data Access

3.1   Universal Data Model

Since context awareness is one of the key characteristics of ubiquitous computing, several studies examined the management of context information in ubiquitous applications. To date, however, no satisfactory context data model for heterogeneous data management has been found. Ontology represented in logic would be our choice, but is hardly considered practical so far.

We have defined a new simple context data model for context information that we have called UDM (Universal Data Model). It is similar to OEM [14], a semi-structured database model, in that context information is denoted as an edge-labeled graph. Although we developed UDM for PLUE, it can be used for other ubiquitous programming environments. Its main concepts are described below.

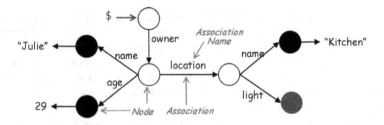

Fig. 3. Context data for the SmartRoom Application

- **Nodes:** Each node in UDM represents an entity, such as a person, place, task, service, and so on.
- **Associations:** An association is a labeled directed edge. It presents the relationship between nodes. Some associations change with time. In Fig. 3, the location of a person varies whenever he/she moves to a different place.

Fig.3 is an example of a simple UDM model that shows that "29-year-old Julie is in a kitchen that has a light fixture". As you can see, UDM provides a very easy way to describe the context.

PLUE provides facilities to access context data represented in UDM. PLUE programs can handle any data from various sources in a uniform format. 'UDM bindings' provide a transparent view of the context data from heterogeneous data sources. When a new data source is added, a corresponding UDM binding should also be supported to map from the native data into a UDM view and vice versa.

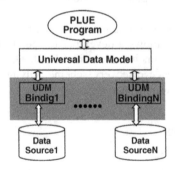

Fig. 4. Context data integration using UDM bindings

Fig. 4 shows the data flow among data sources, UDM bindings, and PLUE programs. Our current version of PLUE provides built-in bindings for XML documents, Unix/Linux/Windows file systems, JavaBeans, and annotated plain Java objects.

3.2 Path Expressions

PLUE supports path expressions to retrieve and modify the context data modeled in UDM. A path expression is a sequence of association names starting from a node. By evaluating a path expression, we obtain a set of nodes that are reached through the sequence of associations beginning at the starting node. In PLUE, the starting node is denoted by the '$' symbol. It points to the root context node for a PLUE application. For instance, in Fig. 3, the path expression "$.owner.location.name" points to the valued node whose value is "Kitchen". The meaning of the expression is "the name of the place where the owner is currently located."

Using path expressions, a PLUE application is able to reach all the necessary context information, such as the name of the person who executes this application, the address of the owner's location, and other application-specific data.

PLUE supports a set of sophisticated path expressions to query the interesting data. These expressions are highly expressive, but they are still simple and easy to describe. We categorize them as shown in the following examples:

Basic path expressions
A UDM node may have more than one departing edge with the same tag. A path expression will return multiple values in that case.

- $.owner.location: is the single value for the location
- $.owner.location.residents: is a set of multiple values when multiple residents are present in a location.
- $.owner.location.'temporal residents during a month'.id: is the id of the multiple temporal residents that are present in a location. (a quoted string in an association name is useful for a long sentence with spaces)

Selective association traversal
PLUE assigns orders sequentially for departure edges with the same tag that leave from a single UDM node. Specifically, the ordinals or the ranges of ordinal numbers can confine a multi-valued path expression. The following examples assume a multi-valued association 'children' from the location of the owner.

- $.owner.location.children[2]: Of the multiple associations tagged with **'children'**, the second one is selected.
- $.owner.location.children[2-4]: Of the multiple associations tagged with **'children'**, the second, third, and fourth are selected.
- $.owner.location.children[4-]: Of the multiple associations tagged with **'children'**, the ones whose ordinal numbers are larger than four are selected.
- $.owner.location.children[1,4-5,9]: Of the multiple associations tagged with **'children'**, the ones whose ordinal numbers are 1, 4, 5, and 9 are selected.

Conditional path traversal
Selection on multiple associations with a shared name is done based on matching values, as is done in database queries. When a comparison is made between multiple values and a scalar or between two sets of multiple values, the condition will be true for at least one case.

- $.owner.location.residents[.name=='Tom']: retrieves people who are at the same place as the owner and whose names are 'Tom'.
- $.owner.location.residents[.name=='Tom' && .age=='10]: retrieves 10-year-old Tom from among the residents who are at the same place as the owner.

Wildcards

Traversing an anonymous edge is denoted by a wildcard ('*') in a path expression. '**' denotes any number of anonymous edges. This enables edge selection even when the programmer does not know the exact path. '%' is used for a wild card character in an association name.

- $.owner.location.*.id: the nodes that are reachable from $.owner.*some_anony-mous_link*.id.
- $.owner.**.id: the nodes of the set of 'id' links that are reachable from $.owner
- $.owner.location.pa%.id: the nodes of the set of 'id' links that are reachable from $.owner.location and links whose names are prefixed with "pa".

Built-in functions

Our current version of PLUE supports two built-in functions that transform multiple values to a single value.

- exists($.owner.location.parent): true if the cardinality of $.owner.location.parent is not 0.
- count($.owner.location.parent): the cardinality of $.owner.location.parent

4 Task Description

4.1 State Transitions

Ubiquitous computing applications, like other user-centric services, are usually designed based on preconceived corresponding scenarios. For instance, a smart conference room would be built for a scenario where conferences are managed automatically. The flow of an example scenario is as shown in Fig. 5.

In PLUE programs, all of the work that must be done for a scenario is called a '*task*'. For programmers, a PLUE task is much like a Java class with methods, instance variables, and inner classes. Since a task forms a sequence of actions with patterns that are a kind of finite state automaton, a task definition is augmented with a flow description using '*states*' and '*transitions*'.

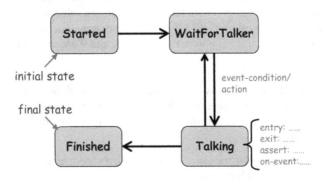

Fig. 5. The flow of a smart conference room scenario

A '*state*' has a duration for which some property in the context must remain constant. A PLUE state consists of four parts – *the entry, the exit, asserts*, and *on-event-rules*. The *entry* part initializes the state. The variables used in the state are initialized and resources are prepared. *Assert* phrases are conditions that are true for the duration of the current state of the task.

On-event-rule phrases describe the actions to be taken when specific events occur. The *exit* part describes the work that must be done before the task transits to other states. The keywords 'initial' and 'final' are attached to the initial and final states, respectively. Currently, we have implemented only one state for each. The entry and exit phrases can be omitted if no action needs to be specified while entering/exiting the state. A state can have multiple asserts and on-event rules.

Fig. 6 depicts a code fragment of a PLUE program, showing that the state 'Talking' describes a situation where a speaker is giving a talk in a conference. The entry part of this state prepares the presentation foils for him on the screen in the conference room. If any transition occurs, then the exit phrase sets the current speaker to the next speaker. The assert phrase ensures that the platform light is turned off while the speaker is talking.

```
state Talking{
  entry
  {$.platform.slideshow.slide_path=$.current.material;}
  exit { $.current=$.current.next; }
  assert $.platform.light==false;
  on event VoiceReceived(e)
      condition(e.speech =='next')
        { $.platform.slideshow.next();}
}
```

Fig. 6. An example of a state definition: state 'Talking'

If the speaker says "*next*", then the next slide is shown. Note that a task writer can assign event variables to their target event names. These variables can then be used in on-event rules. In the example, the event variable "e" is bound to an event named "VoiceReceived". PLUE supports seven built-in event types: TagEntered, TagLeft, UserEntered, UserLeft, SpeechReceived, PropertyChanged, and TimeExpired. However, task writers could add any new event types that would be necessary to develop their tasks. The 'condition' clause expresses the condition for which a rule is invoked. Path expressions, the event variable, and the usual Java comparators can appear as well. The braced body denotes the action part of the on-event rule.

A '*transition*' describes the actions taken during the transition from the current state into the next state when the event satisfying the corresponding conditions occurs. The transition consists of a from-state, a to-state, the 'on-event/condition', and the action. The 'on-event /condition' includes the transition condition, as well as what must be executed during the transition. This is similar to the on-event rules for a state.

```
transition WaitForTalker -> Talking{
    on event VoiceReceived(e)
      condition (e.speech=='Start presentation'){
        $.current = $.conference.first;
        $.room.tts.speak("Start");
    }
}
```

Fig. 7. An example of a transition definition: from 'WaitForTalker' to 'Talking'

Fig. 7 describes the transition from the WaitForTalker state to the Talking state. If the chairman says *"Start presentation"*, then the data for the first speaker is prepared and a TTS (Text-To-Speech) system says *"Start"* to those present while the transition is made.

A PLUE task is modularized into states and their transitions. If an event occurs in the current state and it satisfies the condition of any transition, then the current state is changed to the next state in the transition. Since massive events and fluctuating situations in ubiquitous environments can be directly modeled in PLUE, it is easier for the programmers to write and maintain application programs for ubiquitous computing.

Fig. 8 depicts a part of a task with two states and a transition. 'Rule-based programming' for proactive services in context-aware applications is achieved by using on-event rules and asserts in states and transitions in PLUE. On-event rules and transitions are only invoked when the required events are received. The actions of assert phrases are invoked when the required conditions occur. Path expressions are used extensively to express such ECA rules and asserts.

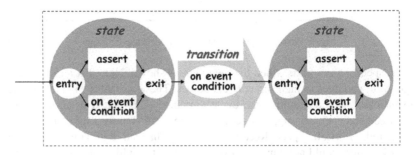

Fig. 8. Transition of states while a task is running

4.2 Context Management

Context information gained from path expressions is manipulated extensively in the entry/exit phrases and rule descriptions that are contained in a task definition. Such information is usually calculated with other values and modified by assignment in a C-like program. In addition, it is more difficult to handle a path expression that returns a multi-value like a set, a list, and a bag. PLUE supports tools that make it easier to process path expressions.

- *<path expression> <op> <scalar value>*
- When *<path expression>* results in value nodes, PLUE allows basic operations to be conducted on the path expression. Our current version of PLUE supports +,-,*, and / with integer values, and + for string concatenation. If *<path expression>* has multiple values, each value will undergo an operation *<op>* with a *<scalar value>* that will then be merged into the resulting set. These expressions, simple path expressions, and values are collectively called 'complex path expressions'.
- *<path expression>* = *<complex path expression>*
- When *<path expression>* results in a value node, it will update the value. If *<path expression>* has multiple values, the right side should have multi-values. All of the departing edges of the resulting nodes of *<path expression>* will be replaced with the new ones.
- *<path expression>* <= *<complex expression>*
- The result of *<complex expression>* will be added as departing edges to the resulting nodes of *<path expression>*.
- *<path expression>* = nil
- PLUE supports a special keyword nil to clear the departing edges of the resulting nodes of *<path expression>*.
- foreach (*<var>* = *<path expression>* : [*<condition on the var>*]) *<action on the var>*
- The foreach statement can be used as an iterator for multiple edges. *<var>* is the usual variable name that is prefixed with a '$' for discrimination with other Java variables. In the above example, since the location 'e.location' has more than one light, the variable $light points to each element of the set of lights. If the light that is referenced by the variable $light is off, ('light.power==false'), then action will be taken on it.
- foreach *<var>* in (select *<path expression>* from *<path expression>* where *<path expression>* *<op>* *<complex path expression>*)
- Like object database query languages [15], a 'select-from-where' clause is provided in this special foreach-statement. Since a select-from-where statement can also be expressed with the usual path expressions, programmers can choose not to use this version of a foreach-statement.

This language extension is preprocessed into a plain Java program before compilation. Every new feature is similar to a plain Java expression and would therefore be familiar to Java programmers. The following example shows an on-event rule in PLUE that ensures that at least one light is on whenever a person enters the kitchen. A variable for a path expression ('$light') and a Java variable ('flag') both appear in the foreach statement.

```
on event UserEntered(e)
condition ( e.platform.name == 'Kitchen') {
   boolean flag = false;
   foreach ($light=e.platform.light:
                $light == false && flag == false) {
      $light = true;
      flag = true;
   }
}
```

5 Implementation

A PLUE task program developed with a context data model is basically put into a PLUE Preprocessor and translated into Java code and an XML file. Rules are translated into a code fragment that generates rule objects and registers them with the Rule Processor. The path expressions are converted into a composition of appropriate API calls to the underlying Path Expression Processor. As a result, any Java compiler can compile the generated Java code into Java byte code.

The loader module creates a task object from the Java byte code and the XML file and then it delivers it to the State Transition Machine dedicated to the task. Fig. 9 depicts the processing flow of a PLUE task.

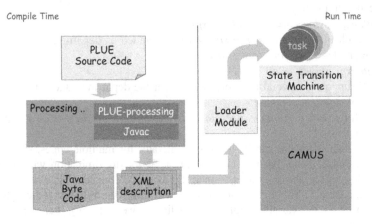

Fig. 9. PLUE architecture

```
<?xml version="1.0" encoding="EUC-KR"?>
<task name= "ConfAssistant" >
    ...
<state name = "Talking"  >
    <entry name= "stTalking$entry" />
    <exit name= "stTalking$exit" />
    <assert name = "stTalking$assertECA1" />
    <rule name = "rule0" >
        <event name = "VoiceReceived" />
        <condition >
            <![CDATA[ e.speech=='next' ]]>
        </condition >
        <action name = "stTalking$rule0Action" />
    </rule>
</state>
<transition from = "Talking" to = "WaitForTalker" >
    <rule name = "rule3" >
        <event name = "VoiceReceived" />
        <condition >
            <![CDATA[ e.speech=='end' ]]>
    ...
<action name ="trTalkingWaitForTalker$rule3Action"/>
    </rule>
</transition>
```

Fig. 10. Translated XML document for the state 'Talking' (in part)

The PLUE Preprocessor, based on JavaCC 4.0 beta 1 [16] for parsing, inputs a PLUE program and outputs new Java byte code and an XML file. Each tag in the XML file corresponds to a PLUE language feature, such as '<task>', '<state>', '<entry>', '<exit>', and '<assert>'. The 'name' attribute of '<task>' or '<state>' represents the name of the task (or the state). The name attribute of '<entry>', '<exit>', '<assert>', or '<action>' is for the method name in the Java byte code that describes the corresponding behaviour. Fig. 10 is an example of the XML file that is generated for the state 'Talking' that was introduced above.

At run time, the Loader Module registers the states and transitions of the task with the State Transition Machine for the task. The State Transition Machine executes the entry phrases of the initial state of the task and runs the state transition machine until it encounters the exit phrase of the final state. When an outside event occurs, the Rule Processor selects the related on-event rules or transitions in the task by checking the on-clause and the condition-clause of the rules. While the action part of the matched rule is being executed, it interacts with the Path Expression Processor and the remote services, as shown in Fig. 11.

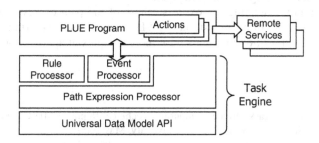

Fig. 11. Interactions with CAMUS

This approach with XML file generation achieves a kind of separation of concerns between PLUE Preprocessor and State Transition Machine, but imposes runtime overhead. As an alternative, we are currently developing Java API for registering and loading tasks directly from the translated PLUE program, which enables getting rid of the intermediate XML description.

6 Discussion and Conclusions

Traditional programming languages are not sufficient for ubiquitous application programming because they cannot manage the various types of data and dynamic changes that occur in real-world scenarios. However, relatively less interest is given to programming paradigms for ubiquitous environments.

This paper describes an object-oriented language named 'PLUE (a Programming Language for Ubiquitous Environments)' that will help programmers write ubiquitous applications. PLUE supports ECA (event-condition-action) rules and finite state automata-based (FSA-based) interactive responses to dynamic situations. It also allows the manipulation of UDM (Universal Data Model) data in the form of conventional path expressions. We expect that PLUE will facilitate the rapid prototyping of ubiquitous applications and will help to accelerate the deployment of ubiquitous computing.

Some commonly used concepts for data processing are reflected in the context management of PLUE. The idea for the powerful, but succinct, path expressions in PLUE comes from the query languages for XML [6]. Select-from-where clauses in PLUE are similar to query languages for OODBMS [13].

Although PLUE provides powerful expressions to develop context-aware applications, the preprocessing based extension to a common language may give rise to complications in using an IDE (Integrated Development Environment) tool, such as Eclipse or JBuilder. To overcome this limitation, we have also provided an annotation-based rule description. Based on Java 1.5 program annotations and the APT tool (annotation processing tool) [17], task rules are translated to work as normal Java code.

PLUE is now deployed on top of CAMUS (a Context-Awareness Middleware for URC Systems), the ubiquitous middleware system running in the Ubiquitous Dream Hall [2]. However, any PLUE applications could be ported on other ubiquitous middleware systems in a straightforward manner.

We are currently extending the expressiveness of the path expressions to handle ontology data derived from an external OWL resource and exploring methods of extending the state transition mechanism for more complex ubiquitous applications.

References

1. Wang Z, Garlan D, Task-Driven Computing, Technical Report, CMU-CS-00-154, School of Computer Science, Carnegie Mellon University, May 2000
2. Banavar G, Beck J, Gluzberg E, Munson J, Sussman JB, Zukowski D. Challenges: an application model for pervasive computing. In *Mobile Computing and Networking*, pages 266-274, 2000
3. H. Kim*, Y.-J. Cho*, S.-R. Oh, CAMUS: A Middleware Supporting Context-aware Services for Network-based Robots, In Proc. of IEEE Workshop on Advanced Robotics and its Social Impacts (ARSO '05)
4. Ubiquitous Dream Hall, http://www.ubiquitousdream.or.kr/, 2005
5. Java Remote Method Invocation (Java RMI), http://java.sun.com/products/jdk/rmi/
6. W3C XML Query (XQuery), http://www.w3.org/XML/Query, 2005
7. Lopez de Ipina D, An ECA Rule-Matching Service for Simpler Development of Reactive Applications, *IEEE. Distributed Systems*, Vol. 2, 2001
8. Yau SS, Karim F, Wang Y, Wang B, Gupta SKS. Reconfigurable Context-Sensitive Middleware for Pervasive Computing, *IEEE Pervasive Computing*, Vol. 1, Issue 3, July 2002
9. Rodríguez M, Favela J, Preciado A, Vizcaíno A. An Agent Middleware for Supporting Ambient Intelligence for Healthcare, In Proc. of ECAI 2004 Second Workshop on Agents Applied in Health Care, Aug 2004
10. Rakotonirainy A. Context-Oriented Programming for Pervasive Systems, Technical Report, University of Queensland, Sep 2002
11. Cardelli L, Gordon AD. Mobile ambients. *Theoretical Computer Science*, 240(1): 177-- 213, 2000

12. Grimm R, Davis J, Lemar E, MacBeth A, Swanson S, Anderson T, Bershad B, Borriello G, Gribble S, Wetherall D. System support for pervasive applications. *ACM Transactions on Computer Systems*, 22(4):421-486, Nov 2004

13. Ranganathan A, Chetan S, Al-Muhtadi J, Campbell RH, Mickunas MD. Olympus: A High-Level Programming Model for Pervasive Computing Environments, In Proc. of International Conference on Pervasive Computing and Communications (PerCom 2005), Kauai Island, Hawaii, March 8-12, 2005

14. Papakonstantinou Y, Garcia-Molina H, Widom J. Object exchange across heterogeneous information sources. In Proceedings of IEEE International Conference on Data Engineering (ICDE), pages 251--260, Taipei, Taiwan, Mar 1995

15. Cattell RGG, Barry DK, Berler M, Eastman J, Jordan D, Russell C, Schadow O, Stanienda T, Velez F, The Object Data Standard: *ODMG 3.0*, ISBN 1-55860-647-4, Academic Press, 2000

16. JavaCC Home, https://javacc.dev.java.net/, 2004

17. Annotation Processing Tool (apt), http://java.sun.com/j2se/1.5.0/docs/guide/apt/, 2004

JSense - Prototyping Sensor-Based, Location-Aware Applications in Java

Silvia Santini, Robert Adelmann, Marc Langheinrich,
Georg Schätti, and Steven Fluck

Institute for Pervasive Computing
ETH Zurich, 8092 Zurich, Switzerland
{santini, adelmann, langheinrich}@inf.ethz.ch,
{schaetti, stfluck}@student.ethz.ch

Abstract. Creating applications based on data from individual sensor nodes is typically a two-tiered process: Firstly, a (potentially large) number of sensor nodes is deployed in order to gather comprehensive datasets. After analyzing the collected data, algorithms are then installed on the individual nodes and iteratively fine-tuned using a collect-and-analyze procedure. This approach is not only time consuming, but also prone to errors: the two separate steps of data collection and data analysis complicate algorithm development; the absence of programming abstractions in embedded systems programming languages often introduces hard-to-detect runtime errors; and the lack of modern integrated development environments (IDEs) does not allow for quick trial-and-error prototyping. To mitigate those effects, we have developed JSense – a hardware abstraction layer for modern sensor nodes that allows for Java-based access to all sensor and actuator controls. It supports an IDE-based centralized development cycle with real-time debugging of a particular sensor environment, as well as the use of not-yet-available sensor and actuator hardware on each node, such as positioning information. Using JSense, designers of sensor-based environments can quickly try out a combination of situations and observe in real-time the data collection processes of their nodes, while programmers are able to prototype applications in their favorite Java-IDE in a hardware independent fashion, even taking into account not-yet-deployed node hardware.

1 Introduction

Sensor-based applications form the backbone of the field commonly known as ubiquitous computing or ambient intelligence. Without sensors, popular visions of "an environment recognising and responding to the presence of individuals in an invisible way" [1] will hardly be possible. Wireless sensor nodes such as Berkeley's MICA motes [2] or ETH Zurich's BTnodes [3] are envisioned to become both considerably smaller and cheaper, thus eventually allowing "an end-user buying a collection of sensor nodes and gateways, powering them up, and sprinkling them – literally and figuratively – within an environment"[4]. However, even if such motes would cost cents, not dollars, and even if they would be small enough to

H.Y. Youn, M. Kim, and H. Morikawa (Eds.): UCS 2006, LNCS 4239, pp. 300–315, 2006.

be "sprinkled" into our environment, it is far from clear how an end-user would actually go about *programming* these systems to do what she or he wants. This is because wireless sensor nodes today largely remain within the realm of embedded systems programming – typically requiring: intimate knowledge of the hardware being used (in order to correctly read out sensor values and communicate them wirelessly); the means to perform *in-system-programming*[1] (in order to upload new programs); experience with embedded debugging tools; and proficiency in low-level programming languages such as assembler or C.

Even if a user would fit this description, the development of a particular application would most likely still be tedious: Uploading programs to dozens of nodes, as well as debugging them individually, is a time consuming process. Moreover, due to the lack of abstractions in typical embedded system programming languages such as standard C, the likelihood for non-trivial runtime errors such as invalid pointers, improper stack management, or memory leaks significantly increases. Last but not least, the lack of direct control over individual nodes typically leads to a non-integrated (hence suboptimal) design process, where a first stage collects a multitude of sensory information (often spatially and temporally over- or undersampled) while a second stage is used to separately design an application on top of such datasets.

In this paper, we describe a Java-based network interface to wireless sensor nodes that significantly simplifies the design and development cycle for wireless sensor node applications. Our system, called JSense, works by deploying a small hardware-specific access and control layer on each individual sensor node. One or more gateway nodes can than be controlled via a set of common Java APIs to read out or send commands to each individual node, thus providing programmers with a Java-based direct access interface to their sensors. JSense's Java-based approach not only supports an "armchair" development-cycle (i.e., programmers can collect and analyze data, and eventually reprogram their sensor-based application from within their favorite Java-IDE), but also improves code portability and quality through the use of Java's high-level programming abstractions.

In addition to providing an easy-to-use sensor and actuator interface, JSense's hardware abstraction layer also supports the inclusion of *external sensors*, i.e., sensory information attributed to an individual node yet not collected by its own sensors. Examples for such an external sensor would be temperature information from an infrared camera picture, or a node's location determined with the help of an external positioning system. External sensors further simplify the development of sensor-based applications, as they not only allow for the inclusion of yet-to-be-released hardware (e.g., a GPS-enabled BTnode) but also transparently support the use of multiple sensor technologies (e.g., UWB, GPS, ultrasound) for performance comparison or across different environments (e.g., indoor vs. outdoor).

---

[1] In-system-programming describes the process of directly storing a program on an embedded microchip's flash memory, e.g., using a serial cable and a corresponding hardware programming device.

After briefly describing the main challenges related to the development of sensor-based applications and our concrete hardware setup in sections 2 and 3, we will present the JSense architecture and its implementation details in section 4. Section 5 will contrast our approach to existing development environments, while section 6 concludes with a summary and an outlook on future work.

2   Developing Sensor-Based Applications

Sensor-based applications use measurements from real-world sensor deployments to offer a particular service, e.g., a motion detection measurement might be used to automatically switch on the lights when a person enters a room. Using multiple sensors (both in terms of numbers and in terms of sensor types) can often significantly improve such an application, e.g., a co-located light sensor might help our motion sensor from above decide whether there is actually a need for lighting during daytime. Developing such a simple application on a typical sensor platform would require the developer to learn not only the basics of embedded systems programming (i.e., hardware-near programming languages such as C, microcontroller memory management, and in-system programming), but also the accompanying APIs of the employed sensors and may be even the platform's radio module. It is widely recognized that the absence of a common, extendible, and easy-to-use programming interface for accessing real-world sensors still represents a major burden for a rapid prototyping of sensor-based applications [4,5,6,7].

A typical approach to simplify the initial development of such applications is the use of a simulator: instead of having to deal with the intricacies of actual sensor hardware, the developer can use abstract sensor nodes with simulated sensor readings that can quickly be programmed and debugged. While simulations are a powerful tool for evaluating preliminary design and configuration choices, they often fail to capture the complex, real-time interactions between the application software and the faulty-prone, physical sensors. In order to build reliable sensor-based applications, real-world deployments must be an integral part of the development cycle [4,5].

So what do we need to support application developers in deploying their ideas onto actual sensor platforms, so that they can quickly try out a variety of approaches to provide higher-level services from low-level sensor data? Based on our own experiences in teaching sensor-based application development to students, as well as by reviewing a number of state-of-the-art development environments [4,5,7,8,9], we have distilled five core requirements:

1. *Hardware Abstraction:* Instead of requiring developers to learn about embedded systems programming (which entails both hardware and software concepts), they should be able to simply query a particular sensor on a particular node, or set a node's actuator (e.g., an LED), through a high-level, unified API.
2. *Integrated Design Process:* In order to avoid a suboptimal, decoupled design process (i.e., separate stages for data collection and algorithm design/testing),

the framework should allow near real-time gathering and analysis of collected sensor readings. This allows developers to receive direct feedback on algorithm design under controllable real-world conditions.

3. *Centralized Programming Environment:* While sensor-based applications will ultimately need to be distributed onto individual sensor nodes, the process of programming and debugging sensor nodes one by one is time consuming and error prone. Instead, developers can greatly benefit from a centralized programming environment that lets them (virtually) upload new program versions in an instant and quickly observe the results.

4. *High-Level Programming Language:* Embedded microcontrollers are typically programmed using the low-level C language, as it allows for a direct control of the individual IC registers and flags. In contrast to higher-level languages such as Ada or Java, however, low-level languages fail to support reliability and maintainability, nor do they try to address the compile-time detection of errors [10,11]. Providing developers with a Java-interface would thus not only improve the code quality, but also lower the barrier of entry, as an increasing number of universities, colleges, and secondary schools have since long adopted Java as the programming language for their introductory computer science courses [12].

5. *Location Information:* In most sensor-based applications scenarios – from large scale environmental monitoring [13] to smart-buildings applications [14] – reported measurements are often useless if they are not accompanied by a corresponding (absolute or relative) sensor position. In the smart room example cited above, the controlled light switch must obviously be the one that is co-located with the light and motion sensors. An application thus greatly benefits from having direct access to the geometric or symbolic [15] coordinates of the sensors within the actual deployment area.

With these five requirements in mind, we have developed JSense, a Java-based direct access and control interface to common sensor platforms. Like a number of similar rapid prototyping environments for sensor nodes (which we will discuss in detail in section 5 below), JSense aims at speeding up the prototyping phase of sensor-based applications by providing a high-level API for programming heterogenous sensor platforms. As we will describe in details in section 4, the JSense API provides a set of basic programming primitives for activating and deactivating sensors, importing sensor data streams, and eventually set parameters like sampling frequencies or actuators states. Unlike many other approaches, however, JSense provides an application developer with an easy-to-use *Java* interface, which – due to its popularity as a programming language in universities and colleges [12] – offers a significant potential to use JSense specifically as an educational tool, e.g., in tutorials accompanying courses in embedded systems, sensor networks, or ubiquitous computing. The adoption of Java as a programming language also facilitates the use of external data processing tools (e.g., Matlab) that already offer Java bindings, thus further improving applications development.

Secondly, JSense explicitly supports the use of *location information* on the sensor node. In many experimental settings, location data is typically retrieved from an external database, where the position of the single sensing devices is registered during deployment. This solution not only seriously limits reconfigurability, but also makes the system prone to inaccuracies, as sensors could be moved and thus would invalidate the information in the database. However, as only few of today's popular sensor platforms supports location sensing, JSense provides the concept of *external sensors* in order to allow developers to seamlessly use third-party positioning systems (e.g., GPS or Cricket, but also optical systems based on fiducial markers) as if the positioning data would be generated by the actual sensor platform.

Before describing the JSense architecture in detail (and in particular its Java-interface and location data support), we will briefly describe our particular hardware setup, i.e., the sensor platform and localization system that we have used to develop our initial prototype of JSense: The Tmote Sky sensor platform and the Ubisense location system.

3   JSense Hardware Setup

In the context of this work we use the term *sensor platforms* to refer to a device endowed with one or more sensors and/or actuators, some computational capabilities, and means for wireless communication. A sensor platform can thus consist of a single, stand-alone temperature or orientation sensor [16], or be a more complex device that offers a range of sensing capabilities [3,17,18].

One popular sensor platform family – the Berkeley MICA motes – is based on work originally done at UC Berkeley and Intel Research [19]. Its latest generation is the "Tmote Sky" sensor mote, which is developed by Moteiv, a UC Berkeley spin-off company [20]. It features an IEEE 802.15.4 compliant radio transceiver; built-in temperature, light and humidity sensors; and three LEDs. The Tmote Sky platform can be programmed using "TinyOS", a component-based, open-source operating system widely used for research in wireless embedded systems [21,22]. Applications on top of TinyOS are developed through composition of independent modules, which must be written using "NesC", an extended dialect of the C programming language [23]. TinyOS has already been ported to a large number of hardware platforms and is therefore widely used within the sensor network community for research and development. Due to the popularity of both TinyOS and the Berkeley motes family, we have started our initial development of JSense using the Tmote Sky sensor platform. While programming the Tmote Sky motes is well supported by the (mote-specific) NesC programming language, it is still hampered by the general drawbacks of C-programming, as well as the difficulties of learning the needed TinyOS programming paradigm.

Although some commercially available platforms also integrate positioning devices, such as GPS receivers [24,18] wireless sensor platforms typically do not feature any integrated positioning devices, due to their high costs and significant energy requirements. However, as we pointed out in the previous section, the ability to retrieve position information is often crucial in order to validate sensor-based application design and system configuration. We have thus incorporated the ability to include *external sensors* when modeling a sensor platform in JSense, i.e., sensors that operate independently of the actual sensor platform used, but which can be correlated with individual nodes such that they form a single, virtual node. We use this mechanism to incorporate location information from an external positioning system directly into the representation of every single Tmote Sky, making it appear as if this sensor platform would already be equipped with such a positioning technology.

The particular location system we use is based on ultra wide band (UWB) technology, which promises energy-efficient, accurate positioning in both indoor and outdoor settings. Systems that use this technology for getting 3-dimensional indoor positioning information are already commercial available, like, e.g., the Ubisense system [25]. We have installed a set of Ubisense sensors in our student lab, which are able to report the geometrical coordinates of corresponding Ubisense *tags* (i.e., small UWB radio beacons) with an accuracy of up to 30 cm in 3D. We thus enhanced the sensing capabilities of the Tmote Sky platform by attaching a Ubisense tag to the sensor node, and then provided the necessary Java software interface to our JSense architecture in order to integrate positioning information into the regular Tmose Sky sensor readings (i.e., temperature, light, and humidity). JSense in effect allows application developers to use this compound platform as a unique, homogenous entity.

The next section will explain in more detail how our JSense architecture combines the measurements collected by the Tmote Sky sensing devices with the position information computed by the Ubisense location system.

4   The JSense Architecture

The first core component of JSense's two-tiered architecture sketched in figure 1, is implemented through so-called *Virtual Platforms*. As we will detail in section 4.2 Virtual Platforms (VP) are software entities accessible through a standardized Java API that virtually bind together a compound of different sensor platforms. In our prototypical implementation, for example, a VP combines a Tmote Sky sensor node and the correspondent affixed Ubisense tag in a unique virtual sensor platform.

JSense's second core component consists in a lightweight, platform-specific, hardware access and control layer, that shields the application developer from the nasty hardware-specific details of the sensor platforms. This framework, described in more detail in section 4.1 below, enables remote access to the sensing devices available on the physical hardware platforms and is easily extendible due to its component-based architecture.

4.1   Local Command Execution: The Hardware Abstraction Layer

For enabling ease of access to the sensing devices of a sensor platform, JSense provides a hardware-specific access and control layer, the so-called Hardware

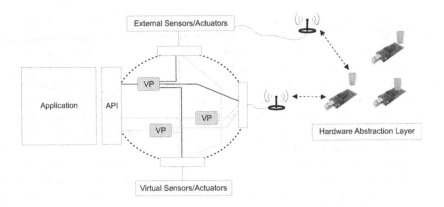

Fig. 1. The JSense architecture

Abstraction Layer (HAL). The HAL runs on the specific platform it has been written for and uses a pluggable-module approach, where each sensor or actuator is accessed through an individual driver module. The HAL is not only responsible for scheduling and executing hardware access (using the sensor specific modules) but also for managing the received access requests and returning the adequate sensor responses. The existence of this abstraction layer allows the application developer to issue remote access requests that will be received and executed on the target platform, while the correspondent sensing results will be back-forwarded to the remote system, e.g., a desktop PC.

Figure 2 shows the implementation of JSense's Hardware Abstraction Layer on the Tmote Sky sensor platform. Its lightweight, easy-to-extend implementation is based on three main components. The *SensorComm* component manages the communication with the remote system: it is responsible for receiving remotely issued commands and forwarding them (after adequate unmarshalling) to the *Sensor-Logic* component. Commands typically have the form "get current value of sensor X" or "perform X on actuator Y". In order to reduce, when possible, the communication overhead, commands that need to be executed periodically can be issued by the remote system as periodic access requests. This requests will perform sensor/actuator access with the specified frequency and for the desired time frame.

The duty of scheduling sensor/actuator access is taken over by the *SensorLogic* component, which handles commands coming from the *SensorComm* component and either executes them immediately or provides the adequate scheduling for periodic execution, as illustrated in figure 3. When a command needs to be executed (thus, a sensor need to be read or an actuator to be set), the *Sensor-Logic* component activates the correspondent sensor- or actuator-specific module, which is responsible for the actual physical access to the hardware device. The compound of these modules constitutes the third logic component of our HAL. Please note that enhancing the sensor platform with additional sensors and/or actuators, just requires adding to the JSense'S framework the correspondent sensor-/actuator-specific physical access modules and registering them to the *SensorLogic* component.

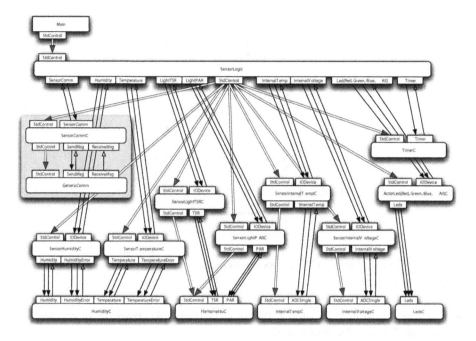

Fig. 2. Component model of the **JSense**'s Hardware Abstraction Layer for the Tmote Sky sensor platform

Access request responses sent through the *SensorComm* component are received by a Tmote Sky node connected to a remote system (e.g., a desktop PC) through a USB serial port. This node acts as a gateway between the sensor deployment and the desktop PC by transferring received radio packets to the *SerialForwarder*, a Java application that is part of the TinyOS tool-chain. The *SerialForwarder* listens for TinyOS packets on a serial port and forwards them over a local TCP network socket, thus allowing more than one application to send and receive packets to and from the "gateway" Tmote Sky.

The current **JSense**'s HAL implementation for the Tmote Sky sensor platform, allows for an easy and efficient access to the physical sensors and actuators, generating a 63kB footprint on the 1MB external flash memory module of the Tmote Sky platform. This footprint includes both the operating system's proprietary modules and the **JSense**'s HAL components for accessing the platform's built-in sensors and actuators.

4.2 Remote Access: **JSense**'s Virtual Platforms

As mentioned earlier in this section, a Virtual Platform is a software entity that virtually binds together a compound of different real sensor platforms. Figure 4 shows that this virtual entity typically integrates one or more target platforms and eventually external and virtual sensors. We refer to a *target platform*

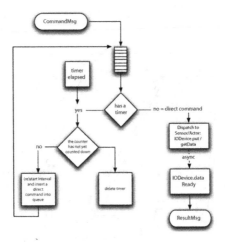

Fig. 3. Scheduling of sensors/actuators access as implemented by the *SensorLogic* component

as a sensor platform that runs a **JSense**'s Hardware Abstraction Layer, for instance, the Tmote Sky sensor node.

The possibility to add external sensors to a target platform represents a powerful feature of the **JSense** system, as it allows for incorporating functioning sensor hardware that is not (yet) integrated into the target platform. We assume that external sensors can communicate independently over a wireless channel, or at least can be assessed from the outside (e.g., using a camera-picture or a microphone array). For instance, a location sensor can be "attached" to a target platform in order to enable prototyping of location-aware, sensor-based applications. Due to the often significant power, cost and size requirements of location sensors such as GPS receivers or UWB tags, these devices are typically not integrated on common sensor node platforms (such as MICA-motes or BTnodes). However, using the VP abstraction we can easily integrate a target platform with an external GPS module or a UWB-tag, allowing the application developer to access these devices as they were built-in sensors of the target platform, thus completely hiding the existence of an external positioning system from our development cycle. This not only provides us with a unified access and control framework to heterogenous sensor platforms, but also allows for the simultaneous use of multiple technologies, thus offering a precious tool for e.g., performance comparisons.

Target platforms can be integrated not only with external, but also with so-called *virtual* sensors. These represent devices that either cannot be purchased (e.g, for cost or availability reasons) or even do not yet physically exist. In both cases, the virtual sensor simulates the existence of a real sensor. In effect, using the concept of virtual sensors, we can develop sensor-based applications also integrating yet-to-be-released or yet-to-be-operational sensing devices, significantly shortening the development cycle.

Once sensing devices have been associated to a certain VP, JSense provides a transparent access to the physical hardware through a standardized Java API. The development of an application that makes use of the deployed sensor hardware is therefore reduced to the compilation of a standard Java program that access the correspondent VPs. For the application programmer, a VP is represented by a Java object that provides methods for a direct access to its sensors and actuators.

The VP abstraction supports the development and implementation of both *distributed* Java applications (i.e., each virtual node is a separate thread with individual code) and *centralized* applications (i.e., virtual nodes are simply objects that can be queried and accessed from a central program). This allows developers a gentle learning curve into sensor-based application development, as one can quickly prototype a centralized application, and then gradually distribute it onto individual nodes.

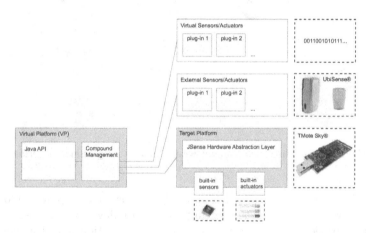

Fig. 4. A JSense Virtual Platform as a compound of a target platform, external and virtual sensors

We would like to point out that integrating new external sensor and actuator systems into JSense requires writing the appropriate Java bindings and registering them as plug-in components using methods provided by the JSense Java API. For instance, the Ubisense UWB location system has been integrated in JSense by implementing a software layer that enables a Java-based access to the most relevant functionalities of the Ubisense native C++ libraries through a dedicated socket-connection.

4.3 JSense Enabled Systems

The JSense system is in general very well suited for centralized implementation and testing of applications requiring on-line processing of real-world sensor data. For this kind of applications, the enrichment of sensor readings with the correspondent location information represents in many cases a mandatory feature. For this reason, the JSense system provides the Ubisense UWB-based location system as an external sensor integrating the Tmote Sky sensor node platform.

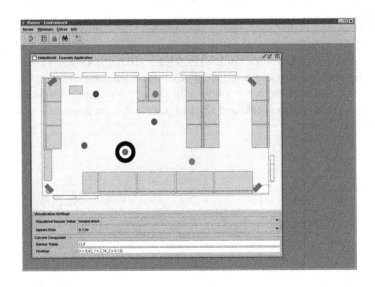

Fig. 5. Application development using JSense: the graphical interface

A set of 6, Ubisense-integrated, Tmote Sky sensor nodes deployed in our student lab, provided the hardware setting for prototyping our first, 'hello-world'-style JSense-based application. The developed application aimed at collecting temperature readings (with an update rate of 0.1 Hz) from the deployed nodes. The temperature data and the correspondent position information from the Ubisense system could be visualized through a simple graphical interface (see figure 5) and were logged in a protocol file for off-line inspection. Figure 6 shows the simple Java program that it was necessary to write for implementing the described application. As it can be seen from the code, accessing sensor or actuators on the target platform or adding an external sensor to a VP, require just simple Java method calls.

Thus, using JSense a first prototype of a sensor-based, location-aware application can be written and tested in Java, having all the benefits of unrestricted system resources and integrated development environments. On this level, the logical correctness of the approach can be tested and the general functioning in combination with real sensor data can be assured – with basic Java knowledge being the only required skill for the application developer.

```
1   import jSense.*;
2   import jSense.Sensors.*;
3   import jSense.Actuators.*;
4   import jSense.ExternalSystems.*;
5   import tools.protocol.*;

6   public class JSenseDemo implements VPListener {

7     private VirtualPlatform vp;

8     TemperatureSensor tempSensor;
9     LEDActuator ledActuator;
10    LocationSensor locationSensor;

11    Protocol protocol;

12    public JSenseDemo() {
13      // create a new virtual platform associated to a TMoteSky node (logical adress 1):
14      vp = new VirtualPlatform(new TMoteSkyPlatform(1));

15      // add components: (UbiSense tag number 016-000-003-180)
16      ExternalSystem localizationSensor = new UWBLocationSensor("016-000-003-180");
17      vp.add(localizationSensor);

18      // create shortcuts to the used sensors and acuators:
19      tempSensor=(TemperatureSensor)((TMoteSkyPlatform)vp.getPlatform()).getTempSensor();
20      ledActuator=(LEDActuator)((TMoteSkyPlatform)vp.getPlatform()).getLEDActuator();
21      locationSensor=(UWBLocationSensor)(vp.getExternalSystems().elementAt(0));

22      // initialize the protocol system:
23      protocol = new Protocol("c:/temperature_readings.txt");
24      protocol.setTimeStampsEnabled(true);
25    }

26    public void directAccessExample() {
27      // get the current temperature value:
28      float temperature = tempSensor.getTemperature();
29      // turn the first LED on:
30      ledActuator.setLED(0, true);
31    }

32    public void eventBasedAccessExample() {
33      vp.subscribe(this);
34      // get 100 temperature readings every 1000 ms, starting now (0 ms):
35      vp.issueTask(new SensorReadingTask(tempSensor,0,100,1000));
36    }

37    /** This method is called if the VP receives a message regarding an issued task*/
38    public void resultReceived(Result result) {
39      if (result.getSensor() instanceof TemperatureSensor) {
40        TemperatureSensor tempSensor = (TemperatureSensor) result.getSensor();
41        // write the obtained values into the protocol file, incuding the current system time:
42        protocol.println("temperature:"+tempSensor.getTemperature()+
43                         "at position:"+locationSensor.getPosition());
44      }
45    }

46    public static void main(String[] args) {
47      JSenseDemo demo = new JSenseDemo();
48      demo.directAccessExample();
49      demo.eventBasedAccessExample();
50    }
51  }
```

Fig. 6. JSense enabled, sensor-based application written as a standard Java program. Using the JSense package, sensors and actuators can be accessed through simple methods calls.

5   Related Work

Due to the growing interest in wireless sensor applications, researcher have put considerable effort in the development of tools for allowing easy development and prototyping of wireless, sensor-based systems. For instance, a number of interesting approaches like TASK [4], EES [5] and SNACK [7], have been proposed within the sensor networks research community.

The "Tiny Application Sensor Kit" (TASK) provides sensor networks end-users with a set of graphical tools for facilitating deployment and inspection of environmental monitoring systems. It has been successfully used in real-world experiments and complies with the need of end-users providing, among others, ease of software installation, simple deployment tools for sensor placement, reconfigurability and ease of integration with data analysis tools. TASK has been specifically designed for low data rate environmental monitoring applications and relies on the TinyDB query processor [26]. The data collected in the context of TASK-enabled real-world experiments has been made publicly available [27] and serves as a benchmark for evaluating data processing techniques for sensor networks [28,29]. Unlike JSense, TASK does not support easy extendability of the sensor platform and is specifically designed for inexpert computer users, rather than for application developers that are familiar with high-level programming languages like Java. The same considerations apply for the Extensible Sensing System (EES), that has been used to collect micro-climate data from large scale (> 100 nodes) outdoor deployments. Unlike TASK, the sensor nodes in ESS are heterogeneous and run a proprietary "Data Sampling Engine" rather than TinyDB.

One of the approaches we retain to be more closely related to our work is the "Sensor Network Construction Kit" (SNACK). SNACK is a NesC-based system that aims at providing a set of efficient, high-level service libraries to support sensor network application development. However, while SNACK uses a proprietary component composition language that the application developer must eventually learn from scratch, JSense applications can be written using standard Java programming.

Other interesting systems, which are to some respect related to our work are "Marionette" [8] and "IrisNet" [9]. Marionette is a tool for interactive sensor network application development. It provides remote access to wireless embedded devices through a Phyton-based client and allows to monitor and change at runtime the state of a sensor node. The Marionette architecture promises to become a powerful tool for developing and debugging sensor network applications, but it addresses expert programmers that can understand and properly manage NesC modules, rather than Java developers, as JSense does. The IrisNet architecture aims at providing the missing software components necessary to support the realization of a "Worldwide Sensor Web", in which users can access a plethora of distributed, remote sensor systems through the internet. IrisNet holds distributed databases to store sensor data across the network and uses XML to query these databases. Sensors send their data to a so-called *Sensing Agents* (SA) that pre-processes the data and updates the sensor database distributed throughout the network. IrisNet's main purpose is also the provision of means for a unified access interface to real-world sensors, but while JSense mainly accesses local sensors, reachable through a one-hop, wireless communication channel, IrisNet uses the world wide web infrastructure for accessing remotely located sensors.

Researchers at Sun Microsystems Laboratories recently announced a project that aims at realizing a sensor development kit called Sun SPOT (Small Programmable Object Technology) [6]. A Sun SPOT platform is based on a 32 bit ARM CPU and an 11 channel 2.4 GHz wireless transceiver and is equipped with temperature, light and motion sensors. The Sun SPOT system does not need to rely on an operating system like TinyOS: it features the so-called "Squawk VM", a Java Virtual Machine mainly written in Java (only the interpreter and the garbage collector are written in C) that acts as an operating system running "on the bare metal" of the hardware platform. Applications building upon the Sun SPOT platform can be completely written in Java, using the native libraries of the Squawk Java VM. Since it is Java-based, the Sun SPOT will be easily integrable in our JSense system, and will thus constitute an additional sensor platform to experiment with. However, even if the the Sun SPOT technology is envisioned to enable rapid prototyping of some wireless sensor-based applications, it is still unclear if and how this technology would be mature enough to be extended to other hardware platforms. For instance, consider that while the Tmote Sky platform features $10kB$ of RAM and $1MB$ of flash memory, the Squawk VM has a $80kB$ footprint on the RAM and additional $270kB$ of libraries need to be loaded on the flash memory. Moreover, while considerable effort has been spent in the wireless sensor community to minimize cost of sensor platforms, a Sun SPOT development kit containing two wireless sensors, a base station and the software development tools will be available for about \$500. Three Tmote Sky nodes can be purchased for less than half of this money.

6   Conclusions

Today's means of designing, developing, and deploying sensor-based applications lack in flexibility, reliability, and convenience, thus seriously hampering sensor-based application development [4]. With JSense, we have presented a rapid prototyping environment for wireless sensor-based applications that offers developers not only a convenient Java interface for direct access and control of individual sensor nodes, but which also seamlessly integrates external sensor information, such as positioning data, in order to better design and inspect location-dependent sensor applications.

The support for Java programming puts sensor-based application development within the reach of millions of Java programmers and is especially relevant in the educational domain, where Java is often preferred over languages like C or C++ for introductory programming classes [12]. The seamless inclusion of location information as part of a Virtual Platform offers the promise of a much faster and more exact design cycle, as sensor readings can be directly correlated with a sensed position, alleviating the need for manual location measurements or fixed sensor locations.

JSense represents a first step towards a much simpler access to sensor-based applications, yet much needs to be done before we can use JSense to develop complex real-world applications. In particular, we kept the JSense Java API very simple in order to get a first, working prototypical implementation of the system. On the basis of this first experience, we are currently redesigning the sensor programming interface in order to allow more powerful querying primitives than single-value or periodic sensor queries. An almost trivial extension, for example, is to include support for spatial queries, i.e., based on a nodes location, as JSense's virtual platforms already support positioning information "natively".

Obviously, JSense will also benefit from extending it to run on a larger number of sensor platforms, e.g., the BTnodes. We are currently planning to release JSense as an open-source project in order to simplify the addition of different hardware. By using JSense in a number of student projects within our lab, we also hope to gain more insights into the practical uses (and shortcomings) of our system.

References

1. Ahola, J.: Ambient Intelligence. ERCIM News (47) (2001)
2. Estrin, D., Culler, D., Pister, K., Sukhatme, G.: Connecting the Physical World with Pervasive Networks. Pervasive Computing **1**(1) (2002) 59–69
3. Beutel, J., Kasten, O., Mattern, F., Römer, K., Siegemund, F., Thiele, L.: Prototyping Wireless Sensor Network Applications with BTnodes. In: Proceedings of the First European Workshop on Wireless Sensor Networks (EWSN'04). Number 2920 in LNCS, Berlin, Germany, Springer-Verlag (2004) 323–338
4. Buonadonna, P., Gay, D., Hellerstein, J.M., Hong, W., Madden, S.: TASK: Sensor Network in a Box. In: Proceedings of the Second IEEE European Workshop on Wireless Sensor Networks (EWSN'05), Istanbul, Turkey (2005)
5. Guy, R., Greenstein, B., Hicks, J., Kapur, R., Ramanathan, N., Schoellhammer, T., Stathopoulos, T., Weeks, K., Chang, K., Girod, L., Estrin, D.: Experiences with the Extensible Sensing System ESS. Technical Report 01-310-825-3127, UCLA Center for Embedded Network Sensing (2006)
6. Sun Microsystems Laboratories: The Sun SPOT Project. (Project Website: www.sunspotworld.com)
7. Greenstein, B., Kohler, E., Estrin, D.: A Sensor Network Application Construction Kit (SNACK). In: Proceedings of the Second ACM Intl. Conf. on Embedded Networked Sensor Systems (SenSys'04), Baltimore, MD, USA, ACM Press (2004)
8. Whitehouse, K., Tolle, G., Taneja, J., Sharp, C., Kim, S., Jeong, J., Hui, J., Dutta, P., , Culler, D.: Marionette: Using RPC for Interactive Development and Debugging of Wireless Embedded Networks. In: Proceedings of the Fifth Intl. Symposium on Information Processing in Sensor Networks (IPSN'06), Nashville, TN, USA, ACM Press (2006) 416–423
9. Gibbons, P., Karp, B., Ke, Y., Nath, S., Seshan, S.: IrisNet: An Architecture for a Worldwide Sensor Web. IEEE Pervasive Computing **2**(4) (2003) 22–33
10. Wheeler, D.A.: Ada, C, C++, and Java vs. the Steelman. Ada Letters **XVII**(4) (1997) 88–112
11. Martin, P.: Java, the Good, the Bad, and the Ugly. SIGPLAN Notices (1998)

12. Roberts, E.: Resources to Support the Use of Java in Introductory Computer Science. In: Proceedings of the 35th SIGCSE Technical Symposium on Computer Science Education (SIGCSE'04), New York, NY, USA, ACM Press (2004) 233–234
13. Szewczyk, R., Mainwaring, A., Polastre, J., Culler, D.: An Analysis of a Large Scale Habitat Monitoring Application. In: Proceedings of the Second ACM Intl. Conf. on Embedded Networked Sensor Systems (SenSys'04), Baltimore, MD, USA (2004)
14. Holmquist, L., Gellersen, H., Kortuem, G., Antifakos, S., Michahelles, F., Schiele, B., Beigl, M., Maze, R.: Building Intelligent Environments with Smart-Its. IEEE Computer Graphics and Applications 24(1) (2004) 56–64
15. Becker, C., Dürr, F.: On Location Models for Ubiquitous Computing. Personal and Ubiquitous Computing 9(1) (2005) 20–31
16. Xsens Ltd.: Motion Technologies. (Company Website: www.xsens.com)
17. Polastre, J., Szewczyk, R., Culler, D.: Telos: Enabling Ultra-Low Power Wireless Research. In: Proceedings of the Fourth Intl. Symposium on Information Processing in Sensor Networks: Special Track on Platform Tools and Design Methods for Network Embedded Sensors (IPSN/SPOTS'05), Los Angeles, CA, USA (2005)
18. Crossbow Technology Inc.: Solutions for Wireless Sensor Networks. (Company Website: www.xbow.com)
19. Szewczyk, R., Polastre, J., Mainwaring, A.M., Culler, D.E.: Lessons from a Sensor Network Expedition. In: Proceedings of the First European Workshop on Wireless Sensor Networks (EWSN'04). Number 2920 in LNCS, Berlin, Germany, Springer-Verlag (2004) 307–322
20. Moteiv Corporation: Accelerating Sensor Networking. (Company Website: www.moteiv.com)
21. Hill, J., Szewczyk, R., Woo, A., Hollar, S., Culler, D.E., Pister, K.S.J.: System Architecture Directions for Networked Sensors. In: Proceedings of the Ninth Intl. Conf. on Architectural Support for Programming Languages and Operating Systems (ASPLOS-IX), Cambridge, MA, USA, ACM Press (2000) 93–104
22. TinyOS: An Open-Source Operating System Designed for Wireless Embedded Sensor Networks. (Project Website: www.tinyos.net)
23. Gay, D., Levis, P., von Behren, R., Welsh, M., Brewer, E., Culler, D.: The nesC Language: A Holistic Approach to Networked Embedded Systems. In: Proceedings of the ACM SIGPLAN Conference on Programming Language Design and Implementation, San Diego, CA, USA (2003)
24. Wildlife Computers: Innovative Tags for Innovative Research. (Company Website: www.wildlifecomputers.com)
25. Ubisense Ltd.: The Ubisense UWB Location System. (Company Website: www.ubisense.net)
26. Madden, S.R., Franklin, M.J., Hellerstein, J.M., Hong, W.: TinyDB: An Acquisitional Query Processing System for Sensor Networks. ACM Transactions on Database Systems 30(1) (2005) 122–173
27. Intel Research Laboratories Berkeley: Intel Lab Data. (Project Website: berkeley.intel-research.net/labdata/)
28. Deshpande, A., Guestrin, C., Madden, S., Hellerstein, J., Hong, W.: Model-Driven Data Acquisition in Sensor Networks. In: Proceedings of the 30th Intl. Conf. on Very Large Data Base (VLDB'04), Toronto, Canada (2004)
29. Santini, S., Römer, K.: An Adaptive Strategy for Quality-Based Data Reduction in Wireless Sensor Networks. In: Proceedings of the 3rd Intl. Conf. on Networked Sensing Systems (INSS'06), Chicago, IL, USA (2006)

Estimation of the Number of Competing Stations Applied with Central Difference Filter for an IEEE 802.11 Network

Jang-Sub Kim[1], Hojin Shin[1], Dong-Ryeol Shin[1], and Woo-Gon Chung[2]

[1] School of Information and Communication Engineering,
Sungkyunkwan University,
300 ChunChun-Dong, JangAn-Gu, Suwon, Korea 440-746
{jangsub, hjshin, drshin}@ece.skku.ac.kr
[2] Computer Science Dept. CSU at Bakersfield, USA
wchung@csub.edu

Abstract. The ubiquitous computing environments requires integration of a variety of current and future wired and wireless networking technologies to support seamless computing and communication environments for user applications. WLAN also need to be a part of a seamless communication infrastructure, as they can be used either as a wireless extension of wired networks or peer-to-peer networks. This paper proposes a new methodology to estimate the number of competing stations in an IEEE 802.11 network. Due to nonlinear nature of measurement model, an iterative nonlinear filtering algorithm, called the "Central Difference Filter" (CDF), is employed. The CDF can provide a better alternative to nonlinear filtering than the conventional extended Kalman filter (EKF) since it avoids errors associated with linearization. This approach shows both high accuracy as well as prompt reactivity to changes in the network occupancy status. Specially, our proposed algorithm is more improved performance in non saturated conditions than the EKF. Numerical results show that it provides a more viable means for estimation of the number of competing stations in IEEE 802.11 network than estimators based on the EKF.

Keywords: Competing Stations Estimation, Central Difference Filter, Extended Kalman Filter, IEEE 802.11 WLAN, Distributed Coordination Function.

1 Introduction

A variety of current and future wired and wireless networking technologies can be transformed into seamless communication environments supporting future ubiquitous computing. The integration of WLAN (Wireless LAN)s and Mobile cellular networks has recently evolved into hot issue. By supporting Mobile IP, WLAN can meet demands for expanded wireless access coverage while maintaining continuous connectivity from one WLAN to another or from one WLAN to 3G cellular networks. Mobile technologies such as GSM (Global System for Mobile Communications), GPRS (General Packet Radio Service), UMTS (Universal Mobile Telecommunication System) and IS-95 A/B and cdma2000 provide high-mobility but with less data

H.Y. Youn, M. Kim, and H. Morikawa (Eds.): UCS 2006, LNCS 4239, pp. 316–330, 2006.

transmission bandwidth to mobile users over a wide coverage area. On the other hand, WLAN technologies such as IEEE 802.11 and European HiperLAN are gaining popularity, as they provide low-cost, high data bandwidth but with less mobility for the localized hot spots. For the hot spot area such as a building, a station or an airport, it is normally covered by a number of networks. Mobile cellular networks and WLANs will complement each other to provide ubiquitous high-speed wireless Internet connectivity to mobile users. Therefore, it is important to consider dual mode users roaming in between Mobile cellular networks and WLANs. Like this, WLAN technology also need to be a part of a seamless communication infrastructure, as they can be used either as a wireless extension of wired networks or peer-to-peer networks.

In this paper, in order to maximize the WLAN system performance, we propose an improved estimation of the number of competing stations applied with Central Difference Filter (CDF). Wireless LAN (WLAN) provides a resolution to realize mobile Internet, and IEEE 802.11 Wireless LAN (WLAN) has emerged as one of the most deployed wireless access technologies. In the IEEE 802.11 Medium Access Control (MAC) layer protocol, the basic access method is the distributed coordination function (DCF) which is based on the mechanism of carrier sense multiple access with collision avoidance (CSMA/CA). The performance strongly depends on the number of competing stations. In infrastructured 802.11 networks, the information available at the AP (Access Point) is limited to the number n of "associated" stations, a number which may be very different from the number of competing stations.

The ability to acquire knowledge of n leads to several implications. Firstly, it has been shown [1] [2] that, in order to maximize the system performance, the backoff window should be made depend upon n. Indeed, the knowledge of n has several possible practical implications also in currently deployed 802.11 networks. The 802.11 standard is designed to allow both basic access and RTS/CTS access modes to coexist. The standard suggests that the RTS/CTS access model should be chosen when the packet payload exceeds a given RTS threshold. However, it has been shown [3] that the RTS threshold which maximizes the system throughput is not a constant value, but significantly depends on the number n of competing stations. Specifically, as the number of stations in the network increases, the Basic Access becomes ineffective and it results convenient to switch to the RTS/CTS mode even in the presence of short packets. Clearly, this operation requires each station to be capable of estimating n. Secondly, in cellular-like 802.11 scenario, the estimated knowledge of traffic load and number of stations sharing an 802.11 cell might effectively derive load-balancing and handover algorithms to achieve better network resource utilization. In this point a view, it is important to estimate the knowledge of the number n of competing stations in not only IEEE 802.11 network but also wireless technologies. Thus, we focus on the accuracy of estimator for track/estimate the number of competing stations. In this paper, to improve the performance of competing stations estimation for IEEE 802.11 network, we introduce an efficient technique to estimate the number of competing stations. This technique is based on the SUF that provides an improvement in the accuracy and stability more than the conventional EKF.

The Kalman filtering is known as a recursive optimum approximation to the optimum MMSE solutions [4]. A central and vital operation performed in the Kalman filter is the propagation of a Gaussian random variable (GRV) through the state and measurement models. In the EKF, the state distribution is approximated by a GRV, which is then propagated analytically through the first-order linearization of the nonlinear system. This can introduce large errors in the true posterior mean and co-variance of the transformed GRV, which may lead to sub-optimal performance and sometimes divergence of the filter. Giuseppe Bianchi paper [5] was presented based on the EKF-based estimator. Since EKF-based estimator is frequently divergence in non saturated conditions, we proposed a new mechanism to more efficiency, accuracy and convergence than the EKF-based estimator.

A new filtering called UT (Unscented Transform) has been employed to tackle the nonlinearity and shown its effectiveness in terms of the divergence reduction or error propagation [6]. The UF (using UT) addresses this problem by using a deterministic sampling approach. The state distribution is again approximated by a GRV, but is now represented using a minimal set of carefully chosen sample points. All the itera-tive solutions including Kalman filters appeared in the literature necessarily assume that the unknown parameters are Gaussian distributed. These sample points com-pletely capture the true mean and covariance of the GRV, and when propagated through the true nonlinear system, captures the posterior mean and covariance accu-rately to the 3rd order (Taylor series expansion) for any nonlinearity. The EKF, in contrast, only achieves first-order accuracy. Remarkably, the computational complex-ity of the UF is the same order as that of the EKF [6]. Moreover, we will apply the scaled unscented transform (SUT) [7] that describes a generalisation of the unscented transformation (UT) which allows sigma points to be scaled to an arbitrary dimension. In this paper, we called "Scaled Unscented Filter" (SUF). We adapted a new way of parameterization for Gaussian variables and instead, applied the extended Kalman filtering. Instead of approximating the nonlinearity by linearization as in the EKF, the SUT [7] parameterizes the Gaussian distribution and directly apply to the nonlinear function in the measurement model.

To relate this sample-based (*sigma point*) approach the EKF, we consider expand-ing the nonlinear function by polynomial approximations based on *Sterling's interpo-lating formulas*. This filter is called CDF. This filter can interpret as a Taylor series expansion where the derivatives are replaced by central differences which rely on functional evaluations. The CDF and the SUF simply retain a different subset. It is shown in [8] that the CDF has marginally higher theoretical accuracy than the SUF in the higher terms of Taylor series expansion, but we've found in practice that both the CDF and SUF perform equally well with negligible difference in estimation accuracy. The CDF as proposed estimator does, however, have a smaller absolute error in the fourth order term and also guarantees positive semi-definiteness (PSD) of the poste-rior covariance. In contrast, the SUF may result in a non-positive semi-definite co-variance, which is compensated for using two additional heuristic scaling parameters [8]. Additional advantage of the CDF over the SUF is that it only uses a single scalar scaling parameter, the central difference half-step size h, as opposed to the three (α, β, κ) that the SUF uses. From this fact, the CDF has smaller degree of freedom than the SUF. Thus the proposed estimator can easily control more than the SUF. Both filters generate estimates that are clearly superior to those calculated by a conven-tional EKF.

In summary, it is the purpose of this paper to improve the previous development of estimators to estimate of the number of competing stations in an IEEE 802.11 net-work. While the work shown in [5] used the EKF as competing stations estimators, we employ a recently introduced filtering such as the CDF to give more improved performance than the EKF.

The rest of this paper is organized as follows. Section 2 introduces the state-space model that will be used throughout the paper and a description of problem formulation. Section 3 provides a description of the EKF, and the CDF modified and applied to competing stations estimation in IEEE 802.11 network. The results of the performance from computer simulations are given in Section 4. Finally, Section 5 provides concluding remarks.

2 Problem Formulation

2.1 State Space Model

In this section, we show that, starting from the model proposed in [5], it is immediate to derive a formula that explicitly relates the number of competing stations to a performance figure that can be measured run-time by each station. We consider a scenario composed of a fixed number n of contending stations, each operating in saturation conditions. Channel conditions are ideal: no hidden stations and no packet corruption is considered.

From [5], we provide an explicit expression of n versus the conditional collision probability p as follows:

$$n = f(p) = 1 + \frac{\log(1-p)}{\log\left(1 - \frac{2(1-2p)}{(1-2p)(W+1) + pW(1-(2p)^m)}\right)} \tag{1}$$

where n is the number of competing stations, p is the conditional collision probability, m and W are the known and constant backoff parameters.

Since the conditional collision probability p can be independently measured by each station by simply monitoring the channel activity, if follows that each station can estimate the number of competing stations. Specifically, each individual station can efficiently measure p as follows. Since in each busy slot an eventual packet transmission would have failed, the conditional collision probability can be obtained by counting the number of experience collisions, C_{coll}, as well as the number of observed busy slots, C_{busy}, and dividing this sum by the total number B of observed slots on which the measurement is taken,

$$p_{measurement} = \frac{C_{busy} + C_{coll}}{B} \tag{2}$$

If, at time l, there are $n(l)$ stations in the system, then, the conditional collision probability can be obtained as $h(n(l))$, where h is the inverse function of (1). We can thus rewrite the measurement model $p(l)$ as follows:

$$p(l) = f^{-1}(n(l)) + v(l) = h(n(l)) + v(l) \tag{3}$$

where, $h(n(l)) = f^{-1}(n(l))$, based on the [5] consideration, $v(l)$ is a binomial random variable with zero mean and variance:

$$R(l) = Var[v(l)] = \frac{h(n(l))[1 - h(n(l))]}{B} \tag{4}$$

The system state is trivially represented by the number $n(l)$ of stations in the network a discrete time l. In most generality, the network state evolves as:

$$n(l) = n(l-1) + w(l) \tag{5}$$

where the number of stations $n(l)$ in the system at time l is given by the number of stations at time $l-1$ plus a random variable $w(l-1)$ which accounts for stations that have activated and/or terminated in the last time interval. where $w(l)$ is process noise with mean of zero and covariance matrix $Q(l)$.

2.2 Our Goal

Equation (5) and (3) thus provide a complete description of the state model for the system under consideration. Hence, our goal is to find the estimator $E\{n(l) | p^l\}$ with estimated error covariance given by

$$\Phi_{nn} = E\left\{\left[n(l) - \hat{n}(l|l)\right]\left[n(l) - \hat{n}(l|l)\right]^T | p^l\right\} \tag{6}$$

where $p^l \in \{p(l), p(l-1), \cdots, p(1)\}$ is the set of received samples up to time l.

3 The Central Difference Filter (CDF)

The major shortcomings of the EKF have limited first-order accuracy of propagated means and covariances resulting from a first-order truncated Taylor-series linearization method. The EKF also have to the need to analytical calculate Jacobians. These considerations motivate the development of the CDF in IEEE 802.11 competing stations estimation.

3.1 Extended Kalman Filter

Because IEEE 802.11 measurement models are nonlinear, we cannot use the KF. The EKF has probably had the most widespread use in nonlinear estimation, and we briefly explain the EKF. EKF has been the solution to the MMSE estimation in the nonlinear state transition and/or the nonlinear measurement models. In order to retain the simple and strong predictor-corrector solution structure for the Kalman filter for the models which is obtained again from the linearity and Gaussian assumption, the

EKF takes the linear approximation by the Taylor series expansion of the nonlinear models. Taylor series expansion of the nonlinear functions h around the estimates $\hat{n}(l+1\,|\,l)$ of the states $n(l+1)$ can be expressed as

$$p = h(\overline{n}(l+1)) = h(\overline{n}(l+1\,|\,l)) + \nabla h\big|_{n(l+1)=\overline{n}(l+1|l)} (n(l+1) - \overline{n}(l+1\,|\,l)) + \cdots \qquad (7)$$

Using only the linear expansion terms, it is easy to derive the following update equations. A full derivation of the EKF recursions is beyond the scope of this paper, but time update and measurement update form based on the state-space equations (5) and (3) are listed in Table 1 [4].

Table 1. Conventional Extended Kalman Filter

Model	$n(l+1) = n(l) + w(l)$
	$p(l) = h(n(l)) + v(l)$
Time Update	$\overline{n}(l+1\,|\,l) = \overline{n}(l)$
	$\Phi_{nn}(l+1\,|\,l) = \Phi_{nn}(l) + Q(l+1)$
Measurement Update	$K(l+1) = \Phi_{np}(l+1\,|\,l)\Phi_{vv}^{-1}(l+1\,|\,l)$
	$\overline{n}(l+1) = \overline{n}(l+1\,|\,l) + K(l+1)v(l+1\,|\,l)$
	$\Phi_{nn}(l+1) = \Phi_{nn}(l+1\,|\,l) - K(l+1)\Phi_{vv}(l+1\,|\,l)K^T(l+1)$

where

$$\overline{p}(l+1\,|\,l) = h(\overline{n}(l+1\,|\,l))$$
$$v(l+1\,|\,l) = p(l+1) - \overline{p}(l+1\,|\,l)$$
$$\Phi_{vv}(l+1\,|\,l) = H\Phi_{nn}(l+1\,|\,l)H^H + R(l+1)$$

where K is known as the Kalman gain, Q is the variance of the process noise, R is the variance of the measurement noise, $H \triangleq \nabla h\big|_{n(l+1)=\overline{n}(l+1|l)}$ is the Jacobians of the measurement model, v is the innovation.

The EKF approximates the state distribution using a Gaussian random variable, which is then propagated analytically through the first-order linearization of the nonlinear system. The EKF does not take into account the second and higher order terms in mean and fourth and higher order terms in the covariance are negligible. These approximations can introduce large errors in the true posterior mean and covariance of the transformed random variable in many practical situations, leading to suboptimal performance and divergence of the filter.

3.2 The Scaled Unscented Filter (SUF)

The main idea of the SUF is as follows: Instead of linearizing the nonlinear function through a truncated Taylor-series expansion at a single point (mean value of the random variable), we rather linearize the function through a linear regression between d points drawn from the prior distribution of the random variable, and the true nonlinear functional evaluations of those points. Since this approach takes into account the statistical properties of the prior random variable, the resulting linearization error tends to be smaller than that of a truncated Taylor-series linearization. A good approximation to this approach, but with greatly decreased complexity is the SUF developed by Julier and Uhlmann [6]. The scaled unscented transformation (SUT) is a key method for calculating the statistics of a random variable, which undergoes a nonlinear transformation and builds on the principle that it is easier to approximate a probability distribution than an arbitrary nonlinear function. The SUT is a method to efficiently compute the first two moments of a random variable undergoing an arbitrary non-linear transformation. The SUT compute a set of $d = 2\eta + 1$ weighted σ-points $S = \{w^{(i)}, n^{(i)}\}$ (such that $\sum_{i=1}^{d} w^{(i)} = 1$) that exactly capture the mean and covariance of n, i.e.

$$\sum_{i=1}^{d} w_m^{(i)} n^{(i)} = \overline{n} \tag{8}$$

$$\sum_{i=1}^{n} w_m^{(i)} (n^{(i)} - \overline{n})(n^{(i)} - \overline{n})^T = \Phi_{nn}$$

where n is a random variable with mean $\overline{n}$ and covariance Φ_{nn}.

These sigma vectors are propagated through the nonlinear function,

$$p^{(i)} = h(n^{(i)}) \quad i = 1, \cdots, d \tag{9}$$

The mean and covariance for p are approximated using a weighted sample mean and covariance of the posterior sigma points,

$$\overline{p} \approx \sum_{i=1}^{d} w_c^{(i)} p^{(i)} \tag{10}$$

$$\Phi_{pp} \approx \sum_{i=1}^{d} w_c^{(i)} \{p^{(i)} - \overline{p}\}\{p^{(i)} - \overline{p}\}^T$$

Although the SUT transform bears a superficial resemblance to particle filter (or Monte Carlo methods), there is a fundamental difference. The points are not drawn at random, as they are in Monte Carlo methods, but are deterministically chosen to exactly capture the mean and covariance of the variable to undergo the transformation. The PF do need to use a large number of particles for accurate and robust operation, often making their use computationally expensive.

The necessary statistical information capture by the SUF is the first and second order moments of $p(n)$. The number of sigma points required is $d = 2\eta + 1$ where η is the dimension of n. It can be shown [8] that matching the moments of n accurately up to the η th order implies that the capture is propagated through the nonlinear function mean and covariance. See [8] for more details on how the sigma points are calculated as a solution to equation (11). The resulting set of σ-points and weights utilized by the SUF are

$$n^{(0)}(l\,|\,l) = \bar{n}(l\,|\,l) \tag{11}$$

$$n^{(i)}(l\,|\,l) = \bar{n}(l\,|\,l) + (\sqrt{(\eta+\lambda)\Phi_{nn}(l\,|\,l)})_i \quad i = 1,\dots,\eta$$

$$n^{(i+\eta)}(l\,|\,l) = \bar{n}(l\,|\,l) - (\sqrt{(\eta+\lambda)\Phi_{nn}(l\,|\,l)})_i \quad i = 1,\dots,\eta$$

$$w_m^{(0)} = \lambda/(\eta+\lambda)$$

$$w_c^{(0)} = \lambda/(\eta+\lambda) + (1-\alpha^2+\beta)$$

$$w_m^{(i)} = w_c^{(i)} = 1/\{2(\eta+\lambda)\} \quad i = 1,\cdots,2\eta$$

where, $\kappa \in \Re$, $(\sqrt{(\eta+\kappa)\Phi_{nn}(l\,|\,l)})_i$ is the i th row or column of the matrix square root of $(\eta+\kappa)\Phi_{nn}(l\,|\,l)$ and $w^{(i)}$ is the weight that associated with the i th point. $\lambda = \alpha^2(\eta+\kappa)-\eta$ is a scaling parameter and $\theta = \sqrt{(n+\lambda)}$. α is a positive scaling parameter which can be made arbitrarily small to minimize higher order effects(e.g. $1e-2 \le \alpha \le 1$). κ is a secondary scaling parameter which is usually set to either 0 or $3-\eta$. β is an extra degree of freedom scalar parameter used to incorporate any extra prior knowledge of the distribution of n (for Guassian distributions, $\beta = 2$ is optimal).

A block diagram illustrating the steps in performing the SUT in shown in Fig. 1.

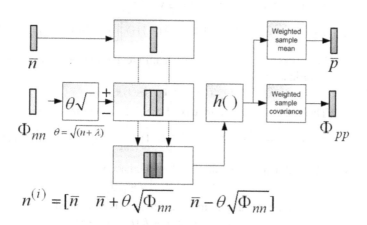

Fig. 1. Block diagram of the SUT

The deceptively simple approach taken with the SUT results in approximations that are accurate to the third order for Gaussian inputs for all nonlinearities. For non-Gaussian inputs, approximations are accurate to at least the second-order, with the accuracy of third and higher order moments determined by the choice of α and β.

The precise implementation of SUF in IEEE 802.11 competing stations estimation is given by:

Step 1)   The sigma point is calculated as

$$n^{(i)}(l) = [\bar{n}(l\,|\,l) \quad \bar{n}(l\,|\,l)+\theta\sqrt{\Phi_{nn}(l\,|\,l)+Q} \quad \bar{n}(l\,|\,l)-\theta\sqrt{\Phi_{nn}(l\,|\,l)+Q}]$$

Step 2)   The SUF time updates as follows

① The transformed set is given by instantiating each point through the pro cess model

$$n^{(i)}(l+1|l) = n^{(i)}(l|l)$$

② The predicted mean is computed as

$$\bar{n}(l+1|l) = \sum_{i=0}^{2\eta} w_m^{(i)} n^{(i)}(l+1|l)$$

③ The predicted covariance is computed as

$$\Phi_{nn}(l+1|l) = \sum_{i=0}^{2\eta} w_c^{(i)} \left[n^{(i)}(l+1|l) - \bar{n}(l+1|l) \right] \left[n^{(i)}(l+1|l) - \bar{n}(l+1|l) \right]^T$$

④ Instantiate each of the prediction points through the observation model

$$p^{(i)}(l+1|l) = h(n^{(i)}(l+1|l))$$

⑤ The predicted observation is calculated by

$$\bar{p}(l+1|l) = \sum_{i=0}^{2\eta} w_c^{(i)} p^{(i)}(l+1|l)$$

Step 3)   The SUF measurement updates as follows

① The innovation covariance is given by

$$\Phi_{pp}(l+1) = \sum_{i=0}^{2\eta} w_c^{(i)} \left[p^{(i)}(l+1|l) - \bar{p}(l+1|l) \right] \left[p^{(i)}(l+1|l) - \bar{p}(l+1|l) \right]^T$$

② Since the observation noise is additive and independent, the innovation covariance is

$$\Phi_{vv}(l+1) = \Phi_{zz}(l+1) + R$$

③ The cross-covariance matrix of x and z, is determined by

$$\Phi_{np}(l+1) = \sum_{i=0}^{2\eta} w_c^{(i)} \left[n^{(i)}(l+1|l) - \bar{n}(l+1|l) \right] \left[p^{(i)}(l+1|l) - \bar{p}(l+1|l) \right]^T$$

④ The Kalman gain matrix can be found according to

$$K(l+1) = \Phi_{np}(l+1) / \Phi_{vv}(l+1)$$

⑤ The update mean (parameter estimated) is calculated

$$\bar{n}(l+1) = \bar{n}(l+1|l) + K(l+1)v(l+1)$$
$$v(l+1) = p(l+1) - \bar{p}(l+1|l)$$

⑥ The update covariance (error covariance matrix are updated) is also pro vided by

$$\Phi_{nn}(l+1) = \Phi_{nn}(l+1|l) - K(l+1)\Phi_{pp}(l+1)K^T(l+1)$$

In the SUF where the SUT is employed in the prediction stages follows the given nonlinear function, no harmful loss in the above is expected. It is not necessary to calculate the Jacobian (and Hessian if 2nd order approximation in the Taylor series) and the prediction stage only consists of standard linear algebra operations (matrix square root, etc). The superior performance of the SUF over that of the EKF has been reported in numerous publications including [9].

3.3 The Central Difference Filter (CDF)

To relate this sample-based approach to the EKF, we consider expanding the nonlinear function by polynomial approximations based on interpolating formulas. One such formula is Sterling's interpolation formula, which, if we are restricted to first and second-order polynomial approximations gives the following approximation

$$p = h(n) \tag{12}$$

$$\approx h(\overline{n}) + \Delta_n h'_{CD}(n)\,|_{n=\overline{n}} + 1/2 \cdot \Delta_n^2 h''_{CD}(n)\,|_{n=\overline{n}}$$

where

$$h'_{CD}(n) = \frac{h(n+g) - h(n-g)}{2g}$$

$$h''_{CD}(\mathbf{x}) = \frac{h(n+g) + h(n-g) - 2h(n)}{g^2}$$

One can thus interpret above equation as a second order Taylor series expansion where the derivatives are replaced by central differences which only rely on functional evaluations. This formulation was the basis of Norgaard's [10] recent derivation of the divided difference filter as well a Ito and Xiong's [11] central difference filter. These two filters are essentially identical. The CDF was developed in this manner, careful analysis of the Taylor series expansion of both the CDF and the SUF approximations, show that both approaches are essentially the same [8]. Even though this approach is not explicitly derived starting from the statistical linear regression rationale, it can be shown [12] that the resulting Kalman filter again implicitly employs WSLR-based linearization. The resulting set of sigma-points for the CDF is once again $d = 2\eta + 1$ points deterministically drawn from the prior statistics of n, i.e.

$$n^{(0)}(l\,|\,l) = \overline{n}(l\,|\,l) \tag{13}$$

$$n^{(i)}(l\,|\,l) = \overline{n}(l\,|\,l) + (\sqrt{g^2 \Phi_{nn}(l\,|\,l)})_i \quad i = 1,...,\eta$$

$$n^{(i+\eta)}(l\,|\,l) = \overline{n}(l\,|\,l) - (\sqrt{g^2 \Phi_{nn}(l\,|\,l)})_i \quad i = 1,...,\eta$$

$$w_m^{(0)} = (g^2 - \eta)/g^2$$

$$w_c^{(0)} = 1/(4g^2)$$

$$w_m^{(i)} = 1/(2g^2) \qquad i = 1,\cdots,2\eta$$

$$w_c^{(i)} = (g^2 - 1)/(4g^2) \qquad i = 1,\cdots,2\eta$$

It is shown in [12] that the CDF has marginally higher theoretical accuracy than the SUF in higher order terms of the Taylor series expansion, but we've found in practice that both the CDF and the SUF perform equally well with negligible difference in estimation accuracy. One advantage of the CDF over the SUF is that it uses only a single scalar scaling parameter, the central difference half-step size g, as opposed to the three (α, β, κ) that SUF uses. Once again this parameter determines the spread of the sigma-points around the prior mean. For Gaussian priors, its optimal value is $\sqrt{3}$.

The complete CDF algorithm that updates the mean $\bar{n}$ and P_{nn} of the Gaussian approximation to the posterior distribution of the states is given by subsection B but only difference is that the sigma point is calculated as

$$n^{(i)}(l) = [\bar{n}(l\mid l) \quad \bar{n}(l\mid l) + \sqrt{g^2(\Phi_{nn} + Q)} \quad \bar{n}(l\mid l)) - \sqrt{g^2(\Phi_{nn} + Q)}]$$

The remaining procedure is a repeated implementation of subsection B. For precise implementation of the CDF in an IEEE 802.11 network given by :

Step.1)   The sigma point is calculated as using eq. 18

$$n^{(i)}(l) = [\bar{n}(l\mid l) \quad \bar{n}(l\mid l) + \sqrt{g^2(\Phi_{nn} + Q)} \quad \bar{n}(l\mid l)) - \sqrt{g^2(\Phi_{nn} + Q)}]$$

Step.2)   The CDF time updates as follows

① The transformed set is given by instantiating each point through the process model

$$n^{(i)}(l+1\mid l) = n^{(i)}(l\mid l)$$

② The predicted mean is computed as

$$\bar{n}(l+1\mid l) = \sum_{i=0}^{2\eta} w_m^{(i)} n^{(i)}(l+1\mid l)$$

③ The predicted covariance is computed as

$$\Phi_{nn}(l+1\mid l) = \sum_{i=0}^{2\eta} w_m^{(i)} \left[n^{(i)}(l+1\mid l) - \bar{n}(l+1\mid l) \right]\left[n^{(i)}(l+1\mid l) - \bar{n}(l+1\mid l) \right]^T$$

④ Instantiate each of the prediction points through the observation model

$$p^{(i)}(l+1\mid l) = h(n^{(i)}(l+1\mid l))$$

⑤ The predicted observation is calculated by

$$\bar{p}(l+1\mid l) = \sum_{i=0}^{2\eta} w_c^{(i)} p^{(i)}(l+1\mid l)$$

Step.3)   The CDF measurement updates as follows

① The innovation covariance is given by

$$\Phi_{pp}(l+1) = \sum_{i=0}^{2\eta} w_c^{(i)} \left[p^{(i)}(l+1\mid l) - \bar{p}(l+1\mid l) \right]\left[p^{(i)}(l+1\mid l) - \bar{p}(l+1\mid l) \right]^T$$

② Since the observation noise is additive and independent, the innovation covariance is

$$\Phi_{vv}(l+1) = \Phi_{zz}(l+1) + R$$

③ The cross-covariance matrix of x and z, is determined by

$$\Phi_{np}(l+1) = \sum_{i=0}^{2\eta} w_c^{(i)} \left[n^{(i)}(l+1\mid l) - \bar{n}(l+1\mid l) \right]\left[p^{(i)}(l+1\mid l) - \bar{p}(l+1\mid l) \right]^T$$

④ The Kalman gain matrix can be found according to

$$K(l+1) = \Phi_{np}(l+1)/\Phi_{vv}(l+1)$$

⑤ The update mean (parameter estimated) is calculated

$$\bar{n}(l+1) = \bar{n}(l+1\mid l) + K(l+1)v(l+1)$$

$$v(l+1) = p(l+1) - \bar{p}(l+1\mid l)$$

⑥ The update covariance (error covariance matrix are updated) is also pro
vided by

$$\Phi_{nn}(l+1) = \Phi_{nn}(l+1 \mid l) - K(l+1)\Phi_{pp}(l+1)K^T(l+1)$$

Step.2 and 3 stages are time update and measurement update in the Kalman update rule (Table. 1), respectively. Strictly speaking, we say that the main difference between EKF and CDF is whether use sigma points or not. And SUF and CDF perform equally well in estimation accuracy. Because both filters are derived by analytically derived 1st and 2nd order derivatives in the Taylor series expansion. But the EKF is to the nature of the 1st order Taylor series linearization. Thus, SUF and CDF are clearly superior to the EKF. And one advantage of the CDF over the SUF is that it only uses a single scalar scaling parameter, as opposed to the three.

4 Simulation

We now examine the performance of the CDF for making competing stations estimates for an IEEE 802.11 network. We compare the CDF-based estimator with an estimator based on the EKF [5].

In applications of the Kalman filter, it is generally assumed that $w(l)$ is a stationary process with a given constant variance Q. The tuning of the Kalman filter is then performed by appropriately selecting this variance. We choice the process noise covariance was $Q = 0.1$ for convergence in non saturated conditions. The three parameters (α, β, and κ) of the SUF estimator are assume to $\alpha = 1$, $\beta = 2$, and $\kappa = 0$. The central difference half-step size is assume to $g = \sqrt{3}$. One aspect about using the CDF is that they require proper initialization. Regarding the initial conditions, quick convergence is guaranteed when the initial error variance Φ_0 is set to a large value (in our numerical results, we have used $\Phi(0) = 100$). In these conditions, The initial estimate of the state is not relevant, and can be set to any value (we use $n(0) = 1$).

The ability of the estimator to track the number of competing stations is shown in Fig. 2 in saturated network conditions. In this figure, we have simulated a scenario in which the number of stations in the network increases in steps (5, 30, 25, 15 and 10 stations). As the figure indicates, the estimator/tracker is able to accurately track the number of competing stations. Although unrealistic, this scenario allows to prove that our proposed estimation technique is able to track abrupt variations in the network state, while keeping a very high level of accuracy in the estimation more than EKF.

Fig. 3 show the behavior of the proposed estimation technique when the stations are not in saturated conditions. EKF and CDF parameter are the same as that used in the previous figure. In particular, figure 3 reports a simulation run for a network scenario of 20 stations. Packets arrive to each station according to a Poisson process, whose rate is initially set to be lower than the saturation throughput. The arrival rate is subsequently increased so that, at the end of the simulation time, all stations are in saturation conditions. In the non saturated regime, the number of stations attempting to transmit a packet shows fairly large and fast fluctuations, as highlighted by the dashed plot in figure 3. In convergence case, the CDF and EKF are able to slowly follow these fast fluctuations. They both technique is able to roughly track abrupt variations, while our proposed technique keeping a similar level of accuracy in the estimation with EKF. Is case of the EKF-based estimator converge, the CDF-based estimator's performance of accuracy is similar with the EKF-based estimator.

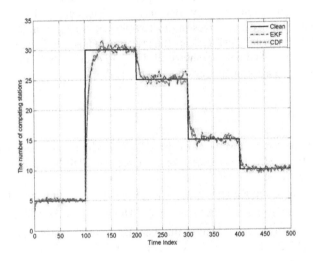

Fig. 1. CDF estimation in saturated network conditions

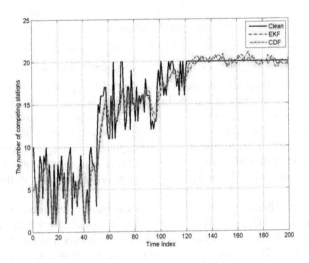

Fig. 2. CDF estimation in non saturated network conditions

To further quantify the performance of the estimator, the MSE (Mean Square Error) from simulation of the estimator is presented. The MSE was computed for the estimates as follows:

$$MSE_n(m) = \frac{1}{N_s} \sum_{i=1}^{N_s} |\mathbf{n} - \hat{\mathbf{n}}^{(i)}|^2 \tag{14}$$

where $\hat{\mathbf{n}} = [\hat{n}(1)\, \hat{n}(2) \cdots \hat{n}(l)]$ denote the MSE of the competing stations estimation, iteration 1 until l of the estimator. N_s is the number of ensemble samples used to form the MSE.

Table 1. MSE and variance of ensenble samples for the CDF and the EKF

Network conditions	MSE		Variance	
	EKF	CDF (SUF)	EKF	CDF (SUF)
Saturated	3.3992	3.4493 (3.1306)	0.0151	0.0168 (0.0136)
Non saturated	124.9055	2.1980 (2.2587)	13214.32	0.0071 (0.0073)

Table 1 shows the MSE of ensemble samples for the estimates of the competing stations. The number of ensemble samples was chosen to be $N_s = 300$. The MSE terms defined in (14) were computed for the parameter estimates from during 500 and 200 seconds of the filter in saturated condition and non saturated conditions, respectively. The MSE and Variance of the CDF-based estimator is smaller than that of the EKF-based estimator. Specially, in non saturated conditions with fast fluctuations, since the EKF that does not take into account above the second order terms of means and covariances, it is frequently divergence, but the CDF is not happen once. In Monte Carlo simulations with run of 300, the number of divergence is 160 of 300 (about 54%). Thus, EKF-based estimator can introduce large errors, leading to worse performance than the CDF. Our proposed CDF is an excellent performance in non saturated conditions of IEEE 802.11 network, compared with the EKF.

By comparing the CDF estimator with the EKF one, we see that our proposed mechanism appears to provide an improved estimation in both saturated and nonsaturated regimes, although the different level of accuracy can be fully appreciated only in the saturated and non saturated regime.

5 Conclusions

This paper has described a new class of EKF. The result in efficient implementations, have better numerical properties and provide improved performance relative to EKF parameter estimation without the need to analytical calculate Jacobians. We have presented a parameter estimator based on the CDF that is capable of estimating the number of competing stations in both saturated and non saturated regimes IEEE 802.11 network. The CDF can provide a better alternative to nonlinear filtering than the EKF since it has better numerical efficiencies. Computer simulations also show that it provides a more viable means of tracking time-varying amplitudes and delays in IEEE 802.11 network than the EKF.

References

1. G. Bianchi, L. Fratta, M. Oliveri, "Performance Evaluation and Enhancement of the CSMA/CA MAC Protocol for 802.11 Wireless LANS", Proc. PIMRC 1996, October 1996, Taipei, Taiwan, pp.392-396.
2. F. Cali, M. Conti, E. Gregori, "Dynamic Tuning of the IEEE 802.11 Protocol to Achieve a Theoretical Throughput Limit", Trans. On Networking, Vol. 8, No. 6, December 2000, pp. 785-799.
3. G. Bianchi, "Performance Analysis of the IEEE 802.11 Distributed Coordination Function", IEEE Journal of Seleted Areas in Telecommunications, Wireless series, Vol 18, no. 3, March 2000, pp.535-547.
4. Anderson, B. D. and Moore, J. B. Optimal Filtering, Prentice-Hall, New Jersey, 1979
5. Giuseppe Bianchi, Ilenia Tinnirello, "Kalman Filter Estimation of the Number of Competing Terminals in an IEEE 802.11 network", IEEE Infocom 2003.
6. S. J. Julier and J. K. Uhlmann, "A New Extension of the Kalman Filter to Nonlinear Systems," In Proc. Of AeroSense: The 11th Int. Symp. On Aerospace/Defence Sensing, Simulation and Controls., 1997.
7. S. J. Julier, "The Scaled Unscented Transformation," Proceedings of American Control Conference 2002, Vol. 6, pp. 4555-4559, May 2002.
8. R. van der Merwe and E. Wan. "Efficient Derivative-Free Kalman Filters for Online Learning." In Pro. of ESANN, Bruges, April 2001.
9. S. J. Julier, and J. K. Uhlmann, "A Consistent, Debiased Method for Converting Between Polar and Cartesian Coordinate Systems," in The Proceedings of AeroSense: Acquisition, Tracking and Pointing XI. 1997, vol.3086, pp. 110-121, SPIE.
10. N. Norgaard, N. K. Poulsen, and O. Ravn, "Advances in Derivative-Free State Estimation for Nonlinear Systems," Tech. Rep. IMM-REP-1998-15, Tech. Univ. of Denmark, 2000.
11. Kazufumi Ito and Kaiqi Xiong. "Gaussian Filters for Nonlinear Filtering Problems." IEEE Trans. Automatic Control, 45(5), May 2000, pp. 910-927.
12. T. Lefebvre, H. Bruyninckx, and J. De Schutter, Comment on' A new Method for the Nonlinear Transformation of Means and Covariances in Filters and Estimators'. IEEE Trans. Automatic Control, 47(8), Aug 2002.

An Emergency Message Propagation Method in Highway Traffic

Sukdea Yu[1], Moonkun Lee[2], and Gihwan Cho[2]

[1] Dept. of Computer Statistic & Information, Univ. of Chonbuk, 664-14 1ga Duckjin-Dong,
Duckjin-Gu, Jeonju, Jeonbuk 561-756 South Korea
sdyu@chonbuk.ac.kr
[2] R.C. for Advanced CIST, Division of Electronic & Information Engineering, Univ. of
Chonbuk, 664-14 1ga Duckjin-Dong, Duckjin-Gu, Jeonju, Jeonbuk 561-756 South Korea
{moonkun, ghcho}@chonbuk.ac.kr

Abstract. This paper presents an intelligent vehicle safety system, constructed by exchanging emergency-related information such as urgency stop, traffic accident, and obstacles between vehicles. In the majority of vehicle safety communication applications, an emergency message is propagated in the form of broadcasts. However, this causes numerous problems, such as massive radio collision, multi-hop propagation and fast relay. This paper presents a selective message forwarding method by proposing a stem and branch structure based on prospected positions. The logical structure makes it possible to assign a representative vehicle to relay an emergency message among the different level of wireless radio coverage. The proposed scheme improves the efficiency of message transmission with the selective priority for forwarding messages by distance. The structure also limits the number of broadcasting hops. The proposed method is evaluated using a network simulator.

Keywords: Broadcasting, Stem and Branch, Selective Forwarding, Highway Traffic, Vehicle Safety Communications.

1 Introduction

Highways were created to enable high speed transportation. However, various hazardous factors may result in casualties when drivers do not notice hazardous factors or cannot react in time to these hazardous factors. The rapid speed and well-guided road situation sometimes distract the driver's attention. In these situations, the driver can easily experience a rear-end collision when an event suddenly occurs. The danger of rear-end collision is greater in the vehicles that follow after the collision, than vehicles close to the collision. If these collisions occur consecutively, chain collision may occur.

In emergency situations, a driver typically relies on the tail brake light of the car immediately ahead to decide his or her braking action. Under typical road situations, this is not always the best collision avoidance strategy, for various reasons. This is particularly true in many situations where vehicles need to have an extended range of awareness beyond that which drivers can immediately see or autonomous safety

H.Y. Youn, M. Kim, and H. Morikawa (Eds.): UCS 2006, LNCS 4239, pp. 331–343, 2006.
© Springer-Verlag Berlin Heidelberg 2006

systems can detect. In many cases, driver's reaction time typically ranges between 0.7 and 1.5 seconds [1]. According to OFCOM's investigation reports, if drivers have a 1 second composure time, before reacting to traffic danger situation, the 90% of rear-end collision accidents can be reduced [2,3]. Chain collisions can potentially decrease, or their severity can be reduced, by lowering the delay between the occurrence time of an emergency event and the time at which the vehicles behind are informed of the event [4].

Broadcast service is important for all kinds of networks. Whether a new message needs to be sent to all participants across the network or a destination's location is unknown, broadcasting is a necessary condition [5]. If vehicles run on the same road, these vehicles do not have a pre-relationship with each other. Therefore, the broadcasting service is useful in the inter-vehicle communication. Inter-vehicle communication makes use of a successive broadcasting (that is, flooding) method to extend transmission coverage, as the simple broadcasting considers 1-hop propagation. However, a simple flooding method drops bandwidth efficiency dramatically and results in frequent message collisions, when the density of vehicles is high [5]. Therefore, a number of inter-vehicle communication methods attempt to overcome those problems by considering the direction of the message forwarding or using the selective re-broadcasting method [5-7].

This paper deals with a kind of the selective re-broadcasting. It makes use of the position of a vehicle for selecting an effective representative vehicle, which relays emergency messages. The message's sender informs the receivers of an ideal position included in the sending message. This is called a PP (Prospected Position). The vehicle s receiving the broadcast, defer the re-forwarding during the proportional delay time that is obtained by the difference from its current position to the PP. A selected vehicle with the shortest delay re-forwards the message. The procedure of re-forwarding is discarded when receiving the same message as that received prior. As a result, only one vehicle relays the emergency event among vehicles included in the same wireless coverage; therefore, broadcasting overhead for vehicle safety is dramatically reduced.

The remainder of this paper is organized as follows. Section 2 presents work relating to selective re-broadcasting; section 3 contains the procedure and protocol steps; section 4 presents the simulation model, the results and the analysis of the proposed approach; the last section concludes this paper and discusses future research.

2   Related Works

There is much research in the area of the V2V (Vehicle-to-Vehicle) communication [8]. The majority of traditional protocols make use of location information to exchange vehicles' current locations periodically with neighbor nodes. These operations require numerous wireless resources and are unrealistic due to the vehicles' high mobility. Therefore, the majority of vehicle safety-related protocols make use of the directional forwarding protocol, for propagating information. Those protocols use the inefficient random position selection method, because exchanging position information is not usually required.

Representative directional broadcasting methods for inter-vehicle communication are NB (Naïve Broadcast) forwarding [9] and IB (Intelligent Broadcast) forwarding [10]. NB forwarding only considers message arrival direction, however, IB forwarding considers additional factors, such as implicit acknowledgment, message history and random duration for re-broadcasting.

The NB forwarding method serves as a baseline packet-routing mechanism for the target of the cooperative collision avoidance application. As soon as an emergency event is detected, the detecting vehicle periodically transmits a CW (Collision Warning) message [9]. Upon receiving the message, the vehicle decides to actuate related devices and start generating its own CW messages. Vehicles ignore the message if it comes from behind the vehicle.

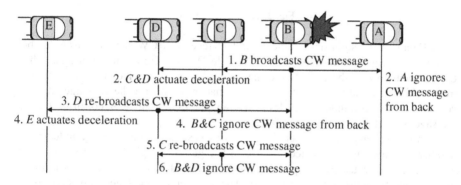

Fig. 1. NB forwarding

Figure 1 describes the procedure of NB forwarding. If vehicle B detects an emergency event, the vehicle creates a CW message and broadcasts this message. Vehicle A and C receive the message. However, vehicle A ignores the message, as it arrives from behind. Upon receiving the message, vehicle C and D actuate deceleration and try to re-broadcast the message. If vehicle D attempts to re-broadcast first, vehicle B and C ignore the message that came from behind. Although message receptions are duplicated, all receiving vehicles must perform re-transmission. Because vehicle C did not attempt to re-broadcast, vehicle C subsequently performs re-broadcasting. Vehicle B ignores the message because the message was received from behind, and vehicle D ignores the message because the message had already been re-broadcasted. However, NB leads to excessive message forwarding, which escalates message collisions for the 802.11 MAC [10].

To avoid these problems, the IB forwarding method uses the implicit acknowledgment-based message generation and transmission strategy. After starting broadcasts, if the event source and relay vehicles receive the same message from behind, it is inferred that at least one vehicle at the back has received the message and will be responsible for propagating the message along the range. The receiving vehicles, except the relaying node, regard message duplication as a stop-sign for the re-broadcasting process. This operation is a of role of implicit acknowledgment method.

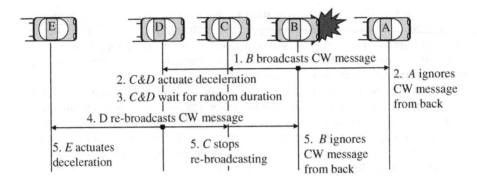

Fig. 2. The IB forwarding

In Figure 2, as soon as vehicle C and D receive a CW message from B, both vehicles wait for a random duration. If vehicle D has a shorter duration than vehicle C, then vehicle D re-broadcasts the message. Vehicle C receives the same message from behind, indicating that other vehicles had re-broadcast the message. It forces vehicle C to discontinue the re-broadcasting process. Vehicle B confirms that the message was relayed back successfully.

With this scheme, the protocol can improve system performance by reducing the number of messages injected within a range of a given emergency event. Nevertheless, because relaying vehicles are selected randomly, the possibility of unnecessary transmission is very high. The number of message relay hops is not bounded for the similar reasons.

3 Stem and Branch Protocol

Vehicles that are running on the highway can exchange safety related information with each other in the wireless coverage area. A vehicle that senses a hazardous event creates a warning message and broadcasts this message. As it is different from the wired communication, several vehicles may simultaneously receive the message at the same time using wireless communication. The receiving vehicles re-broadcast the message in order to pass the information to distant vehicles.

3.1 Basic Structure

The proposed method uses a selective re-broadcasting to raise the efficiency of message transmission. The receiving vehicles are given an order for re-broadcasting, according to their positions. A vehicle with high priority re-broadcasts the message. The remaining vehicles notice the fact that the message is already re-broadcasted by other vehicle and stop re-broadcasting process.

The messages are re-broadcasted to limited hop distance that is defined at protocol's definition. Vehicles that have an opportunity of re-broadcasting become the representative on the same hop. If it compares the structure of message propagation with the tree's structure, that is as following. The vehicle that generates the message is the root of tree, and vehicles that re-broadcast the message are the branch point, the line which connects those points becomes the stem of tree. That is to say, the stem consists of stem vehicles which re-broadcast the message. Remained vehicles become branch vehicle. Figure 3 illustrates the structure, which is defined as the SNB (Stem aNd Branch) structure.

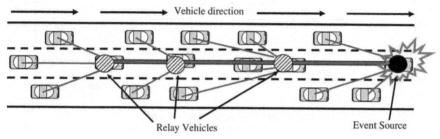

Fig. 3. The SNB structure

Stem vehicles take a responsibility that they must forward to backward. Branch vehicles potentially are candidate who becomes a stem vehicle. However, this structure is created whenever a message is issued by real-time; it is not a fixed structure because vehicles are moving around. With this structure, the logical vehicle groups are easily organized based on radio coverage. The SNB structure has advantages in highway environment; the efficiency of broadcasting can be raised and the number of broadcasting hop can be bounded as applying the logical structure.

3.2 Stem Vehicle Selection

The PP (Prospected Position) is established near the stable signal distance, so that a stem vehicle may not be selected in unstable boundary line or near source vehicle. Normally, the strength of radio signal is inverse proportion in distance square. The PP is the most suitable position of forwarder to which a current vehicle considers. The position is located on the opposite direction where the current vehicle advances toward and is assigned between current position and radio boundary line within the stable signal distance. The reason that the PP is established on less than radio boundary line is to reduce messages damages and heighten messages receptions. The stable signal distance is about 150~225 meter in open field considering 802.11 Wireless LAN. Inter-stem distance refers to distance between successive PPs. The inter-stem distance may not be fixed one; the distance can be changed according to situation of road. The inter-stem distance can be established longer to rural road and shorter to urban road, respectively.

Vehicles that locate around the PP become potential candidates of the stem vehicle. Considering the singular situation of road - serialized nodes' arrangement, similar moving direction and speed - even if any vehicle which locates around the PP becomes stem vehicle, it does not influence performance greatly. However, the nearest vehicle is more suitable as candidate of stem vehicle. Our work takes into account this point to find better candidate. The competition problem which potentially can be happened is solved by the distance between the PP and the current vehicle's position.

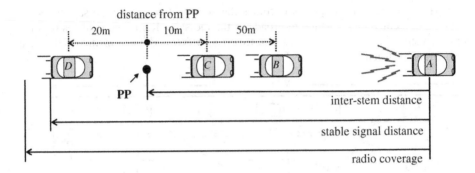

Fig. 4. The next stem vehicle selection

Figure 4 illustrates a next stem vehicle selection. Vehicle *C* which has the shortest distance from the PP is selected by the next stem vehicle. The next stem vehicle defers re-broadcasting for delay time commensurately that is acquired by distance with the PP. According to the duration of the delay time, each vehicle's priority is given itself naturally. Each vehicle re-broadcasts the received message after latency time as much as the distance. When another vehicle re-broadcasts the same message already, the others discontinue their re-broadcasting processes and covert into reception stand-by mode. If a vehicle that has the highest priority order does not attempt normally to re-broadcast because of its own problem, the other vehicle which has next priority order re-broadcasts the message. Through this backup function, the proposed scheme heightens transmission reliability. This re-broadcasting is repeated up to the hop limitation.

3.3   SNB Protocol Description

The proposed protocol uses a selective re-broadcasting scheme to propagate emergency-related information to the rear vehicles effectively. In the proposed protocol, it is assumed that all vehicles equipped with a locating system, i.e., such as GPS obtain location information with some accuracy. Each vehicle uses its position, speed and direction for stem vehicle selection.

It is the most important function to select the vehicle which re-broadcasts the received message. Therefore, the protocol description shows the procedural message re-forwarding steps. It uses the inner product of two vehicle's directional vector for classifying vehicles on the same road [6].

Protocol steps:
   1) Source vehicle does broadcasting a message which includes the position, the next PP, the direction vector.
   2) If the message arrived from the same road's vehicle, message duplication is checked.
   3) If the message is validate, reception is logged, and the procedure of message re-broadcasting is triggered, if not, the message is discarded.
   4) If the procedure starts, the delay time and the PP are calculated.

5) The re-broadcasting is deferred for the calculated delay time. If any duplicated messages are received while the delay time expires, the message is broadcasted immediately.

6) Re-broadcasting process is repeated to the hops that TTL value permits.

If a new message arrives at the current vehicle, the directional vector which is stamped in the message is compared with the current vehicle's directional vector. If the message arrived from other road, then the message is discarded. In the case that the message arrived from the vehicle on the same road, the duplicated reception of message is checked with message's source ID and message sequence number. If the message is new, the message is conveyed to the upper application. And then, the message's TTL is checked. If the TTL is under 1, the message might not be re-broadcasted. Otherwise, that is, if the TTL is more than or equal to 1, the re-broadcasting procedure is started. When the procedure begins, the node calculates the next PP and the delay time. After rebuilding the message which will be re-broadcasted, the broadcasting must be deferred during the delay time. If the vehicle does not receive any of the same messages during the delay time, the message may be re-broadcasted. When the vehicle receives the same messages during the delay time, the procedure of re-broadcasting that was scheduled before the message is canceled.

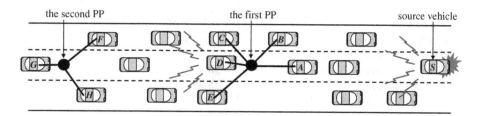

Fig. 5. Example of the SNB protocol

Figure 5 shows an example of emergency message broadcasting scenario with SNB protocol. Assume that vehicle S recognizes a hazard and issues an emergency event. First, S calculates the first PP to make an emergency message and broadcasts the message. All vehicles that receive the message actuate the related device to decelerate themselves, and calculate their delay times. The first PP was established among vehicle A, B, C, D and E, the D is the nearest vehicle with the PP; the D has the shortest delay time. The D modifies the message with its status during its delay time. If the D's delay time is expired, the D tries to re-broadcast the message. After the D succeeds in transmission, other vehicles including A, B, C and E could receive the D's transmission. Because the same message was re-broadcasted by other vehicle already, those vehicles give up re-broadcasting. Vehicles that receive the message that D transmits calculate distance from the second PP. Because G is the nearest vehicle with PP, G performs the re-broadcasting to next hop.

4 Simulation and Performance Analysis

4.1 Simulation Environment

The simulation has been implemented in NS-2 (version 2.29) [11]. The proposed protocol was designed for highway scenario. Every vehicle goes straight on the same road, and don't change direction during simulation time. But all vehicles depart at different position, and change speed as time goes periodically. The speed steps that each vehicle uses are 80Km/hr (22.22m/s), 100Km/hr (27.78m/s) and 120Km/hr (33.33m/s). So the topology of vehicles changes continuously. Vehicles do not change moving direction during simulation. The number of lanes is four. So, higher speed vehicles may progress passing lower speed vehicles. In simulation, a certain vehicle belonging to forefront group creates and broadcasts emergency event occasionally until 5 hops distance.

Table 1. Simulation parameters

Parameter	Value
Number of vehicles	10~100
Vehicle's speed	80~120Km/hr
Simulation area	2500meter * 2500meter
Number of emergency event	10 events
MAC protocol	802.11 MAC
Emergency message size	200bytes
Intelligent broadcast random duration	0~10msec
Delay per meters for SNB	0.5msec
Wireless coverage	250meter
Emergency message's TTL	5 hop
Simulation time	30 seconds

The SNB protocol has been analyzed for its performance with NB protocol [9] and IB protocol [10]. Also, to analyze SNB protocol's characteristics, the distance between stem vehicles has been established by 150m and 200m each in the protocol. The parameters used for the simulation are listed in Table 1. All protocols use 802.11 MAC as layer 2 MAC protocol. And, every emergency message size is fixed by 200 bytes. The IB protocol also has a random value for waiting other vehicle's broadcasting. The proposed protocol calculates its delay time by distance from the PP (Prospected Position). The protocol sets the delay time by 0.5msec per meter.

The simulation results have been analyzed in terms of following four performance criteria:

- The number of sent packets: the total number of sent packets to evaluate the network's complexity.
- The percentage of effective packets: the percentage of the number of effective packets to the number of received packets to evaluate wireless bandwidth utility.

- The average duration time of complete propagation: the average duration time of message for completing propagation to evaluate message propagation rapidity.
- The maximum coverage: the average maximum coverage after completing propagation.

4.2 Performance Evaluation

Figure 6 depicts the number of sent packets with respect to the number of vehicles. The number of sent packets increases commensurately with number of vehicles in the NB (Naïve Broadcasting) and the IB (Intelligent Broadcast with implicit acknowledgement). But, the number of sent packets is almost fixed regardless of the number of vehicles in SNB150 (the inter-stem vehicle distance is 150m) and SNB200 (the inter-stem vehicle distance is 200m). But, according to my behind simulation's results, the number of sent packets had stopped in double degree of SNB protocol if random duration is increased from 0msec to 100msec in the IB. Because the proposed protocol does not use random value in selection of vehicles to re-broadcast but uses the logical priority, packet collision decreases remarkably. In case of assigning delay time per meter by 0.1msec, the number of sent packets increased about double in the proposed scheme.

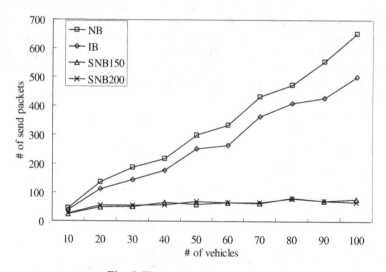

Fig. 6. The number of sent packets

Figure 7 shows the percentage of effective packets. The effective packet means that the packet is not duplicated. Once receiving a new message, every vehicle discards the messages which are duplicated. Of course, the first duplication is very important for implicit acknowledgment. So, the percentage of effective packet may not pass over maximum 50% for reliability. As the number of vehicles increases, the number of effective packets increases proportionally, but the number of received packets increases exponentially. The percentage of effective packets decreases by increasing the number

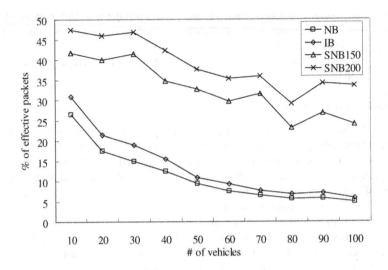

Fig. 7. The percentage of effective packet

of vehicles. As seen in Figure 7, all protocol is apt to drop the percentage as the number of vehicles increases. The NB and IB show the characteristics of typical flooding methods.But, SNB150 and SNB200 are approximating to 30~45%. Because the SNB200 has longer distance per hop than the SNB150, – it means that more vehicles receive same message at once - the SNB200 is more efficient. The SNB protocols are heightening the bandwidth efficiency by the packet that is less than IB or NB, and improves the availability of wireless resources maximally.

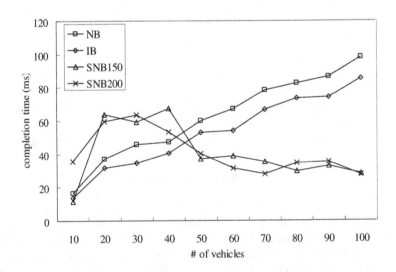

Fig. 8. The average duration for completing propagation

Figure 8 describes the average duration time for completing whole propagation. The duration time means the time that message broadcasting no longer happened in the propagation area. In case of low vehicle density, the completion time is short in the NB and IB protocol, because the number of sent messages is low and the possibility of message collision is low. But the completion time is longer in the SNB protocols, because the gap among vehicles is wide and the delay time is determined based on distance. When the number of vehicles is 10, the inter-vehicular gap is so wide that the message is not conveyed to the last hop. So, most protocols have short duration time in that situation. In case of high vehicle density, the number of vehicles increases, the completion times of the NB and IB increase steadily. On the contrary, the completion time decreases steadily in SNB protocols. The reason that the completion time decrease in the SNB protocols is that the delay time is low, because the distance between the PP and the adjacent vehicles is short. The SNB protocol's completion time begins to become lower than NB and IB, when the distance between vehicles decreases by 35meter.

Figure 9 shows the maximum propagation coverage of event message. The emergency message's TTL is limited to five hops. Therefore, the re-broadcasting of message could be repeated up to five times. When the radio transmission range is supposed by 250meter, the theoretical maximum propagation range is about 1250meter. But, according to simulation results, most protocols show the range about 1000meter. The SNB150 protocol shows shorter maximum propagation range because the re-broadcasting vehicles are chosen in shorter position than radio range. SNB225 protocol (stem vehicle distance is 225meter) is measured to examine characteristics of SNB protocol little more. According to simulation results, the maximum propagation range increased about 1150meter in the SNB225 protocol.

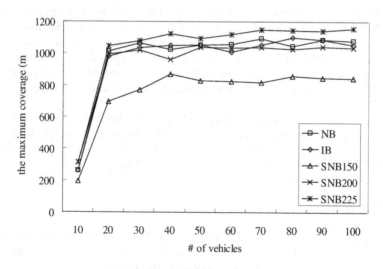

Fig. 9. The maximum coverage

4.3 Discussion

Wireless network technologies (i.e. 5.9 GHz DSRC [9]) for vehicle safety communication have the similar characteristics to 802.11 Wireless LAN transmissions by CSMA. Therefore, transmission delay can be emerged as the number of packet increases. Also, bandwidth efficiency can be dramatically dropped because of repeating send-receive beyond necessity. The proposed protocol is an emergency message propagation protocol for highway vehicle safety communication.

According to simulation results, the proposed SNB protocols are similar with the existing protocols in transmission properties aspect, such as transmission delay, transmission range. But the number of packets that use for this performance is extremely lower. In efficiency aspect, the SNB protocols show near optimal performance. The density of vehicles increases, the SNB protocol shows better performance, unlike existing protocols whose performances grow worse. In addition, the protocol includes an implicit acknowledgment function that is offered in the IB, the forwarding reliability is highly improved. When a vehicle which with the highest priority does not re-broadcast timely because of its own problems, the next prior vehicle performs re-broadcasting. This is a kind of guaranteed function.

The SNB150 and SNB200 protocols show similar performance, but maximum propagation ranges are different. Shortening the inter-stem vehicle distance, an effect that transmission radius decreases appears and the transmission efficiency drops a little. When the vehicle speed is relatively low or the highway is jammed, unnecessary transmission can be reduced by decreasing the inter-stem distance.

5 Conclusion

The proposed scheme is a kind of priority-based selective re-forwarding for highway traffic situation. The proposed protocol raised the wireless broadcasting efficiency epochally using distance-based priority method for relay vehicle selection instead of using random method. Using the proposed method, it can conserve costly wireless bandwidth maximally as well as lower packet collision possibility by decreasing the number of sent messages. If the proposed protocol is used, broadcasting hop can be bounded, unlike existing broadcasting protocol, because enough propagation range can be guaranteed.

In the results of simulation, the proposed method is better than other methods for vehicle safety communication in the number of sent packets and the transmission efficiency. Specially, the number of transmission packets to propagate emergency information is kept almost changeless as the vehicle density increases.

References

1. Yang, X., Lui, J., Zhao, F., Vaidya, N.H.: A Vehicle-to-Vehicle Communication Protocol for Cooperative Collision Warning. Proc. of the 1st IEEE Int'l. Conf. on Mobile and Ubiquitous System Networking and Services (2004) 114-123
2. The Office of Communication in UK, http://www.ofcom.gov.uk/

3. Scherrer, D.: Short Range Devices, Radio Frequency Identification Devices, Bluetooth, Ultra Wideband Systems, Automotive Short Range Radars, Overview and Latest Developments. OFCOM (2003)
4. Xu, Q., Sengupta, R., Jiang, D.: Design and Analysis of Highway Safety Communication Protocol in 5.9 GHz Dedicated Short-Range Communication Spectrum. Proc. of the 57th IEEE VTC (2003) 2451-2455
5. Sun. M.T., Feng, W.., Lai, T.H., et al.: GPS-Based Message Broadcast for Adaptive Inter-Vehicle Communications. Proc. of the 52nd IEEE VTC (2000) 2685-2692
6. Fukuhara, T., Warabino, T.: Broadcast Methods for Inter-Vehicle Communications System. Proc. of IEEE Wireless Communications and Networking Conference (2005) 2252-2257
7. Torrent-Moreno, M., Jiang, D., Hartenstein, H.: Broadcast Reception Rates and Effects of Priority Access in 802.11-Based Vehicular Ad-Hoc Networks. Proc. of the 1st ACM Int'l Conf. on Vehicular Ad hoc Networks (2004) 10-18
8. Hasegawa, T., Mizui, K., Fujii, H., Seki, K.: A Concept Reference Model for Inter-Vehicle Communications (Report2). Proc. of IEEE ITS (2004) 810-815
9. ASTM Int'l: Standard Specification for Telecommunications and Information Exchange Between Roadside and Vehicle Systems - 5GHz Band Dedicated Short Range Communications (DSRC) Medium Access Control (MAC) and Physical Layer (PHY) Specifications. ASTM E2213-03 (2003)
10. Biswas, S., Tatchikou, R., Dion, F.: Vehicle-to-Vehicle Wireless Communication Protocols for Enhancing Highway Traffic Safety. IEEE Communications Magazine, Vol. 44, Issue 1, (2006) 74-82
11. Network Simulator Version 2.29, http://www.isi.edu/nsnam/ns/

UbiComm: An Adaptive Vertical Handoff Decision Scheme for Heterogeneous Wireless Networks*

Wonjun Lee[1,**], Eunkyo Kim[2] Jieun Yu[1], Donghwan Lee[1], Jihoon Choi[1], Joongheon Kim[3], and Christian K. Shin[4]

* Dept. of Computer Science and Engineering, Korea University, Seoul, Korea
wlee@korea.ac.kr
* LG Electronics Institute of Technology, LG Electronics, Seoul, Korea
* Digital Media Research Lab., LG Electronics, Seoul, Korea
* State University of New York (SUNY), Geneseo, NY, USA

Abstract. Vertical handoff will be essential for the next generation heterogeneous wireless networks. We propose an *Adaptive Vertical Handoff Decision Scheme* called *UbiComm* to avoid unbeneficial handoffs in the integrated WiBro and WLAN networks. If the mobile node (MN)'s velocity is high and moving pattern is irregular, more unnecessary handoffs can occur. Therefore, MN's velocity and moving pattern are the important factors of our handoff decision scheme. In order to avoid unbeneficial handoff the *UbiComm* adjusts the dwell time adaptively, and it also predicts the residence time in the target network. In addition, *UbiComm*'s adaptive dwell timer makes a MN receive service of a better network as long as possible. The simulation results show that the reduction of unnecessary handoffs proposed in *UbiComm* improves the MN's throughput.

1 Introduction

Recent wireless networks have various characteristics in terms of latency, bandwidth, frequency and coverage. Wireless networks can be divided into two groups; one that provides high bandwidth and small coverage (e.g. WLAN), and one that provides low bandwidth and wide coverage (e.g. WWAN) [1]. The vertical handoff, which is the roaming technology among different types of networks, has been studied in order to satisfy the demand on QoS as well as wide coverage. For example, an MN equipped with both WWAN and WLAN interfaces can perform vertical handoff to WLAN hotspot while receiving the service of WWAN. As a result, the MN's overall throughput is improved. There has been little research on handoffs between WiBro and WLAN. In this paper, we deal with vertical handoffs between WLAN and WiBro (which is a type of WMAN).

For vertical handoff, it is important to determine when a MN should perform handoff and to which network a MN should perform handoff. Despite the increased

---

* This research was supported by the Ministry of Information and Communication, Korea under ITRC program supervised by IITA, IITA-2005-(C1090-0501-0019).
** Corresponding author.

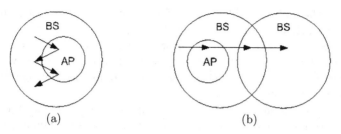

Fig. 1. Unbeneficial vertical handoff: (a) MN's ping-pong movement and (b) MN's movement at high speed.

in research on the received signal strength (RSS)-based and the utility-based vertical handoff algorithms in recent years, few have attempted to focus on factors on mobile node condition such as velocity and moving pattern. However, if factors on the MN's mobile condition are not considered, unbeneficial handoffs can be triggered frequently without any gain in such situations depicted in Figure 1.

In Figure 1, smaller circles are networks that provide better utility than larger ones. Hence, a MN prefers smaller networks. The first example shows a situation that a MN keeps handing off between the two base stations back and forth (ping-pong effect [3]) while keeping ping-pong movement [2] near the edge of two networks. Frequent handoffs cause packet loss/delay, decrease throughput, and increase the signaling overhead. The second example shows that a MN travels at high speeds around the edge of the small network. In these two cases, performing vertical handoff to smaller networks is unnecessary since a MN leaves it after a short period of time.

For the reasons stated above, we propose an *adaptive vertical handoff decision scheme for heterogeneous wireless networks*, called *UbiComm*, not only to avoid unnecessary and unbeneficial handoffs and ping-pong effect, but also to provide better service to loss and delay sensitive applications. The handoff decision algorithm of *UbiComm* uses an *adaptive dwell timer* and *predictive residence time* in the target network to avoid unbeneficial handoffs. The adaptive dwell timer adjusts the length of timeout according to the ping-pong movement pattern. The predictive residence time in the target network is used to check if the target network could compensate for the handoff delay to the applications.

The remainder of this paper is organized as follows. Section 2 reviews related work. Section 3 describes the architecture for performing vertical handoff. In Section 4, an adaptive handoff decision mechanism, i.e., *UbiComm* is proposed. In Section 5, *UbiComm* is evaluated compared to previous handoff decision algorithms through simulation. Finally, the conclusion is drawn in Section 6.

2   Related Work

Traditionally, homogeneous networks have used the RSS as the main factor of the handoff decision. However, the vertical handoff decision needs to consider more factors other than the RSS because networks have different characteristics.

Therefore, the policy-enabled handoff decision algorithm using the utility function with various factors was proposed in [4]. Factors used with the RSS include service types, monetary cost, network conditions, system performance, mobile node conditions, etc. [5]. It performs handoff to the best network determined by the utility function. Such policy-based handoff decision algorithms can be used to provide QoS to users.

In a homogeneous environment, the ping-pong effect is a phenomenon that rapidly repeats handoff between two base stations [6]. In a heterogeneous environment, the ping-pong effect occurs if factors for the handoff decision are changing rapidly and a MN performs handoff as soon as the MN detects the better network [7]. The dwell timer scheme has been used to avoid such ping-pong effect. It starts to work when the handoff condition is first satisfied. If the handoff condition persists during the dwell time, the MN performs handoff to the target network after the dwell timer is expired. Otherwise the MN resets the dwell timer [8]. Consequently, a MN doesn't perform handoff until the target network becomes stable. Ping-pong effect can also occur if the speed of a MN is high or the moving direction of the MN is irregular. Thus, UbiComm adjusts the length of the dwell time adaptively according to the MN's ping-pong movement.

In [9], a MN selects a network with the least QoS level from networks that can satisfy QoS requirement of the current application, i.e., a MN does not select the best network. Therefore, the MN remains in the current network as long as the current network satisfies the MN's QoS requirement. When the type of the application used is changed or a MN leaves the current network, the MN attempts to find other networks. The proposed handoff decision algorithm in [9] can avoid ping-pong effect since it is based on the need of the application and not the RSS of the network. However, UbiComm provides the handoff decision scheme that can avoid ping-pong effect as well as select the best network.

3   Interworking Architecture Between WiBro and WLAN

Previous vertical handoff studies have been mainly carried out over the integrated WLAN and WWAN networks. The next generation network will be a convergence of various wireless networks. Our approach described in this paper uses for the first time the integrated environment of WiBro and WLAN networks. WiBro (Wireless Broadband Internet), a type of WMAN (Wireless Metropolitan Area Network), has been proposed and standardized in Korea. WiBro is compatible with 802.16e and will become commercialized in 2006. WiBro has medium characteristics between WWAN and WLAN in terms of bandwidth (3Mbps/user), coverage (1km) and mobility support ($\leq$ 60km/h) [10]. Therefore, a MN can handoff to WiBro when leaving WLAN, and handoff to WWAN when leaving WiBro for maintaining connection during data communication. Figure 2 shows the proposed interworking architecture between WiBro and WLAN. It is a tightly-coupled architecture where WLAN is connected to WiBro core network. In this architecture, seamless vertical handoff is possible between WiBro and WLAN. A dual-mode MN has two interfaces; one for WiBro and the other for

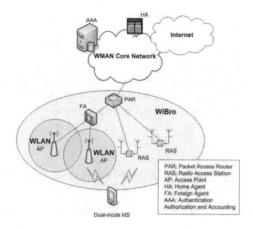

Fig. 2. Interworking network architecture between WiBro and WLAN

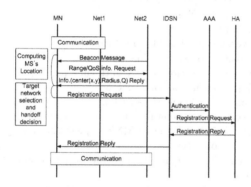

Fig. 3. Proposed handoff procedure

WLAN. Figure 3 shows that we add process of requesting and replying network's information, i.e., QoS and location information, to existing handoff procedure in order to support *U*biComm. If a MN receives a beacon message from network2 during communication with network1, it requests range and QoS information of network2. A MN decides to perform handoff to network2 based on the information of network2 and the location of the MN. The MN needs to inform HA of the current network through PAR after handoff.

4 *U*biComm: Proposed Vertical Handoff Mechanism

First, assumption and notations for *U*biComm are described in section 4.1 and 4.2 respectively. Section 4.3 shows three processes of *U*biComm in detail. The basic operation of handoff decision algorithm in *U*biComm is shown as pseudo code in section 4.4.

4.1   Assumption

We use the following assumptions for our proposed algorithm. Each network area is a circle. Each MN knows the degree of QoS factors of applications. Each network can provide information about its location (i.e., center location) and available resources (i.e., degree of QoS factors). How to detect a MN's location and its moving direction is not covered in this scheme.

4.2   Notations

The following Table 1 presents main symbols for describing UbiComm.

Table 1. Symbols used for description of UbiComm

Symbol	Description
$LUTO$	Location Update Timeout
v_t	Speed of MN at time t
$V_{default}$	Default speed of MN
V_t	Average speed of MN until time t
d_t	Direction of MN at time t
D_t	Average direction of MN until time t
α	Exponential smoothing factor
f_t	Ping-pong flag at time t (0 or 1)
F_t	Average ping-pong flag until time t (0 or 1)
$u_{j,i}$	The satisfied degree of MN's request (network j, QoS factor i)
U_j	Utility of network j
T_RES_{target}	Predictive residence time in the target network
DT	Dwell timer
γ	Utility ratio of current network to the target network

4.3   Algorithm

UbiComm consists of three processes as described in this section. The *periodic location update* process detects the location of a MN periodically according to velocity of the MN. Values used in the handoff decision are also updated periodically. The *target network selection* process selects a network providing the maximum utility. Based on the information obtained from the above two processes, the *handoff decision* process determines when a MN should perform handoff. In the *handoff decision* process, while utility-based handoff is triggered if the handoff is beneficial based on predictive residence time in the target network, RSS-based handoff is triggered if the MN leaves the current network.

Periodic Location Update. A MN's location can be detected periodically using either GPS or a location detection schemes, which use signals received from more than three networks.

Location Update Timeout ($LUTO$) is set based on the MN's current velocity. The higher the velocity is, the shorter the $LUTO$ is. Equation (1) sets $LUTO$ at time t using the default, upper bound, and lower bound values of $LUTO$.

$$LUTO_t = \min[LUTO_{ubound}, \max(LUTO_{lbound}, \beta \cdot LUTO_{default})], \qquad (1)$$

where current speed of MN is V_t and $\beta = \frac{V_{default}}{V_t}$.

In addition to updating the MN's location, weighted average velocity, direction, and ping-pong movement flag are calculated every $LUTO$ times for the handoff decision as follows.

A MN's weighted average velocity V_t and direction D_t at time t are used to obtain the predictive residence time in the handoff decision process. In (2), weighted average V_t and D_t at time t are calculated by using the real values of velocity v and direction d for the previous intervals. When $\alpha = 0.5$, the weight affects the 4-5 latest v and d data. The length of interval between t and $t - 1$ equals $LUTO_{t-1}$.

$$V_t = (1 - \alpha)v_t + \alpha(1 - \alpha)v_{t-1} + \alpha^2(1 - \alpha)v_{t-2} + \cdots + \alpha^k(1 - \alpha)v_1 \qquad (2)$$
$$D_t = (1 - \alpha)d_t + \alpha(1 - \alpha)d_{t-1} + \alpha^2(1 - \alpha)d_{t-2} + \cdots + \alpha^k(1 - \alpha)d_1$$

To detect a MN's movement pattern, direction d_t at current time t is compared to direction d_{t-1} at time $t - 1$ (i.e., previous $LUTO$ interval) every $LUTO$ times while storing the direction value at time t. In (3), if there is a considerable change of more than 90 degrees between d_t and d_{t-1}, flag f_t is set to 1 since the probability of a ping-pong movement is high. The flag At is set to the weighted average of f_t so that the ping-pong flag F_t keeps a value of 1 during several intervals after $f_t = 1$ and presents ping-pong movement. F_t is used to adjust the dwell timer adaptively in the handoff decision process.

$$f_t = \begin{cases} 1 \text{ if } d_t \geq d_{t-1} + 90° \\ 0 \text{ otherwise} \end{cases} \qquad (3)$$

$$A_t = (1 - \alpha)f_t + \alpha(1 - \alpha)f_{t-1} + \alpha^2(1 - \alpha)f_{t-2} + \cdots + \alpha^k(1 - \alpha)f_1$$

$$F_t = \begin{cases} 1 \text{ if } A_t > 0 \\ 0 \text{ otherwise} \end{cases}$$

Target Network Selection. The target network is the network that provides the maximum utility among detected ones except the current network. After receiving QoS information from each network, utilities of networks are calculated using the MN's request level $((R_1, R_2, \ldots, R_n)$ and available level in network j $(A_{j,1}, A_{j,2}, \ldots, A_{j,n})$ in terms of QoS factor $(1, 2, \ldots, n)$ such as data rate and mobility support.

Equation (4) presents $u_{j,i}$, which is the satisfied degree of MN's request level in network j in terms of each QoS factor i.

$$u_{j,i} = \min[1, \frac{A_{j,i}}{R_i}] \qquad (4)$$

The importance of each QoS factor becomes different according to MN's application. Thus, utility of network j, U_j, is calculated using weight in (5).

$$U_j = \frac{1}{n} \sum_{i=1}^{n} w_i \cdot u_{j,i},$$ (5)

where w_i is the weight of QoS factor i ($0 \leq w_i \leq 1$). As a result, $0 \leq$ utility of network $j \leq 1$.

Handoff Decision. Although the target network provides better utility than the current network, the handoff to the target network becomes unbeneficial if the predictive residence time in the target network is smaller than the delay caused by the handoff process. Thus, the handoff decision has to take into account both utility and residence time. MN's predictive residence time in the target network (T_RES_{target}) can be calculated by using MN's movement direction, velocity, and the range of the target network. On the other hand, although the current network provides maximum utility, handoff to the target network has to be performed if RSS of current one is lower than the threshold. Consequently, handoff occurs when one of the following conditions lasts until the dwell timer expires. "Make Up Time" means the amount of time needed to make up the loss due to handoff delay.

- $(Utility_{current} < Utility_{target})$ and $(RSS_{target} > TH_{target})$ and $(T\_RES_{target} > HandoffDelayTime + MakeUpTime)$
- $RSS_{current} < TH_{current}$

A dwell timer is a smoothing technique for ping-pong effect, cutting too frequent sequential handoffs [3]. It starts to work from the first time that one of above conditions is satisfied. We propose an adaptive dwell timer that can adjust timer duration according to the situation of MN and the network. If utility of the target network is much better than the current one, a dwell timer is shortened, and if movement direction is irregular (ping-pong movement), the dwell timer is extended. The dwell timer has the value of the upper bound $DT_{ubound,j}$, the lower bound $DT_{lbound,j}$ and the default $DT_{defualt,j}$ that depend on the MN's velocity. In consideration of utility and ping-pong movement, equation (6) sets the dwell timer.

$$DT_t = \min[DT_{ubound}, \max(DT_{lbound}, (1 + F_t) \cdot \gamma \cdot DT_{default})],$$ (6)

where F_t is the ping-pong flag (0 is not ping-pong; 1 is ping-pong) and $\gamma = \frac{U_{current}}{U_{target}}$.

4.4   Basic Operations of *Ubi*Comm Handoff Decision Algorithm

Algorithm 1 shows the whole structure of *Ubi*Comm handoff decision algorithm in pseudo code. First of all, utilities of the current network and the target network are compared. Secondly, a dwell timer starts if the conditions such as RSS and T_RES are satisfied. A MN handoffs to the target network only if the condition persists until the dwell timer expires. Otherwise the MN stays in the current network.

Algorithm 1 UbiComm Handoff Decision

1: **loop**
2:    location update periodically
3:    **if** $Utility_{current} > Utility_{target}$ {detect better network} **then**
4:       **if** $RSS_{target} < Threshold_{target}$ and $T\_RES_{target} > handoffdelaytime + makeuptime$ {beneficial handoff?} **then**
5:          Start adaptive dwell timer
6:          **if** condition persists until timer expires **then**
7:             Handoff to target network
8:          **else**
9:             reset dwell timer
10:          **end if**
11:       **else**
12:          stay in current network
13:       **end if**
14:    **else if** $RSS_{current} > Threshold_{current}$ {current network is weak} **then**
15:       Start adaptive dwell timer
16:       **if** condition persists until timer expires **then**
17:          Handoff to target network
18:       **else**
19:          reset dwell timer
20:       **end if**
21:    **end if**
22: **end loop**

---

5   Simulation Results

We have performed ns-2 simulation [11] with three scenarios for testing various aspects of the proposed protocol. In the first scenario, we compared a fixed dwell timer to an adaptive dwell timer using the utility ratio when a MN passes the center of WLAN slowly. In the second scenario, we compare a fixed dwell timer to an adaptive dwell timer using T_RES when a MN passes the edge of WLAN rapidly. When there are MN's quick ping-pong movements across the edge of WiBro and WLAN, we compared RSS with an adaptive dwell timer in the third scenario. We assume that the utility ratio of WLAN to WiBro is a fixed value of 2 in the simulation. The IEEE 802.11a standard is used for WLAN and a simple link adaptation is applied [12]. The traffic used in the simulation is non-real time data service with TCP (selective ACK). The simulation parameters of the scenarios used are shown in Table 2.

Table 2. Simulation parameters of each scenario

Parameter	Scenario 1	Scenario 2	Scenario 3
Radius to RSS threshold	20m	20m	20m
γ (utility ratio)	2	2	2
Link adaptation	802.11a	802.11a	802.11a
MN's speed (m/s)	1 m/s	5 m/s	5 m/s
Movement pattern	Line	Line	Ping-pong

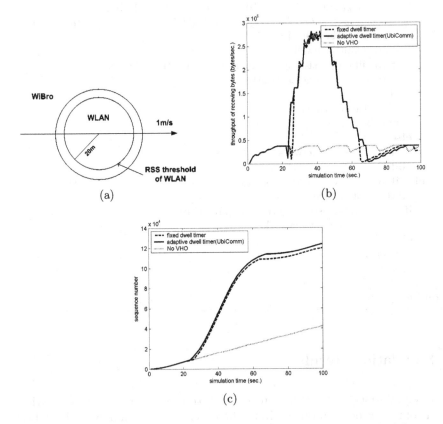

Fig. 4. Scenario 1: (a) a MN passes over WLAN with radius 20m at 1m/s, (b) through-put vs. simulation time, and (c) sequence number vs. simulation time.

5.1   Scenario 1: Adaptive Dwell Timer's Behavior when MN passes the Center of WLAN at Slow Speed

Figure 4(a) shows that a MN passes the center of WLAN (802.11a) at slow speed (1m/s). If fixed dwell time is 4 seconds, UbiComm's adaptive dwell time is adjusted to 2 seconds and 8 seconds during handoff to WLAN and leaving

WLAN respectively. Therefore, the adaptive dwell timer, i.e. *U*biComm scheme, can receive WLAN's service for longer duration.

Variations of the throughput are presented in Figure 4(b) in order to observe handoff time according to handoff decision algorithms. At around 20 seconds, *U*bi-Comm performs an earlier handoff to WLAN from WiBro than the fixed dwell timer scheme. At around 70 seconds, *U*biComm performs a later handoff to WiBro than the fixed dwell timer scheme. Because link adaptation occurs while in motion, the closer a MN is to WLAN's AP, the higher the throughput the MN gains. The No VHO (not to perform vertical handoff) scheme shows TCP behavior (selective ACK) of receiving WiBro service with constantly low throughput.

Variations of the sequence number are shown in Figure 4(c) to show the cumulative amount of received packets for certain elapsed time periods. *U*biComm has the largest number of received packets since it has the longest service time of WLAN. *U*biComm has 3,900 packets more than the fixed dwell timer scheme after 100 seconds. No VHO scheme receives much smaller number of packets than the other vertical handoff schemes.

5.2 Scenario 2: Use of T_RES when MN passes over the Edge of WLAN at Rapid Speed

Figure 5(a) depicts the scenario 2 where a MN passes the point 19m away from WLAN's AP at 5m/s (18km/h). The predictive dwell time (T_RES) in WLAN is 2.56 seconds. However, handoff delay + makeup time is more than 10 seconds on the assumption that the vertical handoff delay is 0.5 second and the packet loss fraction at handoff is 0.5. If T_RES is shorter than handoff delay + makeup time, *U*biComm doesn't perform vertical handoff to the preferred network because continuous handoffs for short time cause a ping-pong effect. *U*biComm is compared with the fixed dwell timer scheme (dwell time = 2 seconds without using T_RES) as follows.

In figure 5(b), the fixed dwell timer scheme performs a vertical handoff to WLAN at 32 seconds after dwell time of 2 seconds. After receiving WLAN service for very short time, the MN handoffs to WiBro again at 34.56s after dwell time 2 seconds. However, *U*biComm does not handoff to WLAN due to short T_RES. In Figure 5(c), the fixed dwell timer scheme performs unbeneficial handoffs, and, as a result, has much packet loss without being able to make up the loss quickly enough. Therefore,, the number of received packets using the fixed dwell timer becomes less than *U*biComm that avoids handoffs.

In Figure 5(d), the number of cumulative received packets after 100 seconds is compared based on the total time receiving WLAN service. No VHO scheme receives 42280 packets after 100 seconds regardless of residence time in WLAN. The fixed dwell timer scheme without using T_RES has smaller number of received packets than No VHO scheme where residence time in WLAN is less than 8 seconds. *U*biComm takes T_RES into account for the handoff decision. Consequently, *U*biComm does not perform handoffs to WLAN if T_RES is less than 8 seconds, and it performs handoffs only if T_RES is more than 9 seconds. As a result, it avoids unnecessary handoffs that can degrade performance.

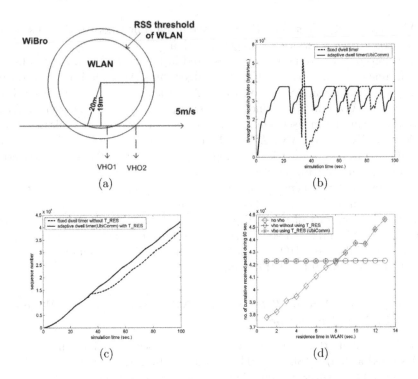

Fig. 5. Scenario 2: (a) a MN passes the point 19-20m away from WLAN's AP at 5m/s, (b) throughput vs. simulation time, (c) sequence number vs. simulation time, and (d) comparison of number of cumulative received packets with different T_RES

5.3 Scenario 3: Adaptive Dwell Time's Behavior when MN has Ping-pong Movement Pattern and High Speed

Figure 6(a) shows scenario 3 where a MN starts to show ping-pong movement before the MN enters WLAN with the MN's velocity of 5m/s (18km/h). In scenario 3, a MN's residence time in WLAN RSS threshold is 3 seconds whenever a MN enters WLAN. If the change in the MN's direction is more than 90 degrees, *Ubi*Comm checks the ping-pong flag and makes the previous dwell time 2 times longer. Therefore, 2 second dwell time in scenario 2 is adjusted to 4 seconds, and the MN does not handoff in scenario 3. The fixed dwell timer and the *Ubi*Comm have the same performance if the dwell time is fixed as more than 4 seconds. However, the fixed dwell timer scheme performs handoffs if dwell time is fixed as less than 4 seconds. The RSS-based handoff decision scheme always performs handoff whenever a MN passes the RSS threshold. The *Ubi*Comm and the RSS-based schemes are compared as follows.

Figure 6(b) shows the sudden changes of throughput of the RSS-based handoff decision scheme that performs a total of 4 handoffs. The RSS-based scheme receives WLAN's service for very short time. *Ubi*Comm avoids vertical handoffs because of the ping-pong movement, and continues to receive WiBro's service. In

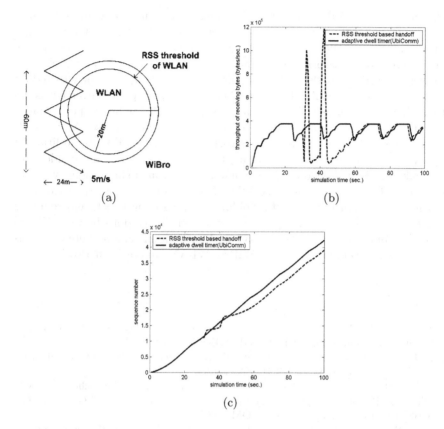

Fig. 6. Scenario 3: (a) a MN's ping-pong movement over the edge of WLAN and WiBro at 5m/s, (b) throughput vs. simulation time, and (c) sequence number vs. simulation time

Figure 6(c), the RSS-based scheme receives packets quickly right after handoff to WLAN. However, the RSS-based scheme receives fewer packets than *U*biComm after 100 seconds because it has more packet loss due to continuous handoffs of for short duration.

6   Conclusion and Future Work

Performing vertical handoffs to the network of better performance results in better throughput. However, frequent handoffs of short time period cause more packet loss/delay, and, as a result, decrease the overall throughput. The ping-pong effect, which is a phenomenon that repeats handoffs between two base stations, results from short residence time in the preferred network. Therefore, we have investigated the cause of the short residence time (i.e. MN's high speed and ping-pong movement), and we have proposed *U*biComm which is an improved handoff decision algorithm that avoids the ping-pong effect. The fixed dwell timer scheme used to avoid the ping-pong effect cannot handoff to the preferred network quickly even if it has sufficiently long dwell time. On the other hand, the ping-pong effect occurs if it has short dwell time of receiving service from the preferred network early. However, *U*biComm adjusts the dwell time adaptively according to the MN's mobility. The dwell time doubles to reduce the probability of performing handoffs when a MN's ping-pong movement is detected. The dwell time is reduced if the target network has better performance than current network, and the dwell time is increased otherwise. As a result, a MN receives service of the better network as long as possible. In addition, if the predictive residence time in the target network is shorter than handoff delay + make up time, *U*biComm avoids handoffs. Through simulations, we have shown that *U*biComm is a more flexible scheme than the fixed dwell timer by increasing the overall throughput, avoiding the ping-pong effect, and reducing unbeneficial handoffs. In this paper, we focused on the handoffs between WiBro and WLAN, but *U*biComm can also be used for handoffs among heterogeneous networks, such as cellular networks, WiBro, WLAN, and other networks.

References

[1] M. Stemm, R. H. Katz: Vertical handoffs in wireless overlay networks. ACM Mobile networks and applications (ACM MONET) (1998).

[2] R. Hsieh, Z. G. Zhou, A. Senevirante: S-MIP: A Seamless Handoff Architecture for Mobile IP. in Proc. IEEE INFOCOM (2003).

[3] M. Ylianttila, M. Pande, J. Makela, P. Mahonen: Optimization Scheme for Mobile Users Performing Vertical Handoffs between IEEE 802.11 and GPRS/EDGE networks. in Proc. IEEE GLOBECOM (2001).

[4] H. J. Wang, R. H. Katz, and J. Giese: Policy-enabled Handoffs across Heterogeneous Wireless Networks. in Proc. the IEEE Workshop on Mobile Computing Systems and Applications (WMCSA) (1999).

[5] J. McNair, F. Zhu: Vertical Handoffs in Fourth-Generation Multinetwork Environments. IEEE Wireless Communications (2004).

[6] G. P. Pollini: Trends in Handover Design. IEEE Communications Magazine (1996).

[7] W-T. Chen, J-C. Liu, H-K. Huang: An Adaptive Scheme for Vertical Handoff in Wireless Overlay Networks. in Proc. IEEE ICPADS (2004).

[8] M-H. Ye, Y. Liu, H-M. Zhang: The Mobile IP Handoff between Hybrid Networks. in Proc. PIMRC (2002).

[9] W-T. Chen, Y.Y. Shu: Active Application Oriented Vertical Handoff in Next-Generation Wireless Networks. in Proc. IEEE WCNC (2005).

[10] TTA: Specifications for 2.3GHz band Portable Internet Service - Physical and Medium Access Control Layer. TTAS.KO-06.0082 (2005).

[11] A. Gurtov: NS2 Simulation Tests for Modeling Wireless Links. Technical Report, University of Helsinki (2003).

[12] D. Qiao and S. Choi: Fast-Responsive Link Adaptation for IEEE 802.11 WLANs. in Proc. IEEE ICC (2005).

Reducing Location Update Cost Using Multiple Virtual Layers in HMIPv6

Jongpil Jeong, Min Young Chung, and Hyunseung Choo*

Intelligent HCI Convergence Research Center
Sungkyunkwan University
440-746, Suwon, Korea +82-31-290-7145
{jpjeong, mychung, choo}@ece.skku.ac.kr

Abstract. Hierarchical Mobile IPv6 (HMIPv6) guarantees to reduce handoff latency, because the MN only registers the new addresses at mobility anchor point (MAP) when the MN moves around access routers (ARs) in the same MAP domain. HMIPv6 still has packet loss problem when the MN moves from one MAP to another. In this paper, a novel location update scheme which further reduces signaling traffic for location update by employing virtual MAP (VMAP) on top of overlapped MAP in HMIPv6, is proposed. This proposed scheme significantly improves performance compared to HMIPv6, in terms of location update rate per user. Also it makes the mobile nodes (MNs) moving around the boundary ARs of adjacent MAP's become to move within a VMAP. It is certain that this scheme reduce the network resources efficiently by reason of removing the location update. In conclusion, this scheme greatly reduces the packet loss and delay, due to Inter-MAP handoff not occurring.

1 Introduction

Mobile IPv6 (MIPv6) [1,2] of Internet Engineering Task Force (IETF) Mobile IP Working Group [4], is the main protocol supporting IP mobility [3]. This protocol provides connectivity with the Internet from the MN's movement. When the MN moves away from its home link, it configures a new care-of-address (CoA) at a visited network. The MN registers new CoA at the Home Agent (HA) and the Correspondent Node (CN) to indicate its current location. However, MIPv6 has weak points, such as handoff latency resulting from movement detections, IP address configurations and location updates which is unacceptable in real-time application.

The purpose of Hierarchical Mobile IPv6 (HMIPv6) [5] is to reduce the amount of signaling to CNs and the HA. However, this does not satisfy the requirements of real-time services which are susceptible to delay, because HMIPv6 also uses MIPv6 for Inter-MAP handoff. Furthermore, HMIPv6 is managed by several MAPs to solve the Single Point of Failure (SPOF) and bottleneck state of traffic. Thus, Inter-MAP handoff is increasingly expanding.

---

* Corresponding author.

H.Y. Youn, M. Kim, and H. Morikawa (Eds.): UCS 2006, LNCS 4239, pp. 357–367, 2006.

In this paper, the Inter-MAP handoff scheme is proposed, in order to improve HMIPv6 performance. This scheme is based on a virtual layer employing the VMAP (virtual MAP). The virtual layer consists of virtual MAP's, each of which is managed by a VMAP. This proposed scheme significantly improves performance compared to HMIPv6, for location update rate per users. The proposed scheme allows the mobile terminals moving around the boundary ARs of adjacent MAP's to move within either a VMAP or an overlapped region. This greatly reduces the packet loss and delay, due to the Inter-MAP handoff not occurring.

This paper is organized as follows. In Section 2, we reviewed the analytic models for location update, the basic operation of HMIPv6 and its MAP discovery. The motivation of this work and the new proposed scheme is presented in Section 3 based on HMIPv6. In Section 4, the performance of the proposed scheme is evaluated. Finally, this paper is concluded in Section 5, presenting future direction.

2   Related Works

This section provides a brief overview of analytic approaches for performance improvement of mobile network. Recently, Xie et al. proposed an analytic model for regional registration [6], which is a derivative of a hierarchical mobility management scheme [7]. The proposed analytic model focuses on the determination of the optimal size of regional networks, given the average location update and packet delivery costs. In this study, the existence of one-level regional networks is assumed where there is a single Gateway Foreign Agent (GFA).

In addition, Woo proposed an analytic model, in order to investigate the performance of Mobile IP regional registration [8]. In [8], Woo measured registration delay and CPU processing overhead loaded on the mobility agents to support regional registration. Although this model is a well-defined analytic model, it is based on MIPv4 and not MIPv6. Furthermore, in this study, a spatial-oriented Internet architecture was used for performance analysis. Currently, the Internet is based on the spatial-oriented location area model, which specifies that the distance between two end points situated on the Internet is unrelated to the geographic locations of these two points. However, the ARs used in next-generation wireless and mobile networks may utilize a cellular architecture, in order to maximize utilization of the limited radio resources. Therefore, it is more appropriate to analyze network performance in the context of IP-based cellular networks [9].

HMIPv6 [5] is the extension of MIPv6 and IPv6 Neighbor discovery protocols to support local mobility. Therefore, the introduction of a hierarchy only makes sense if the MAP is located between the MN and HA/CNs. It also reduces the signaling traffic for handoff due to transmitting a BU (Binding Update) regardless of the number of CNs. MN receive the Router Advertisement (RA) having the MAP information from AR. This creates the Regional Care-of-Address (RCoA) and On-link Care-of-Address (LCoA) with received MAP and AR's subnet prefix,

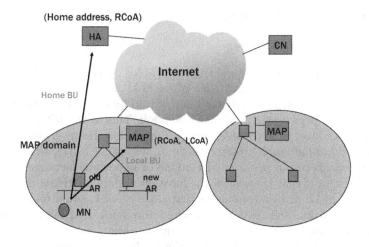

Fig. 1. HMIPv6 Operation

registering them to MAP and HA/CNs. In the case of moving the ARs in the same MAP, MN only registers a changed LCoA to MAP. The MAP intercepts all packets directed to MN in MAP, performing the local HA's role that encapsulates and delivers them.

Fig.1 depicts the basic operations which are performed in HMIPv6. An MN entering a MAP domain will receive RA message containing information on one or more local MAPs. Then, the MN selects the most suitable MAP by a number of criteria (distance, mobility, preference, *etc.*). However, the question of how to select a MAP is the beyond the scope of this paper. We simply assume that a specific MAP selection scheme is used and that the MN sends a BU message to the selected MAP. The MN can bind its current location (*i.e.*, LCoA) with an address on the MAP's subnet (*i.e.*, RCoA). Acting as a local home agent (HA), the MAP will receive all packets on behalf of the MNs it is serving and will decapsulate and forward them to the MN's current address. If the MN changes its current address within a local MAP domain, it only needs to register the new address to the MAP. The RCoA does not change as long as the MN moves within the MAP domain. This makes the MN's mobility transparent to the correspondent nodes (CNs).

The MAP option newly reconfigured for MN to recognize the MAP, to configure the RCoA and to receive the necessary information of basic HMIPv6 operation. The Preference field is 4 bit and indicates the MAP preference. It also consists of a Valid Lifetime field, Distance field, Global IP Address field and several flags. MAP discovery is the procedure of discovering the MAP for ARs and acquiring the MAP subnet prefix. It is possible to pre-configure the Routers for MAP options from MAP to MN over the specified interfaces. All ARs in the same MAP are configured for receiving MAP options with the same MAP address.

3   The Proposed Scheme

3.1   Virtual Layer Scheme

The proposed scheme is configured to receive MAP options from all the adjacent MAPs, for ARs in the boundary area of its MAP. In addition, when a MN is connecting with a boundary area's AR in the overlapped MAP, it should perform MAP switching prior to the Inter-MAP handoff. This MAP switching performs identical procedures to Inter-MAP handoff operation. However, no packet loss occurs or additional handoff latency occurs, because of MAP switching on receiving the packet from previous MAP. One of important facts motivating the proposed design is that the cost of the location update for HA is much greater than that of MAP. A disadvantage is that since every location request in addition to the location registration, is serviced through a HA, in addition to the HA being overloaded with database lookup operation, the traffic on the links leading to the HA is heavy. Therefore, the traffic required for updating HA is required to be minimized, and the principle employed in the proposed scheme is to distribute the signaling traffic heading to HA and MAPs.

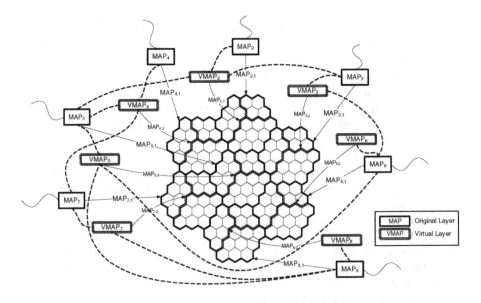

Fig. 2. Proposed Virtual Layer Structure

The enhanced location management scheme proposed in this paper employs virtual layer in part as presented in Fig. 2. Layer-2 MAPs represented as thick lines are in a virtual layer. It can be observed that the entire area is partitioned into seven MAP's ($MAP_2 \sim MAP_8$), which are drawn by dotted MAP boundary lines. In addition, this scheme combines three neighboring MAP's as an expanded cluster in the original layer, an expanded MAP. As previously mentioned, each

MAP has an associated VMAP. This original layer of MAP's is called Layer-1 and the expanded MAP's overlap each other. It is important to note that another portion of the area exists, using bold lines as mentioned above, which is in a virtual layer and are called in Layer-2. Each MAP of Layer-2 also has a VMAP. Each virtual MAP, which is of equal size, is laid upon the center of the combined three MAP's of each expanded MAP. As a result, the mobile terminals' moving around the boundary ARs of adjacent MAP's increasingly move within either a virtual MAP or an overlapping region. VMAPs, which manage the original layer, take charge of the management for the entire area. However, MAPs, which manage the virtual layer, take charge of the management for the partial areas. In what follows, $MAP_{i,j}$ the MAP_i of Layer-j, are denoted. For example, $MAP_{5,1}$ consists of part of $MAP_{2,2}$, $MAP_{4,2}$, and $MAP_{9,1}$. The MAP of Layer-2 is connected to three VMAPs representing the MAP's of Layer-1. For example, MAP_5 is connected to $VMAP_2$, $VMAP_4$ and $VMAP_5$. The proposed structure effectively avoids the ping-ponging effect, occurring when a mobile user travels along the boundary of two adjacent MAP's and distributes the location update signaling traffic over many ARs using the virtual layer.

3.2   Operational Mechanism

The proposed scheme can be implemented by assigning a unique ID to each MAP of Layer-1 and 2. It is important to note that the proposed scheme covers the service area with homogeneous MAP's. The original MAP's are partially overlapped with the MAP's of the virtual layer, and expanded clusters combine three neighboring MAP's in the original layer so they overlap each other. The ARs of layer-1 used to be entirely in one, two, or three MAP's, and the ARs of layer-2 managed by two or three MAP's. Even though each AR belongs to one, two, or three MAP's, the mobile user in an AR registers with only one MAP at any moment. The preference field of MAP options is used to cache the location information of each ARs in the MAP domain. If they are delivered the preference field values of MAP options to all ARs of the same MAP domain, they have exactly the same value. As ARs own location is close to the boundary AR from the center AR, the preference field value is reduced by 1 and then delivered to MN over the Router Advertisement (RA). MN recognizes that it arrived at the boundary ARs of MAP, using the preference field value from AR.

If two MAPs domains overlap other boundary ARs, AR_5, AR_6 and AR_7 receive all the MAP options that are composed MAP_1 and $VMAP_1$. The preference field of MAP options is used for caching AR's location information in the MAP domain and AR transmits the preference field value through Router Advertisement (RA) to MN after decreasing by 1. MN is going to obtain a response that is the value of a preference field, and then obtains boundary ARs. In Fig. 3, when AR_6 is moved to an area of AR_7, Intra-MAP handoff occurs and has received a packet coming from CN through MAP_1 and AR_7 (path 1). AR_7 is located at the outer AR in the overlapping area, so MN is going to turn into its own MAP from MAP_1 to $VMAP_1$. MN transmits Local Binding Update (LBU) to $VMAP_1$, then obtains an Ack, and transmits BU again to HA/CNs. After

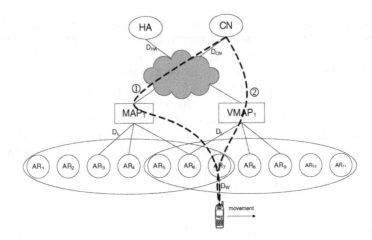

Fig. 3. Operation Procedure

CN receives BU, it transmits data packets with Ack to MN through AR_7 and $VMAP_1$ (path 2). AR_7 does not initiate Inter-MAP handoff if it does not move to AR_5, because AR_7 is located inside of the domain. Considering all of ARs incurring additional overhead for MAP switching are located in MAP domain, the main problem of HMIPv6, SPOF and traffic bottleneck state, are going to have a solution, therefore it can prevent performance downgrade using Inter-MAP handoff.

4   Performance Evaluation

This section presents processing of two kinds of performance analysis in the proposed scheme. First, comparison between the proposed scheme and HMIPv6 for Inter-MAP handoff, is presented. Second, a formula of Average Inter-MAP handoff latency and Total Average handoff latency will be obtained. The handoff latency can be multiplied respectively after an average Intra-MAP handoff probability and Inter-MAP handoff probability occurs, through movement and modeling of handoff procedures. The process for performance comparison when obtaining each value of proposed scheme and HMIPv6 is presented.

4.1   Inter-MAP Handoff Performance Comparison

This consists of topology identical to Fig. 3, for performance comparing of Inter-MAP handoff from the proposed scheme and HMIPv6. AR_5, AR_6, and AR_7 have received all MAP options from MAP_1 and $VMAP_1$. As already mentioned, if the mobile node moves AR_6 to AR_7, and processes the local binding update to MAP_1 in AR_7, then the mobile node in AR_7 is going to process MAP selection algorithm and MAP switching. Parameters for performance evaluation are defined in Table 1.

Table 1. Parameters for Performance Analysis

Parameter	Time
L2 Handoff Latency (Wireless LAN)	80 ms
Receipt of Router Advertisement (Mobility Detection)	20 ms
D_W (Wireless Part Delay)	2 ms
D_L (Wired Part Delay	10 ms
D_{CN} (Delay among MAP and CN)	50 $\sim$ 130 ms

In this case, for performance comparison the following is assumed. First, On-link CoA Test and Return Routability Test are compared. This does not consider operation time for security in local BU and global BU. Second, it does not consider Duplicated Address Detection (DAD) operation in Address Auto-configuration (AA). Third, if CN delivers packets to MN directly without the HA, mobile node would transmits a binding update to CN first, after checking the local BU. Therefore, if a mobile node does not require the response acknowledgement message, the BA will not return and will transmit data packets with the request. Fourth, CN always transmits packets for moving MN during performance analysis. Fifth, Intra-MAP handoff and MAP switching is always completed during mobile node and stays with a single AR.

In case of moving AR_6 to AR_7, HMIPv6 is $2(D_W+D_L)$ for Intra-MAP handoff latency, proposed scheme is identical. In case of moving AR_7 to AR_8, HMIPv6 is $2(2D_W + 2D_L + D_{CN})$ for Inter-MAP handoff latency, the proposed scheme is $2(D_W + D_L)$ for Intra-MAP handoff latency.

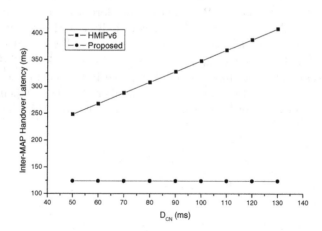

Fig. 4. Inter-MAP Handoff Latency Comparison

As presented in Fig. 4, Inter-MAP handoff latency is identical with Intra-MAP handoff latency for the proposed scheme, these are always the same values regardless of D_{CN} value. Otherwise, HMIPv6 handoff latency is larger, according to D_{CN} because the Inter-MAP handoff latency time should process a local binding update and additional BU to CNs.

4.2 Total Average Handoff Latency

The proposed scheme is only able to improve performance of Inter-MAP handoff. Therefore, it is required to grasp all Inter-MAP handoff probability, in order to decide improvement of the proposed scheme exactly. Given the MAP's radius, Inter-MAP handoff probability is obtained through mobility modeling, and the general formula of average Inter-MAP handoff latency is created after multiplying it by the handoff latency value. In addition, in the same manner, the average Intra-MAP handoff latency is obtained, the sum of the two values and the general formula of total average handoff latency is then obtained. For the proposed scheme, after Inter-MAP and Intra-MAP handoff latency value is input in this general formula. Average Inter-MAP handoff latency and total average handoff latency can be calculated, comparing these values. In this paper, the Markov Chain [10] used for handoff procedures is modified for the Location Update procedures, five formulas are also derived from this Markov Chain. For modeling of border crossing to be used for handoff procedures, the following is assumed.

1. MN's moving direction is distributed equally to $[0,2\pi)$ in AR.
2. Residence time is when MN remains in AR, and has negative exponential distribution.
3. All ARs have identical shape and size, form an adjacent area with each other, and are approximately a circular shape.

The Border-crossing rate can be calculated when MN moves away from MAP [11], as $V_{MAP} = \frac{\pi V}{4R_{MAP}}$. where, R_{MAP} is MN's average movement velocity and is the radius of the circular MAP. Similarly, the Border-crossing rate when MN moves away from AR, is $V_{AR} = \frac{\pi V}{4R_{AR}}$. Accordingly, the MN always passes by AR when it crosses MAP and the rate of crossing only AR's border in the same MAP, is calculated [10] as $V_{AR\_in\_MAP} = V_{AR} - V_{MAP} = \frac{\pi V(R_{MAP}-R_{AR})}{4R_{AR}\cdot R_{MAP}}$.

The MN's handoff procedures are modeling the Imbedded Markov Chain as Fig. 5. Markov chain's state is defined as the number of visiting ARs in the same MAP for MN. In other words, it means the number of Intra-MAP handoff until Inter-MAP handoff.

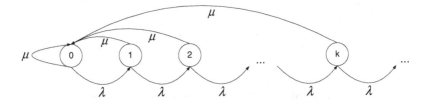

Fig. 5. Markov Chain for Handoff Procedure

where, $\lambda(= V_{AR\_in\_MAP})$ is the transition rate, moving from state k to $k+1$ (Intra-MAP handoff) and $\mu(= V_{MAP})$ is the transition rate, moving from state k to state 0 (Inter-MAP handoff) for MNs.

The steady state probability (P_k) of State k using the global balance equation is $P_0 = \frac{\mu}{\mu+\lambda}$, $P_k = (\frac{\mu}{(\mu+\lambda)})^k P_0 = (1-P_0)^k P_0$. The Inter-MAP handoff probability is $\alpha = P_0 \times 1 = \frac{\mu}{\mu+\lambda} = \frac{R_{AR}}{R_{MAP}} = AMR$. Where, AMR is the ratio for the radius of MAP and AR. Similarly, the Average Intra-MAP handoff probability is $\beta = \sum_{k=1}^{\infty}(1-P_0)^k P_0 = \frac{1}{P_0} - 1 = \frac{R_{MAP}}{R_{AR}} - 1$.

For the topology shown in Fig. 3, the Average Inter-MAP handoff latency is found my multiplying the average Inter-MAP handoff probability by Inter-MAP handoff latency, and the average Intra-MAP handoff latency is achieved similarly. Therefore, the total average handoff latency (L_{T_Av}) is the sum of average Inter-MAP handoff latency (αL_R) and average Intra-MAP handoff latency (βL_A). Handoff latency for the HMIPv6 and proposed scheme are compared in Table 2.

Table 2. Handoff Latency Comparison for HMIPv6 and Proposed schemes

-	HMIPv6	Proposed
αL_R	$AMR(2D_{CN} + 48)$	$24AMR$
βL_A	$24(\frac{\cdot}{AMR} - 1)$	$24(\frac{\cdot}{AMR} - 1)$, $(\Theta L_R = L_A = 2D_W + 2D_L)$
L_{T_Av}	$AMR(2D_{CN} + 48) + 24(\frac{\cdot}{AMR} - 1)$	$24AMR + 24(\frac{\cdot}{AMR} - 1)$

Fig. 6 presents the appearance of average Inter-MAP handoff latency according to the AMR and D_{CN} value. For HMIPv6, average Inter-MAP handoff latency increases in proportion to the D_{CN} value, however, the proposed scheme always has same average Inter-MAP handoff latency for all D_{CN} values. As reviewed earlier, in the case of the Inter-MAP handoff of HMIPv6,the Local BU and Global BU are performed respectively. However, in the case of the proposed

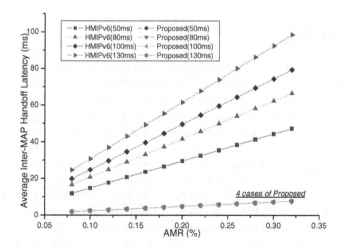

Fig. 6. Average Inter-MAP handoff latency

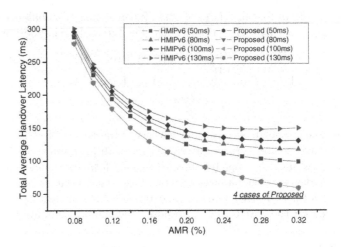

Fig. 7. Total Average handoff latency

scheme, a local BU is always required, this local BU does not change latency according to D_{CN}, which is the distance between MAP and CNs.

AMR's value is the ratio of MAP's radius to AR's radius, actually average Inter-MAP handoff probability based on the formulas as mentioned earlier. When the AMR value close to 1, Inter-MAP handoff probability is greater for HMIPv6 and the proposed scheme, and the Inter-MAP handoff latency also increases. Therefore, when the AMR value is close to 1, there is greater Inter-MAP handoff latency improvement in the proposed scheme.

As presented in Fig. 7, when AMR is 0.32, average handoff latency improved between 40.3% and 55% in accordance with D_{CN}. However, when AMR is 0.08, it is only improved between 5.4% and 9.3%. There is reason to rapidly increase the Inter-MAP handoff probability when there are too many ARs in MAP.

5   Conclusion

In this paper, an efficient location update scheme employing a partial virtual layer to reduce the update signaling traffic in HMIPv6, is proposed. The system has a two-layer architecture and is configured by homogenous MAP's. Conceptually, the proposed scheme is a combination of grouping, overlapping, and local updating in MAP. This scheme yields significant performance improvement over the overlapping and fully virtual layer scheme in terms of the average location update rate per user. Moreover, the new method offers considerable enhancement in utilizing the network resources which otherwise will be wasted by mobile users causing frequent update in HMIPv6. The signaling traffic concentrated on boundary ARs in the HMIPv6 is also distributed to many ARs.

In addition to the mobile users at the boundary ARs, the location update is required to consider other factors such as mobility pattern, dwell time, call to movement ratio, and so on. The relationship between the factors will be investigated, and included in the model of the update rate. This will present good measure by which efficient location management policy can be derived.

Acknowledgment

This research was supported by Ministry of Information and Communication, Korea under ITRC IITA-2005-(C1090-0501-0019) and grant No. R01-2006-000-10402-0 from the Basic Research Program Korea Science and Engineering Foundation of Ministry of Science & Technology.

References

1. D. Johnson, C. Perkins, and J. Arkko, "Mobility Support in IPv6," IETF RFC 3775, June 2004.
2. H. Soliman, "Mobile IPv6 - Mobility in a Wireless Internet," Addison Wesley, 2004.
3. I. F. Akyildiz, et al., "Mobility Management in Next-Generation Wireless Systems," Proceedings of the IEEE, Vol. 87(8), pp. 1347-1385, August 1999.
4. IETF Mobile IP Working Group: http://www.ietf.org/html.charters/mip6-charter.html
5. H. Soliman and K. E1-Malki, "Hierarchical Mobile IPv6 mobility management(HMIPv6)," IETF RFC 4140, August 2005.
6. E. Gustafsson, A. Jonsson, and C. Perkins, "Mobile IPv4 Regional Registration," IETF Internet-Draft, November 2005.
7. J. Xie and I. F. Akyildiz, "A Distributed Dynamic Regional Location Management Scheme for Mobile IP," IEEE Transactions on Mobile Computing, Vol. 1, No. 3, July 2002.
8. M. Woo, "Performance Analysis of Mobile IP Regional Registration," IEICE Transactions on Communications, Vol. E86-B, No. 2, February 2003.
9. S. Pack and Y. Choi, "A Study on Performance of Hierarchical Mobile IPv6 in IP-based Cellular Networks," IEICE Transactions on Communications, Vol. E87-B, No. 3, pp. 462-469, March 2004.
10. Z. D Wu, "An Efficient Method for Benefiting the New Feature of Mobile IPv6," Proceeding of IASTED, pp.65-70, October 2002.
11. J. H. Schuringa, "Performance Modeling of Location Management Strategies in Mobile Networks," Master Thesis, Dept. of Computer Science, University of Twente, 1995.

Design and Emulation of Integration Framework for Heterogeneous Wireless PAN Networks

In-Yeup Kong[1] and Won-Joo Hwang[2,*]

[1] Department of Computer Eng.
Pusan National University
leafgirl@pusan.ac.kr
[2] Department of Information and Communications Eng.
Inje University
Tel.: +82-55-320-3847; Fax: +82-55-322-6275
ichwang@inje.ac.kr

Abstract. WPANs (Wireless personal area networks) vary greatly by nature with regard to requirements such as data rate, coverage, subscriber volume, and supported mobile velocity. Mobile devices with multiple network interfaces are very common and to make these multi-mode devices communicate with any WPAN device at anytime, anywhere, a framework for heterogeneous wireless networks is essential. Therefore, we propose an integration framework that handle heterogeneous WPAN protocols simultaneously in a unified ways. In this paper, we explain the requirements and detailed design of our framework, and then present the emulation test results.

Keywords: Heterogeneous WPAN, Integration, Framework, Convergence.

1 Introduction

Advanced wireless networks and portable devices are making ubiquitous networking a reality. Wireless networks vary greatly by nature with regard to data rate, coverage, subscriber volume, supported mobile velocity, anti-interference, and suitable transmitting environment [1]. Nowadays, it is very common to have one mobile device equipped with multiple network interfaces, e.g. a mobile phone have CDMA, Bluetooth, and IrDA. Users with those devices may demand heterogeneous services at anytime, anywhere. To satisfy this growing demand, a framework for heterogeneous wireless networks is needed. Frameworks that integrate heterogeneous wireless networks for coexistence mechanisms [2], service architecture [3], seamless roaming [4], resource allocation [5], adaptive connectivity management [1], and mobility management [6] have been proposed already in the literature. However, a framework for converging mixed WPANs has not been proposed until now. Hence, we design and emulate a framework to integrate heterogeneous WPANs. This framework can handle three kinds of WPAN protocols simultaneously in a unified ways, so it makes the development of variable WPAN services easy.

This paper is organized as follows. In section 2, we summarize the existing convergence techniques for wireless networks. In section 3, we show the integration

---

* Corresponding author.

H.Y. Youn, M. Kim, and H. Morikawa (Eds.): UCS 2006, LNCS 4239, pp. 368–383, 2006.

framework for WPANs. In section 4, we explain the design for the middleware in details and, in section 5, we verify our design using emulation tests. Finally, in section 6, we conclude our work and refer further works.

2 Convergence of Heterogeneous Wireless Networks

Previous studies in heterogeneous wireless networks have focused on adaptive connectivity management [1], coexistence mechanisms [2], service architecture [3], seamless roaming [4], resource allocation [5], and mobility management [6]. Reference [1] presents the design and implementation of connectivity management middleware (CMM), which is a channel-based architecture for context-aware connectivity management. In the case of network awareness, the platform provides interfaces for applications to query network QoS and availability status, as well as connection events. As for adaptive resource management, channel-based transport services for seamless access switching and disconnection treatment is provided based on a policy mechanism. In [2], they find that the efficiency of the "channel classification" sub-process in non-collaborative mechanisms is by and large ignored in the literature. Then, they propose a customized channel classification process, thereby simplifying the time and space complexity of the said mechanism.

Reference [3] proposes innovative services and architectures that can achieve enhanced security, energy efficiency, and just-for-you and just-in-time content delivery. Since the state-of-the-art technologies do not appropriately cover the needs required for 4G environment, a context-sensitive service discovery that can operate in a wireless as well as in a wired network environment, ranging from local to global distances, is described and applied to the case of the proposed services.

The authors in [4] propose a global mobility management framework to support seamless roaming across cellular and WLAN. Highlights of the framework include a robust architecture for mobility management for varying user mobility spans, provisioning for QoS mapping, intersystem message translation, and mechanisms in the WLAN to support user-subscribed services. Performance aspects related to handoff delays, data redirection, and processing overheads are presented. In [6], the definition of NMM (Network-Layer Mobility Management) is given and the framework of NMM for the convergence of the heterogeneous wireless networks is presented. Its structure and function model were also given.

Reference [5] proposes a novel resource allocation framework to cope with the time-varying channel conditions, co-channel interferences, and different QoS requirements in various kinds of services. A simple feedback mechanism is developed to report the system with the users' QoS satisfaction levels and channel conditions. Then the system will then adapt its resource allocation strategy according to the users' feedbacks to favor the users with the bad QoS satisfaction levels or the good channels.

3 Requirements for the Framework in Heterogeneous WPANs

3.1 Heterogeneous WPANs

As shown in Figure 1, multi-mode device means that the device with multiple interfaces is capable of communication over heterogeneous WPANs.

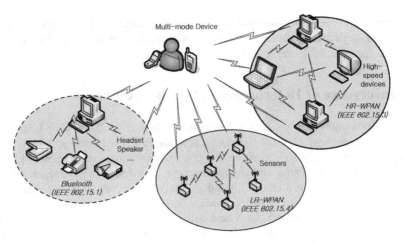

Fig. 1. Heterogeneous WPANs

Basically, WPANs support wireless interconnection and communication in short range (< 10m) for variable devices such as computers, peripherals, cellular phone, and appliances. In Figure 1, there are various devices with different WPAN interface depending on requirements of user or device, as well as cost. These WPANs are based on IEEE 802.15 standards: IEEE 802.15.1 [7], IEEE 802.15.3 [8] and IEEE 802.15.4 [9]. Their industry market consortiums are Bluetooth, WiMedia, and ZigBee (from here, for simplicity, we call each WPAN technique as Bluetooth, WiMedia, and ZigBee respectively.).

Bluetooth [7] replaces the wired connection among devices in short range (10~100m). This device is small sized, low cost, and low powered. It supports both asynchronous connection-less (ACL) links and synchronous connection-oriented (SCO) links. WiMedia [8] is a high-speed multimedia communication specifically for devices such as digital camera, digital TV, mp3 player, CD players, and multimedia PC. It includes the concept of guaranteed time shots to enable the QoS. Its data rate varies from 11Mbps to 55Mbps. ZigBee [9] is a lower data rate (20~25kbps) which is lower than bluetooth. Its characteristics include long battery lifetime, very low cost, and simple connectivity within the range below 10m. The major application areas are wide-range applications such as perception system for emergency situation, interactive security system and home automation using wireless sensors.

3.2 Technical Requirements for the Framework

In the framework, users are able to connect various WPANs using multi-mode WPANs devices. However they do not need to know more about network configuration or addressing. That is, user can communicate with any target devices regardless of current status and changes of underlying WPANs. To support this, the framework discovers available networks, devices and services within the device's radio range, and then notifies the user of that information. In the viewpoints of the devices, the devices require multi-mode WPAN interfaces and its driver module inside of them to enable services, anytime and anywhere. In addition the devices have to be designed for its extendibility if other networks will be added in the system. Finally, for the point of view of service, the framework provides mandatory service, which is common for various WPANs. Moreover, it provides a method where developers can add or modify services easily, according to their requirements, WPAN's own characteristics, or the changes in WPANs. To do this, from requirement analysis to the end of design, we consider these technical requirements for high reusability and scalability continuously.

4 WPAN Integration Framework

4.1 Top-Level Design

The architecture of the framework is shown in Fig. 2.

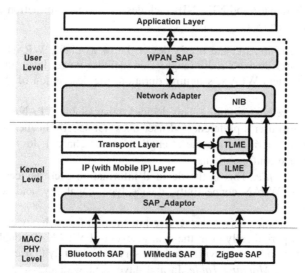

- WPAN_SAP: Wireless Personal Area Network Service Access Point
- NIB: Network Information Base
- TLME: Transport Layer Management Entity
- ILME: Internet Layer Management Entity

Fig. 2. The architecture of the framework for multi-mode WPAN device

To obtain the advantages of modulated design, our framework has layered architecture (Fig. 2). We consider future ALL-IP networks in this paper. So, this framework is based on legacy TCP/IP protocol suit including 5 additional modules to enable the communication over heterogeneous WPANs: WPAN_SAP module, Network Adaptor module with NIB, TLME module, ILME module, and SAP_Adaptor module. In the user level, the framework provide WPAN_SAP module for users to access variable WPAN devices. This module includes common WPAN SAP that covers all kind of parameters for each function. When user calls the primitive of WPAN_SAP module, the Network Adaptor module decides the WPAN connectivity internally. NIB enables this decision, because it manages WPANs, devices, and services. It is updated by TLME module, ILME module and SAP_Adaptor module. In the kernel level, there are helper module for transport layer and internet layer: TLME module and ILME module, respectively. The framework can know the session information from TLME module, and the addressing and movement detection information from ILME module. The SAP_Adaptor module in the kernel level maps user request from WPAN_SAP module to a specific WPAN SAP. To do this, SAP_Adaptor module interacts with Network Adapter module for the mapping decision. In the MAC/PHY level, there are heterogeneous SAPs for Bluetooth, WiMedia, and ZigBee. From subsection 4.2 to 4.5, we show the detailed design for each module.

4.2 Network Adaptor Module with NIB

Network Adaptor decides the kind of WPAN and service information for target device from user's request and NIB. NIB includes following information about WPAN devices and their services.

- *WPAN Profile*. Let the user's device know available WPAN configuration within user device's radio range. This includes power level, identifier of coordinator and WPAN, scanning duration, the description of WPAN, and so on.
- *WPAN Preference Policy*. This decides the available WPAN connectivity according to user's preference. If user does not specify his/her preference, the decision criteria can be the strength of radio channel, loss rate, or default preference configuration.
- *Device Profile*. This is the detailed information each devices. The kind of available WPAN connectivity, device type, capability, and service list are included.
- *Service Profile*. This is the service information for each device, which is discovered periodically or at the change event of WPAN. Through this profile, the framework can provide available services currently to user.
- *Addressing Mapping Table*. In high-layer's view, addressing is based on IP addressing, on the other hand, in low-layer's view, addressing is based on WPAN-specific addressing. Therefore, this table manages the mapping between IP addresses and WPAN addresses.

4.3 SAP_Adaptor Module

User calls the primitive of WPAN_SAP module to communicate with target WPAN device.If user's device wants to transfer a data to target WPAN device, it will always call the "WP_DataTansferReq" primitive (referred in section 4.4) regardless WPAN connectivity of target device. Then the kind of WPAN is decided by Network_Adaptor module internally and SAP_Adaptor module maps that request to MAC SAP of corresponding WPAN. To explain the adaptation from WPAN_SAP module to SAP of each WPAN, first of all, we show the architecture including MAC/PHY SAP for each WPAN from the definition of standards.

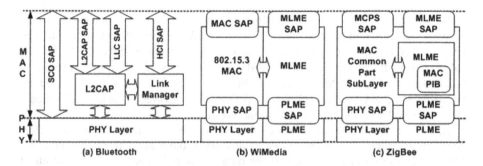

Fig. 3. Architecture of WPAN MAC/PHY including SAP

As shown in Fig. 3 (a), in case of the Bluetooth, there are 4 SAPs. SCO SAP provides the access for connection-oriented links, and L2CAP SAP provides link control and discovery for control capability. Moreover, HCI SAP controls the host internally, provides the interfaces for discovery or modification of physical information to control and manage the links. An example of L2CAP SAP, primitives for server operation is difference from the primitives for client operation. Table 1 shows the primitives under the client operation. We use these primitives for accessing MAC/PHY layer of each WPAN.

Table 1. L2CAP SAP primitives (in case of client operation)

Function	Primitives	Description
Client SAP interface (Upper-layer) to L2CAP request		
Connection Establishment	L2CA_ConnectReq	Connection establishment request to peer (in ACL links)
Configuration	L2CA_ConfigReq	Re-configuration of the channels by high-layer
Connection Termination	L2CA_DisconnectReq	Connection termination request to the peer
Writing data	L2CA_DataWrite	Transmission of a data
Reading data	L2CA_DataRead	Reception of a data
Group Management	L2CA_GroupCreate	Creation of a group
	L2CA_GroupClose	Destroy of a group
	L2CA_GroupAddMember	Addition a member to a group
	L2CA_GroupRemoveMember	Deletion a member from a group
	L2CA_GroupMembership	Discovery of group membership
Ping	L2CA_Ping	Reply request for Echo message
Information Retrieval	L2CA_InfoReq	Request for detailed information
Connectionless Communication	L2CA_DisableCLT L2CA_EnableCLT	Enabling or Disabling of connectionless communication
L2CAP to client SAP interface (Upper-layer) action		
Connection Establishment	L2CA_ConnectCfm L2CA_ConnectCfmNeg	Confirmation for connection establishment request
Configuration	L2CA_ConfigCfm L2CA_ConfigCfmNeg	Confirmation for configuration request
Connection Termination	L2CA_DisconnectCfm	Confirmation for connection termination request

Next, in case of the WiMedia, it includes management plane for each layer, as well as basic network protocol including PHY and MAC layers. If LLC is used, then Frame Convergence sublayer is used. In management plane, there exists MLME (MAC Layer Management Entity) and MLME SAP for the MAC layer, and similarly PLME (Physical Layer Management Entity) and PLME SAP for the MAC layer. WiMedia MAC SAP includes following primitives as showed in table. The architecture of the ZigBee is the same as that of the WiMedia.

As shown above, the architecture of each WPAN is similar with some differences among them. For example, let's think about the case of transfer a data. All WPAN has the primitive to support the data transfer. In case of the Bluetooth, it has L2CA_DataWrite and L2CA_DataRead primitive, and in case of the WiMedia, it has MAC-ASYNC-DATA primitive for asynchronous data, and MAC-ISOCH-DATA primitive for isochronous data. In the case of the ZigBee, it has MCPS-DATA primitive for data transfer, and MCPS-PURGE primitive to let high-layer read data stored data in transaction queue. Although there is the common primitive in each WPAN, their in/out parameters are different from each other, due to their own characteristics.

For example, if we think about writing and reading the frame data, then parameters for Bluetooth's primitive are as follows.

- CID: channel identifier to represent local endpoint of communication channel
- Length: the size of buffer that transmitted data is stored
- OutBuffer: the address for buffer that transmitted data is stored
- InBuffer: the address for buffer that received data is stored
- Size: byte counts for transmitted or received data
- Result: result code for data transfer

Next, parameters for WiMedia's primitive are as follows.

- TrgtID: identifier for target device that accepts the request
- OrigID: identifier for source device that requests
- Priority: priority of the data (from 0 to 7)
- ACKPolicy: ACK policy
  - IMM_ACK: send ACK immediately when receiving
  - NO_ACK: ACK is not transferred
  - DLY_ACK: Delayed ACK. If receive buff is full, the ACK is sent.
- StreamIndex: index of stream for this transfer
- TransmissionTimeout: maximum time to transfer the data successfully (unit: milliseconds)
- Length: total length (unit: octets)
- Data: length of only data
- ResultCode: result code for the request such as success, transfer timeout, failed delayed ACK, invalid ACK policy, and invalid stream.

Finally, parameters for ZigBee's primitive are as follows.

- SrcAddrMode: address type of the source device (16-bit short address, and 64-bit extended address)

- SrcPANId: 16-bit PAN identifier for the source device
- SrcAddr: address for the source device
- DstAddrMode: address type of the destination device
- DstPANId: 16-bit PAN identifier for the destination device
- DstAddr: address for the destination device
- msduLength: length of transmitted or received data (unit: octets)
- msdu: transmitted or received data
- msduHandle: handle for transmitted or received data
- TxOptions: transmission options (ACKed transmission, the transmission gua ranteed time slots, the indirect transmission, and the secured transmission)
- status: result code for the request

As explained above, each WPAN has its own characteristics, SAP, and parameters. Therefore, we need the middleware for abstraction of underlying networks, which provides simple and common interfaces to users. That is our WPAN_SAP module and we present it in following subsection.

4.4 WPAN_SAP Module

The WPAN_SAP module provides 14 common primitives for user application as follows:

- *Connection primitive.* This includes connection request, connection confirmation (positive/negative), connection response (positive/negative), indication of connection request from peer, timeout for connection acceptance, and the creation of SCO connection (in case of the Bluetooth). For the WiMedia, it also has the management function for streams. On the other hand, ZigBee supports the function for guaranteed time slots.
- *Disconnection primitive.* This includes disconnection request, disconnection confirmation (positive/negative), disconnection response (positive/negative), indication of disconnection request from peer, and the termination of SCO connection (in case of the Bluetooth).
- *Configuration primitive.* This includes configuration request, confirmation and response, as well as reset function for the device. Moreover, for the Bluetooth, it can control the operation parameters such as page timeout, class of device, local name, and flow control of SCO link.
- *DataTransfer primitive.* This includes the function for transmitting and receiving a data. Detailed transfer mode is different among heterogeneous WPANs.
- *Scan primitive.* This supports local and remote scan for wireless channel. Specially, in case of the Bluetooth, we can read or change the scan mode, duration, and scan activity.
- *Information primitive.* This supports the information retrieval and notification. The information retrieval includes the remote peer name, piconet information, piconet services, and application-specific information.

- *Synchronization primitive.* In case of the Bluetooth, this is for reading the clock offset with piconet coordinator. In case of the WiMedia and the ZigBee, this performs the synchronization process and notifies the loss of the synchronization.
- *PowerManagement primitive.* This is for saving the limited power. So it includes reading and changing the transmission power level, as well as the management for power-saving mode.
- *Security primitive.* This primitive is for security function such key management, secured message, authentication, and authorization.
- *EventHandler primitive.* This primitive gathers the event from the peer and notifies that to the framework.
- *Piconet primitive.* This primitive is related on the life cycle of the piconets.
- *Association primitive.* This primitive is related on the association and disassociation of the piconets.
- *ChannelManagement primitive.* This primitive manages the communication channel among devices.

These primitives are defined as the methods of CWPAN_SAP_APIs class in Fig. 4.

```
enum NET_TYPE {BLUETOOTH, WIMEDIA, ZIGBEE};
class CWPAN_SAP_APIs {
        ...
        uint_2octets WP_ConnectionReq (NET_TYPE net_type,
                CONNECTION_PARAM_PTR param);
        uint_2octets WP_StreamReq (NET_TYPE net_type,
                STREAM_PARAM_PTR param);
        uint_2octets WP_DisconnectionReq (NET_TYPE net_type,
                DISCONNECTION_PARAM_PTR param);
        uint_2octets WP_ConfigueReq(NET_TYPE net_type,
                CONFIG_PARAM_PTR param);
        uint_2octets WP_DataTransferReq (NET_TYPE net_type,
                DATA_TRANSFER_PARAM_PTR param);
        uint_2octets WP_ScanReq (NET_TYPE net_type,
                SCAN_PARAM_PTR param);
        uint_2octets WP_InformationReq (NET_TYPE net_type,
                INFORMATION_PARAM_PTR param);
        uint_2octets WP_SynchronizationReq (NET_TYPE net_type,
                SYNCHRONIZATION_PARAM_PTR param);
        uint_2octets WP_PowerManagementReq (NET_TYPE net_type,
                POWER_MANAGEMENT_PARAM_PTR param);
        uint_2octets WP_SecurityReq (NET_TYPE net_type,
                SECURITY_PARAM_PTR param);
        uint_2octets WP_EventHandlerReq (NET_TYPE net_type,
                EVENT_HANDLER_PARAM_PTR param);
        uint_2octets WP_PiconetReq (NET_TYPE net_type,
                PICONET_PARAM_PTR param);
        uint_2octets WP_AssociationReq (NET_TYPE net_type,
                ASSOCIATION_PARAM_PTR param);
        uint_2octets WP_ChannelManagementReq (NET_TYPE net_type,
                CHANNEL_MANAGEMENT_PARAM_PTR param);
};
```

Fig. 4. Prototype for basic methods of WPAN_SAP_APIs class

```
#define uint_1octet    unsigned char
#define uint_2octets   unsigned int

typedef struct
{
          uint_2octets          PSM;
          uint_6octets          BD_ADDR;
          uint_1octet           Identifier;
          uint_2octets          LCID;
          uint_2octets          Result;
          uint_2octets          Status;
          uint_2octets          Packet_Type;
          uint_1octet           Page_Scan_Repetition_Mode;
          uint_1octet           Page_Scan_Mode;
          uint_2octets          Clock_Offset;
          uint_1octet           Allow_Role_Switch;
          uint_2octets          Connection_Handle;
          uint_1octet           Role;
          uint_2octets          Conn_Accepted_Timeout;
} CONNECTION_PARAM, *CONNECTION_PARAM_PTR;
```

Fig. 5. The structure definition for in/out parameters of Connection primitive

As shown in Fig. 4, the common primitives have the similar prototype. Data type for first input parameter is NET_TYPE as defined in first line in Fig. 4. This value is decided by Network Adaptor module. To make common access method regardless the specific WPAN characteristics, we define input parameters that cover all attributes for heterogeneous WPANs as the structure for each primitive. According to target WPAN connectivity, some attributes of the structure are used as input parameter, another attributes are used as output parameter or other parameters are not used if needed. For example, Figure 5 shows the structure for in/out parameters of Connection primitive.

Each element in Figure 5 can be used as input parameter or output parameter as situation demands. For example, if we try to connect to target device using Connection primitive, and that device is Bluetooth device, the structure is used as shown in Table 2 and Table 3.

Table 2. Input parameters for Connection primitive (a part of parameters)

Parameter	Type	Values	Description
PSM	2octets	Any value	PSM (protocol / service multiplexer)
BD_ADDR	6octets	Any value	Address for target device
Identifier	1octet	Any value	Identifier to L2CA_ConnectInd event
LCID	2octets	Any value	Channel identifier of local endpoint

Table 2. *(continued)*

Parameter	Type	Values	Description
Response	2octets	0x0000	Successful connection establishment
		0x0001	Connection is pending.
		0x0002	Connection refused – PSM is not supported.
		0x0003	Connection refused –blocking due to security reason
		0xEEEE	Connection timeout.
		0xXXXX	Other response code
Status	2octets	0x0000	No detailed information
		0x0001	Authorization pending
		0x0002	Reason for refuse
		0xXXXX	Other response code
Connection_Handle	2octets	0x0020	HV1
		0x0040	HV2
		0x0080	HV3
Role	1octet	0x00	Mater for this connection
		0x01	Slave for this connection
Conn_Accepted_Timeout	2octets	0xXXXX	Timeout for acceptance

Table 3. Output parameters for Connection primitive

Parameter	Type	Values	Description
LCID	2octets	0xXXXX	If Result is '0', it means channel identifier for local endpoint. Otherwise, it will be '0'.
Result	2octets	In case of the request, it will be one of 0x0000, 0x0001, 0x0002, 0x0003, and 0xEEEE. In case of the response, it will be one of 0x0000 and 0x0001.	
Status	2octets	0x0000	No detailed information
		0x0001	Authentication pending
		0x0002	Authorization pending
Reason	1octet	0x0D–0x0F	Reason for refuse
Conn_Accepted_Timeout	2octets	0xXXXX	Timeout for acceptance

4.5 TLME/ILME Module

TLME module manages the information about session between the user device and the target device. This information includes identifier of the session, the status of session, some timeout values, and so on. ILME module manages the information about addressing and mapping of between IP addresses and WPAN addresses. Moreover, using movement detection of Mobile IP, the framework will know the movement of user device or the changes in addresses. For enough addressing space for scalability, IPv6 with Mobile IPv6 will be used for near future.

5 Emulation Tests

We can not use real hardware including multiple WPAN interfaces yet. So, we perform the emulation instead of real implementation at the moment. The emulation scenario is shown in Fig. 6.

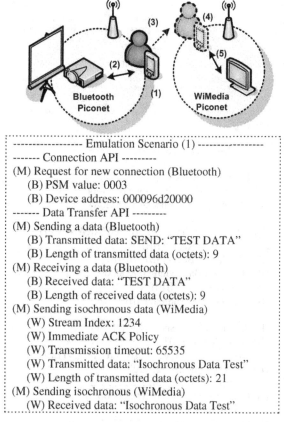

```
------------------ Emulation Scenario (1) -----------------
------- Connection API ---------
(M) Request for new connection (Bluetooth)
    (B) PSM value: 0003
    (B) Device address: 000096d20000
------- Data Transfer API ---------
(M) Sending a data (Bluetooth)
    (B) Transmitted data: SEND: "TEST DATA"
    (B) Length of transmitted data (octets): 9
(M) Receiving a data (Bluetooth)
    (B) Received data: "TEST DATA"
    (B) Length of received data (octets): 9
(M) Sending isochronous data (WiMedia)
    (W) Stream Index: 1234
    (W) Immediate ACK Policy
    (W) Transmission timeout: 65535
    (W) Transmitted data: "Isochronous Data Test"
    (W) Length of transmitted data (octets): 21
(M) Sending isochronous (WiMedia)
    (W) Received data: "Isochronous Data Test"
```

Fig. 6. 1st emulation scenario and its execution logs

In execution logs, (M) means that user's request occurred by calling the primitive of WPAN_SAP module. (B), (W) and (Z) denote that the SAP primitive of the Bluetooth, WiMedia, and ZigBee respectively, is called. First emulation scenario is testing the function of the connection establishment, data transfer, and movement of the user

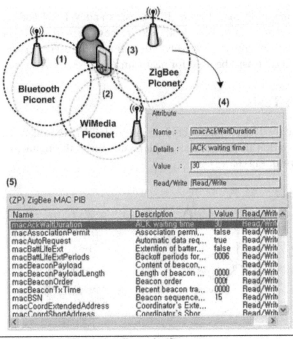

------------- Emulation Scenario (2) ----------------

------- Configuration API ---------
(M) Request for Flow Specification (Bluetooth)
     (B) Requested Flow Spec. is as follows
     (B) Flow Identifier: 03
     (B) Flow Service Type: FLOW_GUARANTEED
     (B) Flow TokenRate: ffffffff
     (B) Flow TokenBucketSize: ffffffff
     (B) Flow PeakBandwidth: 00000000
     (B) Flow Latency: ffffffff
     (B) Flow DelayVariation: ffffffff

     (B) Permitted Flow Spec. is as follows
     (B) Flow Identifier: 03
     (B) Flow Service Type: FLOW_GUARANTEED
     (B) Flow TokenRate: 22222222
     (B) Flow TokenBucketSize: 22222222
     (B) Flow PeakBandwidth: 00000000
     (B) Flow Latency: 22222222
     (B) Flow DelayVariation: 22222222

Read attributes from WiMedia/ZigBee MAC PIB

------- Configuration API ---------
(M) Change MAC PIB Configuration (ZigBee)
     (Z-ZP) MAC PIB Configuration is changed (ZigBee)

Fig. 7. 2nd emulation scenario and its execution logs

device. Under first emulation scenario we consider the case that the user communicates with Bluetooth device, and moves to the WiMedia network. First of all, user device makes the connection with the Bluetooth device. To do this, Connection primitive is called, and then L2CA_ConnectReq primitive of the Bluetooth SAP is called internally (1). For transferring multimedia data, DataTransfer primitive is called, and then L2CA_DataWrite and L2CA_DataRead primitive of the Bluetooth SAP are called (2). Due to user movement, the connection with the Bluetooth device will be lost (3). In the space where user moves, there is the WiMedia piconet with multimedia devices. After detecting the movement through the Mobile IP, the frame work of the user device discovers available devices and services. Then it finds new target device suitable for the user's application (4). Data is then transferred to the new target device using the DataTransfer primitive. Actually, the ISOCH_DATA_WRITE and ISOCH_DATA_READ primitive of the WiMedia SAP is called (5).

Second emulation scenario is shown in Fig. 7. In execution log, (Z-ZP) means that the information about the ZigBee protocol is changed.

Using second emulation scenario, we test the configuration for the Bluetooth flow, WiMedia PIB (Protocol Information Base: detailed information of the protocol) and ZigBee PIB. These tests call the Configuration primitive in general, at user's point of view. However, detailed settings of in/out parameters are different to each other. First of all, in case of the Bluetooth, we can request the flow specification for the target device, and receive the permission for that request (1). This includes flow identifier, service type, token rate, peak bandwidth, and delay variation as shown in Fig. 7. Next, the framework reads the PIB attributes of the WiMedia and the ZigBee (2 and 3). To read the value of specific attribute, the MLME_GET primitive of the corresponding WPAN SAP is called. Similarly, to write the value of specific attribute, the MLME_SET primitive of the corresponding WPAN SAP is called. In this example, we change the value of macAckWaitDuration attribute from default value of '55' to '30', and then the MLME_SET primitive of the corresponding WiMedia SAP is called. Changed value is shown in (5).

Third emulation scenario is as showed in Fig. 8.

In third scenario, user's device has been synchronized with ZigBee piconet using the Synchronization primitive. First, MLME_SYNC primitive of the ZigBee SAP is called (1). Next, the device receives a notification that the synchronization is lost from low-layer. This event is known through MLME_SYNC_LOSS_IND primitive of the ZigBee SAP (2). The device scans the wireless channels, where it finds the WiMedia piconet. To make the synchronization with the WiMedia piconet, Synchronization primitive is also called. Afterwards, MLME_SYNCH primitive of the WiMedia SAP is called (3). In this trial, if the synchronization request failed, it should retry. If the synchronization request is successful on the subsequent trials, the device will have the information such as the identifier, description, and the duration of channel scan for available piconet (4).

Other scenarios include various cases, for example:

- When devices providing the service requested by a user are more than one device, the framework chooses the best device among those devices automatically according to user's preference or signal strength of each WPAN connection.

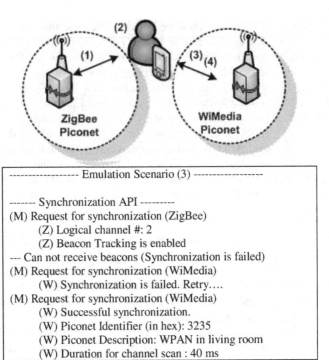

```
----------------- Emulation Scenario (3) ------------------

------- Synchronization API ---------
(M) Request for synchronization (ZigBee)
        (Z) Logical channel #: 2
        (Z) Beacon Tracking is enabled
--- Can not receive beacons (Synchronization is failed)
(M) Request for synchronization (WiMedia)
        (W) Synchronization is failed. Retry....
(M) Request for synchronization (WiMedia)
        (W) Successful synchronization.
        (W) Piconet Identifier (in hex): 3235
        (W) Piconet Description: WPAN in living room
        (W) Duration for channel scan : 40 ms
```

Fig. 8. 3rd emulation scenario and its execution logs

- For ubiquitous healthcare, any problem in transferring information from a monitoring device occurs, the framework notices this event to the user. And it checks the network connectivity and tries to use available WPAN connection.
- For multimedia service, the difference of each WPAN's capability has an effect on the quality of service. When WPAN connectivity is changed according to the user's movement, the framework provides the service considering the difference.
- When WPAN capability of a device is changed, the device reports the change to the framework, and then the device's profile in the framework is changed.

6 Conclusion

Evolution of the WPANs for ubiquitous computing varies according the service characteristics, and requirements. This trend results in mixed networks that consist of heterogeneous WPANs. There are existing works to converge these heterogeneous characteristics of the network, however, they just focus on coexistence mechanisms, service architecture, seamless roaming, resource allocation, adaptive connectivity management, and mobility management. The framework to converge heterogeneous WPANs at a unified view has not been proposed yet. Thus, we propose the said framework according to IEEE standards and perform the emulation to verity our design. In further works, we plan to enhance our emulation by adding more convenient editing for the emulation environments and scenario. Finally, at the time that we can use real multi-mode WPAN device, we will implement our module inside the kernel.

References

[1] Jun-Zhao Sun; Riekki, J.; Jurmu, M.; Sauvola, J., "Adaptive connectivity management middleware for heterogeneous wireless networks", IEEE Wireless Communications, Vol. 12, Issue 6, pp. 18 – 25, Dec. 2005.

[2] Yu-Kwong Kwok; Chek, M.C.-H., "Design and evaluation of coexistence mechanisms for Bluetooth and IEEE 802.11b systems", Proceeding of the 15th IEEE International Symposium on Personal, Indoor and Mobile Radio Communications (PIMRC), Vol.3, pp. 1767 – 1771, Sept. 2004.

[3] Frattasi, S.; Olsen, R.L.; De Sanctis, M.; Fitzek, F.H.P.; Prasad, R., "Heterogeneous Services and Architectures for Next-Generation Wireless Networks", Proceeding of the 2nd International Symposium on Wireless Communication Systems, pp. 213 – 217, Sept. 2005.

[4] Shenoy, N.; Montalvo, R., "A framework for seamless roaming across cellular and wireless local area networks", IEEE Wireless Communications, Vol. 12, Issue 3, pp. 50 – 57, June 2005.

[5] Han, Z.; Wang, Z.J.; Liu, K.J.R., "A resource allocation framework with credit system and user autonomy over heterogeneous wireless network", IEEE Global Telecommunications Conference (GLOBECOM), Vol.2, pp. 977 – 981, Dec. 2003 Page(s):

[6] Ruijun Feng; Wenan Zhou; Ningning Liu; Jianwen Huang; Junde Song, "A network-layer mobility management framework for the convergence of heterogeneous wireless networks", Proceeding of the 9th Asia-Pacific Conference on Communications (APCC), Vol.2, pp. 635 – 638, Sept. 2003.

[7] LAN/MAN Standards Committee of the IEEE Computer Society, Part 15.1: Wireless Medium Access Control (MAC) and Physical Layer (PHY) Specifications for Wireless Personal Area Networks (WPANs), pp. 1 ~ 1196, May 2002.

[8] LAN/MAN Standards Committee of the IEEE Computer Society, Part 15.3: Wireless Medium Access Control (MAC) and Physical Layer (PHY) Specifications for High Rate Wireless Personal Area Networks (WPANs), pp. 1 ~ 324, Sep. 2003.

[9] LAN/MAN Standards Committee of the IEEE Computer Society, Part 15.4: Wireless Medium Access Control (MAC) and Physical Layer (PHY) Specifications for Low-Rate Wireless Personal Area Networks (LR-WPANs), pp. 1 ~ 679, Oct. 2003.

Heterogeneous Routing Protocol Coordinator for Mobile Ad Hoc Networks*

Namhi Kang, Seongil Yoo, Younghan Kim**, Souhwan Jung, and Kihun Hong

Ubiquitous Network Research Center in Soongsil University
Sangdo 5-Dong 1-1, Dongjak-Ku, 156-743 Seoul, South Korea
nalnal@dcn.ssu.ac.kr, nowdob@dcn.ssu.ac.kr, yhkim@dcn.ssu.ac.kr,
souhwanj@ssu.ac.kr, kihum@cnsl.ssu.ac.kr

Abstract. Lots of routing protocols have been proposed in the literatures to overcome several challenges in ad hoc networks. The fundamental point we consider in this paper is that most of such protocols are generally based on the assumption that mobile nodes are functionally equivalent to each other in computing power and memory space. Moreover, all of the mobile nodes are required to use a common routing protocol to communicate with each other. However, such assumptions do not reflect the real world, even further the future oriented ubiquitous world. The ubiquitous paradigm requires networking technologies to support the heterogeneity including various capabilities to compute, amounts of storage, radio interfaces, patterns of mobility and others. In real scenario, for instance, some nodes may not want to relay packets for others owing to their power constraints. Also there might be nodes employing different routing protocols in a single communication zone. To cover some of these cases, this paper proposes a simple but efficient approach called HRPC (Heterogeneous Routing Protocol Coordinator) that works well in our previously proposed MANET architecture. HRPC is not a stand-alone routing protocol but a coordinating module for support bridging functionality between heterogeneous routing protocols in MANET. This paper also gives HRPC implementation and its demonstration results, where DYMO and OLSR routing protocols are used as an exemplified scenario to evaluate the operability of HRPC.

1 Introduction

Mobile ad hoc networking is currently regarded as one of the most promising solutions to support the future oriented ubiquitous paradigm from the aspect of construction time and cost efficiency. However, there are several challenges to practically deploy it into the real field. Most challenges (e.g. scalability, load balancing, reliability etc.) are related to the difficulty in routing because MANET is self-organized without any support of a centralized coordinator or pre-installed

---

* This research is supported by the ubiquitous Autonomic Computing and Network Project, the Ministry of Information and Communication (MIC) 21st Century Frontier R&D Program in Korea.
** Corresponding author.

H.Y. Youn, M. Kim, and H. Morikawa (Eds.): UCS 2006, LNCS 4239, pp. 384–397, 2006.

infrastructure [1]. Therefore, routing schemes used in conventional wired network can not work well in ad hoc networks.

Routing in packet networks generally consists of the route discovery phase and maintenance phase. The main difference between wired and wireless network appears in the latter rather than the former. In wired network, on one hand, the processing of route maintenance is activated once a link is broken. The link breakage is generally caused by the fault of router along the path or serious buffer overflows owing to the congestion at an intermediate router. On the other hand, the maintenance processing in wireless networks, especially in multi-hop based mobile wireless network, is very frequently and randomly activated. In this kind of networks, not to mention the faults as in wired network, link can be broken in several reasons, for instance changes in topology caused by the node mobility, switching to power saving mode (i.e. sleep mode or turn off the power) at any intermediate node on the path. Therefore it is a challenge to find and maintain a stable route in MANET, further, it becomes more difficult to solve as the scale of network increases [2].

To overcome (at least reduce) those shortcomings, lots of routing protocols have been proposed in the literatures [3]. In particular, many research results have shown that clustering approach is a good solution to enhance the scalability of MANET [4], [5], [6]. Moreover, in order to maximize the gains of clustering, most studies (e.g. [7], [8] and [9]) typically used a hybrid routing protocol based on the hierarchical network architecture. In such schemes, researchers have commonly assumed that mobile nodes are homogeneous and all of nodes in the same communication domain use a common routing protocol. However, such assumptions may not be adaptable to the real scenario. As time goes by, mobile devices are going to be heterogeneous in several aspects such as computing power, amount of memory, video/audio capabilities, operating system, communication interfaces and others. In addition, each of them prefers to install a single or at most two dominant routing protocols according to their capabilities of computing and memorizing.

Despite the trends of great generality, there is a common requirement that is the increasing desire to communicate with each other for sharing information without any restriction such as time and place, the kind of device system, the type of wireless technology, and so on. It might be a trivial scenario that a powerful laptop needs to communicate with a small device equipped with very low computing power and limited storage. More badly, the small device is not equipped with the routing protocol that the laptop uses. Up to our best knowledge, no previous work can solve this scenario. In this sense, this paper is intended to find a solution that allows mobile nodes to communicate with each other even though they are equipped with heterogeneous routing protocols in a single communication domain.

The organization of this paper is as follows. Section 2 presents network models, where nodes are required to be equipped with two different routing protocols. In section 3, we give the problem statements that might be occurred in the network models described in section 2. Afterwards, we give the proposed HRPC and its operation in section 4. Section 5 presents the HRPC implementation and its experimental test results. Finally, section 5 concludes this paper.

2   Network Model

The proposed HRPC can be deployed into a cluster-based MANET, where a cluster head node is equipped with the HRPC module. In this section, we first describe the cluster based MANET and then give an advanced model of the architecture called u-Zone based MANET.

2.1   Cluster-Based MANET

The communication in MANET only relies on mutual and cooperative routing functionalities of ordinary nodes without any specific relaying devices. Moreover, network topology can be unpredictably changed over time due to the mobility of nodes. These make a flat ad hoc network difficult to be deployed into a large scale network. Cluster-based MANET architecture is regarded as an alternative solution to the scalability problem. The result of [10] has shown that clustering reduces the routing overhead by a factor of $O(1/M)$, where M is the cluster size.

In such architecture, the mobile nodes are logically partitioned into a set of clusters and a cluster head node is elected for each cluster by predefined algorithm. The cluster head node binds ordinary nodes in his cluster to perform routing procedures that include management of cluster members, routing information distribution, and communication management. The limitation is the cluster head election overhead because all nodes must exchange information to elect a cluster head in addition to the routing procedure itself. Furthermore a cluster head should be reelected whenever the network topology of a cluster is changed. In some scenarios, it results in very high overhead owing to the frequent changes in topology. To reduce the overheads presented in cluster-based MANET, Zone-based Hierarchical Link State Routing Protocol (ZHLS) was proposed, where the network is divided into non-overlapping zones and there is no zone head [9]. However, ZHLS requires that all nodes are equipped with GPS like system.

2.2   Semi-infrastructured MANET

All of cluster-based schemes have a common limitation from the practical usage point of view. They assumed that all nodes are functionally equivalent as well as they are kindly willing to become a head node. In real life, however, most nodes do not want to become a header node because they may not want to spend their power to forward/relay packets of other nodes. On the contrary, in many cases, they become a selfish node resulting in breakage of a route. The u-Zone based MANET that we have introduced in [13] is a solution to the problem.

As shown in Fig. 1, we borrowed the concept of cluster based routing protocols. That is, MANET is divided into a set of u-Zones and a u-Zone Master (u-ZM) is assigned for each of the u-Zones. The u-ZM is not an ordinary node (i.e. neither a source nor a sink node) but a super node having high computing power and robust electrical power. For example, a service provider (e.g. a committee of workshop or manager of event) can install u-ZMs within the expected communication space. A u-ZM assists its member nodes in most of routing functionalities such as gathering and/or relaying routing information so that the proposed architecture can reduce lots of overburden of ordinary nodes and the amount of control packets necessary to maintain both route and cluster.

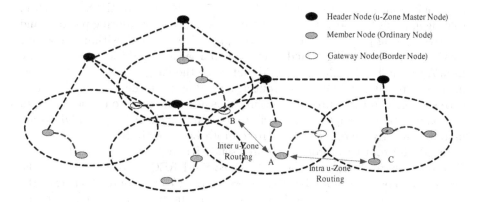

Fig. 1. Network model

The u-ZM is different from a fixed network device such as AP or BS in other wireless networks. The u-ZM is an assistant device to reduce routing overheads of mobile nodes as does a cluster head in cluster-based approaches. But, the AP or BS is the main device; therefore, failure of such a device results in breakdown of the network. Besides, in AP/BS based network, all data must go through the AP/BS even though a receiver is placed within the transmission coverage of a source. In the proposed network, however, if a source has routing information to the receiver then he can send data directly. Hence the proposed architecture is regarded as a semi-infrastructured MANET.

Two or more u-Zones are connected with each other by direct wireless links between u-ZMs. Such a wireless back bone (WBB) offers reliable communication and reduction in hop counts from a source to a particular destination. The decreased number of hops is desirable since larger hop counts results in worse performance in wireless communication. Moreover, it offers spatial reuse resulting in enhanced performance of overall network by assigning different radio channel or frequency to WBB from one used for links within a zone. If the WBB is not used, traffic may concentrate on just a few nodes resulting in a long end-to-end delay due to congestion at the nodes and a high energy consumption of the nodes.

2.3   Routing Protocol

MANET routing protocols are generally divided into three categories; proactive, reactive, and hybrid routing protocols. In proactive routing protocols, the routes are immediately available because all nodes contain routing table showing direction to all possible destinations. Therefore, lots of control packets are necessary to keep track of up-to-date network topology. To eliminate the overheads, reactive routing protocols have been proposed. Unlike proactive schemes, a route is discovered when a source has packets to send in an on-demand way. Such routing protocols also introduce lots of control packets, especially route request query packets that are to be flooded throughout the network.

In cluster-based MANET, researchers typically employed a hybrid approach into their routing protocols such as HARP [7], ZRP [8] and ZHLS [9]. Hybrid routing approach exploits the advantages of both proactive routing protocol and reactive routing protocol. They utilized a proactive approach within a zone (see route from A to B in Fig.1) and a reactive approach beyond the zone (see route from A to C in Fig.1). That is, hybrid routing methodology consists of two levels: intra zone routing and inter zone routing according to the destination's location corresponding to the source (i.e. within the same zone or beyond the Zone). In this paper, we also employ the hybrid routing approach. DYMO and OLSR are used as a reactive and proactive routing protocol respectively.

In DYMO routing protocol, a source sends RREQ message toward the destination node to discover a route [11]. Once the RREQ message arrives at the destination node, it responds RREP message back to the source node over the discovered path by unicasting. During such a route discovery process, intermediate nodes (i.e. nodes that relay the RREQ and RREP message) update its routing table based on the routing information that is present in those two messages for each direction.

Optimized Link-State Routing protocol (OLSR) obtains routing information for all nodes by periodically exchanging control packets [12]. The primary advantage of the proactive approach is that delay required to setup a connection is lower than that of a reactive approach. On the other hand, proactive routing approach introduces more control overheads because it must broadcast control packets to all nodes in the network periodically. Multipoint relays (MPR) has been presented to alleviate the control overheads by propagating the topology information via only selected nodes. Additionally, complexity and lack of mobility support are regarded as disadvantages of OLSR.

3   Problem Statement

This section describes a set of problems that are possibly occurred in MANET. In hybrid routing approach as described in section 2, a proactive routing protocol is used within a zone and a reactive routing protocol is used to discover a route to the destination which is placed at different zone from the source. Despite the efficiency of such a hybrid approach, it is of no use in the case, where a node can not execute both two routing protocols at the same time owing to the limitation of its capability (e.g. low CPU and small space of memory). A node employing a reactive routing protocol only, for instance, can not figure out the network topology composed of a set of nodes running a proactive routing protocol (i.e.

within a zone). We divide such problem set into two parts; intra-zone and inter-zone problem.

3.1   Intra-zone Routing Problem

Fig. 2 shows three cases that any existing routing algorithm can not support, where two different routing protocols (i.e. proactive and reactive routing protocol) are supposed to be used.

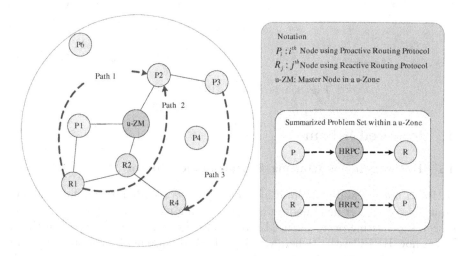

Fig. 2. Intra-zone HRPC processing

We note here that the *Path 1* of Fig. 2 can not be solved even though HRPC is properly installed. But any other scheme proposed so far also can not solve the problem. The last two problems (i.e. *Path 2* and *Path 3*) that can be solved by HRPC are simplified into two cases as follows (we show the cases in the box at the right hand side of Fig. 2).

– A *proactive node* needs to communicate with a *reactive node* within a zone.
– A *reactive node* needs to communicate with a *proactive node* within a zone.

3.2   Inter-zone Routing Problem

In the proposed MANET architecture (see subsection 2.2), WBB is used to enhance the reliability and performance. Hence, the set of intermediate u-ZMs (i.e. $\{u - ZM_k\}$) are simply regarded as a virtual link form the ingress u-ZM to the egress u-ZM as shown in Fig. 3. For example, an intermediate uZM that receives a control packet addressed to the destination retransmits the packet on the link connected to the next-hop u-ZM of the WBB. Similarly to the intra-zone problem, there are two cases possibly occurred in the MENET as follows.

– A *proactive node* needs to communicate with a *reactive node* beyond a zone.
– A *reactive node* needs to communicate with a *proactive node* beyond a zone.

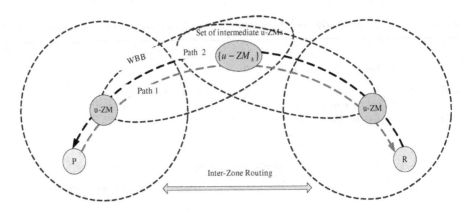

Fig. 3. Inter-zone HRPC processing

4   Proposed Scheme

4.1   Heterogeneous Routing Protocol Coordinator

HRPC is not a stand-alone routing protocol but a coordinator module running on u-ZM (or cluster head node) for support bridging functionality between heterogeneous routing protocols in MANET. The flow diagram illustrated in Fig. 4 shows how HRPC works, where OLSR and DYMO are used for a proactive and reactive routing protocol respectively.

Once a packet arrives at HRPC of u-ZM, HRPC first checks whether it is a control packet (see the left side of Fig. 4) or not (see the right side of Fig. 4). If the packet is identified as a control message then HRPC distinguish which routing protocol can use the packet. Afterwards the control packet is handled by the specification of the distinguished routing protocol (i.e. either DYMO or OLSR). In the next subsection, we discuss the HRPC operations in detail.

4.2   HRPC Processing

As described in section 3, two cases are enough to show the funtional operability of HRPC.

- Reactive node (DYMO) $\longrightarrow$ u-ZM (HRPC) $\longrightarrow$ Proactive node (OLSR)

When the DYMO module of u-ZM receives a route request message (RREQ), it first looks up the destination in its routing table (RT_{DYMO} shown in Fig. 6). If it can finds an available path (i.e. next hop toward the destination), it generates a route reply (RREP) to send it back to the RREQ requestor. Otherwise, it queries to the HRPC module to look up the destination in RT_{HRPC} table which is coupled with RT_{OLSR} table (both routing tables are also illustrated in Fig. 6). If the destination node using OLSR is resided in the same zone with the route requestor, OLSR module of u-ZM definitely knows the routing information owing

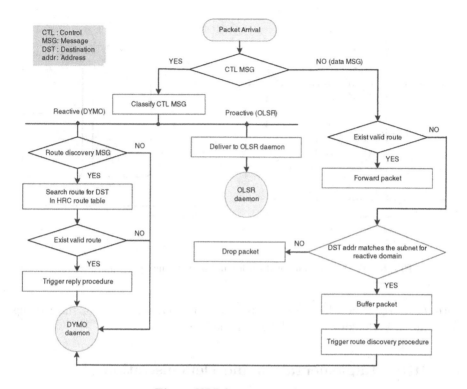

Fig. 4. HRPC processing flow

to the table driven manner of OLSR routing protocol. Hence, the u-ZM can send a route reply (RREP) back to the requestor. If there is no information, the u-ZM broadcasts the RREQ to his zone to find the destination that must be use DYMO as a routing protocol. Also the RREQ is forwarded to the next hop u-ZM to discover the destination beyond the zone. The final u-ZM which includes the destination node as a member node in its zone can generate RREP in the same way to the case of intra-zone.

- Proactive node (OLSR) ⟶ u-ZM (HRPC) ⟶ Reactive node (DYMO)

In order to enable OLSR nodes to discover a DYMO node, HRPC utilizes *"Host and Network Association (HNA)"* message of OLSR which is defined for providing OLSR MANET with connectivity to external network. Once a node receives a HNA message, it is able to create a routing entry for its routing table by using the network address and netmask conveyed in the HNA message thereafter the originator of HNA message operates as a gateway for the external network. In our scheme, u-ZM is the originator of the HNA message. In case there is no routing information in the RT_{OLSR} of u-ZM, then HRPC activates DYMO module to start a route discovery process. After getting RREP from the destination node, the u-ZM updates its routing table which is synchronized

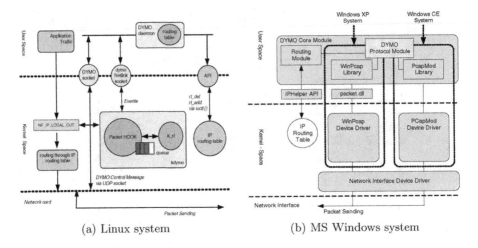

Fig. 5. DYMO implementation for heterogeneous operating system

with RT_{OLSR}. Now, the u-ZM is able to inform OLSR nodes of the routing information by looking up the DYMO node in RT_{HRPC}.

5 HRPC Implementation and Demonstration

This section first describes the implementation of HRPC and then shows experimental results. To demonstrate the HRPC, we have ported a freely available implementation of OLSR [14] and implemented our own version of DYMO as a proactive and a reactive routing protocol respectively. The selected OLSR daemon is well structured and can be applied into various platforms (e.g. GNU/Linux, Windows, FreeBSD, etc). The OLSR daemon is completely compatible with RFC 3626 and supports both IPv4 and IPv6.

The DYMO implementation was based on the specification of the earlier version of Internet-Drafts [11] posted at MANET working group in IETF. In particular, to support heterogeneous mobile nodes, the DYMO have been implemented not only on the Linux system but also on the Windows based systems (Windows XP for a laptop and Windows CE for a PDA) as shown in Fig. 5.

5.1 HRPC Implementation

The HRPC module resides in the kernel space of Linux operating system as a daemon process. Three different ways are possible to implement it into kernel; Snooping, kernel modification and Netfilter framework. Advantages and disadvantages of each of such three methodologies were described in [15]. We decided to use Netfilter which is a raw framework consisting of a set of hooks inside the Linux kernel. The hooks are generally regarded as specified points along a handling flow of packets (there are 5 hooks for IPv4). A protocol (or a developer)

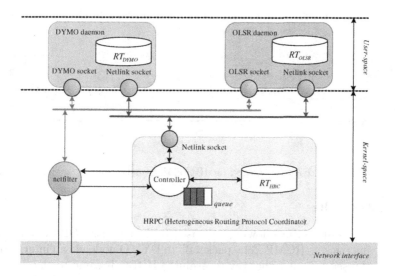

Fig. 6. HRPC module diagram

is allowed to define its own functionalities and then attach them to each of such points. Fig. 6 illustrates the simplified module architecture of HRPC.

HRPC holds its own routing table (see RT_{HRPC} in Fig. 6) and collects topological information from both OLSR and DYMO routing tables (see also RT_{OLSR} and RT_{DYMO} respectively in Fig. 6). Hence, the maintenance of RT_{HRPC}, for example addition and deletion of routing table entries, are tightly coupled with both routing protocols. Like most routing protocol implementations (e.g. AODV-UU [16], AODV-UCSB [17]), both RT_{OLSR} and RT_{DYMO} are placed at the user space so that we have utilized the Netlink socket to enable inter-communication between kernel and user space. Netlink socket is commonly used IPC (Inter-Process Communication) facilities and follows the functionalities of standard socket APIs. In addition to the Netlink socket, each of both routing protocols creates their own socket to send/receive control messages.

5.2 Test Environment

We have evaluated the operations of HRPC module using the network topology as shown in Fig. 7.

The testbed was comprised of three laptops equipped with IEEE 802.11b wireless chipset. All laptops were Linux system and their communication state was set to ad hoc mode. Each of three nodes employed one or more routing protocols as follows.

– Node employing DYMO as a reactive routing protocol
– Node employing OLSR as a proactive routing protocol
– u-Zone Master node employing HRPC, DYMO and OLSR protocols

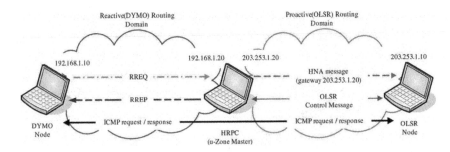

Fig. 7. Testbed for HRPC demonstration

5.3   Test Results

We show the results of the following two cases. In the first case, OLSR node wants to send "ping packets (ICMP Echo packets)" to DYMO node via an intermediate u-ZM. In the second case, the way to evaluate HRPC is same to the first case but the packets are delivered in a reverse way. In both cases, u-ZM informs that it is the gateway by means of OLSR HNA message as the first step.

- case 1: OLSR node $\longrightarrow$ HRPC (u-ZM) $\longrightarrow$ DYMO node

Fig. 8 and Fig. 9 show the results of the first case. We have utilized a network protocol analyzer called Ethereal [18] to monitor the packets over time from the source to the destination. Fig. 8 is a snapshot of the monitoring outputs of Ethereal running at the source, where both the ping request and the reply

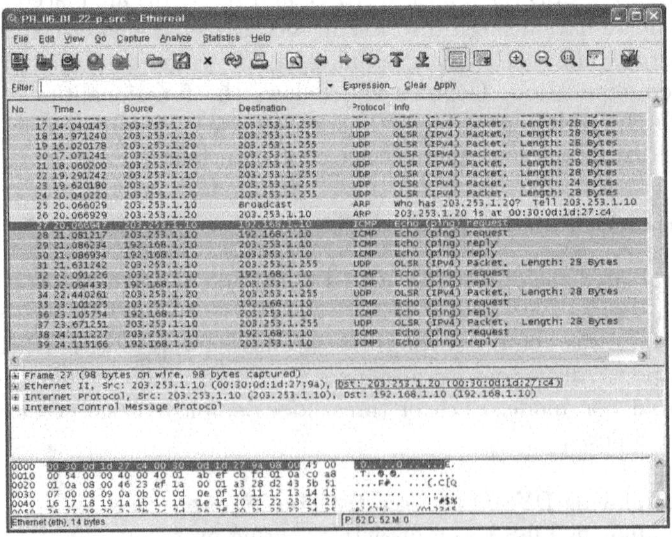

Fig. 8. Test result for case 1 (snapshot at proactive source node)

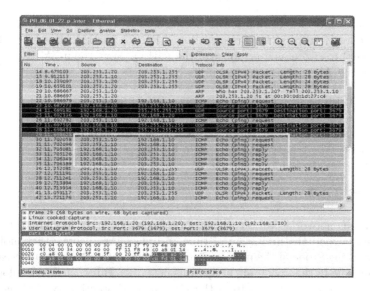

Fig. 9. Test result for case 1 (snapshot at u-ZM)

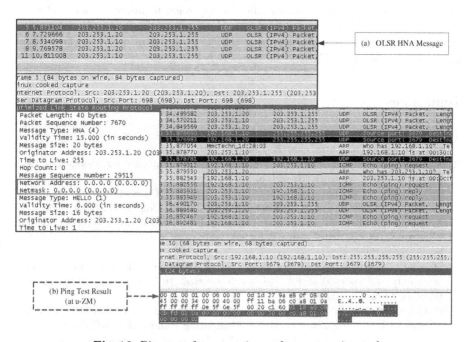

Fig. 10. Ping test from reactive node to proactive node

packets are shown. Like Fig. 8, Fig. 9 also shows the deliveries of echo packets but the figure was taken at the u-ZM.

OLSR sends ICMP echo request packet to u-ZM then the u-ZM hooks the packet to determine the next processing by means of Netfilter. Afterwards, the

u-ZM aware that the destination is not an OLSR node so that it activates a
route discovery process (i.e. broadcasting a RREQ packet). The DYMO node
sends RREP to u-ZM as a response of the RREQ. Now, the u-ZM is capable of
sending the ICMP packets queued in its buffer.

- case 2: DYMO node $\longrightarrow$ HRPC (u-ZM) $\longrightarrow$ OLSR node

As described above, the way to demonstrate the second case are similar to
the first case. The test result is shown in Fig. 10.

6   Conclusion

In ubiquitous networks, various types of communication devices are to be interconnected beyond the limitation of time and place. We believe that mobile ad
hoc networking is one of the most promising technologies playing an increasingly
important role in the upcoming ubiquitous networks. But such a technology still
introduces several challenges from the viewpoint of practicality. Among those,
the primary focus of the paper was on the heterogeneity of nodes. More specifically, the paper has presented an efficient approach to allow mobile nodes to
communicate each other regardless of the type of routing protocols. We have
shown in this paper that the proposed HRPC running on u-ZM works well in
the u-Zone based MANET.

References

1. IETF MANET (Mobile Ad hoc Networks) Working Group, Available URL:
   http://www.ietf.org/html.charters/manet-charter.html
2. X. Hong, K. Xu and M. Gerla. Scalable Routing Protocols for Mobile Ad Hoc
   Networks. IEEE Network Magazine, Vol.16, 2002.
3. E. M. Royer, S. Barbara and C.K. Toh. A Review of Current Routing Protocols
   for Ad hoc Mobile Wireless Networks. IEEE Personal Communications, 1999.
4. A. Iwata, C. Chiang, G. Pei and M. Gerla, Scalable Routing Strategies for Ad Hoc
   Wireless Networks, IEEE Journal on Selected Areas in Communications, Vol. 17,
   No. 8, Aug. 1999.
5. Myeong L. Lim and Chansu Yu, Does Cluster Architecture Enhance Performance
   Scalability of Clustered Mobile Ad Hoc Networks?, In Proc. of the Int'l. Conf. on
   Wireless Networks, June 2004.
6. B. Lee, C. Yu and S. Moh, Issues in Scalable Clustered Network Architecture for
   Mobile Ad Hoc Networks, The Mobile Computing Handbook, CRC Press, 2005.
7. N. Navid, W. Shiyi, and C. Bonnet, HARP: Hybrid Ad hoc Routing Protocol, In
   Proc. of IST, 2001.
8. Z. J. Haas and M. R. Pearlman. The Zone Routing Protocol (ZRP) for Ad Hoc
   Networks. IETF Internet Draft, 1998.
9. M. Joa-Ng and I. Lu, A Peer-to-Peer Zone-Based Two-Level Link State Routing
   Protocol for Ad Hoc Wireless Networks, Journal of Communications and Networks,
   Vol. 4, No. 1, Mar. 2002.

10. H. Wu and A. Abouzeid, Cluster-based Routing Overhead in Networks with Unreliable Nodes, In Proc. of IEEE WCNC04, Mar. 2004.
11. I. Chakeres, E. Belding-Royer and C. Perkins. Dynamic MANET On-demand (DYMO) Routing. IETF Internet Draft, (Work in Progress) 2006.
12. T. Clausen, and P. Jacquet, Optimized Link State Routing Protocol (OLSR), IETF RFC 3626, 2003.
13. N. Kang, I. Park, and Y. Kim. Secure and Scalable Routing Protocol for Mobile Ad-hoc Networks, Lecture Notes in Computer Science, Vol 3744, Oct. 2005.
14. OLSR daemon(olsrd), Available URL: http://www.olsr.org
15. I. Chakeres and E. Belding-Royer. AODV Routing Protocol Implementation Design, In Proc. of WWAN, Mar. 2004.
16. H. Lundgren, D. Lundberg, J. Nielsen, E. Nordstroem, and C. Tschudin. A Large-scale Testbed for Reproducible Ad hoc Protocol Evaluations. In Proc. of IEEE WCNC, Mar. 2002.
17. I. Chakeres. AODV-UCSB Implementation from University of California Santa Barbara, Available URL: http://moment.cs.ucsb.edu/AODV/aodv.html.
18. Ethereal: network protocol analyzer, Available URL: http://www.ethereal.com/

DynaMoNET: Dynamic Multi-homed IPv6 Mobile Networks with Multiple Mobile Routers

Won-Tae Kim

Embedded SW Division, ETRI, 161 Gajeong-Dong, Yuseong-gu, Daejeon, 305-700, Korea
wtkim@etri.re.kr

Abstract. DynaMoNET is designed for a multihomed moving network which has various MANETs interconnected through WPAN interfaces. Each MANET has a mobile router, e.g. a cellular phone which can work as a root MR in DynaMoNET. The essential technologies for DynaMoNET include handover protocol in heterogeneous networks, network switchover algorithm considering multiple decision factors, root MR election process based on token-based algorithm, fast root MR discovery algorithm and fault avoidance mechanism to support reliable Internet connectivity. In addition DynaMoNET handles multiple HAs model, i.e. (n, n, n) model. Finally the system design of a mobile router is suggested in order to make relationship between the key components.

Key words: Network mobility, heterogeneous networks, fault tolerance.

1 Introduction

The evolution speed toward beyond third generation (B3G) network has been accelerated by the development of various advanced access technologies including infrastructure and ad hoc modes. The needs for seamless connectivity are issued by mobile users who want to enjoy ubiquitous computing and communication services, i.e. computing and communication at any time, in any place and with any devices.

In ubiquitous environment, fine grain services to support seamless mobility in complex heterogeneous networks will be the most essential issue. IETF Mobile IPv6 (MIPv6) will be a suitable solution for global mobility support of devices scattered around us. Network mobility, however, can not be enough served by MIPv6 because MIPv6 manage only terminal mobility [1-3]. IETF *NEMO* (Network Mobility) WG has made effort on network mobility with various scenarios [4][5]. As access networks evolve, moving networks and mobile terminals use multiple network interfaces. As a result, the network technologies related with multiple network interfaces come to be very critical issues which includes vertical handover based on multiple factors, load sharing or MR (Mobile Router) synchronization, fault detection and avoidance, and HA synchronization [5]. The issues will be actively investigated in *monami6* (Mobile Nodes and Multiple Interfaces in IPv6) WG in IETF as well as in *NEMO* WG. *Monami6* WG especially focuses on multihomed device and network support by extending MIPv6 and NEMO protocols.

Recently several researches on multihomed network mobility have been made to solve the issues mentioned above [6-10]. *Cho* proposes the authentication mechanism

H.Y. Youn, M. Kim, and H. Morikawa (Eds.): UCS 2006, LNCS 4239, pp. 398–413, 2006.

of neighbor MR and registration process in case of multiple MRs [11]. In addition load balancing can be achieved by adopting HA-based load sharing mechanism with latency-based approach. *Song* introduces a decision making process integrated with AHP (Analytic Hierarchy Process) and GRA (Grey Relation Analysis) [12]. *Paik* addresses many issues in multihomed NEMO and gives analysis of influence of network mobility with multiple MRs on load sharing and session preservation [13].

Our special interesting is concentrated on nested mobile ad hoc networks (MANET) dynamically composed of MANETs visiting a mobile network. Let's assume that MANETs in small size, e.g. WPAN (Wireless Personal Area Network) with a cellular phone as a MR, assemble and make a larger MANET moving together. They can elect one or multiple root MRs within the moving network in order to serve as egress network interfaces. The relationship between MANETs is not client/server but peer to peer, i.e. equivalent to each other. Any of the MRs in the moving network can be a root MR and the number of root MRs are not restricted to support the others by the reasons of load balancing and fault avoidance. As a result, the NEMO can be conceived as a mobile node which has dynamically changeable network capability. The architecture, therefore, proposed in this paper is named DynaMoNET (Dynamic Mobile Network). DynaMoNET will address vertical handover algorithm in heterogeneous network models, MR election algorithm among multiple MRs, fast MR discovery algorithm, fault avoidance and protocol for seamless Internet connectivity. However, route optimization for pinball routing of nested NEMO and ad hoc routing protocol itself are out of scope of this paper.

The organization of this paper is as follows: Section 2 designs the architecture of DynaMoNET including interworking model of heterogeneous mobile networks. And handover procedure based on 'NEMO basic support protocol' will be given for two networking model, e.g. (n, 1, 1) and (n, n, n) model. The notation of (n, n, n) model means the set of {multiple MRs, multiple HAs, multiple MNPs (Mobile Network Prefixes)}. One of the essential features of multihomed NEMO, fault avoidance mechanism based on token, will be introduced as well. In section 3, the detail development mechanisms will be described for the introduced features of DynaMoNET including the system architecture of a MR, network switchover algorithm, token-based MR selection algorithm and fast MR discovery algorithm. After evaluating the features of DynaMoNET, we will give the conclusive remarks.

2. DynaMoNET Architecture

2.1 Design Considerations

Some issues are discussed for the design of an efficient multihomed NEMO [14]. With considering the issues, key design requirements of DynaMoNET are extracted as follows:

(1) Mobility protocol should consider multiple HAs and multiple MNPs, i.e. (n, n, n) model including single HA and single MNP, i.e. (n, 1, 1) model.
(2) Network switchover algorithm must consider multi-optional preferences of users or service policies.

(3) Fault tolerant mechanism based on available multi-paths should be taken into consideration.

(4) Multiple MRs can be fairly used as an external connection interface in order to overcome the limitation of mobile devices, e.g. battery power.

(5) Fast MR discovery algorithm in a moving network should be independent to ad hoc routing protocol.

2.2 DynaMoNET Overview

The interconnection between heterogeneous networks with different technologies can be achieved by IP based protocol, e.g. MIPv6, NEMO and monami6. There can be various service models related with MRs and MNPs. In this paper, we have interesting on (n, 1, 1) and (n, n, n) models as an extended network model of (n, 1, 1). We don't, however, consider HA synchronization in (n, *, *) model [14]. MR synchronization can be performed by means of token-based root MR selection algorithm which will be explained in later sections.

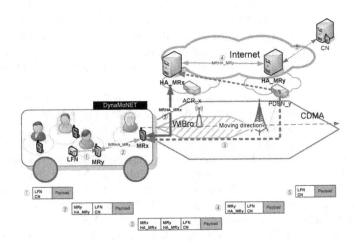

Fig. 1. DynaMoNET (n, 1, 1) model

Figure 1 shows (n, 1, 1) model which is a very simple architecture in terms of handover protocol. When mobile users with WPAN (Wireless Personal Area Network) get on a bus which has no network interfaces to the Internet, they will make a MANET in the vehicle and automatically elect root MR among them like figure 1. The elected MR will perform as a default router for the MANET to the Internet.

The packet formats for IP tunneling operation between LFN (Local Fixed Node), e.g. a digital camera with Bluetooth, and a corresponding node (CN) are shown at the bottom of figure 1. Since the depth of nested networks is 2 in this case, the tunnel header is encapsulated in double times. Figure 2 says the handover protocol in the scenario. When MRx detects availability of networks and makes decision of switching over to one of the networks, it performs MIPv6 binding update (BU) to its home agent (HA) which is the integrated mobility agent between CDMA and WiBro networks, i.e. (n, 1, 1) model. After the registration process is done, MRx releases the previous one. The support of simultaneous multiple paths on different network interfaces is out of scope of this research. Since MIPv6 can not support multiple CoAs at the same time, it is permitted that only one interface can be used as an egress interface in (n, 1, 1) model. However, *Wakikawa* suggests the modification on HA and caches to support multiple CoAs [15]. Since there are no changes of MNPs assigned to MRy, the nodes inside DynaMoNET do not need to update their CoAs (Care of Addresses). If the digital camera works as a VMN (Visiting Mobile Node) instead of a LFN, one more tunnel should be made between VMN and its HA or the CN.

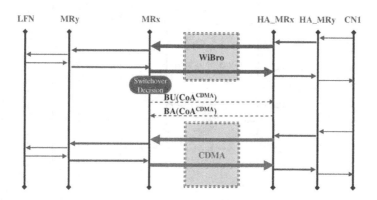

Fig. 2. Handover protocol in (n, 1, 1) model

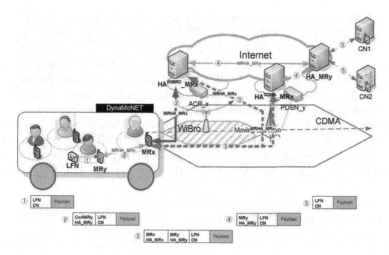

Fig. 3. DynaMoNET (n, n, n) model

Figure 3 and figure 4 show the service scenario and handover protocol of (n, n, n) model respectively. Let's assume that HAs of a MR are independent to each other and MNPs under control of each HA are different in our (n, n, n) model. As mentioned above, HA synchronization for the same MNP is out of our research scope in this paper. Multiple HAs assigns a HoA (Home Address) per interface in a MR and each HoA is registered with each authorized HA respectively. In DynaMoNET architecture, HoA of one network interface should be able to be assigned to the other network interface so that seamless connectivity can be achieved on handover process. Since the protocol, i.e. MIPv6, allows the operation in which multiple HoAs can be assigned to a network interface, this mechanism can be fallen into implementation issue.

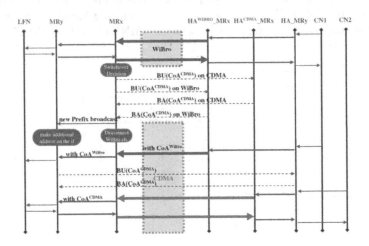

Fig. 4. Handover protocol in (n, n, n) model

When MRx decides to switch over to the new network, it sends BU (CoA^{CDMA}) messages to both HA^{CDMA}_MRx and HA^{WIBRO}_MRx before it releases the connection of the previous network, i.e. WiBro. By this operation, HA^{WIBRO}_MRx forwards all traffic for MRx toward the new CoA, i.e. CoA^{CDMA} over CDMA networks not over WiBro. The CDMA interface of MRx should be able to have the HoA from HA^{WIBRO}_MRx so as to permit the tunneled packets from CoA^{CDMA} with HA^{WIBRO}_MRx. After MRx disconnects WiBro connection, the existing connection between LFN and CN1 will continue to flow over CDMA networks as shown in figure 4. On receiving router advertisement with a new MNP, MRy generates a new CoA and tries to register the new CoA with HA_MRy. If a new CN2 tries to communicate with LFN, the new path will pass through HA^{CDMA}_MRx with CoA^{CDMA}.

2.3 Network Switchover Mechanism

The network switchover or handover of a root MR is an important feature of DynaMoNET for seamless Internet connectivity. The existing research suggested an intelligent multi-optional network decision algorithm based on AHP (Analytic Hierarchy Process) and GRA (Grey Relational Analysis) [12]. It analyses the relationship between multiple factors which affects the decision of an optimal network and evaluates each options, e.g. UMTS and WLAN, in terms of GRC (Gray Relational Coefficient). It neither considers the ping-pong problem or back-and-forth problem of mobile nodes nor takes RSS factor into the multiple factors of AHP, such as throughput, BER (Bit Error Rate), security level, and cost per packet. The algorithm simply decides if WLAN is available or not because of ubiquity of CDMA networks. If WLAN is available, it calculates GRC for the available options. However, RSS should be included to make decision of an optimal network. And hysteresis function (terminal_speed) is especially adopted for ping-pong problem. The solution will be introduced in the other paper in detail. Since the solution was developed and validated for a key component of dual-mode terminal software platform, i.e. CDMA-WiBro dual-mode platform in our research, this paper uses the result of the research as shown in figure 5 and figure 6.

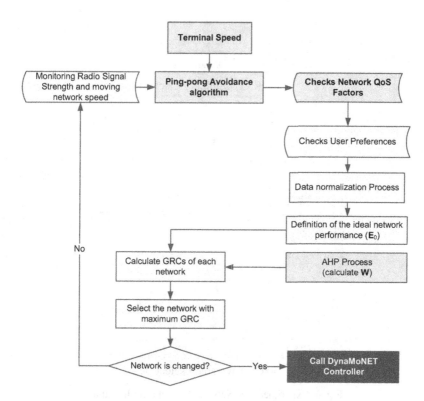

Fig. 5. Network Switchover algorithm with multi-optional preferences

2.4 DynaMoNET MR System

A MR system of DynaMoNET consists of 5 modules as shown in figure 5 which includes DynaMoNET controller, MR Election Module (MEM), Fast Route Discovery (FRD), Network Switchover Decision module (NSD) and DynaMoNET handover protocol. In network convergence layer it has network status monitor module (NSM), tunnel interface manager (TIM), network device manager (NDM) and multiple HoA manager (MHM).

```
1. Initial selected network (1: CDMA, 2:WiBro, 3: NONE) : )1
2-1. Normalized Radio Signal strength of CDMA (0 - 7) = 5
2-2. Normalized Radio Signal strength of WiBro (0 - 7) = 2
3. The Speed of Mobile Terminal : (1)10 (2)60 (3)120 (4)250 (5
4. Which network selection service do you want?

(1) Only RSS(Radio Signal Strenth) based Network selection
(2) Cost based Network selection
(3) Throughput based Network selection
(4) Security based Network selection
(5) Channel Reliability

Select service which you want (1-5): 1
################# GRC on CDMA and WiBro #################

   GRC of CDMA:          1
   GRC of WiBro:       0.5

Multi-demensional parameters of CDMA and WiBro
|=============================|=========||========|
|                             |  CDMA   |  WiBro  |
|-----------------------------|---------|---------|
|Normalized RSS               |  5.00   |  2.00   |
|Bandwidth (Mbps)             |  0.70   |  1.50   |
|Delay (msec)                 |100.00   | 10.00   |
|Radio BER                    |1.00e-03 |1.00e-04 |
|Security Level               |  1.00   |  3.00   |
|Packet Cost (Won)            | 30.00   | 10.00   |
|=============================|=========||========|
Keep CDMA network interface
###################################################################
```

(a) RSS-weighted selection

```
1. Initial selected network (1: CDMA, 2:WiBro, 3: NONE) : )1
2-1. Normalized Radio Signal strength of CDMA (0 - 7) = 7
2-2. Normalized Radio Signal strength of WiBro (0 - 7) = 3
3. The Speed of Mobile Terminal : (1)10 (2)60 (3)120 (4)250 (5
4. Which network selection service do you want?

(1) Only RSS(Radio Signal Strenth) based Network selection
(2) Cost based Network selection
(3) Throughput based Network selection
(4) Security based Network selection
(5) Channel Reliability

Select service which you want (1-5): 2
################# GRC on CDMA and WiBro #################

   GRC of CDMA:       0.5155
   GRC of WiBro:      0.8065

Multi-demensional parameters of CDMA and WiBro
|=============================|=========||========|
|                             |  CDMA   |  WiBro  |
|-----------------------------|---------|---------|
|Normalized RSS               |  7.00   |  3.00   |
|Bandwidth (Mbps)             |  1.50   |  1.50   |
|Delay (msec)                 | 10.00   | 20.00   |
|Radio BER                    |1.00e-05 |1.00e-04 |
|Security Level               |  1.00   |  3.00   |
|Packet Cost (Won)            | 30.00   | 10.00   |
|=============================|=========||========|
WiBro Network is selected and change to WiBro
###################################################################
```

(b) Cost-weighted selection

Fig. 6. Experiments of Network Switchover algorithm

DynaMoNET controller manages all the control modules and receives L2 triggering events from NSM. The triggering can be implemented as polling based mechanism for NSM, however event-based or interrupt-based mechanism is much more efficient in terms of computing power efficiency. After receiving events, it notifies NSD which performs the network selection algorithm as described in section 2.3. If the result of the calculation says change of network attachment, NSD calls DynaMoNET controller to switchover to the triggered network. From this point, handover protocol can be performed under the control of DynaMoNET controller as shown in figure 2 and figure 4. The management of DynaMoNET covers dynamic tunnel interfaces, network device management and multiple HoAs control on each network interfaces.

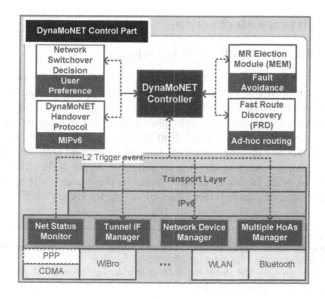

Fig. 7. DynaMoNET MR System Architecture

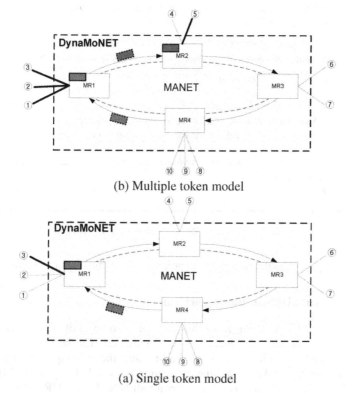

(b) Multiple token model

(a) Single token model

Fig. 8. Token-based control model

3   Fault Tolerance Mechanisms

3.1   Logical Ring Topology for Root MR Selection

This section explains a logical ring mechanism for management of root MR candidates which can be a root MR or multiple root MRs in DynaMoNET. There are two types of token models as shown in figure 8. Token means the right to work as a root MR in a DynaMoNET domain. If there is single token in a logical ring as shown figure 8 (a), only one MR, i.e. MR1 can be a root MR in the network. In this case MR1 comes to be a primary MR which can generate tokens in order to support QoS and fault tolerance. If there are multiple tokens in the ring as shown in figure 8 (b), there are the same numbers of root MRs. In this case MR1 works as the primary MR as well. Figure 9 shows the algorithm of establishment of a logical ring for DynaMoNET.

Establishment of Logical Ring

MEM initializes data structures for DynaMoNET;
MEM of the primary MR makes logical ring map based on link local addresses;
Sets the first root MT as the primary MR ;

Sets τ_{MR} to a fixed period;

while(TRUE) {
        MEM broadcasts solicit_root_MR over ad hoc network;
        Receives candidate_root_MR messages;

        Set $N_{candidates}$ to the number of messages;

        Registers the link local addresses with candidate root MR table;

        if ($N_{candidates}$ is changed) {

        for (i =0; i < $N_{candidates}$; i++){
         Sorts candidate root MR table by addressing order;
         Makes unidirectional linked list in candidate root MR table;
         }
        MEM reliably sends the updated map to all candidates' link local
        addresses ;
        }
}

Fig. 9. The algorithm for establishment of logical ring

where $N_{candidates}$ means the number of candidate MRs which want to be root MRs

3.2   Token-Based MR Selection Algorithm

The token-based MR selection algorithm can solve some fault states. Let's assume that MR1 detects the lack of egress network bandwidth. The best way for this is to make another paths which can load sharing with the existing path. The primary MR generates multiple tokens until the congestion is solved. The primary MR has the right to delete tokens which was released by a root MR. A root MR with a token can release the token when the traffic level goes down under a threshold level within some period. The released token goes around along the logical ring and arrives at MR1 which decides to delete the token or not. Figure 10 gives the algorithm implementing the above operations. We define three possible fault states as follows:

1) Traffic overload makes packet overflow or packet loss
2) The shortage of battery capacity
3) The breakdown of network devices

Token Control Algorithm for Fault Avoidance

while(TRUE) {
Monitors fault conditions;

if ($\Delta_i < \lambda_i$ or $C_{MR} < T_{MR}$ or $RSS_{active\_if} = 0$) set fault_state to TRUE;

if(fault_state == TRUE) {
switch(policy) {
case SINGLE_ROOTMR:

> *Sends token to P_{next} node;*
>
> *Waits for response from P_{next} until the reserved time;*
> *if no response within the timer) retransmits 3 times;*
> *else received positive response from P_{next} or others next to P_{next} &*
>> *prefix broadcast from the answerer then break;*

case MULTI_ROOTMR:
> *switch(fault_option){*
>> *case **TRAFFIC_OVERLOAD**:*
>>
>> *Generates a new token & N_{token} ++;*
>>
>> *Sends the token to P_{next} node;*
>>
>> *Waits for response from P_{next} until the reserved time;*
>> *if(no response within the timer) retransmits 3 times;*
>> *else received positive response from P_{next} or others next to P_{next} &*
>>> *prefix broadcast from the answerer then break;*
>> *case **BREAKDOWN_NETIF**:*
>> *case **SHORTAGE_BATTERY**:*
>>
>> *Sends token to P_{next} node;*
>>
>> *Waits for response from P_{next} until the reserved time;*
>> *if(no response within the timer) retransmits 3 times;*
>> *else received positive response from P_{next} or others next to P_{next} &*
>>> *prefix broadcast from the answerer then close all egress network interfaces;*
>> *break;*
>> *}*
> *}*

}

Fig. 10. Token Control Algorithm for Fault Avoidance

where, N_{token} : The number of generated tokens by the primary MR which is a root MR, and the default value of N_{token} is 1

P_{next} : The pointer (link local address) for the next node in a logical ring topology

$P_{previous}$: The pointer (link local address) for the previous node in a logical ring topology

λ_i : Incoming traffic rate on i^{th} network interface

Δ_i : The threshold bandwidth of ith network interface on a root MR

C_{MR} : Available Battery capacity of root MR

T_{MR} : The threshold battery capacity

RSS_{active_if} : Radio signal strength of active interfaces

3.3 Fast Root MR Discovery Algorithm

There are very interesting phenomena in which specific some nodes have the traffic favoritism, i.e. taking almost chances to serve requests from others. Through analyzing the patterns of network traffic, it is generally known that most traffic of a node is concentrated on a few particular nodes [16]. FRD (Fast Route Discovery) algorithm is devised to fast find the route to root MRs which have the traffic favoritism in DynaMoNET.

FRD can be combined with reactive ad hoc routing protocol, e.g. Ad-hoc On-Demand Distance Vector (AODV) or Dynamic Source Routing (DSR) since this algorithm is not a fundamental routing protocol but a supplementary algorithm to improve the base routing algorithm. The essential difference from native ad hoc routing mode is that the additional RREQ (Route Request) message is added to the ad hoc routing protocol in order to fast explore path for nodes with traffic favoritism. There are two additional fields in each destination entry in the routing table: the Counter and the Is_Sel_RREQ. Each node examines the packet type when transmitting the packet. If it is the data packet, the Counter value for the destination increases. Therefore, the number of packets transmitted to a destination is easily grasped. Note that the Counter value does not increase for control messages such as RREQ or RREP. Increasing the Counter value for the control packet disturbs the analysis of the traffic pattern. The maximum number of selected nodes with traffic favoritism is controlled by a variable, MAX_NUM_FRD.

Let RREQ_Entry_Selection_Time and Sel_RREQ_Time be the periods to select the frequently accessed nodes and to send the additional RREQ messages, respectively. Each host searches the Counter values in its routing table entries and determines the RREQ_Entry_Number nodes with the largest values. The Is_Sel_RREQ values of these nodes are set to one. Each node sends additional RREQ messages to the destination nodes every Sel_RREQ_Time if the Is_Sel_RREQs corresponding to those nodes are one. Then, the Counter values in the routing entries are initialized to zero in order to rapidly adapt to the changes of network. These procedures are consecutively repeated every *RREQ_Entry_ Selection_Time*. By doing so, the packet is sent faster and is more stable for most frequently accessed destinations.

Since root MRs, as mentioned above, natively have traffic favoritism in a DynaMoNET, they have the highest priority as selected nodes in this algorithm. When an elected MR broadcast router advertisement into the network, each MR makes an entry for the MR, if necessary, and sets *Is_Sel_RREQ* flag without concerns of *Counter value*. Of course, the number of the root MRs should be counted in *MAX_NUM_FRD*. If there is a late selected root MR and slot for the root MR is occupied, then *Is_Sel_RREQ* flag of a normal MR or a node with lowest *Counter value* should be reset instead of the late joined root MR.

4 Simulation Study

In section 3, the token-based MR selection algorithm was proposed to support fault tolerance to a DynaMoNET domain. If a DynaMoNET suffers from buffer overflow or packet loss caused by traffic overload in a root MR, additional new root MRs must be selected as the algorithm. In case of traffic overload condition, the optimum number of root MRs is so important factors in order to save entire network energy and keep the network reliability as well. Root MRs forward the packets from its DynaMoNET toward the Internet via theirs own infrastructure network interfaces. While internal MRs in a DynaMoNET are interconnected with WPAN and establish MANET domain, root MRs use infrastructure network interfaces, e.g. CDMA or WiBro. As a result, there is asymmetric energy consumption between root MRs and internal MRs in a DynaMoNET [17]. Therefore, the network total energy consumption must be considered for selecting additional MRs in order to avoid the traffic overload. In this section, the simulation about selecting optimum number of root MR is considered for reducing packet loss and packet overflow and minimizing network total energy consumption.

Table 1. The simulation environment

ITEMS	VALUE
Simulation tool	NS-2
MANET MAC	IEEE 802.11
Bandwidth of external network interface	2Mbps
Packet size	1024 bytes
Radio coverage range of MANET	50m
Simulation Area	500m x 500m
Traffic pattern	Constant bit rate
Number of nodes	30
Number of network interfaces	2

Table 1 shows the network simulation environment for a DynaMoNET. The total number of nodes in the network and the number of nodes selected as root MR is determined to meet the optimum ratio considering packet loss and energy consumption. It is necessary that the total number of node and the number of node selected as root MR are constituted to optimum rate for reducing packet loss and energy consumption. We define ρ factor to show simulation results according to the ratio of the number of root MRs to the number of the internal MRs.

$$\rho = \frac{\text{The number of selected root MRs}}{\text{The number of other MRs excluding the root MRs}} \times 100(\%) \quad (1)$$

In order to find the optimum number of root MRs, energy consumption and packet loss are under consideration with various ρ rates, e.g. 5%, 20%, 40% and 60% respectively. Figure 11 shows the simulation results of total energy consumption according to the ρ values. As the root MRs need more energy consumption than other MRs to interconnect the moving network with the Internet, the cases with higher ρ value consumes much more energy level than the ones with lower ρ rate. In terms of network lifetime, high energy consumption has an effect on the network lifetime.

Figure 12 gives the simulation result of packet loss amount in terms of network reliability according to the ρ rates. With higher ρ rate, because traffic processed by root MR is reduced, possibility to be in fault state gets lower. Therefore network reliability is enhanced with higher ρ rate. As a result of the simulations, all of network energy consumption and network reliability can be considered in terms of the number of root MRs. If many root MRs are elected in order to increase the reliability as designed in the fault tolerant algorithm, the energy

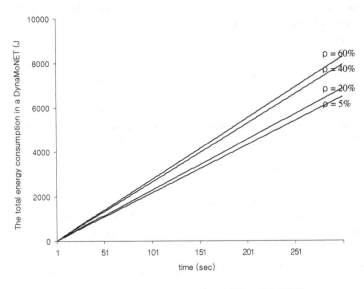

Fig. 11. Total energy consumption of DynaMoNET

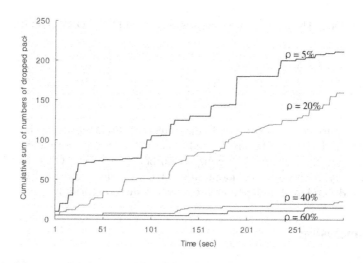

Fig. 12. Packet loss amount in terms of ρ

consumption will increase and the lifetime of the entire network will linearly decrease as the number of the root MRs selected in a DynaMoNET. Meanwhile, the network reliability does not increase as the number of root MRs. In case of this simulation, the network reliability or packet loss rate comes to be stable as the value of ρ approaches to 40%. Therefore, the optimum rate of ρ for network reliability is around 40% at the expense of entire network energy.

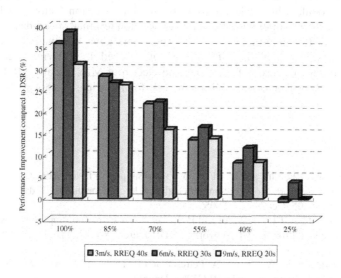

Fig. 13. The performance enhancement in terms of delivery delay(%)

Table 2. The performance comparison between FRD-AODV and FRD-DSR

	100%	80%	70%	55%	40%	25%	Average
3m/sec 40s	0.34	0.32	0.82	1.08	-0.95	3.02	0.771667
6m/sec 30s	0.98	0.58	0.84	0.84	-0.26	0.8	0.63
Average	0.66	0.45	0.83	0.96	-0.605	1.91	0.700833

As mentioned in section 3.3, the effect of FRD needs to be proved in a DynaMoNET domain. Figure 13 and table 2 show the performance enhancement by FRD and the performance comparison between FRD-AODV and FRD-DSR, respectively. As a result the adoption of FRD can enhance the delivery delay time in DynaMoNET with independent to ad hoc routing algorithm.

5 Conclusion

In this paper we proposed a novel moving network architecture, DynaMoNET, which aims to solve the problems of moving ad hoc networks with multiple network interfaces. There are some key issues in DynaMoNET in order to support seamless Internet connectivity: handover protocol in heterogeneous networks, vertical handover algorithm considering multiple decision factors, root MR election algorithm, fast root MR discovery algorithm and fault avoidance mechanism.

Handover protocol is designed based on NEMO basic support protocol, which does not consider multiple network interfaces and multiple HAs environment. DynaMoNET addresses the problems by adopting multiple CoAs registration mechanism. The handover protocol is triggered by the decision from network switchover module which takes account of multiple decision factors, such as RSS, bandwidth, BER, Cost per packet and etc. In addition terminal speed-based hysteresis value is used for ping-pong problem. There are always reliability problem in unreliable networks like ours. Therefore, token-based logical ring mechanism is adopted in order to improve fault states and elect root MRs. Finally FRD algorithm was introduced so that normal MRs can seek for the route to root MRs as fast as possible.

References

[1] D. Johnson, C. Perkins and J. Arkko, "Mobility Support in IPv6," RFC 3775, June 2004.
[2] T. Ernst, ""Network Mobility Support Goals and Requirements," IETF draft-ietf-nemo-requirements-05, October 24, 2005.
[3] H. Y. Jung, E. A. Kim, J. W. YI and H. H. Lee, "A Scheme for Supporting Fast Handover in Hierarchical Mobile IPv6 Networks," ETRI Journal, vol.27, no.6, Dec. 2005, pp.798-801.
[4] V. Devarapalli, R. Wakikawa, A. Petrescu and P. Thubert, "Network Mobility (NEMO) Basic Support Protocol," IETF RFC3963, January 2005.
[5] H.-Y. Lach, C. Janneteau, A. Petrescu, "Network mobility in beyond-3G systems," IEEE Communications Magazine, Volume 41, issue 7, July 2003 Page(s):52 – 57.

[6] C. Ng, E. Paik, T. Ernst, M. Bagnulo, "Analysis of Multihoming in Network Mobility Support," IETF draft-ietf-nemo-multihoming-issues-04, October 24, 2005.

[7] R. Wakikawa, T. Yokota, K. Tasaka, H. Horiuchi, K. Uehara and J. Murai, "Experimentation of networked vehicle with multihomed mobile router," VTC-2005-Fall, Volume 1, 28-25 Sept., 2005 Page(s):334 – 338.

[8] P. E. Engelstad, A. Tonnesen, A. Hafslund and G. Egeland, "Internet connectivity for multi-homed proactive ad hoc networks," IEEE International Conference on Communications Volume 7, 20-24 June 2004 Page(s):4050 – 4056.

[9] S. Kashihara, T. Nishiyama, K. Iida, H. Koga, Y. Kadobayashi and S. Yamaguchi, "Path selection using active measurement in multi-homed wireless networks," Applications and the Internet, 2004. Proceedings. 2004 International Symposium on 2004 Page(s):273 – 276.

[10] N. Montavont, T. Noel and T. Ernst, "Multihoming in nested mobile networking," SAINT 2004 Workshops on 26-30 Jan. 2004 Page(s):184 – 189.

[11] S. H. Cho, J. K. Na and C. K. Kim, "A dynamic load sharing mechanism in multihomed mobile networks," ICC 2005 16-20 May 2005 Page(s):1459 - 1463 Vol. 3.

[12] Q. Song and A. Jamalipour, "Network selection in an integrated wireless LAN and UMTS environment using mathematical modeling and computing techniques," IEEE Wireless Communications, Volume 12, Issue 3, June 2005 Page(s):42 – 48.

[13] E. K. Paik, H. S. Cho, T. Ernst and Y. H. Choi, "Load sharing and session preservation with multiple mobile routers for large scale network mobility," The proceedings of AINA 2004: Page(s):393 - 398 Vol.1.

[14] N. Montavont , R. Wakikawa, T. Ernst, C. Ng and K. Kuladinithi, "Analysis of Multihoming in Mobile IPv6," IETF draft-montavont-mobileip-multihoming-pb-statement-05.txt, October 27, 2005.

[15] R. Wakikawa, K. Uehara and T. Ernst, "Multiple Care-of Addresses Registration," IETF draft-wakikawa-mobileip-multiplecoa-04.txt, june 2005.

[16] A.-L. Barabasi, "LINKED," Penguin, June 2003.

[17] Benjie Chen, Kyle Jamieson, Hari Balakrishnan, and Robert Morris, "Span: An Energy-Efficient Coordination Algorithm for Topology Maintenance in Ad Hoc Wireless Networks", 2001 ACM.

Fast IPv6 Address Auto-configuration Using Proxy for Mobile Environment*

Dongkeun Lee and Keecheon Kim[**]

Dept. of Computer Science & Engineering, Konkuk University
Gwang-Jin Gu, Seoul, Korea
{dklee, kckim}@konkuk.ac.kr

Abstract. IPv6 stateless address auto-configuration scheme is very useful in mobile environment like as Mobile IPv6 network. Using address auto-configuration, mobile node can configure global address and access Internet when it moves away from home network. In some mobile environment, how-ever, DAD procedure for auto-configuration might not be applicable. For ex-ample, in mobile ad-hoc network, DAD procedure using timeout cannot reliably detect the absence of a duplicate address. In this paper, we propose new IPv6 addressing mechanism and address auto-configuration scheme using proxy. A proxy, in our scheme, can allocate global addresses to other IPv6 nodes. Our so-lution uses a stateful approach, but the solution is lighter and faster than DHCPv6. Our scheme is flexible and efficient, as shown by simulation.

1 Introduction

A mobile node visiting foreign network needs to be configured with a global address in order to access Internet. So IPv6 address auto-configuration is a very useful mecha-nism in mobile environment. Typically, dynamic configuration in a wired network is accomplished by using Dynamic Host Configuration Protocol (DHCPv6 [1]). This requires a centralized server to provide dynamic address assignment and maintenance for the network. If there is no DHCPv6 server, a mobile node can be configured with a new global address using IPv6 stateless auto-configuration mechanism [2]. This mechanism allows a node to pick a tentative address randomly and then use a Dupli-cate Address Detection(DAD) procedure to detect duplicate addresses. The DAD procedure uses timeouts. In some mobile environment, however, timeout approach in DAD may decrease the performance of IPv6.

For example, in Hierarchical Mobile IPv6 Mobility Management (HMIPv6) [3], two DAD procedures are needed. One is for LCoA and the other is for RCoA. Hence, when a mobile node enters into a new MAP domain, it must wait at least two DAD times in order to send a binding update to a home agent or correspondent nodes. This waiting time may disturb the seamless communication.

Another example is a mobile ad-hoc networks(MANET). MANETs are envisioned to have dynamic, sometimes rapidly changing, random, multi-hop topologies which

---

* This research was supported by the Brain Korea 21 project.
** Corresponding author.

H.Y. Youn, M. Kim, and H. Morikawa (Eds.): UCS 2006, LNCS 4239, pp. 414–427, 2006.

are likely composed of relatively bandwidth-constrained wireless links [4]. Significant research in this area has been focused on the design of efficient routing protocols such as DSDV [5], AODV [6], etc. The majority of routing protocols assume that mobile nodes in ad hoc networks are configured with IP addresses before they begin communications in the network. Thus, Auto-configuration is a desirable goal in implementing MANET [7].

IPv6 stateless address auto-configuration can be used in MANET. This mechanism uses timeouts. In ad-hoc networks, however, message delay cannot be bounded. Thus the use of timeouts cannot reliably detect the absence of a message. Such unreliability can lead to a situation in which the duplicate addresses go undetected [8].

Another challenging issue in MANET rises in connecting to the Internet through the nodes of ad-hoc network [9]. This MANET topology could be an ordinary situation if we think of our real life depending on the Internet.

In this paper, we propose a new IPv6 addressing mechanism using proxy. A proxy can be configured by static or dynamic manners. Our solution uses a stateful approach. Proxies have available global addresses and allocate these addresses to other nodes. This scheme is lighter and faster than DHCPv6.

This paper is organized as follows. In section 2, related works are presented. Our proxy based IPv6 addressing scheme is described in section 3 and its application for MANET is presented in section 4. IPv6 address auto-configuration for HMIPv6 is presented in section 5. We show performance of our scheme in section 6. Finally, conclusion with future research works are presented in section 7.

2 Related Work

2.1 Address Auto-configuration for Ad-Hoc Networks

The IETF zeroconf working group already standardized a stateless auto-configuration mechanism for IPv6 [2]. However, this protocol was not designed for mobile ad hoc networks. In the wireless ad-hoc network, we cannot determine how many nodes will exist, and how long will it take for DAD messages to be returned to the originate node. Hence, DAD waiting time is a big problem of this standard.

DAD based on the stateless auto-configuration in MANET is presented in [7], in which addresses are randomly selected. Duplicate Address Detection(DAD) is performed by each node to guarantee the uniqueness of the selected address. However, this approach uses timeouts, so it has DAD timeout bound problem. The scheme in [7] supports both IPv4 and IPv6.

There is another DAD process to compensate the DAD time. Weak Duplicate Address Detection [8] aims at lowering the overhead needed for the DAD by integrating it with the routing protocol. Weak DAD is an approach to prevent a packet from being routed to a wrong destination, even if duplicate addresses exist. In weak DAD, the nodes do the DAD process with direct linkable nodes first. After that, with the aids of routing protocol, node can detect duplicate address with itself from others. This system is based on the use of a single key that is assigned to each node. Nodes in the network are identified not only by the IP address, but also additionally by a key. If two nodes with the same address choose the same key, a conflict is not detectable because the key is only generated once by each node.

The MANETconf [10] presents an address assignment scheme for ad hoc networks based on a distributed mutual exclusion algorithm that treats IP addresses as a shared resource. In this work, each node maintains a list of all IP addresses in use in the network. A new node obtains an IP address through an existing node in the network. Assignment of a new address requires an approval from all other known nodes in the network. When the network partition is detected, every node in each partition cleans up the addresses in other partitions, and then the nodes agree on a unique identifier for the network. When partitions merge, nodes are required to exchange the set of allocated addresses in each partition. MANETconf produces complex and bandwidth-consuming process by maintaining common address pool information depending on the mobility parameters and also requires the use of timeouts for several operations. In contrast to this approach, our solution does not require each node to maintain and exchange a list of all IP addresses and it is much simpler. Our solution can work in the presence of partitions without requiring any special procedure to detect the partitions or merging of partitions.

3   New IPv6 Addressing Scheme Using Proxy

3.1   Basic Idea

Our proposal enables a node to auto-configure an unique IPv6 global address fast. In our proposal, an address allocation server allocates global addresses to other IPv6 nodes with its network prefix and manages the allocated addresses. The address allocation server is a router and it manages the whole address space which has network prefix of its own.

When a new node wants to have a global address, it requests an available global IPv6 address to the allocation server. We call this address request message as Address_Request message and call response message to this request as Address_Reply message. Address_Reply message has an unique IPv6 address allocated by the server to the requester.

In most cases, there are many hops between a requesting node and the allocation server. For a rapid address allocation, we introduce proxy nodes that execute the address allocation on behalf of the allocation server. With proxy nodes, a requesting node can send an Address_Request messages to the proxy node, and then the proxy node replies with a new IPv6 global address to that node. In this procedure, the distance between the proxy node and the requesting node is so close, so the mobile node can get a global IPv6 address more rapidly.

3.2   Address Allocation

In order to allocate the addresses, we use new IPv6 addressing format that has three parts, Global Network Prefix, Proxy ID and Host ID. Network Prefix is identical as general IPv6 prefix[12]. Interface ID field in normal IPv6 address is divided into two parts, Proxy ID and Host ID. Proxy ID is allocated by the address allocation server and is used as proxy address. Host ID is used as free space and the proxy can allocate addresses within this space to other nodes. Fig. 1 represents the addressing architecture for ad-hoc networks.

Global Network Prefix	Proxy ID	Host ID (Free Space)

Fig. 1. Addressing architecture for ad-hoc networks

For example, if we assume that the prefix length of the address allocation server is 64bits and the length of Proxy ID is 48 bits, Host ID can have 16 bits length. These values of length are included in Address_Reply messages.

When the allocation server allocates the new address, it selects an unused value as Proxy ID and sets the value of Host ID as 0. Thus, if the address that is allocated from the allocation server is 3ffe:2e01:2b:1111:2222:2222:2222:0000, the first 64bits, 3ffe:2e01:2b:1111:, is a global network prefix and the second 48bits, 2222:2222:2222, is Proxy ID. These two parts are fixed by the allocation server. The last 16bits, 0000, is the free space.

The new node who receives this address from the allocation server becomes a proxy node, and it can allocate an address to another node by using free space of Host ID from 3ffe:2e01:2b:1111:2222:2222:2222:0001 to 3ffe:2e01:2b:1111:2222:2222: 2222:FFFF.

As usual, the proxy node uses the first free address as its own node address. And the address, which all bits of Host ID are set to 0, must be used as a proxy multicast address.

In above example, 3ffe:2e01:2b:1111:2222:2222:2222:0001 is used as a proxy's address and 3ffe:2e01:2b:1111:2222:2222:2222:0000 is used as a proxy multicast address. The proxy multicast address is used for address management.

4   Fast Address Allocation for MANET Using Proxy

4.1   Ad-Hoc Node Advertisement

We consider a MANET topology in which all the nodes in MANET want to connect to the Internet through a special node called Internet gateway. The Internet gateway acts as a default router for the MANET. As mentioned in [9], connecting MANET to the Internet through the nodes of an ad-hoc network is seriously required.

In such configuration, Internet gateway acts as address allocation server and allocates the addresses to other ad-hoc nodes and manages the allocated addresses.

In order to obtain information of Internet Gateway and neighboring nodes, the nodes in ad-hoc network use Ad-hoc Node Advertisement messages. Internet Gateway's Router Advertisement messages cannot be transmitted over multi-hop link. For that reason, the Internet Gateway's neighbors include the received Router Advertisements in its Ad-hoc Node Advertisement messages and periodically broadcast these messages to its neighbors. If a node receives an Ad-hoc Node Advertisements from its neighbors, it extracts the Router Advertisement message from the received message and then broadcasts the Router Advertisement to its neighbors using Ad-hoc Node Advertisements.

Ad-hoc Node Advertisement message contains its lifetime, preference, and Internet Gateway's advertisement message. Link-local address is used for source address of Ad-hoc Node Advertisement. Preference is a value of hop counts from Internet Gateway. This message is limited by one-hop range.

All nodes in ad-hoc network broadcast Ad-hoc Node Advertisement messages periodically or non-periodically. When a node receives a Router Solicitation message form its neighbor nodes, it sends its Ad-hoc Node Advertisement immediately in order to inform Internet Gateway's information to neighbor nodes.

After a node assigns a link-local address to its interface, it starts to broadcast Ad-hoc Node Advertisement to its neighbor nodes using all nodes multicast address. If the node doesn't configure a global address yet, it sets *preference* field in its Ad-hoc Node Advertisements to maximum value in order to inform its neighbor nodes that it cannot send messages beyond one hop yet.

A new node selects an initiator that has the smallest value in the *preference* field of Ad-hoc Node Advertisement message among its neighboring nodes. We explained more about Ad-hoc Node Advertisement message in [11].

4.2 Address Allocation Procedure

When a new node enters into an ad-hoc network, it first creates its IPv6 link-local address and performs DAD procedure as described in [2]. And then, in order to auto-configure its global IPv6 address, it requests an available global IPv6 address to the Internet gateway.

But without a global address, if it isn't directly linked with the gateway, the new node cannot send an address request message to the gateway using ad-hoc routing protocol. An ad-hoc node without a global address cannot send a packet through multi-hop. Hence, a new node entering the network chooses a reachable MANET node that can perform an address allocation for itself.

For example, the new node i selects neighboring node j as an initiator and then sends an Address_Request message to the initiator node j. On receiving the Address_Request message from i, node j forwards this message to the Internet gateway and receives an Address_Reply message including the available global address from the gateway. Finally node j delivers the received Address_Reply message to node i, and node i configures the address included in the received Address_Reply message as its global address.

The proposed approach is flexible enough to be integrated with many different ad-hoc routing protocols.

The procedure of determining a proxy node in MANET is simple. If a new node receives an Address_Reply from the Internet gateway, it becomes a proxy node automatically and can allocate the addresses to other nodes like as mentioned in section 3.

If a node becomes a proxy, the node should send periodic Proxy_Advertisement message to its neighboring nodes. This message is limited by one-hop range. Actually, Proxy_Advertisement and Ad-hoc Node Advertisement are the same message.

When a new mobile node that needs to acquire a global IPv6 address selects an initiator, it sends Address_Request to the initiator. If the initiator knows that there is at least one proxy node within one hop area from itself from the periodic Proxy_Advertisement messages by neighbor nodes, it sends the received

Address_Request to one of proxy nodes that exist within one hop area from itself. And then the proxy allocates a new address to the new mobile node.

If there is no proxy node, the initiator sends the received Address_Request to the Internet Gateway with IPv6 hop by hop option which can be understood by proxies. In this case, if at least one proxy exists in the path from the initiator to the Gateway, the proxy seizes the request packet and sends a reply with an available global address to the initiator. In this way, the new mobile node can get a global IPv6 address faster than getting it from the Gateway. The address received from the proxy is a single address, thus the new node cannot become a proxy node. If there is no proxy in the path, the request packet is delivered to the Gateway, and the Gateway allocates new address set for the new node and sends reply message. In this case, the new node becomes a proxy node.

In an ad-hoc network, mobile node can move any direction. Therefore, proxy nodes may huddle up in the edge of ad-hoc network or leave the ad-hoc network. As a result new nodes that need an IPv6 address can't find any proxy node. So, general node must be able to become a proxy node in order to achieve the high performance of this address allocation scheme.

If a general node that already configured IPv6 address doesn't receive any Proxy_Advertisement message during some period, it sends a Proxy_Address_Request message to the Gateway in order to become a proxy. When the Gateway receives this message, it allocates a new proxy address space to that node. This process is identical with allocating a new proxy address space to a new mobile node. And then the node becomes a proxy node and it can allocate addresses within its address space to other nodes. In this way, proxy nodes can be distributed equally in ad-hoc network.

4.3 Address Management in MANET

The Internet Gateway allocates the addresses from its address space. So, it should do the address management to prevent the loss of addresses. When the Internet Gateway allocates a new address to a new node(i.e. proxy node), it records this address with its lifetime. This lifetime is included in Address_Reply message, thus the proxy node is able to know its lifetime.

In our solution, the proxy node should send Address_Refresh message to the Gateway before the end of its lifetime. Then the Gateway extends the lifetime of the proxy node and reply to the proxy node with Refresh_Reply message containing the extended lifetime. If the Gateway does not receive any refresh request message from the proxy node before the lifetime expires, the Gateway multicasts the Refresh_Request message using the proxy multicast address to the ad-hoc network. In this case, all bits in Host ID of destination address are set to 0. This address indicates that all nodes that have the identical Proxy ID with the requested destination address must receive the packet and respond to the Gateway using Address_Refresh.

If the Gateway does not receive any reply message for the Refresh_Request message before timeout, it decides that there is no node using that address space, and removes the proxy address space from the table. This address space can be reallocated to the other nodes later.

If a Gateway receives reply messages from any node, it knows that there is no proxy node but some nodes are using the proxy address space. In this case, the

Gateway should not remove the proxy address space from the table. In order to reduce the request and reply messages, the Gateway may select a tentative proxy node among the responding nodes and sends Refresh_Reply message to the tentative node. If a node is selected as a tentative proxy node, it cannot allocate addresses to other nodes, but it must send periodic Address_Refresh messages to the Gateway in order to prevent the gateway from sending additional Refresh_Request messages. When a proxy node(or a tentative proxy node) receives Refresh_Reply message with an extended lifetime, it must multicast Refresh_lifetime message using its proxy multicast address to the ad-hoc network in order to inform the other nodes in the group that the lifetime is extended.

Our address management uses timeout approach, so the Gateway might not receive any proper Address_Refresh message within timeout even if at least one node that sends the Address_Refresh message exists in ad-hoc network. Thus the Gateway must set timeout long enough for receiving reply and perform refresh request procedure again before it reallocates the recollected addresses to other nodes.

The state transition diagram of an ad-hoc node is depicted in Fig. 2. When a new mobile node enters in ad-hoc network and does not configure global address yet, it is in 'INIT' state. And then the node is in 'General' state if it receives a global address from a proxy. 'Proxy' state represents the proxy node and 'Tentative Proxy' state represents the tentative proxy node.

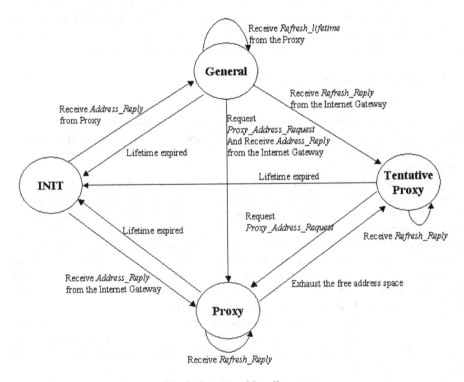

Fig. 2. State transition diagram

5 Fast Address Allocation for HMIPv6

5.1 Address Allocation for Mobile Node

Fast address allocation scheme using a proxy can be applied to HMIPv6. Hierarchical mobility management for Mobile IPv6 is designed to reduce the amount of signaling between the mobile node, its correspondent nodes, and its home agent. However, two DAD processes for LCoA and RCoA in HMIPv6 may disturb a seamless communication of mobile node. Using proxy scheme, we can remove DAD process for RCoA, thus increase HMIPv6 performance.

Using a proxy scheme in HMIPv6 is simple. MAP(Mobility Anchor Point) acts as an address allocation server and ARs(Access Routers) act as proxies. ARs in MAP domain have free address spaces allocated by MAP. In contrast to auto-configuration in MANET, free address spaces in ARs are pre-configured statically.

When a MAP advertises its RA(Router Advertisement) message and MAP option, it adds a new flag to RA message in order to inform that it can act as an address allocation server, so the new node must request a new address to the MAP. This flag must be included in ARs' RA messages, too.

When a new mobile node enters into a MAP domain, it receives a RA from its AR and it knows that it must configure RCoA using proxy scheme. So, it first auto-configures an LCoA as described in [3] and then requests an RCoA to its AR using Address_Request message. The AR selects a new unique address in its address space and allocates this address to the new node by Address_Reply message. When the new node receives the address from the AR, it sets this address as RCoA and sends a binding update to the MAP with the LCoA and the RCoA.

In HMIPv6, MAP must perform DAD for the received RCoA in Binding Updates message on behalf of the new node. However, in our solution, RCoA of the new node is unique, so DAD is not necessary. In our scheme, only one DAD for LCoA is required.

If a new node attaches directly to the MAP, it will require an address to the MAP. But the MAP will not allocate proxy address space to the new node, instead it will allocate an ordinary single address. In other words, in HMIPv6, all proxy nodes must be configured statically, thus there are no dynamically allocated proxy nodes.

In HMIPv6, a new node configures LCoA before configuring RCoA, and it receives RCoA to its AR not to the MAP, thus in contrast to the address allocation for MANET, address allocation for HMIPv6 does not require an initiator node.

5.2 Address Management in HMIPv6

In MANET, proxies are mobile nodes, but in HMIPv6, proxies are static routers. So, MAP does not need to manage addresses allocated to proxies. Instead, MAP manages addresses allocated to mobile nodes using Mobile IPv6 Binding Updates.

All mobile nodes which configured RCoA in MAP domain must perform a binding updates to the MAP with its RCoA and LCoA. Whenever a mobile node changes its point of attachment, it sends binding updates message to the MAP. Even if the mobile node does not change its point of attachment, it must sends binding updates message to the MAP before its lifetime is expired. Thus, if the lifetime of mobile node which is registered in MAP's binding cache is expired, the MAP can assume that the mobile node moves out of its MAP domain.

When the MAP knows that a mobile node's lifetime was expired, it finds the proxy AR who allocated address to the mobile node by proxy id of the address, and informs the absence of the mobile node to the AR. Eventually, address management in HMIPv6 is performed by each proxy ARs.

6 Performance Evaluation

6.1 Address Allocation for MANET

The primary goal of the simulation is to gather statistics regarding delays in getting global address. Especially, we focus on effectiveness of using proxies. We assume that nodes are moving according to a random waypoint mobility model [13]. In our simulation environment, we set the pause time to be 10 seconds and the node speeds to be randomly distributed between 2 and 10m/s. Nodes move in a square area. Networks of the maximum size of 30, 50 and 100 nodes were investigated.

Our simulation scenario starts with only one static node, Internet Gateway, and adds other mobile nodes in the simulation area at 2, 100 and 200 seconds in simulation time. Every nodes can move to anywhere in the test area so that the network partition and merger may occur often during the simulation. Parameters used in the simulation are displayed in Table 1. We used ns-2 simulator to perform simulation and analyze the performance.

Table 1. Simulation parameters

Parameters	Values
Total Number of Nodes	30, 50, 100, 150, 200
Simulation Area	500m x 500m, 750m x 750m, 1000m x 1000m, 1200m x 1200m, 1500m x 1500m
Advertisement Interval	3000ms
Ad-hoc Routing Protocols	AODV, DSDV
MAC	802.11
Transmission Range	100m

When a new node recognize ad-hoc network by receiving an advertisement message, it sends AREQ and receive AREP. We evaluated this round trip time as global address allocation latency. In order to verify the efficiency of proxy, we compared the performance of proxy scheme with the performance of non-proxy scheme.

Without a proxy, every new node must receive an available global address from the Internet Gateway. Non-proxy scheme can be a good substitution for DHCPv6 or other ad-hoc auto-configuration schemes.

Fig. 3 shows the address allocation latency of each node in the ad-hoc network. Figure (a) and (b) shows comparison between AODV and DSDV. Figure (a) shows address allocation latency until a new node which receives a global address from it sends an AREQ message. Figure (b) shows latency when a new node which receives a global address from it comes into the simulation area. When a new node enters into the simulation area, it may participate in ad-hoc network immediately or not. Fig. 3 (a) and (b) represent our proxy scheme can be applied in different ad-hoc routing protocol and produce good performance.

Fig. 3 (c) and (d) show address allocation latency comparison between proxy scheme and non-proxy scheme using AODV when the total number of nodes in simulation area is 50 and 100. At first, when there are few proxy nodes in ad-hoc network, the effect of having proxies is small. But when there are some proxy nodes in ad-hoc network, the effect of proxies in allocating address to new mobile nodes is increasing. When a proxy node is located uniformly and if more nodes exist in an ad-hoc network, we get better performance.

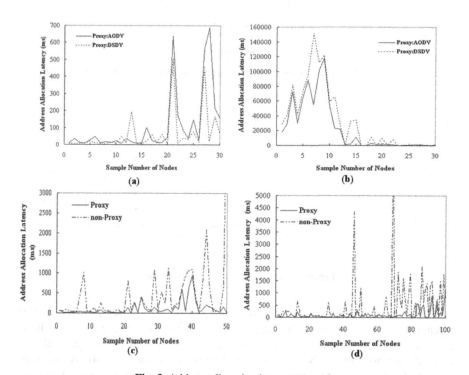

Fig. 3. Address allocation latency per node

In fig. 3. (c) and (d), some nodes take a great deal of time to receive addresses. It means that network partitioning now happen. After the network partitions, ad-hoc routing delay may increase. Thus, the allocation latency may increase too. However, in the proxy scheme, a new node can acquire an address from the proxy nodes which exists in the same partition without additional routing delay.

Some nodes using proxy scheme take longer time compared with non-proxy scheme. By analyzing the log data, we can explain the reason. First, there are some delays in ad-hoc routing and MAC 802.11 because of congestion in proxy. Second, the information of proxy node in initiator is expired. So hop counts between proxy node and the initiator are more than one hop. This situation occurs because lifetime of proxy advertisement is longer than the interval of proxy advertisement. Fig. 4 shows address allocation latency comparison when the total number of nodes in simulation area is 200.

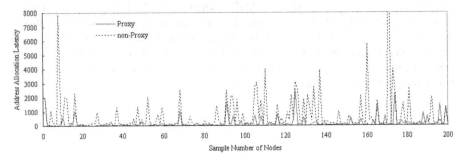

Fig. 4. Address allocation latency per node, number of nodes: 200

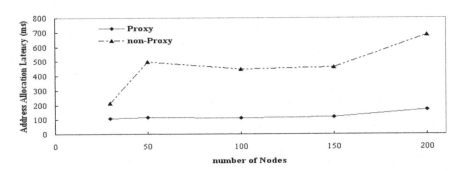

Fig. 5. Average address allocation latency

Fig. 5 shows the average address allocation latency of the networks using AODV. In general, as more nodes are included in the network, the average node density of one node increases too. So, the allocation latency does not increase dramatically. In proxy scheme, we can see the average allocation increases more slowly. As the number of nodes increase, the number of proxies increases too. Thus, proxy nodes are distributed equally in ad-hoc network. As a result, the address allocation latency does not increase a lot.

According to the simulation results, we know that the proposed solution in this paper gets more flexible and scalable as the size of ad-hoc network increases.

6.2   Address Allocation for HMIPv6

The primary goal of the simulation in HMIPv6 is to measure TCP stream when using our proxy scheme. Appling a proxy scheme, we don't need to perform DAD for RCoA.

Fig. 6 shows a simulation network and Table 2 represents the simulation parameters. We simulated that MN(Mobile Node) starts TCP session with CN(Correspondent Node) at 4 seconds and move to a foreign network at 5 seconds during the simulation. Beginning the TCP session, MN starts sending some amount of data to CN. The maximum segments size is 1024 bytes. We assume there is no transmission error. We used OMNet++ [14] to perform a simulation and analyze the performance of our solution.

Table 2. TCP simulation parameter

Parameters	Values
DAD Timeout	1 second
DAD Retries	1
TCP Application	FTP
TCP Algorithm	TCP Reno
TCP MSS	1024
TCP Advertised Window Size	14336 # 14*mss

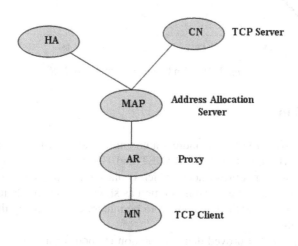

Fig. 6. Simulation network

Fig. 7 shows the simulation results. In order to show the status of TCP session, we printed the sending sequence number of MN. In order to compare the results, we simulated three situations. One is that MN stays at home network during TCP session. The others are that MN moves to a foreign network and starts HMIPv6 with or without proxy scheme.

The dotted line on the top by circle represents the send sequence of MN at home network. Our TCP application repeatedly sends some amount of data and stops for a while. So, we can see the results as fig. 7.

In fig. 7, mobile node at foreign network suffers data loss for long latency of binding updates whether using proxy scheme or not. With proxy, however, mobile node can continue TCP session with minimum latency. Otherwise, without proxy, it is hard to continue TCP session. TCP application in mobile node does not know that MN is moving, thus if there is no acknowledgement for some period, TCP session will be closed.

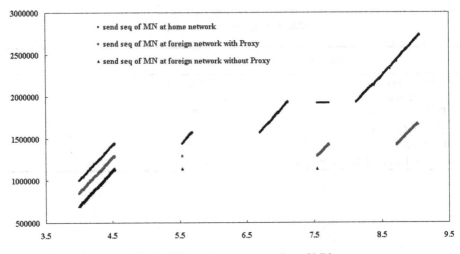

Fig. 7. TCP send sequence number of MN

7   Conclusion

This paper proposes a fast IPv6 address auto-configuration scheme using a proxy for IPv6 mobile environment such as MANET and HMIPv6. Since a new node gets a global IP address from a proxy node, which is placed near the new node, we can improve the performance of auto-configuration as shown in our simulations. Moreover, the proposed protocol is flexible enough to be integrated with many different ad-hoc routing protocols.

In this paper, we just proved that our solution is good for mobile environment, but proxy scheme can be applied to a wired network as well. Actually, we expect our proxy scheme to replace DHCPv6 in many situations.

Acknowledgement

This research was supported by the MIC(Ministry of Information and Communication), Korea, under the ITRC(Information Technology Research Center) support program supervised by the IITA(Institute of Information Technology Assessment).

References

1. R. Droms, J. Bound, B. Volz, T. Lemon, C. Perkins, and M. Carney: Dynamic Host Configuration Protocol for IPv6 (DHCPv6). Request for Comments 3315. Internet Engineering Task Force (2003)
2. S. Thomson, T. Narten: IPv6 Stateless Address Autoconfiguration. Request for Comments 2462. Internet Engineering Task Force (1998)
3. H. Soliman, C. Castelluccia, K. El Malki, and L. Bellier: Hierarchical Mobile IPv6 Mobility Management (HMIPv6). Request for Comments 4140. Internet Engineering Task Force (2005)
4. S. Corson, J. Macker: Mobile Ad hoc Networking (MANET): Routing Protocol Performance Issues and Evaluation Considerations. Request for Comments 2501. Internet Engineering Task Force (1999)
5. C. Perkins, P. Bhagwat: Highly Dynamic Destination-Sequenced Distance-Vector Routing (DSDV) for Mobile Computers. In Proceedings of the ACM SIGCOMM'94 Conference on Communications Architectures, Protocols and Applications (1994)
6. Charles Perkins, Elizabeth Royer: Ad Hoc On-Demand Distance Vector Routing. In Proceedings of the 2nd IEEEWorkshop on Selected Areas in Communication (1999) 90–100
7. C.E. Perkins, J.T. Malinen, R. Wakikawa, E.M. Belding-Royer, and Y. Sun: IP Address Autoconfiguration for Ad Hoc Networks. Internet Draft. Internet Engineering Task Force (Work in Progress) (2001)
8. N. H. Vaidya: Weak Duplicate Address Detection in Mobile Ad Hoc Networks. In Proceedings of the 3rd ACM International Symposium on Mobile Ad Hoc Networking and Computing (MobiHoc'02) (2002) 206–216
9. Y.Sun, E. M. Belding-Royer, C. Perkins: Internet Connectivity for Ad hoc Mobile Networks. Intenational Joulnal of Wireless Information Networks special issue on Mobile Ad hoc Networks (2002)
10. S. Mesargi, R. Prakash: MANETconf: Configuration of Hosts in a Mobile Ad Hoc Network. In Proceedings of the IEEE Conference on Computer Communications (INFOCOM) (2002)
11. Dongkeun Lee, Jaepil You, Keecheon Kim, Kyunglim Kang: IPv6 Stateless Address Autoconfiguration in Mobile Ad-Hoc Network. Advanced Web and Network Technologies, and Applications(APWeb 2006). Lecture Notes in Computer Science, Vol. 3842. Springer-Verlag, Berlin Heidelberg New York (2006) 360–367
12. R. Hinden, S. Deering,: IP Version 6 Addressing Architecture. Request for Comments 3513, Internet Engineering Task Force (2003)
13. J. Broch, D. A. Maltz, D. B. Johnson, Y.-C. Hu, J. Jetcheva: A Performance Comparison of Multihop Wireless Ad Hoc Network Routing Protocols. In Proceedings of the 4th ACM/IEEE International Conference on Mobile Computing and Networking (MobiCOM'98) (1998) 85–97
14. András Varga.: The OMNeT++ Discrete Event Simulation System. In the Proceedings of the European Simulation Multiconference (2001)

Parametric Routing for Wireless Sensor Networks

Yeultak Sung and Hojung Cha

Department of Computer Science, Yonsei University
Seodaemum-gu, Shinchon-dong 134, Seoul 120-749, Korea
{uniarel, hjcha}@cs.yonsei.ac.kr

Abstract. Developing an ideal routing protocol that satisfies various wireless sensor network applications is difficult due to their different requirements. In this paper, we propose a parametric routing protocol that considers performance parameters such as time, reliability, and energy to satisfy various circumstances of wireless sensor network applications. Based on a geographic algorithm, the proposed protocol calculates each node's routing costs for three performance parameters and negotiates to select the next node. The framework supports adaptive service as well as scalability because the mechanism requires only neighboring nodes' information. The experiment shows that the proposed protocol provides adaptive services for various sensor networks applications.

1 Introduction

Applications in wireless sensor networks are developed in diverse fields; hence specifically-designed routing protocols for each application are required. For instance, object tracking applications such as Countersniper System [1] or Cricket System [2] need a real-time routing protocol, whereas a structural monitoring application [3] requires a reliable network protocol and an energy-efficient routing protocol is necessary for an environment monitoring system. One protocol in wireless sensor networks may not operate properly in another application.

Popular operating systems in wireless sensor networks such as TinyOS [4] and SOS [5] use a single image or loadable module to install software on sensor hardware. TinyOS is compiled with all required libraries, including a routing protocol and the single image, is generated. SOS offers a loadable module technique to install libraries efficiently. For those operating systems, application developers should understand details of the routing protocol. Moreover, they probably design and implement their own routing protocols. Thus, a general protocol considering various domains and simple APIs is required.

In this paper, we propose a parametric routing protocol that considers several performance domains such as time, reliability, and energy consumption. For the time domain, the protocol calculates a cost between the current node and the destination, the distance between the next node and the destination, and packet delay time. A link quality indicator, transmission success ratio, and buffer overflow are used for reliability. The protocol predicts a node's lifetime, based on battery residual, cutoff voltage and energy consumption rate. The key of the proposed parametric routing is the negotiation algorithm. When an application sets parameters using simple APIs ("care" or

H.Y. Youn, M. Kim, and H. Morikawa (Eds.): UCS 2006, LNCS 4239, pp. 428–439, 2006.

"don't care"), the current node selects the next one using the negotiation algorithm. Therefore, the proposed routing protocol operates different applications with desirable performance. Moreover, removing reinstallation of routing protocol reduces overhead for the code dissemination.

The remainder of the paper is organized as follows. Section 2 discusses related work. In Section 3, the details of parametric routing are introduced. The experimental results are discussed in Section 4. Finally, Section 5 concludes the paper with a discussion of future work.

2 Related Work

Routing protocols in wireless sensor networks have general requirements such as real-time, reliability, energy efficiency, depending on the characteristics of applications. Much research on routing protocols [6]-[13] has been conducted to satisfy these requirements, but they hardly cover all three requirements.

Protocols considering only one of those requirements are as follows. SPEED [6] and RAP [7] focus on time domain only. SPEED selects the next node in terms of speed estimation calculated by the distance from the current node to the destination, the distance from the next node to the destination, and transmission delay. It also provides a backpressure technique to prepare the failure of the next node. RAP is designed for burst real-time traffic. The mechanism calculates a cost from the distance from the current node to the destination, deadline and packet traveling time from the source to the current node. Thus, a packet traveling a longer distance receives higher priority. Woo et al. [8] propose a reliable routing protocol that calculates an average of transmission success ratio over a certain time period to select the next node. ReIn-ForM [9] is a multi-path routing providing reliability. A user selects a reliability level and the protocol estimates a number of next nodes satisfying users' expectation. Energy aware routing mainly focuses on maximizing the network lifetime. Chung's protocol [10] decides a path, based on the Bellman-Ford Algorithm, with transmission energy and residual energy. LEACH [11] is proposed to reduce transmission power by data aggregation and rotating a role of cluster header. However, the cluster structure causes other problems.

From the QoS point of view, some research has dealt with two domains. MMSPEED [12] is a routing protocol deliberating both time and reliability issues. The main idea to select a next relay node is adopted from SPEED [4] and ReInForM [9]. An energy-aware QoS routing protocol [13] sets a path depending on the energy consumption factors. Later, the protocol uses different queues to minimize collision for packets requiring real-time. However, the reliability issue is not considered in the protocol.

3 Parametric Routing Protocol

In this section, we present a parametric routing protocol that considers the key metrics of wireless sensor networks: time, reliability, and power issue. The following sub-sections discuss the system architecture, routing components, and the routing algorithm.

3.1 System Architecture

Fig.1 illustrates the system architecture for the parametric routing protocol. The system consists of user APIs, estimation components, the negotiation protocol, and greedy algorithm, and neighbor table manager. Before sending packets, a user should decide which domains are cared and set parameters through APIs. In order to select candidate nodes, the parametric routing uses the greedy forwarding routing method [14], which selects the nearest node from the destination. The difference between [14] and the greedy forwarding method we use is that the greedy algorithm of the parametric routing chooses multiple nodes that are near the destination. After choosing the candidates, estimation components, which are time, reliability and energy domain, calculate a domain cost based on information from a neighbor table. Finally, negotiation algorithm analyzes the cost of each domain and selects the next relaying node.

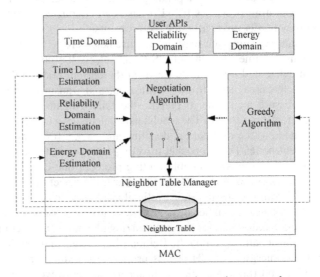

Fig. 1. Architecture for parametric routing protocol

The parametric routing works via negotiation among three independent domains of time, reliability and energy. Hence, the negotiation algorithm should make use of neighbor information, and the neighbor table manger plays the key role. A neighbor table has important information for parametric routing protocol, and the table is handled by the neighbor table manager. The manager periodically monitors the status of its neighbors and stores information in the neighbor table. The detailed scenario is as follows: The manager periodically broadcasts query to one-hop neighbors. Upon receiving the query, the neighbors send a reply message which includes its geographical position, delay time, LQI (Link Quality Indicator) and battery level. The manger node then updates the neighbor table with the new statistics, and provides latest information to the routing module via appropriate function calls shown in Table 1. This mechanism is similar to the beaconing which is commonly found in many routing protocols.

Table 1. Function calls for neighbor table manager

Component of Parametric Routing	Function Calls of NTM	Description
Time Domain Estimator	get_position()	Position of a neighbor node
	get_delay()	Delay time from receiving to sending
Reliability Domain Estimator	get_rate0	Delivery success rate of a neighbor node
	get_lqi()	Link quality of a neighbor node
Energy Domain Estimator	get_battery()	Battery level of a neighbor node

3.2 Routing Components

The negotiation algorithm for parametric routing protocol uses three components: time, reliability, and energy estimation. The estimation component for time uses the idea from SPEED [4]. Fig. 2 and Equation 1 explain how to calculate speed from distance information. Distance is calculated by subtracting the distance Ci to the destination D from the distance source S to destination D. Delay is packet relaying time at Ci.

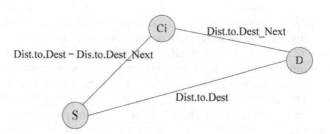

Fig. 2. Measurement distance of SPEED

$$Speed = \frac{Dist.to.Dest - Dist.to.Dest\_next}{delay(C_i)} \tag{1}$$

For reliability, the estimation component uses link quality indicator (LQI) and delivery success rate to select the reliable node as the next node. According to IEEE 802.15.4 [15], LQI is calculated by the ratio of the number of received packets to the error bits. Relay success rate is defined as the ratio of the number of received packets that should be relayed to the number of packets transmitted successfully within a certain time. In Equation 2, a reliable node is calculated by multiplying LQI to delivery success rate. That is, the estimation component considers not only network-wide reliability (LQI) but also local reliability (delivery success rate). Therefore, it accurately estimates the possible packet loss.

$$ReliableMedium = LQI \cdot DeliverySuccessRate \tag{2}$$

The estimation component considering energy uses battery residual to distribute packets to several nodes. Using the battery consumption rate, time to reach the cutoff voltage can be predicted. Based on the previous information, nodes can find the better energy-efficient paths to extend network lifetime.

$$V_{cutoff} = V_{current} - \frac{\Delta V}{\Delta t} \times LifeTime \tag{3}$$

$$LifeTime = \frac{(V_{current} - V_{cutoff}) \times \Delta t}{\Delta V} \tag{4}$$

According to Equation 3, the cutoff voltage is calculated by subtracting predicted voltage consumption from current voltage for remaining lifetime. Equation 4 is derived from Equation 3. Lifetime in Equation 4 is the predicted operating time to send and receive packets. Therefore, finding the node that has the highest lifetime brings the extension of network lifetime.

3.3 Negotiation Algorithm

The application determines the class where each packet should be sent with three parameters. The Application API is defined as *net_set_value (int time, int reliability, int energy)*. The parameters of the function determine each domain to consider. The application uses the function to setup the required domains of following packets. Each parameter is set to CARE or DONT_CARE. Candidate nodes are selected through the geometric forwarding algorithm with its neighbor table. Our algorithm considers the parameters of domain marked CARE and chooses the next node that is superior in CARE domain. On the other hand, the algorithm does not consider the DONT_CARE domain. Hence, a packet including DONT_CARE domains possibly travels good or bad performed nodes to a destination with information about those domains.

In order to process the negotiation, parameters of speed, reliable-medium and lifetime need to be adjusted in to the same metric. We express the performance by calculating the relative proportion of the value to the maximum cost of each domain metric. We use the largest domain value among the candidates as the maximum value of the domain and calculate the proportion P to the basis. Maximum value of candidates is used since the negotiation algorithm is not for guaranteeing the path but for best-effort. Equation 5 shows the calculation for proportion P.

$$P_{domain}(candidate) = \frac{Cost(candidate)}{MaxCost(\forall candidates)} \tag{5}$$

Fig. 3 shows an example of the parametric routing protocol. C1, C2 and C3 represent the candidates selected by the greedy algorithm among the neighbors of S. When the time domain values of candidates are 7, 10 and 4, the speed performance proportion

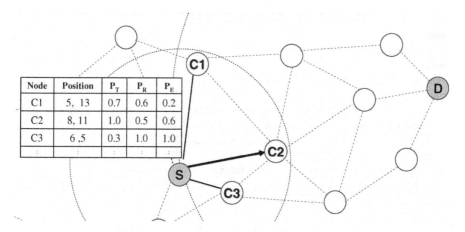

Node	Position	P_T	P_R	P_E
C1	5, 13	0.7	0.6	0.2
C2	8, 11	1.0	0.5	0.6
C3	6 ,5	0.3	1.0	1.0
:	:	:	:	:

Fig. 3. Selection of the next node of parametric routing protocol

P_T of candidates are 7/10, 10/10 and 3/10. Hence, C2 is the most appropriate node in the time domain. P_R and P_E, which represent the performance proportion of reliability and energy domains, are computed using the same method.

Users may set CARE to more than two domains when they want all the CARE domains to be satisfied. However, it is difficult to find a node that guarantees the best performance for all domains. We choose the node that has the largest weight through negotiation.

$$P_{sum}(candidate) = \sum_{i \in domain} P_i(candidate) \tag{6}$$

$$P_{difference}(candidate) = \sum_{i \in domain \cap \{j\}^c} |P_j(candidate) - P_i(candidate)| \tag{7}$$

$$W(candidate) = P_{sum}(candidate) - P_{difference}(candidate) \tag{8}$$

Equation 6 shows the summation of P in CARE domains for a candidate. P_{SUM} is used to find the candidate node that has the highest performance. $P_{difference}$ in Equation 7 is the summation of differences between all of the domains marked to CARE. A node with large difference among its CARE domains makes it difficult to satisfy the user's demand. Equation 8 shows the weight for final node selection. Fig. 4 shows the algorithm to select the next node with the weight. The general idea of the algorithm is to find the node that has high total performance and small performance differences among the domains. The algorithm works properly with one CARE domain since the $P_{difference}$ would be 0 in this case.

Suppose a user sets all the domains to CARE in the situation described in Fig. 3. P_{SUM} of each candidate is calculated as $P_T(C1) + P_R(C1) + P_E(C1) = 1.5$, $P_T(C2) + P_R(C2) + P_E(C2) = 2.1$ and $P_T(C3) + P_R(C3) + P_E(C3) = 2.3$. $P_{difference}$ of each candidate is calculated as $P_T(C1) - P_R(C1) + P_T(C1) - P_E(C1) P_R(C1) - P_E(C1) = 1.0$,

```
FOR each candidates in candidate list
begin
  FIND the maximum cost in each domain;
end
FOR each candidates in candidate list
begin
  P_domain := cost of each domain / maximum cost of each domain;
  CHOOSE a domain D1 which is marked CARE
  FOR each domain D2 which is marked CARE
  begin
    P_sum(candidate) := P_sum(candidate) + P_D2(candidate);
    P_difference(candidate) := P_difference(candidate) + P_D1(candidate) -
    P_D2(candidate);
  end
  W(candidate) := P_sum(candidate) - P_difference(candidate);
end
FIND a next node in candidates having the maximum W randomly;
```

Fig. 4. Negotiation Algorithm of Parametric Routing

$P_T(C2) - P_R(C2) + P_T(C2) - P_E(C2) + P_E(C2) - P_R(C2) = 1.0$ and $P_R(C3) - P_T(C3) + P_E(C3) - P_T(C3) + P_E(C3) - P_R(C3) = 1.4$. The final weights of each candidate are $W(C1) = 0.5$, $W(C2) = 1.1$ and $W(C3) = 0.9$. According to these results, our algorithm chooses C2 as the next node. The candidate C2 has higher performance on time domain and lower performance on reliability and energy domains than C3. However, the difference of total performance between C2 and C3 is insignificant and the domain performances of C2 are even.

The proposed parametric routing protocol provides various parameters for setting up the packets' requirements and operates appropriately for demands of various applications of wireless sensor networks through negotiation algorithm. The protocol is scalable because it selects candidates based on greedy forwarding algorithm.

4 Experiments

In this section, we validate the negotiation algorithm and analyze the path of packets delivery by actual experiments. We use RETOS [16] on Tmote Sky from Moteiv. RETOS is an operating system that is currently being developed in our laboratory. For updating neighbor table, a query is sent every 30 seconds by the table manger. The application changes the parameters in every second as shown in Table 2 and sets the cut-off voltage to 2V. The nodes are arbitrarily deployed in 4x4 grids. The length of each side of the little squares is 30cm. To prevent one hop communication between node number 1 and node number 6, we adjust the RF power to -35dBm. The minimum value of delta-V, in Equation 4, is set to 0.001 to prevent it from reaching 0. We analyze the experimental results of the proposed parametric routing for each domain and the effect of the negotiation. In the experiment, the situation has four different requirements. Packets are transmitted from node number 6 to the sink node.

Table 2. Delay time and success rate of each requirement

Requirement	Delivery time	Delivery Success Rate
(Time, Reliability, Energy)	(ms)	(%)
(CARE, DONT_CARE, DONT_CARE)	7.91	77
(DONT_CARE, CARE, DONT_CARE)	8.17	90
(DONT_CARE, DONT_CARE, CARE)	8.62	91
(CARE, CARE, CARE)	8.18	86

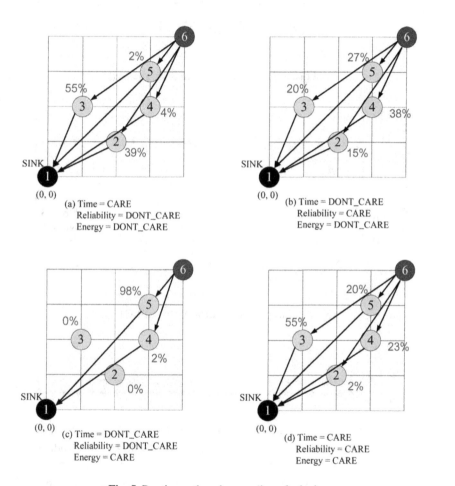

Fig. 5. Routing path and proportion of relaying

Fig. 5 (a) shows the packet path when the time domain is set to CARE. Most packets are sent to nodes 2 and 3, which are the farthest nodes from node 6. However, the delivery time of each node is continually changed, as shown in Fig. 6 (a). Although node 5 is closer to node 6 than nodes 2 and 3, it is selected as next node of node

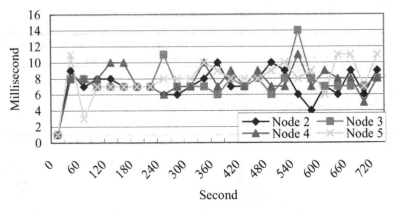

(a) Variation of delay time vs. a period

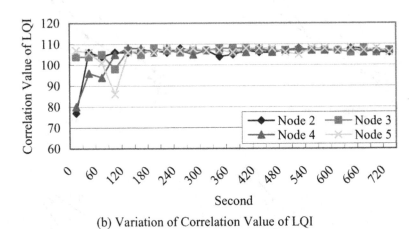

(b) Variation of Correlation Value of LQI

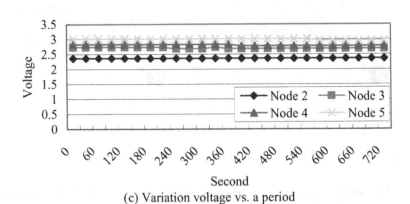

(c) Variation voltage vs. a period

Fig. 6. Battery level is stable, but LQI and delivery time continually change

number 6 because it has a significantly smaller packet delivery delay time. Node number 4 has less selectivity because it is close to node 6 and generally has a similar delay time as compared to the other nodes.

Fig. 5 (b) shows the result when the reliability domain is set to CARE. The decisive factor for the performance cost is LQI since the relay success rate in the node is 100%. As shown in Fig. 6 (b), the quality of the link begins to stabilize after 120 seconds. The nodes are evenly selected as the next node. Fig. 5 (c) shows the routing path that considers the remaining battery power. Most of packets are transmitted to node number 4 because it has the highest battery power. Few packets are delivered to node number 5 in the period of 570 seconds. This is because the delta-T in Equation 4 of node 5 grows relatively bigger than that of node 4 by the voltage drop of node 5. The delivery path is return to node number 4 after the period. Fig. 5 (d) shows the result when all the domains are set to CARE. Since node number 3 has good performance in the time and reliability domains and normal performance in the energy domain, more than half of the packets are sent to node 3. Table 2 shows the effect of the experiment. When the time domain is considered, the delivery time is relatively low because the SPEED algorithm considers not only the distance but also time. Since the algorithm does not consider the quality of link, relative success rate decreases. When all of the domains are considered, the delivery time is similar and the success rate is lower than the cases just considering the reliability domain. The delivery time is longer and success rate is higher than the case when the time domain is considered. According to Table 2, general performance is decreased when all domains are considered; however, we can see that node number 2 is excluded as a next node because it has the lowest battery power. In other words, the negotiation operates properly.

5 Conclusion and Future Work

The proposed parametric routing offers the best-effort service when applications have a request in one domain and adaptive service when applications have requirements in two or three domains by means of computing cost in time, reliability and energy domains that applications generally request. Thus, the application programmer is relieved from developing their own routing protocols, and it is cost effective to disseminate code because parametric routing can support three domains and be loaded on a sensor node as a module. The parametric routing recognizes the state of nodes in the networks, real-time packets are transmitted fast, packets for reliability are transmitted more reliably and energy aware packets are transmitted following a path that consists of nodes having enough energy. If a packet requires "care" about all domains, parametric routing negotiates with them and offers appropriated service. The negotiation algorithm we proposed can be applied to more parameters. Thus, parametric routing is possibly expended with a cost estimation algorithm of a domain that sensor network applications require is newly suggested.

In our future work, we plan to study how differentiated service for the time and reliability domain can be supported precisely by packets having different requirements in the same network, such as periodic and alert packets of an application, and fill the buffer of a node. One possible approach is priority based multiple queues.

Acknowledgements

This work was supported by the National Research Laboratory (NRL) program of the Korean Science and Engineering Foundation (2005-01352) and the ITRC Program (MMRC) of IITA, Korea.

References

1. Ledeczi A., Volgyesi P., Maroti M., Simon G., Balogh G., Nadas A., Kusy B., Dora S., Pap G.: Multiple Simultaneous Acoustic Source Localization in Urban Terrain. IPSN 05, CD-Rom, Los Angeles, CA, (2005).
2. Nissanka B. Priyantha, Anit Chakraborty, Hari Balakrishnan: The Cricket location-support system, Proceedings of the 6th annual international conference on Mobile computing and networking. Boston, Massachusetts, United States, (2000).
3. N. Xu, S. Rangwala, K. K. Chintalapudi, D. Ganesan, A. Broad, R. Govindan, and D. Estrin: A wireless sensor network for structural monitoring. Proceedings of the 2nd international conference on Embedded networked sensor systems (SenSys), (2004).
4. Philip Levis, Sam Madden, David Gay, Joe Polastre, Robert Szewczyk, Alec Woo, Eric Brewer and David Culler: The Emergence of Networking Abstractions and Techniques in TinyOS. Proceedings of the First USENIX/ACM Symposium on Networked Systems Design and Implementation (NSDI), (2004).
5. Chih-Chieh Han, Ram Kumar Rengaswamy, Roy Shea, Eddie Kohler and Mani Srivastava: SOS: A dynamic operating system for sensor networks. Proceedings of the Third International Conference on Mobile Systems, Applications, and Services (Mobisys), (2005).
6. T. He et al.: SPEED: A stateless protocol for real-time communication in sensor networks. Proceedings of the International Conference on Distributed Computing Systems, Providence, RI, (2003).
7. C. Lu, B. M. Blum, T. F. Abdelzaher, J. A. Stankovic, and T. He: RAP: A Real-Time Communication Architecture for Large-Scale Wireless Sensor Networks. Proceedings of IEEE Real-Time and Embedded Technology and Applications Symposium (RTAS 2002), San Jose, CA, (2002).
8. B. Deb, S. Bhatnagar, and B. Nath: ReInForM: Reliable Information Forwarding Using Multiple Paths in Sensor Networks. Proceedings of IEEE International Conference on Local Computer Networks, pp. 406–415, (2003).
9. Alec Woo, Terence Tong, David Culler: Taming the underlying challenges of reliable multihop routing in sensor networks. Proceedings of the 1st international conference on Embedded networked sensor systems, Los Angeles, California, USA, (2003).
10. J.-H. Chang and L. Tassiulas: Maximum Lifetime Routing in Wireless Sensor Networks. IEEE Transactions on Networking VOL. 12, NO. 4 (2004).
11. 11 W. Heinzelman, A. Chandrakasan, and H. Balakrishnan,: Energy-Efficient Communication Protocols for Wireless Microsensor Networks. Proceedings of Hawaaian Int'l Conf. on Systems Science, (2000).
12. E. Felemban, C.-G. Lee, E. Ekici, R. Boder, and S. Vural: Probabilistic QoS Guarantee in Reliability and Timeliness Domains in Wireless Sensor Networks. Proceedings of IEEE INFOCOM 2005, Miami, FL, USA, (2005).

13. K. Akkaya and M. Younis: An Energy-Aware QoS Routing Protocol for Wireless Sensor Networks. Proceedings of the IEEE Workshop on Mobile and Wireless Networks (MWN 2003), Providence, RI, (2003).

14. B. Karp and H. Kung: GPSR: greedy perimeter stateless routing for wireless networks. In Mobile Computing and Networking, pages 243-254, (2000).

15. IEEE std. 802.15.4 - 2003: Wireless Medium Access Control (MAC) and Physical Layer (PHY) specifications for Low Rate Wireless Personal Area Networks (LR-WPANs) .

16. H. Kim and H. Cha: Towards a Resilient Operating System for Wireless Sensor Networks. Proceedings of the 2006 USENIX Annual Technical Conference, Boston, NY, USA, (2006).

Analyzing the Effect of a Block FEC Algorithm's Symbol Size on Energy Consumption in Wireless Sensor Networks

Jong-Suk Ahn[1], Young-Su Lee[1],
Jong-Hyuk Yoon[1], and Kang-Woo Lee[2]

[*] Department of Computer Engineering, Dong-Guk University, Seoul, South Korea[**]
{jahn, diwkd, ronaldo}@dongguk.edu
[*] Department of Information and Communication Engineering,
Dong-Guk University, Seoul, South Korea
klee@dongguk.edu

Abstract. This paper evaluates the effect of a block Forward Error Correction (FEC) algorithm's symbol size on power consumption in wireless sensor networks (WSN). The WSN channels exhibit frequent bursty errors with a high average Bit Error Rate (BER) due to low transmission power, random deployment, and moving intermediate objects obstructing WSN communications. For resisting against the bursty errors, WSN would adopt a block FEC algorithm that restores more tainted bits than other kinds of FEC algorithms as errors become burstier since it recovers errors symbol-by-symbol not bit-by-bit. Even when the same amount of bits are allocated for FEC code, different FEC symbol size meaning different number of FEC symbols vary the packet error rate and the transmission energy over a given WSN. They also affect the computational energy since their decoding and encoding complexities depend on the number of FEC symbols per packet. The analytical evaluation based on long-term sensor traffic traces indicates that the appropriate FEC symbol size saves a sensor node's energy consumption by up-to 85 % comparing to other sizes.

1 Introduction

Recently sensor network researchers propose various power-conserving algorithms to reduce the power waste of sensor networks to extend sensor node's life due to the difficulty of replacing their battery. Much research for efficiently achieving reliable transmission over wireless sensor channels, especially, have been actively conducted since frequent retransmissions of packets due to their corruption dissipate a large amount of energy. One technique for accomplishing reliable transmission against the noisy channels would be the adoption of an appropriate

[**] This work is in part supported by a grant (5NK0503502) from the basic research program of Korea Science and Engineering Foundation (KOSEF) and a grant (2005-0211-0) from SEOUL METROPOLITAN GOVERNMENT.

H.Y. Youn, M. Kim, and H. Morikawa (Eds.): UCS 2006, LNCS 4239, pp. 440–453, 2006.

FEC algorithm since the hybrid technique [1], [2], combining FEC and Automatic Request (ARQ) algorithms is more effective at reducing the number of retransmissions than ARQ technique alone, over prolonged bursty error channels. During this persisted error interval, the repeated retransmission without FEC codes would be useless since all subsequently retransmitted packets are likely to be corrupt as the previous one.

The FEC algorithm, however, deteriorates the performance when the inappropriate amount of FEC code is attached comparing to the channel BER [3]. It, furthermore, degrades the performance by selecting an unsuitable symbol size when it is a block FEC algorithm. Note that among diverse kinds of FEC algorithms, WSN prefer the linear or block FEC algorithm which effectively deals with short-term bursty errors. It is due to that with a given amount of FEC check bits, the block FEC algorithm recovers errors symbol-by-symbol, not bit-by-bit regardless of how many bits are stale in each error symbol. It leads to that as far as errors tend to grouped together, the block FEC algorithm tends to correct more error bits.

When the FEC symbol size in Reed-Solomon (RS) algorithm [4], one of representative block algorithms is s bits, the maximum size C_{size} of its codeword that it generates is $2^s - 1$ symbols or $(2^s - 1) * s$ bits. The codeword consisting of a pair of user data to protect and their corresponding FEC code also known as check bits is represented as (C_{size}, D_{size}) where D_{size} is the size of the user data. In this instance, the FEC code of $C_{size} - D_{size}$ symbols corrects as many as $(C_{size} - D_{size})/2$ error symbols since RS algorithm requires two FEC symbols to correct one error symbol.

When RS algorithm generates its FEC code for a packet, the FEC symbol size s affects the power consumption for successfully transmitting a packet even when it reserves the same amount of bits since s varies two energy-related metrics, the complexity of encoding and decoding the FEC code and the number of retransmissions. The computation complexity of synthesis and analysis of the packet FEC code is exponentially proportional to s while the number of retransmissions grows as s becomes smaller when channel errors are burstier. Note that the small s is effective at the uniformly distributed errors than the large one since a packet holds many codewords each of which independently restores its errors. Conversely, the large s outperforms over bursty errors since the FEC code is more likely to collectively cooperate to recover errors occurred in any part of the packet.

This paper analyzes the impact of the FEC symbol size on the computation energy and transmission energy based on wireless channels modeled as a uniform distribution and packet traces collected from real WSN channels. The trace-based analyses show that the total power expenditure widely varies by 85 % maximally depending on the FEC symbol size of RS algorithm.

This paper is organized as follows. Section 2 and 3 analytically estimate the power demand of FEC code computations and transmissions respectively as a function of the FEC symbol size. Section 4 experimentally calibrates the total power consumption based on channels modeled with real WSN traces. Section 5

finally summarizes some observations from our experiments and presents our
to-do-list.

2   The Effect of the FEC Symbol Size on Computation Power

This section estimates the amount of power that sensor nodes consume to encode and decode RS check bits. The power demand by RS algorithm is known
to be determined by the total codeword length n and the check-bit length t as
shown in (1) [5] where E_{add} and E_{mult} represent the energy spent for executing one addition and one multiplication instruction respectively. Note that (1)
only accommodates the power consumption of the FEC decoder since the power
necessary for the FEC encoder is assumed to be negligible.

$$E_{dec} = (2nt + 2t^2) * (E_{add} + E_{mult}) . \quad (1)$$

Table 1 measures the actual power consumption of TIP50CM [6] exhibiting
the same performance as Moteiv Telos [7] when it executes RS program [8] to
encode and decode five different RS codewords depicted in Fig. 1 where n and u in
$RS(n, u)$ represent the total codeword size and the data size in the unit of symbols
respectively. TIP50CM employs TI's MSP430f149 low-power processor requiring
3 V voltage and $240\,\mu$A current for processing one instruction. For evaluating
the actual power in Table 1, we measure the encoding or decoding time t_{proc} of
RS program for each different number of errors by counting the internal clock
counter of TIP50CM. And we compute the total energy to spend by (2) under the
assumption that each instruction's execution consumes almost the same amount
of voltage and current regardless of the instruction type. This assumption is
known to be true when processors like TIP50CM adopt the pipeline technique.

$$E = V \cdot I \cdot t_{proc} . \quad (2)$$

Table 1 indicates that the encoding energy of the RS program is comparable
to the decoding energy differently from the assumption for (1) [5]. It is only
less two times maximally than the decoding one in all error cases. Table 1 also
describes the total decoding energy monotonically increases as the number of
error symbols, the size of codewords, and the number of corrupt symbols grows
even though the energy for uncorrectable errors is slightly less than one for the
maximum correctable number of error symbols.

Since different FEC symbol sizes produce different codeword sizes, they require different packet formats to accommodate a fixed amount of data. For the
fair comparison of energy consumption as a function of FEC symbol size, we assume one possible hypothetical packet configuration shown in Fig. 2 which fixes
the amount of FEC code depicted by gray boxes to 11-byte and the size of user
payload described by white boxes to 69-byte. Note that since the packet size,
80-byte in this example is not the multiples of codewords of every symbol size,
the total amount of check bits and user data in Fig. 2 are not the same. The

Table 1. Energy consumption for encoding and decoding RS code

RS code	The number of error symbols	Encoding time (sec)	Decoding time (sec)	Encoding energy (mJ)	Decoding energy (mJ)
(15, 13)	0	0.2561	0.3266	0.1844	0.2352
	1	0.2561	0.4566	0.1844	0.3288
	uncorrectable	0.2561	0.3215	0.1844	0.2315
(31, 27)	0	0.4860	0.5946	0.3499	0.4281
	1	0.4860	0.7208	0.3499	0.5290
	2	0.4860	0.8444	0.3499	0.6080
	uncorrectable	0.4860	0.6717	0.3499	0.4836
(63, 55)	0	0.7820	0.9544	0.5631	0.6872
	1	0.7820	1.0753	0.5631	0.7743
	2	0.7820	1.1865	0.5631	0.8543
	3	0.7820	1.3030	0.5631	0.9382
	4	0.7820	1.4253	0.5631	1.0262
	uncorrectable	0.7820	1.2775	0.5631	0.9198
(127, 115)	0	1.2219	1.4381	0.8798	1.0354
	1	1.2219	1.5896	0.8798	1.1445
	2	1.2219	1.7240	0.8798	1.2413
	3	1.2219	1.8633	0.8798	1.3416
	4	1.2219	2.0075	0.8798	1.4454
	5	1.2219	2.1565	0.8798	1.5527
	6	1.2219	2.3104	0.8798	1.6635
	uncorrectable	1.2219	2.2175	0.8798	1.5966
(255, 245)	0	2.1638	2.4350	1.5579	1.7532
	1	2.1638	3.4301	1.5579	2.4697
	2	2.1638	3.4220	1.5579	2.4639
	3	2.1638	3.5982	1.5579	2.5907
	4	2.1638	3.5980	1.5579	2.5906
	5	2.1638	3.5981	1.5579	2.5906
	uncorrectable	2.1638	3.3896	1.5579	2.4405

check-bit of $Symbol_8$ is, for example, 80-bit while that of $Symbol_7$ is 84-bit. We believe that these slight differences would insignificantly affect the validity of our energy analysis.

When the codeword size C_{size} is less than the given packet size P_{size}, a packet needs to concatenate several codewords enough to cover the packet's user payload as in $Symbol_4$, $Symbol_5$, and $Symbol_6$ of Fig. 2. Note that $symbol_i$ means i-bit FEC symbol size. When C_{size} is greater than P_{size} as in the last block of the three upper symbol sizes, $Symbol_7$, $Symbol_8$, and $Symbol_9$ in Fig. 2, the t FEC code is generated from the remaining data or $P_{size} - t$ user data. For the encoding computation, we assume that the packet holds $C_{size} - P_{size} - t$ null data even though these null data are not actually delivered. The FEC decoder at

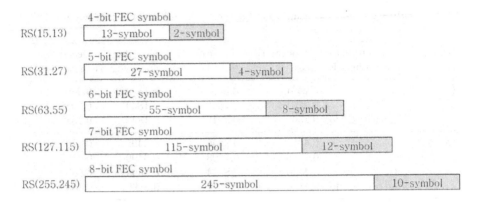

Fig. 1. Codeword configurations for five different FEC symbol sizes

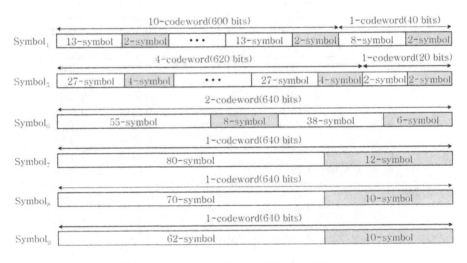

Fig. 2. Packet configurations for six different FEC symbol sizes

receivers verifies the transferred FEC codeword after padding the same amount of null data. In $Symbol_7$, for instance, it attaches null data of 35 symbols (= $((2^7 - 1) - 80 - 12)$) for checking the transmitted 12-symbol FEC code.

Figure 3 displays the encoding energy E_{enc} and three average decoding energy per packet, $E_{dec\_no\_error}$ for no-error state, $E_{dec\_correctable\_error}$ for correctable-error state, and $E_{dec\_uncorrectable\_error}$ for uncorrectable-error state. Since numerous cases belong to these two correctable error and uncorrectable error state, (3) and (4) at first compute two average process time $t_{correctable}$ and $t_{uncorrectable}$ by summing each case's processing time multiplied by each case's occurrence probability. When a packet contains n codewords and each codeword repairs t stale symbols maximally in (3), the total process time of a correctable case where the number of codewords holding 0, 1, 2, ..., t corrupt symbols are $k_0, k_1, ..., k_t$

respectively would be $k_0 t_0 + k_1 t_1 + \ldots + k_t t_t$ where t_i represents the recovery time of $i(0 \leq i \leq t)$ corrupt symbols within a codeword. Note that each k_i can range from 0 to n while $k_0 + k_1 + \ldots + k_t$ should be equal to n. Since the sum of all these correctable cases is $(t+1)^n$ and the number of occurrences corresponding to this case is $C_n^{k_0} * C_{n-k_0}^{k_1} * \ldots * C_{n-k_0-k_1-\ldots-k_{t-1}}^{k_t}$ equivalent to the number of ways to orderly pick up $k_0, k_1, \ldots, k_t$, sequentially out of n codewords, the probability of this case is $(C_n^{k_0} * C_{n-k_0}^{k_1} * \ldots * C_{n-k_0-k_1-\ldots-k_{t-1}}^{k_t})/(t+1)^n$. Note that C_n^k is the combination operator implying the number of choosing k out of n distinct objects.

Differently from (3), (4) shows that $t_{uncorrectable}$ consists of two terms, the time to correct j codewords contaminated with the repairable number of error symbols where j ranges from 0 to $n-1$ and t_{t+1} to process the uncorrectable $(j+1)$-th codeword. Note that RS program terminates its decoding operation as soon as it meets the first uncorrectable codeword. The first term of (4) averages the recovery time of j correctable codewords by multiplying $1/n$ after summing all delays for recovering j correctable codewords when j spans from 0 to $n-1$.

$$t_{correctable} = \sum_{k_t=0}^{n-(k_0+k_1+\ldots+k_t)} \cdots \sum_{k_2=0}^{n-(k_0+k_1)} \sum_{k_1=0}^{n-k_0} \sum_{k_0=0}^{n-1}$$

$$\frac{C_n^{k_0} * C_{n-k_0}^{k_1} * \ldots * C_{n-k_0-k_1-\ldots-k_{t-1}}^{k_t}}{(t+1)^n}(k_0 t_0 + k_1 t_1 + \ldots + k_t t_t) \qquad (3)$$

$$\text{where } k_0 + k_1 + \ldots + k_t = n .$$

$$t_{uncorrectable} = \frac{1}{n}\sum_{j=0}^{n-1}\left(\sum_{k_t=0}^{j-(k_0+k_1+\ldots+k_t)} \cdots \sum_{k_2=0}^{j-(k_0+k_1)} \sum_{k_1=0}^{j-k_0} \sum_{k_0=0}^{j} \right.$$

$$\left. \frac{C_j^{k_0} * C_{j-k_0}^{k_1} * \ldots * C_{j-k_0-k_1-\ldots-k_{t-1}}^{k_t}}{(t+1)^n}(k_0 t_0 + k_1 t_1 + \ldots + k_t t_t) \right) + t_{t+1} \qquad (4)$$

$$\text{where } k_0 + k_1 + \ldots + k_t = j .$$

Figure 3 displays that E_{enc} almost linearly increases in proportional to the symbol size, resulting in 68 % difference between 4-bit and 8-bit symbol sizes since the user data to process is almost equivalent even though the amount of user data to process exponentially grows as FEC symbol size expands. Figure 3 also confirms that each RS decoding time continues to increase as a function of FEC symbol size as the encoding energy. It also illustrates that $E_{dec\_correctable\_error}$ is 28 % at least larger than $E_{dec\_no\_error}$ at all symbol sizes since the rectification of errors requires more code lines to run. It finally indicates that $E_{dec\_uncorrectable\_error}$ is little less than $E_{dec\_no\_error}$ at $Symbol_4$ since RS code finishes its recovery operation as soon as it reaches the uncorrectable codeword without checking the remaining ones in Fig. 2. As the number of codewords packed in the packet diminishes, $E_{dec\_uncorrectable\_error}$ becomes similar to $E_{dec\_correctable\_error}$.

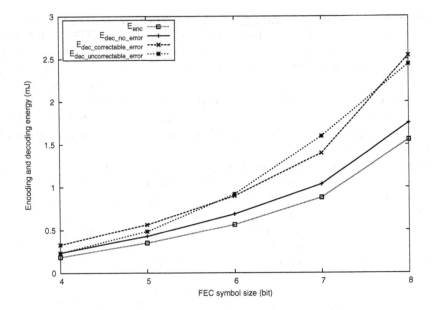

Fig. 3. Energy consumption of encoding and decoding

3   The Effect of the FEC Symbol Size on Energy Consumption for Transmission

This section analytically analyzes the effect of the FEC symbol size on transmission energy over wireless channels modeled with a uniform error distribution. At first, (5) specifies the relation between the FEC symbol error probability P_f and transmission symbol error probability P_e when an FEC symbol is composed of c transmission symbols. Note that wireless networks tend to modulate several consecutive bits into one transmission symbol for speedup. Equation (5) indicates that a FEC symbol is contaminated when any transmission symbol out of c ($= m/h$) transmission symbols is corrupted where one transmission and FEC symbol are h and m bits respectively. In TIP50CM, for example, h is 2-bit since it employs offset-DQPSK (Differential Quadrature Phase Shift Keying) for modulation and m is a variable generally greater than 2-bit. P_e is analytically calculated as in (6) [9] where E_b, M, and N_0 denote energy per bit, the degree of modulation, and white noise's energy respectively.

$$P_f = 1 - (1 - P_e)^c .$$

(5)

$$P_e = 2Q\left(\sqrt{\frac{2hE_b}{N_0}} * \sin\left(\frac{\pi}{M}\right)\right) .$$

(6)

Equation (7) and (8) compute the probability P_c of successfully recovering a packet by RS algorithm when the size of one packet is n symbols including

t-symbol FEC code. When $n \le (2^m - 1)$, P_c is the probability that the number of corrupt symbols is less than $t/2$ out of n symbols. When $n > (2^m - 1)$, P_c is the probability that the number of corrupt symbols is less than $t/2d$ in each codeword since t FEC symbols are assumed to be equally assigned over d ($= n/(2^m - 1)$) codewords for their check bits. When d is not an integer, the check-bit size of the last codeword needs to be appropriately determined like 2 symbols at $Symbol_5$ in Fig. 2. In this case, the probability of recovering the last codeword should be computed separately and multiplied with the recovery probabilities of the previous codewords. For example, P_c of $Symbol_5$ in Fig. 2 would be $(6.77 * 10^{-1})^4 * (9.77 * 10^{-1})$ since the repair probabilities of the first 4 codewords and the last one are $(6.77 * 10^{-1})^4$ and $9.77 * 10^{-1}$ respectively when P_e is $2.63 * 10^{-2}$.

$$P_c = \sum_{k=0}^{t/2} C_n^k * P_f^{\ k} * (1 - P_f)^{n-k} \qquad \text{when } n \le 2^m - 1. \quad (7)$$

$$P_c = \left(\sum_{k=0}^{t/2d} C_{n/d}^k * P_f^{\ k} * (1 - P_f)^{n/d-k} \right)^d \qquad \text{when } n > 2^m - 1. \quad (8)$$

Equation (9) computes the average number of retransmissions R for a packet's successful receipt by summing k-retransmission expectation values over k ranging from 0 to infinite. The expectation of k-retransmission is a multiplication of k-retransmission probability $P_c * (1 - P_c)^k$ with $k + 1$ transmissions.

$$R = P_c * \sum_{k=0}^{\infty} \left((k + 1) * (1 - P_c)^k \right) = \frac{1}{P_c}. \quad (9)$$

Equation (10) [10], [11] presents the transmission energy spent for R-time retransmissions when the transmission symbol's size is h bits. Its two terms denote the initial energy for activating a transceiver chip and the energy for R-time retransmissions where each abbreviation P_{MOD}, P_{FS}, P_{tx}, B, and N represents modulation energy, frequency synthesis energy, radiated energy, symbol transmission ratio, and packet size in bits. And α and β are the energy ratio of modulation and frequency synthesis between M-ary and binary PSK modulation technique. Table 2 specifies each parameter's value for TIP50CM.

$$E_{M-ary}(\frac{E_b}{N_0}, B \cdot h) = P_{FS} \cdot T_{start} + R \cdot ((\alpha \cdot P_{MOD} + \beta \cdot P_{FS} + P_{tx}(\frac{E_b}{N_0}, B \cdot h)) \cdot \frac{N}{B \cdot h}). \quad (10)$$

Figure 4 displays the retransmission energy of TIP50CM E_{M-ary} as a function of P_e and the FEC symbol size m which is calculated by applying the values in Table 2 to (10) when packets shown in Fig. 2 are assumed to be continuously sent over wireless channels with six P_e's. Each P_e is the threshold probability for each codeword at six m's, at which packets of Fig. 2 become uncorrectable. Since a packet is uncorrectable if any codeword is tainted beyond its recovery

Table 2. CC2420 parameters

variable	value
P_{FS}	10 mW
T_{start}	1 ms
P_{MOD}	2 mW
P_{tx}	0.000181 mW
α	2.0
β	1.75
B	640 symbol/sec
N	640 bits
h	2 bits

capability, this threshold probability P_e is the probability satisfying $n * P_f = n * (1 - (1 - P_e)^c) = t/2$. The P_e is analytically calculated as in (11).

$$P_e = 1 - (1 - t/2n)^{1/c} . \tag{11}$$

Figure 4 implies that the larger FEC symbol sizes tend to consume more energy for retransmission at any P_e since symbols with larger sizes are more likely to be infected under the uniform error distribution. The aggregation of check bits of several codewords into one codeword at large FEC symbol sizes to collectively remedy any error is not advantageous under this uniform error distribution. Figure 4 also shows that E_{M-ary} fluctuates more significantly at $Symbol_4$, $Symbol_8$, and $Symbol_9$ while it becomes rather constant at the other ones when P_e changes from $3.39 * 10^{-2}$ to $2.26 * 10^{-2}$. For example, E_{M-ary} of

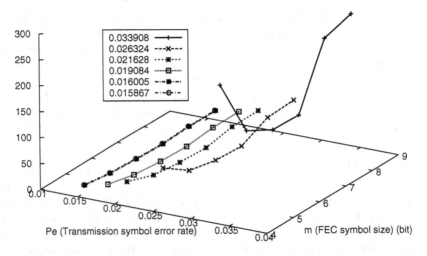

Fig. 4. Average energy of retransmissions as a function of transmission P_e and m

$Symbol_4$ abruptly lowers from 268.4 mW to 25.5 mW while E_{M-ary} of $Symbol_6$ slightly changes from 121.8 mW to 15.3 mW. It is because that around these rates the number of corrupt symbols in $Symbol_8$ and $Symbol_9$ rapidly changes due to their P_f's abrupt transition under this uniform assumption while in $Symbol_4$, the number of fatally infected codewords significantly varies since $Symbol_4$ has more codewords than any symbol size in Fig. 2.

4   The Effect of the FEC Symbol Size on Energy in Real Sensor Networks

This section estimates the extra energy consumption of a sensor node by the introduction of RS algorithm in real sensor networks. The energy calculation bases on traffic traces collected from sensor networks where a sender continuously transmits 80-byte packets with the speed of 160 byte-per-second to its receiver which is 10-meter apart on line-of-sight. Figure 5 and 6 illustrate five burst length and run length Complementary Cumulative Distribution Function (CCDF) graph averaging three traces with five different signal powers. Each trace is measured for 3-hour from 1 p.m. to 4 p.m. in the corridor where pedestrian traffic tends to be heavy. Fig. 5 and 6 indicate that these two metrics are not inversely proportional to signal power in this network as predicted in [12] since our channels are rather heavily influenced by the small-scale fading effect caused by people traffic. The burst lengths at $3.16 * 10^{-1}$ mW signal power, for

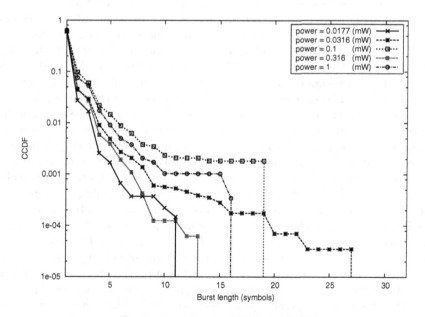

Fig. 5. Burst length CCDF of a WSN

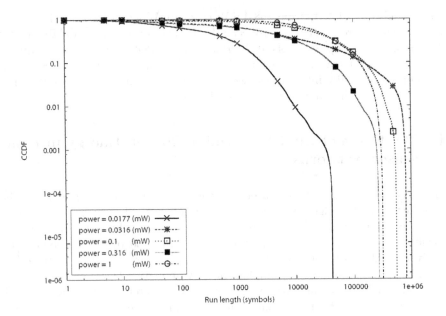

Fig. 6. Run length CCDF of a WSN

example, are generally smaller than those at 1 mW. Figure 5 and 6 finally show that the lengths of 95% bursts and 90% runs are less than 4-bit and 1000-bit.

Figure 7 depicts two graphs representing the retransmission ratio and the energy expenditure ratio for one-bit transmission including encoding and decoding energy at five different FEC symbol sizes. The retransmission ratio is the total retransmitted packet count at one FEC symbol size in Fig. 2 divided by the maximum resent packet count among the five symbol sizes while the energy ratio is the ratio of the total energy per bit at one FEC symbol size to the largest one. For Fig. 7, packets are simulated to be orderly infected as like packets recorded in the 15 traces whose burst and run CCDF are depicted in Fig. 5 and 6 and the energy for encoding, sending, and decoding each packet is computed by (12). Note that the average BER, the total number of corrupt packets, and the total number of simulated packets for 15 traces are $4.7*10^{-3}$, $1.8*10^4$, and $2.97*10^5$ respectively.

Equation (12) divides the total energy required for encoding, sending, decoding packets as many as ones in the traces by the total number of bits successfully transmitted excluding the retransmitted packets and their FEC code. In (12), each abbreviation Pkt_{total}, E_{dec}, E_{enc}, E_{send}, $Total\_Timeout$, E_{listen}, $Pkt_{total\_success}$, Pkt_{size} corresponds to the total number of simulated packets, energy for decoding a packet, energy for encoding a packet, energy for sending a packet, total timeout time, energy for listening per second, the number of packets successfully received, the packet size in bits respectively. The energy for decoding and encoding is computed by inferring to Table 2 based on the degree of each packet's contamination. The energy for transmitting packets is divided into two

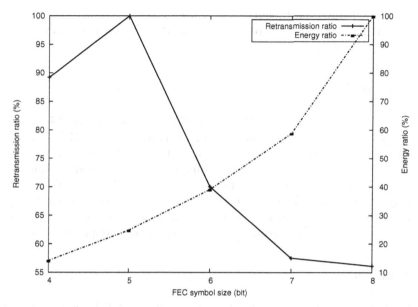

Fig. 7. Retransmission and energy ratio of the performance of each FEC symbol size

terms, E_{send} for sending packets and E_{listen} for waiting for acknowledgement packets for the timeout interval. This transmission energy computation assumes that the propagation and transmission delay of acknowledgement packets are ignorable and the retransmission timer's timeout is fixed with 75 msec specified in [13]. We also assume that TIP50CM adopts 1.8 V and 8 different current values 9.55, 9.9, 10.45, 11, 12.5, 15, 15.7, 17.4 mA for driving its transceiver as like the experiments for collecting 15 traces and 1.8 V and 18.8 mA [14], [15] for listening per one second.

Based on these values, the average energy for sending one packet, listening during the same interval as the transmission delay of one packet, encoding one packet, and decoding one packet are $5.8 * 10^{-2}$, $8.6 * 10^{-2}$, $7.07 * 10^{-1}$, $8.27 * 10^{-1}$ mW respectively. Note that the adopted RS code is quite complicated so that the decoding and encoding the FEC code of a packet is more expensive than its transmission energy. The transmission energy of one packet at 5-bit symbol size, for example, only amounts to 15 % of the computational energy for encoding and decoding.

$$E_{perbit} = \frac{(Pkt_{total} \cdot (E_{dec} + E_{enc}) + Pkt_{total} \cdot E_{send} + Total\_Timeout \cdot E_{listen})}{Pkt_{total\_success} \cdot Pkt_{size}}$$

$$(12)$$

Figure 7 confirms that the appropriate selection of FEC symbol size can save much energy over this wireless channel. As shown in Fig. 7, for example, the small FEC symbol size requires less energy than the large one even though the small one retransmits more packets over this wireless channel with the light BER. $Symbol_4$, for example, consumes 85 % energy less than $Symbol_8$ due to its low

computation energy even though packets are retransmitted more by 33 % than
$Symbol_8$. It is due to that the retransmission energy is negligible comparing to
the computational energy.

5 Conclusions

This paper analyzes the effect of various FEC symbol sizes in RS algorithm
on energy consumption in sensor networks comprised with TIP50CM nodes.
The experiments based on traces indicate that the appropriate selection of a
FEC symbol size causes 85 % energy consumption difference and the small FEC
symbol size is more efficient over wireless sensor channels with the light BER,
specially when the encoding and decoding operations of the FEC code is quite
expensive. As future research, we will actually measure the real sensor node's
energy waste due to FEC algorithms when sensor nodes adopt 802.11 code.

References

1. A. Levisianou, C. Assimakopoulos, F.-N. Pavlidou, and A. Polydoros, "A recursive
   IR protocol for multicarrier communications", Proceedings of the 6-th International
   OFDM-Workshop, pp. 22-1–22-4, September, 2001.
2. L. Zhao, J. W. Mark, and Y. C. Yoon, "A combined link adaptation and incremental
   redundancy protocol for enhanced data transmission", Proceedings of the GLOBE-
   COM 2001, pp. 25–29, November, 2001.
3. J. S. Ahn, S. W. Hong, and J. Heidemann, "An adaptive FEC code control algorithm
   for mobile wireless sensor networks", JCN, VOL. 7, NO. 4, pp. 489–499, December,
   2005.
4. I. S. Reed, and G. Solomon, "Polynomial codes over certain fields", Soc. Ind. Appl.
   Math., Proceedings of the GLOBECOM 2001, pp. 8:300–304, June, 1960.
5. Y. Sankarasubramaniam, I. F. Akyildiz, and S. W. McLaughlin, "Energy efficiency
   based packet size optimization in wireless sensor networks", Proceedings of the
   1-st IEEE International Workshop on Sensor Network Protocols and Applications
   (SNPA), pp. 1–8, May, 2003.
6. http://www.maxfor.co.kr.
7. http://www.moteiv.com.
8. S. Rockliff, "Reed-Solomon (RS) codes" program, 1989, http://www.eccpage.com.
9. T. S. Rappaport, "Wireless communications principles and practice", Prentice
   Hall, Upper Saddle River, NJ, 2002.
10. A. Wang, S. H. Cho, C. G. Sodini, and A. P. Chandrakasan, "Energy Efficient Mod-
    ulation and MAC for Asymmetric RF Microsensor Systems", Proceedings of Inter-
    national Symposium on Low Power Electronics and Design (ISLPED), pp. 106–111,
    August, 2001.
11. H. Karl, and A. Willing, "Protocols and Architectures for Wireless Sensor Net-
    works", WILEY, 2005.
12. D. Ganesan, B. Krishnamachari, A. Woo, D. Culler, D. Estrin, and S. Wicker,
    "Protocols and Architectures for Wireless Sensor Networks", Technical Report
    UCLA/CSDTR 02-0013, February, 2002.
13. http://www.tinyos.net

14. B. Bougard, D. Daly, A. P. Chandrakasan, F. Catthoor, and W. Dehaene, "Energy Efficiency of the IEEE 802.15.4 Standard in Dense Wireless Microsensor Networks: Modeling and Improvement Perspectives", Proceedings of Design, Automation and Test in Europe (DATE), pp. 196–201, March, 2005.
15. http://www.chipcon.com/files/CC2420_Data_Sheet_1_3.pdf

Minimum Dominating Sets for Solving the Coverage Problem in Wireless Sensor Networks

Babak Pazand and Amitava Datta

School of Computer Science & Software Engineering
The University of Western Australia
35 Stirling Highway, Crawley
W.A. 6009, Australia
{babak, datta}@csse.uwa.edu.au

Abstract. One of the major requirements for new wireless sensor networks is to extend the lifetime of the network. Node scheduling techniques have been used extensively for this purpose. Some existing approaches rely mainly on location information through GPS devices for designing efficient scheduling strategies. However, integration of GPS devices with sensor nodes is expensive and increases the cost of deployment dramatically. In this paper we present a location-free solution for node scheduling. Our scheme is based on a graph theoretical approach using *minimum dominating sets*. We propose a heuristic to extract a collection of dominating sets. Each set comprises of a group of working nodes which ensures a high level of network coverage. At each round, one set is responsible for covering the sensor field while the nodes in other sets are in sleep mode. We evaluate our solution through simulations and discuss our future research directions.

1 Introduction

In recent years, deployment and importance of wireless sensor networks have grown rapidly. Advances in wireless communication features and micro-sensing technologies play a key role in this growth. A wireless sensor network includes a collection of battery-powered and wireless-connected [1] tiny sensor nodes which are capable of monitoring a region of interest. These low-cost and low-power sensor nodes collect and process environmental data locally and transmit them to the base station over a wireless channel. Transmission of packets is accomplished through multi-hop communication based on the position of sensor nodes.

In most applications, placement of sensor nodes cannot be pre determined [2]. For instance, suppose we need a wireless sensor network in order to detect the fire in thousands of hectares of bush land. In this case and in many similar cases, not only deterministic positioning of numerous nodes is costly, but in some situations it is not feasible due to harsh conditions in remote areas. Therefore, dense deployment of sensor nodes which have been spread randomly is the only practical and preferred way of deployment in many circumstances. However, this kind of deployment has an obvious problem in covering the sensing area.

H.Y. Youn, M. Kim, and H. Morikawa (Eds.): UCS 2006, LNCS 4239, pp. 454–466, 2006.

Coverage is one of the most important metrics for evaluating the quality of service (QoS) in wireless sensor networks. A region in a sensor field is considered as a covered region if every point in this area is in the sensing radius of one or more sensors [1]. However, it is important to consider how efficiently the sensor field is covered by the deployed sensors.

Researchers have investigated two different aspects of the coverage problem. One aspect considers the efficiency of coverage of a deployment region in terms of the percentage of the total area covered. Several algorithms propose solutions for discovering blind spots in the sensor field as well as determining the number of necessary sensor nodes to cover an area without any blind spots in the coverage. Another aspect of the coverage problem is to explore how to reduce the redundancy in the coverage. The same area of a sensor field may be covered by more than one sensor node in a dense deployment and the aim is to ensure that not more than one node covers a particular area at any time, increasing sensing efficiency. We consider the coverage problem from this sensing efficiency point of view.

We consider a uniform random distribution of numerous sensor nodes across a physical environment. The disorganized arrangement of sensor nodes results in inefficiency of coverage and wastes energy which is the most vital resource. One of the most effective solutions for this problem is a node scheduling approach. Generally, a scheduling approach selects a subset of all the deployed nodes to sense and cover the deployment region on behalf of other redundant nodes. In this paper we propose a solution for the node scheduling problem based on a graph theoretic formulation. We utilize the minimum dominating set technique to eliminate redundancy in sensing and to improve the lifetime of the network. This approach generates a number of dominating sets of sensor nodes. At each time slice, nodes of one set are responsible for monitoring the sensor field while the other nodes are in sleep mode. Then at the next time slice, these nodes go to sleep mode and another set becomes active. Each dominating set contains a small number of nodes with a good coverage of the sensor field. This fact allows us to have more sets and improve the lifetime of the wireless sensor network.

The rest of the paper is organized as follows. Section 2 gives an overview of related work in the literature. In Section 3 and 4 we describe the coverage problem in details and explain our scheduling approach. In section 5, we propose our solution for node scheduling. Simulation results are shown in section 6. Finally, we conclude with some remarks in Section 7.

2   Related Work

To date researchers have proposed several solutions for the coverage problem. These methods can be classified into *location aware* and *location independent* schemes. In the following we review the related work in each class briefly.

Location aware techniques utilize the precise position information of each node to select one or more subset of sensor nodes. Most of these schemes need to have the exact geographic coordinates of sensors. Therefore, they require that each node is equipped with a GPS (Global Positioning System) device. These approaches can guarantee 100% coverage without any blind spot. However, GPS units consume a lot of energy and increase the cost of wireless sensor networks significantly. Following are the related researches which assume the existence of location information. Meguerdichian *et al.* [3] define the worst case coverage as the problem of having breach regions, areas with zero coverage. They combine computational geometry techniques such as Voronoi diagram and Delaunay triangulation with graph search methods to solve the coverage problem. Slijepcevic *et al.*[4] present a heuristic that divides the nodes into mutually exclusive sets. At any time slot only one set is active and covers the sensor field completely. In the protocol by Tian and Georganas [5], each node utilizes its local neighbor information to schedule its on-duty and off-duty time while preserving the original coverage. In order to extract several subsets of nodes, a method is proposed based on ILP (Integer Linear Program) formulation in [6].

In Location free schemes, nodes obtain relative location information by sending control messages to their neighbors. Then a centralized or distributed algorithm selects a group of nodes as the active nodes at each time slice. Location independent schemes fail to ensure 100% network coverage and may introduce more overhead on the network. However, they extend lifetime of the network considerably without additional cost. PEAS [7] is a well known algorithm for node scheduling without location information. It comprises of two main components, probing and adaptive sleeping. Each node wakes up at the time which has been determined by the adaptive sleeping module. Then, it probes its vicinity to find out the situation of its neighboring working nodes. If there is no active node in the probe range, it turns itself into a working node. Otherwise it goes to the sleep mode. In [8, 9] k-coverage is defined as the problem of selecting at least k out of n sensor nodes to cover the monitored area. Then Yen *et al.*[10] consider the problem of assessing k-coverage as the coverage problem. They propose a mathematical expression to formulate the expected coverage by considering the deployment area, number of nodes and sensory range. They further present the application of this argument by devising a node scheduling scheme. In [11], Wu and Ssu assume that each node has its own neighbor table to keep the record of its neighbor nodes and their distances. Distance between nodes is calculated based on the signal strength of received hello messages. Then, each sensor node makes use of its neighbor table and different timers to determine its eligibility to be active or inactive. Also, each inactive node is responsible for finding out the blind spots in its range.

3   Problem Definition

As we mentioned earlier, disorganized placement of sensor nodes is the most preferred way of deployment for many applications. Due to unplanned nature of this kind of deployment, a wireless sensor network might face large scattered areas or sensing holes which decrease the reliability of the network drastically. In order to overcome this shortcoming, sensor nodes have to be spread densely. Moreover, fault tolerance is an important feature of every wireless sensor network and to achieve that, nodes have to be deployed heavily. However, dense deployment has its own drawbacks. Although it minimizes the uncovered area and increases the reliability, it maximizes the redundancy which decreases the energy efficiency significantly. We refer to this behavior as the coverage problem. Figure 1 shows the dense deployment of nodes and the resulting overlapped sensing regions which are the intersections between circles. Each circle denotes the sensing range of a node.

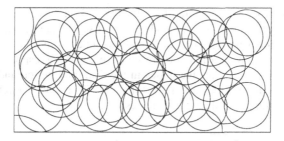

Fig. 1. Dense deployment of sensor nodes results in numerous redundancy

As can be seen, a large number of sub-regions in the sensor field are covered by too many sensors instead of one or two nodes. In order to have a more detailed view, we used a test to obtain the redundancy of 100 nodes in a 50m*50m area with sensing radius of 10m. Figure 2 is a cumulative distribution function which shows the distribution of the number of overlapped sensor nodes. It shows that nearly 10% of the deployment region is covered by 4 or less overlapped nodes and clearly illustrates that more than 10 overlapped nodes cover almost 50% of the sensor field.

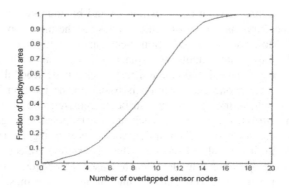

Fig. 2. Cumulative distribution function of overlapped sensor nodes

Sensing same regions of physical environment by many sensor nodes results in wastage of energy. This behavior conflicts with the most important requirement of a wireless sensor network which is power efficiency. Thus, it is essential to have a mechanism to eliminate high redundancy while preserving an acceptable level of network coverage.

4 Node Scheduling

Obviously, in a wireless sensor network with large number of overlapped nodes, turning off some redundant nodes does not affect the overall functionality of the network [5]. As a result, devising a robust activity scheduling technique for sensor nodes is one of the most useful approaches to extend the lifetime of a network. *Node scheduling* is the process of deciding the off-duty and on-duty cycle for each sensor node. It determines the eligibility of a node to be active or inactive. At each time slice, selected working nodes perform the sensing tasks on behalf of other redundant nodes. Therefore, only a small proportion of representative nodes are responsible to cover the sensor field. Figure 3 illustrates the nodes in their on-duty period and there is a reasonable amount of redundancy for fault tolerance. The shaded circles in Figure 3 denote the sensing ranges of the on-duty nodes.

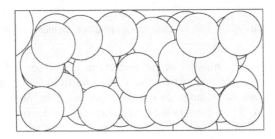

Fig. 3. At each round one subset of nodes is responsible for covering the sensor field

In fact, there are three crucial issues which should be addressed properly by any scheduling scheme. First and foremost, which nodes are the most appropriate ones to be active nodes? Moreover, is the selection mechanism relatively cheap in terms of packet overhead? Last, when should we replace one set of active nodes by another set? In the literature, we have different classifications for node scheduling algorithms. As we mentioned earlier, one classification is based on the location information of nodes. Also, node scheduling algorithms can be categorized into centralized or distributed ones. In distributed approaches, each node is responsible to gather information of its adjacent sensor nodes. Then, it determines its working status in an autonomous manner. While in centralized schemes, the base station collects node information and decides the operational mode of each sensor. Moreover, [10] suggests another classification which is coordinated or uncoordinated schemes. A coordinated approach requires that sensor nodes establish their operational mode based on collaboration with their neighbors. Whereas in an uncoordinated approach, there is no need for communication between nodes and each node acts independently.

5 Proposed Solution

We assume dense uniform distribution of sensor nodes which have been spread randomly. Our node scheduling scheme is an uncoordinated and centralized approach. It neither utilizes location information nor distance information. Also, nodes may have their sensing range and transmission ranges either the same or unequal. The proposed approach is based on the Minimum Dominating Set concept and it comprises of three phases. Phase one is to find out nodes' neighbors and corresponding graph of the network. Next stage is dedicated to discovering a collection of different dominating sets of sensor nodes. Finally, phase three exploits these dominating sets to schedule the node activities.

5.1 Constructing Graph of the Network

In this phase, nodes have to detect the existence their neighbors without location information. Thus, each node broadcasts a "HELLO beacon" and waits to receive "REPLY messages" from its recipients. When a node discovers its neighbors, it sends the collected information back to the base station. Then, base station constructs the graph of the network and represents it by an adjacency matrix. This matrix serves as an input for the second phase.

5.2 Determining Minimum Dominating Sets

Suppose $G = (V, E)$ is an undirected graph. A *Dominating Set* of G is a subset of vertices, $V' \subseteq V$ such that for all $u \in V - V'$ there is a $v \in V'$, for which $(u, v) \in E$. Then, a dominating set that has the least cardinality amongst the other sets is called *Minimum Dominating Set* (MDS). Figure 4 shows a simple graph and its equivalent MDS. The determination of a minimum dominating set is a *NP-Hard* problem and hence we use a heuristic solution for determining minimum dominating sets.

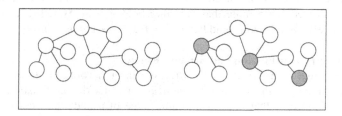

Fig. 4. Graph and its Minimum Dominating Set (MDS)

Let $S = \{s_1, s_2 .... s_n\}$ indicates the entire collection of sensor nodes and $L = \{l_1, l_2 .... l_m\}$ refers to the links between nodes. Then $G = (S, L)$ is the graph which represents the wireless sensor network. Our goal is to determine $M = \{M_1, M_2 .... M_k\}$, a collection of MDSs of graph G. The proposed approach is targeted to maximize the cardinality of M and to minimize the cardinality of members of it. Phase two of our solution is dedicated to obtain these MDSs. We propose two different heuristics. The first algorithm considers that sensing range is equal to transmission range and the second algorithm assumes that these ranges are different.

5.2.1 Same Transmission and Sensing Range

First, the scheme uses the adjacency matrix to choose the sensor node p with the highest number of neighbors. This node p becomes the first member of M_1, the first dominating set. Then, all the neighbors of p are excluded from the next selections. Again, the heuristic searches the adjacency matrix for the node with the second highest neighbors, it is selected as the second member of M_1 and similarly all its neighbors will be omitted from the next rounds. This process continues until all the nodes are processed. Then, after determining M_1, all of its members are excluded from calculation of next sets. Subsequently, the above process is repeated to obtain members of M_2, M_3, ..., M_k, the k dominating sets.

Ideally, intersection of members of M should be empty. However, it is not feasible in real world. Discovering MDS is a *NP-Hard problem* and we are using only a heuristic solution. This implies that in most cases, i.e. complex graphs like dense wireless sensor networks, the calculated MDS may not dominate 100% of the graph. In order to tackle this issue, we analyze the union of members of an MDS and their neighbors, if the resulting set does not cover the sensor field reasonably, we add more nodes to an MDS to improve its coverage. Consequently, this approach adds some sensor nodes in the MDS which is not unique to it and has been selected for another MDS. Moreover, some nodes are located close to the borders of the sensor field and their sensing ranges usually do not overlap with other nodes (*border effect*). Therefore, the first MDS will have all these border nodes. This inclusion causes lack of border nodes in next MDSs and increases the number of sensing holes in them significantly. We address this problem by including the border nodes in all MDSs. We consider a parameter which is called *Repeated Ratio* to asses the efficiency of each MDS.

$$\text{Repeated Ratio} = \frac{\text{Number of non unique nodes}}{\text{Total number of nodes}} \times 100\% \tag{1}$$

By considering a threshold of 20% based on our experimental results, each MDS which has Repeated Ratio more than this threshold will be excluded from M. This means that an effective MDS should have more than 80% unique sensor nodes.

5.2.2 Different Transmission and Sensing Range

The sensing range of nodes in some wireless sensor networks is smaller than the transmission range. We propose a different heuristic to tackle this situation. The main problem in this case is that the transmission range of a node does not give a good indication of its sensing range as the sensing range is smaller. If we apply the heuristics of the previous section and exclude all the neighbors of a node from the MDS, there will be large sensing holes in the network. Hence, we use a different approach for constructing the MDS in this case. First, similar to the previous approach the scheme selects the node p which has the most neighbors, followed by choosing one of its neighbors randomly. These nodes become the first members of M_1. Then, Each adjacent node i of node p is examined by equation 2, if it complies with the condition, node i will be chosen as the next member of M_1.

$$2 \leq \text{Neighbors of node } i \text{ in } Mj \leq F \tag{2}$$

The parameter F is directly related to the density of the network. It has been determined based on our simulation results. Table 1 shows values of F for different densities.

Table 1. Relation between density and parameter F

Density (nodes per square meter)	F
$0.02 \leq density < 0.06$	2
$0.06 \leq density < 0.08$	3
$density \geq 0.08$	4

The intuitive meaning of equation 2 is that a node is chosen as a member of M_l if it does not have a large number of neighbors in that set. When all the neighbors of node p are checked, the selected nodes are excluded from further selections. Then, the scheme chooses the node with the second highest number of neighbors and repeats the above procedure for it. Finally, the selected nodes in each round form M_l and they are ignored for the selection of next MDS.

The above process will be replicated to discover all the MDSs. Subsequently, boundary nodes are added to each member of M and inefficient MDSs are omitted from M.

5.3 Scheduling Minimum Dominating Sets

Phase three is the simplest part of our scheme. In fact, the computed MDSs are scheduled to cover the network. At each round, one MDS is selected to sense the entire deployment region independently. Then, at the next round working nodes in current active MDS go to sleep mode and on-duty cycle of nodes in another MDS begins. Each round should be reasonably long to improve the resulting overhead.

6 Simulation Results

In this section we evaluate the performance of the proposed scheme by using our network simulator written in C++. The sensor field is a 50*50 square meter area. We consider different densities by deployment of 100, 150, 200, 250 and 300 sensor nodes distributed uniformly and randomly. Nodes have the same sensing range which is fixed to 10 meters. Although transmission ranges of nodes are equal, one scenario considers it equal to sensing range and the other one uses 20 meter transmission range for each node. Each scenario is simulated 10 times and the average results are calculated. The performance is assessed based on four metrics. These are *Coverage Ratio*, *Saved Energy*, number of MDSs and their cardinality.

In order to compute the coverage ratio we divide the deployment area to 1*1 meter cells. Uncovered cells are those in which zero or less than 50% of their area have been covered. Furthermore, cells which have 50% to 100% of their areas covered are treated as covered cells. Figure 5 illustrates covered and uncovered cells for node i.

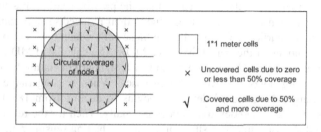

Fig. 5. Coverage calculation for each node

After calculating coverage of each node, the coverage ratio of the network is determined as:

$$\text{Coverage Ratio} = \frac{\sum_{i=1}^{n} \text{Coverd cells of node } i}{\text{Total cells}} \times 100\% \tag{3}$$

In equation 3 we count overlapped covered cells as one cell. Figure 6 depicts the number of MDSs and their average node number when sensing range is equal to transmission range. According to the graph, there is a steady increase in number of sets from 3 to 8 between 100 and 300 deployed nodes. Moreover, the most important fact is the average number of nodes, which is considerably low. It shows that for different densities, only 15% to 6% of nodes are active at each round. By taking into account that there can be up to 8 rounds, we can expect high level of energy savings.

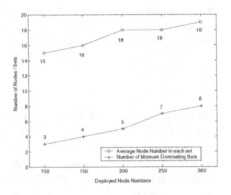

Fig. 6. Number of MDSs and their node numbers when transmission range is equal to sensing range

We propose a different approach in case of having different sensing and transmission ranges. Figure 7 illustrates the result of our simulation for this approach. As can be seen, number of MDSs increased slightly from 2 sets in 100 deployed nodes to 4 sets in a dense deployment. Also, the average number of nodes rose relatively sharply, from 21 to 43 sensor nodes, apart from in 300 deployed nodes where it fell to 41 sensor nodes. Although the results are weaker than the previous case, it has to be considered that nodes are consuming less energy due to their reduced sensing ranges.

As we discussed earlier, sensing holes are those cells which have not been covered by any working nodes of the currently active MDS. The calculated MDSs differed in the number of uncovered cells. Figure 8 shows the standard deviation between MDSs in terms of sensing holes for two different cases. When sensing range is equal to transmission range, the standard deviation begins to decline from 18.01 in 100 deployed nodes to 3.52 in 200 deployed nodes gradually. Then for the rest of the densities it remained almost same. The situation in case of having sensing range as half the transmission range was completely different. The standard deviation fluctuated over different densities with maximum number of 53.01 to 17.53. In this case, first MDSs

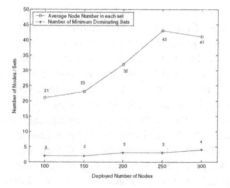

Fig. 7. Number of MDSs and their node numbers when sensing range is half the transmission range

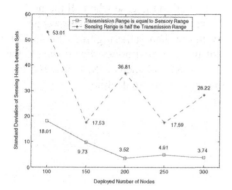

Fig. 8. Standard deviation of sensing holes between MDSs

had less sensing holes while it increased rapidly over the next calculated MDS. This behavior was the main reason to have less number of dominating sets compared to the case when nodes have the same sensing and transmission ranges.

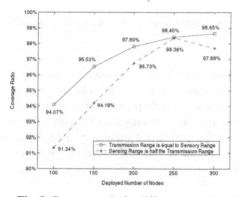

Fig. 9. Coverage ratio for different node densities

Figure 9 shows the coverage ratio which is one of the most important metrics to evaluate the performance of redundancy elimination schemes. In the case of having equal transmission range and sensing range, our scheme obtained very good result with 94% of coverage for the least dense network, up to more than 98% of coverage for higher densities. In case of different sensing and transmission ranges, our approach achieved slightly less coverage, 91% for 100 deployed nodes and reached up to 98% of coverage for deployment of 250 sensor nodes.

Finally, the next graphs illustrate the most interesting result of our node scheduling scheme which is the amount of saved energy. For this metric, we ran the simulation for 5000 seconds and calculated the total amount of spent energy by all the working nodes. Nodes are working in CSMA mode. Figure 10 presents the outcome when transmission range is equal to sensing range and both are 10 meters. According to the graph, our MDSs consume almost 1/5 to 1/13 of the energy for different densities compared to the case when all the nodes are working all the time. One might assume that MDSs with average 15 nodes (for 100 deployed nodes) should consume nearly 1/7 of the total power compared to the case when all the nodes are working. However, in the case of having same transmission and sensing range, nodes in an MDS fail to provide full connectivity in our data gathering tree. We solve this issue by increasing the transmission range of unconnected nodes. For instance, the average transmission range for MDSs with 15 nodes is 16 meters. Nevertheless, by increasing the density, this average transmission range starts to decline.

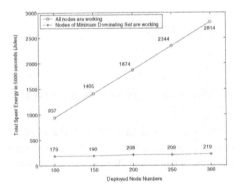

Fig. 10. Total spent energy in 5000 seconds. Transmission range is 10 meters and Sensing range is 10 meters.

Figure 11 shows similar data when the transmission range is not equal to the sensing range. In this case transmission range and sensing range are 20 and 10 meters respectively. Although, nodes in MDSs provide full connectivity, they consume more power due to their higher transmission range. As the graph shows, MDSs use roughly 1/5 to 1/7 of the total energy during our simulation time. Also, we need to consider that the number of MDSs in this case is lower than the previous case which results in lower saving of energy.

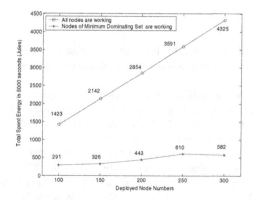

Fig. 11. Total spent energy in 5000 seconds. Transmission range is 20 meters and Sensing range is 10 meters.

7 Conclusion and Future Work

In this paper we proposed a solution to address the coverage problem in terms of redundancy. We eliminated redundancy by presenting a heuristic for node scheduling based on Minimum Dominating Sets approach. In case of having sensing range equal to transmission range, we could extract between 3 to 8 independent sets with very small number of working nodes in each of them. These numbers were 2 to 4 sets, when sensing range was half the transmission range. These dominating sets were scheduled to cover the monitored area. We measured the total accumulated energy and they could consume nearly 1/5 to 1/13 of the total energy compared to the case when all the nodes are working. By taking into account the number of sets, we can expect considerable network lifetime extension while preserving up to 98% of network coverage.

In comparison with other location-free solutions, we argue that PEAS [7] is strongly mixed with medium access control layer because of its probing component, but our approach is independent of MAC. In other words our scheduling sits above the MAC layer. However, PEAS can work in harsh environments with a lot of node failures and the inclusion of this feature is a part of our future work. Also, Triangular [11] approach considers distance information by using bidirectional antenna. This device increases the cost of sensor nodes remarkably, while our approach utilizes the simplest form of sensor node hardware.

Our future work will improve some shortcomings of the proposed scheme, when sensing range is not equal to transmission range. This includes reducing the high amount of standard deviation between MDSs in terms of sensing holes. Also, fluctuations of this metric between different densities should be addressed. These improvements will lead to more dominating sets in case of different sensing range and transmission range.

References

1. Y. Shang, W. Ruml, Y. Zhang, M. Fromherz. Localization from Connectivity in Sensor Networks. IEEE Transcations on Paralllel and Distributed Systems, vol. 15, no. 11, November 2004.
2. I. F. Akyildiz, W. Su, Y. Sankarasubramaniam, and E. Cayirci. A survey on sensor networks. IEEE Communications Magazine, vol. 40, no. 8, pp. 102--114, August 2002.
3. S. Meguerdichian, F. Koushanfar, M. Potkonjak, and M. B. Srivastava. Coverage problems in wireless ad-hoc sensor networks. in Proc. IEEE Infocom, pp. 1380—1387, 2001.
4. S. Slijepcevic, M. Potkonjak. Power efficient organization of wireless sensor networks. In IEEE Int'l Conf. on Communications (ICC), pages 472-476, 2001.
5. D. Tian and N. D. Georganas, A Coverage-Preserving Node Scheduling Scheme for Large Wireless Sensor Networks, Proc. ACM Workshop on Wireless Sensor Networks and Applications, Atlanta, October 2002.
6. S. Meguerdichian, M. Potkonjak. Low Power 0/1 Coverage and Scheduling Techniques in Sensor Networks. UCLA Technical Report 030001, January 2003.
7. F. Ye, G. Zhong, J. Cheng, S. Lu, L. Zhang. PEAS: A Robust Energy Conserving Protocol for Long-lived Sensor Networks. in: Proceedings 23rd International Conference on Distributed Computing Systems, pp. 28-37, 2003.
8. C.-F. Huang, Y.-C. Tseng. The coverage problem in a wireless sensor network, in: ACM International Workshop on Wireless Sensor Networks and Applications, pp. 115–121, 2003.
9. G. Xing, X. Wang, Y. Zhang, C. Lu, R. Pless, C. Gill. Integrated coverage and connectivity configuration for energy conservation in sensor networks. ACM Trans. Sensor Networks, In Press.
10. L. Yen, C. W. Yu, Y. Cheng. Expected k-coverage in wireless sensor networks. Elsevier Ad Hoc Networks Journal, In Press.
11. T-T. Wu, K-F. Ssu. Determining active sensor nodes for complete coverage without location information. Intl. J. Ad Hoc and Ubiquitous Computing, vol. 1, no. 1/2, pp. 38-46, 2005.

A Simple Scheme with Low Energy consumption for Coverage Maintenance in Wireless Sensor Networks

Sung Ho Hwang[1], Minsu Kim[1], and Tae-young Byun[2]

[1] School of ECE, Georgia Tech, USA
[2] School of CICE, Catholic University of Daegu, Korea
{sungho, kiunsen}@ece.gatech.edu, tybyun@cu.ac.kr

Abstract. An effective approach for energy conservation in wireless sensor networks is scheduling sleep intervals for redundant nodes, while guaranteeing continuous services with the remaining active nodes. For the sensor networks to operate successfully, the active nodes must maintain sensing coverage. In this paper, we present the design and analysis of a novel scheme that can adaptively configure a network to achieve entire coverage. This work differs from the existing coverage maintenance schemes in several ways: 1) We propose a novel scheme of configuring active nodes from all given nodes; 2) We provide simple coverage model to calculate the number of active nodes satisfying the coverage; and 3) Our scheme performs well without any location information, so it can be easily used in hostile environments which requires a fast network configuration. We demonstrate the capability of our scheme in terms of coverage configuration through simulations.

Keyword: Energy consumption, Coverage, and Wireless Sensor Networks.

1 Introduction

One of the goals of Ubiquitous computing is to make it possible for users to provide the service by any device, anytime and anywhere with minimum user interference in their environment. All devices in Ubiquitous computing are able to continuously communicate to each other through wireless network which enables small range wireless network with low power, such as Wireless Sensor Network (WSN). Recently WSN is recognized as the one of the core technology to realize Ubiquitous computing, and various researches related WSN have been studied by many scientists and researchers.

A WSN generally consists of tiny sensing devices, deployed in a region of interest. Each device has processing and wireless communication capabilities, which enable it to gather information from the environment and to generate and deliver report messages to the remote sink node. The sink node aggregates and analyzes the report message received and decides whether there is an unusual or concerned event occurrence in the deployed area. Considering the limited capabilities and vulnerable nature of an individual sensor, a WSN has a large number of sensors deployed in high density and thus redundancy can be exploited to increase data accuracy and system reliability. In a WSN, energy source provided for sensors is usually battery type,

H.Y. Youn, M. Kim, and H. Morikawa (Eds.): UCS 2006, LNCS 4239, pp. 467–477, 2006.

which has not yet reached the stage for sensors to operate for a long time without recharging. Moreover, sensors are often intended to deploy in remote or hostile environment, such as a battlefield or desert; it is undesirable or impossible to recharge or replace the battery power of all sensors. Therefore, the design for energy efficient power consumption without sacrificing system reliability is one important challenge to the design of a large wireless sensor network.

In WSN, all nodes share common sensing tasks. This implies that not all sensors are required to perform the sensing task during the whole system lifetime. Turning off some nodes does not affect the overall system function as long as there are enough working nodes to assure it. Therefore, if we can schedule sensors to work alternatively, the system lifetime can be prolonged correspondingly; i.e. the system lifetime can be prolonged by exploiting redundancy.

Most prior work has treated the problem of sensing coverage and network connectivity separately to design the scheme for efficient power consumption. Only few studies have handled the coverage and connectivity problem jointly. Also, current studies mainly focused on a data-aggregated routing algorithm [1],[2],[4] and energy efficient MAC protocols [6],[8]. However, for more inherent solution to reduce energy consumption problem, the application level should be also considered [9][12]. These approaches require exactly location information of either neighboring nodes or all nodes in sensing field. However, the location information may not be always available.

In this paper, we propose a simple scheme with low power consumption considering coverage problem without using any location information. Proposed scheme can configure a set of active nodes from randomly deployed nodes, which performs without any location information. To this configuration, the active node set should have three procedures, i.e., initial, configuring, and normal sensing procedure.

The main contribution of this paper is to provide a distributed scheduling scheme with solving energy consumption with considering coverage problem by using minimum available information.

This paper is organized as follows. Section 2 reviews related works and Section 3 introduces our proposed scheme. In Section 4, simulation results are provided, and finally, Section 5 presents our conclusions.

2 Related Works

A WSN generally is assumed to operate over the coverage guarantees. As mentioned above, most studies have treated the problem of sensing coverage and network connectivity separately.

In recent years, several important theoretical evaluations of coverage maintenance have been studied. In [14], D. Tian et al. has proposed a distributed node scheduling scheme to decide which node can be turned off without affecting the sensing coverage, where global coverage is achieved by making use of the geometric relationships between the sensing regions of the nodes. Also, in [16], Y. Zou et al. have suggested distributed node scheduling algorithms with location information of its own and 1-hop neighbors. In addition, they consider bakeoff and token passing scheme to decide the role/state of nodes (i.e. sleeping, sensing, or routing) in a distributed manner. X. Wang et al. distinguish connectivity from sensing and determine the configuration of the nodes with both communication connectivity and sensing coverage as considerations in [15].

These approaches above mentioned require exactly location information of either neighboring nodes or all nodes in sensing field. In WSN, the exact location information of sensor node may not be always available in real sensor field.

A number of studies for analyzing the distributed algorithms of a connected dominating set (CDS) have been performed. In [2], Gao et al. present a randomized algorithm for maintaining a CDS with low overhead. The algorithm assumes the grid partition of the coverage and selects a small number of cluster heads. Y. Wang et al. suggest a geometric spanner algorithm that can be implemented in a distributed manner in [4]. In [3], Alzoubi et al. describe a distributed algorithm for constructing a minimum connected dominating set (MCDS) with a constant approximation ratio of the minimum possible and linear time complexity.

The above algorithms provide the theoretical limits and bounds of what is achievable with coverage maintenance. However, there is poor correlation between the spatial distance and reception rate, so assumptions based on geographic proximity between nodes do not necessarily hold in practice. Furthermore, the radio propagation is not circular, presenting non-isotropic properties. Therefore, the approximations under these assumptions may cause serious problems with algorithms that assume bidirectional connectivity [13].

Another approach in reducing energy consumption has been to adaptively control the transmit power of the radio. The lazy scheduling proposed in Prabhakar et al. [9] transmits packets with the lowest possible transmit power for the longest possible time such that delay constraints are still met. Ramanathan and Rosales-Hain [10] proposed some distributed heuristics to adaptively adjust node transmit powers in response to topological changes caused by mobile nodes. This work assumes that a routing protocol is running at all times and provides basic neighbor information that is used to dynamically adjust transmit power. While power control can be very useful, particularly in asymmetric networks such as cellular telephony, their advantages are less pronounced in sensor networks [5]. In Xu et al. [11], GAF nodes use geographic location information to divide the network into fixed square grids. Nodes in each grid alternate between sleeping and listening, and there is always one node active to route packets per grid. Chen et al. [12] proposed SPAN, an energy efficient algorithm for topology maintenance, where nodes decide whether to sleep or join the backbone based on connectivity information supplied by a routing protocol. Our scheme does not depend on routing information nor need to modify the routing state; it decides whether to generate a report message or not based on adaptive report probability. In addition, our work does not presume a particular model of fairness or network capacity that the application requires.

3 Proposed Scheme

As mentioned before, we propose a simple scheme with low power consumption considering coverage without using any location information. For this, we first have to get the set of active nodes from randomly deployed nodes. To derive the set size of active nodes, we provide a simple coverage model.

3.1 Simple Coverage Model

Prior to introducing our simple coverage model, we describe assumptions and notations. First, we assume that all sensor nodes are equipped with the same hardware, software and initial energy, and only the number of neighbors is available information. In other words, each node does not have its neighbors' location. We present the surveillance field by a two-dimension grid, whose dimension is given as X x Y [meters^2]. Let $m = X$ x Y, i.e., there are total m grid points in the field. Let $\zeta = \{g_1, g_2, ..., g_m\}$ be the set of all grid points. Let g_i is the location vector for grid point g_i. i.e., $g_i = <x_i, y_i>$, where x_i and y_i are the coordinates. We use S to denote the set of n sensor nodes that have been placed in the sensor field, i.e., $|S| = n$. A node with id k is denoted with s_k ($s_k \in S$, $1 \leq k \leq n$). Let l_k be the location vector of node k and let L = $\{l_1, ..., l_n\}$. Let N_k be the neighbor set of node s_k. Assume that all sensor nodes are equipped with the same type of sensing and communication hardware, i.e., they have the same sensing and communication range, r, both in meters. Let $d_{kl} = \|l_k - l_l\|$ be the distance between nodes s_k and s_l, and $d^{ik} = \|g_i - l_k\|$ be the distance between grid point g_i and sensor node s_k.

We denote the *sensing ratio* that a target at grid point g_i is detected by at least one node with p_s, where

$$p_s = \frac{|\varsigma \setminus \varsigma_0|}{m},\qquad(1)$$

where ζ_0 denotes the set of grids that there is no sensor node within the distance r.

The coverage probability is used to demonstrate the performance of the proposed scheme. We also denote the *local coverage* that the set of grids within the covered area of the node s_k with ζ^k, where

$$\varsigma^k = \{g^i \mid d^{ik} < r, 1 \leq i \leq m\}.\qquad(2)$$

As mentioned earlier, the node whose own local coverage is entirely sponsored by its active neighbors can stay in INACTIVE state without loss of the area of sensing field.

Now, we investigate the relationship between the local coverage and the number of neighbors. We can write the problem as "when a node can sleep?" Each node should decide whether its local coverage can be fully sponsored or not, using only the number of active neighbors. We represent the area of sponsored local coverage of a node with a neighbor located in the distance of d as $\omega(d)$. In addition, let $\Gamma(j)$ and $p_{sl}(j)$ be the mean sponsored area and the probability of sponsored area of local coverage of a node with j neighbors, respectively. Let $p_{ul}(j) = 1 - p_{sl}(j)$. Then, we can easily see that

$$p_{sl}(j) = \frac{\Gamma(j)}{\pi r^2}.\qquad(3)$$

Based on Equation (4), we can rewrite the problem as "when $p_{ul}(j)$ becomes 0?" To solve this problem, we calculate first $\Gamma(j = 1)$ as follows:

$$\Gamma(j = 1) = \int_0^r \frac{2\pi x \omega(x)}{\pi r^2} dx.\qquad(4)$$

Using (3), (4) and (5), we can simply get $p_{ul}(1) = 0.41$. In addition, $p_{ul}(j = 2)$ can be calculated by

$$p_{ul}(j=2) = p_{ul}(j=1) - p_{ul}(j=1)p_{sl}(j=1).   \qquad (5)$$

Then, we can obtain $p_{ul}(j=k)$ as follows:

$$p_{ul}(j=k) = 1 - p_{ul}(j=1)^k.   \qquad (6)$$

When k is equal to 4, p_{sl} is about 0.96. It means that a node with 4 neighbors can be sponsored its local coverage by its neighbors. In other words, when a node with 4 active neighbors goes to the sleep state, only 4% of its own local coverage would be uncovered. Intuitively, this 4 % uncovered area would not be accumulated if the number of nodes is increased. This property is also shown in our simulation results.

3.2 Node Activity Configuration Scheme

We propose to decide the role of individual node with only the number of neighbors in a fully distributed manner. We assume that each node hears the neighbors' HELLO messages, and maintains neighbors' states. In our coverage model, we investigate the relationship between sponsored local coverage and the number of active neighbors. Therefore, each node can decide its own role using its own active neighbors' information and the results of our model.

Therefore, node scheduling process may be performed at every start of sensing period, and can be summarized as the following three pseudo codes for each node:

```
Initial procedure:
(1)  turns on the radio
(2)  estimates the number of total neighbors(N_x)
(3)  if N_x differs from the value of the previous period,
         a. performs configuration procedure
(4)  else
         a. performs normal procedure

Configuration procedure:
(1)  calculates the length of sensing interval (χ)
(2)  contends with its own neighbors and investigates the
     winners (N_a^k)
(3)  if wins the contention
         a. selects its own sensing time
         b. performs sensing (active)
         c. sleep after completing the sensing and reporting
(4)  else
         a. turns off the radio (inactive)
         b. tries to the next contention

Normal procedure:
(1)  if its own sensing time
         a. performs sensing (active)
         b. sleep after completing the sensing and reporting
(2)  else
         a. turns off its radio (inactive)
         b. contends with its own neighbors
```

Initial procedure is performed by all sensors at every start of sensing repetition interval, and configuration procedure is performed when N_a^k has changed due to newly added or disabled (due to power exhaustion) nodes. In the configuration procedure, we compute the length of the sensing interval, denoted by χ, as follows

$$\chi = \left\lfloor \frac{N_k}{N_{th}^a} \right\rfloor, \tag{7}$$

where N_{th}^a is the threshold value of the active number of neighbors that node s_k can fall into sleeping.

The contention method can be token passing, random backoff, or probabilistic scheme, and so on. In this contention, the winner can sleep when $N_{th}^a \leq N_a^k$. Otherwise, the winner begins to sense and report the gathered information to the sink at every χ^{th} frame. This cycle is the sensing time of the node, denoted by t_k. The loser should contend with the other losers in next frame until wins. The nodes that have not been a winner during χ frames can select random number in range of 1 and χ. Then, the node begins to perform sensing and reporting task.

Sensing degree, denoted by ζ_D, can be obtained by

$$SD = \sum_{k=0}^{n} \frac{|\varsigma^k|}{m}. \tag{8}$$

4   Simulations

In this paper, we evaluate the performance of the proposed scheme with simulations by varying the map size (100~500m) of sensor field and sensor nodes are deployed in a square space (100 x 100) as shown in Fig. 1. The coordinates of all nodes are randomly selected in sensor field. All sensor nodes are assumed to have the same sensing and communication range. The number of nodes are generated by $k = \pi r^2 (|s|-1)/m$.

For feasibility of simulations, we divide the space into 1m×1m unit grids as shown Fig.1. We assume an event occurs in each grid, with the event source located at the center of the grid.

To calculate sensing coverage, we investigate how many original nodes and how many active nodes can detect every event. In the simulations, we compute the area of circular regions that completely fit into the network, and the regions outside of the edges of the network are not considered. The simulated coverage is calculated by the ratio of the covered grids on the entire sensing field.

In this proposed scheme, each node has to decide its role individually with only the number of neighbors because it is not necessary exact position of neighbor nodes. That is to say, the state of each node is decided in a distributed manner.

Fig. 1. grid representation of 100 X 100 sensing field

In Fig. 2, we observe the relation between the ratio of coverage in different map size and the number of neighbors according to increase the number of entire nodes. For this experiment, we change the number of entire nodes by varying the map size form 100 x 100 to 500 x 500.

As shown in Fig. 2, the coverage ratio of simulation (sim_cov) is almost similar to the coverage ratio of analysis (ana_cov) model regardless of map size and the coverage ratio is about 96% when the average number of neighbors is 4. That is, that means that the average coverage is guaranteed over 96% when the average number of active neighbors is 4 in high density environment.

We can also see that the number of active node remain constant over different deployed the number of entire nodes when the sensing range and deployed area are varied. Proposed scheme can be easily applied to various MAC level for power saving approaches because the calculation of idle node is very easy using our scheme

These trends can be observed more precisely as illustrated in Fig. 3.

In Fig. 3, we observe the phase transition curve of the coverage ratio by increasing the number of active neighbors. As above mentioned, this figure shows that the average coverage is 96% when the number of active neighbors, denoted with D_1 in Fig. 3, is 4 (i.e. $D_1=4$).

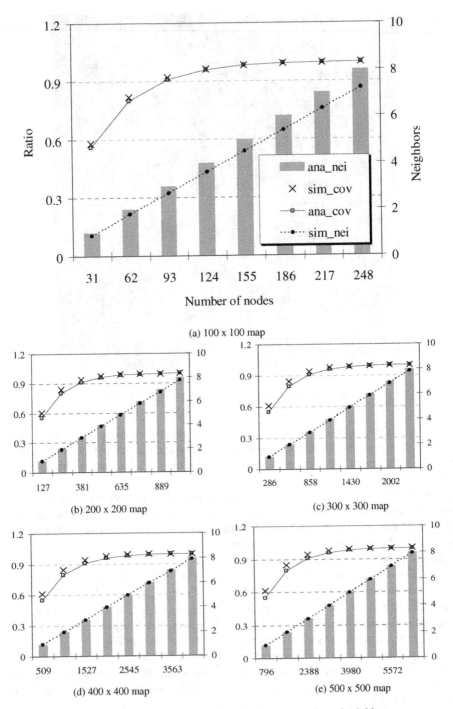

(a) 100 x 100 map

(b) 200 x 200 map

(c) 300 x 300 map

(d) 400 x 400 map

(e) 500 x 500 map

Fig. 2. Coverage ratio and number of nodes vs. number of neighbors

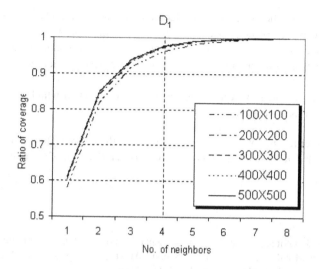

Fig. 3. Ratio of coverage vs. number of neighbors

Table 1. Coverage ratio vs. node density ($r = 16$)

Node density	Frame (χ)		
	1	2	3
100	0.856047	0.952808	0.978567
200	0.823276	0.956346	0.987592
300	0.790469	0.946907	0.989562
400	0.784575	0.947001	0.988882

We let each node decide whether to report or not based on its report probability. The decision of each node is visible to the neighbors. The nodes, which make decisions later, cannot see the nodes that have been turned off before. The current sensing coverage by active nodes is compared with the original one where all nodes are active. As shown in Fig. 3, the coverage ratio will approach to the numerical results regardless of increasing the size of map.

Table 1 summarizes coverage vs. the number of subsets which it gets to experiments. When the deployed node number is more than 100, the total coverage ratio reaches almost 100 % with three distinct subsets. It means that active nodes set of entire nodes can monitor almost full area coverage by proposed scheme.

5 Conclusions

This paper presents a simple scheme with energy consumption for coverage maintenance, which will be able to use in for power saving policy at the node level.

With the proposed scheme, each node decides its sensing activity (i.e. active/sleep) using proposed policy of node itself without any location information. In this paper, the performance of proposed scheme is investigated via simulations, and the results verify that the proposed scheme provides comparable performance with the results of analytical model.

In the future, we plan to experiment on sensor networks in which the sensing and transmission radius are different.

Acknowledgment. This work was supported by the Korea Research Foundation Grant funded by Korean Government (MOEHRD) (No. D00362 (M01-2004-000-20297-0)).

References

[1] J. Gao, L.J. Guibas, J. Hershburger, L. Zhang, and A. Zhu, "Geometric Spanner for Routing in Mobile Networks," Proc. Second ACM Symp. Mobile Ad Hoc Networking and Computing (MobiHoc 01), pp. 45-55, Oct. 2001.

[2] J. Gao, L.J. Guibas, J. Hershburger, L. Zhang, and A. Zhu, "Discrete and Computational Geometry," Proc. Second ACM Symp. Mobile Ad Hoc Networking and Computing (MobiHoc 01), vol. 30, no. 1, pp. 45-65, 2003.

[3] K.M. Alzoubi, P.-J. Wan, and O. Frieder, "Message-Optimal Connected-Dominating-Set Construction for Routing in Mobile Ad Hoc Networks," Proc. Third ACM Int'l Symp. Mobile Ad Hoc Networking and Computing (MobiHoc), June 2002.

[4] Y. Wang and X.-Y. Li, "Geometric Spanners for Wireless Ad Hoc Networks," Proc. 22nd Int'l Conf. Distributed Computing Systems (ICDCS 2002), July 2002.

[5] A. Cerpa, N. Busek, and D. Estrin, "SCALE: A Tool for Simple Connectivity Assessment in Lossy Environments," Technical Report CENS Technical Report 0021, Center for Embedded Networked Sensing, Univ. of California, Los Angeles, Sept. 2003.

[6] K. Sohrabi and G. Pottie, "Performance of a Novel Self-Organization Protocol for Wireless Ad Hoc Sensor Networks," Proc. IEEE Vehicular Technology Conf., Sept. 2000.

[7] W. Ye, J. Heidemann, and D. Estrin, "An Energy-Efficient MAC Protocol for Wireless Sensor Networks," Proc. 21st Ann. Joint Conf. IEEE Computer and Comm. Soc. (INFOCOM), pp. 1567-1576, June 2002.

[8] R. Zheng, J.C. Hou, and L. Sha, "Asynchronous Wakeup for Ad Hoc Networks," ACM Int'l Symp. Mobile Ad Hoc Networking and Computing, June 2003.

[9] B. Prabhakar, E. Uysal-Biyikoglu, and A.E. Gamal, "Energy-Efficient Transmission over a Wireless Link Via Lazy Packet Scheduling," Proc. 20th Ann. Joint Conf. IEEE Computer and Comm. Soc. (INFOCOM), pp. 386-394, Apr. 2001.

[10] R. Ramanathan and R. Rosales-Hain, "Topology Control of Multihop Wireless Networks Using Transmit Power Adjustment," Proc. 19th Ann. Joint Conf. IEEE Computer and Comm. Soc. (INFOCOM), pp. 404-413, Mar. 2000.

[11] Y. Xu, J. Heidemann, and D. Estrin, "Geography-Informed Energy Conservation for Ad Hoc Routing," Proc. Seventh Ann. ACM/IEEE Int'l Conf. Mobile Computing and Networking (MobiCom), pp. 70-84, July 2001.

[12] B. Chen, K. Jamieson, H. Balakrishnan, and R. Morris, "Span: An Energy-Efficient Coordination Algorithm for Topology Maintenance in Ad Hoc Wireless Networks," Proc. Seventh Ann. ACM/IEEE Int'l Conf. Mobile Computing and Networking (MobiCom), pp. 85-96, July 2001.

[13] A. Cerpa and D. Estrin, "ASCENT: Adaptive Self-Configuring sEnsor Networks Topologies," IEEE Transaction on Mobile Computing and Networking, vol. 3, issue. 3, pp. 272-285, July 2004.
[14] D. Tian and N.D. Georganas, "A Node Scheduling Scheme for Energy Conservation in Large Wireless Sensor Networks," Wireless Comm. and Mobile Computing, vol.3, pp. 271-290, 2003.
[15] Xiaorui Wang, Guoliang Xing, Yuanfang, Chenyang Lu, Robert Pless and Christopher Gill, "Integrated Coverage and Connectivity Configuration in Wireless Sensor Networks," ACM SenSys '03, pp.: 28 – 39, November, 2003.
[16] Yi Zou and Krishnendu Chakrabarty, "A Distributed Coverage- and Connectivity-Centric Technique for Selecting Active Nodes in Wireless Sensor Networks," IEEE Transactions On Computers, vol. 54, No. 8, August 2005.

Spectrum Sensing Method for Increasing the Spectrum Efficiency in Wireless Sensor Network

Ning Han, Sung Hwan Shon, Jong Ok Joo, and Jae Moung Kim

Graduate school of IT & Telecommunications Inha University, 253 Yonghyun-dong,
Nam-gu Incheon 402-751, Korea
neil_han@china.com, kittisn@naver.com, joojoo@mic.go.kr,
jaekim@inha.ac.kr
http://witlab.inha.ac.kr

Abstract. As the spectral recourses are limited, the spectrum efficiency is more important for the design of wireless sensor network. In this paper, a spectral correlation based detection method for spectrum sensing is proposed to increase the spectrum efficiency in wireless sensor network. The signal of interests is modeled as a cyclostationary random process, therefore, the spectral correlation function could be used, and a squared coherence function is used as the decision criterion. Simulations are made based on the 4-FSK signal. The results verify that the proposed method outperforms the conventional energy detection.

Keywords: wireless sensor network, spectrum sensing, energy detection, spectral correlation, spectral coherence function.

1   Introduction

Wireless sensor network is made up of many small sensor nodes and one or more base station called sink [1]. It consists of the processing unit with limited computational power and limited memory sensors, a communication device, and a power supply. The base stations are the most important components of the wireless sensor network with much more computational, energy and communication resources. They act as a gateway between sensor nodes and the end users. Wireless sensor network consists of the individual nodes that is capable of interacting with the environment by sensing or controlling the physical parameters each have to collaborate to fulfill their tasks. A single node is capable of doing so. Sensors and control devices due to the battery constraints has a limited amount of delay and low energy consumption. They are self organizing and deployed within their application areas. In wireless sensor network, the redundant nodes are deployed to protect against the node failure. Power conservation is the main concern for the network life time. Network capable of multi-hop reduces the overall network power consumption. It has vast areas of applications such as in the Disaster relief application, Environmental control and biodiversity mapping, telemetric, medicine and health care etc. Transceiver is available for different carrier frequencies. Both a transmitter and a receiver are required in a sensor node. The essential task is to convert a bit stream coming from a microcontroller (or a sequence of bytes or frames) and convert them to and from radio waves. The

H.Y. Youn, M. Kim, and H. Morikawa (Eds.): UCS 2006, LNCS 4239, pp. 478 – 488, 2006.

Transceiver supports the modulation schemes such as the on/off- keying, ASK, FSK or similar scheme.

Our limited spectral resources have been used sufficiently, especially the frequencies below 3GHz. In fact, a certain number of frequency bands are underutilized in spectacularly times and locations. As the sensor node increased, frequency resource going drop off. In addition, conventional energy detection method has problem that it could not be operated in low SNR situation. Under this circumstance, an efficient spectrum utilization technology is in great need. The essential stage for increasing the spectrum efficiency is the spectrum sensing, in which the spectrum environment is recognized by the elements of the senor network. In this paper, we mainly discuss the applicable methods for spectrum sensing, we proposed a spectral correlation based detection method which could be used to increase the spectrum efficiency in wireless sensor network.

In the second section, we introduce the detection model which is valid for both conventional method and proposed method. And then, we proposed a spectral correlation based detection method which is explained in details in section three and section four. The expression of False alarm probability and threshold are derived. Simulation results are shown and analyzed in the fifth section. At last, this paper is concluded in the last section.

2 Detection Model

Detection in spectrum sensing is a procedure to search the empty frequency bands for sensor network elements. As explained, there are limited spectral recourses; therefore, the detection procedure is essential for increasing the efficiency of the wireless sensor network. Different kind of modulated signal are used in wireless sensor network, such as OOK, ASK and FSK. The OOK signal is simple and easy to be implemented, while FSK has better performance in the presence of interference with implementation difficulties. However, ASK is more robust against OOK and is easier to implement with a low cost. The typical 4-FSK is shown in figure 1. In the following section of this paper, we will use this signal as an example for wireless sensor network.

The purpose of detection is to learn the environment of the sensors and find the empty frequency bands for operating. It is obviously a simple binary hypothesis detection problem. The two hypotheses which are defined as H_0 and H_1 are modeled as:

(1) H_0: the frequency band is empty and the received signal is noise only:

$$y(t) = n(t). \tag{1}$$

(2) H_1: the frequency band is occupied and the received signal is transmitted signal interfered by noise.

$$y(t) = x(t) + n(t). \tag{2}$$

where x(t), y(t) and n(t) denote the transmitted signal, the received signal and the noise respectively. This binary hypothesis test is valid for the following sections of this paper.

For the design of detector, various measurements are made based on different techniques first, and then the criterion is derived according to the measurement to make the decision whether H_0 or H_1 occurs.

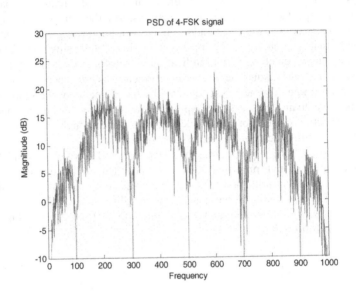

Fig. 1. Power spectrum density of 4-FSK signal

3 Energy Detection Method

The classical method for signal detection is referred to as energy detection was first proposed by Urkowitz in 1967. This method is also known as radiometry which based on energy measurement. The general block diagram for energy detection described in [2] is shown in figure 2. The main parts of energy detector are a noise pre-filter, a square law device and an integrator

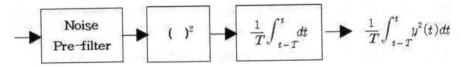

Fig. 2. Energy detection procedure

Energy of the received signal is measured in the observation interval. The notation used in this paper is the same as that in [2]. According to the comparison result between the measured energy and the predefined threshold, decision is made by the detector.

As explained in [2], the test statistic can be expressed by:

$$W = \sum_{i=1}^{2TB} \frac{r_i^2}{2B\sigma^2} \tag{3}$$

where T and B are the observation interval and channel bandwidth, respectively. σ^2 is noise power measured in bandwidth. r_i is the sampled received signals.

Under the hypotheses H_0, which means no signal was transmitted in the detected band, W is the summation of the squares of the 2TB Gaussian random variables with zero mean and unity variance, and takes the form

$$W = \sum_{i=1}^{2TB} \frac{n_i^2}{2B\sigma^2} \tag{4}$$

it has a chi-square distribution with 2TB degrees of freedom. The corresponding false alarm probability for energy detection is:

$$P_{fa} = \Pr\{W > TH | H_1\} = \Pr\{\chi_{2TB}^2 > TH\} \tag{5}$$

where χ_{2BT}^2 indicates a chi-square variable with 2BT degrees of freedom and TH is the detection threshold which is used to decide the detection results. When the false alarm probability of the detector is determined, the corresponding threshold can be calculated by the inverse chi-square process.

As the statistic of the transmitted signal is not known to the sensor itself, an exact expression for the test statistic W under hypotheses H_1 cannot be concluded. However, in [2], this test statistic was shown under the assumption that the input with a deterministic signal present is Gaussian but not zero mean.

Considering that the energy detector only measures the energy of the received signal in the observation interval, the performance will degrade in the low SNR. The straightforward influence to the spectrum efficiency of entire system will be significant. Therefore, a better detector should be implemented.

4 Proposed Detection Method

Generally, the signal of interest is modeled as a stationary random process. However, in most of the modern communication systems, the signal of interest can be modeled as a cyclostationary random process instead. Under this assumption, another catalog of signal detection methods could be explored; even the signal classification can be realized under certain circumstances. In this paper, we proposed a spectral correlation based detection method for WSN. The proposed detector is explained in detail as well as the decision criterion. The concept of cyclostationary theory described by [3][4][5] will be introduced briefly in this section.

A process, for instance X(t), is said to be cyclostationary in the wide sense if its mean and autocorrelation are periodic with some period, say T [3]:

$$m_X(t+T) = m_X(t) . \tag{6}$$

$$R_X\left(t+T+\frac{\tau}{2},t+T-\frac{\tau}{2}\right) = R_X\left(t+\frac{\tau}{2},t-\frac{\tau}{2}\right) \tag{7}$$

$R_x(t+\tau/2, t-\tau/2)$, which is a function of two independent variables, t and τ, is periodic in t with period T for each value of τ.

The spectral correlation function which is also known as the cyclic spectral density function could be measured by the normalized correlation between two spectral components of x(t) at frequencies (f+α/2) and (f-α/2) over an interval of length Δt.

$$S_{xT}^{\alpha}(f)_{\Delta t} = \frac{1}{\Delta t}\int_{-\Delta t/2}^{\Delta t/2}\frac{1}{\sqrt{T}}X_T(t,f+\alpha/2)\cdot\frac{1}{\sqrt{T}}X_T^*(t,f-\alpha/2)dt \tag{8}$$

In (8) the spectral of x(t) over the time interval [t-T/2,t+T/2] is defined by:

$$X_T(t,v) = \int_{t-T/2}^{t+T/2}x(u)e^{-j2\pi vu}du \cdot \tag{9}$$

The ideal measurement of the SCF for the received signal x(t) is given by:

$$S_x^{\alpha}(f) = \lim_{T\to\infty}\lim_{\Delta t\to\infty}S_{xT}^{\alpha}(f)_{\Delta t}\cdot \tag{10}$$

In order to generate the SCF, the procedure in figure 3 can be used. [6]

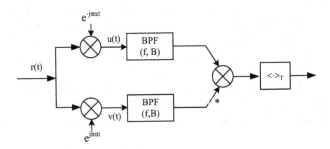

Fig. 3. Spectral correlation function generation

The spectral correlation characteristic of the cyclostationary signals provides us a richer domain signal detection method. By searching the cyclic frequencies of different kinds of modulated signals the detection can be accomplished. Also, information such as the carrier frequency, chip rate could be calculated according to the cyclic frequencies. The spectral correlation of 4-FSK signal is plotted as shown in figure 4. The cyclic frequencies are f_c, $2f_c$ and $3f_c$. Meanwhile, the spectral correlation of ASK signal is plotted in figure 5 as well with cyclic frequency equal to $2f_c$. Here, f_c denotes the carrier frequency.

Another reason why spectral correlation based method is attractive in the area of signal detection is that it is robust against random noise and interference. Spectral correlation of random noise is shown in figure 6. It is obviously to be obtained the spectral correlation is significant large when cyclic frequency equals to zero comparing to that of other values.

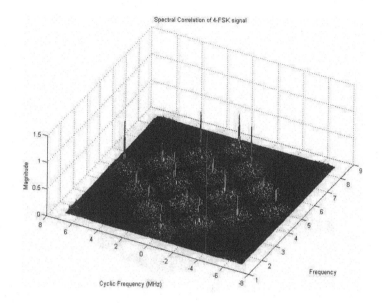

Fig. 4. SCF of 4-FSK signal

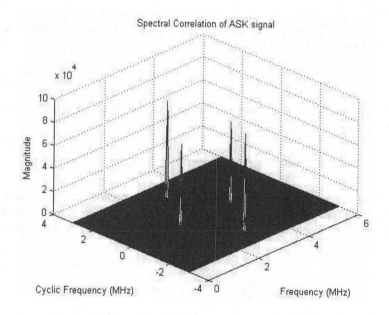

Fig. 5. SCF of ASK signal

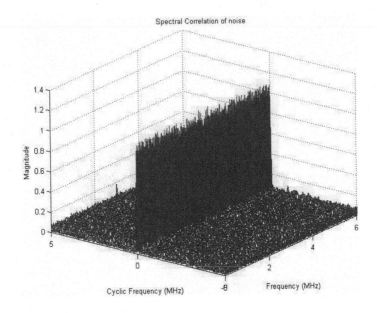

Fig. 6. SCF of random noise

The SCF of the received signal, denoted by $S_r^\alpha(f)$, is calculated, we will make the decision based on it. The energy in the frequency interval F is measured. The test statistic W is expressed as:

$$W = \sum_{i=1}^{F} S_r^2(f) \cdot \qquad (11)$$

Here we propose to use the coherence function as the detection criteria, which is defined in [3] by:

$$C_r^\alpha(f) = \frac{S_r^\alpha(f)}{\sqrt{S_r(f+\alpha/2)S_r(f-\alpha/2)}} \qquad (12)$$

We find that the two terms in the denominator can be treated as filtered from two channels. We proposed to use the modified coherence function named magnitude-squared coherence function which is verified and derived well in [4]. This function is defined as:

$$C_r^\alpha(f) = \frac{\left(S_r^\alpha(f)\right)^2}{S_r(f+\alpha/2)S_r(f-\alpha/2)} \qquad (13)$$

The probability distribution for $C_r^\alpha(f)$ which is also derived in [4] is

$$\Pr\{C < TH\} = 1 - (1-TH)^{N-1} \, for \quad 0 \le TH \le 1 \quad N \ge 2 \qquad (14)$$

Therefore the false alarm probability is:

$$P_{fa}\{C > TH | H_o\} = (1 - TH)^{N-1} \, for \quad 0 \le TH \le 1 \quad N \ge 2 \tag{15}$$

As stressed in [4], the reason why we can use this probability distribution in stead of the conditional probability distribution is because either $S_r(f + \alpha/2)$ or $S_r(f - \alpha/2)$ is a Gaussian random variable under the hypotheses H_0 in our case. With the derived expression of false alarm probability, we can determine the threshold for the detection probability independent of the input signal.

5 Simulation Results

In order to verify the performance of the proposed method, computer simulations are made. The Receiver operating characteristic (ROC) is considered as the main performance evaluation parameter and various ROC curves are shown for both methods in AWGN.

In figure 7, the ROC for the conventional energy detection is shown in different SNR levels. When the transmitted signal power is comparable to the noise power, the performance is poor. With the existence of strong transmitted signal, whose power is as 10 times larger than that of noise, the energy detection performs efficiently. This verifies why energy detection is generally used in strong signal detection.

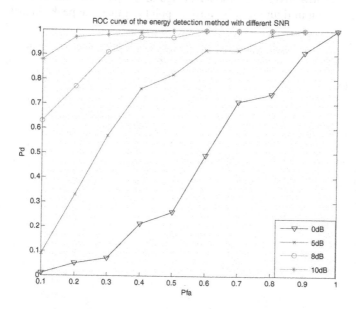

Fig. 7. ROC curve of energy detection method with different SNR

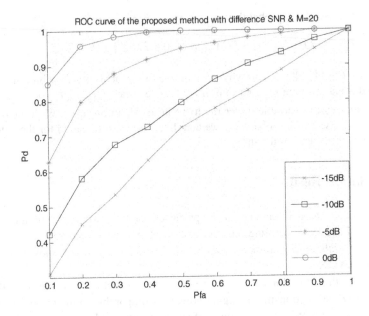

Fig. 8. ROC curve of proposed method with different SNR (M=20)

In the case of low SNR level, the advantage of the proposed method can be seen obviously as shown in figure 8. It is worth to point out that, the peak characteristic of

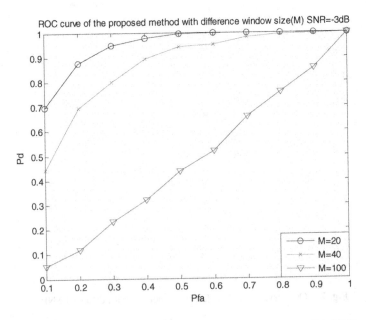

Fig. 9. ROC curve of proposed method with different window size (M) (SNR=-3db)

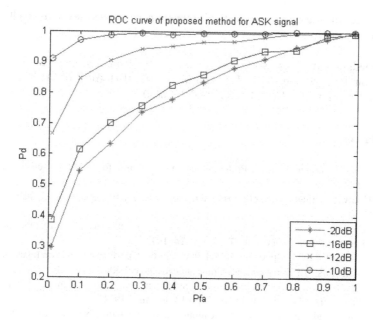

Fig. 10. ROC curve of proposed method with different SNR

the SCF of signal should be considered. As the peaks contain most of the power, therefore the smaller the observation window, the better the performance will be. The ROC curve of the proposed method with various value of window size M is shown in figure 9. As we predicted, the narrow window increases the detection probability in the same SNR level. The detection probability increases linearly as the window size reach to 100 samples. Therefore, the detector efficiency can be increased significantly by applying a narrow window to contain the peaks.

As ASK signal is also used in WSN, we show the performance of our proposed method with ASK signal. As shown in figure 10, it is similar to the performance of 4-FSK signal. It proves that the proposed method is valid for detecting WSN signals, therefore could be used to increase the spectral efficiency in WSN.

Our proposed detection method works efficient when a priori information of cyclic frequencies of the received signals is known. In practical, the cyclic frequency for signal used in the WSN is considered to be known in the sensors.

6 Conclusions

In this paper we proposed a spectral correlation based detection method for spectrum sensing which could be used to increase the spectral efficiency in wireless sensor network. By measuring the squared coherence function, the false alarm probability and the related threshold are shown based on the study of [7]. 4-FSK signal based computer simulations show that the proposed method works efficient in the low SNR level in which the energy detection method does not work well. The detection performance of the proposed method relies on the SNR level as well as the observation window size.

Acknowledgement. This work was supported by Korea Science & Engineering Foundation through the NRL Program(M1060000019406J000019410) and Basic Research Program grant No.R01-2006-000-10266-0.

References

1. Holger Karl, Andreas Willig : Protocols and Architectures for Wireless Sensor Networks. England, 2005.
2. B H.Urkowitz : Energy detection of unknown deterministic signals, Proc. IEEE, vol. 55, pp.523-531, 1967.
3. W.A. Gardner, L.E. Franks : Characterization of cyclostationary random signal processes, IEEE Trans. Inform Theory, vol. IT-21, pp4-14, 1975.
4. W.A. Garnder, C. M. Spooner: Signal interception : performance advantages of cyclic-feature detectors, IEEE transactions Communications, vol.40, pp149-159.
5. W.A. Gardner : Exploitation of spectral redundancy in cyclostationarity signals, IEEE Signal Processing Magazine, vol.8, no.2, pp.14-36, April 1991.
6. Ning Han, SungHwan Shon, JaeHak Chung, JaeMoung Kim : Spectral Correlation Based Signal Detection Method for Spectrum Sensing in IEEE 802.22 WRAN systems, The 6th ICACT, Korea, Feb, 2006.
7. A.H.Nuttall : Invariance of distribution of coherence estimate to second-channel statistics, IEEE Transactions of Acoustics, Speech, and Signal Processing, vol. ASSP-29, no.1, pp.120-122, February 1981.

Algorithm for the Predictive Hibernation of Sensor Systems

Hyo Jong Lee

Division of Electronics and Information Engineering
Research Center of Industrial Technology, Chonbuk National University,
Jeonju City, Jeonbuk Prov., 561-756, Korea
hlee@chonbuk.ac.kr

Abstract. As key technologies of sensor network have been deployed to various applications, such as ubiquitous computing and mobile computing, the importance of sensor network were recognized. Because most sensors are battery operated, the constrained power of sensors is a serious problem. If data containing small error is tolerable to users, the sensor data can be sampled discretely. An efficient power conserving algorithm is presented in this paper. By observing the trend of the sensor data, it was possible to predict the time that exceeds the specified maximum error. The algorithm has been applied to various sensor data including synthetic data. Compared to the regular sensors which do not adapt the proposed algorithm, the proposed sensors in this paper shows that the sensor's life time can be increased up to six folds within the range of 1% tolerable data error.

1 Introduction

As the VLSI technology advances continuously, the new simple yet powerful computing environments are being developed. The development introduces higher performance in processor, memory, and radio components with relatively low price. Consequently ubiquitous computing encompasses a wide range of researches, such as mobile computing, distributed computing, and sensor networking. A sensor network, which takes low cost, is advantageous and efficient to measure environment parameters [1] including temperature, sound, vibration, motion, pollutants and traffic condition. Thus a sensor network could be applied to the ubiquitous computing effectively.

The application areas of sensor network vary from personal to governmental usages. Madden et. al. [2] summarized application examples, such as monitoring building integrity [3] and ecological effects [4, 5]. Berkeley's smartdust [6] and Systronix's JStamps [7] are good running examples. Many scientists anticipate sensor network to provide easily accessible and high quality information by taking advantage of the rapidly developing semiconductor technology. They will perform their responsibilities with more accuracy and robustness.

Most sensors are typically battery operated to compute, probe and transmit data. Due to its limited size, the power source is always constrained. Several

H.Y. Youn, M. Kim, and H. Morikawa (Eds.): UCS 2006, LNCS 4239, pp. 489–499, 2006.

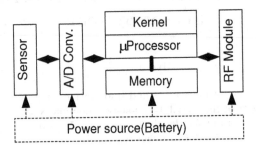

Fig. 1. Architecture of sensor system

methods have been introduced to minimize power consumption [8, 9]. An efficient power management can reduce its consumption by setting idle components into lower power state [10]. The key factors in saving energy are not only the frequency of idle states, but also the duration of each idle state. Let's consider a typical sensor. Figure 1 shows a typical sensor architecture. A sensor system contains microprocessor, small memory, kernel, sensor module, and RF module. Kernel controls each component through micro-device drivers. The kernel decides which component is idle and places the component into either lower power states or off-mode.The questions are how to find out the optimal duty cycle and when it is best to put a module into an idle state. If the idle time is too short, the system will not save power by setting the modules as idle state. The system will suffer with the consequence of latency caused by state transition. The overall system performance will be also degraded due to retrials of sender sensors. A sensor with small duty cycle, but long idle time cannot collect accurate data because it simply miss important data change, if any, during the long idle time.

There is trade-off between data quality and power consumption of sensors. Sensor network may produce data of higher quality with more power consumption. The power conserving methods for sensors have been researched based on either statistical observation or circuit design technology.

The objective of this research is to find the optimal duration of idle time of a sensor. The algorithm has been simulated to measure the life-time power of sensor battery. A noble power-conserving method, which is suitable for wireless sensor networks is proposed. It provides the longest life time of sensors, while the accuracy of collected data is satisfied within a specified tolerable error.

The remainder of the paper is organized as follows: Section 2 defines the problem. Section 3 describes the power conservation model in detail. Next, the performance of the algorithm has been described in Section 4. Finally, Section 5 concludes the paper.

2   Problem Description

The most commonly adapted sensor network is a multi-hop wireless network with no fixed infrastructure. In order to find an optimal method to conserve power for a single sensor, a number of sensors are limited to one in our problem.

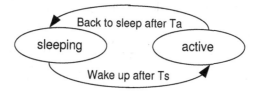

Fig. 2. System model

A target sensor is which keeps sending data to its leader or server. The collected data should be processed in real-time instead of batch mode. This is necessary to handle most of sensor data to prevent disaster or propagate to required next action.

Each module of a sensor may be in different states, such as *active, idle or sleep*. Assuming sensor nodes sends data to its server only, a sensor node is in one of two states, *sleeping* and *active*. Figure 2 shows the state diagram of the described sensor system model. Initially a sensor starts from the *active* state. When its state is *active* the sensor probes first. Then, the sensor processes data and decides whether it needs to send data to a server or not. It also needs to estimates next idle time. The *active* state lasts for constant time T_a every case. T_a is a preset value that depends on a specific sensor.

When its state is *sleeping*, the processor goes to sleep and every other module is off. Even the sensor may be off. The power consumption is minimized in this state. The sleeping time T_s is calculated, while it was in *active* mode. If the sleeping time T_s is too large, a new sleeping time is set to predefined heartbeat interval, T_h. Thus, the relationship of $T_s \leq T_h$ is always valid. The power consumption of *sleeping* state may differ depending on the number of off-modules. In our problem, *sleeping* represents a complete off state. Its consumed power is assumed to be 10mW per unit time. In this case the processor itself enters sleep mode, while the power of all other modules is turned off.

The relationship between data quality and the level of power conservation is investigated in this paper. The goal is to find the maximal life time of a sensor node, while data from the sensor is accurate within a tolerable error, ϵ. The detailed algorithm to achieve the goal is described in Section 3.

It is necessary to define a quality function $\mathcal{Q}$ to measure errors The error can be express with distance between actual values and approximate values. The simple quality function can be defined using $\mathcal{D}_4$ distance as following:

$$\mathcal{D}_4(d - d_s) = \frac{1}{n} \sum^{n} (|d - d_s|)$$

However, a commonly used distance function is Euclidean distance $\mathcal{D}_e$ [11] because of its capability to distinguish maximum boundary, such as:

$$\mathcal{D}_e(d - d_s)^2 = \frac{1}{n} \sum^{n} (d - d_s)^2$$

Thus, the quality function Q is defined as:

$$Q(D - D_s) = \frac{1}{\sqrt{n}} \sqrt{\sum^{n} (D - D_s)^2} \tag{1}$$

3   Power Conservation Model

The only possible way to save power consumption from sensors is to predict how long the current data will stay within a specified error tolerance. If the probability that the sensed value stays is high, the sensor should go to *sleeping* mode; otherwise, it should stay in *active* mode. The principle of data sample is described in the following section before we explain the algorithm.

3.1   Piecewise Approximation

The piecewise constant approximation [12] [13] was developed during the Quality-Aware Sensor Architecture project at UC Irvine. It was designed to work for batch-mode for archival data instead of real-time data compression. Figure 3 shows pseudocode of batch-PMC algorithm.

What the algorithm does is, it examines the sensor values. If the range between the mean value and the sensor data is less than or equal to ϵ, it updates the partial sum(psum) and mean value. If the range of the sensor data exceeds ϵ, then the value and its time step are transmitted to a server. The algorithm continues to

---

```
procedure BPMC
input: sensor data D =< d[1], d[2], ... >, tolerance ε
output: Compressed data D_s which satisfies D_s ≤ D ± ε
01    i, k ← 1
02    mean ← d[1]
03    psum ← 0
04    while (more archival data)
05        if abs(d[i] - mean) > ε
06            append(mean, i − 1) to a list
07            psum ← 0
08            mean ← d[i]
09            k ← 1
10        else
11            psum ← psum + d[i]
12            mean ← psum/k
13            k ← k + 1
14        end
15        i ← i + 1
16    end.
```

Fig. 3. Pseudocode of Batch-mode PMC

compress the next set of sample from the changed time step. It is proved that no other data set exists, which satisfies the given constrained error ϵ [13].

The problem of this algorithm is that it lacks of real-time processing. A sensor has to wait to decide when the error of the data becomes larger than the constrained error in the algorithm. For example, a set of sensor data is within the constrained error for one day, the final value is appended to a list after the examining of one data data. Again it is good for archival purpose, but it needs to be modified to work for real-time manner.

3.2 Real-Time PMC

A real-time PMC has been developed from the batch-mode PMC to work with real-time data. The modified real-time PMC is displayed in Figure 4.

---

procedure RPMC
input: sensor data $D = < d[1],\ d[2], ... >$, tolerance ϵ
output: Transmit data D_s which satisfies $D_s \leq D \pm \epsilon$
```
01    i, k ← 1
02    threshold ← d[1] ±ε
03    transmit (threshold, i − 1)
04    psum ← 0
05    while (sensor is on)
06      if abs(d[i] - threshold) > ε
07        threshold ← d[i] ±ε
08        transmit(threshold, i − 1) to a server
09        psum ← 0
10        mean ← d[i]
11        k ← 1
12      else
13        psum ← psum + d[i]
14        threshold ← psum/k ±ε
15        k ← k + 1
16      end
17      i ← i + 1
18    end.
```

Fig. 4. Pseudocode of Real-time PMC

In the real-time PMC mean value is adjusted with ϵ at line 02 and 07 according to data change direction. When a new value is out of the error range and its value is *greater* than the mean value, a new mean value will be adjusted by adding ϵ to move upwardly. If a new value is *smaller* than the mean value, a new mean value will be adjusted by subtracting ϵ to lower the current mean value.

A sensor generates data continuously in the real world. However, power can be conserved by omitting redundant data. The algorithm in the real-time PMC needs to update the mean value constantly. It means that significant amount of power is consumed for redundant data. In the extreme case, 90% of total energy of the sensor is wasted in waiting or sending redundant data [6]. A statistical approach to remove the redundant data is explained in the following section.

3.3   Prediction Model

There are some researches done about predicting behaviors of sensor networks [8, 14]. They tried to model each state from sensor network. Even if a complicated model is built for a specific sensor network, the model will not work properly when its behavior does not follow exactly with the model, which is common in the real world. The complicated algorithm does not reward the efforts that has been made.

In this paper a very simple statistical information is adapted to model sleeping behavior of a sensor. It is reasonable to assume that every data changes within a certain range. The boundary of temperature, humidity, salinity, location and many more parameters are restricted within a limited time range. If the range is long enough, then distribution of each sensor readings may be assumed to be a normal distribution.

The mean μ and variance σ for N data D, which is large enough, is defined as follows:

$$\mu = \frac{\Sigma D}{N}, \qquad \sigma^2 = \frac{\Sigma(D - \mu)^2}{(N - 1)}$$

Since a sensor sends data indefinitely, it is necessary to define a memory size for calculations. If the sensor has a memory block of size B for parameter calculation, the memory can be operated as a queue, which has FIFO property. We can assume that the prediction model of the sleeping time starts after the buffer is filled initially.

If the calculation for μ and σ is performed for each data, the complexity is $O(N^2)$. Mean and variance for incoming sensor data can be calculated based on the previous parameter values to save excessive computational time. If a current and a new mean, and a current and new variance are noted as μ^-, μ^+, σ^2_- and σ^2_+, the new mean and variance μ^+ and σ^2_+ can be derived from simple arithmetic processes. The following formulas satisfy $O(1)$ complexity.

$$\mu^+ = B \cdot \mu^- - d_s^- + \frac{d_s^+}{B} \tag{2}$$

where B, d_s^- and d_s^+ are, respectively, a queue size, the oldest data to be removed from the queue, and a new data to be stored into a queue. The current and new variances are defined:

$$\sigma^2_- = \frac{1}{B-1}[\Sigma(d_s - \mu^-)^2] =$$

$$\frac{1}{B-1}[(d_s[i] - \mu^-)^2 + (d_s[i+1] - \mu^-)^2 + \cdots + (d_s[k] - \mu^-)^2]$$

$$\sigma_+^2 = \frac{1}{B-1}[\Sigma(d_s - \mu^+)^2] =$$

$$\frac{1}{B-1}[(d_s[i+1] - \mu^+)^2 + \cdots + (d_s[k] - \mu^+)^2 + (d_s[k+1] - \mu^+)^2]$$

k here represents the last index of the current queue, which is equal to the buffer size $B - 1$. Since only a single new data is inserted to the queue each time, a relationship, $\mu^+ \simeq \mu^-$ should hold. Therefore, the final new variance is defined as follows:

$$\sigma_+^2 = \sigma_-^2 - \frac{1}{B-1}[(d_s^- - \mu^-)^2 + (d_s^+ - \mu^+)^2] \qquad (3)$$

Both μ and σ represent distribution of momentum locally. If the memory block size B is either too big or too small, they may not be useful to represent overall sensor data correctly. If B is too small, then it may not represent correct distribution. If B is too large, then the sensor may not be able to hold the memory, although it provides better stabilization.

Given momentum of distribution, the probability distribution function of continuous distribution is approximated in asymptotic manner as follows:

$$P(x) = Z(x) - \frac{1}{6}\frac{\mu}{\sigma^3}Z^3(x) + \cdots \qquad (4)$$

where $Z(x) = \frac{1}{\sigma\sqrt{2\pi}}e^{-(x-\mu)^{\cdot}/2\sigma^{\cdot}}$.

The probability function simply states how frequently the value can occur. It is logical to reason that the value of higher probability will be sensed frequently. In that case the value with higher frequency will last longer than the one with lower frequency.

Another behavior of a sensor is that the value is changed with momentum. Most sensor values move upward or downward slowly in a long time range. However, one of our data set, *relative humidity*, which is described in the next section, is an exception; it suddenly drops at a certain time step. The derivative and acceleration of changing values are good measurement tools for the behavior. If the derivative of values are assumed to be constant, i.e., no acceleration is found, the exact time to reach the thresholding from the current value can be predictable. In the real world, however, the behavior of sensor data are fluctuating irregularly.

Our goal is to predict the optimal sleeping time for a sensor. The sleeping time T_s can be modeled empirically based on observation described above. The derivative becomes a major factor in estimating T_s. However, the acceleration of change and the probability of the value should be also considered. If the acceleration becomes large, sleeping time becomes shorter. The sleeping time of sensor reading value x is formulised as follow:

$$T_s = \frac{\epsilon}{(Der - Acc/\alpha)} + Prob(x) \cdot \beta \qquad (5)$$

where Der and Acc represent derivative and acceleration of data change, α and β are constant real numbers. It is found that the good range of α and β are [1.5 ~ 2.5] and [8 ~ 12], respectively.

Figure 5 shows the ratio of sleeping time to total time of four different data set for different heartbeats. The data set is explained in the next section. Heartbeat was set at 40 and 20 for the top and bottom plot, respectively. They look similar, although the ratio is slightly higher for the heartbeat of 40. However, data set of *processor list* is clearly better in the lower heartbeat.

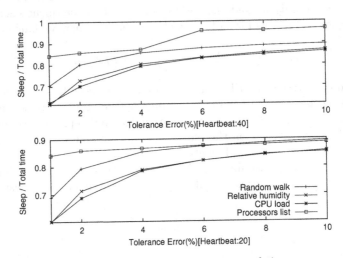

Fig. 5. Ratio of sleeping time to total time

4   Performance Analysis

The proposed model has been implemented to verify the proposed idea. The results show the algorithm is capable to handle various data sets. In this section, experimental environment and result are described.

4.1   Simulator

A distributed sensor network simulator has been implemented with Java language. Each individual system may represent a single sensor node or multiple nodes. Each node has a simulated sensor, memory, and processor. One of the nodes is defined as a permanent server. The main tasks of the server is 1)to set up the connection for the requested sensor, 2)to receive and store sensor data, and 3)to monitor the functionality of the sensors. It can allow the same physical node to be connected to the server with different sensor identification numbers. Whenever a connection is requested, the server creates a new thread so that the other sensor can still communicate with the server.

A sensor node is defined as a logical node, such that, multiple sensors can be created within a single physical node. Three major components, a sensor module, a communication module, and processor module are built inside each sensor. The sensor module probes data continuously while the node is awake. Data set can be random walk, number of processes, average load of the system, and number of characters in the processes' list. A new synthetic sensor data can be programmed easily. The communication module has the *sender* and *receiver* threads. It can send data to a server or other sensors. The main function of the processor module is to calculate statistical information, such as μ and σ, and estimate the ideal sleeping time T_s. In this paper it is assumed that a single sensor communicates with a server. Thus, it has only two states, *sleeping* and *active*.

4.2   Quality Measurement

Four data sets, random walk, relative humidity, average CPU load, and processes list have been collected and used for the experiment. The compression ratio of real-time PMC have been measured and compared with same results from batch-mode PMC. Figure 6 and Figure 7 show similar ratio of compression for four data sets.

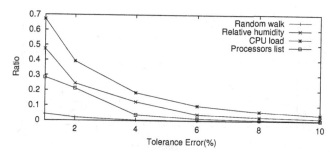

Fig. 6. Compression performance of Batch-mode PMC

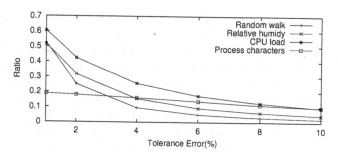

Fig. 7. Compression performance of Real-time PMC

4.3   Power Conservation

In this section power conservation has been estimated under simplified conditions. It is not realistic to calculate exact amount of power conservation with simulation. The power consumption for the active and sleeping sensor are assumed to be about 1000mW and 10mW, respectively. Assuming that the voltage

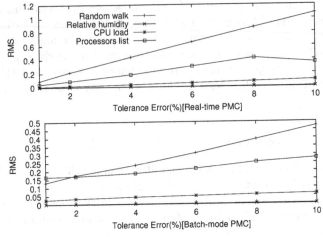

Fig. 8. Error of prediction

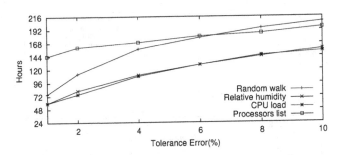

Fig. 9. Relative sensor life-hours

of the sensors is 1.3V, the consumed current per unit second for the active and sleeping sensors are 800mA and 8mA, respectively.

Figure 9 displays the lasting of sensors of different data sets. In the figure the life time of a normal sensor, without using real-time PMC, is assumed to be as 24 hours. That is, the x-axis represents the life hours of a normal sensor without any PMC. The same amount of power is applied to the sensor with the real-time PMC to measure relative life hours of sensors. The life time of sensors with real-time PMC is clearly improved compared with the normal sensors. The life time is increased 247% ~ 600% for 1% of error. The life time is increased up to 862% for 10% of error.

5   Conclusion

A new modified piecewise approximation is proposed to predict sleeping time of sensors. The sensor values are estimated immediately after reading. Then, the sensor continues to examine whether the error of new data is larger than the given tolerable error. If it is not larger, then the sensor enters into a sleeping state for a certain amount of period. If the error is larger than the tolerance, the sensor sends a new data after adjustment, then enters into a sleep state.

The key idea of power conservation is to calculate the appropriate sleeping time. An efficient formula is derived based on statistics of distributed values. The sleeping time is dependent on the derivative and the acceleration of data change. The probability of measured value is also affective to the sleeping time. The formula introduced in this paper estimates sleeping time according to the specified tolerable error. The dramatic power conservation is achieved in the case of sensors with the power conserving formula. The life span of sensors can be increased from 247% to 600% with 1% of error tolerance. The rate of power conservation becomes higher with greater error tolerance.

References

1. G.J. Pottie and W. J. Kaiser, "Wireless Integrated Network Sensors," *Communications of the ACM*, vol. 43, no. 5, pp. 51–58, 2000.
2. S. Madden, Michael J. Franklin, Joseph M. Hellerstein, and Wei Hong, "Tag: A Tiny Agregation Service for Ad-hoc Sensor Networks," in *Fifth USENIX Symposium on Operating Systems Design and Implementation (OSDI)*, Boston, Dec 2002.
3. UC Berkeley, "Smart Buildings Admit Their Faults," 2001.
4. A. Cerpa, J Elson, D. Estrin, L Girod, M. Hamilton, and J Zhao, "Habitat Monitoring: Application Driver for Wireless Communications Technology," in *Workshop on Data Communications in Latin America and the Caribbean(ACM SIGCOMM 2001)*, 2001.
5. A. Mainwaring, J. Polastre, R. Szewczyk, and D. Culler, "Wireless Sensor Networks for Habitat Monitoring," in *Workshop on Sensor Networks and Applications*, 2002.
6. J. Hill and D. Culler, "A Wireless Embedded Architecture for System-level Optimization," Oct 2002.
7. Systronix, "Jstamp Technical Data," 2002.
8. T. Simmunic, L. Benini, P. Glynn, and G. De Micheli, "Event-driven Power Management," *IEEE Transaction on Computer Aided Design of Integrated Circuits Systems*, vol. 20, no. 7, pp. 840–857, 2001.
9. N. Bulusu, D. Estrin, L. Girod, and J. Heidemann, "Scalable Coordination for Wireless Sensor Networks:Self-configuring Localization Systems," in *6th International Symposium on Communication Theory and Applications(ISCTA'01)*, Ambleside, UK, July 2001.
10. L. BEnini and G. De Micheli, *Dynamic Power Management:Design Techniques and CAD Tools*, Kluwer Academic Publishers, 1997.
11. L. Gao and X. S. Wang, "Continually Evaluating Similarity-based Pattern Queries on a Streaming Time Series," in *ACM SIGMOD 2002*, 2002, pp. 370–381.
12. Kaushik Chakrabarti, Eamonn Keogh, and S. Mehrotra, "Locally Adaptive Dimensionality Reduction for Indexing Large Time Series Database," *ACM Transactions on Database Systems*, vol. 27, no. 2, pp. 188–228, jun 2002.
13. I. Lazaridis and S. Mehrotra, "Capturing Sensor-Generated Time Series with Quality Guarantees," 2003.
14. Amit Sinha, "Dynamic Power Management in Wireless Sensor Networks," *IEEE Design & Test of Computers*, vol. 18, no. 2, pp. 62–74, 2001.

Encapsulation and Entity-Based Approach of Interconnection Between Sensor Platform and Middleware of Pervasive Computing

Shinyoung Lim and Abdelsalam (Sumi) Helal

Mobile and Pervasive Computing Laboratory
Computer & Information Science and Engineering Department
College of Engineering, University of Florida
P.O. Box 116120, Gainesville FL 32611, USA
{lim, helal}@cise.ufl.edu
www.ctia.ufl.edu

Abstract. In this paper, we present a unique mechanism that enables seamless interconnection and scalability of the interface between the sensor platform layer and the middleware layer in pervasive computing. The disadvantages of using one-to-one hard coding for various device drivers and firmware for interfacing sensor platform and middleware layers are primarily a lack of flexibility and scalability when the system changes environments. The encapsulation of access point of the sensor platform layer provides developers and designers with an effective way of interconnecting and scaling up with diverse and various kinds of sensors and actuators. In this paper, we define encapsulation of the access point of the sensor platform layer. The module for encapsulating the detected sensor data is called 'context representer'. The context representer converts detected sensor data to raw context. For interconnecting with the sensor platform layer and the middleware layer, 'entity manager' module in the middleware layer for each entity of context representer is defined. The entity manager is for transforming the raw context to a general context. Then, the middleware is able to interact with context-aware applications according to the reasoning with context in the middleware layer, upper layer requests and lower layer status, without being influenced by a change of sensor node and sensor platform environments. We present the encapsulation mechanism and entity manager for efficient interfacing and scalability of context-aware applications and compare them with other approaches.

1 Introduction

Pervasive computing is considered a comprehensive autonomous computing paradigm for the next generation computing environments [1]. One of major advantages in pervasive computing is the capability of building intelligent spaces, where people and environments can interact naturally and autonomously based on the situational contexts. A smart home is one of the most tangible scenarios for pervasive computing applications, and several projects have been proposed to construct a

H.Y. Youn, M. Kim, and H. Morikawa (Eds.): UCS 2006, LNCS 4239, pp. 500–515, 2006.

framework for the smart home [2, 3, 15]. In the smart home, various services are automatically and intelligently provided to the users without the users necessarily being aware of them.

Currently, some computer scientists considered that machines could understand contexts of situation relating to human beings. Thus, some definitions and operational methods for context-awareness have been proposed. Based on the methods, various context-aware applications have been designed, but their applications tend to become significantly more complicated as the number of applications increase. In utilizing various contexts, such applications require several modules to sense environmental data, collect and maintain the sensed data, and derive contexts from the sensed data. Thus, a well-defined context service framework is essential for the efficient design of applications using contexts. Recently, several research papers proposing toolkits and middleware for building context-aware applications have been introduced. From these approaches, users can design context-aware applications more easily. However, most of them are lacking in reusability, scalability and interoperability of applications is still high. Specifically, they do not have any method for efficiently maintaining the plethora of sensed data.

In this paper, we propose an encapsulation and entity manager (EEM)-based context service framework that is required to design applications for work on the smart home. The EEM is constructed as layered components that will satisfy certain degrees of requirements of applications, sensors and actuators. It also categorizes and maintains the collected data according to semantic entities. Such an entity manager-based algorithm and layered architecture can improve the reusability, scalability and interoperability of the contexts and reduce the time required to collect necessary contexts. It also allows developers to design lightweight context-aware applications quickly. Eventually, context-aware applications will be able to focus on adjusting behaviors based on contexts generated by the EEM. Experiment results show that the EEM can reduce the complexity of an application by more than 70%. Also, it improves feasible delivery time and has better response time than the other context service models. In this paper, section 2 introduces related work; section 3 provides a description of the raw context by encapsulating sensor data; section 4 provides a description of the generalization of context by entity manager-based aggregation; section 5 covers implementation; and section 6 provides a performance evaluation and comparison. The conclusion is presented in Section 7.

2   Related Work

There have already been several studies undertaken on the development and implementation of context-aware applications. Context Toolkit [4] is an example of the pioneering work done this area. The Context Toolkit suggests a well-defined conceptual framework that supports context-aware applications and provides several software components, which can aggregate and manage sensed data. Thus, developers can rapidly make context-aware applications by adopting the Context Toolkit.

After the advent of the Context Toolkit, a number of other research projects were completed. Some modify architectural features, others improve performance, and still others leverage emerging technologies such as semantic web and grid computing. CIS [5] (Contextual Information Service), a part of the Aura project [6], provides users with a convenience interface for obtaining contextual information. It adopts the concept of databases and provides an SQL-like query language because users are familiar with retrieving information from databases. Thus, users can access contexts as if they were using databases. Semantic Space [7] has a similar conceptual framework to that of Context Toolkit and enhances software components by using emerging technologies. It provides RDF query and ontology-based context representation. Ubi-UCAM (Unified Context-Aware Application Model) shares object-oriented unified contexts. It suggests a method to represent basic context based on 5W1H (who, when, where, what, why, and how), and can provide higher-level contexts by composition of basic contexts [8]. Other research on context-aware computing suggests additional context framework and software components [9, 10, 12, 13, 14].

The proposed EEM framework resembles these frameworks in that it provides contextual information to context-aware applications. While the prior research does not specify any method for efficiently maintaining the plethora of sensed data and does not reflect varying degrees of requirements for applications, we introduce a unique mechanism to resolve such problems by providing both raw context, which is an outcome of the encapsulation mechanism in the sensor platform layer, and generalized context, which is not affected by any applications, through an entity manager-based aggregation of raw context. In this paper, we assume the service environments to include various sensors, sensor platforms, actuators, a home area network and home server for the specific service scenario of watching a movie in the home.

3   Raw Context by Encapsulation of Sensor Information

To begin with, the concepts and characteristics of the EEM need to be discussed. We adopt the concept model of multi-layered context, where contexts are provided with various degrees to satisfy application requirements. Figure 1 shows multi-layered contexts of the proposed context service framework. It is hierarchically divided into 4 layers, i.e., raw contexts, general contexts, application-specific context, and inferred context. Higher-level context can be formed by composition of lower-level contexts.

In this paper, the raw context is a primitive form of contexts. Various sensors do the generation of raw context. For instance, a bundle of raw context that provides bundled sensor data, such as sensed temperature from a thermometer or an object's position from location sensors. General context is the smallest unit that can have a useful meaning. It is defined as a collection of raw contexts that are related to a specific entity. The application-specific contexts contain the composed contexts that are required for a specific application. Some parts of general contexts, or raw contexts, are composed as an application-specific context.

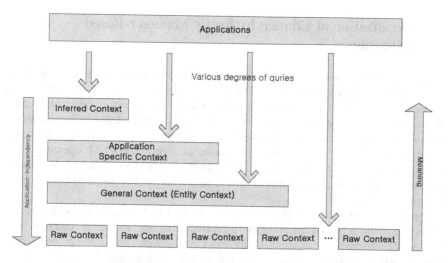

Fig. 1. The Concept of Multi-layered Contexts

Finally, inferred context is a context inferred by an inference algorithm for a specific situational context. However, it is different from application-specific contexts in terms of contexts, which are not simply a collection of lower-level contexts. This approach can provide two benefits; the variety and scalability of application programming requirements. In general, applications require various levels of contexts, from raw contexts to inferred contexts. In our framework, contexts are frequently transformed and modified. For example, additional information is added to a raw context, two contexts can be merged into one, and some information can be extracted from a single context. Because XML is a well-structured format and provides convenient APIs, we adopted the XML format to represent context. We defined the schema of context compatible with RDF (Resource Description Framework) [11] to raise interoperability, scalability and reusability of the context model. Figure 2 shows an example of context.

```
<?xml version="1.0"?>
<edf:entity id="livingRoom"
   xmlns:edf="http://icta.cise.ufl.edu/entity-vocabulary">
<edf:Description about="temperature">
     <edf:Defaults degree="80" />
</edf:Description>
<edf:Description about="humidity">
     <edf:Defaults degree="75" />
   </edf:Description>
   .

   .
  </edf>
```

Fig. 2. Example of the General Context

4 Generalization of Context by Entity Manager-Based Aggregation

Context can have a meaning only if the subject of a context is specified. For instance, suppose that a location sensor is used to position a location. We are not interested in the location of the location sensor itself. If someone or something being attached to the location sensor, the location information is considered to dedicate to a subject of meaningful value and then, we can use the sensed location. Here, entity is defined as an object, which can be a subject of a context. Thus, the EEM aggregates raw contexts and categorize them according to entities to generate and update general context. A sophisticated algorithm to find a particular entity related to the incoming raw context is required.

Figure 3 shows the overall architecture of the EEM, which comprises of five components. It is based on the multi-layered concept and each component is responsible for forming context in its associated layer. The *context representer* generates raw context by wrapping sensed data with XML format. The *entity manager* aggregates raw contexts and categorizes them according to entities, so that it generates general context. The *application-specific context manager* generates application-specific context by composing general contexts, and the *inference module* can generate inferred context based on application-specific contexts and knowledge of application. In addition to the above four modules, *channel manager* is needed to control the flow of contexts between components. In this paper, we focus only on the context representer and entity manager for efficient interconnection between sensor platform layer and middleware layer of pervasive computing system.

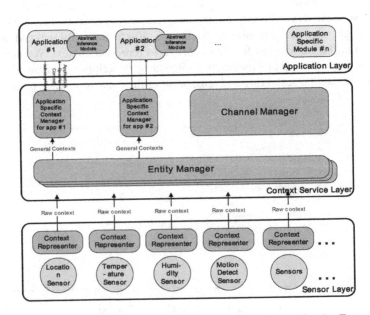

Fig. 3. Architectural overview of the proposed EEM-based Context Service Framework

The basic role representer is to wrap sensor data with a uniform interface. Sensors are varied from a physical thermometer to weather forecasting devices and they have different interfaces. Thus, it is too hard for upper-level components or applications to understand interfaces of various sensors. The context representer wraps sensor data with XML-based interface and formats of sensor data according to the XML schema. Therefore, upper-level components can obtain the raw context only by retrieving XML messages regardless of types of sensors. As we define the raw context has meta-data such as sensed time and valid period of the raw context by adding elements, the raw context can provide more accuracy and validity.

Figure 4 shows an example of raw context. All data, including both sensed data and meta-data in raw context, are expressed with 'edf:description' elements. If role attribute is marked as 'meta', it is meta-data.

```
<?xml version="1.0"?>
<edf:sensor id="lightSensor"
   xmlns:edf="http://icta.cise.ufl.edu/entity-vocabulary"
   ref="http://icta.cise.ufl.edu/sensor/lightSensor_type12">
<edf:Description about="brightness" role="main">
      <edf:Defaults degree="65" />
</edf:Description>
<edf:Description about="DetectionTime" role="meta">
      <edf:Defaults location="20060415123000" />
</edf:Description>
<edf:Description about="TimeToLive" role="meta">
      <edf:Defaults location="100" />
   </edf:Description>
  </edf>
```

Fig. 4. An example of raw context

The entity manager generates and maintains general context by aggregating raw contexts and categorizing them by entities. For this, the entity manager includes a sophisticated categorization algorithm to find a particular entity, which is related to the incoming raw contexts and additional data structures. Figure 5 shows the internal diagram of the entity manager.

The entity manager comprises of an event processor, event buffers, a sensor registry, and an entity registry. All sensors are registered to the sensor registry. The sensor registry maintains ID, type, and location of sensors in the smart home. It classifies sensors into three types, i.e., predefined sensor, entity detector, and location-based sensor. The predefined sensors are sensors those are defined and registered individually for special purposes, i.e., for people with special needs. The entity detectors are various types of sensors attached to the objects excluding location sensors. For instance, RFID reader, temperature sensor, humidity sensor, or acoustic sensor can be an entity detector.

When a raw context comes to the entity manager, it is regarded as an event. The entity manager can extract information from the raw context, generate an event, and then store it in the event buffer. An event includes 4 parameters, i.e., sensor ID, sensed data, detection time, and valid period. Now, the event processor dispatches the event and processes it by following the algorithm shown in Figure 6.

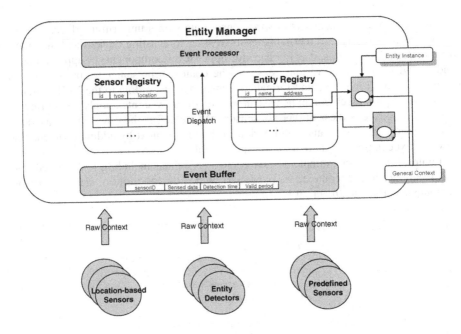

Fig. 5. Component diagram of the Entity Manager

First of all, it checks the type of the sensor by scanning the sensor registry. If the type of the sensor is predefined sensor, it can easily find the related entity because the subject of data from the sensor is already defined. It is the reason why the sensor is called predefined sensor. As a consequence, we can find the proper entity on entity registry and update its general context by using sensed data. Every entity has an XML document which represents the general context of the entity. Entity detector is the sensor that can identify entities. For example, RFID reader attached to the moving chair of the person with special needs can be an entity detector.

Basically, it provides not only the unique identification of the entity, but also can infer the location of the entity based on the location of the sensor. Thus, if an event occurs from the entity detector, the event processor can modify the location of the entity. If it cannot find the entity on the entity registry, event processor creates an instance of the entity and registers it into the entity registry. Finally, if the type of the sensor is location-based sensor, the subject of sensed data is determined by matching the location of the sensor with the location of entities. Assume a scale that can measure body weight. When the scale sensed a body weight, the sensed data is subjected to the entity, which has same location with the scale.

Thus, if an event is coming from the location-based sensor, the event processor finds the entity that has the same location as the sensor, and updates the general context of the entity by using sensed data. As shown in Figure 2, a general context includes information from multiple sensors related to an entity.

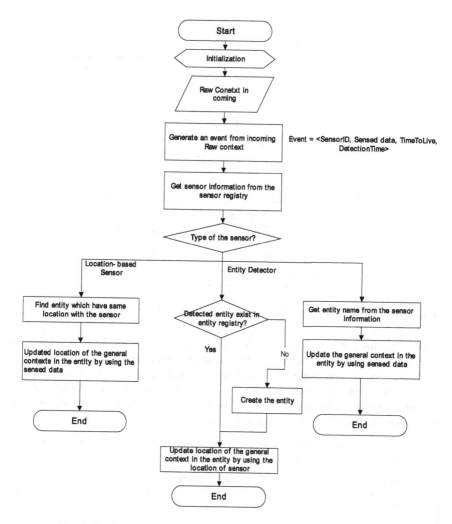

Fig. 6. Operational flow of Generating and Updating a General Context

5 Implementation

Applications can retrieve general contexts by connecting the entity manager and raw contexts by connecting context representers. For example, assume an intelligent home theater application, which can control environments according to the user and user's situational status. Figure 7 shows a home theater service scenario utilizing the EEM-based context service framework, which depicts components functioning in the application and interactions between components. In this scenario, user 'Lim' watches the movie 'Matrix3' with his home theater system in his livingRoom. To detect the contexts for the application, the light sensor, the RFID, the video device, the motion detect sensor, and the location sensor continuously sense the contexts.

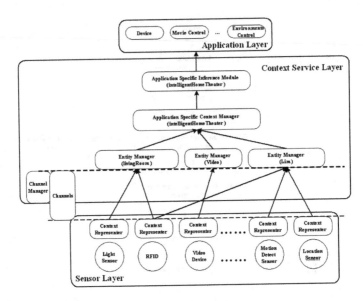

Fig. 7. Home Theater service scenario utilizing EEM-based Context Service Framework

The entity managers for the 'livingRoom', 'Video', and user 'Lim' aggregate the raw contexts from the sensors through the channels managed by the channel manager. The application specific context manager maintains the application specific contexts formed by the general contexts to handle the request of the application and the application specific inference module infers the situational contexts or the inferred contexts using the application specific contexts.

```xml
<?xml version="1.0"?>
<edf:entity id="lightSensor"
   xmlns:edf="http://icta.cise.ufl.edu/entity-vocabulary"
   ref="http://icta.cise.ufl.edu/sensor/lightSensor_type12">
<edf:Description about="location">
     <edf:Defaults location="livingRoom" />
   </edf:Description>
   <edf:Description about="brightness">
     <edf:Defaults degree="50" />
   </edf:Description>
</edf>

<?xml version="1.0"?>
<edf:entity id="movementSensor_202"
   xmlns:edf="http://icta.cise.ufl.edu/entity-vocabulary"
   ref="http://icta.cise.ufl.edu/sensor/movementSensor_livingroom">
   <edf:Description about="movement">
     <edf:Defaults location="4_3" status="sit" />
   </edf:Description>
</edf>
```

Fig. 8. Raw Contexts from a light sensor and a movement sensor

```
<?xml version="1.0"?>
<edf:entity id="Lim"
   xmlns:edf="http://icta.cise.ufl.edu/entity-vocabulary"
ref="http://icta.cise.ufl.edu/temporary-testing/video/spv20060415">
<edf:Description about="movement">
     <edf:Defaults status="sit" />
   </edf:Description>
   <edf:Description about="location">
     <edf:Defaults name="livingRoom">
   </edf:Description>
 </edf>

 <?xml version="1.0"?>
 <edf:entity id="video"
   xmlns:edf="http://icta.cise.ufl.edu/entity-vocabulary"
   id="spDemoDevice_110"
   ref="http://icta.cise.ufl.edu/temporary-testing/video/spv20060415">
   <edf:Description about="status">
     <edf:Defaults  status="play"  screen="16:9  wide"  audiodecode="dolby
digital"
         volume="12" />
   </edf:Description>
   <edf:Description about="content">
     <edf:Defaults movie="matrix3"
        ref="http://ictacise.ufl.edu/temporary-testing/matrix3-
movieguide.xml" />
   </edf:Description>
 </edf>

 <?xml version="1.0"?>
 <edf:entity id="livingRoom"
   xmlns:edf="http://icta.cise.ufl.edu/entity-vocabulary">
   <edf:Description about="People">
     <edf:Defaults number="1">
       <edf:Detail about="Person" who="Lim" />
     </edf:Defaults>
   </edf:Description>
   <edf:Description about="brightness">
     <edf:Defaults degree="50" />
   </edf:Description>
   <edf:Description about="device">
     <edf:Defaults id="spDemoDevice_110" name="video"
        ref="http://icta.cise.ufl.edu/temporary-testing/video/spv20060415"
/>
   </edf:Description>
 </edf>
```

Fig. 9. General Contexts about Lim, Video, and Livingroom

Figures 8 and 9 show several contexts generated by the context engine for the intelligent home theater application. Figure 8 shows the raw context format based on the XML technology, and 'edf' is the 'entity description framework' based on the RDF. The upper XML message on Figure 8 means that the degree of 'lightSensor' in the living room is 50. Moreover, the bottom message shows that the 'movementSensor' senses 'sit' status at location '4_3'.

General contexts are those categorized raw contexts collected for each entity. In this example, the specific user 'Lim', the 'video device', and the 'living room' are the entities. Figure 9 presents the case of general contexts. The beginning of message in Figure 9 shows contextual information related to user 'Lim', and the middle of message in Figure 9 shows the contextual information about device 'video' which can be referenced at 'http://icta.cise.ufl.edu/video/spv10311254'. Currently, the device plays 'matrix3' with '16:9 wide' screen and 'dolby digital' audio method. The bottom part in Figure 9 contains the general context of the 'livingRoom' entity. In this 'livingRoom', there are a person named 'Lim', and a 'video' device, which has id 'spDemoDevice_110'. Moreover the degree of its brightness is 50.

6 Performance Evaluation and Comparison

The implementing and experimental environments are AMD Athlon XP2500, 512 MB RAM, Windows XP, JESE 1.4.2_05 SDK and Eclipse 3.0.1. In this paper, our evaluation metrics are confined to the delivery time of sensed data and the average response time to retrieve a context between sensor platform and middleware of pervasive computing. To measure such metrics of the EEM, we deploy implemented components as shown in Figure 10. All components of the EEM are located in a machine named home server, and each sensor and application are placed in different machines. All machines are connected with local area network. Applications communicate with application specific context manager (ASCM) by using RMI calls and sensors send the data to the context representer (CR) by using TCP/IP socket API. Communication between components in home server also performed via RMI calls.

Also, we compare the EEM with two other context service models. One is single application model where an application includes all components to handle contexts

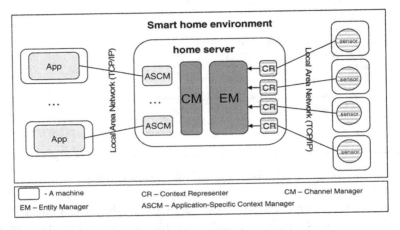

Fig. 10. Experimental Environment

like centralized application system. The other is Context Toolkit, which is a well-known context-aware application development kit. We deploy two models similar to our context service as shown in Figure 11.

6.1 Delivery Time

Delivery time refers to the time spent delivering data from specific sensor to an application. It is especially important in contextual information services because they have to guarantee that the information is provided to the applications in a pre-specified time period. Figure 12 show the delivery time from a sensor to an application in the EEM. It consists of three parts, including two communication parts and one processing part. The first part of the delivery time is the time of transmission of the sensed data from the sensor to the server where the context representer resides. Then, the datum is sequentially processed and formed as raw context, general context and application-specific context. The final part of the delivery time is the time taken to transmit the application-specific context to the application layer. The communication parts do not reflect any characteristics of the context service itself, but depends on the network status.

Processing time is determined by the operational characteristics of context services. Based on the sensed data, the EEM creates contexts as XML documents. Thus, most of processing time is to parse XML documents and to handle information in XML trees. Also, it includes local RMI invocation time between components. According to our experiments, such a processing time does not exceed 10ms and the total delivery time is about 15ms in our experimental environments as shown in Figure 10. We repeat the same experiment over the 1,000 times and obtain a mean value to guarantee high confidence interval. Specifically, 15ms of delivery time is quite feasible because valid

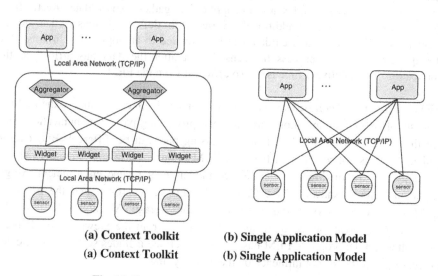

(a) Context Toolkit   **(b) Single Application Model**

Fig. 11. Two-context service models for comparison

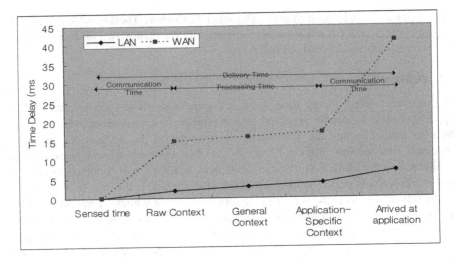

Fig. 12. Time delay of the EEM

time period of sensed data takes generally a couple of seconds. We also perform same test on the WAN environment, where sensors and applications are located in different spaces, which are far from the EEM. Dotted line in Figure 12 shows the delivery time of the test in WAN environment. In this case, communication environments dominate delivery time. But, the processing time is not different from the LAN case because processing is performed only in a computer system.

EEM vs. Single Application Model: Naturally, the delivery time for a single application model is fastest because the application gathers sensed data directly from the sensors. There is no additional overhead in delivering sensed data to an application. In this case, sensed data can be provided to an application in 5ms. But, the application has to process the sensed data after the data has arrived at the application. Thus, delivery time is not so different from the EEM.

EEM vs. Context Toolkit: Delivery time in Context Toolkit is similar to the EEM. It consists of two communication parts and one processing part. Communication parts are the same with the EEM and the processing part can be different. But, overall delivery time is not so different from the EEM in our experiments. Figure 13 shows the delivery time of three context service models in the same environment. Single application model shows 9.7ms, Context Toolkit shows 16ms, and the proposed EEM-based context service shows 15.7ms on the average. All models have similar delivery time and those are quite feasible. Finally, from the viewpoint of delivery time, although the proposed EEM-based context service includes several complicated processing, but it does not influence on the delivery time.

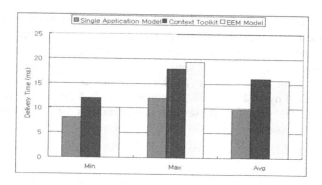

Fig. 13. Delivery time of three context models

6.2 Response Time

Response time is defined as the period the application waits for the data from the sensors. It seems to be similar to delivery time, but the meaning is quite different. Response time is regarded as the actual waiting time of applications in various situations, whereas delivery time can show only simple processing time of given components. For instance, response time can be the time it takes for sensors to send the required data, sensed data, to the application. This means response time can be influenced by the complexity of the system, i.e. various system parameters such as the number of sensors and applications. We compare the response time of three models while changing the complexity of the system.

EEM vs. Single Application Model: Basically, the EEM can provide better response time than the single application model because sensed data are already collected in the EEM and the requests of application are processed in the context service. Namely, the application do not concern about sensors. However, response time of single application model requires more than double of delivery time. And single application model is sensitive to the number of sensors and applications. When the number of applications increases, race condition occurs between applications using same sensors, so that response time can be degraded. Also, when the number of sensors used for an application increases, the overhead of application also increases because the application has to communicate with all the sensors directly and process sensed data by itself. As a consequence, the response time is degraded.

EEM vs. Context Toolkit: As Context Toolkit has a similar architecture with the EEM, it also does not concern about sensors, but just communicates with aggregators that already collect the necessary sensed data. However, Context Toolkit is also sensitive to the number of sensors and applications because it does not maintain generalized context. Typically, an aggregator in Context Toolkit is assigned to an application to collect relevant contexts, which are required to the application. Therefore, when the number of applications increases, there can be a race condition between aggregators, which use same widgets. Therefore, response time can be degraded. But the EEM maintains and provides generalized-level of context by the entity manager, so that the race condition occurs less even though the number of applications increases. Figure 14 shows the comparison in response times of each context frameworks. We measure the response time while changing the number of applications and the number of sensors and repeat same test over 1,000 times to verify the complexity by way of response time. As shown in the figure 14, response time of the EEM is lower than Context Toolkit by about 20% and lowers than single application model by 55% when we run simultaneously 5 application programs based on 15 sensors. The gap of response time is increased as the number of sensors and applications increases.

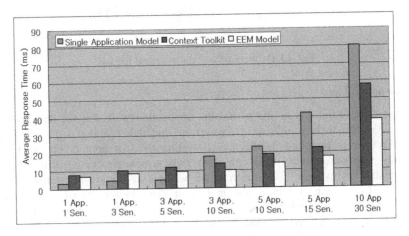

Fig. 14. Response time according to the number of sensors

7 Conclusions

In this paper, we proposed an encapsulation and entity manager-based context service to support context-aware applications in the smart home. It can provide various levels of context and categorize and maintain the collected data according to semantic entities. Thus, with the EEM model, applications can focus on adjusting their behaviors to the environment based on given contexts from the EEM. The result of experiment on delivery time and response time shows that the EEM can provide feasible delivery time and better response time than other context service models from the viewpoint of interconnection between sensor platform and middleware of pervasive computing.

References

[1] M. Weiser, "The computer for the 21st Century," *Scientific American*, 265(3), 66-75.
[2] B. N. Schilit, N. L. Adams, R. Want, "Context-aware computing applications," *Proc. of Workshop on Mobile computing systems and applications.*, Santa Cruz, CA. Dec. 1994.
[3] B. Brumitt, B. Meyers, J. Krumm, A. Kern, and S. Shafer. "EasyLiving: Technologies for intelligent environments," *Proc. of Second International Symposium on Handheld and Ubiquitous Computing, HUC 2000*, pp. 12-29, Bristol, UK, September 2000.

[4] A. K. Dey, D. Salber, and G. D. Abowd, "A Conceptual Framework and a Toolkit for Supporting the Rapid Prototyping of Context-Aware Applications," *Human Computing Interaction*, Vol. 16, pp. 97-166, 2001.

[5] G. Judd, P. Steenkiste, "Providing Contextual Information to Ubiquitous Computing Applications," *Proc. of the First IEEE International Conference on Pervasive Computing and Communications (PerCom'03)*, 2003.

[6] J. P. Sousa and D. Garlan, "Aura: an Architectural Framework for User Mobility in Ubiquitous Computing Environments," *Proc. of the 3rd Working IEEE/IFIP Conference on Software Architecture*, pp 29-43, Aug. 2002.

[7] X. Wang, J. Dong, C. Chin, and S. R. Hettiarachchi, "Semantic Space: An Infrastructure for Smart Spaces," IEEE Pervasive Computing, pp 32-39, Jul. 2004.

[8] S. Jang and W. Woo, "Ubi-UCAM: A Unified Context-Aware Application Model," *Lecture Notes in Artificial Intelligence*, Vol. 2680, Springer-Verlag, Berlin Heidelberg New York (2003), pp. 178-189.

[9] A. Ranganathan and R. Campbell, "An infrastructure for context-awareness basd on first order logic," Personal Ubiquitous Computing, 2003.

[10] T. Winograd, "Architecture for Context," *Human Computing Interaction*, Vol. 16, pp. 401-419, 2001.

[11] "RDF (Resource Description Framework) online at http://www.w3.org/TR/rdf-syntax-grammar/," *World Wide Web Consortium*, 10 February 2004.

[12] J. I. Hong and J. A. Landay, "An Infrastructure Approach to Context-Aware Computing," *Human Computing Interaction*, Vol. 16, pp. 287-303, 2001.

[13] H. Lei, D. Sow, J. Davis II, G. Banavar, and M. Ebling, "The Design and Applications of a Context Service," Mobile Computing and Communications Review, Vol. 6, No. 4, pp. 45-55, 2002.

[14] A. Harter, A. Hopper, P. Steggles, A. Ward, and P. Webster, "The Anatomy of a Context-aware Application," *Proc. of MOBICOM 1999*, Seattle, WA, August 1999.

[15] S. Lee and T. Chung, "System Architecture for Context-Aware Home Application," *Proc. of Second IEEE workshop on Software Technologies for Future Embedded and Ubiquitous Systems*, Vienna, Austria, May 11-12, 2004.

Feature Selection and Activity Recognition from Wearable Sensors

Susanna Pirttikangas[1,2], Kaori Fujinami[2], and Tatsuo Nakajima[2]

. Department of Electrical and Information Engineering,
University of Oulu, Finland
. Department of Computer Science, Waseda University, Japan
msp@ee.oulu.fi, {fujinami, tatsuo}@dcl.info.waseda.ac.jp

Abstract. We describe our data collection and results on activity recognition with wearable, coin-sized sensor devices. The devices were attached to four different parts of the body: right thigh and wrist, left wrist and to a necklace on 13 different testees. In this experiment, data was from 17 daily life examples from male and female subjects. Features were calculated from triaxial accelerometer and heart rate data within different sized time windows. The best features were selected with forward-backward sequential search algorithm. Interestingly, acceleration mean values from the necklace were selected as important features. Two classifiers (multilayer perceptrons and kNN classifiers) were tested for activity recognition, and the best result (90.61 % aggregate recognition rate for 4-fold cross validation) was achieved with a kNN classifier.

1 Introduction

Our system of identifying the user of a sentient artefact was presented in [3]. The system recognised the user's activity from wearable sensors (on the right wrist and thigh, triaxial acceleration signals) with a neural network and combined the information of the state-of-use of an artefact to an activity with a linkage condition (sitting activity linked to a chair, walking activity linked to a door), and in this way identified the wearer as the user of the artefact. In the case of multiple users doing the same activity, the identity of each user was verified with correlation analysis between the artefact's and user's acceleration signals. In the experiment, we studied the activities typing, sitting and walking from two different users.

This paper expands our research and explores the activity recognition of 13 different users and 17 different activities from wearable sensors as a classification problem. We describe our sensor device and some data collection issues. The goal is to find the best discriminative features that will be fast to calculate to enable prompt processing of information from multiple sources. Our sensory device can be programmed so that only the essential data is sent to a data analysing terminal. This setting requires fast processing, since the amount of data and traffic is very high as most artefacts and users will be equipped with sensor devices.

H.Y. Youn, M. Kim, and H. Morikawa (Eds.): UCS 2006, LNCS 4239, pp. 516–527, 2006.
© Springer-Verlag Berlin Heidelberg 2006

We calculate several features from triaxial acceleration data from four wearable sensory devices. Also heart rate mean values are calculated. The feature set is pruned with a forward-backward search [4] where we utilise a kNN classifier to select the best features. We will also test different lengths of time window sizes for feature calculation in order to find a good accuracy in recognition and minimum delay of the final answer for the user. The analysis involves testing two different classifiers, a multilayer perceptron (MLP) and a kNN classifier for activity recognition.

2   Related Work

Activity recognition from wearable acceleration sensors is a current research problem. The most comprehensive study to date is presented in [1], where 5 biaxial accelerometers were attached to the hip, right wrist, left elbow, left thigh and right ankle of a testee. The authors studied 20 different activities from 20 different users, achieving a 84 % overall recognition rate with a decision tree. For some activities, such as walking, running, and standing still, a user-specific training data is reported not to have been required to reach over 80 % recognition accuracy. Furthermore, the authors emphasise the importance of natural, non-laboratory data collection. Their approach has guided us in the data collection phase as described in section 3.2. A summary of activity recognition research can be found in their paper.

The best placements for wearable acceleration sensors was sought for in [7]. For lower body, the sensors attached to the ankle or hip (also the thigh gave good results) are the best in complex situations, such as walking up or down the stairs. The analysis on upper body sensor placement is confused by the fact that the user had to carry an iPAQ to annotate their data. In [1], the dominant wrist and thigh of the user were found to be the best placements for acceleration sensors. Based on these findings, we attached the acceleration sensors on the right and left wrists and on the right thigh. Also, we attached one sensor device into necklaces worn by the testees, as it is a natural placement for, for example, sensor embedded jewellery or name tags.

Cluster precision for evaluating the best features for discriminating activitities with acceleration data has been applied in [5]. The most discriminative features are from FFT, although different components of FFT and different time window lengths are required to separate different activities. The authors also found that variance of acceleration is more accurate than the mean value. However, their data set includes only the data of two persons in the activities of walking, standing, jogging, skipping, hopping and riding a bus. The paper also lists the most frequently used features in activity analysis from acceleration signals, including the correlations between different axes of acceleration as well as the mean and standard deviation.

Depending on the system's sampling frequence, the lag of processing the FTT and saving the results into a buffer can be quite high [8] (more than ten seconds in [8], 6.7 seconds in [1]). In our system, the delay of processing must be as short as possible, since in our experience the user expects an artefact to act as a kind of a switch to an action (imagine pressing the remote control buttons). Therefore, instead of using FFT features, we calculate mean crossing values within a time window for the study. We also test the correlation between the x and y axes of each acceleration signal and the mean and standard deviation values.

3   Data

3.1   The Sensor Device

To test our activity recognition and the utilisation of sentient artefacts, we used our own sensor node named Cookie (Figure 1 (a)). Cookie is a 50 EUR cent-sized wireless sensor node that is extensible for nine types of sensors and can communicate with any device that is capable of Bluetooth v1.1 Serial Port Profile. The main board of Cookie consists of a Bluetooth module, 2-axis linear accelerometer, compass and ambient light sensor. The extensions include e.g. a heart rate sensor, force sensor and 3-axis linear accelerometer.

Fig. 1. The Cookie attached with three axis accelerometers (a) and placements of Cookie (b)

In this experiment, four Cookies were attached, one to each of the following locations: right wrist, left wrist, right thigh and necklace, as depicted in Figure 1 (b). All the triaxial accelerometer sensors from each Cookie and the heart rate sensor on the right wrist were utilised here.

Raw data was acquired on the node (acceleration sampled 64 times at 200kHz) and the averaged value was sent to a data collecting terminal at every 100 msec at 9600bps. For tests performed outside the permises of our laboratory, the data collecting terminal was worn by the user (Sony VAIO Type-U running Windows XP SP2 with USB-Bluetooth dongle).

3.2   Semi-naturalistic Data Collection

To achieve as natural a setting as possible for the data collection, a semi-naturalistic data collection schema, as suggested in [1], was applied. The semi-naturalistic data collection aims at minimising the possible disturbance of outside observers and the awareness of perfoming some specified activity (leading to unnatural behaviour).

In [1], the users were given a worksheet describing an obstacle course of activities to be performed. The users wrote down the starting and ending time on the worksheet and, therefore, no research observation was needed. We did not, however, find the approach of using a workheet very feasible, so we built two different kinds of user interfaces to help annotate the data and describe the obstacles for the testees. These interfaces support the labelling of different activities (time stamp labels), syncronising the data and organising it.

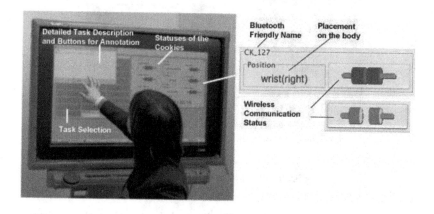

Fig. 2. The touch screen-based user interface

Figure 2 presents the obstacles in a large touch screen as tasks. When the user selects a task, a detailed description of the obstacle is given. Each task description GUI includes a button for labeling a starting time and ending time for the activity. On the right in Figure 2, the statuses of all wearable Cookies are shown. Thus, if the Bluetooth connection is lost, the testee will be able to contact the researchers and the loss of data is prevented. We also added a sound feature for the interface: a sound is played to indicate the success of time stamping each time a task is started and ended. Furthermore, after one minute, a sound is played to inform the user about the time spent in an activity. The minimum of one minute of data were collected for each activity. The user interface is bilingual (Japanese and English) and example tasks are shown in Table 1.

Table 1. Examples of the task descriptions

Task 1   Clean the white board with the brush.
Task 2   Sit down and read a newspaper. Read at least one whole article
         from the paper.
Task 3   Stand still for a minute
Task 4   Sit down to the sentient chair and relax
Task 5   Sit down, switch on the TV with the remote control and watch some TV
...   ...
Task 14: Walk up the stairs (at least to the 3th floor)
...   ...
Task 17: Ride around the laboratory with a bicycle

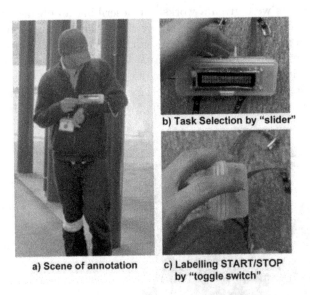

a) Scene of annotation   b) Task Selection by "slider"

c) Labelling START/STOP by "toggle switch"

Fig. 3. The wearable user interface

A wearable user interface (Figure 3) with a slider to select the description of each task was built for tasks performed outdoors or not in the vicinity of the screen (Figure 2). The time stamps are here labelled with a toggle switch on the right side of the interface. The interface shows a short description of each task in English, and it also informs the user if the Bluetooth connection is lost.

Both interfaces record the test details in a log file, from where they are easy to extract. The placements of the Cookies, as well as the data file name associated to each Cookie, is logged. Furthermore, the time stamps for the beginning and ending time of each activity and a short description of the tasks are saved.

The data were collected from 13 testees, 9 males and 4 females, aged from 22 to 32. The users were given a brief introduction of the obstacles and the equipment, and the users performed the tasks and labelled the activities with time stamps on their own, utilising the built interfaces. In some cases, a researcher was observing the activities and in one case, a video recording was made. The testee indicated

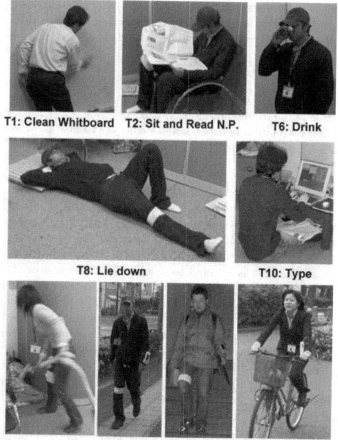

T1: Clean Whitboard   T2: Sit and Read N.P.   T6: Drink

T8: Lie down   T10: Type

T9: Vacuum Clean T11: Walk T13: Descend Stairs T17: Bike

Fig. 4. Pictures from data collection tasks

that this did not affect his behaviour. Pictures from the data collection are shown in Figure 4.

3.3   Feature Selection

Regarding an online setting including several Cookies that send data continuously to a data processing terminal, the design of the activity recognition system should remain simple and the lag affected by feature calculation and traffic should be small. As described in section 3.1, the Cookie is extensible to various types of sensors and can be programmed so that not all of the data are sent. We must, therefore, select the most important information from each Cookie to be sent. The delay and traffic will decrease if we can find a small subset of the most important (in view of recognition accuracy) features.

From each Cookie, we calculated only features that are fast to process in a short time window: each axis (3D) acceleration mean and standard deviation values, correlation coefficients between the x and y axes of acceleration, and mean crossing values for each axis acceleration. Furthermore, the heart rate mean from the Cookie placed on the right wrist was calculated. The tested features are listed below:

acceleration mean (x, y, z axes)
acceleration standard deviation (x, y, z axes)
acceleration correlation between x and y axis (x, y axes)
acceleration mean crossing (x, y, z axes)
heart rate mean

The features mentioned above were tested with forward-backward search [4], which is a well-known feature selection algorithm. With this procedure, a subset of best (giving the best classification result) features can be determined for the final analysis. In forward search (FS), every feature is tested for the classification one by one, and the best is selected to a subset of best features. The features that remain are then tested with the selected one, and the best one is selected to the subset and so forth. The procedure starts from one feature. The FS finds the best single features but does not find the best combination subset.

Backward search (BS) starts with classifying all features and removing the one that is lowering the classification result. In forward-backward combination, two features are selected with FS and one is removed with BS. The classification is usually done with a simple classifier, such as kNN, which was also used in this procedure. We utilised Matlab technical language to process the data and calculate the features and the LNKnet [6] pattern recognition software for other analyses.

3.4 Testing and Training

[1] state that the individual variation in body worn acceleration may be dominated by strong commonalities between people in activity patterns. Therefore, we combined all the data from different testees into one data set. The data were divided and synchronized based on the labelled time stamps to different activities, and the evaluations of the activity recognition algorithms were done with 4-fold cross validation.

From the beginning of each activity, 50 samples (5 seconds) were removed, because in some cases the starting of an activity after reading the task description and labelling the data takes a while (e.g. moving away from the screen towards the white board). Furthermore, if the time spent on an activity exceeded five minutes, the data were truncated to get as homogenous (in view of number of examples) data set as possible. Several MLP and kNN classifiers were tested for activity recognition as described in the following. The 17 activities studied are shown in Figure 6.

4 Results

4.1 Features

Three separate feature selection tests were made. In the first experiment, the mean, the standard deviation and the mean crossing values of each acceleration signal were calculated in windows of five samples (0.5 seconds). The mean values of heart rate from the right wrist were also included in the feature set. The number of features was then 37. Forward-backward search was applied, and the final feature set consisted of 19 features. No mean crossing values nor heart rate means were in this group, but all of the mean values of each acceleration signal from each Cookie (except necklace mean acceleration y) were included.

Table 2. The selected features for activity recognition

Cookie	RightWrist	LeftWrist	Thigh	Necklace
	mean X	mean X	mean X	mean X
	mean Y	mean Y	mean Y	mean Y
	mean Z	mean Z	mean Z	mean Z
		std X		
	std Y			
	std Z		std Z	

Another experiment was made with a window size of 7 samples (0.7 seconds), and this time the correlations between the x and y axis accelerometers were included into the feature set (now 28 features). All the means from all the Cookies were present in the final subset. The standard deviations from the right wrist (y, z), left wrist y, and thigh (y, z) were also included (a total of 18 features). The correlations were not included in the subset of best features.

Finally, we made one more feature selection from the mean and standard deviation values of each Cookie's accelerometer data. This time, the window length was five and the feature set included 25 features (note that the HR mean value was tested again). The final 16 features selected are presented in Table 2. The standard deviations (y, z) of the dominant wrist (all of the testees were right handed) are included. It is expected that in the case of left handed people, the standard deviations (y, z) of the left wrist would be present, but we cannot answer this question with this data.

As the mean values of the necklace were included in all of the best subsets, we made a test (with window length of seven samples) where only the mean and standard deviation information from three Cookies, i.e. the right wrist, left wrist and thigh, were included. We compared the test results with and without the necklace features and noticed that when removing the necklace information, the classification error of "sit and read a newspaper", "sit and relax", "sit and watch TV" and "lie down" was increased considerably. The highest increase of confusion was between

"sit and read a newspaper" and "brush teeth"
"sit and read a newspaper" and "sit and relax"
"sit and read a newspaper" and "sit and watch TV"
"sit and read a newspaper" and "lie down"

This result suggests that the necklace helps in detecting certain kind of movement of the upper body while seated.

4.2   Time Window

With the selected feature set presented in Table 2, experiments were made to test a suitable time window for the feature calculation. We tested windows of 1, 2, 5, 7, 10 and 15 samples (from 100 msec to 1.5 seconds) for both MLP and kNN. The results can be seen in Figure 5. The best result was achieved with the kNN classifier for the window length of 10 (1 second), giving a 90.61 % recognition accuracy.

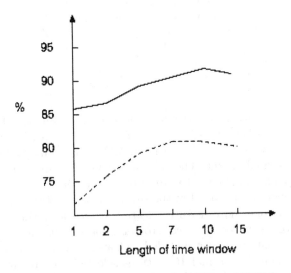

Fig. 5. Classification results in percents for the MLP and kNN for different time windows (x axis). The dashed line represents the results for the MLP.

The aggregate confusion matrix for the 17 activities and the best classification result (kNN, time window 1 second) with 4-fold cross -validation is shown in Figure 6.

4.3   Simplifying the Problem

A sentient artefact is usually developed to achieve a specific task and, therefore, the state-of-use of an artefact can be a cue to infer the user's activity [2].

0	1	2	3	4	5	6	7	8	9	10	11	12	13	14	15	16	< classified as
336	2	2	1	0	5	14	0	7	0	0	1	1	2	1	0	0	0=clean whiteboard
4	352	0	5	10	4	0	1	10	0	1	1	1	0	0	0	1	1=read a newspaper
4	0	379	0	3	1	0	0	1	0	0	0	0	1	1	0	0	2=stand still
2	7	0	370	3	3	0	2	1	1	0	0	1	0	0	0	0	3=sit and relax
1	10	1	1	357	5	0	0	12	3	0	0	0	0	0	0	0	4=sit and watch TV
2	3	1	1	2	336	4	0	8	8	3	3	0	5	1	0	1	5=drink
4	0	0	0	0	5	378	0	2	0	0	0	0	0	0	0	0	6=brush teeth
0	5	0	1	1	0	0	340	2	1	0	0	0	0	0	0	0	7=lie down
7	16	2	0	6	17	0	0	302	0	9	14	8	4	2	0	3	8=vacuum clean
0	1	0	2	0	4	0	1	0	369	0	0	0	0	0	0	2	9=type
0	1	0	0	0	1	1	0	2	0	307	30	18	0	0	0	0	10=walk
0	0	0	0	0	1	0	0	3	1	35	221	17	1	0	0	0	11=climb stairs
0	1	0	0	0	0	0	0	0	0	36	26	176	1	0	0	0	12=descend stairs
3	0	4	0	1	4	2	0	5	0	0	0	2	235	12	0	1	13=elevator Up
1	1	1	0	0	0	0	0	2	0	0	0	0	16	196	0	0	14=elevator Down
0	0	0	0	0	0	0	0	0	0	0	0	0	0	0	148	0	15=run
0	0	0	0	0	1	0	0	0	0	0	0	1	1	0	0	343	16=cycle

Fig. 6. The aggregate confusion matrix of 4-fold crossvalidation for kNN classifier based on semi-naturalistic data from 13 subjects

In our system to identify the user of an sentient artefact, the linkage condition activity-artefact, such as vacuum cleaning-vacuum cleaner, is the unifying element between an artefact and the user. However, the activity needs not to be this detailed, but could be e.g. cleaning-vacuum cleaner. If the linkage condition is satisfied, the more accurate activity for the wearer can then be determined from the artefact.

To simplify the recognition problem, we unified the activity classes vacuum clean and clean whiteboard to an activity clean. We also unified the classes sit and read newspaper, sit and relax, sit and watch TV and type into the activity sit. The activities stand, elevator Up and elevator Down are replaced simply with the activity stand. Climbing and descending stairs is now stairs. There are thus nine (9) different activities to be recognised. The scalability of the system is improved considerably if only the basic activities are modeled. This way, when new elements (artefacts) are added to the environment, only a new linkage condition needs to be added.

The best selected features and window size of seven (as no considerable improvement in classification accuracy from seven to ten samples with these features in Figure 5) samples were utilized to train a kNN and a MLP classifier to identify the nine activities. The recognition accuracies were 89.76 % and 92.89 % for the MLP and kNN, respectively.

4.4 Discussion

The features selected are the most commonly used features for activity recognition, but as a contradiction to the work in [5], the mean values of acceleration signals were the most important features instead of standard deviations. Furthermore, the correlation and mean crossing values of acceleration signals or heart rate means were not included in the subset of best features in any of the tests performed in this investigation.

The most interesting finding in feature selection was the importance of the necklace features. It is easy to embedd sensory devices to a necklace, which can also have some aesthetic value. The necklace features were found to escpecially improve the discrimination of different sitting activities (sitting and relaxing as opposed to sitting and reading a newspaper, for example). Otherwise, the importance of the thigh and the dominant wrist, as stated in [1] and [7], was confirmed.

The best recognition accuracy was achieved with a time window of ten samples (1 sec) to enable over 90 % recognition accuracy, but the results for the window sizes of five and seven were not considerably lower. When testing different time windows, the results from MLP were weaker than from kNN, but the fact that the features were selected with the latter is, naturally, an advantage to it.

In our final test, we unified the information of different activites that involved sitting into a class titled `sitting`, activities that involved standing into `standing` and activites that involved cleaning into `cleaning`. The final number of activities to be recognised was considerably lower (from 17 to nine) and the final classification result was much better (92.89 %).

5   Conclusions and Future Work

We described here the development of an activity recognition system starting from semi-naturalistic data collection to feature selection and finally proceeded to recognising different activities. The aim was to find a good set of features that enable fast processing of information giving an acceptable recognition rate.

Two different kinds of user interfaces were built for assisting the collection, synchronisation and management of data. The interfaces were found to be very useful and can be applied in any data collection task that involves a Bluetooth based device.

In our analysis, we provided a minimal feature set needed for the recognition of different activities occurring in daily life. The system's sensory device can be programmed to send only some of the data to a data analysing terminal and find the minimum set of features to enable the decrease of both computing time and traffic in the system. The features were tested with two classifiers (MLP and kNN) and the recognition accuracy for 17 activities was 90.61% in the best case. The necklace features were also found to be important in the recognition tasks. It remains to be studied whether the activity recognition algorithm for the nine basic activities studied in section 4.3 will still need these features to be present.

The ideal situation for a calm environment is that recognition accuracy could be increased up to near 100 %. To enable this, either the recognition capability of the machine learning algorithm must be made better or the other elements of the environment should be utilised in the recognition. Our vision is that the higher level context (from cleaning to vacuum cleaning, for example) will come from the artefact the wearer is using.

Our ongoing research addresses testing the combination of artefacts and wearable devices in the real world. We have already implemented the system proposed in [3]. Our future research includes the trade off analysis between the recognition accuracy and delay for the final answer. Furthermore, we are studying the situation of unknown (for the system) activity or inaccurate decision by the system and attempts to recover from such situations by rejection analysis.

Acknowledgments

This work was partially funded by the Academy of Finland, Finnish Funding Agency for Technology and Innovation and companies.

References

[1] L. Bao and S. S. Intille. Activity recognition from user-annotated acceleration data. In *Proc. Int. Conf. Pervasive Computing (Pervasive 2004)*, pages 1–17, 2004.

[2] K. Fujinami and T. Nakajima. Sentient artefact: Acquiring user's context through daily objects. In *Proc. 2nd Int. Workshop Ubiquitous Intelligence and Smart Worlds (UISW2005)*, pages 335–344, 2005.

[3] K. Fujinami, S. Pirttikangas, and T. Nakajima. Who opened the door?: Towards the implicit user identification for sentient artefacts. In *Adjunct Proc. Int. Conf. Pervasive Computing, (Pervasive 2006)*, pages 107–111, 2006.

[4] Fukunaga. *Introduction to Statistical Pattern Recognition*. Academic Press, 1990.

[5] T. Huynh and B. Schiele. Analyzing features for activity recognition. In *Proc. Joint Conf. Smart Objects and Ambient Intelligence (sOc-EUSAI '05)*, pages 159–163, 2005.

[6] L. Kukolich and R. Lippmann. Lnknet user's guide, August 1999. http://www.ll.mit.edu/IST/lnknet/ (available on 18.4.2006).

[7] B. S. N. Kern and A. Schmidt. Multi-sensor activity context detection for wearable computing. In *Ambient Intelligence*, volume 2875/2003, pages 220–232, 2003.

[8] T. Yamabe, A. Takagi, and T. Nakajima. Citron: A context information acquisition framework for personal devices. In *Proc. the 11th IEEE Int. Conf. Embedded and Real-Time Computing Systems and Applications (RTCSA '05)*, pages 489–495, 2005.

Portable Device for Bi-emotional State Identification Using Heart Rate Variability

Sun K. Yoo[1], ChungKi Lee[1,2], GunKi Lee[3], ByungChae Lee[4], KeeSam Jeong[4], and YoonJung Park[1,5]

[1] Dept of Medical Engineering, College of Medicine, Yonsei University, Seoul, Korea
sunkyoo@yumc,yonsei.ac.kr
[2] Human Identification Research Center, Yonsei University, Seoul, Korea
nolegal@yumc.yonsei.ac.kr
[3] Depart of Electronic Engineering. Gyeongsang National University, Korea
gklee@nongae.gsnu.ac.kr
[4] Dept of Medical Information System, Yongin Songdam College, Gyeonggi, Korea
bclee@ysc.ac.kr , ksjeong@ysc.ac.kr
[5] Center for Signal Processing Research, Yonsei University, Seoul, Korea
shydeng@yumc.yonsei.ac.kr

Abstract. For the Ubiquitous computing system, a well designed computer interface should have the ability of making the user feel comfortable so as to encourage user performance. In order to do this, systems should be able to identify the emotional state of the user. Thus, the identification of the user's emotional state is of importance in developing context-related devices, which offer the optimal feedback to the user depending on the user's emotional state. Those devices require portability and continuous measurement for daily use, which is particularly essential for an ubiquitous healthcare device. In this paper, the portable device for bi-emotional state identification was designed using heart rate variability (HRV) extracted from beat-to-beat photoplethysmography (PPG) waveforms. A portable wrist-band type PPG measuring device was equipped with a Bluetooth communication interface to provide mobility. HRV was estimated from smoothed differentiated PPG waveforms by the absolute value of the successive beat-to-beat interval difference. Two emotional states are artificially induced by a composed video clip, and then validated by the self-assessment Manikin method. The designed device was then applied to a respiration training device to adjust the balance level of the autonomous nervous system throughout the respiration pager, whose level changes in proportion to the estimated ratio between negative and positive emotional states. Experimentation using 19 male and six female participants demonstrated the feasibility of a ubiquitous emotional feedback control device.

1 Introduction

In the ubiquitous environment, a computer system exists at all places and times of human life with features that satisfy a person's need of being comfortable and convenient. However, there are times when people do not desire to have this service provided to them constantly. Therefore, we have improved ubiquitous service to provide feedback to the user only when he or she requests it or when absolutely

H.Y. Youn, M. Kim, and H. Morikawa (Eds.): UCS 2006, LNCS 4239, pp. 528–536, 2006.

necessary. To realize the emotional consideration of ubiquitous service, we will use simple and quantitative measurements to evaluate human emotion. Also, in the future, we must be able to compute real-time changes in human emotion. Currently, there are other researchers who are working on similar studies. Rosalind W. Picard (Massachusetts Institute of Technology) used volunteers to classify eight different emotions using a portable device. The result of her studies showed 81% accuracy [1][12]. Picard's findings show high accuracy, but the eight emotion classifications used are ambiguous and the number of sample volunteers from which she recorded data was too few. Since two or three volunteers were used, it is too difficult to make a generalization about Picard's results. She also devised a device for emotion identification which measures the changes in ANS(Autonomous nervous system) including respiration, Galvanic Skin Resistance(GSR), temperature, blood volume pressure (BVP), heart rate (from BVP), and electromyogram(EMG). Since it used many parameters, it could achieve high identification accuracy, but it also increased the computational complexity and the cost.[18] Another researcher, R. Sinha, tested only two emotions, fear and anger [2][4][5]. Using six parameters (HR, GSR, finger temperature, blood pressure, electro-oculogram, and facial EMG), Sinha also showed high accuracy in his results. However, he used too many parameters in his experiment, which resulted in a complicated bio-signal measurement. Furthermore, Sinha did not use a portable device. To improve on these previous studies, clear definitions of each human emotion are required. Also, we must reduce the differences in cultural physiological response. In order to globally classify an emotion, we must select an acceptable parameter and develop a simple hardware device with intractable software. Photoplethysmography (PPG) can be used to extract heart rate and is better suited for the simplification of the sensor module. Heart rate variability (HRV) contains abundant information on the status of the autonomic nervous system and can be derived from ECG or PPG measurements[11][14]. Degrees of the sympathetic and parasympathetic nervous system activities can be measured. Therefore, using nervous system information, an emotional state can be predicted[7][8][9][13][15]. In this paper, using one bio-signal (PPG-HRV), we will show the effects of the emotion interactive ubiquitous service.

2   Materials and Methods

In our research, we did experiments on 25 healthy people (19 males, 6 females). The mean age of the participants was twenty-five years with a standard deviation of four years. Before commencing the experiment, we asked the participants about their smoking, drug, alcohol, disease, and sleep history. The participants were asked to minimize their physical movement during experimentation. The experiment was performed at Severance Hospital in a small room of about three meters by three meters in size. Each participant was given about 15 minutes of rest time before the experiment began. Using a video projector, we showed an emotion inducing video on a forty inch screen. Table 1 shows the experimental protocol used. This table also describes the expected response of the participant after watching the videos. We showed two videos, a Korean variety show program (positive emotion) and a collection of murder and suicide clips (negative emotion). Each video lasted ten minutes. Each participant was given the same amount of time to watch the videos. We emphasized finding valence differences between participants during the experiment.

Table 1. Experimental protocol: video type and expected responses

Emotion	Time (min)	Video	Description	Expected Response	
				Arousal	Valence
Positive	10	Variety Show	Happiness, Uplifting	Don't care	Very Positive
Negative	10	Murder, suicide	Passive, Anger, Want to Avoid	Don't care	Very Negative

After watching the video, each participant was given a self evaluation. This self evaluation tool, called the Self-Assessment Manikin (SAM), was originally employed by Lang [3]. Figure 1 shows the SAM. Figure 1(a) demonstrates different facial expressions with the expressions going from sad to happy starting from the left. In Figure 1 (a), the participant can select his or her feeling after watching the video clip. Figure 1(b) shows the participant's arousal level, from calm to excited, starting from the left. Each of the video materials was supposed to induce an opposite emotional state. Most of the participants chose the negative section in the SAM after watching the video clip that induces a negative emotion.

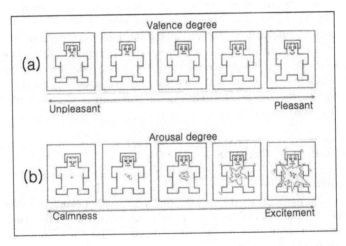

Fig. 1. Emotion assessment using the Self-Assessment Manikin (SAM)

The changes in emotion reflect changes in the bio-signal, and the changes in bio-signal indicate that there are changes in the ANS. It is well known that emotional stimuli can have a great effect on the activity of the ANS. Using the information we obtain from the signal PPG, we can estimate the emotional state of the participant. The PPG was measured from the index finger using the infrared sensor method. The

PPG signal results from activities in the ANS (both the sympathetic nerve and vagal nerve) and HRV (heart rate variability), which is an important factor to estimate emotion[11][14].

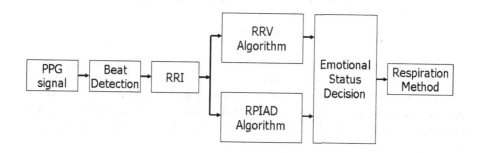

Fig. 2. PPG signal Processing

Figure 2 demonstrates the entire sequence of PPG signal processing, which is composed of acquisition, heart beat-detection, emotional status decision, and respiration method. HRV data was extracted from the PPG signal. Then, we applied the RPIAD algorithm to the absolute value of successive RR interval differences [10] that have a low computational complexity. This allows us to extract the change in emotional state in real-time. Through the infrared sensor, the measured PPG signal is converted to a RR interval (RRI) using a beat detection algorithm. After achieving the RRI we used the RR variability (RRV) algorithm to determine HR change, and adapted the RPIAD algorithm to measure mental stress. Because HR changes continuously, we have to calculate HR of schedule section. The RRV algorithm functions as a low pass filter, which uses a moving average [10].

$$RRV(i) = \frac{1}{k}\sum_{n=1}^{k} RRI(i - n + 1)$$

$$where \quad k=10$$

Wang originally developed the RPIAD algorithm to measure mental stress. [10] One important characteristic of this algorithm is that one can obtain HRV frequency analysis in real-time since the computational complexity is low. The RPIAD is a square root of the product of RRI and the absolute value of the successive RRI difference. The RPIAD equation is shown below.

$$RPIAD(n) = \sqrt{RRI(n) \times |RRI(n) - RRI(n-1)|}$$

Smoothing was performed again to obtain the SRPIAD (smoothed RPIAD) value. Empirically, a P-value of 10 was chosen for this paper. If the P-value is too small, the filtered signal will remain too sensitive so that an emotional state can not be seen clearly. Otherwise, if the P-value is too large, the time delay of the result will also increase.

$$SRPIAD(n) = \sum_{k=1}^{p} a(k) \times RPIAD(n-k)$$

$$where, \quad a(k) = 1/p$$

Studies of human emotion that use bio-signals have to consider various problems. First, data obtained from a participant vary due to emotional state. Because a bio-signal is non-linear and non-stationary even during the same emotional state, we removed the difference between inter-emotional states, to show the difference during emotion state change. We also removed variability for the current emotional state.

$$NSRPIAD(n) = SRPIAD(n) / \overline{SRPIAD(rest0)}$$

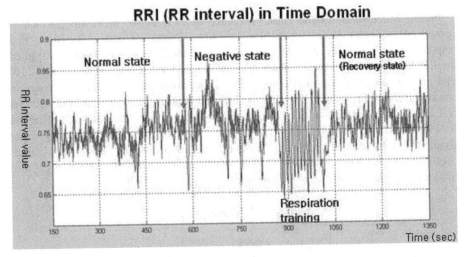

Fig. 3. Typical example of RR interval signal according to emotional state over time

Table 2. The mean of the LF/HF ratio and Standard deviation by emotional state

Emotion state	Normal state (positive state)	Negative state	Normal state (Recovery state)
Mean of LF/HF ratio	1.03	4.64	1.44
Standard deviation of LF/HF	0.19	2.46	0.25

Low Frequency/High Frequency: LF/HF

Figure 3 shows changes of the RRI signal with emotional state. The x-axis shows the time domain and y-axis shows the signal amplitude. Figure shows the change in RRI during stimulation and respiration training. Figure 3 also demonstrates that respiration training can balance emotion change. Table 2 shows the effect of respiration training by a typical method that analyzes the state of the ANS [6][16]. An inference from Table 2 shows that respiration training helps to balance the ANS.

3   Results

3.1   Self Evaluation for Emotion Stimulus

Table 3 shows the results from the SAM. After the experiment, each participant was supposed to produce a SAM regarding their emotional state. We assessed the emotion state scores, and then the participants estimated their scores. The second column from the right shows the average and distribution over for all participants. The SAM result yielded an average arousal of -0.24, close to calm, during positive stimulation and the average valence score was 1, close to happy. For negative video clip, the average arousal was 0.36, close to excitation, and the average valence was -1.72, close to very unhappy. Thus we could see that the participants on average reacted positively during positive video stimulus and negatively for negative stimulus.

Table 3. Results of SAM and the emotion state estimation

Type of stimulation	Type of assessment	SCORE					AVERAGE SCORE	Emotion state
		-2	-1	0	1	2		
Positive	Arousal	0	9	13	3	0	-0.24	Calm
	Valence	0	0	7	11	7	1	Happy
Negative	Arousal	0	4	8	13	0	0.36	Excitation
	Valence	18	7	0	0	0	-1.72	Very Unhappy

3.2   Interactive Portable Hardware Device

Figure 4 (a) shows the developed wrist type potable hardware device. This device is operated by Bluetooth communication. Figure 4 (b) shows the device in use. Once the program and device are set up, the PPG signal is obtained and then transmitted to the main computer. The architecture of the portable device is shown in Figure 4 (c). The PPG sensor used in this experiment was a reflective type, consisting of a LED and a photo detector. The raw data were converted into digital signals at a sampling rate of 500Hz. The PPG signal was preprocessed by filtering the low and high frequency components. An Atmel ATMEGA32 microcontroller was selected for our study, since it has many I/O ports and a plentiful amount of flash memory. These conditions are suitable to determine real time emotional state identification.

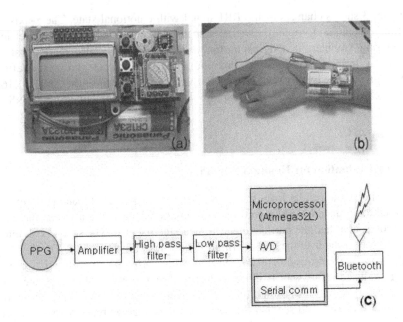

Fig. 4. Portable Hardware device & architecture (PPG sensor, filters, microprocessor, and Bluetooth)

3.2 Interactive Biofeedback Software

The systems shown in Figure. 4 and 5 operate in real time. The system in Figure. 5 can adjust the balance of the ANS using respiration training. SRPIAD data can determine heart rate and its variability. Imbalance of ANS regards that broken if

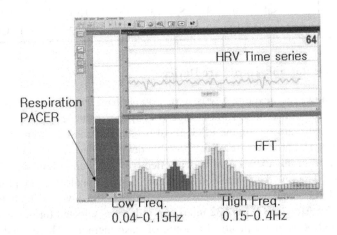

Fig. 5. Feedback software system for balancing the Autonomic Nerve System (ANS)

SRPIAD was small or large than range value. Most of the participants achieved a balanced state of the ANS through respiration training. When a participant observes negative stimuli, balance of the ANS is lost and respiration changes slowly. This program can show balance of the sympathetic nerve and parasympathetic nerve by the ratio of HF (High Frequency: 0.04~0.15Hz) and LF (Low Frequency: 0.15~0.4Hz) domains. Then participants can then recover the ANS balance again. However, recovery time differs between participants.

4 Conclusions

Preceding this study, there were several papers issuing the portable devices for detecting emotions. Rosalind W.Picard has devised a measuring system, an augmentation of Thad Starner's design. This device can measure the changes in ANS (Autonomous Nervous System) including respiration, skin conductivity (GSR), temperature, blood volume pressure (BVP), heart rate (from BVP), and EMG (electromyogram, for muscular electrical activity). Of course, all measurement doesn't cause any pain of subject. With those many bio parameters, they could achieve high accuracy of emotion identification.[17] However, the thing important is that the features of the sensor information should be considered salient, both to reduce the amount of data that is stored and transmitted, and to improve the analysis of the data[17]. So through this study, we tried to develop a portable device for bi-emotional state identification only with heart rate variability. We developed a potable device, which is applied to respiration training software to adjust the balance level of the ANS. The devices should be easy to use and light. The greater number of biological signal parameters results higher accuracy, but at a cost of greater power requirements since more variables result in higher computational complexity for emotion extraction. In addition, measuring numerous parameters limits human behavior too strictly, which results in a negative feeling. This is against the concept of ubiquitous service. To avoid this, we should consider which and how many parameters will be required for emotion estimation. Thus, we finally selected HRV since this parameter is very easy to measure. Also, HRV works well for estimating the bi-emotional state. Therefore, we expect that HRV and this device can be used as a core technology for ubiquitous health care and other areas.

Acknowledgments

This work was supported by the Ministry of Commerce and the Industry & Energy (Korea) under Grant 2004-00609 (Development of New Technologies for Mental Health Promotion and Interface of the Elderly)

References

1. Rosalind W. Picard, Elias Vyzas, Jennifer Healey: Toward Machine Emotional Intelligence: Analysis of Affective Physiological State, IEEE Transactions on Pattern Analysis and Machine Intelligence, Vol. 23, No. 10. October (2001)

2. R.Sinha O. Parsons: Multivariate response patterning of fear and anger, Cognition and Emotion, Vol. 10, no. 2, pp. 173-198, (1996)
3. Lang P J, Bradley,□.M & Cuthbert , B,N NIMH: Center for the Study of Emotion and Attention, "international Affective Picture System (IAPS)" Technical Manual and Affective Ratings (1995)
4. Christine Laetitia Lisetti, Fatma Nasoz.: Using Noninvasive Wearable Computers to Recognize Human Emotions form Physiological Signals, EURASIP Journal on Applied Signal Processing, 11, 1672-1687 (2004)
5. Jiapupan and Willis J. Tompkins: A Real Time QRS Detection Algorithm, IEEE Transactions on Biomedical Engineering Vol. BME-32, No. 3, March (1985)
6. Mika P. Tarvainen, Perttu O. Ranta-aho, and PasiA. Karjalainen: An advanced detrending method with application to HRV analysis, IEEE Trans Biomed Eng, 49(2): 172-175, (2002)
7. R.W. Levenson, P. Ekman, and W.V. Friesen: Voluntary facial action generates emotion-specific autonomic nervous systemactivity, Psychophysiology, Vol. 27, pp.363-384 (1990)
8. John T. Cacioppo, Gary G. Berntson, Jeff T. Larsen, Kirsten M. Poehlmann, Tiffany A. Ito " The psychophysiology of Emotion "The handbook of emotion, 2nd. Edition (pp. 173-191). New York: Guilford Press
9. Andreassi, J. L Psychophysiology human behavior and physiological response, Lawrence Erlbaum Associates, New Jersey (2000)
10. F. Wang, K Sagawa, H. Inooka, : Time domain HRV index for accessment of Dynamic stress, Computers in Cardiology (1998)
11. K.H. Kim, S.W. Bang, S.R. Kim: Emotion recognition system using short-term monitoring of physiological signals, Medical & Biological Engineering &Computing, Vol. 42, 419-427 (2004)
12. R.W. Picard, Affective Computing, MIT Press, London, England, (1997)
13. Yoon-Ki Min, Soon-Cheol Chung, Byung Chan Min (2005) Physiological Evaluation on Emotional Change Induced by Imagination. Psychophysiology and Biofeedback, Vol. 30, No 2, June 2005
14. Sun. K. Yoo et al,(2005) Neural Network Based Emotion Estimation using Heart Rate Variability and Skin Resistance, ICNC 2005 LNCS 3610, pp 818-824, 2005
15. Shusterman, V., Barnea, O.(1995) Analysis of skin-temperature variability compared to variability of blood pressure and heart rate, IEEE Ann Conf. Engineering Medicine Biology Society, pp 1027-1028
16. Task Force of The European Society of Cardiology and The North American Society of Pacing and Electrophysiology: Heart rate variability, Standards of measurement, physiological interpretation, and clinical use, American Heart Association Inc. European Society of Cardiology (1996)
17. R.W. Picard, Jennifer Healey, Affective Wearables, IEEE Proceedings of the First International Symposium on Wearable Computers October, 1997 ISWC'97

An Optimizing Authenticated Key Exchange Protocol for Self-organizing Sensor Networks

Eun-Jun Yoon and Kee-Young Yoo*

Department of Computer Engineering, Kyungpook National University,
Daegu 702-701, South Korea
Tel.: +82-53-950-5553; Fax:+82-53-957-4846
ejyoon@infosec.knu.ac.kr, yook@knu.ac.kr

Abstract. In 2003, Huang et al. proposed an authenticated key exchange (AKE) protocol for secure communications between a sensor and a security manager based on elliptic curve cryptography in a self-organizing sensor network. In 2005, Tian et al., however, showed that a security manager will learn the long-term private key of a sensor after having one normal run of the protocol with the sensor. Then they proposed an improvement which solves the problem. The current paper, however, demonstrates neither protocol provides perfect forward secrecy, and presents an improved protocol in order to address this problem. Not only is the computational cost of the proposed AKE protocol less than that of both protocols, the number of steps in communication is one fewer than conventional protocols and only needs three steps.

Keywords: Cryptography, Sensor network, Key exchange protocol, Secure communication, Self-organizing.

1 Introduction

Self-organizing sensor networks [1] are emerging and being put into practice for many new applications. This type of network can usually be set up quickly and inexpensively using low-cost and ultra low-power sensors. Target applications include battlefield services, rescue missions, nature research projects, etc. The self-organizing model can be further divided into two cases [1][2]. In the non-uniform self-organizing model the network may contain two types of nodes: full functional devices (FFD) with high energy, power, and storage capabilities; and the restricted functional devices (RFD), which are typical low-capability sensor nodes. In the uniform self-organizing model, all nodes are assumed to be restricted functional devices. A RFD plays on the role of an end device, such as a low-power sensor, while a FFD takes the role of a coordinator, a router, or a security manager. A security manager in a cluster is responsible for installing symmetric link keys to individual sensors such that these sensors can communicate with each other securely in the cluster. To establish these link keys for a sensor, the security manager must first establish an initial session key with the

---

* Corresponding author.

H.Y. Youn, M. Kim, and H. Morikawa (Eds.): UCS 2006, LNCS 4239, pp. 537–546, 2006.

sensor. The initial session key is then used to build a secure channel in which link keys are subsequently installed into the sensor by the security manager.

In 2003, Huang et al. [3] proposed an efficient initial session key establishment protocol which provides key exchange and mutual authentication between a sensor node and a security manager. When compared with other public key-based authenticated key exchange (AKE) protocols, their protocol provides a smaller key length, faster processing speed, and smaller communication overhead because their protocol is based on elliptic curve cryptography [4]. When implemented, the total processing time on a 10MHz sensor is only 760ms. In 2005, Tian et al. [5], however, showed that a security manager can learn the long-term private key of a sensor after having one normal run of the protocol with the sensor. Then they proposed an improvement which solves the improvement which solves the problem and makes all of their security claims hold again. Neither protocol, however, is appropriate for uniform self-organized sensor networks [1], since they assume the existence of full-functional devices and do not provide perfect forward secrecy [10][12]. Achieving the required security level is more difficult in the uniform model, since one can only rely on low-capability devices. In this paper, we are concerned with key management in uniform self-organizing sensor networks [1][2]. Therefore, the current paper demonstrates that neither protocol provides perfect forward secrecy; then an improved protocol is presented in order to address this problem. Not only is the computational cost of the proposed AKE protocol less than that of both protocols, the number of steps in communication is one fewer than conventional protocols and only needs three steps.

The remainder of the paper is organized as follows: Section 2 briefly reviews two AKE protocols. Then Section 3 demonstrates its security weaknesses. Our proposed protocol is presented in Section 4. In Sections 5 and 6, we analyze the security and efficiency of our proposed protocol, respectively. Our conclusions are presented in Section 7.

2   Review of Two AKE Protocols

This section briefly reviews both Huang et al.'s [3] and Tian et al.'s AKE protocols [5]. Some of the notations used in this paper are defined as follows:

- C: an elliptic curve defined over $GF(p)$.
- P: a base point of large order n on C. It is assumed that the elliptic curve discrete logarithm problem (ECDLP) [4][7][8] in this group is intractable.
- CA: a system-wide trusted party called Certificate Authority.
- U, V: a sensor and a security manager, respectively.
- q_{CA}, Q_{CA}: the private/public key pair of CA, where q_{CA} is a random integer and $Q_{CA} = q_{CA}P$.
- $H(\cdot)$: a secure one-way hash function which maps finite binary strings to integers in the range $[2, n-2]$.
- $KDF(\cdot)$: a secure key derivation function.
- $MAC(\cdot)$: a message authentication code function.

- $||$: the conventional binary string concatenation operator.
- $k \in N$: a system-wide security parameter.

2.1   Huang et al.'s AKE Protocol

There are two phases in Huang et al.'s AKE protocol. In the first phase, each party (e.g. a sensor or a security manager) in the system communicates securely with the CA through an out-of-band channel and gets a certificate. In the second phase, a sensor and a security manager carry out an AKE protocol for establishing an initial session key.

Phase 1: Certificate Generation. The certificate generation mechanism is based on an elliptic curve implicit certificate scheme [6]. The steps of establishing a long-term public key pair for sensor U are described as follows. The entire process must be carried out through a secure and authenticated channel such as an out-of-band interface with the identities of the communicating parties verified.

(1) (Public Key Pair Contribution Generation) U picks a random integer g_U, computes $G_U = g_U P$, and sends G_U and his identity ID_U to CA.
(2) (Certificate Generation) If both G_U and ID_U are valid, CA picks a random integer g_{CA}, computes $G_{CA} = g_{CA}P$, and $B_U = G_U + G_{CA}$. CA sets the implicit certificate IC_U as $IC_U = (Q_{CA}, ID_U, B_U, t_U)$, where t_U denotes the certification expiration date. CA computes $e_U \leftarrow H(IC_U)$ and $s_U = g_{CA}e_U + q_{CA} \bmod n$. The user then sends s_U and IC_U to U.
(3) (Certificate Verification and Public Key Pair Generation) U computes $e_U \leftarrow H(IC_U)$ and his or her long-term private/public key pair (q_U, Q_U) as $q_U = s_U + g_U e_U \bmod n$ and $Q_U = q_U P$. Then, he checks if $Q_U \stackrel{?}{=} e_U B_U + Q_{CA} \bmod n$. If the condition holds, U accepts the certificate. Otherwise, s/he rejects.

In the same way, V gets an implicit certificate $IC_V = (Q_{CA}, ID_V, B_V, t_V)$ and a long-term public key pair (q_V, Q_V).

Phase 2: The AKE Protocol for Initial Session Key. After generating certificates and public key pairs, sensor U and security manager V carry out the following protocol to establish an initial session key. The session key is used to set up a secure channel for V to install link keys to U. Figure 1 shows the Huang et al.'s AKE protocol.

(1) $U \rightarrow V$: $IC_U = (Q_{CA}, ID_U, B_U, t_U)$
    $V \rightarrow U$: $IC_V = (Q_{CA}, ID_V, B_V, t_V)$
    U and V exchange their implicit certificates. The content of the certificate is verified on the other side that includes the certificate format, expected device identity, and the validity period. The public keys of the counter-party are also obtained from the certificates: V obtains U's public key Q_U as $H(IC_U)B_U + Q_{CA}$. Similarly, U obtains V's public key Q_V as $H(IC_V)B_V + Q_{CA}$. If

anything goes wrong, the protocol is terminated. Note that $Q_U = q_U P$ and $Q_V = q_V P$.

(2) $U \rightarrow V: D_U = H(c_U||r)P, (c_U||r) \oplus (d_U Q_V).x$

   U randomly picks a k-bit integer cU and a $(160 - k)$-bit integer r, computes $d_U = H(c_U||r)$, $D_U = d_U P$, $R = d_U Q_V$, and sends D_U and $T = (c_U||r) \oplus R.x$ to V, where $R.x$ denotes the x coordinate of R.

(3) $V \rightarrow U: y = Enc_{c_U}(ID_V||c_V)$

   V computes $R = q_V D_U$, $m = T \oplus R.x$ and checks if $D_U \overset{?}{=} H(m)P$. If yes, V obtains c_U as the most significant k bits of m; otherwise, the protocol is terminated. V then generates a k-bit random number c_V and sends $y = Enc_{c_U}(ID_V||c_V)$ to U, where Enc_{c_U} is some secure symmetric key encryption function under the key c_U. V also computes $MacK||SessionK = KDF(c_U||c_V||ID_U||ID_V)$. V then destroys c_U and c_V. Here, the lengths of $MacK$ and $SessionK$ should be at least k bits long.

(4) $U \rightarrow V: z = q_U H(MacK) + d_U \bmod n$

   U decrypts y and checks if the plaintext is ID_V followed by some number. If the check fails, the protocol is terminated. Otherwise, U denotes the number which follows ID_V as c_V. U then computes $MacK||SessionK = KDF(c_U||c_V||ID_U||ID_V)$ and sends $z = q_U H(MacK) + d_U \bmod n$ to V. U then destroys c_U and c_V.

(5) $V \rightarrow U: z' = MAC_{MacK}(ID_V||ID_U)$

   After V receives z, he checks if $zP \overset{?}{=} H(MacK)Q_U + D_U$. If the check fails, the protocol is terminated. Otherwise, V sends $z' = MAC_{MacK}(ID_V||ID_U)$ to U.

(6) U check if z' is valid. If not, the protocol is terminated. The initial session key established by U and V is $SessionK$.

2.2   Tian et al.'s Improved AKE Protocol

Tian et al. showed than Huang et al.'s key establishment protocol suffers from a serious problem. That is, the security manager V can easily learn the long-term private key of the sensor U after launching a normal run of the protocol with U. In Huang et al.'s AKE protocol, V's attack proceeds as follows:

(1) In Step (3) of Huang et al.'s AKE protocol, after V computes $m = T \oplus R.x$, V obtains c_U and r. V can then compute $d_U = H(c_U||r)$.

(2) In Step (5) of Huang et al.'s AKE protocol, after V receives $z = q_U H(MacK) + d_U \bmod n$, s/he can find out the value of U's private key q_U as $q_U = (z - d_U)(H(MacK))^{-1} \bmod n$.

Tian et al. also proposed an improvement of Huang et al.'s protocol that can withstand their suggested attack. That is, Tian et al. slightly improved the AKE protocol in which the security manager V cannot get U's private key q_U, unlike Huang et al.'s protocol. The steps of Tian et al.'s improved AKE protocol are almost the same as those of Huang et al.'s protocol, except for Steps (2) and (3). In Step (2) of Tian et al.'s AKE protocol, they specified that U chooses d_U

Shared Information: $\{E, P, Enc_K(\cdot), KDF(\cdot), MAC(\cdot), H(\cdot)\}$
Information held by Sensor U: $\{ID_U, q_U, Q_U, IC_U, IC_V, Q_V\}$
Information held by Security Manager V: $\{ID_V, q_V, Q_V, IC_V, IC_U, Q_U\}$

Sensor U		**Security Manager V**
Randomly choose c_u (k bits) and r (160 - k bits)		
$d_U \leftarrow H(c_U\|r)$		
$D_U \leftarrow d_U P$		
$R \leftarrow d_U Q_V$		
$T \leftarrow (c_U\|r) \oplus R.x$	$\xrightarrow{\{D_U, T\}}$	$R \leftarrow q_V D_U$
		$m \leftarrow T \oplus R.x$
		Check $D_U \doteq H(m)P$
		Obtain c_U from m
		Randomly choose c_V (k bits)
Decrypt y	$\xleftarrow[\{y\}]{MacK\|SessionK \leftarrow KDF(c_u\|c_V\|ID_U\|ID_V)}$	$MacK\|SessionK \leftarrow KDF(c_u\|c_V\|ID_U\|ID_V)$
Check ID_V		$y \leftarrow Enc_{c_U}(ID_V\|c_V)$
$MacK\|SessionK \leftarrow KDF(c_u\|c_V\|ID_U\|ID_V)$		
$z \leftarrow H(MacK)q_U + d_U (mod n)$	$\xrightarrow{\{z\}}$	Check $zP \doteq H(MacK)Q_U + D_U$
Check $z' \doteq MAC_{MacK}(ID_V\|ID_U)$	$\xleftarrow{\{z'\}}$	$z' \leftarrow MAC_{MacK}(ID_V\|ID_U)$

Shared Session key = $SessionK$

Fig. 1. Huang et al.'s AKE Protocol

randomly instead of deriving it from c_U and r. Consequently, V does not check whether $D_U = H(m)P$ in Step (3). Figure 2 shows Tian et al.'s improved AKE protocol.

3 Perfect Forward Secrecy Problem of Two AKE Protocols

This section shows that neither Huang et al.'s and Tian et al.'s AKE protocols provide perfect forward secrecy. Perfect forward secrecy is a very important security requirement for evaluating a strong protocol. A protocol with perfect forward secrecy assures that even if one entity's long-term key (e.g. user password) is compromised, it will never reveal the session keys used before. For example, the well-known Diffie-Hellman key agreement scheme can provide perfect forward secrecy.

Neither AKE protocols, however, provide perfect forward secrecy because once the long-term private key q_V of the security manager V is disclosed, all previous fresh session keys $MacK\|SessionK \leftarrow KDF(c_U\|c_V\|ID_U\|ID_V)$ will be opened and hence previous communication messages will be learned.

In the two AKE protocols, suppose an attacker E obtains the long-term private key q_V from the compromised security manager and intercepts transmitted values (D_U, T, y), from an open network, where $D_U = d_U P$, $T = (c_U\|r) \oplus R.x$ and $y = Enc_{c_U}(ID_V\|c_V)$. It is easy to obtain the information since it is exposed

Shared Information: $\{E,\ P,\ Enc_K(\cdot),\ KDF(\cdot),\ MAC(\cdot),\ H(\cdot)\}$
Information held by Sensor U: $\{ID_U,\ q_U,\ Q_U,\ IC_U,\ IC_V,\ Q_V\}$
Information held by Security Manager V: $\{ID_V,\ q_V,\ Q_V,\ IC_V,\ IC_U,\ Q_U\}$

Sensor U		Security Manager V

Randomly choose c_u (k bits) and r (160 - k bits)
Randomly choose d_U
$D_U \leftarrow d_U P$
$R \leftarrow d_U Q_V$
$T \leftarrow (c_U \| r) \oplus R.x$

$\xrightarrow{\quad \{D_U, T\} \quad}$

$R \leftarrow q_V D_U$
$m \leftarrow T \oplus R.x$
Obtain c_U from m
Randomly choose c_V (k bits)
$MacK \| SessionK \leftarrow KDF(c_U \| c_V \| ID_U \| ID_V)$
$y \leftarrow Enc_{c_U}(ID_V \| c_V)$

Decrypt y

$\xleftarrow{\quad \{y\} \quad}$

Check ID_V
$MacK \| SessionK \leftarrow KDF(c_U \| c_V \| ID_U \| ID_V)$
$z \leftarrow H(MacK)q_U + d_U \pmod{n}$

$\xrightarrow{\quad \{z\} \quad}$

Check $zP \overset{\cdot}{=} H(MacK)Q_U + D_U$

Check $z' \overset{\cdot}{=} MAC_{MacK}(ID_V \| ID_U)$

$\xleftarrow{\quad \{z'\} \quad}$

$z' \leftarrow MAC_{MacK}(ID_V \| ID_U)$

Shared Session key = $SessionK$

Fig. 2. Tian et al.'s AKE Protocol

over an open network. Then E can compute $R = d_U Q_V = D_U q_V$ by using D_U and q_V. Then, E can get c_U from T by computing $T \oplus R.x$, where $R.x$ denotes the x coordinate of R. By using c_U, E can decrypt y and get c_V. Finally, E can compute the shared session key $MacK \| SessionK \leftarrow KDF(c_U \| c_V \| ID_U \| ID_V)$ by using c_U and c_V. Neither Huang et al.'s and Tian et al.'s AKE protocols provide perfect forward secrecy.

4   Proposed Optimizing AKE Protocol

This section proposes an optimized AKE protocol that can provide perfect forward secrecy. Unlike both AKE protocols than can perform six rounds, the proposed AKE protocol reduces one round than both protocols. The first phase (certificate generation) is the same as both AKE protocol. Figure 3 shows the second phase (AKE protocol for initial session key) in which a sensor and a security manager carry out an AKE protocol to establish an initial session key. The proposed initial session key generation phase requires only five rounds and works as follows:

Phase 2: The AKE Protocol for Initial Session Key. After generating certificates and public key pairs, sensor U and security manager V carries out the following protocol to establish an initial session key. The session key will be used to set up a secure channel for V to install link keys to U.

(1) $U \to V$: $IC_U = (Q_{CA}, ID_U, B_U, t_U)$
     $V \to U$: $IC_V = (Q_{CA}, ID_V, B_V, t_V)$
     U and V exchange their implicit certificates. The content of the certificate is
     verified at the other side and includes the certificate format, expected device
     identity, and the validity period. The public keys of the counter-party are also
     obtained from the certificates; V obtains U's public key Q_U as $H(IC_U)B_U +$
     Q_{CA}. Similarly, U obtains V's public key Q_V as $H(IC_V)B_V + Q_{CA}$. If
     anything goes wrong, the protocol is terminated. Note that $Q_U = q_U P$ and
     $Q_V = q_V P$.

(2) $U \to V$: $y = Enc_R(ID_U \| D_U)$
     U randomly picks d_U, computes $D_U = d_U P$, $R = q_U Q_V = q_U q_V P$, and
     sends $y = Enc_R(ID_U \| D_U)$ to V, where Enc_R is some secure symmetric key
     encryption function under the key R.

(3) $V \to U$: D_V, $z = MAC_{MacK}(ID_v \| ID_U)$
     V computes $R = q_V Q_U = q_V q_U P$, decrypts y, and check if the plaintext
     is ID_U followed by some number. If the check fails, the protocol is ter-
     minated. Otherwise, V denotes the number which follows ID_U as D_U. V
     then randomly picks d_V, and computes $D_V = d_V P$, $K = d_V D_U = d_V d_U P$
     and $MacK \| SessionK = KDF(K \| ID_U \| ID_V)$. V then sends D_V and $z =$
     $MAC_{MacK}(ID_V \| ID_U)$ to U. Then V destroys d_V, R, and K.

(4) $U \to V$: $z' = MAC_{MacK}(ID_U \| ID_V)$
     U computes $K = d_U D_V$ and $MacK \| SessionK = KDF(K \| ID_U \| ID_V)$. U
     then checks if $z \overset{?}{=} MAC_{MacK}(ID_v \| ID_U)$. If the check fails, the protocol is
     terminated. Otherwise, U sends $z' = MAC_{MacK}(ID_U \| ID_V)$ to V. Then U
     destroys d_U, R and K.

(5) U check if $z' \overset{?}{=} MAC_{MacK}(ID_U \| ID_V)$ is valid. If not, the protocol is termi-
     nated. The initial session key established by U and V is $SessionK$.

5   Security Analysis

This section analyzes the security of the proposed AKE protocol. First, we define the security terms [7][8][9][10][11][12] needed to conduct an analysis of the
proposed protocol. They are as follows:

Definition 1. *The elliptic curve discrete logarithm problem (ECDLP) is as
follows; given a public key point $V_i = k_i P$, it is hard to compute the secret key
k_i.*

Definition 2. *The elliptic curve Diffie-Hellman problem (ECDHP) is as follows; given point elements aP and bP, it is hard to find abP.*

Definition 3. *A secure one-way hash function $y = H(x)$ is one where given x
to compute y is easy and given y to compute x is hard.*

The following six security properties [9][10][12] must be considered for the proposed protocol: a replay attack, an impersonation attack, a known-key security,

Shared Information: $\{E, P, Enc_K(\cdot), KDF(\cdot), MAC(\cdot), H(\cdot)\}$
Information held by Sensor U: $\{ID_U, q_U, Q_U, IC_U, IC_V, Q_V\}$
Information held by Security Manager V: $\{ID_V, q_V, Q_V, IC_V, IC_U, Q_U\}$

Sensor U		Security Manager V
Randomly choose d_U		
$D_U \leftarrow d_U P$		
$R \leftarrow q_U Q_V$		$R \leftarrow q_V Q_U$
$y \leftarrow Enc_R(ID_U \| D_U)$	$\{y\}$ $\longrightarrow$	
		Decrypt y
		Check ID_U
		Randomly choose d_V
		$D_V \leftarrow d_V P$
		$K \leftarrow d_V D_U$
		$MacK \| SessionK \leftarrow KDF(K \| ID_U \| ID_V)$
$K \leftarrow d_u D_V$	$\xleftarrow{\{D_V, z\}}$	$z \leftarrow MAC_{MacK}(ID_V \| ID_U)$
$MacK \| SessionK \leftarrow KDF(K \| ID_U \| ID_V)$		
Check $z \overset{\cdot}{=} MAC_{MacK}(ID_V \| ID_U)$		
$z' \leftarrow MAC_{MacK}(ID_U \| ID_V)$	$\{z'\}$ $\longrightarrow$	Check $z' \overset{\cdot}{=} MAC_{MacK}(ID_U \| ID_V)$
	Shared Session key $= SessionK$	

Fig. 3. Proposed AKE Protocol

a session key security, an explicit key confirmation, and perfect forward secrecy. Regarding the above mentioned definitions, the following is used to analyze the six security properties of the proposed protocol.

(1) *The proposed protocol can resist a replay attack:* Attacker E can intercept all transmission values $\{y, D_V, z, z'\}$ and can use them to impersonate U (or V) when sending the next key agreement message. For a random challenge, however, d_U and d_V, which are separately generated by U and V, are different every time. Since U and V always verify the integrity of the fresh session key $SessionK$ by checking z and z' in Steps (4) and (5), the replayed messages can be detected by U and V, respectively.

(2) *The proposed protocol can resist an impersonation attack:* Due to the use of implicit certificates, attacker E cannot successfully execute an impersonation attack. During the key establishment phase, U uses the implicit certificate of V and the public key of the CA to reconstruct the public key Q_V of node V. At the end of the key establishment phase, when V uses its private key q_V for the construction of the $ECDH$ key R, verifies y and returns D_V and z. U will have implicit assurance that it is talking to V and that all information included in the certificate is genuine (i.e. signed by the CA).

(3) *The proposed protocol provides known-key security:* Known-key security means that each run of a key agreement protocol between two entities U and V should produce unique secret keys; such keys are called session keys. Knowledge of a session key $SessionK$ and the random values d_U and d_V

will not help in computing the other session keys $MacK \| SessionK' = KDF(K' \| ID_U \| ID_V)$. This is because without knowing d'_U and d'_V, it is impossible to compute the other secret value K'.

(4) *The proposed protocol provides session key security:* Session key security means that at the end of the key exchange, the session key is not known by anyone but U and V. This in because the random values d_U and d_V are protected by the $ECDHP$ and the secure one-way hash function. Only U and V know about $K = d_U d_V P$ and this information is nor revealed to anybody else.

(5) *The proposed protocol provides explicit key confirmation:* It should be confirmed to a legitimate user participating in the protocol that he or she actually shares a common secret session key with an entity with which communication is intended. The proposed protocol includes the session key in z and z', in order to confirm the keys.

(6) *The proposed protocol provides perfect forward secrecy:* Perfect forward secrecy means that if the long-term private keys of one or more entities are compromised, the secrecy of previous session keys, which was established by honest entities, is not affected. If the the long-term private keys of two entities U and V are compromised, an attacker will not be able to determine the session key K for the past sessions or to decrypt them, since the attacker is still faced with the $ECDHP$.

6   Efficiency Analysis

The followings are used to analyze the efficiency properties in the proposed protocol.

(1) *The proposed protocol uses a low computational load:* In general, a protocol requires a low computational load that can be borne by even low-power devices such as sensors. In the key establishment phase, the proposed protocol requires a total of six exponentiation operations, six hash operations, and one symmetric key encryption operation. Note D_U, R, and y are computed by pre-computation manner. U performs pre-computation in the idle time of the last running period. The pre-computation reduces time and computational load during the key agreement protocol execution. More specifically, a random number d_U is selected, and then $D_U = d_U P$, R, y are calculated by this pre-computation phase to execute the key agreement protocol.

(2) *The proposed protocol uses a minimum number of message exchanges:* In terms of network resource efficiency and network delay, there should be as few communication rounds as possible. Therefore, the number of messages that are exchanged between U and V should be kept to a minimum. Both Huang et al.'s and Tian et al.'s protocols require four steps in order to perform mutual authentication and key establishment, while the proposed protocol requires only three steps.

(3) *The proposed protocol uses a minimum communication bandwidth:* The protocol message should be as short as possible. Among the four messages,

two are hash output bits, one is random number bits, and the other is the encryption output bit of ID_U and D_U.

7 Conclusion

The current paper demonstrated that neither Huang et al.'s and Tian et al.'s protocols provide perfect forward secrecy; then an improved protocol is presented in order to address this problem. Not only the computational cost of the proposed AKE protocol is less than that of both protocols, the number of steps in communication is one fewer than conventional protocols and only three steps.

Acknowledgements

This work was supported by grant No. R01-2006-000-10614-0 from the Basic Research Program of the Korea Science & Engineering Foundation.

References

1. Eschenauer, L., Gligor, V.D.: A Key-Management Scheme for Distributed Sensor Networks. Proc. of 9th CCS ACM conference. (2002) 41-47
2. IEEE Std. 802.15.4-2003.: IEEE Standard for Information Technology - Telecommunications and Information Exchange Between Systems - Local and Metropolitan Area Networks - Specific Requirements - Part 15.4: Wireless Medium Access Control (MAC) and Physical Layer (PHY) Specifications for Low Rate Wireless Personal Area Networks (WPANS). (2003)
3. Huang, Q., Cukier, J., Kobayashi, H., Liu, B., Zhang, J.: Fast Authenticated Key Establishment Protocols for Self-Organizing Sensor Networks. In Proc. of the Second ACM International Conference on Wireless Sensor Networks and Applications. ACM Press. (2003) 141-150
4. Menezes, A.: Elliptic Curve Public Key Cryptosystems. Kluwer Academic Publishers. (1993)
5. Tian, X., Wong, D.S., Zhu, R.W.: Analysis and Improvement of an Authenticated Key Exchange Protocol for Sensor Networks. IEEE Communication Letters. Vol. 9. No. 11. (November 2005) 970-972
6. Struik, R., Rasor, G.: Mandatory ECC Security Algorithm Suite. Submissions to IEEE P802.15 Wireless Personal Area Networks. (Mar. 2002)
7. Miller, V.: Uses of Elliptic Curves in Cryptography. Proceedings of Crypto'85. Santa Barbara. USA. (1986) 417-426
8. Koblitz, N.: Elliptic Curve Cryptosystems. Mathematics of Computation. Vol. 48. (1987) 203-209
9. Boyd, C., Mathuria, A.: Protocols for Authentication and Key Establishment. Springer-Verlag. (2003)
10. Menezes, A.J., Oorschot, P.C., Vanstone, S.A.: Handbook of Applied Cryptograph. CRC Press. New York. (1997)
11. Diffie, W., Hellman, M.: New Directions in Cryptography. IEEE Transaction on Information Theory. Vol. IT-22. No. 6. (1976) 644-654
12. Schneier, B.: Applied Cryptography-Protocols. Algorithms and Source Code in C. 2nd edi. John Wiley & Sons Inc. (1995)

Author Index

Adelmann, Robert 300
Ahn, Jong-Suk 440
An, Sunshin 210

Baek, Eui-Hyun 225
Baik, Doo-Kwon 1
Balfanz, Dirk 73
Begole, James "Bo" 82
Beigl, Michael 254
Byun, Tae-young 467

Cha, Hojung 428
Cho, Eun-Sun 286
Cho, Gihwan 331
Cho, Jaejoon 210
Cho, Kenta 98
Choi, Hyun Il 41
Choi, Jihoon 344
Choi, Soo-Mi 73
Choi, Yoo-Joo 73
Choo, Hyunseung 357
Chung, Min Young 357
Chung, Woo-Gon 316

Dannhäuser, Günter 129
Datta, Amitava 454
Decker, Christian 254

Fluck, Steven 300
Fujinami, Kaori 270, 516

Han, Ning 478
Hattori, Masanori 98
Helal, Abdelsalam (Sumi) 500
Hong, Kihun 384
Hwang, Sung Ho 467
Hwang, Won-Joo 368

Igaki, Hiroshi 13
Ikonen, Veikko 57

Jeong, Dongwon 1
Jeong, Jongpil 357
Jeong, KeeSam 528
Ji, Youngmin 210
Jin, Guang-yao 200

Jing, Yixin 1
Joo, Jong Ok 478
Jung, Souhwan 384
Jung, Youna 171

Kaasinen, Eija 57
Kang, Chang-Deok 225
Kang, Namhi 384
Kargl, Frank 129
Kashihara, Shigeru 239
Kawsar, Fahim 270
Kim, Dae Hwan 41
Kim, Eunkyo 344
Kim, Hyun 286
Kim, Jae Moung 478
Kim, Jang-Sub 316
Kim, Jihoon 28
Kim, Jin Hyung 41
Kim, JinHyung 1
Kim, Joongheon 344
Kim, Keecheon 414
Kim, Minkoo 171
Kim, Minsoo 171
Kim, Minsu 467
Kim, Min-Young 286
Kim, Shin-Dug 225
Kim, Won-Tae 398
Kim, Younghan 384
Kong, In-Yeup 368
Kortuem, Gerd 183
Krohn, Albert 254
Kunze, Kai 82
Kwon, Ohbyung 28

Langheinrich, Marc 300
Lee, ByungChae 528
Lee, ChungKi 528
Lee, Donghwan 344
Lee, Dongkeun 414
Lee, Eunseok 158
Lee, GunKi 528
Lee, Hoon-Ki 225
Lee, Hyo Jong 489
Lee, Jee-Hyong 158

Lee, Jungtae   171
Lee, Kang-Woo   286, 440
Lee, Moonkun   331
Lee, Seunghwa   158
Lee, Wonjun   344
Lee, Young-Su   440
Lim, Sangsoon   210
Lim, Shinyoung   500
Lu, Xiao-yi   200

Matsumoto, Ken-ichi   13
Mitsui, Kohei   13

Nagler-Ihlein, Jürgen   129
Nakajima, Tatsuo   270, 516
Nakamura, Masahide   13
Ngoh, Lekheng   119
Ni, Hongbo   119
Niemelä, Marketta   57

Ohsuga, Akihiko   98
Oie, Yuji   239
Okamoto, Masayuki   98
Okamoto, Yuzo   98

Park, Joo-Kyoung   225
Park, Kyung-Lang   225
Park, Myong-Soon   200
Park, Seong-Ook   111
Park, YoonJung   528
Partridge, Kurt   82
Pazand, Babak   454
Pirttikangas, Susanna   516

Riedel, Till   254

Santini, Silvia   300
Schätti, Georg   300
Schlott, Stefan   129
Schmidtke, Hedda R.   144
Seong, Nak-Seon   111
Sheridan, G. Jennifer   183
Shin, Christian K.   344
Shin, Dong-Ryeol   316
Shin, Hojin   316
Shon, Sung Hwan   478
Sung, Yeultak   428

Takemura, Kentaro   13
Tsukamoto, Kazuya   239

Van Kleek, Max   82

Waldeck, Carsten   73
Woo, Woontack   144

Yamaguchi, Takeshi   239
Yamasaki, Tomohiro   98
Yoo, Kee-Young   537
Yoo, Seongil   384
Yoo, Seong Joon   73
Yoo, Sun K.   528
Yoon, Eun-Jun   537
Yoon, Jong-Hyuk   440
Yu, Jieun   344
Yu, Sukdea   331

Zhang, Daqing   119
Zhou, Xingshe   119
Zimmer, Tobias   254

Lecture Notes in Computer Science

For information about Vols. 1–4136

please contact your bookseller or Springer

Vol. 4239: H.Y. Youn, M. Kim, H. Morikawa (Eds.), Ubiquitous Computing Systems. XVI, 548 pages. 2006.

Vol. 4238: Y.-T. Kim, M. Takano (Eds.), Management of Convergence Networks and Services. XVIII, 604 pages. 2006.

Vol. 4228: D.E. Lightfoot, C.A. Szyperski (Eds.), Modular Programming Languages. X, 415 pages. 2006.

Vol. 4227: W. Nejdl, K. Tochtermann (Eds.), Innovative Approaches for Learning and Knowledge Sharing. XVII, 721 pages. 2006.

Vol. 4224: E. Corchado, H. Yin, V. Botti, C. Fyfe (Eds.), Intelligent Data Engineering and Automated Learning – IDEAL 2006. XXVII, 1447 pages. 2006.

Vol. 4223: L. Wang, L. Jiao, G. Shi, X. Li, J. Liu (Eds.), Fuzzy Systems and Knowledge Discovery. XXVIII, 1335 pages. 2006. (Sublibrary LNAI).

Vol. 4222: L. Jiao, L. Wang, X. Gao, J. Liu, F. Wu (Eds.), Advances in Natural Computation, Part II. XLII, 998 pages. 2006.

Vol. 4221: L. Jiao, L. Wang, X. Gao, J. Liu, F. Wu (Eds.), Advances in Natural Computation, Part I. XLI, 992 pages. 2006.

Vol. 4219: D. Zamboni, C. Kruegel (Eds.), Recent Advances in Intrusion Detection. XII, 331 pages. 2006.

Vol. 4217: P. Cuenca, L. Orozco-Barbosa (Eds.), Personal Wireless Communications. XV, 532 pages. 2006.

Vol. 4216: M.R. Berthold, R. Glen, I. Fischer (Eds.), Computational Life Sciences. XIII, 269 pages. 2006. (Sublibrary LNBI).

Vol. 4213: J. Fürnkranz, T. Scheffer, M. Spiliopoulou (Eds.), Knowledge Discovery in Databases: PKDD 2006. XXII, 660 pages. 2006. (Sublibrary LNAI).

Vol. 4212: J. Fürnkranz, T. Scheffer, M. Spiliopoulou (Eds.), Machine Learning: ECML 2006. XXIII, 851 pages. 2006. (Sublibrary LNAI).

Vol. 4211: P. Vogt, Y. Sugita, E. Tuci, C. Nehaniv (Eds.), Symbol Grounding and Beyond. VIII, 237 pages. 2006. (Sublibrary LNAI).

Vol. 4209: F. Crestani, P. Ferragina, M. Sanderson (Eds.), String Processing and Information Retrieval. XIV, 367 pages. 2006.

Vol. 4208: M. Gerndt, D. Kranzlmüller (Eds.), High Performance Computing and Communications. XXII, 938 pages. 2006.

Vol. 4207: Z. Ésik (Ed.), Computer Science Logic. XII, 627 pages. 2006.

Vol. 4206: P. Dourish, A. Friday (Eds.), UbiComp 2006: Ubiquitous Computing. XIX, 526 pages. 2006.

Vol. 4205: G. Bourque, N. El-Mabrouk (Eds.), Comparative Genomics. X, 231 pages. 2006. (Sublibrary LNBI).

Vol. 4203: F. Esposito, Z.W. Ras, D. Malerba, G. Semeraro (Eds.), Foundations of Intelligent Systems. XVIII, 767 pages. 2006. (Sublibrary LNAI).

Vol. 4202: E. Asarin, P. Bouyer (Eds.), Formal Modeling and Analysis of Timed Systems. XI, 369 pages. 2006.

Vol. 4201: Y. Sakakibara, S. Kobayashi, K. Sato, T. Nishino, E. Tomita (Eds.), Grammatical Inference: Algorithms and Applications. XII, 359 pages. 2006. (Sublibrary LNAI).

Vol. 4199: O. Nierstrasz, J. Whittle, D. Harel, G. Reggio (Eds.), Model Driven Engineering Languages and Systems. XVI, 798 pages. 2006.

Vol. 4197: M. Raubal, H.J. Miller, A.U. Frank, M.F. Goodchild (Eds.), Geographic, Information Science. XIII, 419 pages. 2006.

Vol. 4196: K. Fischer, I.J. Timm, E. André, N. Zhong (Eds.), Multiagent System Technologies. X, 185 pages. 2006. (Sublibrary LNAI).

Vol. 4195: D. Gaiti, G. Pujolle, E. Al-Shaer, K. Calvert, S. Dobson, G. Leduc, O. Martikainen (Eds.), Autonomic Networking. IX, 316 pages. 2006.

Vol. 4194: V.G. Ganzha, E.W. Mayr, E.V. Vorozhtsov (Eds.), Computer Algebra in Scientific Computing. XI, 313 pages. 2006.

Vol. 4193: T.P. Runarsson, H.-G. Beyer, E. Burke, J.J. Merelo-Guervós, L. D. Whitley, X. Yao (Eds.), Parallel Problem Solving from Nature - PPSN IX. XIX, 1061 pages. 2006.

Vol. 4192: B. Mohr, J.L. Träff, J. Worringen, J. Dongarra (Eds.), Recent Advances in Parallel Virtual Machine and Message Passing Interface. XVI, 414 pages. 2006.

Vol. 4191: R. Larsen, M. Nielsen, J. Sporring (Eds.), Medical Image Computing and Computer-Assisted Intervention – MICCAI 2006, Part II. XXXVIII, 981 pages. 2006.

Vol. 4190: R. Larsen, M. Nielsen, J. Sporring (Eds.), Medical Image Computing and Computer-Assisted Intervention – MICCAI 2006, Part I. XXXVVIII, 949 pages. 2006.

Vol. 4189: D. Gollmann, J. Meier, A. Sabelfeld (Eds.), Computer Security – ESORICS 2006. XI, 548 pages. 2006.

Vol. 4188: P. Sojka, I. Kopeček, K. Pala (Eds.), Text, Speech and Dialogue. XIV, 721 pages. 2006. (Sublibrary LNAI).

Vol. 4187: J.J. Alferes, J. Bailey, W. May, U. Schwertel (Eds.), Principles and Practice of Semantic Web Reasoning. XI, 277 pages. 2006.

Vol. 4186: C. Jesshope, C. Egan (Eds.), Advances in Computer Systems Architecture. XIV, 605 pages. 2006.

Vol. 4185: R. Mizoguchi, Z. Shi, F. Giunchiglia (Eds.), The Semantic Web – ASWC 2006. XX, 778 pages. 2006.

Vol. 4184: M. Bravetti, M. Núñez, G. Zavattaro (Eds.), Web Services and Formal Methods. X, 289 pages. 2006.

Vol. 4183: J. Euzenat, J. Domingue (Eds.), Artificial Intelligence: Methodology, Systems, and Applications. XIII, 291 pages. 2006. (Sublibrary LNAI).

Vol. 4182: H.T. Ng, M.-K. Leong, M.-Y. Kan, D. Ji (Eds.), Information Retrieval Technology. XVI, 684 pages. 2006.

Vol. 4180: M. Kohlhase, OMDoc – An Open Markup Format for Mathematical Documents [version 1.2]. XIX, 428 pages. 2006. (Sublibrary LNAI).

Vol. 4179: J. Blanc-Talon, W. Philips, D. Popescu, P. Scheunders (Eds.), Advanced Concepts for Intelligent Vision Systems. XXIV, 1224 pages. 2006.

Vol. 4178: A. Corradini, H. Ehrig, U. Montanari, L. Ribeiro, G. Rozenberg (Eds.), Graph Transformations. XII, 473 pages. 2006.

Vol. 4177: R. Marín, E. Onaindía, A. Bugarín, J. Santos (Eds.), Current Topics in Aritficial Intelligence. XIII, 621 pages. 2006. (Sublibrary LNAI).

Vol. 4176: S.K. Katsikas, J. Lopez, M. Backes, S. Gritzalis, B. Preneel (Eds.), Information Security. XIV, 548 pages. 2006.

Vol. 4175: P. Bücher, B.M.E. Moret (Eds.), Algorithms in Bioinformatics. XII, 402 pages. 2006. (Sublibrary LNBI).

Vol. 4174: K. Franke, K.-R. Müller, B. Nickolay, R. Schäfer (Eds.), Pattern Recognition. XX, 773 pages. 2006.

Vol. 4173: S. El Yacoubi, B. Chopard, S. Bandini (Eds.), Cellular Automata. XV, 734 pages. 2006.

Vol. 4172: J. Gonzalo, C. Thanos, M. F. Verdejo, R.C. Carrasco (Eds.), Research and Advanced Technology for Digital Libraries. XVII, 569 pages. 2006.

Vol. 4169: H.L. Bodlaender, M.A. Langston (Eds.), Parameterized and Exact Computation. XI, 279 pages. 2006.

Vol. 4168: Y. Azar, T. Erlebach (Eds.), Algorithms – ESA 2006. XVIII, 843 pages. 2006.

Vol. 4167: S. Dolev (Ed.), Distributed Computing. XV, 576 pages. 2006.

Vol. 4166: J. Górski (Ed.), Computer Safety, Reliability, and Security. XIV, 440 pages. 2006.

Vol. 4165: W. Jonker, M. Petković (Eds.), Secure, Data Management. X, 185 pages. 2006.

Vol. 4163: H. Bersini, J. Carneiro (Eds.), Artificial Immune Systems. XII, 460 pages. 2006.

Vol. 4162: R. Královič, P. Urzyczyn (Eds.), Mathematical Foundations of Computer Science 2006. XV, 814 pages. 2006.

Vol. 4161: R. Harper, M. Rauterberg, M. Combetto (Eds.), Entertainment Computing - ICEC 2006. XXVII, 417 pages. 2006.

Vol. 4160: M. Fisher, W.v.d. Hoek, B. Konev, A. Lisitsa (Eds.), Logics in Artificial Intelligence. XII, 516 pages. 2006. (Sublibrary LNAI).

Vol. 4159: J. Ma, H. Jin, L.T. Yang, J.J.-P. Tsai (Eds.), Ubiquitous Intelligence and Computing. XXII, 1190 pages. 2006.

Vol. 4158: L.T. Yang, H. Jin, J. Ma, T. Ungerer (Eds.), Autonomic and Trusted Computing. XIV, 613 pages. 2006.

Vol. 4156: S. Amer-Yahia, Z. Bellahsène, E. Hunt, R. Unland, J.X. Yu (Eds.), Database and XML Technologies. IX, 123 pages. 2006.

Vol. 4155: O. Stock, M. Schaerf (Eds.), Reasoning, Action and Interaction in AI Theories and Systems. XVIII, 343 pages. 2006. (Sublibrary LNAI).

Vol. 4154: Y.A. Dimitriadis, I. Zigurs, E. Gómez-Sánchez (Eds.), Groupware: Design, Implementation, and Use. XIV, 438 pages. 2006.

Vol. 4153: N. Zheng, X. Jiang, X. Lan (Eds.), Advances in Machine Vision, Image Processing, and Pattern Analysis. XIII, 506 pages. 2006.

Vol. 4152: Y. Manolopoulos, J. Pokorný, T. Sellis (Eds.), Advances in Databases and Information Systems. XV, 448 pages. 2006.

Vol. 4151: A. Iglesias, N. Takayama (Eds.), Mathematical Software - ICMS 2006. XVII, 452 pages. 2006.

Vol. 4150: M. Dorigo, L.M. Gambardella, M. Birattari, A. Martinoli, R. Poli, T. Stützle (Eds.), Ant Colony Optimization and Swarm Intelligence. XVI, 526 pages. 2006.

Vol. 4149: M. Klusch, M. Rovatsos, T.R. Payne (Eds.), Cooperative Information Agents X. XII, 477 pages. 2006. (Sublibrary LNAI).

Vol. 4148: J. Vounckx, N. Azemard, P. Maurine (Eds.), Integrated Circuit and System Design. XVI, 677 pages. 2006.

Vol. 4147: M. Broy, I.H. Krüger, M. Meisinger (Eds.), Automotive Software - Connected Services in Mobile Networks. XIV, 155 pages. 2006.

Vol. 4146: J.C. Rajapakse, L. Wong, R. Acharya (Eds.), Pattern Recognition in Bioinformatics. XIV, 186 pages. 2006. (Sublibrary LNBI).

Vol. 4144: T. Ball, R.B. Jones (Eds.), Computer Aided Verification. XV, 564 pages. 2006.

Vol. 4143: R. Lämmel, J. Saraiva, J. Visser (Eds.), Generative and Transformational Techniques in Software Engineering. X, 471 pages. 2006.

Vol. 4142: A. Campilho, M. Kamel (Eds.), Image Analysis and Recognition, Part II. XXVII, 923 pages. 2006.

Vol. 4141: A. Campilho, M. Kamel (Eds.), Image Analysis and Recognition, Part I. XXVIII, 939 pages. 2006.

Vol. 4139: T. Salakoski, F. Ginter, S. Pyysalo, T. Pahikkala, Advances in Natural Language Processing. XVI, 771 pages. 2006. (Sublibrary LNAI).

Vol. 4138: X. Cheng, W. Li, T. Znati (Eds.), Wireless Algorithms, Systems, and Applications. XVI, 709 pages. 2006.

Vol. 4137: C. Baier, H. Hermanns (Eds.), CONCUR 2006 - Concurrency Theory. XIII, 525 pages. 2006.